English Letters (continued)

p probability of some outcome given that the null hypothesis is true   **14.6**

Pr( )   probability of the outcome in parentheses   **8.7**

r sample correlation coefficient   **6.3**

$s_{y|x}$ standard error of estimate   **7.4**

SP_{xy} sum of products   **6.5**

SS sum of squares   **4.5**

s sample standard deviation   **4.5**

s_D sample standard deviation of difference scores   **15.5**

$s_{\bar{x}}$ estimated standard error of the mean   **13.6**

$s_{\bar{x}_1 - \bar{x}_2}$ estimated standard error of the difference between two sample means   **14.5**

$s_{\bar{D}}$ estimated standard error of the mean difference scores   **15.5**

s^2 sample variance   **4.5**

s_p^2 pooled sample variance   **14.5**

T Wilcoxon T test for ranked data   **20.4**

t t ratio   **13.3**

U Mann-Whitney U test for ranked data   **20.3**

X any unspecified observation or score   **3.3**

$\bar{X}$ sample mean   **3.3**

$\bar{X}_1 - \bar{X}_2$ difference between two sample means   **14.3**

Y a score paired with X **6.2**

Y' predicted score   **7.3**

z $\begin{cases}\text{standard score} \quad \textbf{5.2} \\ z \text{ ratio} \quad \textbf{10.2}\end{cases}$

z' transformed standard score   **5.7**

STATISTICS

Ninth Edition

Robert S. Witte
Emeritus, San Jose State University

John S. Witte
University of California, San Francisco

WILEY

JOHN WILEY & SONS, INC.

VICE PRESIDENT & EXECUTIVE PUBLISHER	Jay O'Callaghan
EXECUTIVE EDITOR	Christopher T. Johnson
ASSISTANT EDITOR	Eileen McKeever
SENIOR PRODUCTION EDITOR	Nicole Repasky
MARKETING MANAGER	Danielle Torio
SENIOR DESIGNER	Madelyn Lesure
SENIOR PHOTO EDITOR	Hilary Newman
PRODUCTION MANAGEMENT SERVICES	Aptara®, Inc.
MEDIA EDITORS	Lynn Pearlman/Bridget O'Lavin
COVER PHOTO	M.C. Escher's "Circle Limit III" ©2009 The M.C. Escher Company—Holland. All rights reserved.
COVER DESIGNER	M77 Design
COVER IMAGE	M.C. Escher's "Circle Limit III" ©2009 The M.C. Escher Company—Holland. All rights reserved. www.mcescher.com

This book was set in Times Roman by Aptara®, Inc. and printed and bound by R.R. Donnelley/Crawfordsville. The cover was printed by R.R. Donnelley/Crawfordsville.

This book is printed on acid free paper. ∞

To order books or for customer service please, call 1-800-CALL WILEY (225-5945).

ISBN-13 978-0-470-39222-5

Printed in the United States of America
10 9 8 7 6 5 4 3 2

Library of Congress Cataloging-in-Publication Data

Witte, Robert S.
  Statistics/Robert S. Witte, John S. Witte. — 9th ed.
    p. cm.
  Includes index.
  ISBN 978-0-470-39222-5 (cloth)
  1. Statistics. I. Witte, John S. II. Title.
  QA276.12.W57 2010
  519.5—dc22

2009009729

To Doris

Preface

....

TO THE READER

Students often approach statistics with great apprehension. For many, it is a required course to be taken only under the most favorable circumstances, such as during a quarter or semester when carrying a light course load; for others, it is as distasteful as a visit to a credit counselor—to be postponed as long as possible, with the vague hope that mounting debts might miraculously disappear. Much of this apprehension doubtless rests on the widespread fear of mathematics and mathematically related areas.

This book is written to help you overcome any fear about statistics. Unnecessary quantitative considerations have been eliminated. When not obscured by mathematical treatments better reserved for more advanced books, some of the beauty of statistics, as well as its everyday usefulness, becomes more apparent.

You could go through life quite successfully without ever learning statistics. Having learned some statistics, however, you will be less likely to flinch and change the topic when numbers enter a discussion; you will be more skeptical of conclusions based on loose or erroneous interpretations of sets of numbers; you might even be more inclined to initiate a statistical analysis of some problem within your special area of interest.

TO THE INSTRUCTOR

Largely because they panic at the prospect of any math beyond long division, many students view the introductory statistics class as cruel and unjust punishment. A half-dozen years of experimentation, first with assorted handouts and then with an extensive set of lecture notes distributed as a second text, convinced us that a book could be written for these students. Representing the culmination of this effort, the present book provides a simple overview of descriptive and inferential statistics for mathematically unsophisticated students in the behavioral sciences, social sciences, health sciences, and education.

PEDAGOGICAL FEATURES

- Basic concepts and procedures are explained in plain English, and a special effort has been made to clarify such perennially mystifying topics as the standard deviation, normal curve applications, hypothesis tests, degrees of freedom, and analysis of variance. For example, the standard deviation is more than a formula; it roughly reflects the average amount by which individual observations deviate from their mean.
- Unnecessary math, computational busy work, and subtle technical distinctions are avoided without sacrificing either accuracy or realism. Small

batches of data define most computational tasks. Single examples permeate entire chapters or even several related chapters, serving as handy frames of reference for new concepts and procedures.

- Each chapter begins with a preview and ends with a summary, lists of important terms and key equations, and review questions.

- The two-color format highlights topic headings and important formulas, keys step-by-step computational instructions to actual computations, and adds an extra dimension to illustrations.

- Key statements appear in bold type, and step-by-step summaries of important procedures, such as solving normal curve problems, appear in boxes.

- Important definitions and reminders about key points appear in page margins.

- Scattered throughout the book are examples of computer outputs for three of the most prevalent programs: Minitab, SPSS, and SAS. These outputs can be either ignored or expanded without disrupting the continuity of the text.

- Questions are introduced within chapters, often section by section, as Progress Checks. They are designed to minimize the cumulative confusion reported by many students for some chapters and by some students for most chapters. Each chapter ends with Review Questions.

- Questions have been selected to appeal to student interests: for example, probability calculations, based on design flaws, that re-create the chillingly high likelihood of the *Challenger* shuttle catastrophe (8.14, page 190); a *t* test analysis of global temperatures to evaluate a possible greenhouse effect (13.7, page 281); and a chi-square test of the survival rates of cabin and steerage passengers aboard the *Titanic* (19.14, page 445).

- Appendix B supplies answers to questions marked with asterisks. Other appendices provide a practical math review complete with self-diagnostic tests, a glossary of important terms, and tables for important statistical distributions.

INSTRUCTIONAL AIDS

An electronic version of an instructor's manual accompanies the text. The instructor's manual supplies answers omitted in the text (for about one-third of all questions), as well as sets of multiple-choice test items for each chapter, and a chapter-by-chapter commentary that reflects the authors' teaching experiences with this material. Instructors can access this material in the Instructor Companion Site at http://www.wiley.com/college/witte, or obtain a hard copy or a CD from their Wiley sales representative. The multiple-choice test items are also available on request as a computerized test bank that, once installed on either a PC or a Mac, can be used to generate customized exams.

An electronic version of a student workbook, prepared by Beverly Dretzke of the University of Minnesota, also accompanies the text. Self-paced and self-correcting, the workbook contains problems, discussions, exercises, and tests that supplement the text. Students can access this material in the Student Companion Site at http://www.wiley.com/college/witte.

The Web site at http://www.wiley.com/college/witte also links to statistically relevant Internet sites, including many student-friendly, interactive demonstrations, such as the effect of outliers on correlation coefficients and the effect of population shape and sample size on sampling distributions. References to these sites, designated as an "Internet Demonstration" or an "Internet Site," are scattered throughout the book. The Web site for the book also supplies explanatory comments to ease the transition to these sites. Students with access to the Internet are encouraged to explore these sites; they are enlightening and entertaining. However, they can be ignored—whether by choice or necessity—without destroying the continuity of the book.

A current list of all detected errors can be accessed by clicking on "Textbook Corrections" in the Student Companion Site at http://www.wiley.com/college/witte.

CHANGES IN THIS EDITION

- A new section (11.11) on using power curves to find an appropriate sample size.
- An expansion of the discussion of Cohen's guidelines for effect size, including a new figure (14.4) that illustrates the separation between pairs of normal curves for selected effect sizes.
- A new section (19.12) on using the odds ratio to understand the importance of statistically significant chi-square tests.
- Chapter summaries have been expanded, whenever appropriate, to include a list of key equations.
- Questions, examples, and computer outputs have been updated.

USING THE BOOK

The book contains more material than is covered in most one-quarter or one-semester courses. Various chapters can be omitted without interrupting the main development. Typically, during a one-semester course we cover the entire book except for analysis of variance (Chapters 16, 17, and 18) and tests of ranked data (Chapter 20). An instructor who wishes to emphasize inferential statistics could skim some of the earlier chapters, particularly *Normal Distributions and Standard Scores (z)* (Chapter 5), and *Regression* (Chapter 7), while an instructor who desires a more applied emphasis could omit *Populations, Samples, and Probability* (Chapter 8) and *More about Hypothesis Testing* (Chapter 11).

ACKNOWLEDGMENTS

The authors wish to acknowledge their immediate family: Doris, Steve, Faith, Mike, Sharon, Andrea, Phil, Katie, Keegan, Camy, Brittany, Brent, Kristen, Scott, Joe, John, Jack, Carson, Sam, Margaret, and Gretchen. The first author also wishes to acknowledge his brothers and sisters: Henry, the late Lila, J. Stuart, A. Gerhart, and Etz; deceased parents: Henry and Emma; and all friends and relatives, past and present, including Arthur, Betty, Bob, Cal, David, Ellen, George, Grace, Harold, Helen, John, Joyce, Kayo, Kit, Mary, Paul, Ralph, Ruth, and Suzanne.

Numerous helpful comments were made by those who reviewed the current and previous editions of this book: John W. Collins, Jr., Seton Hall University; Jelani Mandara, Northwestern University; L. E. Banderet, Northeastern University; S. Natasha Beretvas, University of Texas at Austin; Patricia M. Berretty, Fordham University; David Coursey, Florida State University; Shelia Kennison, Oklahoma State University; Melanie Kercher, Sam Houston State University; Jennifer H. Nolan, Loyola Marymount University; and Jonathan C. Pettibone, University of Alabama in Huntsville. Kevin Sumrall, Montgomery College Sky Chafin, Grossmont College Christine Ferri, Richard Stockton College of NJ Ann Barich, Lewis University.

Excellent editorial support was supplied by the people at John Wiley & Sons, Inc., most notably by Eileen McKeever, and by the folks at Aptara® Inc., most notably by Helen Greenberg and Jackie Henry.

Contents

PART 2 Inferential Statistics: Generalizing Beyond Data   171

STATISTICS

Ninth Edition

Introduction

Preview

Statistics deals with variability. You're different from everybody else (and, we hope, proud of it). Today differs from both yesterday and tomorrow. In an experiment designed to detect whether psychotherapy improves self-esteem, self-esteem scores will differ among subjects in the experiment, whether or not psychotherapy improves self-esteem.

*Beginning with Chapter 2, **descriptive statistics** will provide tools, such as tables, graphs, and averages, that help you describe and organize the inevitable variability among observations. For example, self-esteem scores (on a scale of 0 to 50) for a group of college students might approximate a bell-shaped curve with an average score of 32 and a range of scores from 18 to 49.*

*Beginning with Chapter 8, **inferential statistics** will supply powerful concepts that, by adjusting for the pervasive effects of variability, permit you to generalize beyond limited sets of observations. For example, inferential statistics might help us decide whether—after an adjustment has been made for background variability (or chance)—an observed improvement in self-esteem scores can be attributed to psychotherapy rather than to chance.*

Chapter 1 provides an overview of both descriptive and inferential statistics, and it also introduces a number of terms—some from statistics and some from math and research methods—with which you already may have some familiarity. These terms will clarify a number of important distinctions that will aid your progress through the book.

1.1 WHY STUDY STATISTICS?

You're probably taking a statistics course because it's required, and your feelings about it may be more negative than positive. Let's explore some of the reasons why you should study statistics. For instance, recent issues of a daily newspaper carried these items:

- The annual earnings of college graduates exceed, *on average,* those of high school graduates by $30,000.
- On the basis of existing research, there is *no evidence of a relationship* between family size and the scores of adolescents on a test of psychological adjustment.
- Heavy users of tobacco suffer *significantly* more respiratory ailments than do nonusers.

Having learned some statistics, you'll not stumble over the italicized phrases. Nor, as you continue reading, will you hesitate to probe for clarification by asking, "Which *average* shows higher annual earnings?" or "What constitutes a *lack of evidence* about a relationship?" or "How many more is *significantly more* respiratory ailments?"

A statistical background is indispensable in understanding research reports within your special area of interest. Statistical references punctuate the results sections of most research reports. Often expressed with parenthetical brevity, these references provide statistical support for the researcher's conclusions:

- Subjects who engage in daily exercise score higher on tests of self-esteem than do subjects who do not exercise [$p < .05$].
- Highly anxious students are perceived by others as less attractive than nonanxious students [$t\,(48) = 3.21, p < .01, d = .42$].
- Attitudes toward extramarital sex are dependent on socioeconomic status [$\chi^2\,(4, n = 185) = 11.49, p < .05, \phi_c^2 = .03$].

Having learned some statistics, you will be able to decipher the meaning of these symbols and consequently read these reports more intelligently.

Sometime in the future—possibly sooner than you think—you might want to plan a statistical analysis for a research project of your own. Having learned some statistics, you'll be able to plan the statistical analysis for modest projects involving straightforward research questions. If your project requires more advanced statistical analysis, you'll know enough to consult someone with more training in statistics. Once you begin to understand basic statistical concepts, you will discover that, with some guidance, your own efforts often will enable you to use and interpret more advanced statistical analysis required by your research.

1.2 WHAT IS STATISTICS?

It is difficult to imagine, even as a fantasy exercise, a world where there is no variability—where, for example, everyone has the same physical characteristics, intelligence, attitudes, etc. Knowing that one person is 70 inches tall, and has an intelligence quotient (IQ) of 125 and a favorable attitude toward capital punishment, we could immediately conclude that everyone else also has these characteristics. This mind-numbing world would have little to recommend it, other than that there would be no need for the field of statistics (and a few of us probably would be looking for work).

Descriptive Statistics

Descriptive Statistics

The area of statistics concerned with organizing and summarizing the inevitable variability in collections of actual observations or scores.

Statistics exists because of the prevalence of variability in the real world. In its simplest form, known as **descriptive statistics,** *statistics provides us with tools—tables, graphs, averages, ranges, correlations—for organizing and summarizing the inevitable variability in collections of actual observations or scores.* Examples are:

1. a tabular listing, ranked from most to least, of the total number of romantic affairs during college reported anonymously by each member of your stat class;

2. a graph showing the annual change in global temperature during the last 30 years;

3. a report that describes the average difference in grade point average (GPA) between college students who regularly drink alcoholic beverages and those who don't.

Inferential Statistics

Inferential Statistics

The area of statistics that provides tools for generalizing beyond collections of actual observations.

Statistics also provides tools—a variety of tests and estimates—for generalizing beyond collections of actual observations. This more advanced area is known as **inferential statistics.** Tools from inferential statistics permit us to use a relatively small collection of actual observations to evaluate, for example:

1. a pollster's claim that an overwhelming majority of all U.S. voters favor stronger gun control laws;

2. a researcher's hypothesis that, on average, meditators report fewer headaches than do nonmeditators;

3. an assertion about the relationship between job satisfaction and overall happiness.

In this book, you will encounter the most essential tools of descriptive statistics (Part 1), beginning with Chapter 2, and those of inferential statistics (Part 2), beginning with Chapter 8.

Progress Check *1.1 Indicate whether each of the following statements typifies descriptive statistics (because it describes sets of actual observations) or inferential statistics (because it generalizes beyond sets of actual observations).

(a) Students in my statistics class are, on average, 20 years old.

(b) The population of the world is approaching 7 billion (that is, 7,000,000,000 or 1 million multiplied by 7000).

(c) Either four or eight years have been the most frequent terms of office actually served by U.S. presidents.

(d) Sixty-four percent of all college students favor right-to-abortion laws.
Answers on page 488.

1.3 MORE ABOUT INFERENTIAL STATISTICS
Populations and Samples

Population

Any complete collection of observations or potential observations.

Sample

Any smaller collection of actual observations from a population.

Inferential statistics is concerned with generalizing beyond sets of actual observations, that is, with generalizing from a sample to a population. In statistics, a **population** refers to *any complete collection of observations or potential observations,* while a **sample** refers to *any smaller collection of actual observations drawn from a population.* In everyday life, populations often are viewed as collections of real objects (people, whales, automobiles), while in statistics, populations may be viewed more abstractly as collections of properties or measurements (the ethnic backgrounds of people, life spans of whales, gas mileage of automobiles).

Depending on your perspective, a given set of observations can be either a population or a sample. For instance, the weights reported by 53 male statistics students in Table 1.1 can be viewed either as a population, because you are concerned about exceeding the load-bearing capacity of an excursion boat (chartered by the 53 students to celebrate successfully completing their stat class!), or as a sample from a population because you wish to generalize to the weights of *all* male statistics students or *all* male college students.

Ordinarily, populations are quite large and exist only as potential observations (for example, the *potential* scores of all U.S. college students on a test that measures anxiety). On the other hand, samples are relatively small and exist as actual observations (the *actual* scores of 100 college students on the test for anxiety). When using a sample (100 actual scores) to generalize to a population (millions of potential scores), it is important that the sample represent the population; otherwise, any generalization might be erroneous. Although conveniently accessible, the anxiety test scores for the 100 students in stat classes at your college probably would not be representative of the scores for all students. If you think about it, these 100 stat students might tend to have either higher or lower

Table 1.1 QUANTITATIVE DATA: WEIGHTS (IN POUNDS) OF MALE STATISTICS STUDENTS							
160	168	133	170	150	165	158	165
193	169	245	160	152	190	179	157
226	160	170	180	150	156	190	156
157	163	152	158	225	135	165	135
180	172	160	170	145	185	152	
205	151	220	166	152	159	156	
165	157	190	206	172	175	154	

anxiety scores than those in the target population for numerous reasons including, for instance, the fact that the 100 students are mostly psychology majors enrolled in a required stat class at your particular college.

Random Sampling (Surveys)

Random Sampling

A procedure designed to ensure that each potential observation in the population has an equal chance of being selected in a survey.

Whenever possible, a sample should be randomly selected from a population in order to increase the likelihood that the sample accurately represents the population. **Random sampling** *is a procedure designed to ensure that each potential observation in the population has an equal chance of being selected in a survey.* Classic examples of random samples are a state lottery where each number from 00 to 99 in the population has an equal chance of being selected as one of the five winning numbers or a nationwide opinion survey in which each telephone number has an equal chance of being selected as a result of a series of random selections, beginning with a three-digit area code and ending with a specific seven-digit telephone number.

Random sampling can be very difficult when a population lacks structure (for example, all persons currently in psychotherapy) or specific boundaries (all volunteers who could conceivably participate in an experiment). In this case, a random sample becomes an ideal that can only be approximated—always with an effort to remove obvious biases that might cause the sample to misrepresent the population. For example, lacking the resources to sample randomly the target population of all U.S. college students, you might obtain scores by randomly selecting the 100 students, not just from stat classes at your college but also from one or more college directories, possibly using some of the more elaborate techniques described in Chapter 8. Insofar as your sample only approximates a true random sample, any resulting generalizations should be qualified. For example, if the 100 students were randomly selected only from several public colleges in Northern California, this fact should be noted, and any generalizations to all college students in the United States would be both provisional and open to criticism.

Random Assignment (Experiments)

Estimating the average anxiety score for all college students probably would not generate much interest. Instead, we might be interested in determining whether relaxation training causes, on average, a reduction in anxiety scores between two groups of otherwise similar college students. Even if relaxation training has no effect on anxiety scores, we would expect average scores for the two groups to differ because of the inevitable variability between groups. The question becomes: How should we interpret the apparent difference between the treatment group and the control group? Once variability has been taken into account, should the difference be viewed as real (and attributable to relaxation training) or as transitory (and merely attributable to variability or chance)?

Random Assignment

A procedure designed to ensure that each person has an equal chance of being assigned to any group in an experiment.

College students in the relaxation experiment probably are not a random sample from any intact population of interest, but rather a *convenience sample* consisting of volunteers from a limited pool of students fulfilling a course requirement. Accordingly, our focus shifts from random sampling to the random assignment of volunteers to the two groups. **Random assignment** *signifies that each person has an equal chance of being assigned to any group in an experiment.* Using procedures described in Chapter 8, random assignment should be employed whenever possible. Because chance dictates the membership of both groups, not only does random assignment minimize any biases that might favor one group or another, it also serves as a basis for estimating the role of variability in any observed result. Random assignment allows us to evaluate any finding, such as the actual average difference between two groups, to determine whether this difference is larger than expected just by chance, once variability is taken into account. In other words, it permits us to generalize beyond mere appearances and determine whether the average difference merits further attention because it *probably is real* or whether it should be ignored because it *can be attributed to variability or chance.*

Overview: Surveys and Experiments

Figure 1.1 compares surveys and experiments. Based on random samples from populations, surveys permit generalizations from samples back to populations. Based on the random assignment of volunteers to groups, experiments permit decisions about whether differences between groups are real or merely transitory.

PROGRESS CHECK *1.2 Indicate whether each of the following terms is associated primarily with a survey (S) or an experiment (E).

(a) random assignment

(b) representative

(c) generalization to the population

(d) control group

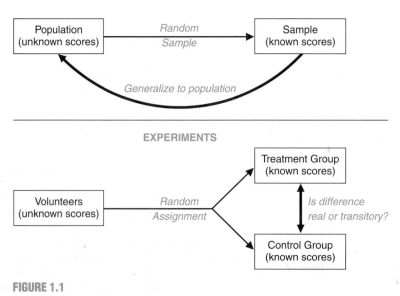

FIGURE 1.1
Overview: surveys and experiments.

(e) real difference

(f) random selection

(g) convenience sample

(h) volunteers

Answers on page 488.

1.4 THREE TYPES OF DATA

Data

A collection of observations or scores in a survey or an experiment

Qualitative Data

A set of observations where any single observation is a word, letter, or numerical code that represents a class or category.

Ranked Data

A set of observations where any single observation is a number that indicates relative standing.

Quantitative Data

A set of observations where any single observation is a number that represents an amount or a count.

Any statistical analysis is performed on **data,** *a collection of actual observations or scores in a survey or an experiment.*

The precise form of a statistical analysis often depends on whether data are qualitative, ranked, or quantitative.

Generally, **qualitative data** consist of words (Yes or No), letters (Y or N), or numerical codes (0 or 1) that represent a class or category. **Ranked data** consist of numbers (1st, 2nd, . . . 40th place) that represent relative standing within a group. **Quantitative data** consist of numbers (weights of 238, 170, . . . 185 lbs) that represent an amount or a count. To determine the type of data, focus on a single observation in any collection of observations. For example, the weights reported by 53 male students in Table 1.1 are quantitative data, since any single observation, such as 160 lbs, represents an amount of weight. If the weights in Table 1.1 had been replaced with ranks, beginning with a rank of 1 for the lightest weight of 133 lbs and ending with a rank of 53 for the heaviest weight of 245 lbs, these numbers would have been ranked data, since any single observation represents not an amount, but only relative standing within the group of 53 students. Finally, the Y and N replies of students in Table 1.2 are qualitative data, since any single observation is a letter that represents a class of replies.

Table 1.2
QUALITATIVE DATA: "HAVE YOU A PROFILE ON FACEBOOK?" YES (Y) OR NO (N) REPLIES OF STATISTICS STUDENTS

Y	Y	Y	N	N	Y	Y	Y
Y	Y	Y	N	N	Y	Y	Y
N	Y	N	Y	Y	Y	Y	Y
Y	Y	N	Y	N	Y	N	Y
Y	N	Y	N	N	Y	Y	Y
Y	Y	N	Y	Y	Y	Y	Y
N	N	N	N	Y	N	N	Y
Y	Y	Y	Y	Y	N	Y	N
Y	Y	Y	Y	N	N	Y	Y
N	Y	N	N	Y	Y	Y	Y
	Y	Y	N				

Progress Check *1.3 Indicate whether each of the following terms is *qualitative* (because it's a word, letter, or numerical code representing a class or category); *ranked* (because it's a number representing relative standing); or *quantitative* (because it's a number representing an amount or a count).

(a) ethnic group

(b) age

(c) family size

(d) academic major

(e) sexual preference

(f) IQ score

(g) net worth (dollars)

(h) third-place finish

(i) gender

(j) temperature

Answers on page 488.

1.5 LEVELS OF MEASUREMENT

Learned years ago in grade school, the abstract statement that $2 + 2 = 4$ qualifies as one of life's everyday certainties, along with taxes and death. However, not all numbers have the same interpretation. For instance, it wouldn't make sense to find the sum of two Social Security numbers or to claim that, when viewed as indicators of academic achievement, two GPAs of 2.0 equal a GPA of 4.0. To clarify further the differences among the three types of data, let's introduce the notion of level of measurement. Looming behind any data, the **level of measurement** *specifies the extent to which a number (or word or letter) actually represents some attribute and, therefore, has implications for the appropriateness of various arithmetic operations and statistical procedures.*

For our purposes, there are three levels of measurement—nominal, ordinal, and interval/ratio—and these levels are paired with qualitative, ranked, and quantitative data, respectively. The properties of these levels—and the usefulness of their associated numbers—vary from nominal, the simplest level with only one property, to interval/ratio, the most complex level with four properties. Progressively more complex levels contain all properties of simpler levels, plus one or two new properties.

> *Level of Measurement*
>
> *Specifies the extent to which a number (or word or letter) actually represents some attribute and, therefore, has implications for the appropriateness of various arithmetic operations and statistical procedures.*

More complex levels of measurement are associated with numbers that, because they better represent attributes, permit a wider variety of arithmetic operations and statistical procedures.

Qualitative Data and Nominal Measurement

If people are classified as either male or female (or coded as 1 or 2), the data are qualitative and measurement is nominal. *The single property of* **nominal measurement** *is classification*—that is, sorting observations into different classes or categories. Words, letters, or numerical codes reflect only differences in kind, not differences in amount. Examples of nominal measurement include classifying mood disorders as manic, bipolar, or depressive; sexual preferences as heterosexual, homosexual, bisexual, or nonsexual; and attitudes toward stricter pollution controls as favor, oppose, or undecided.

A distinctive feature of nominal measurement is its bare-bones representation of any attribute. For instance, a student is either male or female. Even with the introduction of arbitrary numerical codes, such as 1 for male, and 2 for female, it would never be appropriate to claim that, because female is 2 and male is 1, females have twice as much gender as males. Similarly, calculating an average with these numbers would be meaningless. Because of these limitations, only a few sections of this book and Chapter 19 are dedicated exclusively to an analysis of qualitative data with nominal measurement.

Ranked Data and Ordinal Measurement

When any single number indicates only *relative standing,* such as first, second, or tenth place in a horse race or in a class of graduating seniors, the data are *ranked* and the level of measurement is ordinal. *The distinctive property of* **ordinal measurement** *is order*. Comparatively speaking, a first-place finish reflects the fastest finish in a horse race or the highest GPA among graduating seniors. Although first place in a horse race indicates a *faster* finish than second place, we don't know *how much* faster.

Since ordinal measurement fails to reflect the actual distance between adjacent ranks, simple arithmetic operations with ranks are inappropriate. For example, it's inappropriate to conclude that the arithmetic mean of ranks 1 and 3 equals rank 2, since this assumes that the actual distance between ranks 1 and 2 equals the distance between ranks 2 and 3. Instead, these distances might be very different. For example, rank 2 might be virtually tied with either rank 1 or rank 3. Only a few sections of this book and Chapter 20 are dedicated exclusively to an analysis of ranked data with ordinal measurement.*

Quantitative Data and Interval/Ratio Measurement

Often the products of familiar measuring devices, such as rulers, clocks, or meters, *the distinctive properties of* **interval/ratio measurement** *are equal intervals and a true zero*. Weighing yourself on a bathroom scale qualifies as interval/ratio measurement. *Equal intervals* imply that hefting a 10-lb weight

---

*Strictly speaking, ordinal measurement also can be associated with qualitative data whose classes are ordered. Examples of *ordered* qualitative data include the classification of skilled workers as master craftsman, journeyman, or apprentice; socioeconomic status as low, middle, or high; and academic grades as A, B, C, D, or F. It's worth distinguishing between qualitative data with nominal and ordinal measurement because, as described in Chapters 3 and 4, a few extra statistical procedures are available for ordered qualitative data.

while on the bathroom scale always registers your actual weight plus 10 lbs. Equal intervals imply that the difference between 120 and 130 lbs represents an *amount* of weight equal to the difference between 130 and 140 lbs, and it's appropriate to describe one person's weight as a certain amount greater than another's.

A *true zero* signifies that the bathroom scale registers 0 when not in use, that is, when weight is completely absent. Since the bathroom scale possesses a true zero, numerical readings reflect the *total amount* of a person's weight, and it's appropriate to describe one person's weight as a certain ratio of another's. It can be said that the weight of a 140-lb person is twice that of a 70-lb person.

In the absence of a true zero, numbers—much like the exposed tips of icebergs—fail to reflect the total amount being measured. For example, a reading of 0 on the Fahrenheit temperature scale does not reflect the complete absence of heat, that is, the absence of any molecular motion. In fact, true zero equals $-459.4°F$ on this scale. It would be inappropriate, therefore, to claim that 80°F is twice as hot as 40°F. An appropriate claim could be salvaged by adding 459.4°F to each of these numbers: 80° becomes 539.4° and 40° becomes 499.4°. Clearly, 539.4°F is not twice as hot as 499.4°F.

Interval/ratio measurement appears in the behavioral and social sciences as, for example, bar-press rates of rats in Skinner boxes; the minutes of dream-friendly rapid eye movement (REM) sleep among participants in a sleep-deprivation experiment; and the total number of eye contacts during verbal disputes between romantically involved couples Thanks to the considerable amount of information conveyed by each observation, interval/ratio measurement permits meaningful arithmetic operations, such as calculating arithmetic means, as well as the many statistical procedures for quantitative data described in this book.

Measurement of Nonphysical Characteristics

When numbers represent nonphysical characteristics, such as intellectual aptitude, psychopathic tendency, or emotional maturity, the attainment of interval/ratio measurement often is questionable. For example, there is no external standard (such as the 10-lb weight) to demonstrate that the addition of a fixed amount of intellectual aptitude always produces an equal increase in IQ scores (equal intervals). There also is no instrument (such as the unoccupied bathroom scale) that registers an IQ score of 0 when intellectual aptitude is completely absent (true zero).

In the absence of equal intervals, it would be inappropriate to claim that the difference between IQ scores of 120 and 130 represents the same amount of intellectual aptitude as the difference between IQ scores of 130 and 140. Likewise, in the absence of a true zero, it would be inappropriate to claim that an IQ score of 140 represents twice as much intellectual aptitude as an IQ score of 70.

Other interpretations are possible. One possibility is to treat IQ scores as attaining only ordinal measurement—that is, for example, a score of 140 represents more intellectual aptitude than a score of 130—without specifying the actual size of this difference. This strict interpretation would greatly restrict the number of statistical procedures for use with behavioral and social data. A looser (and much more common) interpretation, adopted in this book, assumes that, although lacking a true zero, IQ scores provide a crude measure of corresponding differences in intellectual aptitude (equal intervals). Thus, the difference between IQ scores of 120 and 130 represents a *roughly similar* amount of intellectual aptitude as the difference between scores of 130 and 140.

Insofar as numerical measures of nonphysical characteristics approximate interval measurement, they receive the same statistical treatment as numerical measures of physical characteristics. In other words, these measures support the arithmetic operations and statistical tools appropriate for quantitative data.

At this point, you might wish that a person could be injected with ten points of intellectual aptitude (or psychopathic tendency or emotional maturity) as a first step toward an IQ scale with equal intervals and a true zero. Lacking this alternative, however, train yourself to look at numbers as products of measurement and to temper your numerical claims accordingly—particularly when numerical data only seem to approximate interval measurement.

Overview: Types of Data and Levels of Measurement

Refer to **Figure 1.2** while reading this paragraph. Given some set of observations, decide whether any single observation qualifies as a word or as a number. If it is a word (or letter or numerical code), the data are qualitative and the level of measurement is nominal. Arithmetic operations are meaningless and statistical procedures are limited. On the other hand, if the observation is a number, the data are either ranked or quantitative, depending on whether numbers represent only relative standing or an amount/count. If the data are ranked, the level of measurement is ordinal and, as with qualitative data, arithmetic operations and statistical procedures are limited. If the data are quantitative, the level of measurement is interval/ratio—or approximately interval when numbers represent

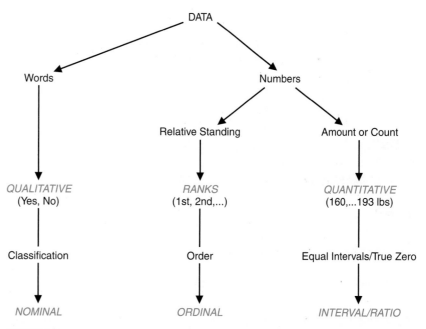

FIGURE 1.2

Overview: types of data and levels of measurement.

nonphysical characteristics—and a full range of arithmetic operations and statistical procedures are available.

Progress Check *1.4 Indicate the level of measurement—*nominal, ordinal,* or *interval/ratio*—attained by the following sets of observations or data. Whenever appropriate, indicate that measurement is only *approximately interval.*

NOTE: Always assign the highest permissible level of measurement to a given set of observations. For example, a list of annual incomes should be designated as interval/ratio because a $1000 difference always signifies the same amount of income (equal intervals) and because $0 signifies the complete absence of income. It would be wrong to describe annual income as ordinal data even though different incomes always can be ranked as more or less (order), or as nominal data even though different incomes always reflect different classes (classification).

(a) height

(b) religious affiliation

(c) score for psychopathic tendency

(d) years of education

(e) military rank

(f) vocational goal

(g) GPA

(h) marital status

      Answers on page 488.

1.6 TYPES OF VARIABLES

General Definition

    Another helpful distinction is based on different types of variables. A **variable** *is a characteristic or property that can take on different values.* Accordingly, the weights in Table 1.1 can be described not only as quantitative data but also as observations for a quantitative variable, since the various weights take on different numerical values. By the same token, the replies in Table 1.2 can be described as observations for a qualitative variable, since the replies to the Facebook profile question take on different values of either Yes or No. Given this perspective, any *single* observation in Tables 1.1 or 1.2 can be described as a **constant,** since *it takes on only one value.*

Discrete and Continuous Variables

    Quantitative variables can be further distinguished in terms of whether they are discrete or continuous. A **discrete variable** *consists of isolated numbers separated by gaps.* Examples include most counts, such as the number of children in a family (1, 2, 3, etc., but never $1\frac{1}{2}$ in spite of how you might occasionally

Variable

A characteristic or property that can take on different values.

Constant

A characteristic or property that can take on only one value.

Discrete Variable

A variable that consists of isolated numbers separated by gaps.

feel about a sibling); the number of foreign countries you have visited; and the current size of the U.S. population. A **continuous variable** *consists of numbers whose values, at least in theory, have no restrictions.* Examples include amounts, such as weights of male statistics students; durations, such as the reaction times of grade school children to a fire alarm; and standardized test scores, such as those on the Scholastic Aptitude Test (SAT).

Continuous Variable

A variable that consists of numbers whose values, at least in theory, have no restrictions.

Approximate Numbers

Numbers that are rounded off, as is always the case with values for continuous variables!

Approximate Numbers

In theory, values for continuous variables can be carried out infinitely far. Someone's weight, in pounds, might be 140.01438, and so on, to infinity! Practical considerations require that values for continuous variables be rounded off. *Whenever values are rounded off, as is always the case with actual values for continuous variables, the resulting numbers are* **approximate,** *never exact.* For example, the weights of the male statistics students in Table 1.1 are approximate because they have been rounded to the nearest pound. A student whose weight is listed as 150 lbs could actually weigh between 149.5 and 150.5 lbs (or between these two numbers with additional zeros, such as 149.500 and 150.500, reflecting the degree of precision of the weighing instrument). In effect, any value for a continuous variable, such as 150 lbs, must be identified with a range of values from 149.5 to 150.5 rather than with a solitary value. As will be seen, this property of continuous variables has a number of repercussions, including the selection of graphs in Chapter 2 and the types of meaningful questions about normal distributions in Chapter 5.

Because of rounding-off procedures, gaps appear among values for continuous variables. For example, because weights are rounded to the nearest pound, no male statistics student in Table 1.1 has a listed weight between 150 and 151 lbs. These gaps are more apparent than real; they are superimposed on a continuous variable by our need to deal with finite (and, therefore, approximate) numbers.

Progress Check *1.5 Indicate whether the following quantitative observations are discrete or continuous.

(a) litter of mice

(b) cooking time for pasta

(c) parole violations by convicted felons

(d) IQ

(e) age

(f) population of your hometown

(g) speed of a jetliner

Answers on page 488.

Independent and Dependent Variables

Unlike the simple studies that produced the data in Tables 1.1 and 1.2, most studies raise questions about the presence or absence of a relationship between two (or more) variables. For example, a psychologist might wish to investigate whether couples who undergo special training in "active listening" tend to have fewer communication breakdowns than do couples who undergo no special training. To study this, the psychologist may expose couples to two different conditions by randomly assigning them either to a treatment group that receives special training in active listening or to a control group that receives no special training. Such studies are referred to as experiments. *An* **experiment** *is a study in which the investigator decides who receives the special treatment.* When well designed, experiments yield the most informative and unambiguous conclusions about cause-effect relationships.

Independent Variable

Since training is assumed to influence communication, it is an independent variable. *In an experiment, an* **independent variable** *is the treatment manipulated by the investigator.*

The impartial creation of distinct groups, which differ only in terms of the independent variable, has a most desirable consequence. Once the data have been collected, any difference between the groups (that survives a statistical analysis, as described in Part 2 of the book) can be interpreted as being *caused* by the independent variable. If, for instance, a difference appears in favor of the active-listening group, the psychologist can conclude that training in active listening causes fewer communication breakdowns between couples. Having observed this relationship, the psychologist can expect that, if new couples were trained in active listening, fewer breakdowns in communication would occur.

Dependent Variable

To test whether training influences communication, the psychologist counts the number of communication breakdowns between each couple, as revealed by inappropriate replies, aggressive comments, verbal interruptions, etc., while discussing a conflict-provoking topic, such as whether it is acceptable to be intimate with a third person. *When a variable is believed to have been influenced by the independent variable, it is called a* **dependent variable.** In an experimental setting, the dependent variable is measured, counted, or recorded by the investigator.

Unlike the independent variable, the dependent variable isn't manipulated by the investigator. Instead, it represents an outcome: the data produced by the experiment. Accordingly, the values that appear for the dependent variable cannot be specified in advance. Although the psychologist suspects that couples with special training will tend to show fewer subsequent communication breakdowns, he or she has to wait to see precisely how many breakdowns will be observed for each couple.

Independent or Dependent Variable?

With just a little practice, you should be able to identify these two types of variables. In an experiment, what is being manipulated by the investigator at the outset and, therefore, qualifies as the independent variable? What is measured, counted, or recorded by the investigator at the completion of the study and, therefore, qualifies as the dependent variable? Once these two variables have been identified, they can be used to describe the problem posed by the

Experiment

A study in which the investigator decides who receives the special treatment.

Independent Variable

The treatment manipulated by the investigator in an experiment.

Dependent Variable

A variable that is believed to have been influenced by the independent variable.

study; that is, does the independent variable cause a change in the dependent variable?*

Observational Studies

Instead of undertaking an experiment, an investigator might simply observe the relation between two variables. For example, a sociologist might collect paired measures of poverty level and crime rate for each individual in some group. If a statistical analysis reveals that these two variables are related or correlated, then, given some person's poverty level, the sociologist can better predict that person's crime rate *or vice versa*. Having established the existence of this relationship, however, the sociologist can only speculate about cause and effect. Poverty might cause crime or vice versa. On the other hand, both poverty and crime might be caused by one or some combination of more basic variables, such as inadequate education, racial discrimination, unstable family environment, and so on. Such studies are often referred to as observational studies. *An* **observational study** *focuses on detecting relationships between variables not manipulated by the investigator,* and it yields less clear-cut conclusions about cause-effect relationships than does an experiment.

To detect any relationship between active listening and fewer breakdowns in communication, our psychologist could have conducted an observational study rather than an experiment. In this case, he or she would have made no effort to manipulate active-listening skills by assigning couples to special training sessions. Instead, the psychologist might have used a preliminary interview to assign an active-listening score to each couple. Subsequently, our psychologist would have obtained a count of the number of communication breakdowns for each couple during the conflict-resolution session. Now data for both variables would have been collected (or observed) by the psychologist—and the cause-effect basis of any relationship would be speculative. For example, couples already possessing high active-listening scores might also tend to be more seriously committed to each other, and this more serious commitment itself might cause both the higher active-listening score and fewer breakdowns in communication. In this case, any special training in active listening, without regard to the existing degree of a couple's commitment, would not reduce the number of breakdowns in communication.

Confounding Variable

Whenever groups differ not just because of the independent variable but also because some uncontrolled variable co-varies with the independent variable, any conclusion about a cause-effect relationship is suspect. If, instead of random assignment, each couple in an experiment is free to choose whether to undergo special training in active listening or to be in the less demanding control group, any conclusion must be qualified. A difference between groups might be due not to the independent variable but to a confounding variable. For instance, couples

---

Observational Study

A study that focuses on detecting relationships between variables not manipulated by the investigator.

---

*For the present example, note that the independent variable (type of training) is qualitative, with nominal measurement, while the dependent variable (number of communication breakdowns) is quantitative. Insofar as the number of communication breakdowns is used to indicate the quality of communication between couples, its level of measurement is approximately interval.

willing to devote extra effort to special training might already possess a deeper commitment that co-varies with more active-listening skills. *An uncontrolled variable that compromises the interpretation of a study is known as a* **confounding variable.** You can avoid confounding variables, as in the present case, by assigning subjects randomly to the various groups in the experiment and also by standardizing all experimental conditions, other than the independent variable, for subjects in both groups.

Sometimes a confounding variable occurs because it's impossible to assign subjects randomly to different conditions. For instance, if we're interested in possible differences in active-listening skills between males and females, we can't assign the subject's gender randomly. Consequently, any difference between these two pre-existing groups must be interpreted cautiously. For example, if females, on average, are better listeners than males, this difference could be caused by confounding variables that co-vary with gender, such as pre-existing disparities in active-listening skills attributable not merely to gender, but also to cultural stereotypes, social training, vocational interests, academic majors, and so on.

Overview: Two Active-Listening Studies

Figure 1.3 summarizes the active-listening study when viewed as an experiment and as an observational study. An experiment permits a decision about whether or not the average difference between treatment and control groups is real. An observational study permits a decision about whether or not the variables are related or correlated.

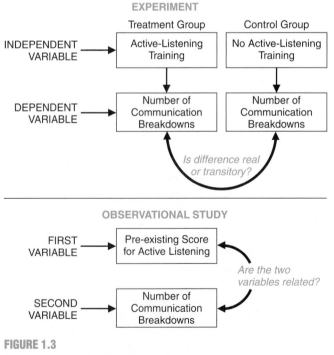

FIGURE 1.3
Overview: two active-listening studies

Progress Check *1.6 For each of the listed studies, indicate whether it is an *experiment* or an *observational study*. If it is an experiment, identify the independent variable and note any possible confounding variables.

(a) years of education and annual income

(b) prescribed hours of sleep deprivation and subsequent amount of REM (dream) sleep

(c) weight loss among obese males who choose to participate either in a weight-loss program or a self-esteem enhancement program

(d) estimated study hours and subsequent test score

(e) recidivism among substance abusers assigned randomly to different rehabilitation programs

(f) subsequent GPAs of college applicants who, as the result of a housing lottery, live either on campus or off campus

Answers on page 488.

1.7 HOW TO USE THIS BOOK

This book contains a number of features that will help your study of statistics. Each chapter begins with a preview and ends with a summary, a list of important terms, and, whenever appropriate, a list of key equations. Use these aids to orient yourself before reading a new chapter and to facilitate your review of previous chapters. Frequent reviews are desirable, since statistics is cumulative, with earlier topics forming the basis for later topics. For easy reference, important terms are defined in the margins. Progress checks appear within chapters, and review questions appear at the end of each chapter. Do not shy away from the progress checks or review questions; they will clarify and expand your understanding as well as improve your ability to work with statistics. Appendix B supplies answers to all questions marked with asterisks, including all progress checks and selected review questions.

The math review in Appendix A summarizes most of the basic math symbols and operations used throughout this book. If you are anxious about your math background—and almost everyone is—check Appendix A. Be assured that no special math background is required. If you can add, subtract, multiply, and divide, you can learn (or relearn) the simple math described in Appendix A. If this material looks unfamiliar, it would be a good idea to study Appendix A within the next few weeks.

An electronic version of a student workbook, prepared by Beverly Dretzke of the Center for Applied Research and Educational Improvement, University of Minnesota, Minneapolis, also accompanies the text. Self-paced and self-correcting, it supplies additional problems, questions, and tests that supplement the text. You can access this material by clicking on the *Student Study Guide* in the Student Companion Site at http://www.wiley.com/college/witte.

The Web site at http://www.wiley.com/college/witte also supplies links to interesting statistical sites on the Internet, including many with interactive demonstrations of basic concepts and procedures. References to these sites, designated as an *Internet Demonstration* or an *Internet Site,* are scattered throughout the book. The Web site for the book also provides explanatory comments to ease the transition to these sites. If you have access to the Internet, do explore these sites; they are enlightening and entertaining. They can, however, be ignored—whether by choice or necessity—without destroying the continuity of the book.

We cannot resist ending this chapter with a personal note, as well as a few suggestions based on findings from the learning laboratory. A dear relative lent this book to an elderly neighbor, who not only praised it, saying that he wished he had had such a stat text many years ago while he was a student at the University of Pittsburgh, but subsequently died with the book still open next to his bed. Upon being informed of this, the first author's wife commented, "I wonder which chapter killed him." In all good conscience, therefore, we cannot recommend this book for casual bedside reading if you are more than 85 years old. Otherwise, read it anywhere or anytime. Seriously, not only read assigned material before class, but also reread it as soon as possible after class to maximize the retention of newly learned material. In the same vein, end reading sessions with active rehearsal: Close the book and attempt to re-create mentally, in an orderly fashion and with little or no peeking, the material that you have just read. With this effort, you should find the remaining chapters accessible and statistics to be both understandable and useful.

Summary

Statistics exists because of the prevalence of variability in the real world. It consists of two main subdivisions: descriptive statistics, which is concerned with organizing and summarizing information for sets of actual observations, and inferential statistics, which is concerned with generalizing beyond sets of actual observations, that is, generalizing from a sample to a population.

Ordinarily, populations are quite large and exist only as potential observations, while samples are relatively small and exist as actual observations. Random samples increase the likelihood that the sample accurately represents the population because all potential observations in the population have an equal chance of being in the random sample.

When populations consist of only limited pools of volunteers, as in many investigations, the focus shifts from random samples to random assignment. Random assignment ensures that each volunteer has an equal chance of occupying any group in the investigation. Not only does random assignment minimize any initial biases that might favor one group over another, but it also allows us to determine whether an observed difference between groups probably is real or merely due to chance variability.

There are three types of data—qualitative, ranked, and quantitative—which are paired with three levels of measurement—nominal, ordinal, and interval/ratio, respectively. Qualitative data consist of words, letters, or codes that represent only classes with nominal measurement. Ranked data consist of numbers that represent relative standing with ordinal measurement. Quantitative data consist of numbers that represent an amount or a count with interval/ratio measurement.

Distinctive properties of the three levels of measurement are classification (nominal), order (ordinal), and equal intervals and true zero (interval/ratio).

Shifts to more complex levels of measurement permit a wider variety of arithmetic operations and statistical procedures.

Even though the numerical measurement of various nonphysical characteristics fails to attain an interval/ratio level, the resulting data usually are treated as approximating interval measurement. The limitations of these data should not, however, be ignored completely when making numerical claims.

It is helpful to distinguish between discrete and continuous variables. Discrete variables consist of isolated numbers separated by gaps, while continuous variables consist of numbers whose values, at least in theory, have no restrictions. In practice, values of continuous variables always are rounded off and, therefore, are approximate numbers.

It is also helpful to distinguish between independent and dependent variables. In experiments, independent variables are manipulated by the investigator, while dependent variables are outcomes measured, counted, or recorded by the investigator. If well designed, experiments yield the most clear-cut information about cause-effect relationships. Investigators may also undertake observational studies in which variables are observed without any intervention. Observational studies yield less clear-cut information about cause-effect relationships. Both types of studies can be weakened by confounding variables.

Important Terms

Descriptive statistics	**Inferential statistics**
Population	**Sample**
Random sampling	**Random assignment**
Data	**Qualitative data**
Ranked data	**Quantitative data**
Level of measurement	**Nominal measurement**
Ordinal measurement	**Interval/ratio measurement**
Variable	**Constant**
Discrete variable	**Continuous variable**
Independent variable	**Dependent variable**
Experiment	**Observational study**
Confounding variable	

REVIEW QUESTIONS

1.7 Indicate whether each of the following statements typifies *descriptive statistics* (because it describes sets of actual observations) or *inferential statistics* (because it generalizes beyond sets of actual observations).

(a) On the basis of a survey conducted by the Bureau of Labor Statistics, it is estimated that 6.1 percent of the entire workforce was unemployed during the last month.

(b)   During a recent semester, the ages of students at my college ranged from 16 to 75 years.

(c)   Recent research suggests that an aspirin every other day reduces the chance of heart attacks (by almost 50 percent) in middle-aged men.

(d)   Joe's GPA has hovered near 3.5 throughout college.

(e)   There is some evidence that any form of frustration—whether physical, social, economic, or political—always leads to some form of aggression by the frustrated person.

(f)   According to tests conducted by the Environmental Protection Agency, the 2008 Toyota Prius should average approximately 46 miles per gallon for combined city/highway travel.

(g)   On average, Babe Ruth hit 32 home runs during each season of his major league baseball career.

(h)   Research on learning suggests that active rehearsal increases the retention of newly read material; therefore, immediately after reading a chapter in this book, you should close the book and try to organize the new material.

(i)   Children with no siblings tend to be more adult-oriented than children with one or more siblings.

1.8   Indicate whether each of the following studies is an experiment or an observational study. If it is an experiment, identify the independent variable and note any possible confounding variables.

(a)   A psychologist uses chimpanzees to test the notion that more crowded living conditions trigger aggressive behavior. Chimps are placed, according to an impartial assignment rule, in cages with either one, several, or many other chimps. Subsequently, during a standard observation period, each chimp is assigned a score based on its aggressive behavior toward a chimplike stuffed doll.

(b)   An investigator wishes to test whether, when compared with recognized scientists, recognized artists tend to be born under different astrological signs.

(c)   To determine whether there is a relationship between the sexual codes of primitive tribes and their behavior toward neighboring tribes, an anthropologist consults available records, classifying each tribe on the basis of its sexual codes (permissive or repressive) and its behavior toward neighboring tribes (friendly or hostile).

(d)   In a study of group problem solving, an investigator assigns college students to groups of two, three, or four students and measures the amount of time required by each group to solve a complex puzzle.

(e)   A school psychologist wishes to determine whether reading comprehension scores are related to the number of months of formal education, as reported on school transcripts, for a group of 12-year-old migrant children.

(f) To determine whether Graduate Record Exam (GRE) scores can be increased by cramming, an investigator allows college students to choose to participate in either a GRE test-taking workshop or a control (non-test-taking) workshop and then compares the GRE scores earned subsequently by the two groups of students.

(g) A social scientist wishes to determine whether there is a relationship between the attractiveness scores (on a 100-point scale) assigned to college students by a panel of peers and their scores on a paper-and-pencil test of anxiety.

(h) A political scientist wishes to determine whether males and females differ with respect to their attitudes toward defense spending by the federal government. She asks each person if he or she thinks that the current level of defense spending should be increased, remain the same, or be decreased.

1.9 If you have not done so already, familiarize yourself with the various appendices in this book.

(a) Particularly note the location of Appendix B (Answers to Selected Questions) and Appendix D (Glossary).

(b) Browse through Appendix A (Math Review). If this material looks unfamiliar, study Appendix A, using the self-diagnostic tests as guides.

PART
1

Descriptive Statistics
Organizing and Summarizing Data

Preview

You probably associate statistics with sets of numbers. Numerical sets—or, more generally, sets of data—usually represent the point of departure for a statistical analysis. While focusing on descriptive statistics in the next six chapters, we'll avoid extensive sets of numbers (and the discomfort they trigger in some of us) without, however, shortchanging your exposure to key statistical tools and concepts. As will become apparent, these tools will help us make sense out of data, with its inevitable variability, and communicate information about data to others.

CHAPTER 2

Describing Data with Tables and Graphs

TABLES (FREQUENCY DISTRIBUTIONS)

GRAPHS

Summary / Important Terms / Review Questions

Preview

A frequency distribution helps us to detect any pattern in the data (assuming a pattern exists) by superimposing some order on the inevitable variability among observations. For example, the appearance of a familiar bell-shaped pattern in the frequency distribution of reaction times of airline pilots to a cockpit alarm suggests the presence of many small chance factors whose collective effect must be considered in pilot retraining or cockpit redesign. Frequency distributions will appear in their various forms throughout the remainder of the book.

Graphs of frequency distributions further aid our effort to detect data patterns and make sense out of the data. For example, knowing that the silhouette of a graph is balanced, as is the distribution of IQs for the general population, or that the silhouette is lopsided, as is the distribution of wealth for U.S. citizens, might supply important clues for understanding the data. Because they vividly summarize information, graphs sometimes serve as the final products of simple statistical analyses.

**Table 2.1
FREQUENCY
DISTRIBUTION
(UNGROUPED DATA)**

WEIGHT	f
245	1
244	0
243	0
242	0
*	
*	
*	
161	0
160	4
159	1
158	2
157	3
*	
*	
*	
136	0
135	2
134	0
133	1
Total	53

Given some data, as in Table 1.1 on page 6, how do you make sense out of them—both for yourself and for others? Hidden among all those observations, is there an important message, possibly one that either supports or fails to support one of your ideas? (Or, more interestingly, is there a difference between two or more sets of data—for instance, between the GRE scores of students who do or do not attend a test-taking workshop; or between the survival rates of coronary bypass patients who do or do not own a dog; or between the starting salaries of male and female executives?) At this point, especially if you are facing a fresh set of data in which you have a special interest, statistics can be exciting as well as challenging. Your initial responsibility is to describe the data as clearly, completely, and concisely as possible. Statistics supplies some tools, including tables and graphs, and some guidelines. Beyond that, it is just the data and you. There is no single right way to describe data. Equally valid descriptions of the same data might appear in tables or graphs with different formats. By following just a few guidelines, your reward will be a well-summarized set of data.

TABLES (FREQUENCY DISTRIBUTIONS)

2.1 FREQUENCY DISTRIBUTIONS FOR QUANTITATIVE DATA

Table 2.1 shows one way to organize the weights of the male statistics students listed in Table 1.1. First, arrange a column of consecutive numbers, beginning with the lightest weight (133) at the bottom and ending with the heaviest weight (245) at the top. (Because of the extreme length of this column, many intermediate numbers have been omitted in Table 2.1, a procedure *never* followed in practice.) Then place a short vertical stroke or tally next to a number each time its value appears in the original set of data; once this process has been completed, substitute for each tally count (not shown in Table 2.1) a number indicating the frequency (f) of occurrence of each weight.

A *frequency distribution* is a collection of observations produced by sorting observations into classes and showing their frequency (f) of occurrence in each class.

When observations are sorted into classes of *single* values, as in Table 2.1, the result is referred to as a **frequency distribution for ungrouped data.**

Not Always Appropriate

The frequency distribution shown in Table 2.1 is only partially displayed because there are more than 100 possible values between the largest and smallest observations. Frequency distributions for ungrouped data are much more informative when the number of possible values is less than about 20. Under these circumstances, they are a straightforward method for organizing data. Otherwise, if there are 20 or more possible values, consider using a frequency distribution for grouped data.

Frequency Distribution

A collection of observations produced by sorting observations into classes and showing their frequency (f) of occurrence in each class.

Frequency Distribution for Ungrouped Data

A frequency distribution produced whenever observations are sorted into classes of single values.

Progress Check *2.1 Students in a theater arts appreciation class rated the classic film *The Wizard of Oz* on a 10-point scale, ranging from 1 (poor) to 10 (excellent), as follows:

3	7	2	7	8
3	1	4	10	3
2	5	3	5	8
9	7	6	3	7
8	9	7	3	6

Since the number of possible values is relatively small—only 10—it's appropriate to construct a frequency distribution for ungrouped data. Do this.

Answer on page 488.

Grouped Data

Table 2.2 shows another way to organize the weights in Table 1.1 according to their frequency of occurrence. When observations are sorted into classes of *more than one value*, as in Table 2.2, the result is referred to as a **frequency distribution for grouped data.** Let's look at the general structure of this frequency distribution. Data are grouped into class intervals with 10 possible values each. The bottom class includes the smallest observation (133), and the top class includes the largest observation (245). The distance between bottom and top is occupied by an orderly series of classes. The frequency (f) column shows the frequency of observations in each class and, at the bottom, the total number of observations in all classes.

Let's summarize the more important properties of the distribution of weights in Table 2.2. Although ranging from the 130s to the 240s, the weights peak in the 150s, with a progressively decreasing but relatively heavy concentration in the 160s and 170s. Furthermore, the distribution of weights is not balanced about its peak, but tilted in the direction of the heavier weights.

A frequency Distribution for Grouped Data

A frequency distribution produced whenever observations are sorted into classes of more than one value.

Table 2.2 FREQUENCY DISTRIBUTION (GROUPED DATA)

WEIGHT	f
240–249	1
230–239	0
220–229	3
210–219	0
200–209	2
190–199	4
180–189	3
170–179	7
160–169	12
150–159	17
140–149	1
130–139	3
Total	53

2.2 GUIDELINES

The "Guidelines for Frequency Distributions" box lists seven rules for producing a well-constructed frequency distribution. The first three rules are essential and should not be violated. The last four rules are optional and can be modified or ignored as circumstances warrant. Satisfy yourself that the frequency distribution in Table 2.2 actually complies with these seven rules.

How Many Classes?

The seventh guideline requires a few more comments. The use of too many classes—as in Table 2.3, in which the weights are grouped into 24 classes, each with an interval of 5—tends to defeat the purpose of a frequency distribution, namely, to provide a reasonably concise description of data. On the other hand,

Table 2.3 FREQUENCY DISTRIBUTION WITH TOO MANY INTERVALS	
WEIGHT	***f***
245–249	1
240–244	0
235–239	0
230–234	0
225–229	2
220–224	1
215–219	0
210–214	0
205–209	2
200–204	0
195–199	0
190–194	4
185–189	1
180–184	2
175–179	2
170–174	5
165–169	7
160–164	5
155–159	9
150–154	8
145–149	1
140–144	0
135–139	2
130–134	1
Total	53

GUIDELINES FOR FREQUENCY DISTRIBUTIONS

Essential

1. Each observation should be included in one, and only one, class.

Example: 130–139, 140–149, 150–159, etc. It would be incorrect to use 130–140, 140–150, 150–160, etc., in which, because the boundaries of classes overlap, an observation of 140 (or 150) could be assigned to either of two classes.

2. List all classes, even those with zero frequencies.

Example: Listed in Table 2.2 is the class 210–219 and its frequency of zero. It would be incorrect to skip this class because of its zero frequency.

3. All classes should have equal intervals.

Example: 130–139, 140–149, 150–159, etc. It would be incorrect to use 130–139, 140–159, etc., in which the second class interval (140–159) is twice as wide as the first class interval (130–139).

Optional

4. All classes should have both an upper boundary and a lower boundary.

Example: 240–249. Less preferred would be 240–above, in which no maximum value can be assigned to observations in this class. (Nevertheless, this type of open-ended class is employed as a space-saving device when many different tables must be listed, as in the *Statistical Abstract of the United States.* An open-ended class appears in the table "Two Age Distributions" in Review Question 2.15 at the end of this chapter.)

5. Select the class interval from convenient numbers, such as 1, 2, 3, . . . 10, particularly 5 and 10 or multiples of 5 and 10.

Example: 130–139, 140–149, in which the class interval of 10 is a convenient number. Less preferred would be 130–142, 143–155, etc., in which the class interval of 13 is not a convenient number.

6. The lower boundary of each class interval should be a multiple of the class interval.

Example: 130–139, 140–149, in which the lower boundaries of 130, 140, are multiples of 10, the class interval. Less preferred would be 135–144, 145–154, etc., in which the lower boundaries of 135 and 145 are not multiples of 10, the class interval.

7. Aim for a total of approximately 10 classes.

Example: The distribution in Table 2.2 uses 12 classes. Less preferred would be the distributions in Tables 2.3 and 2.4. The distribution in Table 2.3 has too many classes (24), while the distribution in Table 2.4 has too few classes (3).

WEIGHT	f
Table 2.4 FREQUENCY DISTRIBUTION WITH TOO FEW INTERVALS	
200–249	6
150–199	43
100–149	4
Total	53

the use of too few classes—as in Table 2.4, in which the weights are grouped into three classes, each with an interval of 50—can mask important data patterns such as the high density of weights in the 150s and 160s.

When There Are Either Many or Few Observations

But there is nothing sacred about 10, the recommended number of classes. When describing large sets of data, you might aim for considerably more than 10 classes in order to portray some of the more fine-grained data patterns that otherwise could vanish. On the other hand, when describing small batches of data, you might aim for fewer than 10 classes in order to spotlight data regularities that otherwise could be blurred. It is best, therefore, to think of 10, the recommended number of classes, as a rough rule of thumb to be applied with discretion.

Gaps between Classes

In well-constructed frequency tables, the gaps between classes, such as between 149 and 150 in Table 2.2, show clearly that each observation or score has been assigned to one, and only one, class. The size of the gap should always equal one **unit of measurement;** that is, it should always equal *the smallest possible difference between scores* within a particular set of data. Since the gap is never bigger than one unit of measurement, no score can fall into the gap. In the present case, in which the weights are reported to the nearest pound, one pound is the unit of measurement, and therefore, the gap between classes equals one pound. These gaps would not be appropriate if the weights had been reported to the nearest tenth of a pound. In this case, one-tenth of a pound is the unit of measurement, and therefore, the gap should equal one-tenth of a pound. The smallest class interval would be 130.0–139.9 (not 130–139), and the next class interval would be 140.0–149.9 (not 140–149), and so on. These new boundaries would guarantee that any observation, such as 139.6, would be assigned to one, and only one, class.

Gaps between classes do not signify any disruption in the essentially continuous nature of the data. It would be erroneous to conclude that, because of the gap between 149 and 150 for the frequency distribution in Table 2.2, nobody can weigh between 149 and 150 lbs. As noted in Section 1.6, a man who reports his weight as 150 lbs actually could weigh anywhere between 149.5 and 150.5 lbs, just as a man who reports his weight as 149 lbs actually could weigh anywhere between 148.5 and 149.5 lbs.

Real Limits of Class Intervals

Gaps cannot be ignored when you are determining the actual width of any class interval. The **real limits** *are located at the midpoint of the gap between adjacent tabled boundaries,* that is, one-half of one unit of measurement below the lower tabled boundary and one-half of one unit of measurement above the upper tabled boundary.

For example, the real limits for 140–149 in Table 2.2 are 139.5 (140 minus one-half of the unit of measurement of 1) and 149.5 (149 plus one-half of the unit of measurement of 1), and the actual width of the class interval would be 10 (from 149.5 − 139.5 = 10).

Unit of Measurement

The smallest possible difference between scores.

Real Limits

Located at the midpoint of the gap between adjacent tabled boundaries.

If weights had been reported to the nearest tenth of a pound, the real limits for 140.0–149.9 would be 139.95 (140.0 minus one-half of the unit of measurement of .1) and 149.95 (149.9 plus one-half of one unit of measurement of .1), and the actual width of the class interval still would be 10 (from 149.95 – 139.95 = 10).

Constructing Frequency Distributions

Now that you know the properties of well-constructed frequency distributions, study the step-by-step procedure listed in the "Constructing Frequency Distributions" box, which shows precisely how the distribution in Table 2.2 was constructed from the weight data in Table 1.1. You might want to refer back to this box when you need to construct a frequency distribution for grouped data.

Progress Check *2.2 The IQ scores for a group of 35 high school dropouts are as follows:

91	85	84	79	80
87	96	75	86	104
95	71	105	90	77
123	80	100	93	108
98	69	99	95	90
110	109	94	100	103
112	90	90	98	89

(a) Construct a frequency distribution for grouped data.

(b) Specify the *real* limits for the lowest class interval in this frequency distribution.

Progress Check *2.3 What are some possible poor features of the following frequency distribution?

ESTIMATED WEEKLY TV VIEWING TIME (HRS) FOR 250 SIXTH GRADERS

VIEWING TIME	f
35–above	2
30–34	5
25–30	29
20–22	60
15–19	60
10–14	34
5–9	31
0–4	29
Total	250

Answers on page 489.

CONSTRUCTING FREQUENCY DISTRIBUTIONS

1. *Find the range,* that is, the difference between the largest and smallest observations. The range of weights in Table 1.1 is $245 - 133 = 112$.

2. *Find the class interval required to span the range* by dividing the range by the desired number of classes (ordinarily 10). In the present example,

$$Class\ interval = \frac{range}{desired\ number\ of\ classes} = \frac{112}{10} = 11.2$$

3. *Round off to the nearest convenient interval* (such as 1, 2, 3, . . . 10, particularly 5 or 10 or multiples of 5 or 10). In the present example, the nearest convenient interval is 10.

4. *Determine where the lowest class should begin.* (Ordinarily, this number should be a multiple of the class interval.) In the present example, the smallest score is 133, and therefore, the lowest class should begin at 130, since 130 is a multiple of 10, the class interval.

5. *Determine where the lowest class should end* by adding the class interval to the lower boundary and then subtracting one unit of measurement. In the present example, add 10 to 130 and then subtract 1, the unit of measurement, to obtain 139—the number at which the lowest class should end.

6. *Working upward, list as many equivalent classes as are required to include the largest observation.* In the present example, list 130–139, 140–149, ... , 240–249, in which the last class includes 245, the largest score.

7. *Indicate with a tally the class in which each observation falls.* For example, the first score in Table 1.1, 160, produces a tally next to 160–169; the next score, 193, produces a tally next to 190–199; and so on.

8. *Replace the tally count for each class with a frequency (f) and show the total of all frequencies.* (Tally marks are not usually shown in the final frequency distribution.)

9. *Supply headings for both columns and a title for the table.*

2.3 OUTLIERS

Outlier
A very extreme score.

Be prepared to deal occasionally with the appearance of one or more *very extreme* scores, or **outliers.** A GPA of 0.06, an IQ of 170, summer wages of $62,000— each requires special attention because of its potential impact on a summary of the data.

Check for Accuracy

Whenever you encounter an outrageously extreme value, such as a GPA of 0.06, attempt to verify its accuracy. For instance, was a respectable GPA of 3.06 recorded erroneously as 0.06? If the outlier survives an accuracy check, it should be treated as a legitimate score.

Might Exclude from Summaries

You might choose to segregate (but not to suppress!) an outlier from any summary of the data. For example, you might relegate it to a footnote instead of using excessively wide class intervals in order to include it in a frequency distribution. Or you might use various numerical summaries, such as the median and interquartile range, to be discussed in Chapters 3 and 4, that ignore extreme scores, including outliers.

Might Enhance Understanding

Insofar as a valid outlier can be viewed as the product of special circumstances, it might help you to understand the data. For example, you might understand better why crime rates differ among communities by studying the special circumstances that produce a community with an extremely low (or high) crime rate, or why learning rates differ among third graders by studying a third grader who learns very rapidly (or very slowly).

Progress Check *2.4 Identify any outliers in each of the following sets of data collected from nine college students.

SUMMER INCOME	AGE	FAMILY SIZE	GPA
$6,450	20	2	2.30
$4,820	19	4	4.00
$5,650	61	3	3.56
$1,720	32	6	2.89
$600	19	18	2.15
$0	22	2	3.01
$3,482	23	6	3.09
$25,700	27	3	3.50
$8,548	21	4	3.20

Answers on page 489.

2.4 RELATIVE FREQUENCY DISTRIBUTIONS

An important variation of the frequency distribution is the relative frequency distribution.

Relative Frequency Distribution

A frequency distribution showing the frequency of each class as a part or fraction of the total frequency for the entire distribution.

Relative frequency distributions show the frequency of each class as a part or fraction of the total frequency for the entire distribution.

This type of distribution allows us to focus on the relative concentration of observations among different classes within the same distribution. In the case of the weight data in Table 2.2, it permits us to see that the 160s account for about one-fourth (12/53 =.23, or 23%) of all observations. This type of distribution is especially helpful when you must compare two or more distributions based on different total numbers of observations. For instance, as in Review Question 2.15, you might want to compare the distribution of ages for 500 residents of a small town with that for the approximately 300 million residents of the United States. The conversion to relative frequencies allows a direct comparison of the shapes of these two distributions without having to adjust for the radically different total numbers of observations.

Constructing Relative Frequency Distributions

To convert a frequency distribution into a **relative frequency distribution,** *divide the frequency for each class by the total frequency for the entire distribution.* **Table 2.5** illustrates a relative frequency distribution based on the weight distribution of Table 2.2. The conversion to proportions is straightforward. For instance, to obtain the proportion of .06 for the class 130–139, divide the frequency

Table 2.5
RELATIVE FREQUENCY DISTRIBUTION

WEIGHT	f	RELATIVE f
240–249	1	.02
230–239	0	.00
220–229	3	.06
210–219	0	.00
200–209	2	.04
190–199	4	.08
180–189	3	.06
170–179	7	.13
160–169	12	.23
150–159	17	.32
140–149	1	.02
130–139	3	.06
Total	53	1.02*

* The sum does not equal 1.00 because of rounding-off errors.

of 3 for that class by the total frequency of 53. Repeat this process until a proportion has been calculated for each class.

Percentages or Proportions?

Some people prefer to deal with percentages rather than proportions because percentages usually lack decimal points. A proportion always varies between 0 and 1, whereas a percentage always varies between 0 percent and 100 percent. To convert the relative frequencies in Table 2.5 from proportions to percentages, multiply each proportion by 100; that is, move the decimal point two places to the right. For example, multiply .06 (the proportion for the class 130–139) by 100 to obtain 6 percent.

Progress Check *2.5 GRE scores for a group of graduate school applicants are distributed as follows:

GRE	f
725–749	1
700–724	3
675–699	14
650–674	30
625–649	34
600–624	42
575–599	30
550–574	27
525–549	13
500–524	4
475–499	2
Total	200

Convert to a relative frequency distribution. When calculating proportions, round numbers to two digits to the right of the decimal point, using the rounding procedure specified in Section A.7 of Appendix A.

Answers on page 489.

2.5 CUMULATIVE FREQUENCY DISTRIBUTIONS

Cumulative frequency distributions show the total number of observations in each class and in all lower-ranked classes.

Cumulative Frequency Distribution

A frequency distribution showing the total number of observations in each class and all lower-ranked classes.

This type of distribution can be used effectively with sets of scores, such as test scores for intellectual or academic aptitude, when *relative standing* within the distribution assumes primary importance. Under these circumstances, cumulative frequencies are usually converted, in turn, to cumulative percentages. Cumulative percentages are often referred to as percentile ranks.

Constructing Cumulative Frequency Distributions

To convert a frequency distribution into a **cumulative frequency distribution,** *add to the frequency of each class the sum of the frequencies of all classes ranked below it.* This gives the cumulative frequency for that class. Begin with the lowest-ranked class in the frequency distribution and work upward, finding the cumulative frequencies in ascending order. In **Table 2.6**, the cumulative frequency for the class 130–139 is 3, since there are no classes ranked lower. The cumulative frequency for the class 140–149 is 4, since 1 is the frequency for that class and 3 is the frequency of all lower-ranked classes. The cumulative frequency for the class 150–159 is 21, since 17 is the frequency for that class and 4 is the sum of the frequencies of all lower-ranked classes.

Cumulative Percentages

As has been suggested, if relative standing within a distribution is particularly important, then cumulative frequencies are converted to cumulative percentages. A glance at Table 2.6 reveals that 75 percent of all weights are the same as or lighter than the weights between 170 and 179 pounds. To obtain this cumulative percentage (75%), the cumulative frequency of 40 for the class 170–179 should be divided by the total frequency of 53 for the entire distribution.

Progress Check *2.6

(a) Convert the distribution of GRE scores shown in Question 2.5 to a cumulative frequency distribution.

(b) Convert the distribution of GRE scores obtained in 2.6(a) to a cumulative percent frequency distribution.

Answers on page 490.

		Table 2.6	
		CUMULATIVE FREQUENCY DISTRIBUTION	
WEIGHT	***f***	**CUMULATIVE *f***	**CUMULATIVE PERCENT**
240–249	1	58	100
230–239	0	52	98
220–229	3	52	98
210–219	0	49	92
200–209	2	49	92
190–199	4	47	89
180–189	3	43	81
170–179	7	40	75
160–169	12	33	62
150–159	17	21	40
140–149	1	4	8
130–139	3	3	6
Total	53		

Percentile Ranks

**Percentile Rank of
an Observation**

*Percentage of scores in the entire
distribution with similar or
smaller values than that score.*

When used to describe the relative position of any score within its parent distribution, cumulative percentages are referred to as percentile ranks. *The* **percentile rank** *of a score indicates the percentage of scores in the entire distribution with similar or smaller values than that score.* Thus a weight has a percentile rank of 80 if equal or lighter weights constitute 80 percent of the entire distribution.

Approximate Percentile Ranks (from Grouped Data)

The assignment of *exact* percentile ranks requires that cumulative percentages be obtained from frequency distributions for ungrouped data. If we have access only to a frequency distribution for grouped data, as in Table 2.6, cumulative percentages can be used to assign *approximate* percentile ranks. In Table 2.6, for example, any weight in the class 170–179 could be assigned an approximate percentile rank of 75, since 75 is the cumulative percent for this class.

Progress Check *2.7 Referring to Table 2.6, find the *approximate* percentile rank of any weight in the class 200–209.

Answers on page 490.

2.6 FREQUENCY DISTRIBUTIONS FOR QUALITATIVE (NOMINAL) DATA

Table 2.7 FACEBOOK PROFILE SURVEY	
RESPONSE	***f***
Yes	56
No	27
Total	83

When, among a set of observations, any single observation is a word, letter, or numerical code, the data are qualitative. Frequency distributions for qualitative data are easy to construct. Simply determine the frequency with which observations occupy each class, and report these frequencies as shown in Table 2.7 for the Facebook profile survey. This frequency distribution reveals that Yes replies are approximately twice as prevalent as No replies.

Ordered Qualitative Data

It's totally arbitrary whether Yes is listed above or below No in Table 2.7. When, however, qualitative data have an ordinal level of measurement because observations can be ordered from least to most, that order should be preserved in the frequency table, as illustrated in Table 2.8, in which military ranks are listed in descending order from general to warrant officer.

Relative and Cumulative Distributions for Qualitative Data

Frequency distributions for qualitative variables can always be converted into relative frequency distributions, as illustrated in Table 2.8. Furthermore, if measurement is ordinal because observations can be ordered from least to most, cumulative frequencies (and cumulative percentages) can be used. As illustrated in Table 2.8, it's appropriate to claim, for example, that a captain has an *approximate* percentile rank of 65 among officers since 65.2 (or 65) is the

Table 2.8
RANKS OF OFFICERS IN THE U.S. ARMY (2008)

RANK	f	PROPORTION	CUMULATIVE PERCENT
General	310	.004*	100.0
Colonel	13,879	.161	99.6
Major	15,706	.183	83.5
Captain	23,859	.277	65.2
Lieutenant	17,867	.208	37.5
Warrant Officer	14,407	.167	16.7
Total	86,028		

* To avoid a value of .00 for General, proportions are carried three places to the right of the decimal point.
Source: http://www.fedstats.gov.

cumulative percent for this class. If measurement is only nominal because observations cannot be ordered, as in Table 2.7, a cumulative frequency distribution is meaningless.

Progress Check *2.8 Movie ratings reflect ordinal measurement because they can be ordered from most to least restrictive: NC-17, R, PG-13, PG, and G. The ratings of some films shown recently in San Francisco are as follows:

PG	PG	PG	PG-13	G
G	PG-13	R	PG	PG
R	PG	R	PG	R
NC-17	NC-17	PG	G	PG-13

(a) Construct a frequency distribution.

(b) Convert to relative frequencies, expressed as percentages.

(c) Construct a cumulative frequency distribution.

(d) Find the *approximate* percentile rank for those films with a PG rating.
    Answers on page 490.

2.7 INTERPRETING DISTRIBUTIONS CONSTRUCTED BY OTHERS

When inspecting a distribution for the first time, train yourself to look at the entire table, not just the distribution. Read the title, column headings, and any footnotes. Where do the data come from? Is a source cited? Next, focus on the form of the frequency distribution. Is it well constructed? For quantitative data, does the total number of classes seem to avoid either oversummarizing or under-summarizing the data?

After these preliminaries, inspect the content of the frequency distribution. What is the approximate range? Does it seem reasonable? (Otherwise, you might be misinterpreting the distribution or the distribution might contain one or more outliers that require special attention.) As best you can, disregard the inevitable irregularities that accompany a frequency distribution and focus on its overall appearance or shape. Do the frequencies arrange themselves around a single peak (high point) or several peaks? (More than one peak might signify the presence of several different types of observations—for example, the annual incomes of male and female wage earners—coexisting in the same distribution.) Is the distribution fairly balanced around its peak? (An obviously unbalanced distribution might reflect the presence of a numerical boundary, such as a score of 100 percent correct on an extremely easy exam, beyond which no score is possible.)

When interpreting distributions, including distributions constructed by someone else, keep an open mind. Follow the above suggestions but also pursue any questions stimulated by your inspection of the entire table.

GRAPHS

Data can be described clearly and concisely with the aid of a well-constructed frequency distribution. And data can often be described even more vividly, particularly when you're attempting to communicate with a general audience, by converting frequency distributions into graphs. Let's explore some of the most common types of graphs for quantitative and qualitative data.

2.8 GRAPHS FOR QUANTITATIVE DATA

Histograms

Histogram

A bar-type graph for quantitative data. The common boundaries between adjacent bars emphasize the continuity of the data, as with continuous variables.

The weight distribution described in Table 2.2 appears as a **histogram** in **Figure 2.1**. A casual glance at this histogram confirms previous conclusions: a dense concentration of weights among the 150s, 160s, and 170s, with a spread in the direction of the heavier weights. Let's pinpoint some of the more important features of histograms.

■ Equal units along the horizontal axis (the *X* axis, or abscissa) reflect the various class intervals of the frequency distribution.

■ Equal units along the vertical axis (the *Y* axis, or ordinate) reflect increases in frequency. (The units along the vertical axis do not have to be the same width as those along the horizontal axis.)

■ The intersection of the two axes defines the origin at which both numerical scales equal 0.

■ Numerical scales always increase from left to right along the horizontal axis and from bottom to top along the vertical axis. It is considered good practice to use wiggly lines to highlight breaks in scale, such as those along the horizontal axis in Figure 2.1, between the origin of 0 and the smallest class of 130–139.

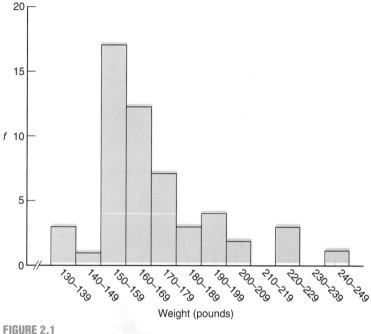

FIGURE 2.1

Histogram.

■ The body of the histogram consists of a series of bars whose heights reflect the frequencies for the various classes. Notice that adjacent bars in histograms have common boundaries that emphasize the continuity of quantitative data for continuous variables. The introduction of gaps between adjacent bars would suggest an artificial disruption in the data more appropriate for discrete quantitative variables or for qualitative variables.

The extensive set of numbers along the horizontal scale of Figure 2.1 can be replaced with a few convenient numbers, as in panel A of Figure 2.2. This concession helps avoid excessive cluttering of the numerical scale.

Frequency Polygons

Frequency Polygon

A line graph for quantitative data that also emphasizes the continuity of continuous variables.

An important variation on a histogram is the **frequency polygon,** or line graph. *Frequency polygons may be constructed directly from frequency distributions.* However, we will follow the step-by-step transformation of a histogram into a frequency polygon, as described in panels A, B, C, and D of Figure 2.2.

A. This panel shows the histogram for the weight distribution.

B. Place dots at the mid-points of each bar top or, in the absence of bar tops, at mid-points for classes on the horizontal axis, and connect them with straight lines. [To find the mid-point of any class, such as 160–169, simply add the two tabled boundaries (160 + 169 = 329) and divide this sum by 2 (329/2 = 164.5).]

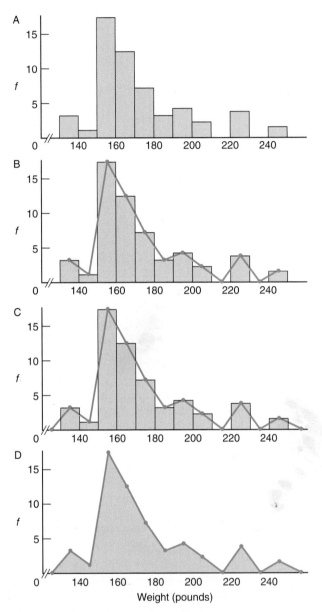

FIGURE 2.2

Transition from histogram to frequency polygon.

C. Anchor the frequency polygon to the horizontal axis. First, extend the upper tail to the mid-point of the first unoccupied class (250–259) on the upper flank of the histogram. Then extend the lower tail to the mid-point of the first unoccupied class (120–129) on the lower flank of the histogram. Now all of the area under the frequency polygon is enclosed completely.

D. Finally, erase all of the histogram bars, leaving only the frequency polygon. Frequency polygons are particularly useful when two or more frequency distributions or relative frequency distributions are to be included in the same graph. See Review Question 2.15.

Progress Check *2.9 The following frequency distribution shows the annual incomes in dollars for a group of college graduates.

INCOME	f
130,000–139,999	1
120,000–129,999	0
110,000–119,999	1
100,000–109,999	3
90,000–99,999	1
80,000–89,999	5
70,000–79,999	7
60,000–69,999	10
50,000–59,999	14
40,000–49,999	23
30,000–39,999	17
20,000–29,999	10
10,000–19,999	8
0–9,999	3
Total	103

(a) Construct a histogram.

(b) Construct a frequency polygon.

(c) Is this distribution balanced or lopsided?
Answers on page 490.

Stem and Leaf Displays

Stem and Leaf Display

A device for sorting quantitative data on the basis of leading and trailing digits.

Still another technique for summarizing quantitative data is a **stem and leaf display.** Stem and leaf displays are ideal for summarizing distributions, such as that for weight data, without destroying the identities of individual observations.

Constructing a Display

The leftmost panel of **Table 2.9** re-creates the weights of the 53 male statistics students listed in Table 1.1. To construct the stem and leaf display for these data, first note that, when counting by tens, the weights range from the 130s to the 240s. Arrange a column of numbers, the stems, beginning with 13 (representing the 130s) and ending with 24 (representing the 240s). Draw a vertical line to separate the stems, which represent multiples of 10, from the space to be occupied by the leaves, which represent multiples of 1.

Table 2.9
CONSTRUCTING STEM AND LEAF DISPLAY FROM WEIGHTS OF MALE STATISTICS STUDENTS

RAW SCORES					STEM AND LEAF DISPLAY	
160	165	135	175			
193	168	245	165	13	3 5 5	
226	169	170	185	14	5	
152	160	156	154	15	2 7 1 7 8 0 2 0 2 6 9 8 2 6 4 7 6	
180	170	160	179	16	0 3 5 8 9 0 0 0 6 5 5 5	
205	150	225	165	17	2 0 0 0 2 5 9	
163	152	190	206	18	0 0 5	
157	160	159	165	19	3 0 0 0	
151	190	172	157	20	5 6	
157	150	190	156	21		
220	133	166	135	22	6 0 5	
145	180	158		23		
158	152	152		24	5	
172	170	156				

Next, enter each raw score into the stem and leaf display. As suggested by the color coding in Table 2.9, the first raw score of 160 reappears as a leaf of 0 on a stem of 16. The next raw score of 193 reappears as a leaf of 3 on a stem of 19, and the third raw score of 226 reappears as a leaf of 6 on a stem of 22, and so on, until each raw score reappears as a leaf on its appropriate stem.

Interpretation

Notice that the weight data have been sorted by the stems. All weights in the 130s are listed together; all of those in the 140s are listed together, and so on. A glance at the stem and leaf display in Table 2.9 shows essentially the same pattern of weights depicted by the frequency distribution in Table 2.2 and the histogram in Figure 2.1. (If you rotate the book counterclockwise one-quarter of a full turn, the silhouette of the stem and leaf display is the same as the histogram for the weight data. This simple maneuver only works if, as in the present display, stem values are listed from smallest at the top to largest at the bottom—one reason why the customary ranking for most tables in this book has been reversed for stem and leaf displays.)

Selection of Stems

Stem values are not limited to units of 10. Depending on the data, you might identify the stem with one or more leading digits that culminates in some variation on a stem value of 10, such as 1, 100, 1000, or even .1, .01, .001, and so on. For instance, an annual income of $23,784 could be displayed as a stem of 23 (thousands) and a leaf of 784. (Leaves consisting of two or more digits, such as 784, are separated by commas.) An SAT test score of 689 could be displayed as a stem of 6 (hundreds) and a leaf of 89. A GPA of 3.25 could be displayed as a stem of 3 (ones) and a leaf of 25, or if you wanted more than a few stems, 3.25 could be displayed as a stem of 3.2 (one-tenths) and a leaf of 5.

Stem and leaf displays represent statistical bargains. Just a few minutes of work produces a description of data that is both clear and complete. Even though rarely appearing in published reports, stem and leaf displays often serve as the first step toward organizing data.

Progress Check *2.10 Construct a stem and leaf display for the following IQ scores obtained from a group of four-year-old children.

120	98	118	117	99	111
126	85	88	124	104	113
108	141	123	137	78	96
102	132	109	106	143	

Answer on page 491.

2.9 TYPICAL SHAPES

Whether expressed as a histogram, a frequency polygon, or a stem and leaf display, an important characteristic of a frequency distribution is its shape. Figure 2.3 shows some of the more typical shapes for smoothed frequency polygons (which ignore the inevitable irregularities of real data).

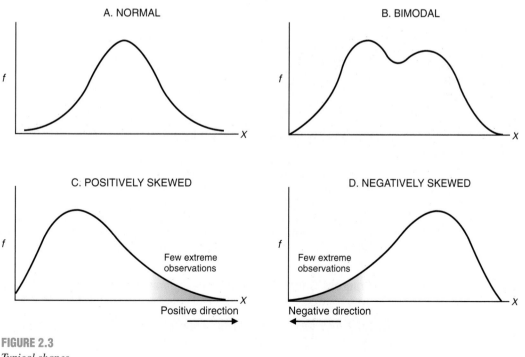

FIGURE 2.3
Typical shapes.

Normal

Any distribution that approximates the normal shape in panel A of Figure 2.3 can be analyzed, as we will see in Chapter 5, with the aid of the well-documented normal curve. The familiar bell-shaped silhouette of the normal curve can be superimposed on many frequency distributions, including those for uninterrupted gestation periods of human fetuses, scores on standardized tests, and even the popping times of individual kernels in a batch of popcorn.

Bimodal

Any distribution that approximates the bimodal shape in panel B of Figure 2.3 might, as suggested previously, reflect the coexistence of two different types of observations in the same distribution. For instance, the distribution of the ages of residents in a neighborhood consisting largely of either new parents or their infants has a bimodal shape.

Positively Skewed

Positively Skewed Distribution

A distribution that includes a few extreme observations in the positive direction (to the right of the majority of observations).

The two remaining shapes in Figure 2.3 are lopsided. A *lopsided distribution caused by a few extreme observations in the positive direction (to the right of the majority of observations), as in panel C of Figure 2.3, is* a **positively skewed distribution.** The distribution of incomes among U.S. families has a pronounced positive skew, with most family incomes under $200,000 and relatively few family incomes spanning a wide range of values above $200,000. The distribution of weights in Figure 2.1 also is positively skewed.

Negatively Skewed

Negatively Skewed Distribution

A distribution that includes a few extreme observations in the negative direction (to the left of the majority of observations).

A *lopsided distribution caused by a few extreme observations in the negative direction (to the left of the majority of observations), as in panel D of Figure 2.3, is* a **negatively skewed** distribution. The distribution of ages at retirement among U.S. job holders has a pronounced negative skew, with most retirement ages at 60 years or older and relatively few retirement ages spanning the wide range of ages younger than 60.

Positively or Negatively Skewed?

Some people have difficulty with this terminology, probably because an entire distribution is labeled on the basis of the relative location, in the positive or negative direction, of a few extreme observations, rather than on the basis of the location of the majority of observations. To make this distinction, always force yourself to focus on the relative locations of the few extreme observations. If you get confused, use panels C and D of Figure 2.3 as guides, noting which silhouette in these two panels best approximates the shape of the distribution in question.

Progress Check *2.11 Describe the probable shape—normal, bimodal, positively skewed, or negatively skewed—for each of the following distributions:

(a) female beauty contestants' scores on a masculinity test, with a higher score indicating a greater degree of masculinity.

(b) scores on a standardized IQ test for a group of people selected from the general population.

(c) test scores for a group of high school students on a very difficult college-level math exam.

(d) reading achievement scores for a third-grade class consisting of about equal numbers of regular students and learning-challenged students.

(e) scores of students at the Eastman School of Music on a test of music aptitude (designed for use with the general population).

Answers on pages 491.

2.10 A GRAPH FOR QUALITATIVE (NOMINAL) DATA

Bar Graph

A bar-type graph for qualitative data. Gaps between adjacent bars emphasize the discontinuous nature of the data.

The distribution in Table 2.7, based on replies to the question "Have you a profile on Facebook?" appears as a **bar graph** in Figure 2.4. A glance at this graph confirms that Yes replies occur approximately twice as often as No replies.

As with histograms, equal segments along the horizontal axis are allocated to the different words or classes that appear in the frequency distribution for qualitative data. Likewise, equal segments along the vertical axis reflect increases in frequency. The body of the bar graph consists of a series of bars whose heights reflect the frequencies for the various words or classes.

A person's answer to the question "Have you a profile on Facebook?" is either Yes or No, not some impossible intermediate value, such as 40 percent Yes and 60 percent No. Gaps are placed between adjacent bars of bar graphs to emphasize the discontinuous nature of qualitative data. A bar graph also can be

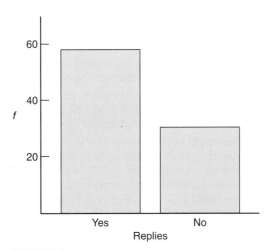

FIGURE 2.4
Bar graph.

used with quantitative data to emphasize the discontinuous nature of a discrete variable, such as the number of children in a family.

Progress Check *2.12 Referring to the box "Constructing Graphs" on page 51 for step-by-step instructions, construct a bar graph for the data shown in the following table:

RACE/HISPANIC ORIGIN OF U.S. POPULATION, 2006 (IN MILLIONS)	
ORIGIN	*f*
African American	38.3
Asian American	16.6
Hispanic	44.3
White	198.7
Total	297.9

Source: 2008 Statistical Abstract of the United States.

Answer on page 491.

2.11 MISLEADING GRAPHS

Graphs can be constructed in an unscrupulous manner to support a particular point of view. Indeed, this type of statistical fraud gives credibility to popular sayings, including "Numbers don't lie, but statisticians do" and "There are three kinds of lies—lies, damned lies, and statistics."

For example, to imply that comparatively many students responded Yes to the Facebook profile question, an unscrupulous person might resort to the various tricks shown in **Figure 2.5**:

- The width of the Yes bar is more than three times that of the No bar, thus violating the custom that bars be equal in width.
- The lower end of the frequency scale is omitted, thus violating the custom that the entire scale be reproduced, beginning with zero. (Otherwise, a broken scale should be highlighted by wiggly lines, as in Figures 2.1 and 2.2.)
- The height of the vertical axis is several times the width of the horizontal axis, thus violating the custom, heretofore unmentioned, that the vertical axis be *approximately* as tall as the horizontal axis is wide. Beware of graphs in which, because the vertical axis is many times larger than the horizontal axis (as in Figure 2.5), frequency differences are exaggerated, or in which, because the vertical axis is many times smaller than the horizontal axis, frequency differences are suppressed.

The combined effect of Figure 2.5 is to imply that virtually all of the students responded Yes. Notice the radically different impressions created by Figures 2.4

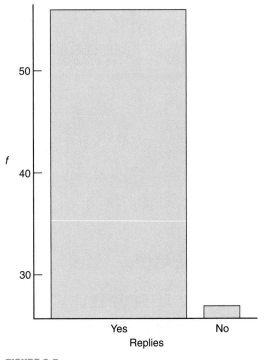

FIGURE 2.5
Distorted bar graph.

and 2.5, even though both are based on exactly the same data. To heighten your sensitivity to this type of distortion and to other types of statistical frauds, read the highly entertaining book by Darrell Huff and Irving Geis, *How to Lie with Statistics* (New York: Norton, 1993).

Progress Check *2.13 Criticize the graphs that appear below and on page 50 (ignore the inadequate labeling of both axes).

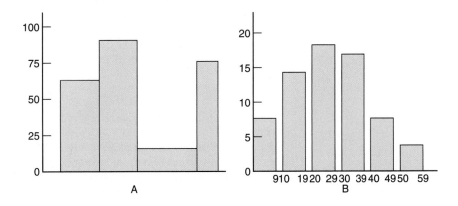

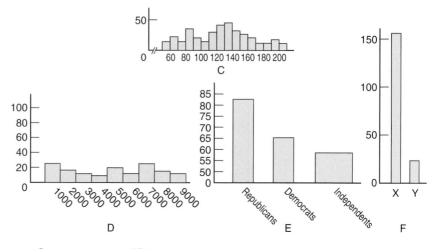

Answers on page 491.

2.12 DOING IT YOURSELF

When you are constructing a graph, attempt to depict the data as clearly, concisely, and completely as possible. The blatant distortion shown in Figure 2.5 can easily be avoided by complying with the several customs described in the preceding section and by following the step-by-step procedure in the box "Constructing Graphs" on page 51. Otherwise, equally valid graphs of the same data might appear in different formats. It is often a matter of personal preference whether, for instance, a histogram or a frequency polygon should be used with quantitative data.

INTERNET DEMONSTRATION
Go to the Web site for this book (http://www.wiley.com/witte/statistics). Click on the *Student Companion Site,* then *Internet Demonstrations,* and finally **Histogram** to see the effect of varying the bar width on the shape of the histogram.

Summary

Frequency distributions organize observations according to their frequencies of occurrence.

Frequency distributions for *ungrouped* data are produced whenever observations are sorted into classes of single values. This type of frequency distribution is most informative when there are fewer than about 20 possible values between the largest and smallest observations.

CONSTRUCTING GRAPHS

1. *Decide on the appropriate type of graph,* recalling that histograms and frequency polygons are appropriate for quantitative data, while bar graphs are appropriate for qualitative data and also are sometimes used with discrete quantitative data.

2. Within the available space, use a ruler to *draw the horizontal axis, then the vertical axis,* remembering that the vertical axis should be about as tall as the horizontal axis is wide.

3. *Identify the string of class intervals that eventually will be superimposed on the horizontal axis.* For qualitative data or ungrouped quantitative data, this is easy—just use the classes suggested by the data. For grouped quantitative data, proceed as if you were creating a set of class intervals for a frequency distribution. (See the box "Constructing Frequency Distributions" on page 33.)

4. *Superimpose the string of class intervals (with gaps for bar graphs) along the entire length of the horizontal axis.* For histograms and frequency polygons, be prepared for some trial and error—use a pencil! Do not use a string of empty class intervals to bridge a sizable gap between the origin of 0 and the smallest class interval. Instead, use wiggly lines to signal a break in scale, then begin with the smallest class interval. Also, do not clutter the horizontal scale with excessive numbers— use just a few convenient numbers.

5. *Along the entire length of the vertical axis, superimpose a progression of convenient numbers,* beginning at the bottom with 0 and ending at the top with a number as large as or slightly larger than the maximum observed frequency. If there is a considerable gap between the origin of 0 and the smallest observed frequency, use wiggly lines to signal a break in scale.

6. Using the scaled axes, *construct bars (or dots and lines) to reflect the frequency of observations within each class interval.* For frequency polygons, dots should be located above the midpoints of class intervals, and both tails of the graph should be anchored to the horizontal axis, as described under "Frequency Polygons" in Section 2.8.

7. *Supply labels for both axes and a title (or even an explanatory sentence) for the graph.*

Frequency distributions for *grouped* data require observations to be sorted into classes of more than one value. This type of frequency distribution should be constructed, step by step, to comply with a number of guidelines. (See the box "Constructing Frequency Distributions" on page 33.) Essentially, a well-constructed frequency distribution consists of a string of non-overlapping, equal classes that occupy the entire distance between the largest and smallest observations.

Very extreme scores, or outliers, require special attention. Given a valid outlier, you might choose to relegate it to a footnote because of its potential for distortion, or you might even concentrate on it as a possible key to understanding the data.

When comparing two or more frequency distributions based on appreciably different total numbers of observations, it is often helpful to express frequencies as relative frequencies.

When relative standing within the distribution is important, convert frequency distributions into cumulative percentages, referred to as percentile ranks. The percentile rank of a score indicates the percentage of scores in the entire distribution with similar or smaller values.

Frequency distributions for qualitative data are easy to construct. They also can be converted into relative frequency distributions and, if the data can be ordered because of ordinal measurement, into percentile ranks.

Frequency distributions can be converted into graphs.

If the data are quantitative, histograms, frequency polygons, or stem and leaf displays are often used. Frequency polygons are particularly useful when two or more frequency distributions are to be included in the same graph.

Shape is an important characteristic of a histogram or a frequency polygon. Smoothed frequency polygons were used to describe four of the more typical shapes: normal, bimodal, positively skewed, and negatively skewed.

Bar graphs are often used with qualitative data and sometimes with discrete quantitative data. They resemble histograms except that gaps separate adjacent bars in bar graphs.

When interpreting graphs, beware of various unscrupulous techniques, such as using bizarre combinations of axes to either exaggerate or suppress a particular data pattern.

When constructing graphs, refer to the step-by-step procedure described in the box "Constructing Graphs" on page 51.

Important Terms

Frequency distribution	**Frequency distribution for ungrouped data**
Frequency distribution for grouped data	
Real limits	**Unit of measurement**
Relative frequency distribution	**Outlier**
Percentile rank	**Cumulative frequency distribution**
Frequency polygon	**Histogram**
Positively skewed distribution	**Stem and leaf display**
Bar graph	**Negatively skewed distribution**

REVIEW QUESTIONS

2.14 Assume that student volunteers were assigned arbitrarily (according to a coin toss) either to be trained to meditate or to behave as usual. To determine whether meditation training (the independent variable) influences GPAs (the dependent variable), GPAs were calculated for each student at the end of the one-year experiment, yielding these results for the two groups:

MEDITATORS			NONMEDITATORS		
3.25	2.25	2.75	3.67	3.79	3.00
3.56	3.33	2.25	2.50	2.75	1.90
3.57	2.45	3.75	3.50	2.67	2.90
2.95	3.30	3.56	2.80	2.65	2.58
3.56	3.78	3.75	2.83	3.10	3.37
3.45	3.00	3.35	3.25	2.76	2.86
3.10	2.75	3.09	2.90	2.10	2.66
2.58	2.95	3.56	2.34	3.20	2.67
3.30	3.43	3.47	3.59	3.00	3.08

(a) What is the unit of measurement for these data?

(b) Construct separate frequency distributions for meditators and for nonmeditators. (First, construct the frequency distribution for the group having the larger range. Then, to facilitate comparisons, use the same set of classes for the other frequency distribution.)

(c) Do the two groups tend to differ? (Eventually, tools from inferential statistics, as described in Part 2, will help you decide whether any apparent difference between the two groups probably is real or merely transitory, that is, attributable to variability or chance. See Review Question 14.15 on page 313.)

*2.15 Are there any conspicuous differences between the two distributions in the following table (one reflecting the ages of all residents of a small town and the other reflecting the ages of all U.S. residents)?

(a) To help make the desired comparison, convert the frequencies (f) for the small town to percentages.

(b) Describe any seemingly *conspicuous* differences between the two distributions.

(c) Using just one graph, construct frequency polygons for the two relative frequency distributions.

NOTE: When segmenting the horizontal axis, assign the same width to the open-ended interval (65–above) as to any other class interval. (This tactic causes some distortion at the upper end of the histogram, since one class interval is doing the work of several. Nothing is free, including the convenience of open-ended intervals.)

Answers on Page 492.

TWO AGE DISTRIBUTIONS		
AGE	**SMALL TOWN** *f*	**U.S. POPULATION (2005)** **(%)**
65–above	105	12
60–64	53	4
55–59	45	5
50–54	40	7
45–49	44	7
40–44	38	8
35–39	31	7
30–34	27	7
25–29	25	7
20–24	20	7
15–19	20	7
10–14	19	7
5–9	17	7
0–4	16	7
Total	500	99%

NOTE: *The top class (65–above) has no upper boundary. Although less preferred, as discussed previously, this type of open-ended class is employed as a space-saving device when, as in the* Statistical Abstract of the United States, *many different tables must be listed.*
Source: 2008 Statistical Abstract of the United States.

2.16 The following table shows distributions of bachelor's degrees earned in 2005–2006 for selected fields of study by all male graduates and by all female graduates.

(a) How many female psychology majors graduated in 2005–2006?

(b) Since the total numbers of male and female graduates are fairly different—504,600 and 676,000—it is helpful to convert first to relative frequencies before making comparisons between male and female graduates. Then, inspect these relative frequencies and note what appear to be the most *conspicuous* differences between male and female graduates.

(c) Would it be meaningful to cumulate the frequencies in either of these frequency distributions?

(d) Using just one graph, construct bar graphs for all male graduates and for all female graduates. **Hint:** Alternate shaded and unshaded bars for males and females, respectively.

BACHELOR'S DEGREES EARNED IN 2005–2006 BY SELECTED FIELD OF STUDY AND GENDER (IN THOUSANDS)		
MAJOR FIELD OF STUDY	MALES	FEMALES
Business	159.7	158.4
Social sciences	80.8	80.7
Education	22.4	84.8
Health sciences	12.9	79.1
Psychology	19.9	68.3
Engineering	67.0	14.6
Life sciences	26.7	42.5
Fine arts	32.1	51.2
Communications	28.1	48.8
Computer sciences	37.7	9.8
English	17.3	37.8
Total	504.6	676.0

Source: 2007 Digest of Educational Statistics at http://nces.ed.gov.

*2.17 Being slightly more complex than previous tables, the following table shows both frequency distributions and relative frequency distributions of race/Hispanic origin for the U.S. population in 1980 and in 2006. It also shows the *frequency (f) change* and the *percent (%) change* of race/Hispanic origin between 1980 and 2006.

(a) Which group changed the most in terms of *actual number* of people?

(b) *Relative* to its size in 1980, which group increased most?

(c) *Relative* to its size in 1980, which group increased less rapidly than the general population?

(d) What is the most striking trend in these data?

Answers on page 492.

RACE/HISPANIC ORIGIN OF U.S. POPULATION (IN MILLIONS)						
	2006		1980		1980–2006	
ORIGIN	f	%	f	%	f CHANGE	% CHANGE
African American	38.3	13%	26.7	12%	11.6	43%
Asian American*	16.6	6%	5.2	2%	11.4	219%
Hispanic	44.3	15%	14.6	6%	29.7	203%
White	198.7	67%	180.1	80%	18.6	10%
Total	297.9	101%	226.6	100%	71.3	31%

* Mostly Asians, but also other races, such as American Indians and Eskimos.
NOTE: The last column expresses the 1980–2006 change as a percentage of the 1980 population for that row.
Source: 2008 Statistical Abstract of the United States.

Describing Data
with Averages

Preview

*Tables and graphs of frequency distributions are important points of departure when attempting to describe data. More precise summaries, such as averages, provide additional valuable information. Long-term investors in the stock market are able to ignore, with only an occasional sleepless night, daily fluctuations in their stocks by remembering that, **on average,** the annual growth rate of stocks during the past 50 years has exceeded by several percentage points that of more conservative investments in bonds. You might stop smoking because, **on average,** non-smokers can expect to live longer than heavy smokers (by as much as 10 years, according to some researchers). You might strengthen your resolve to graduate from college upon hearing that, **on average,** the lifetime earnings of college graduates are almost double those of high school graduates.*

Measures of Central Tendency

Numbers or words that attempt to describe, most generally, the middle or typical value for a distribution.

*Averages consist of numbers (or words) about which the data are, in some sense, centered. Often referred to as **measures of central tendency,** the several types of average yield numbers or words that attempt to describe, most generally, the middle or typical value for a distribution. This chapter focuses on three different measures of central tendency—the mode, median, and mean. Each of these has its special uses, but the mean is the most important average in both descriptive and inferential statistics.*

Mode

The value of the most frequent score.

Bimodal

Describes any distribution with two obvious peaks.

3.1 MODE

The mode reflects the value of the most frequently occurring score.

Table 3.1 shows the number of years served by 20 recent U.S. presidents, beginning with Benjamin Harrison (4 years) and ending with Bill Clinton (8 years). Four years is the modal term, since the greatest number of presidents, 7, served this term. Note that the mode equals 4 years, the *value* of the most frequently occurring term, not 7, the *frequency* with which that term occurred.

It is easy to assign a value to the mode. If the data are organized, as in Figure 3.1, a glance will often be enough. However, if the data are not organized, as in Table 3.1, some counting may be required. The mode is readily understood as the most prevalent or typical value.

More Than One Mode

Distributions can have more than one mode (or no mode at all). Distributions with two obvious peaks, even though they are not exactly the same height, are referred to as **bimodal.** Distributions with more than two peaks are referred to as **multimodal.** The presence of more than one mode might reflect important differences among subsets of data. For instance, the distribution of weights for both male and female statistics students would most likely be bimodal, reflecting the combination of two separate weight distributions—a heavier one for males and a lighter one for females. Notice that even the distribution of presidential terms in Figure 3.1 tends to be bimodal, with a major

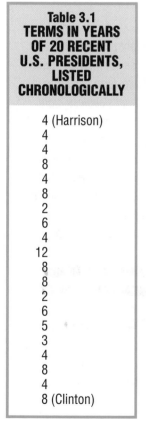

Table 3.1
TERMS IN YEARS OF 20 RECENT U.S. PRESIDENTS, LISTED CHRONOLOGICALLY

4 (Harrison)
4
4
8
4
8
2
6
4
12
8
8
2
6
5
3
4
8
4
8 (Clinton)

Source: The New York Times Almanac (2008).

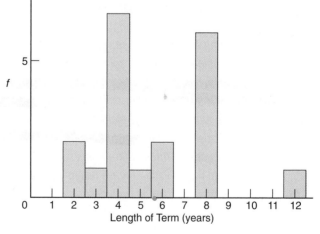

FIGURE 3.1
Distribution of presidential terms.

peak at four years and a minor peak at eight years, reflecting the two most typical terms of office.

Progress Check *3.1 Determine the mode for the following retirement ages: 60, 63, 45, 63, 65, 70, 55, 63, 60, 65, 63.

Progress Check *3.2 The owner of a new car conducts six gas mileage tests and obtains the following results, expressed in miles per gallon: 26.3, 28.7, 27.4, 26.6, 27.4, 26.9. Find the mode for these data.

Answers on page 493.

3.2 MEDIAN

Median

The middle value when observations are ordered from least to most.

> **The median reflects the middle value when observations are ordered from least to most.**

The median splits a set of ordered observations into two equal parts, the upper and lower halves. In other words, the median has a percentile rank of 50, since observations with equal or smaller values constitute 50 percent of the entire distribution.*

Finding the Median

Table 3.2 shows how to find the median for two different sets of scores. The numbers in color squares cross-reference instructions in the top panel with examples in the bottom panel. Study Table 3.2 before reading on.

To find the median, *scores always must be ordered from least to most (or vice versa)*. This task is straightforward with small sets of data but becomes increasingly cumbersome with larger sets of data that must be ordered manually.

When the total number of scores is odd, as in the lower left-hand panel of Table 3.2, there is a single middle-ranked score, and the value of the median equals the value of this score. When the total number of scores is even, as in the lower right-hand panel of Table 3.2, the value of the median equals a value midway between the values of the two middlemost scores. In either case, the value of the median always reflects the *value* of middle-ranked scores, not the *position* of these scores among the set of ordered scores.

The median term can be found for the 20 presidents. First, rank the terms from longest (12 for Franklin Roosevelt) to shortest (2 for Harding and Kennedy), as shown in the left-hand column of Table 3.3. Then, following the instructions in Table 3.2, verify that the median term for the 20 presidents equals 4.5 years, since 4.5 is the value midway between the values (4 and 5) of the two middlemost (10th- and 11th-ranked) terms in Table 3.3.

---

*Strictly speaking, the median always has a percentile rank of *exactly* 50 only insofar as interpolation procedures, not discussed in this book, identify the value of the median with a single point along the numerical scale for the data.

| **Table 3.2** |
| **FINDING THE MEDIAN** |

A. INSTRUCTIONS

1 Order scores from least to most.
2 Find the middle position by adding one to the total number of scores and dividing by 2.
3 *If the middle position is a whole number,* as in the left-hand panel below, use this number to *count* into the set of ordered scores.
4 The value of the median equals the value of the score located at the middle position.
5 *If the middle position is not a whole number,* as in the right-hand panel below, use the two nearest whole numbers to *count* into the set of ordered scores.
6 The value of the median equals the value midway between those of the two middlemost scores; to find the midway value, add the two given values and divide by 2.

B. EXAMPLES

Set of five scores:	Set of six scores:
2, 8, 2, 7, 6	3, 8, 9, 3, 1, 8
1 2, 2, 6, 7, 8	1 1, 3, 3, 8, 8, 9
2 $\dfrac{5+1}{2} = 3$	2 $\dfrac{6+1}{2} = 3.5$
2, 2, 6, 7, 8	
3 1, 2, 3	
4 median = 6	
	1, 3, 3, 8, 8, 9
	5 1, 2, 3, 4
	6 median = $\dfrac{3+8}{2} = 5.5$

Notice that although the values for median and modal presidential terms are quite similar, they have different interpretations. The median term (4.5 years) describes the *middle-ranked* term, while the modal term (4 years) describes the *most frequent* term in the distribution.

Progress Check *3.3 Find the median for the following retirement ages: 60, 63, 45, 63, 65, 70, 55, 63, 60, 65, 63.

Progress Check *3.4 Find the median for the following gas mileage tests: 26.3, 28.7, 27.4, 26.6, 27.4, 26.9.

Answers on page 493.

Table 3.3
TERMS IN YEARS OF 20 RECENT U.S. PRESIDENTS

ARRANGED BY LENGTH	DEVIATION FROM MEAN	SUM OF DEVIATIONS
12	6.40	
8	2.40	
8	2.40	
8	2.40	
8	2.40	21.6
8	2.40	
8	2.40	
6	0.40	
6	0.40	
(mean = 5.60)		0
5	−0.60	
4	−1.60	
4	−1.60	
4	−1.60	
4	−1.60	
4	−1.60	−21.6
4	−1.60	
4	−1.60	
3	−2.60	
2	−3.60	
2	−3.60	

....

3.3 MEAN

The mean is the most common average, one you have doubtless calculated many times.

The mean is found by adding all scores and then dividing by the number of scores.

That is,

$$Mean = \frac{sum\ of\ all\ scores}{number\ of\ scores}$$

To find the mean term for the 20 presidents, add all 20 terms in Table 3.1 $(4 + \ldots + 4 + 8)$ to obtain a sum of 112 years, and then divide this sum by 20, the number of presidents, to obtain a mean of 5.60 years.

There is no requirement that presidential terms be ranked before calculating the mean. Even when large sets of unorganized data are involved, the calculation of the mean is usually straightforward, particularly with the aid of a calculator or computer.

Sample or Population?

Statisticians distinguish between two types of means—the population mean and the sample mean—depending on whether the data are viewed as a **population** (*a complete set of scores*) or as a **sample** (*a subset of scores*). For example, if the terms of the 20 U.S. presidents are viewed as a population, then 5.60 years qualifies as a population mean. On the other hand, if the terms of the 20 U.S. presidents are viewed as a sample from the terms of *all* U.S. presidents, then 5.60 years qualifies as a sample mean. Not only is the present distinction entirely a matter of perspective, but it also produces exactly the same numerical value of 5.60 for both means. Nevertheless, this distinction is introduced here because of its importance in later chapters. *Until then, unless noted otherwise, you can assume that we are dealing with the sample mean.*

Population

A complete set of scores.

Sample

A subset of scores.

Formula for Sample Mean

It's usually more efficient to substitute symbols for words in statistical formulas, including the word formula given above for the mean. When symbols are used, $\bar{X}$ designates the **sample mean,** and the formula becomes

Sample Mean ($\bar{X}$)

The balance point for a sample, found by dividing the sum for the values of all scores in the sample by the number of scores in the sample.

SAMPLE MEAN	
$\bar{X} = \dfrac{\Sigma X}{n}$	(3.1)

and reads: "X-bar equals the sum of the variable X divided by the **sample size n.**" [Note that the uppercase Greek letter sigma (Σ) is read as *the sum of,* not as *sigma*. To avoid confusion, read only the lowercase Greek letter sigma (σ) as *sigma* since it has an entirely different meaning in statistics, as described in Chapter 4.]

Sample Size (n)

The total number of scores in the sample.

In Formula 3.1, the variable X can be replaced, in turn, by each of the 20 presidential terms in Table 3.1, beginning with 4 and ending with 8. The symbol Σ, the uppercase Greek letter sigma, specifies that all scores represented by the variable X be added ($4 + \ldots + 4 + 8$) to find the sum of 112. (Notice that this sum contains the values of *all* scores *including duplications*.) Then divide this sum by n, the sample size—20 in the present example—to obtain the mean presidential term of 5.60 years.

Formula for Population Mean

The formula for the population mean differs from that for the sample mean only because of a change in some symbols. In statistics, Greek symbols usually describe population characteristics, such as the population mean, while English letters usually describe sample characteristics, such as the sample mean. The **population mean** is represented by μ (pronounced "mu"), the lowercase Greek letter *m* for mean,

Population Mean (μ)

The balance point for a population, found by dividing the sum for all scores in the population by the number of scores in the population.

POPULATION MEAN	
$\mu = \dfrac{\Sigma X}{N}$	(3.2)

Population Size (N)

The total number of scores in the population.

where the uppercase letter *N* refers to the **population size.** Otherwise, the calculations are the same as those for the sample mean.

Mean as Balance Point

The mean serves as the balance point for its frequency distribution.

Imagine that the histogram for the terms of the 20 presidents in Figure 3.1 has been constructed out of some rigid material such as wood. Also imagine that, while using only one finger placed under its base, you wish to lift the histogram without disturbing its horizontal balance. To accomplish this, your finger should be at 5.60, the value of the mean, shown as a dot in Figure 3.1. If your finger were to the right of this point, the entire histogram would seesaw down to the left; if your finger were to the left of this point, the histogram would seesaw down to the right.

The mean serves as the balance point for its distribution because of a special property: *The sum of all scores, expressed as positive and negative deviations from the mean, always equals zero.* In the right-hand column of Table 3.3, each presidential term reappears as a deviation from the mean term, obtained by taking each term (including duplications) one at a time and subtracting the mean. Terms above the mean of 5.60 reappear as positive deviations (for example, 12 reappears as a positive deviation of 6.40 from the mean, since 12 − 5.60 = 6.40). Terms below the mean of 5.60 reappear as negative deviations (for example, 2 reappears as a negative deviation of −3.60 from the mean, since 2 − 5.60 = −3.60). As suggested in Table 3.3, when the sum of all positive deviations, 21.6, is combined with the sum of all negative deviations, −21.6, the resulting sum equals zero.

In its role as balance point, the mean describes the single point of equilibrium at which, once all scores have been expressed as deviations from the mean, those above the mean counterbalance those below the mean. You can appreciate, therefore, why a change in the value of a single score produces a change in the value of the mean for the entire distribution. *The mean reflects the values of all scores, not just those that are middle ranked, as with the median, or those that occur most frequently, as with the mode.*

Progress Check *3.5 Find the mean for the following retirement ages: 60, 63, 45, 63, 65, 70, 55, 63, 60, 65, 63.

Progress Check *3.6 Find the mean for the following gas mileage tests: 26.3, 28.7, 27.4, 26.6, 27.4, 26.9

Answers on page 493.

3.4 WHICH AVERAGE?

If Distribution Is Not Skewed

When a distribution of scores is not too skewed, the values of the mode, median, and mean are similar, and any of them can be used to describe the central tendency of the distribution. This tends to be the case in Figure 3.1, where the mode of 4

Table 3.4 INFANT DEATH RATES FOR SELECTED COUNTRIES (2006)	
COUNTRY	**INFANT DEATH RATE***
Sierra Leone	270
Ghana	120
Pakistan	97
Cambodia	82
India	76
South Africa	69
Mexico	35
China	24
Brazil	20
United States	8
Cuba	7
United Kingdom	6
Netherlands	5
Denmark	5
France	5
Israel	5
Germany	4
Japan	4
Sweden	3

* Rates per 1000 live births.
Source: 2008 World Development Indicators.

describes the typical term; the median of 4.5 describes the middle-ranked term; and the mean of 5.60 describes the balance point for terms. The slightly larger mean term is caused by a shift upward in the balance point to compensate for the large positive deviation of 6.40 years for Roosevelt's lengthy 12-year term.

If Distribution Is Skewed

When extreme scores cause a distribution to be skewed, as for the infant death rates for selected countries listed in Table 3.4, the values of the three averages can differ appreciably. The modal infant death rate of 5 describes the most typical rate (since it occurs most frequently, four times, in Table 3.4). The median infant death rate of 8 describes the middle-ranked rate (since the United States, with a death rate of 8, occupies the middle-ranked, or 10th, position among the 19 ranked countries). Finally, the mean infant death rate of 44.47 describes the balance point for all rates (since the sum of all rates, 845, divided by the number of countries, 19, equals 44.47).

Unlike the mode and median, the mean is very sensitive to extreme scores, or outliers. Any extreme score, such as the high infant death rate of 270 for Sierra Leone in Table 3.4, contributes directly to the calculation of the mean and, with arithmetic inevitability, sways the value of the mean—the balance point for the entire distribution—in its direction. In extreme cases, the mean describes the central tendency of a distribution only in the more abstract sense of being the balance point of the distribution.

Interpreting Differences between Mean and Median

Ideally, when a distribution is skewed, report both the mean and the median. Appreciable differences between the values of the mean and median signal the presence of a skewed distribution. If the mean exceeds the median, as it does for the infant death rates, the underlying distribution is positively skewed because of one or more scores with relatively large values, such as the very high infant death rates for a number of countries, especially Sierra Leone. On the other hand, if the median exceeds the mean, the underlying distribution is negatively skewed because of one or more scores with relatively small values. Figure 3.2 summarizes the relationship between the various averages and the two types of skewed distributions (shown as smoothed curves).

INTERNET DEMONSTRATION
Go to the Web site (http://www.wiley.com/college/witte). Click on the *Student Companion Site*, then *Internet Demonstrations*, and finally *Mean and Median* to see how these two averages vary as you change the shapes of histograms.

Progress Check *3.7 Indicate whether the following skewed distributions are positively skewed because the mean exceeds the median or negatively skewed because the median exceeds the mean.

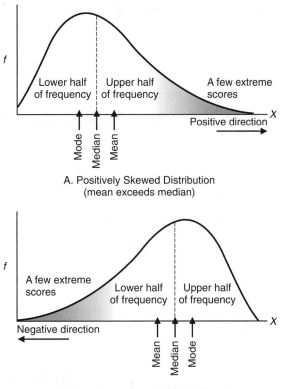

A. Positively Skewed Distribution
(mean exceeds median)

B. Negatively Skewed Distribution
(median exceeds mean)

FIGURE 3.2
Mode, median, and mean in positively and negatively skewed distributions.

(a) a distribution of test scores on an easy test, with most students scoring high and a few students scoring low

(b) a distribution of ages of college students, with most students in their late teens or early twenties and a few students in their fifties or sixties

(c) a distribution of loose change carried by classmates, with most carrying less than $1 and with some carrying $3 or $4 worth of loose change

(d) a distribution of the sizes of crowds in attendance at a popular movie theater, with most audiences at or near capacity

Answers on page 493.

Special Status of the Mean

As has been seen, the mean sometimes fails to describe the typical or middle-ranked value of a distribution. Therefore, it should be used in conjunction with another average, such as the median. In the long run, however, the *mean is the single most preferred average for quantitative data.* After this chapter, it will be used almost exclusively. In the next chapter, the mean serves as a key component in an important statistical measure, the standard deviation. Later, in inferential statistics (Part 2), it emerges as a well-documented measure to be used when generalizing beyond actual scores in surveys and experiments.

Using the Word *Average*

Strictly speaking, an *average* can refer to the mode, median, or mean—or even to some more exotic average, such as the geometric mean or the harmonic mean. Conventional usage prescribes that *average* usually signifies *mean,* and this connotation is often reinforced by the context. For instance, *grade point average* is virtually synonymous with *mean grade point*. To our knowledge, even the most enterprising grade-point-impoverished student has never attempted to satisfy graduation requirements by exchanging a more favorable modal or median grade point for the customary mean grade point. Unless context and usage make it clear, however, it's a good policy to specify the particular average being used, even if it requires a short explanation. When dealing with controversial topics, it is always wise to insist that the exact type of the average be identified.

3.5 AVERAGES FOR QUALITATIVE AND RANKED DATA

Mode Always Appropriate for Qualitative Data

So far, we have been talking about quantitative data for which, in principle, all three averages can be used. But when the data are qualitative, your choice among averages is restricted. *The mode always can be used with qualitative data.* For instance, Yes qualifies as the modal or most typical response for the Facebook profile question (Table 2.7 on page 38). By the same token, it would be appropriate to report that PG is the modal type of rating for recent films shown in San Francisco (Question 2.8 on page 39) and that white is the modal race of Americans (Question 2.12 on page 48).

Median Sometimes Appropriate

The median can be used whenever it is possible to order qualitative data from least to most because the level of measurement is ordinal. It's easiest to determine the median class for ordered qualitative data by using relative frequencies, as in **Table 3.5**. (Otherwise, first convert regular frequencies to relative frequencies.) Cumulate the relative frequencies, working up from the bottom of the distribution, until the cumulative percentage first equals or exceeds 50 percent. Since the corresponding class includes the median and, roughly speaking, splits the distribution into an upper and a lower half, it is designated as the median or middle-ranked class. For instance, the qualitative data in Table 3.5 can be ordered from warrant officer to general. Starting at the bottom of Table 3.5 and cumulating upward (in color), we have a cumulative percent of 37.5 for the class of lieutenant and 65.2 for the class of captain. Accordingly, since it includes a cumulative percent of 50, captain is the median rank of officers in the U.S. Army.

One word of caution when you are finding the median for ordered qualitative data. Avoid a common error that identifies the median simply with the middle or two middlemost classes, such as "between captain and major," without regard to

Table 3.5		
FINDING THE MEDIAN FOR ORDERED		
QUALITATIVE DATA: RANKS OF OFFICERS		
IN THE U.S. ARMY (2008)		
RANK	**%**	**CUMULATIVE %**
General	0.4	
Colonel	16.1	
Major	18.3	
⟨Captain⟩	27.7	+ 37.5 = ⟨65.2⟩
Lieutenant	20.8	+ 16.7 = 37.5
Warrant Officer	16.7	16.7
	100.0	

Source: http://www.fedstats.gov.

the cumulative relative frequencies and the location of the 50th percentile. In other words, *do not treat the various classes as though they have the same frequencies when they actually have different frequencies.*

Inappropriate Averages

Reminder:

Mean cannot be used with qualitative data.

It would not be appropriate to report a median for unordered qualitative data with nominal measurement, such as the ancestries of Americans. Nor would it be appropriate to report a mean for *any* qualitative data, such as the ranks of officers in the U.S. Army. After all, words cannot be added and then divided, as required by the formula for the mean.

Progress Check *3.8 College students were surveyed about where they would most like to spend their spring break: Daytona Beach (DB), Cancun, Mexico (C), South Padre Island (SP), Lake Havasu (LH), or other (O). The results were as follows:

DB	DB	C	LH	DB
C	SP	LH	DB	O
O	SP	C	DB	LH
DB	C	DB	O	DB

Find the mode and, if possible, the median.

Answer on page 493.

Averages for Ranked Data

When the data consist of a series of ranks, with its ordinal level of measurement, the median rank always can be obtained. It's simply the middlemost or average of the two middlemost ranks. For example, imagine that Table 1.1 on page 6 displays not weights for the 53 male statistics students, but only ranks for their weights, beginning with rank 1 for the lightest man (133 lbs) and ending with rank 53 for the heaviest man (245 lbs). Recalling how to find the median when there is an even number of scores, as described in Table 3.2 on page 60, assign the average of the two middlemost ranks (26th and 27th), that is, 26.5, as the median rank.

The mean and modal ranks tend not to be very informative. The mean rank, obtained by summing all ranks and dividing by the number of ranks, always equals the median or middlemost rank. [Calculation of the mean rank also assumes that the level of measurement is interval/ratio, that is, differences between adjacent ranks reflect equal distances (equal intervals) rather than merely more or less (order).]

The modal rank exists only if there is at least one tie in ranks and might not reflect any central tendency. If Table 1.1 had displayed not weights but ranks, the modal rank would have corresponded to the average of the ranks (27th, 28th, 29th, and 30th) for the four men who weigh 165 lbs.

Summary

The mode equals the value of the most frequently occurring or typical score.

The median equals the value of the middle-ranked score (or scores). Since it splits frequencies into upper and lower halves, it has a percentile rank of 50.

The value of the mean, whether defined for a sample or for a population, is found by summing all the scores and then dividing by the number of scores in the sample or population. It always describes the balance point of a distribution, that is, the single point about which the sum of positive deviations equals the sum of negative deviations.

When frequency distributions are not skewed, the values of all three averages tend to be similar and equally representative of the central tendencies within the distributions. When frequency distributions are skewed, the values of the three averages differ appreciably, with the mean being particularly sensitive to extreme scores. Ideally, in this case, report both the mean and the median.

The mean is the preferred average for quantitative data and will be used almost exclusively in later chapters. It reappears as a key component in other statistical measures and as a well-documented measure in surveys and experiments.

Conventional usage prescribes that *average* usually signifies *mean,* but when dealing with controversial topics, it's wise to insist that the exact nature of the average be specified.

Only the mode can be used with all qualitative data. If qualitative data can be ordered from least to most because the level of measurement is ordinal, the median also can be used.

The median is the preferred average for ranked data.

Important Terms

Measures of central tendency	**Bimodal**
Mode	**Median**
Sample	**Population**
Sample mean ($\bar{X}$)	**Population mean (μ)**
Sample size (n)	**Population size (N)**

Key Equation
....

SAMPLE MEAN

$$\bar{X} = \frac{\Sigma X}{n}$$

REVIEW QUESTIONS

NOTE ON COMPUTATIONAL ACCURACY

Answers in Appendix B have been produced by rounding any approximate number two digits to the right of the decimal point, using the rounding procedure described in Section A.7 of Appendix A.

*3.9 To the question "During your lifetime, how often have you changed your permanent residence?" a group of 18 college students replied as follows: 1, 3, 4, 1, 0, 2, 5, 8, 0, 2, 3, 4, 7, 11, 0, 2, 3, 3. Find the mode, median, and mean.
Answers on page 493.

3.10 During their first swim through a water maze, 15 laboratory rats made the following number of errors (blind alleyway entrances): 2, 17, 5, 3, 28, 7, 5, 8, 5, 6, 2, 12, 10, 4, 3.

(a) Find the mode, median, and mean for these data.

(b) Without constructing a frequency distribution or graph, would you characterize the shape of this distribution as balanced, positively skewed, or negatively skewed?

3.11 In some racing events, downhill skiers receive the average of their times for three trials. Would you prefer the average time to be the mean or the median if usually you have

(a) one very poor time and two average times?

(b) one very good time and two average times?

(c) two good times and one average time?

(d) three different times, spaced at about equal intervals?

*3.12 During a strike by Northwest Airline pilots a number of years ago, the average salary for pilots reported by management was $13,000 higher than that reported by the pilots' union. Given the focus of this chapter, what could be the cause of this discrepancy?
Answer on page 493.

3.13 Garrison Keillor, host of the radio program *A Prairie Home Companion,* concludes each story about his mythical hometown with "That's the news from Lake Wobegon, where all the women are strong, all the men are good-looking, and *all the children are above average.*" In what type of distribution, if any, would

(a) more than half of the children be above average?

(b) more than half of the children be below average?

(c) about equal numbers of children be above and below average?

(d) all the children be above average?

3.14 The mean serves as the balance point for any distribution because the sum of all scores, expressed as positive and negative distances from the mean, always equals zero.

(a) Show that the mean possesses this property for the following set of scores: 3, 6, 2, 0, 4.

(b) Satisfy yourself that the mean identifies the only point that possesses this property. More specifically, select some other number, preferably a whole number (for convenience), and then find the sum of all scores in part (a), expressed as positive or negative distances from the newly selected number. This sum should not equal zero.

3.15 If possible, find the median for the film ratings listed in Question 2.8 on page 39.

3.16 Specify the single average—the mode, median, or mean—described by the following statements.

(a) It never can be used with qualitative data.

(b) It sometimes can be used with qualitative data.

(c) It always can be used with qualitative data.

(d) It always can be used with ranked data.

(e) Strictly speaking, it only can be used with quantitative data.

CHAPTER 4

Describing Variability

Summary / Important Terms / Key Equations / Review Questions

Preview

Averages are important, but they tell only part of the story. Most of us would refuse to forge a swift-flowing stream knowing only that the water depth averages 5 feet.

*Statistics flourishes because we live in a world of variability; no two people are identical, and a few are really far out. When summarizing a set of data, we specify not only measures of central tendency, such as the mean, but also **measures of variability,** that is, measures of the amount by which scores are dispersed or scattered in a distribution. This chapter describes several measures of variability, including the range, the interquartile range, the variance, and most important, the standard deviation.*

Measures of Variability
Measures of the amount by which scores are dispersed or scattered in a distribution.

73

4.1 INTUITIVE APPROACH

You probably already possess an intuitive feel for differences in variability. In **Figure 4.1**, each of the three frequency distributions consists of seven scores with the same mean (10) but with different variabilities. (Ignore the numbers in boxes; their significance will be explained later.) Before reading on, rank the three distributions from least to most variable. Your intuition was correct if you concluded that distribution A has the *least* variability, distribution B has *intermediate* variability, and distribution C has the *most* variability.

If this conclusion is not obvious, look at each of the three distributions, one at a time, and note any differences among the values of individual scores. For distribution A with the least (zero) variability, all seven scores have the same value (10). For distribution B with intermediate variability, the values of scores vary slightly (one 9 and one 11), and for distribution C with most variability, they vary even more (one 7, two 9s, two 11s, and one 13).

Importance of Variability

Variability assumes a key role in an analysis of research results. For example, a researcher might ask: Does fitness training improve, on average, the scores of depressed patients on a mental-wellness test? To answer this question, depressed patients are randomly assigned to two groups, fitness training is given to one group, and wellness scores are obtained for both groups. Let's assume that the mean wellness score is larger for the group with fitness training. Is the observed mean difference between the two groups real or merely transitory? This decision depends not only on the size of the mean difference between the two groups but also on the inevitable variabilities of individual scores within each group.

To illustrate the importance of variability, **Figure 4.2** shows the outcomes for two fictitious experiments, *each with the same mean difference of 2,* but with the two groups in experiment B having less variability than the two groups in experiment C. Notice that groups B and C in Figure 4.2 are the same as their counterparts in Figure 4.1. Although the new group B* retains exactly the same (intermediate)

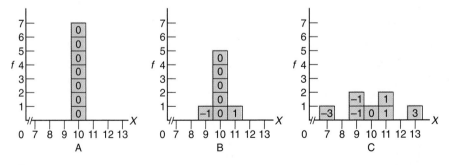

FIGURE 4.1

Three distributions with the same mean (10) but different amounts of variability. Numbers in the boxes indicate distances from the mean.

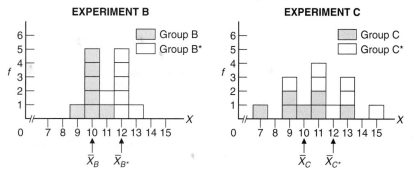

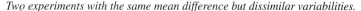

FIGURE 4.2

Two experiments with the same mean difference but dissimilar variabilities.

variability as group B, each of its seven scores and its mean have been shifted 2 units to the right. Likewise, although the new group C* retains exactly the same (most) variability as group C, each of its seven scores and its mean have been shifted 2 units to the right. Consequently, the crucial mean difference of 2 (from $12 - 10 = 2$) is the same for both experiments.

Before reading on, decide which mean difference of 2 in Figure 4.2 is more apparent. The mean difference for experiment B should seem more apparent because of the smaller variabilities within both groups B and B*. Just as it's easier to hear a phone message when static is reduced, it's easier to see a difference between group means when variabilities within groups are reduced.

As described in later chapters, variabilities within groups assume a key role in inferential statistics. Briefly, the smaller variabilities within groups in experiment B translate into *more statistical stability* for the observed mean difference of 2 *when it is viewed as just one outcome among many possible outcomes for repeat experiments.* Therefore, insofar as *similar* (but not necessarily identical) mean differences would reappear in repeat experiments, we can conclude that the observed mean difference of 2 probably reflects a real difference in favor of the treatment in experiment B.

On the other hand, the larger variabilities within groups in experiment C translate into *less statistical stability* for the observed mean difference of 2 when it is viewed as just one outcome among many possible outcomes for repeat experiments. Insofar as *dissimilar* mean differences—even zero or negative mean differences—would appear in repeat experiments, we can conclude that the observed mean difference of 2 *fails* to reflect a real difference in favor of the treatment in experiment C. Instead, since it is most likely a product of chance variability, the observed mean difference of 2 can be viewed as merely transitory and not taken seriously.

Later, Review Question 14.10 on page 311 will permit more definitive conclusions about whether each of the mean differences of 2 for experiments B and C should be viewed as reflecting a real difference or dismissed as merely transitory. These conclusions will require the use of a measure of variability, the standard deviation, described in this chapter, along with tools from inferential statistics described in Part 2.

4.2 RANGE

Exact measures of variability not only aid communication but also are essential tools in statistics. One such measure is the range. *The* **range** *is the difference between the largest and smallest scores.* In Figure 4.1, distribution A, the least variable, has the smallest range of 0 (from 10 to 10); distribution B, the moderately variable, has an intermediate range of 2 (from 11 to 9); and distribution C, the most variable, has the largest range of 6 (from 13 to 7), in agreement with our intuitive judgments about differences in variability. The range is a handy measure of variability that can readily be calculated and understood.

Shortcomings of Range

The range has several shortcomings. First, since its value depends on only two scores—the largest and the smallest—it fails to use the information provided by the remaining scores. Furthermore, the value of the range tends to increase with increases in the total number of scores. For instance, the range of adult heights might be 6 or 8 inches for a half a dozen people, whereas it might be 14 or 16 inches for six dozen people. Larger groups are more likely to include very short or very tall people who, of course, inflate the value of the range. Instead of being a relatively stable measure of variability, the size of the range tends to vary with the size of the group.

4.3 VARIANCE

Although both the range and its most important spin-off, the interquartile range (discussed later in Section 4.7), serve as valid measures of variability, neither is among the statistician's preferred measures of variability. Those roles are reserved for the variance and *particularly for its square root, the standard deviation,* because these measures serve as key components for other important statistical measures. Accordingly, the variance and standard deviation occupy the same exalted position among measures of variability as does the mean among measures of central tendency.

Following the computational procedures described in later sections of this chapter, we could calculate the value of the variance for each of the three distributions in Figure 4.1. Its value equals 0.00 for the least variable distribution, A, 0.29 for the moderately variable distribution, B, and 3.14 for the most variable distribution, C, in agreement with our intuitive judgments about the relative variability of these three distributions.

Reconstructing the Variance

To understand the variance better, let's reconstruct it step by step. Although a measure of variability, the variance also qualifies as a type of mean, that is, as the balance point for some distribution. To qualify as a type of mean, the values of all scores must be added and then divided by the total number of scores. In the case of the variance, each original score is re-expressed as a distance or deviation from the mean by subtracting the mean. For each of the three distributions in Figure 4.1, the face values of the seven original scores (shown as numbers along the X axis) have been re-expressed as deviation scores from their mean of 10 (shown as numbers in the boxes). For example, in distribution C, one score coincides with the mean of 10, four scores (two 9s and two 11s) deviate 1 unit from the mean, and two scores (one 7 and one 13) deviate 3 units from the mean, yielding a set of seven deviation scores: one 0, two –1s, two 1s, one –3, and one 3. (Deviation scores above the mean are assigned positive signs, while those below the mean are assigned negative signs.)

Mean of the Deviations Not a Useful Measure

No useful measure of variability can be produced by calculating the mean of these seven deviations, since, as you will recall from Chapter 3, the sum of all deviations from their mean always equals zero. In effect, the sum of all negative deviations always counterbalances the sum of all positive deviations, regardless of the amount of variability in the group.*

Mean of the Squared Deviations

Before calculating the variance (a type of mean), negative signs must be eliminated from deviation scores. Squaring each deviation—that is, multiplying each deviation by itself—generates a set of squared deviation scores, all of which are positive. (Remember, the product of any two numbers with similar signs is always positive.) Now it's merely a matter of adding the consistently positive values of all squared deviation scores and then dividing by the total number of scores to produce *the mean of all squared deviation scores, also known as the* **variance.**

Weakness of Variance

In the case of the weights of 53 male students in Table 1.1 on page 6, it is useful to know that the mean for the distribution of weights equals 169.51 pounds, but it is confusing to know that, because of the squared deviations, the variance for the same distribution equals 544.29 *squared pounds.* What, you might reasonably ask, are squared pounds?

Variance

The mean of all squared deviation scores.

4.4 STANDARD DEVIATION

To rid ourselves of these mind-boggling units of measurement, simply take the square root of the variance.† This produces a new measure, known as the standard deviation, that describes variability in the original units of measurement. For

---

*A measure of variability, known as the *mean absolute deviation* (or *m.a.d.*), can be salvaged by summing all *absolute* deviations from the mean, that is, by ignoring negative signs. However, this measure of variability is not preferred because, in the end, the simple act of ignoring negative signs has undesirable mathematical and statistical repercussions.

†The square root of a number is the number that, when multiplied by itself, yields the original number. For example, the square root of 16 is 4, since $4 \times 4 = 16$. To extract the square root of any number, use a calculator with a square root key, usually denoted by the symbol $\sqrt{\ }$.

example, the standard deviation for the distribution of weights equals the square root of 544.29 squared pounds, that is, 23.33 pounds.

The variance often assumes a special role in more advanced statistical work, including that described in Chapters 16, 17, and 18. Otherwise, because of its unintelligible units of measurement, the variance serves mainly as a stepping stone, only a square root away from a more preferred measure of variability, the standard deviation, *the square root of the mean of all squared deviations from the mean, that is,*

$$standard\ deviation = \sqrt{variance}$$

Standard Deviation: An Interpretation

> *Standard Deviation*
>
> A rough *measure of the average (or standard) amount by which scores deviate on either side of their mean.*

You might find it helpful to think of the standard deviation as a *rough* measure of the average (or standard) amount by which scores deviate on either side of their mean.

For distribution C in Figure 4.1, the square root of the variance of 3.14 yields a standard deviation of 1.77. Given this perspective, a standard deviation of 1.77 is a rough measure of the average amount by which the seven scores in distribution C (7, 9, 9, 10, 11, 11, 13) deviate on either side of their mean of 10. In other words, the standard deviation of 1.77 is a rough measure of the average amount for the seven deviation scores in distribution C, namely, one 0, four 1s, and two 3s. Notice that, insofar as it is an average, the value of the standard deviation always should be between the largest and smallest deviation scores, as it is for distribution C.

Actually Exceeds Mean Deviation

Strictly speaking, the standard deviation usually exceeds the mean deviation or, more accurately, the mean absolute deviation. (In the case of distribution C in Figure 4.1, for example, the standard deviation equals 1.77, while the mean absolute deviation equals only 1.43.) Nevertheless, it is reasonable to describe the standard deviation as the average amount by which scores deviate on either side of their mean—as long as you remember that an approximation is involved.

Majority of Scores within One Standard Deviation

A slightly different perspective makes the standard deviation even more accessible.

For most frequency distributions, a majority (often as many as 68 percent) of all scores are within one standard deviation on either side of the mean.

This generalization applies to all of the distributions in Figure 4.1. For instance, among the seven deviations in distribution C, a majority of five scores deviate less than one standard deviation (1.77) on either side of the mean.

Essentially the same pattern describes a wide variety of frequency distributions including the two shown in **Figure 4.3**, where the lowercase letter *s* represents the standard deviation. As suggested in the top panel of Figure 4.3, if the distribution of IQ scores for a class of fourth graders has a mean ($\overline{X}$) of 105 and

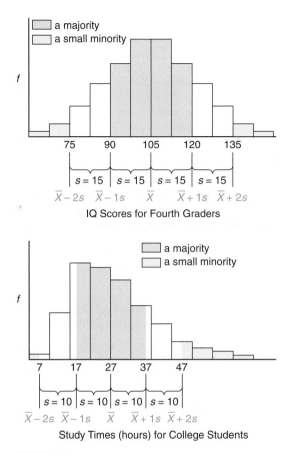

FIGURE 4.3

Some generalizations that apply to most frequency distributions.

a standard deviation (*s*) of 15, a majority of their IQ scores should be within one standard deviation on either side of the mean, that is, between 90 and 120. By the same token, as suggested in the bottom panel of Figure 4.3, if the distribution of weekly study times for a group of college students, estimated to the nearest hour, has a mean ($\overline{X}$) of 27 hours and a standard deviation (*s*) of 10 hours, a majority of their study times should be within one standard deviation on either side of the mean, that is, between 17 and 37 hours.

A Small Minority of Scores Deviate More Than Two Standard Deviations

The standard deviation also can be used in a generalization about the extremities or tails of frequency distributions:

For most frequency distributions, a small minority (often as small as 5 percent) of all scores deviate more than two standard deviations on either side of the mean.

This generalization describes each of the distributions in Figure 4.1. For instance, among the seven deviations in distribution C, none deviates more than two standard deviations ($2 \times 1.77 = 3.54$) on either side of the mean. As suggested in Figure 4.3, relatively few fourth graders have IQ scores that deviate more than two standard deviations ($2 \times 15 = 30$) on either side of the mean of 105, that is, IQ scores less than 75 ($105 - 30$) or more than 135 ($105 + 30$). Likewise, relatively few college students estimate their weekly study times to be more than two standard deviations ($2 \times 10 = 20$) on either side of the mean of 27, that is, less than 7 hours ($27 - 20$) or more than 47 hours ($27 + 20$).

Generalizations Are for All Distributions

These two generalizations about the majority and minority of scores are independent of the particular shape of the distribution. In Figure 4.3, they apply to both the balanced distribution of IQ scores and the positively skewed distribution of study times. In fact, the balanced distribution of IQ scores approximates an important theoretical distribution, the normal distribution. As will be seen in the next chapter, much more precise generalizations are possible for normal distributions.

Progress Check *4.1 Employees of Corporation A earn annual salaries described by a mean of $90,000 and a standard deviation of $10,000.

(a) The majority of all salaries fall between what two values?

(b) A small minority of all salaries are less than what value?

(c) A small minority of all salaries are more than what value?

(d) Answer parts (a), (b), and (c) for Corporation B's employees, who earn annual salaries described by a mean of $90,000 and a standard deviation of $2,000.

Answers on page 493.

Standard Deviation: A Measure of Distance

There's an important difference between the standard deviation and its indispensable co-measure, the mean. *The mean is a measure of position, but the standard deviation is a measure of distance (on either side of the mean of the distribution).* **Figure 4.4** describes the weight distribution for the males originally shown in Figure 2.1. Note that the mean ($\bar{X}$) of 169.51 lbs has a particular position or location along the horizontal axis: It is located at the point, and only at the point, corresponding to 169.51 lbs. On the other hand, the standard deviation (s) of 23.33 lbs for the same distribution has no particular location along the horizontal axis. Using the standard deviation as a measure of distance on either side of the mean, we could describe one person's weight as two standard deviations above the mean, $\bar{X} + 2s$, another person's weight as two-thirds of one standard deviation below the mean, $\bar{X} - \frac{2}{3}s$, and so on.

Value of Standard Deviation Cannot Be Negative

Standard deviation distances always originate from the mean and are expressed as positive deviations above the mean or negative deviations below

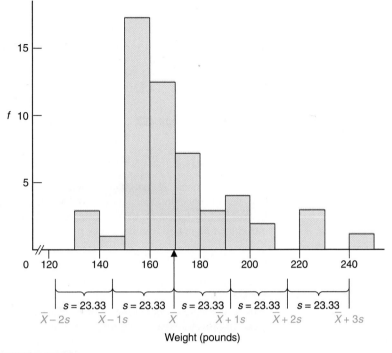

FIGURE 4.4

Weight distribution with mean and standard deviation.

the mean. Note, however, that although the actual value of the standard deviation can be zero or a positive number, it can never be a negative number because any negative deviation disappears when squared. When a negative sign appears next to the standard deviation, as in the expression $\bar{X} - \frac{1}{2}s$, the negative sign indicates that one-half of a standard deviation unit (always positive) must be subtracted from the mean to identify a weight located one half of a standard deviation *below* the mean weight. More specifically, the expression $\bar{X} - \frac{1}{2}s$ translates into a weight of 158 lbs since $169.51 - \frac{1}{2}(23.33) = 169.51 - 11.67 = 157.83$.

Progress Check *4.2 Assume that the distribution of IQ scores for all college students has a mean of 120, with a standard deviation of 15. These two bits of information imply which of the following?

(a) All students have an IQ of either 105 or 135 because everybody in the distribution is either one standard deviation above or below the mean. True or false?

(b) All students score between 105 and 135 because everybody is within one standard deviation on either side of the mean. True or false?

(c) On the average, students deviate approximately 15 points on either side of the mean. True or false?

(d) Some students deviate more than one standard deviation above or below the mean. True or false?

(e) All students deviate more than one standard deviation above or below the mean. True or false?

(f) Scott's IQ score of 150 deviates two standard deviations above the mean. True or false?

Answers on page 493.

4.5 DETAILS: STANDARD DEVIATION

As with the mean, statisticians distinguish between population and sample for both the variance and the standard deviation, depending on whether the data are viewed as a complete set (population) or as a subset (sample). This distinction is introduced here, and it will be very important in inferential statistics.

Sum of Squares (*SS*)

Calculating the standard deviation requires that we obtain first a value for the variance. However, calculating the variance requires, in turn, that we obtain the sum of the squared deviation scores. *The sum of squared deviation scores, or more simply* the **sum of squares**, *symbolized by SS*, merits special attention because it's a major component in calculations for the variance, as well as many other statistical measures. There are two formulas for the sum of squares: the definition formula, which is easier to understand and remember, and the computation formula, which usually is more efficient. In addition, we'll introduce versions of these two formulas for populations and for samples.

Sum of Squares (SS)

The sum of squared deviation scores.

Sum of Squares Formulas for Population

The definition formula provides the most accessible version of the population sum of squares:

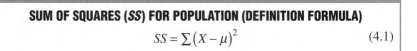

SUM OF SQUARES (*SS*) FOR POPULATION (DEFINITION FORMULA)
$$SS = \sum(X - \mu)^2 \qquad (4.1)$$

where *SS* represents the sum of squares, Σ directs us to sum over the expression to its right, and $(X - \mu)^2$ denotes each of the squared deviation scores. Formula 4.1 should be read as "The sum of squares equals the sum of all squared deviation scores." You can reconstruct this formula by remembering the following three steps:

1. Subtract the population mean, μ, from each original score, *X*, to obtain a deviation score, $X - \mu$.
2. Square each deviation score, $(X - \mu)^2$, to eliminate negative signs.
3. Sum all squared deviation scores, $\Sigma(X - \mu)^2$.

Table 4.1 shows how to use the definition formula to calculate the sum of squares for distribution C in Figure 4.1 on page 74. (Ignore the last two steps in this table until later, when formulas for the variance and standard deviation are introduced.)

The definition formula is cumbersome when, as often occurs, the mean equals some complex number, such as 169.51, or the number of scores is large. In these cases, use the more efficient computation formula:

SUM OF SQUARES (*SS*) FOR POPULATION (COMPUTATION FORMULA)

$$SS = \sum X^2 - \frac{\left(\sum X\right)^2}{N} \qquad (4.2)$$

---

where $\sum X^2$, the sum of the squared X scores, is obtained by *first squaring each X score and then summing all squared X scores;* $(\sum X)^2$, the square of sum of all X

Table 4.1
CALCULATION OF POPULATION STANDARD DEVIATION (σ)
(DEFINITION FORMULA)

A. COMPUTATION SEQUENCE
Assign a value to *N* **1** representing the number of *X* scores
Sum all *X* scores **2**
Obtain the mean of these scores **3**
Subtract the mean from each *X* score to obtain a deviation score **4**
Square each deviation score **5**
Sum all squared deviation scores to obtain the sum of squares **6**
Substitute numbers into the formula to obtain population variance, σ^2 **7**
Take the square root of σ^2 to obtain the population standard deviation, σ **8**

B. DATA AND COMPUTATIONS

X	**4** $X - \mu$	**5** $(X - \mu)^2$
13	3	9
10	0	0
11	1	1
7	−3	9
9	−1	1
11	1	1
9	−1	1

1 $N = 7$ **2** $\sum X = 70$ **6** $SS = \sum (X - \mu)^2 = 22$

3 $\mu = \frac{70}{7} = 10$

7 $\sigma^2 = \frac{SS}{N} = \frac{22}{7} = 3.14$ **8** $\sigma = \sqrt{\frac{SS}{N}} = \sqrt{\frac{22}{7}} = \sqrt{3.14} = 1.77$

scores, is obtained by *first adding all X scores and then squaring the sum of all X scores;* and *N* is the population size.

We'll not attempt to demonstrate that the computation formula, with its more complex expressions, can be derived algebraically from the definition formula. However, Table 4.2 does confirm that the computation formula yields the same sum of squares of 22 for distribution C as did the definition formula in Table 4.1. The tremendous efficiency of the computation formula becomes more apparent when dealing with large sets of scores, as in Review Question 4.12.

Sum of Squares Formulas for Sample

Sample notation can be substituted for population notation in the above two formulas without causing any essential changes:

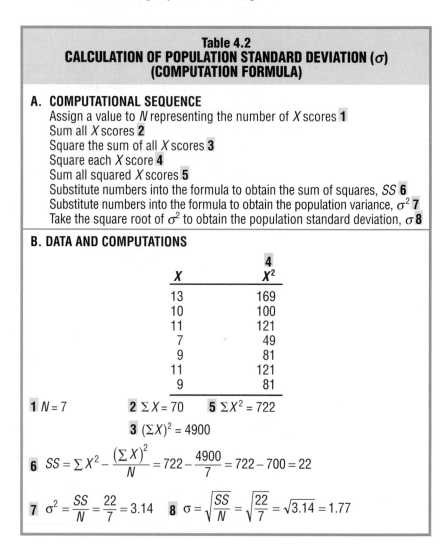

Table 4.2
CALCULATION OF POPULATION STANDARD DEVIATION (σ)
(COMPUTATION FORMULA)

A. COMPUTATIONAL SEQUENCE
Assign a value to *N* representing the number of *X* scores **1**
Sum all *X* scores **2**
Square the sum of all *X* scores **3**
Square each *X* score **4**
Sum all squared *X* scores **5**
Substitute numbers into the formula to obtain the sum of squares, *SS* **6**
Substitute numbers into the formula to obtain the population variance, σ^2 **7**
Take the square root of σ^2 to obtain the population standard deviation, σ **8**

B. DATA AND COMPUTATIONS

X	**4** X^2
13	169
10	100
11	121
7	49
9	81
11	121
9	81

1 $N = 7$ **2** $\Sigma X = 70$ **5** $\Sigma X^2 = 722$

3 $(\Sigma X)^2 = 4900$

6 $SS = \Sigma X^2 - \dfrac{(\Sigma X)^2}{N} = 722 - \dfrac{4900}{7} = 722 - 700 = 22$

7 $\sigma^2 = \dfrac{SS}{N} = \dfrac{22}{7} = 3.14$ **8** $\sigma = \sqrt{\dfrac{SS}{N}} = \sqrt{\dfrac{22}{7}} = \sqrt{3.14} = 1.77$

SUM OF SQUARES (*SS*) FOR SAMPLE (DEFINITION FORMULA)

$$SS = \sum \left(X - \overline{X} \right)^2 \qquad (4.3)$$

(COMPUTATION FORMULA)

$$SS = \sum X^2 - \frac{\left(\sum X \right)^2}{n} \qquad (4.4)$$

---

where $\overline{X}$, the sample mean, replaces μ, the population mean, and n, the sample size, replaces N, the population size. Notwithstanding these two changes in notation, the numerical result for the sample sum of squares (22) is the same as that for the population sum of squares in Tables 4.1 and 4.2. Accordingly, the same symbol, *SS*, will represent the sum of squared deviation scores for both populations and samples.

Standard Deviation for Population (σ)

Recall that, most generally, a mean is defined as the sum of all scores divided by the number of scores. Since the variance is the *mean* of all squared deviation scores, it can be defined as the sum of all squared deviation scores divided by the number of scores:

$$variance = \frac{sum\ of\ all\ squared\ deviation\ scores}{number\ of\ scores}$$

or, in symbols:

VARIANCE FOR POPULATION

$$\sigma^2 = \frac{SS}{N} \qquad (4.5)$$

---

where the squared lowercase Greek letter, σ^2 (pronounced "sigma squared"), represents the population variance, *SS* is the sum of squared deviations for the population, and N is the population size.

To rid us of the bizarre squared units of measurement, take the square root of the variance to obtain the standard deviation, that is,

....

Population Standard Deviation (σ)

A rough measure of the average amount by which scores in the population deviate on either side of their population mean.

STANDARD DEVIATION FOR POPULATION

$$\sigma = \sqrt{\sigma^2} = \sqrt{\frac{SS}{N}} \qquad (4.6)$$

---

where σ represents the **population standard deviation,** $\sqrt{\ }$ instructs us to take the square root of the covered expression, and *SS* and N are defined above.

By referring to the last two steps in either Table 4.1 or 4.2, you can verify that the value of the variance, σ^2, equals 3.14 for distribution C because

$$\sigma^2 = \frac{SS}{N} = \frac{22}{7} = 3.14$$

and that the value of the standard deviation, σ, equals 1.77 for distribution C because

$$\sigma = \sqrt{\frac{SS}{N}} = \sqrt{\frac{22}{7}} = \sqrt{3.14} = 1.77$$

Standard Deviation for Sample (s)

Although the sum of squares term remains essentially the same for both populations and samples, there is a small but important change in the formulas for the variance and standard deviation for samples. This change appears in the denominator of each formula where N, the population size, is replaced not by n, the sample size, but by $n - 1$, as shown:

VARIANCE FOR SAMPLE

$$s^2 = \frac{SS}{n-1} \tag{4.7}$$

STANDARD DEVIATION FOR SAMPLE

$$s = \sqrt{s^2} = \sqrt{\frac{SS}{n-1}} \tag{4.8}$$

Sample Standard Deviation (s)

A rough measure of the average amount by which scores in the sample deviate on either side of their sample mean.

where s^2 and s represent the sample variance and **sample standard deviation,** SS is the sample sum of squares as defined in either Formula 4.3 or 4.4, and n is the sample size.*

The reason for using $n - 1$ will be explained in the next section. But first, spend a few moments studying Tables 4.3 and 4.4, which show the calculations for the sample standard deviation, using the definition and computation formulas for sample sums of squares and a new set of five scores. Notice that, except for changes in notation and the smaller $(n - 1)$ denominator, the computational procedures for the sample standard deviation in Tables 4.3 and 4.4 are the same as those for the population standard deviation in Tables 4.1 and 4.2.

---

*As recommended in the *Publication Manual of the American Psychological Association,* authors of current psychological reports often symbolize the sample standard deviation as SD instead of s and the sample mean as M instead of $\bar{X}$. However, we'll continue to use s and $\bar{X}$, the customary symbols in most statistics texts.

Table 4.3
CALCULATION OF SAMPLE STANDARD DEVIATION (s)
(DEFINITION FORMULA)

A. COMPUTATION SEQUENCE
   Assign a value to n **1** representing the number of X scores
   Sum all X scores **2**
   Obtain the mean of these scores **3**
   Subtract the mean from each X score to obtain a deviation score **4**
   Square each deviation score **5**
   Sum all squared deviation scores to obtain the sum of squares **6**
   Substitute numbers into the formula to obtain the sample variance, s^2 **7**
   Take the square root of s^2 to obtain the sample standard deviation, s **8**

B. DATA AND COMPUTATIONS

X	**4** $X - \bar{X}$	**5** $(X - \bar{X})^2$
7	4	16
3	0	0
1	−2	4
0	−3	9
4	1	1

1 $n = 5$ **2** $\sum X = 15$ **6** $SS = \sum \left(X - \bar{X}\right)^2 = 30$

3 $\bar{X} = \dfrac{15}{5} = 3$

7 $s^2 = \dfrac{SS}{n-1} = \dfrac{30}{4} = 7.50$ **8** $s = \sqrt{\dfrac{SS}{n-1}} = \sqrt{\dfrac{30}{4}} = \sqrt{7.50} = 2.74$

Computational Check

With rare exceptions, the standard deviation should be less than one-half the size of the range, and in most cases, it will be an even smaller fraction (one-third to one-sixth) the size of the range. Use this rule of thumb to detect sizable computation errors. The only foolproof method for detecting smaller errors—whether you're calculating the standard deviation manually or electronically—is to calculate everything twice and to proceed only if your numerical results agree.

Reminder:

*Replace **n** with **n − 1** only when dividing **SS** to obtain s^2 and **s**.*

Progress Check *4.3 Using the definition formula for the sum of squares, calculate the sample standard deviation for the following four scores: 1, 3, 4, 4.

Progress Check *4.4 Using the computation formula for the sum of squares, calculate the population standard deviation for the scores in (a) and the sample standard deviation for the scores in (b).

(a) 1, 3, 7, 2, 0, 4, 7, 3   **(b)** 10, 8, 5, 0, 1, 1, 7, 9, 2

Answers on page 494.

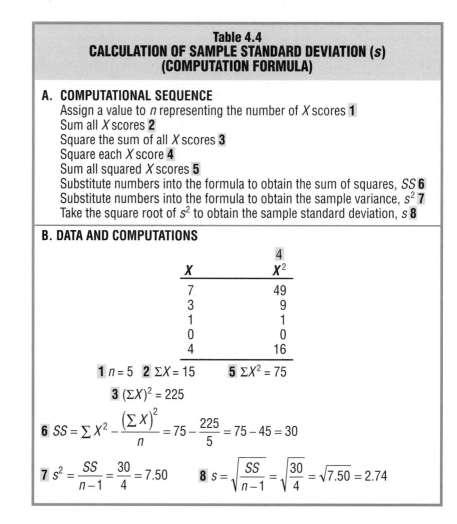

Table 4.4
CALCULATION OF SAMPLE STANDARD DEVIATION (s)
(COMPUTATION FORMULA)

A. COMPUTATIONAL SEQUENCE

Assign a value to n representing the number of X scores **1**
Sum all X scores **2**
Square the sum of all X scores **3**
Square each X score **4**
Sum all squared X scores **5**
Substitute numbers into the formula to obtain the sum of squares, SS **6**
Substitute numbers into the formula to obtain the sample variance, s^2 **7**
Take the square root of s^2 to obtain the sample standard deviation, s **8**

B. DATA AND COMPUTATIONS

X	**4** X^2
7	49
3	9
1	1
0	0
4	16

1 $n = 5$ **2** $\Sigma X = 15$ **5** $\Sigma X^2 = 75$

3 $(\Sigma X)^2 = 225$

6 $SS = \Sigma X^2 - \dfrac{(\Sigma X)^2}{n} = 75 - \dfrac{225}{5} = 75 - 45 = 30$

7 $s^2 = \dfrac{SS}{n-1} = \dfrac{30}{4} = 7.50$ **8** $s = \sqrt{\dfrac{SS}{n-1}} = \sqrt{\dfrac{30}{4}} = \sqrt{7.50} = 2.74$

Why $n - 1$?

Using $n - 1$ in the denominator of Formulas 4.7 and 4.8 solves a problem in inferential statistics associated with generalizations from samples to populations. The adequacy of these generalizations usually depends on *accurately* estimating unknown variability in the population with known variability in the sample. But if we were to use n rather than $n - 1$ in the denominator of our estimates, they would tend to underestimate variability in the population because n is too large. This tendency would compromise any subsequent generalizations, such as whether observed mean differences are real or merely transitory. On the other hand, when the denominator is made smaller by using $n - 1$, variability in the population is estimated more accurately, and subsequent generalizations are more likely to be valid.

Assume that the five scores (7, 3, 1, 0, 4) in Table 4.3 are a random sample from some population whose unknown variability is to be estimated with the sample variability. To understand why $n - 1$ works, let's look more closely at deviation scores. Formula 4.3, the definition formula for the sample sum of squares, specifies that each of the five original scores, X, be expressed as positive or negative deviations from their sample mean, $\bar{X}$, of 3. At this point, a subtle mathematical restriction causes a complication. It's always true, as demonstrated on the left-hand side of Table 4.5, that *the sum of all scores, when expressed as deviations about their own mean, equals zero.* (If you're skeptical, recall the discussion on page 63 about the mean as a balance point that equalizes the sums of all positive and negative deviations.) Given values for *any* four of the five deviations on the left-hand side of Table 4.5, the value of the remaining deviation is not free to vary. Instead, its value is completely fixed because it must comply with the mathematical restriction that the sum of all deviations about *their own mean* equals zero. For instance, given the sum for the four top deviations on the left-hand side of Table 4.5, that is, $[4 + 0 + (-2) + (-3) = -1]$, the value of the bottom deviation must equal 1, as it does, because of the zero-sum restriction, that is, $[-1 + 1 = 0]$. Or since this mathematical restriction applies to *any* four of the five deviations, given the sum for the four bottom deviations in Table 4.5, that is, $[0 + (-2) + (-3) + 1 = -4]$, the value of the top deviation must equal 4 because $[-4 + 4 = 0]$.

If μ is Known

For the sake of the present discussion, now assume that we know the value of the population mean, μ—let's say it equals 2. (Any value assigned to μ other than 3, the value of $\bar{X}$, would satisfy the current argument. It's reasonable to assume that the values of μ and $\bar{X}$ will differ because a random sample exactly replicates its population rarely, if at all.) Furthermore, assume that we take a random sample of $n = 5$ population deviation scores, $X - \mu$. Then these five known

Table 4.5
TWO ESTIMATES OF POPULATION VARIABILITY

WHEN μ IS UNKNOWN $(\bar{X} = 3)$			WHEN μ IS KNOWN $(\mu = 2)$		
X	$X - \bar{X}$	$(X - \bar{X})^2$	X	$X - \mu$	$(X - \mu)^2$
7	$7 - 3 = 4$	16	7	$7 - 2 = 5$	25
3	$3 - 3 = 0$	0	3	$3 - 2 = 1$	1
1	$1 - 3 = -2$	4	1	$1 - 2 = -1$	1
0	$0 - 3 = -3$	9	0	$0 - 2 = -2$	4
4	$4 - 3 = 1$	1	4	$4 - 2 = 2$	4

$$\Sigma(X - \bar{X}) = 0 \quad \Sigma(X - \bar{X})^2 = 30$$

$$df = n - 1 = 5 - 1 = 4$$

$$s^2(df = n - 1) = \frac{\Sigma(X - \bar{X})^2}{n - 1} = \frac{30}{4} = 7.50$$

$$\Sigma(X - \mu) = 5 \quad \Sigma(X - \mu)^2 = 35$$

$$df = n = 5$$

$$s^2(df = n) = \frac{\Sigma(X - \mu)^2}{n} = \frac{35}{5} = 7.00$$

deviation scores will serve as the initial basis for estimating the unknown variability in the population. As demonstrated on the right-hand side of Table 4.5, the sum of the five deviations about μ, that is, $[5 + 1 + (-1) + (-2) + 2]$, equals not 0 but 5. The zero-sum restriction applies only if the five deviations are expressed around *their own* mean, that is, the sample mean, $\overline{X}$, of 3. It does not apply when the five deviations are expressed around *some other* mean, such as the population mean, μ, of 2 for the entire population. In this case, since all five deviations are free to vary, *each* provides valid information about the variability in the population. Therefore, when calculating the sample variance based on a random sample of five population deviation scores, $X - \mu$, it would be appropriate to divide this sample sum of squares by the n of 5, as shown on the right-hand side of Table 4.5.

If μ is Unknown

It would be most efficient if, as above, we could use a random sample of n deviations expressed around the population mean, $X - \mu$, to estimate variability in the population. But this is usually impossible because, in fact, the population mean is unknown. Therefore, we must substitute the known sample mean, $\overline{X}$, for the unknown population mean, μ, and we must use a random sample of n deviations expressed around their own sample mean, $X - \overline{X}$, to estimate variability in the population. Although there are $n = 5$ deviations in the sample, only $n - 1 = 4$ of these deviations are free to vary because the sum of the $n = 5$ deviations from *their own sample mean* always equals zero.

Only $n - 1$ of the sample deviations supply valid information for estimating variability. One bit of valid information has been lost because of the zero-sum restriction when the sample mean replaces the population mean. And that's why we divide the sum of squares for $X - \overline{X}$ by $n - 1$, as on the left-hand side of Table 4.5.

4.6 DEGREES OF FREEDOM (*df*)

Technically, we have been discussing a very important notion in inferential statistics known as degrees of freedom.

Degrees of freedom (df) refers to the number of values that are free to vary, given one or more mathematical restrictions, in a sample being used to *estimate* a population characteristic.

The concept of degrees of freedom is introduced only because we are using scores in a sample to *estimate* some unknown characteristic of the population. Typically, when used as an estimate, not all observed values in the sample are free to vary because of one or more mathematical restrictions. As has been noted, when n deviations about the sample mean are used to estimate variability in the population, only $n - 1$ are free to vary. As a result, there are only $n - 1$ degrees of freedom, that is, $df = n - 1$. One df is lost because of the zero-sum restriction.

If the sample sum of squares were divided by n, it would tend to underestimate variability in the population. (In Table 4.5, when μ is unknown, division by n instead of $n - 1$ would produce a smaller estimate of 6.00 instead of 7.50.) This would occur because, there are only $n - 1$ independent deviations (estimates of variability) in the sample sum of squares. A more accurate estimate is obtained when the denominator term reflects the number of independent deviations—that is, the number of degrees of freedom—in the numerator, as in the formulas for s^2 and s. In fact, we can use degrees of freedom to rewrite the formulas for the sample variance and standard deviation:

VARIANCE FOR SAMPLE

$$s^2 = \frac{SS}{n-1} = \frac{SS}{df} \tag{4.9}$$

STANDARD DEVIATION FOR SAMPLE

$$s = \sqrt{\frac{SS}{n-1}} = \sqrt{\frac{SS}{df}} \tag{4.10}$$

---

where s^2 and s represent the sample variance and standard deviation, SS is the sum of squares as defined in either Formula 4.3 or 4.4, and df is the degrees of freedom and equals $n - 1$.

Other Mathematical Restrictions

The notion of degrees of freedom is used extensively in inferential statistics. We'll encounter other mathematical restrictions, and sometimes more than one degree of freedom will be lost. In any event, however, degrees of freedom (df) always indicate the number of values that are free to vary, given one or more mathematical restrictions, in a set of values used to estimate some unknown population characteristic.

Progress Check *4.5 As a first step toward modifying his study habits, Phil keeps daily records of his study time.

(a) During the first two weeks, Phil's mean study time equals 20 hours per week. If he studied 22 hours during the first week, how many hours did he study during the second week?

(b) During the first four weeks, Phil's mean study time equals 21 hours. If he studied 22, 18, and 21 hours during the first, second, and third weeks, respectively, how many hours did he study during the fourth week?

(c) If the information in (a) and (b) is to be used to estimate some unknown population characteristic, the notion of degrees of freedom can be introduced. How many degrees of freedom are associated with (a) and (b)?

(d) Describe the mathematical restriction that causes a loss of degrees of freedom in (a) and (b).

Answers on page 494.

4.7 INTERQUARTILE RANGE (IQR)

The most important spinoff of the range, the **interquartile range (IQR),** *is simply the range for the middle 50 percent of the scores.* More specifically, the IQR equals the distance between the third quartile (or 75th percentile) and the first quartile (or 25th percentile), that is, after the highest quarter (or top 25 percent) and the lowest quarter (or bottom 25 percent) have been trimmed from the original set of scores. Since most distributions are spread more widely in their extremities than their middle, the IQR tends to be less than half the size of the range.

The calculation of the IQR is relatively straightforward, as you can see by studying Table 4.6. This table shows that the IQR equals 2 for distribution C (7, 9, 9, 10, 11, 11, 13) shown in Figure 4.1.

Not Sensitive to Extreme Scores

A key property of the IQR is its resistance to the distorting effect of extreme scores, or outliers. For example, if the smallest score (7) in distribution C of Figure 4.1 were replaced by a much smaller score (for instance, 1), the value of

---

Table 4.6
CALCULATION OF THE IQR

A. INSTRUCTIONS

1 Order scores from least to most.
2 To determine how far to penetrate the set of ordered scores, beginning at either end, add 1 to the total number of scores and divide by 4. If necessary, round the result to the nearest whole number.
3 Beginning with the largest score, count the requisite number of steps into the ordered scores to find the location of the third quartile.
4 The third quartile equals the value of the score at this location.
5 Beginning with the smallest score, again count the requisite number of steps into the ordered scores to find the location of the first quartile.
6 The first quartile equals the value of the score at this location.
7 The IQR equals the third quartile minus the first quartile.

B. EXAMPLE

1 7, 9, 9, 10, 11, 11, 13
2 $(7 + 1)/4 = 2$
3 7, 9, 9, 10, 11, 11, 13

4 third quartile = 11
5 7, 9, 9, 10, 11, 11, 13

6 first quartile = 9
7 IQR = 11 − 9 = 2

the IQR would remain the same (2), although the value of the original range (6) would be larger (12). Thus, if you are concerned about possible distortions caused by extreme scores, or outliers, use the IQR as the measure of variability, along with the median (or second quartile) as the measure of central tendency.

Progress Check *4.6 Determine the values of the range and the IQR for the following sets of data.

(a) Retirement ages: 60, 63, 45, 63, 65, 70, 55, 63, 60, 65, 63.

(b) Residence changes: 1, 3, 4, 1, 0, 2, 5, 8, 0, 2, 3, 4, 7, 11, 0, 2, 3, 4.

Answers on page 494.

4.8 MEASURES OF VARIABILITY FOR QUALITATIVE AND RANKED DATA

Qualitative Data

Measures of variability are virtually nonexistent for qualitative or nominal data. It is probably adequate to note merely whether scores are evenly divided among the various classes (maximum variability), unevenly divided among the various classes (intermediate variability), or concentrated mostly in one class (minimum variability). For example, if the ethnic composition of the residents of a city is about evenly divided among several groups, the variability with respect to ethnic groups is maximum; there is considerable heterogeneity. (An inspection of county population data from the 2000 census, available on the Internet at http://factfinder.census.gov, reveals that the greatest ethnic variability occurs in large urban counties, such as Bronx County, New York, and San Francisco County, California.) At the other extreme, if almost all the residents are concentrated in a single ethnic group, the variability will be minimum; there is little heterogeneity. (According to the above source, virtually no ethnic variability occurs in sparsely populated rural counties, such as Hooker County, Nebraska, and King County, Texas, with an almost exclusively white population.) If the ethnic composition falls between these two extremes—because of an uneven division among several large ethnic groups—the variability will be intermediate, as is true of many U.S. cities and counties.

Ordered Qualitative and Ranked Data

If qualitative data can be ordered because measurement is ordinal (or if the data are ranked), then it's appropriate to describe variability by identifying extreme scores (or ranks). For instance, the active membership of an officers' club might include no one with a rank below first lieutenant or above brigadier general.

Summary

Measures of variability reflect the amount by which observations are dispersed or scattered in a distribution. These measures assume a key role in the analysis of research results.

The simplest measure of variability, the range, is readily calculated and understood, but it has two shortcomings.

Among measures of variability, the variance and particularly the standard deviation occupy the same exalted position as does the mean among measures of central tendency.

The variance is a type of mean, that is, the mean of all squared deviations about their mean. To avoid mind-boggling squared units of measurement, we take the square root of the variance to obtain the standard deviation.

The standard deviation is a rough measure of the average or typical amount by which scores deviate on either side of their mean.

For most frequency distributions, a majority of all scores are within one standard deviation of their mean, and a small minority of all scores deviate more than two standard deviations on either side of their mean.

Unlike the mean, which is a measure of position, the standard deviation is a measure of distance.

Calculation of either the population standard deviation (σ) or the sample standard deviation (s) requires three steps:

1. Calculate the sum of all squared deviation scores (*SS*) using either the definition or computation formula.
2. Divide the *SS* by *N*, the population size, to obtain the population variance (σ^2) or divide the *SS* by $n-1$, the sample size minus 1, to obtain the sample variance (s^2).
3. Take the square root of the variance to obtain the population standard deviation (σ) or the sample standard deviation (s).

The denominator of the formulas for sample variance and standard deviation reflects the fact that, because of the zero-sum restriction, only $n-1$ of the sample deviation scores provide valid estimates of population variability.

Whenever we estimate unknown population characteristics, we must be concerned about the number of degrees of freedom (*df*) associated with our estimate. Degrees of freedom specify the number of values that are free to vary, given one or more mathematical restrictions. When estimating the population variance and standard deviation, degrees of freedom equal $n-1$.

The interquartile range (IQR) is resistant to the distorting effects of extreme scores.

Measures of variability are virtually nonexistent for qualitative and ranked data.

Important Terms

Measures of variability	**Variance**
Range	**Sum of squares (*SS*)**
Standard deviation	**Sample standard deviation (*s*)**
Population standard deviation (σ)	**Interquartile range (IQR)**
Degrees of freedom (*df*)	

Key Equations
. . . .

STANDARD DEVIATION FOR SAMPLE

$$s = \sqrt{\frac{SS}{n-1}} = \sqrt{\frac{SS}{df}}$$

$$\text{where} \quad SS = \sum X^2 - \frac{(\sum X)^2}{n}$$

REVIEW QUESTIONS

*4.7 For each of the following pairs of distributions, first decide whether their standard deviations are about the same or different. If their standard deviations are different, indicate which distribution should have the larger standard deviation. **Hint:** The distribution with the more dissimilar set of scores or individuals should produce the larger standard deviation regardless of whether, *on average,* scores or individuals in one distribution differ from those in the other distribution.

(a) SAT scores for all graduating high school seniors (a_1) or all college freshmen (a_2)

(b) Ages of patients in a community hospital (b_1) or a children's hospital (b_2)

(c) Motor skill reaction times of professional baseball players (c_1) or college students (c_2)

(d) GPAs of students at some university as revealed by a random sample (d_1) or a census of the entire student body (d_2)

(e) Anxiety scores (on a scale from 0 to 50) of a random sample of college students taken from the senior class (e_1) or those who plan to attend an anxiety-reduction clinic (e_2)

(f) Annual incomes of recent college graduates (f_1) or of 20-year alumni (f_2)
Answers on page 494.

4.8 When not interrupted artificially, the duration of human pregnancies can be described, we'll assume, by a mean of 9 months (270 days) and a standard deviation of one-half month (15 days).

(a) Between what two times, in days, will a majority of babies arrive?

(b) A small minority of all babies will arrive sooner than _____?

(c) A small minority of all babies will arrive later than _____?

(d) In a paternity suit, the suspected father claims that, since he was overseas during the entire 10 months prior to the baby's birth, he could not possibly be the father. Any comment?

4.9 Add 10 to each of the scores in Question 4.3 (1, 3, 4, 4) to produce a new distribution (11, 13, 14, 14). Would you expect the value of the sample standard deviation to be the same for both the original and new distributions? Explain your answer, and then calculate s for the new distribution.

4.10 Add 10 to only the smallest score in Question 4.3 (1, 3, 4, 4) to produce another new distribution (11, 3, 4, 4). Would you expect the value of s to be the same for both the original and new distributions? Explain your answer, and then calculate s for the new distribution.

*4.11 (a) While in office, a former governor of California proposed that all state employees receive the same pay raise of $70 per month. What effect, if any, would this raise have had on the mean and the standard deviation for the distribution of monthly wages in existence before the proposed raise? **Hint:** Imagine the effect of adding $70 to the monthly wages of each state employee on the mean and on the standard deviation (or on a more easily visualized measure of variability, such as the range).

(b) Other California officials suggested that all state employees receive a pay raise of 5 percent. What effect, if any, would this raise have had on the mean and the standard deviation for the distribution of monthly wages in existence before the proposed raise? **Hint:** Imagine the effect of multiplying the monthly wages of each state employee by 5 percent on the mean and on the standard deviation or on the range.

Answers on page 494.

4.12 (a) Using the computation formula for the sample sum of squares, verify that the sample standard deviation, s, equals 23.33 lbs for the distribution of 53 weights in Table 1.1.

(b) Verify that a majority of all weights fall within one standard deviation of the mean (169.51) and that a small minority of all weights deviate more than two standard deviations from the mean.

4.13 In what sense is the variance

(a) a type of mean?

(b) not a readily understood measure of variability?

(c) a stepping stone to the standard deviation?

4.14 Specify an important difference between the standard deviation and the mean.

4.15 Why can't the value of the standard deviation ever be negative?

*4.16 Indicate whether each of the following statements about degrees of freedom is true or false.

(a) Degrees of freedom refer to the number of values free to vary in the population.

(b) One degree of freedom is lost because, when expressed as a deviation from the sample mean, the final deviation in the sample fails to supply information about population variability.

(c) Degrees of freedom makes sense only if we wish to estimate some unknown characteristic of a population.

(d) Degrees of freedom reflect the poor quality of one or more observations.

Answers on page 494.

4.17 Referring to Review Question 2.16 on page 55, would you describe the distribution for all male graduates as having maximum, intermediate, or minimum variability?

Normal Distributions and Standard (*z*) Scores

Summary / Important Terms / Key Equations / Review Questions

Preview

The familiar bell-shaped normal curve describes many observed frequency distributions, including scores on IQ tests, slight measurement errors made by a succession of people who attempt to measure precisely the same thing, the useful lives of 100-watt electric light bulbs, and even the heights of stalks in a field of corn. As will become apparent in later chapters, the normal curve also describes some important theoretical distributions in inferential statistics.

Thanks to the standard normal table, we can answer questions about any normal distribution whose mean and standard deviation are known. In the long run, this proves to be both more accurate and more efficient than dealing directly with each observed frequency distribution. Use of the standard normal table requires a familiarity with z scores. Regardless of the original measurements—whether IQ points, measurement errors in millimeters, or reaction times in milliseconds—z scores are "pure" or unit-free numbers that indicate how many standard deviation units an observation is above or below the mean.

In the classic movie *The President's Analyst,* the director of the Federal Bureau of Investigation, rather short himself, encourages the recruitment of similarly short FBI agents. If, in fact, FBI agents are to be selected only from among applicants who are no taller than exactly 65 inches, what proportion of all of the original applicants will be eligible? This question can't be answered without additional information.

One source of additional information is the relative frequency distribution of heights for the 3091 men shown in **Figure 5.1**. To find the proportion of men who are a particular height, merely note the value of the vertical scale that corresponds to the top of any bar in the histogram. For example, .10 of these men, that is, one-tenth of 3091, or about 309 men, are 69 inches tall.

When expressed as a proportion, any conclusion based on the 3091 men can be generalized to other comparable sets of men, even sets containing an unspecified number. For instance, if the distribution in Figure 5.1 is viewed as representative of all men who apply for FBI jobs, we can estimate that .10 of all applicants will be 69 inches tall. Or, given the director's preference for shorter agents, we can use the same distribution to estimate the proportion of applicants who will be eligible. To obtain the estimated proportion of eligible applicants (.165) from Figure 5.1, add the values associated with the shaded bars. (Only half of the bar at 65 inches is shaded to adjust for the fact that any height between 64.5 and 65.5 inches is reported as 65 inches, whereas eligible applicants must be shorter than *exactly* 65 inches, that is, 65.0 inches.)

The distribution in Figure 5.1 has an obvious limitation: It is based on a group of just 3091 men that, at most, only resembles the distributions for other groups of men, including the group of FBI applicants. Therefore, any generalization will contain inaccuracies due to chance irregularities in the original distribution.

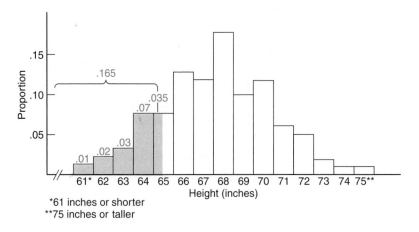

*61 inches or shorter
**75 inches or taller

FIGURE 5.1
Relative frequency distribution for heights of 3091 men.
Source: National Center for Health Statistics, Series 11, No.14.

5.1 THE NORMAL CURVE

More accurate generalizations usually can be obtained from distributions based on larger numbers of men. A distribution based on 30,910 men usually is more accurate than one based on 3091, and a distribution based on 3,091,000 usually is even more accurate. But it is prohibitively expensive in both time and money to survey even 30,910 people. Fortunately, it is a fact that the distribution of heights for all American men—not just 3091 or even 3,091,000—approximates the normal curve, a well-documented theoretical curve.

In **Figure 5.2**, the idealized normal curve has been superimposed on the original distribution for 3091 men. Irregularities in the original distribution, most likely due to chance, are ignored by the smooth normal curve. Accordingly, any generalizations based on the smooth normal curve will tend to be more accurate than those based on the original distribution.

Interpreting the Shaded Area

The total area under the normal curve in Figure 5.2 can be identified with all FBI applicants. Viewed relative to the total area, the shaded area represents the proportion of applicants who will be eligible because they are shorter than exactly 65 inches. This new, more accurate proportion will differ from that obtained from the original histogram (.165) because of discrepancies between the two distributions.

Finding a Proportion for the Shaded Area

To find this new proportion, we cannot rely on the vertical scale in Figure 5.2, because it describes as proportions the areas in the rectangular bars of histograms, not the areas in the various curved sectors of the normal curve. Instead, in Section 5.3 we will learn how to use a special table to find the proportion represented by any area under the normal curve, including that represented by the shaded area in Figure 5.2.

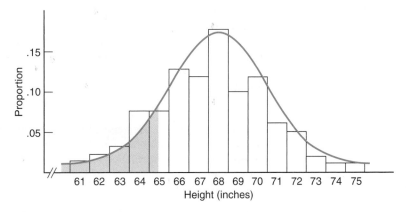

FIGURE 5.2
Normal curve superimposed on the distribution of heights.

Properties of the Normal Curve

Let's note several important properties of the normal curve:

Normal Curve

A theoretical curve noted for its symmetrical bell-shaped form.

- Obtained from a mathematical equation, the **normal curve** is a theoretical curve defined for a continuous variable, as described in Section 1.6, and noted for its symmetrical bell-shaped form, as revealed in Figure 5.2.
- Because the normal curve is symmetrical, its lower half is the mirror image of its upper half.
- Being bell shaped, the normal curve peaks above a point midway along the horizontal spread and then tapers off gradually in either direction from the peak (without actually touching the horizontal axis, since, in theory, the tails of a normal curve extend infinitely far).
- The values of the mean, median (or 50th percentile), and mode, located at a point midway along the horizontal spread, are the same for the normal curve.

Importance of Mean and Standard Deviation

When you're using the normal curve, two bits of information are indispensable: values for the mean and the standard deviation. For example, before the normal curve can be used to answer the question about eligible FBI applicants, it must be established that, for the original distribution of 3091 men, the mean height equals 68 inches and the standard deviation equals 3 inches.

Different Normal Curves

Having established that a particular normal curve has a mean of 68 inches and a standard deviation of 3 inches, we can't arbitrarily change these values, as any change in the value of either the mean or the standard deviation (or both) would create a new normal curve that no longer describes the original distribution of heights. Nevertheless, as a theoretical exercise, it is instructive to note the various types of normal curves that are produced by an arbitrary change in the value of either the mean (μ) or the standard deviation (σ).*

For example, changing the mean height from 68 to 78 inches produces a new normal curve that, as shown in panel A of **Figure 5.3**, is displaced 10 inches to the right of the original curve. Dramatically new normal curves are produced by changing the value of the standard deviation. As shown in panel B of Figure 5.3, changing the standard deviation from 3 to 1.5 inches produces a more peaked normal curve with smaller variability, whereas changing the standard deviation from 3 to 6 inches produces a shallower normal curve with greater variability.

Obvious differences in appearance among normal curves are less important than you might suspect. Because of their common mathematical origin, every normal curve can be interpreted in exactly the same way *once any distance from the mean is expressed in standard deviation units*. For example, .68, or 68 percent of the total area under a normal curve—any normal curve—is within one

---

* Since the normal curve is an idealized curve that is presumed to describe a complete set of observations or a population, the symbols μ and σ, representing the mean and standard deviation of the population, respectively, will be used in this chapter.

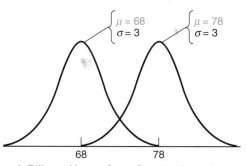
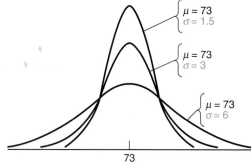

$\begin{cases} \mu = 68 \\ \sigma = 3 \end{cases}$ $\begin{cases} \mu = 78 \\ \sigma = 3 \end{cases}$

$\begin{cases} \mu = 73 \\ \sigma = 1.5 \end{cases}$

$\begin{cases} \mu = 73 \\ \sigma = 3 \end{cases}$

$\begin{cases} \mu = 73 \\ \sigma = 6 \end{cases}$

68   78   73

A. Different Means, Same Standard Deviation   B. Same Mean, Different Standard Deviations

FIGURE 5.3

Different normal curves.

standard deviation above and below the mean, and only .05, or 5 percent, of the total area is more than two standard deviations above and below the mean. And this is only the tip of the iceberg. Once any distance from the mean has been expressed in standard deviation units, we will be able to consult the standard normal table, described in Section 5.3, to determine the corresponding proportion of the area under the normal curve.

5.2 z SCORES

z Score

A unit-free, standardized score that indicates how many standard deviations a score is above or below the mean of its distribution.

A z score is a unit-free, standardized score that, regardless of the original units of measurement, indicates how many standard deviations a score is above or below the mean of its distribution.

To obtain a z score, express any original score, whether measured in inches, milliseconds, dollars, IQ points, etc., as a deviation from its mean (by subtracting its mean) and then split this deviation into standard deviation units (by dividing by its standard deviation), that is,

z SCORE
$z = \dfrac{X - \mu}{\sigma}$ (5.1)

where X is the original score and μ and σ are the mean and the standard deviation, respectively, for the normal distribution of the original scores. Since identical units of measurement appear in both the numerator and denominator of the ratio for z, the original units of measurement cancel each other and the z score emerges as a unit-free or standardized number, often referred to as a standard score.

A z score consists of two parts:

1. a *positive or negative sign* indicating whether it's above or below the mean; and
2. a *number* indicating the size of its deviation from the mean in standard deviation units.

A z score of 2.00 always signifies that the original score is exactly two standard deviations above its mean. Similarly, a z score of -1.27 signifies that the original score is exactly 1.27 standard deviations below its mean. A z score of 0 signifies that the original score coincides with the mean.

Converting to z Scores

To answer the question about eligible FBI applicants, replace X with 65 (the maximum permissible height), μ with 68 (the mean height) and σ with 3 (the standard deviation of heights) and solve for z as follows:

$$z = \frac{65 - 68}{3} = \frac{-3}{3} = -1.00$$

This informs us that the cutoff height is exactly one standard deviation below the mean. Knowing the value of z, we can use the table for the standard normal curve to find the proportion of eligible FBI applicants. First, however, we'll make a few comments about the standard normal curve.

Progress Check *5.1 Express each of the following scores as a z score:

(a) Margaret's IQ of 135, given a mean of 100 and a standard deviation of 15

(b) a score of 470 on the SAT math test, given a mean of 500 and a standard deviation of 100

(c) a daily production of 2100 loaves of bread by a bakery, given a mean of 2180 and a standard deviation of 50

(d) Sam's height of 68 inches, given a mean of 68 and a standard deviation of 3

(e) a thermometer-reading error of -3 degrees, given a mean of 0 degrees and a standard deviation of 2 degrees
Answers on page 495.

Standard Normal Curve

The one tabled normal curve for z scores, with a mean of 0 and a standard deviation of 1.

5.3 STANDARD NORMAL CURVE

If the original distribution approximates a normal curve, then the shift to standard or z scores will always produce a new distribution that approximates the **standard normal curve.** This is the one normal curve for which a table is actually available. It is a mathematical fact—not proven in this book—that the standard normal curve always has a mean of 0 and a standard deviation of 1.

However, to verify (rather than prove) that the mean of a standard normal distribution equals 0, replace X in the z score formula with μ, the mean of any (nonstandard) normal distribution, and then solve for z:

$$\text{mean of } z = \frac{X - \mu}{\sigma} = \frac{\mu - \mu}{\sigma} = \frac{0}{\sigma} = 0$$

Likewise, to verify that the standard deviation of the standard normal distribution equals 1, replace X in the z score formula with $\mu + 1\sigma$, the value corresponding to one standard deviation above the mean for any (nonstandard) normal distribution, and then solve for z:

$$\text{standard deviation of } z = \frac{X - \mu}{\sigma} = \frac{\mu + 1\sigma - \mu}{\sigma} = \frac{1\sigma}{\sigma} = 1$$

Although there is an infinite number of different normal curves, each with its own mean and standard deviation, there is only one *standard normal curve*, with a mean of 0 and a standard deviation of 1.

Figure 5.4 illustrates the emergence of the standard normal curve from three different normal curves: that for the men's heights, with a mean of 68 inches and a standard deviation of 3 inches; that for the useful lives of 100-watt electric light bulbs, with a mean of 1200 hours and a standard deviation of 120 hours; and that for the IQ scores of fourth graders, with a mean of 105 points and a standard deviation of 15 points.

Converting all original observations into z scores leaves the normal shape intact but not the units of measurement. Color-coded observations of 65 inches, 1080 hours, and 90 IQ points all reappear as a z score of −1.00. Verify this by using the z score formula. Showing no traces of the original units of measurement,

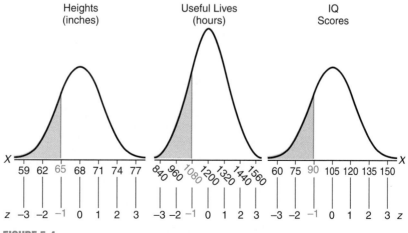

FIGURE 5.4

Converting three normal curves to the standard normal curve.

this z score contains the one crucial bit of information common to the three original observations: All are located one standard deviation below the mean. Accordingly, to find the proportion for the shaded areas in Figure 5.4 (that is, the proportion of applicants who are less than exactly 65 inches tall, or light bulbs that burn for fewer than 1080 hours, or fourth graders whose IQ scores are less than 90), we can use the same z score of -1.00 when referring to the table for the standard normal curve, the one table for all normal curves.

Standard Normal Table

Essentially, the standard normal table consists of columns of z scores coordinated with columns of proportions. In a typical problem, access to the table is gained through a z score, such as -1.00, and the answer is read as a proportion, such as the proportion of eligible FBI applicants.

Using the Top Legend of the Table

Table 5.1 shows an abbreviated version of the standard normal curve, while Table A in Appendix C on page 530 shows a more complete version of the same curve. Notice that columns are arranged in sets of three, designated as A, B, and C in the legend at the top of the table. When using the top legend, all entries refer to the upper half of the standard normal curve. The entries in column A are z scores, beginning with 0.00 and ending (in the full-length table of Appendix C) with 4.00. Given a z score of zero or more, columns B and C indicate how the z score splits the area in the upper half of the normal curve. As suggested by the shading in the top legend, column B indicates the proportion of area between the mean and the z score, and column C indicates the proportion of area beyond the z score, in the upper tail of the standard normal curve.

Using the Bottom Legend of the Table

Because of the symmetry of the normal curve, the entries in Table 5.1 and Table A of Appendix C also can refer to the lower half of the normal curve. Now the columns are designated as A′, B′, and C′ in the legend at the bottom of the table. When using the bottom legend, all entries refer to the lower half of the standard normal curve.

Imagine that the nonzero entries in column A′ are negative z scores, beginning with -0.01 and ending (in the full-length table of Appendix C) with -4.00. Given a negative z score, columns B′ and C′ indicate how that z score splits the lower half of the normal curve. As suggested by the shading in the bottom legend of the table, column B′ indicates the proportion of area between the mean and the negative z score, and column C′ indicates the proportion of area beyond the negative z score, in the lower tail of the standard normal curve.

Progress Check *5.2 Using Table A in Appendix C, find the proportion of the total area identified with the following statements:

(a) above a z score of 1.80

(b) between the mean and a z score of -0.43

(c) below a z score of -3.00

Reminder:

Use of standard normal table always involves z scores.

Table 5.1
PROPORTIONS (OF AREAS) UNDER THE STANDARD NORMAL CURVE FOR VALUES OF z (FROM TABLE A OF APPENDIX C)

A z	B	C	A z	B	C	A z	B	C
0.00	.0000	.5000	0.40	.1554	.3446	0.80	.2881	.2119
0.01	.0040	.4960	0.41	.1591	.3409	0.81	.2910	.2090
•	•	•	•	•	•	•	•	•
						•	•	•
						•	•	•
						•	•	•
•	•	•	•	•	•	•	•	•
						0.99	.3389	.1611
						1.00	.3413 →	.1587
					•	1.01	.3438	.1562
						•	•	•
						•	•	•
•	•	•	•	•	•	•	•	•
0.38	.1480	.3520	0.78	.2823	.2711	1.18	.3810	.1190
0.39	.1517	.3483	0.79	.2852	.2148	1.19	.3830	.1170

(d) between the mean and a z score of 1.65

(e) between z scores of 0 and −1.96

Answers on page 495.

5.4 SOLVING NORMAL CURVE PROBLEMS

Sections 5.5 and 5.6 give examples of two main types of normal curve problems. In the first type of problem, we use a known score (or scores) to find an unknown *proportion*. For instance, we use the known score of 65 inches to find the unknown proportion of eligible FBI applicants. In the second type of problem, the procedure

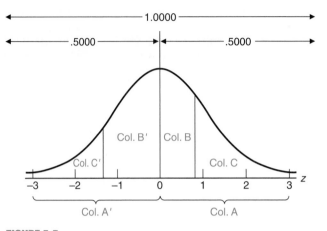

FIGURE 5.5
Interpretation of Table A, Appendix C.

is reversed. Now we use a known proportion to find an unknown *score* (or *scores*). For instance, if the FBI director had specified that applicants' heights must not exceed the 25th percentile (the shortest .25) of the population, we would use the known proportion of .25 to find the unknown cutoff height in inches.

Solve Problems Logically

Do not rush through these examples, memorizing solutions to particular problems or looking for some magic formula. Concentrate on the logic of the solution, *using rough graphs of normal curves as an aid to visualizing the solution.* Only after thinking through to a solution should you do any calculations and consult the normal tables. Then, with just a little practice, you will view the wide variety of normal curve problems not as a bewildering assortment but as many slight variations on two distinctive types.

Key Facts to Remember

Reminder:

z scores can be negative, but not areas under the normal curve.

When using the standard normal table, it is important to remember that for any *z* score, the corresponding proportions in columns B and C (or columns B′ and C′) always sum to .5000. Similarly, the total area under the normal curve always equals 1.0000, the sum of the proportions in the lower and upper halves, that is, .5000 + .5000. Finally, although a *z* score can be either positive or negative, the proportions of area under the curve are always positive or zero but *never* negative (because an area cannot be negative). Figure 5.5 summarizes how to interpret the normal curve table in this book.

5.5 FINDING PROPORTIONS

Example: Finding Proportions for *One* Score

Now we'll use a step-by-step procedure, adopted throughout this chapter, to find the proportion of all FBI applicants who are shorter than exactly 65 inches, given that the distribution of heights approximates a normal curve with a mean of 68 inches and a standard deviation of 3 inches.

1. **Sketch a normal curve and shade in the target area,** as in the left part of **Figure 5.6**. Being less than the mean of 68, 65 is located to the left of the mean. Furthermore, since the unknown proportion represents those applicants who are shorter than 65 inches, the shaded target sector is located to the left of 65.

2. **Plan your solution according to the normal table.** Decide precisely how you will find the value of the target area. In the present case, the answer will be obtained from column C' of the standard normal table, since the target area coincides with the type of area identified with column C', that is, the area in the lower tail beyond a negative z.

3. **Convert X to z.** Express 65 as a z score:

$$z = \frac{X - \mu}{\sigma} = \frac{65 - 68}{3} = \frac{-3}{3} = -1.00$$

4. **Find the target area.** Refer to the standard normal table, using the bottom legend, as the z score is negative. The arrows in Table 5.1 show how to read the table. Look up column A' to 1.00 (representing a z score of -1.00), and note the corresponding proportion of .1587 in column C': This is the answer, as suggested in the right part of Figure 5.6. It can be concluded that only .1587 (or .16) of all of the FBI applicants will be shorter than 65 inches.

A Clarification

Because the normal curve is defined for continuous variables, such as height, the same proportion of .1587 would describe not only FBI applicants who are shorter than 65 inches, but also FBI applicants who are shorter than *or equal to* 65 inches. If you think about it, equal to 65 inches translates into a height of exactly 65 inches, that is, 65.0000 with a string of zeros out to infinity! No measured height can coincide with *exactly* 65 inches since, in theory, however long the string of zeros for someone's height, measurement always can be carried additional steps until a nonzero appears.

Exactly 65 inches translates into a point along the horizontal base of the normal curve. The vertical line through this point defines one side of the desired

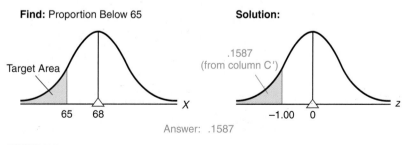

FIGURE 5.6
Finding proportions.

area—the portion below 65 inches—but the line itself has no area. Therefore, when doing normal curve problems, you need not agonize over, for example, whether the desired proportion is below exactly 65 inches or below *and equal to* exactly 65 inches. The answer is the same.

Read Carefully

Carefully read normal curve problems. A single word can change the entire problem as, for example, if you had been asked to find the proportion of applicants who are *taller* than 65 inches. Now we must find the total area to the right, not to the left, of 65 inches (or a z score of -1.00) in Figure 5.6. This requires that we add the proportions for two sectors: the unshaded sector between 65 inches and the mean of 68 inches and the unshaded sector above the mean of 68 inches. To find the proportion between 65 and 68 inches, refer to the standard normal table. Use the bottom legend, as the z score is negative; look up column A′ to 1.00 (representing a z score of -1.00); and note the proportion of .3438 in column B′ (which corresponds to the sector between 65 and 68 inches.) Recalling that .5000 always equals the proportion in the upper half of the curve (above the mean of 68 inches), add these two proportions, $.3438 + .5000 = .8438$, to determine that .8438 of all FBI applicants will be taller than 65 inches.

Reminder about Interpreting Areas

When read from left to right, the X and z scales along the base of the normal curve, as in Figure 5.6, always increase in value. Accordingly, the area under the normal curve to the left of any given score represents the proportion of shorter applicants (or, more generally, smaller or lower scores), and the area to the right of any given score represents the proportion of taller applicants (or larger or higher scores).

Progress Check *5.3 Assume that GRE scores approximate a normal curve with a mean of 500 and a standard deviation of 100.

- **(a)** Sketch a normal curve and shade in the target area described by each of the following statements:

- **(a$_1$)** less than 400

- **(a$_2$)** more than 650

- **(a$_3$)** less than 700

- **(b)** Plan solutions (in terms of columns B, C, B′, or C′ of the standard normal table, as well as the fact that the proportion for either the entire upper half or lower half always equals .5000) for the target areas in part (a).

- **(c)** Convert to z scores and find the proportions that correspond to the target areas in part (a).
  Answers on page 495.

Example: Finding Proportions *between* Two Scores

Assume that, when not interrupted artificially, the gestation periods for human fetuses approximate a normal curve with a mean of 270 days (9 months) and a standard deviation of 15 days. What proportion of gestation periods will be between 245 and 255 days?

1. **Sketch a normal curve and shade in the target area,** as in the top panel of **Figure 5.7**. Satisfy yourself that, in fact, the shaded area represents just those gestation periods between 245 and 255 days.

2. **Plan your solution according to the normal table.** This type of problem requires more effort to solve because the value of the target area cannot be read directly from Table A. As suggested in the bottom two panels of Figure 5.7, the basic idea is to identify the target area with the difference between two overlapping areas whose values can be read from column C′ of Table A. The larger area (less than 255 days) contains two sectors: the target area (between 245 and 255 days) and a remainder (less than 245 days). The smaller area contains only the remainder (less than 245 days). Subtracting the smaller area (less than 245 days) from the larger area (less than 255 days), therefore, eliminates the common remainder (less than 245 days), leaving only the target area (between 245 and 255 days).

3. **Convert X to z** by expressing 255 as

$$z = \frac{255 - 270}{15} = \frac{-15}{15} = -1.00$$

and by expressing 245 as

$$z = \frac{245 - 270}{15} = \frac{-25}{15} = -1.67$$

4. **Find the target area.** Look up column A′ to a negative z score of −1.00 (remember, you must imagine the negative sign), and note the corresponding

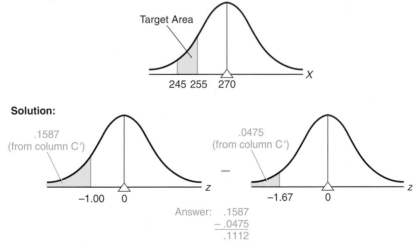

Find: Proportion Between 245 and 255

FIGURE 5.7
Finding proportions.

proportion of .1587 in column C′. Likewise, look up column A′ to a z score of −1.67, and note the corresponding proportion of .0475 in column C′. Subtract the smaller proportion from the larger proportion to obtain the answer, .1112. Thus, only .11, or 11 percent, of all gestation periods will be between 245 and 255 days.

Warning: Enter Table Only with Single z Score

When solving problems with two z scores, as above, resist the temptation to subtract one z score directly from the other and to enter Table A with this difference. Table A is designed only for individual z scores, not for differences between z scores.

Progress Check 5.4 The problem above can be solved in another way, using entries from column B′ rather than column C′. Visualize this alternative solution as a graph of the normal curve, and verify that, even though column B′ is used, the answer still equals .1112.

Example: Finding Proportions *beyond* Two Scores

Assume that high school students' IQ scores approximate a normal distribution with a mean of 105 and a standard deviation of 15. What proportion of IQs are more than 30 points either above or below the mean?

1. **Sketch a normal curve and shade in the two target areas,** as in the top panel of **Figure 5.8**.

2. **Plan your solution according to the normal table.** The solution to this type of problem is straightforward because each of the target areas can be

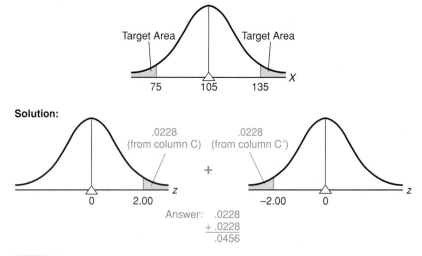

Find: Proportion Beyond 30 Points from Mean

Target Area   Target Area

75   105   135   X

Solution:

.0228   .0228
(from column C) (from column C′)

+

0   2.00   z   −2.00   0   z

Answer: .0228
          + .0228
          .0456

FIGURE 5.8
Finding proportions.

read directly from Table A. The target area in the tail to the right can be obtained from column C, and that in the tail to the left can be obtained from column C′, as shown in the bottom two panels of Figure 5.8.

3. **Convert X to z** by expressing IQ scores of 135 and 75 as

$$z = \frac{135 - 105}{15} = \frac{30}{15} = 2.00$$

$$z = \frac{75 - 105}{15} = \frac{-30}{15} = -2.00$$

4. **Find the target area.** In Table A, locate a z score of 2.00 in column A, and note the corresponding proportion of .0228 in column C. Because of the symmetry of the normal curve, you need not enter the table again to find the proportion below a z score of –2.00. Instead, merely double the above proportion of .0228 to obtain .0456, which represents the proportion of students with IQs more than 30 points either above or below the mean.

Semantic Alert

"*More* than 30 points either above or below the mean" translates into two target areas, one in each tail of the normal curve. "*Within* 30 points either above or below the mean" translates into two entirely new target areas corresponding to the two unshaded sectors in Figure 5.8. Each of these "within" sectors shares a common boundary at the mean, but one sector extends 30 points above the mean and the other sector extends 30 points below the mean.

Progress Check *5.5 Assume that SAT math scores approximate a normal curve with a mean of 500 and a standard deviation of 100.

(a) Sketch a normal curve and shade in the target area(s) described by each of the following statements:

(a_1) *more* than 570

(a_2) *less* than 515

(a_3) *between* 520 and 540

(a_4) between 470 and 520

(a_5) more than 50 points above the mean

(a_6) more than 100 points either above or below the mean

(a_7) within 50 points either above or below the mean

(b) Plan solutions (in terms of columns B, C, B′, and C′) for the target areas in part (a).

(c) Convert to z scores and find the target areas in part (a).
   Answers on page 495.

5.6 FINDING SCORES

So far, we have concentrated on normal curve problems for which Table A must be consulted to find the unknown proportion (of area) associated with some known score or pair of known scores. For instance, given a GRE score of 650, we found that the unknown proportion of scores larger than 650 equals .07. *Now we will concentrate on the opposite type of normal curve problem for which Table A must be consulted to find the unknown score or scores associated with some known proportion.* For instance, given that a GRE score must be in the upper 25 percent of the distribution (in order for an applicant to be considered for admission to graduate school), we must find the unknown minimum GRE score. Essentially, this type of problem requires that we reverse our use of Table A by entering proportions in columns B, C, B′, or C′ and finding z scores listed in columns A or A′.

Example: Finding *One* Score

Exam scores for a large psychology class approximate a normal curve with a mean of 230 and a standard deviation of 50. Furthermore, students are graded "on a curve," with only the upper 20 percent being awarded grades of A. What is the lowest score on the exam that receives an A?

1. **Sketch a normal curve and, on the correct side of the mean, draw a line representing the target score,** as in **Figure 5.9**. This is often the most difficult step, and it involves semantics rather than statistics. It's often helpful to visualize the target score as splitting the total area into two sectors—one to the left of (below) the target score and one to the right of (above) the target score. For example, in the present case, the target score is the point along the base of the curve that splits the total area into 80 percent, or .8000 to the left, and 20 percent, or .2000 to the right. The mean of a normal curve serves as a valuable frame of reference since it always splits the total area into two equal halves—.5000 to the left of the mean and .5000 to the right of the mean. Since more than .5000—that

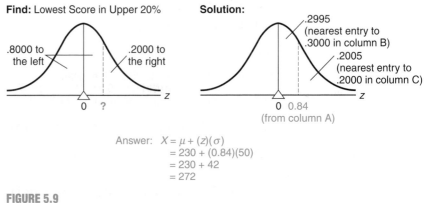

Find: Lowest Score in Upper 20%   **Solution:**

.8000 to the left   .2000 to the right

.2995 (nearest entry to .3000 in column B)
.2005 (nearest entry to .2000 in column C)

0   ?   0   0.84 (from column A)

Answer: $X = \mu + (z)(\sigma)$
= 230 + (0.84)(50)
= 230 + 42
= 272

FIGURE 5.9
Finding scores.

is, .8000—of the total area is to the left of the target score, this score must be on the upper or right side of the mean. On the other hand, if less than .5000 of the total area had been to the left of the target score, this score would have been placed on the lower or left side of the mean.

2. **Plan your solution according to the normal table.** In problems of this type, you must plan how to find the z score for the target score. Because the target score is on the right side of the mean, concentrate on the area in the upper half of the normal curve, as described in columns B and C. The right panel of Figure 5.9 indicates that either column B or C can be used to locate a z score in column A. It is crucial, however, to search for the single value (.3000) that is valid for column B or the single value (.2000) that is valid for column C. Note that we look in column B for .3000, not for .8000. Table A is not designed for sectors, such as the lower .8000, that span the mean of the normal curve.

3. **Find z.** Refer to Table A. Scan column C to find .2000. If this value does not appear in column C, as typically will be the case, approximate the desired value (and the correct score) by locating the entry in column C nearest to .2000. If adjacent entries are equally close to the target value, use either entry—it is your choice. As shown in the right panel of Figure 5.9, the entry in column C closest to .2000 is .2005, and the corresponding z score in column A equals 0.84. Verify this by checking Table A. Also note that exactly the same z score of 0.84 would have been identified if column B had been searched to find the entry (.2995) nearest to .3000. The z score of 0.84 represents the point that separates the upper 20 percent of the area from the rest of the area under the normal curve.

4. **Convert z to the target score.** Finally, convert the z score of 0.84 into an exam score, given a distribution with a mean of 230 and a standard deviation of 50. You'll recall that a z score indicates how many standard deviations the original score is above or below its mean. In the present case, the target score must be located .84 of a standard deviation above its mean. The distance of the target score above its mean equals 42 ($.84 \times 50$), which, when added to the mean of 230, yields a value of 272. Therefore, 272 is the lowest score on the exam that receives an A.

When converting z scores to original scores, you will probably find it more efficient to use the following equation (derived from the z score equation on page 103):

CONVERTING z SCORE TO ORIGINAL SCORE

$$X = \mu + (z)(\sigma) \qquad (5.2)$$

---

in which X is the target score, expressed in original units of measurement; μ and σ are the mean and the standard deviation, respectively, for the original normal curve; and z is the standard score read from column A or A$'$ of Table A. When appropriate numerical substitutions are made, as shown in the bottom of Figure 5.9, 272 is found to be the answer, in agreement with our earlier conclusion.

Comment: Place Target Score on Correct Side of Mean

When finding scores, it is crucial that the target score be placed on the correct side of the mean. This placement dictates how the normal table will be read—whether down from the top legend, with entries in column A interpreted as positive z scores, or up from the bottom legend, with entries in column A′ interpreted as negative z scores. In the previous problem, the incorrect placement of the target score on the left side of the mean would have led to a z score of −0.84, rather than 0.84, and an erroneous answer of 188 (230 − 42), rather than the correct answer of 272 (230 + 42).

To make correct placements, you must properly interpret the specifications for the target score. Expand potentially confusing one-sided specifications, such as the "upper 20 percent, or upper .2000," into "left .8000 and right .2000." Having identified the left and right areas of the target score, which sum to 1.0000, you can compare the specifications of the target score with those of the mean. Remember that the mean of a normal curve always splits the total area into .5000 to the left of the mean and .5000 to the right of the mean. Accordingly, if the area to the left of the target score is more than .5000, the target score should be placed on the upper or right side of the mean. Otherwise, if the area to the left of the target score is less than .5000, the target score should be placed on the lower or left side of the mean.

Example: Finding *Two* Scores

Assume that the annual rainfall in the San Francisco area approximates a normal curve with a mean of 22 inches and a standard deviation of 4 inches. What are the rainfalls for the more atypical years, defined as the driest 2.5 percent of all years and the wettest 2.5 percent of all years?

1. **Sketch a normal curve. On either side of the mean, draw two lines representing the two target scores,** as in **Figure 5.10**. The smaller (driest) target score splits the total area into .0250 to the left and .9750 to the right, and the larger (wettest) target score does the exact opposite.

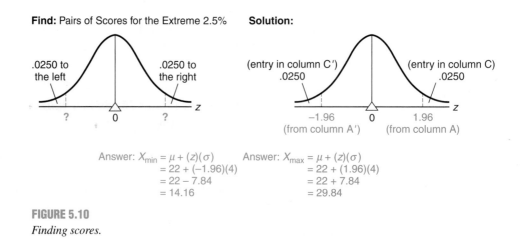

FIGURE 5.10
Finding scores.

2. **Plan your solution according to the normal table.** Because the smaller target score is located on the lower or left side of the mean, we will concentrate on the area in the lower half of the normal curve, as described in columns B′ and C′. The target z score can be found by scanning either column B′ for .4750 or column C′ for .0250. After finding the smaller target score, we will capitalize on the symmetrical properties of normal curves to find the value of the larger target score.

3. **Find z.** Referring to Table A, we can scan column B′ for .4750, or the entry nearest to .4750. In this case, .4750 appears in column B′, and the corresponding z score in column A′ equals −1.96. The same z score of −1.96 would have been obtained if column C′ had been searched for a value of .0250.

4. **Convert z to the target score.** When the appropriate numbers are substituted in Formula 5.2, as shown in the bottom panel of Figure 5.10, the smaller target score equals 14.16 inches, the amount of annual rainfall that separates the driest 2.5 percent of all years from all of the other years.

The location of the larger target score is the mirror image of that for the smaller target score. Therefore, we need not even consult Table A to establish that its z score equals 1.96—that is, the same value as the smaller target score, but without the negative sign. When 1.96 is converted to inches of rainfall, as shown in the bottom of Figure 5.10, the larger target equals 29.84 inches, the amount of annual rainfall that separates the wettest 2.5 percent of all years from all other years.

Comment: Common and Rare Events

In the above problem, we drew attention to the atypical, or rare years, by concluding that 2.5 percent of the driest years registered less than 14.16 inches of rainfall, whereas 2.5 percent of the wettest years registered more than 29.84 inches. Had we wished, we could also have drawn attention to the typical, or common years, by concluding that the most moderate, "middle" 95 percent of all years registered between 14.16 and 29.84 inches of rainfall. The middle 95 percent straddles the line perpendicular to the mean, or 50th percentile, with half, or 47.5 percent, above this line and the other half, or 47.5 percent, below this line.

Later in inferential statistics, we'll judge whether, for instance, an observed mean difference is real or transitory. As you'll see, this decision will depend on whether the one observed mean difference can be viewed as a common outcome or as a rare outcome in the distribution of all possible mean differences that could happen just by chance. Since common events tend to be identified with the middle 95 percent of the area under the normal curve and rare events with the extreme 2.5 percent in each tail, you'll often use z scores of ±1.96 in inferential statistics.

Progress Check *5.6 Assume that the burning times of electric light bulbs approximate a normal curve with a mean of 1200 hours and a standard deviation of 120 hours. If a large number of new lights are installed at the same time (possibly along a newly opened freeway), at what time will

(a) 1 percent fail? (**Hint:** This splits the total area into .0100 to the left and .9900 to the right.)

(b) 50 percent fail?

(c) 95 percent fail?

(d) If a new inspection procedure eliminates the weakest 8 percent of all lights before they are marketed, the manufacturer can safely offer customers a money-back guarantee on all lights that fail before _____ hours of burning time.

Answers on page 495.

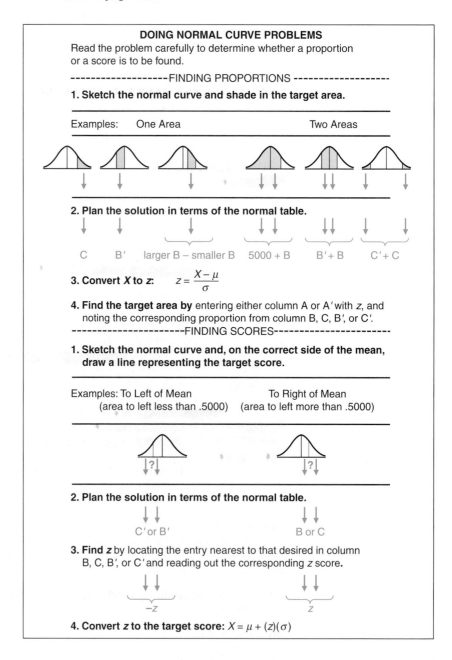

DOING NORMAL CURVE PROBLEMS
Read the problem carefully to determine whether a proportion or a score is to be found.

-------------------FINDING PROPORTIONS--------------------

1. Sketch the normal curve and shade in the target area.

Examples: One Area   Two Areas

2. Plan the solution in terms of the normal table.

C   B′   larger B − smaller B   5000 + B   B′+ B   C′+ C

3. Convert *X* to *z*: $z = \dfrac{X - \mu}{\sigma}$

4. Find the target area by entering either column A or A′ with *z*, and noting the corresponding proportion from column B, C, B′, or C′.

----------------------FINDING SCORES----------------------

1. Sketch the normal curve and, on the correct side of the mean, draw a line representing the target score.

Examples: To Left of Mean   To Right of Mean
          (area to left less than .5000)   (area to left more than .5000)

2. Plan the solution in terms of the normal table.

C′or B′   B or C

3. Find *z* by locating the entry nearest to that desired in column B, C, B′, or C′and reading out the corresponding *z* score.

−z   z

4. Convert *z* to the target score: $X = \mu + (z)(\sigma)$

Guidelines for Normal Curve Problems

You now have the necessary information for solving most normal curve problems, but there is no substitute for actually working problems, such as those offered at the end of this chapter. For your convenience, a complete set of guidelines appears in the "Doing Normal Curve Problems" box on page 118. Before reading on, spend a few moments studying it, and then refer back to it whenever necessary.

5.7 MORE ABOUT z SCORES

z Scores for Non-normal Distributions

z scores are not limited to normal distributions. Non-normal distributions also can be transformed into sets of unit-free, standardized z scores. *In this case, the standard normal table cannot be consulted,* since the shape of the distribution of z scores is the same as that for the original non-normal distribution. For instance, if the original distribution is positively skewed, the distribution of z scores also will be positively skewed. *Regardless of the shape of the distribution, the shift to z scores always produces a distribution of standard scores with a mean of 0 and a standard deviation of 1.*

Interpreting Test Scores

Under most circumstances, z scores provide efficient descriptions of relative performance on one or more tests. Without additional information, it is meaningless to know that Sharon earned a raw score of 159 on a math test, but it is very informative to know that she earned a z score of 1.80. The latter score suggests that she did relatively well on the math test, being almost two standard deviation units above the mean. More precise interpretations of this score could be made, of course, if it is known that the test scores approximate a normal curve.

The use of z scores can help you identify a person's relative strengths and weaknesses on several different tests. For instance, Table 5.2 shows Sharon's scores on college achievement tests in three different subjects. The evaluation of her test performance is greatly facilitated by converting her raw scores into the z scores listed in the final column of Table 5.2. A glance at the z scores suggests that although she did relatively well on the math test, her performance on the English test was only slightly above average, as indicated by a z score of 0.50, and her performance on the psychology test was slightly below average, as indicated by a z score of –0.67.

Table 5.2
SHARON'S ACHIEVEMENT TEST SCORES

SUBJECT	RAW SCORE	MEAN	STANDARD DEVIATION	z SCORE
Math	159	141	10	1.80
English	83	75	16	0.50
Psych	23	27	6	–0.67

Importance of Reference Group

Remember that z scores reflect performance relative to some group rather than an absolute standard. A meaningful interpretation of z scores requires, therefore, that the nature of the reference group be specified. In the present example, it is important to know whether Sharon's scores were relative to those of the other students at her college or to those of students at a wide variety of colleges, as well as to any other special characteristics of the reference group.

Progress Check *5.7 Convert each of the following test scores to z scores:

	TEST SCORE	MEAN	STANDARD DEVIATION
(a)	53	50	9
(b)	38	40	10
(c)	45	30	20
(d)	28	20	20

Progress Check *5.8

(a) Referring to Question 5.7, which one test score would you prefer?

(b) Referring to Question 5.7, if you had earned a score of 64 on some test, which of the four distributions (a, b, c, or d) would have permitted the most favorable interpretation of this score?

Answers on page 495.

Standard Scores

Standard Score

Any unit-free scores expressed relative to a known mean and a known standard deviation.

Whenever any unit-free scores are expressed relative to a known mean and a known standard deviation, they are referred to as **standard scores.** Although z scores qualify as standard scores because they are unit-free and expressed relative to a known mean of 0 and a known standard deviation of 1, other scores also qualify as standard scores.

Transformed Standard Scores

Transformed Standard Score

A standard score that, unlike a z score, usually lacks negative signs and decimal points.

Being by far the most important standard score, z scores are often viewed as synonymous with standard scores. *For convenience, particularly when reporting test results to a wide audience,* z *scores can be changed to* **transformed standard scores,** *other types of unit-free standard scores that lack negative signs and decimal points.* These transformations change neither the shape of the original distribution nor the relative standing of any test score within the distribution. For example, a test score located one standard deviation below the mean might be reported not as a z score of -1.00 but as a T score of 40 in a distribution of T scores with a mean of 50 and a standard deviation of 10. The important point to realize is that although reported as a score of 40, this T score accurately reflects the relative location of the original z score of -1.00: A T score of 40 is located at a distance of one standard deviation (of size 10) below the mean (of size 50). **Figure 5.11** shows the values of some of the more common types of transformed standard scores relative to the various portions of the area under the normal curve.

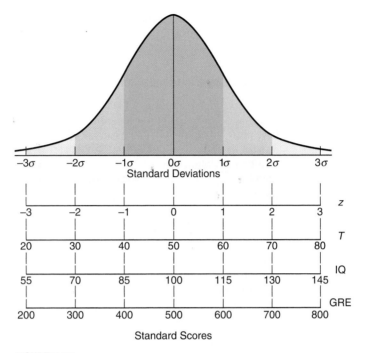

Standard Scores

FIGURE 5.11
Common transformed standard scores associated with normal curves.

Converting to Transformed Standard Scores

Use the following formula to convert any original standard score, z, into a transformed standard score, z', having a distribution with any desired mean and standard deviation.

TRANSFORMED STANDARD SCORE

$$z' = \text{desired mean} + (z)(\text{desired standard deviation}) \qquad (5.3)$$

---

where z' (called *z prime*) is the transformed standard score and z is the original standard score.

For instance, if you wish to convert a z score of -1.50 into a new distribution of z' scores for which the desired mean equals 500 and the desired standard deviation equals 100, substitute these numbers into the above formula to obtain

$$z' = 500 + (-1.50)(100)$$
$$= 500 - 150$$
$$= 350$$

Again, notice that the transformed standard score accurately reflects the relative location of the original standard score of -1.50: The transformed score of 350 is located at a distance of 1.5 standard deviation units (each of size 100) below the mean (of size 500). The change from a z score of -1.50 to a z' score of 350 eliminates negative signs and decimal points without distorting the relative location of the original score, expressed as a distance from the mean in standard deviation units.

Substitute Pairs of Convenient Numbers

You could substitute any mean or any standard deviation in Formula 5.3 to generate a new distribution of transformed scores. Traditionally, substitutions have been limited mainly to the pairs of convenient numbers shown in Figure 5.11: a mean of 50 and a standard deviation of 10 (T scores), a mean of 100 and a standard deviation of 15 (IQ scores), and a mean of 500 and a standard deviation of 100 (GRE scores). The substitution of other arbitrary pairs of numbers serves no purpose; indeed, because of their peculiarity, they might make the new distribution, even though it lacks the negative signs and decimal points common to z scores, slightly less comprehensible to people who have been exposed to the traditional pairs of numbers.

Progress Check *5.9 Assume that each of the raw scores listed below originates from a distribution with the specified mean and standard deviation. After converting each raw score into a z score, transform each z score into a series of new standard scores with means and standard deviations of 50 and 10, 100 and 15, and 500 and 100, respectively. (In practice, you would transform a particular z into only one new standard score.)

	RAW SCORE	MEAN	STANDARD DEVIATION
(a)	24	20	5
(b)	37	42	3

Answers on page 494.

Summary
. . . .

Many observed frequency distributions approximate the well-documented normal curve, an important theoretical curve noted for its symmetrical bell-shaped form. The normal curve can be used to obtain answers to a wide variety of questions.

Although there are infinite numbers of normal curves, each with its own mean and standard deviation, there is only one standard normal curve, with its mean of 0 and its standard deviation of 1. Only the standard normal curve is actually tabled. The standard normal table (Table A in Appendix C), requires the use of z scores, that is, original scores expressed as deviations, in standard deviation units, above or below its mean.

There are two general types of normal curve problems: (1) those that require you to find the unknown proportion (of area) associated with some score or pair of scores and (2) those that require you to find the unknown score or scores associated with some area. Answers to the first type of problem usually require you to convert original scores into z scores (Formula 5.1), and answers to the second type of problem usually require you to translate a z score back into an original score (Formula 5.2).

Even when distributions fail to approximate normal curves, z scores can provide efficient descriptions of relative performance on one or more tests.

When reporting test results, z scores are often transformed into other types of standard scores that lack negative signs and decimal points. These conversions change neither the shape of the original distribution nor the relative standing of any test score within the original distribution.

Important Terms

Normal curve

z score

Standard score

Standard normal curve

Transformed standard score

Key Equations

z SCORE

$$z = \frac{X - \mu}{\sigma}$$

CONVERTING z TO X

$$X = \mu + z\sigma$$

REVIEW QUESTIONS

*5.10 Fill in the blank spaces.

To identify a particular normal curve, you must know the __(a)__ and __(b)__ for that distribution. To convert a particular normal curve to the standard normal curve, you must convert original scores into __(c)__ scores. A z score indicates how many __(d)__ a score is __(e)__ or __(f)__ the mean of the distribution. Although there are infinite numbers of normal curves, there is __(g)__ standard normal curve. The standard normal curve has a __(h)__ of 0 and a __(i)__ of 1.

The total area under the standard normal curve equals __(j)__ . When using the standard normal table, it is important to remember that for any z score, the corresponding proportions in columns B and C (or columns B′ and C′) always sum to __(k)__ . Furthermore, the proportion in column B (or B′) always specifies the proportion of area between the __(l)__ and the z score, while the proportion in column C (or C′) always specifies the proportion of area __(m)__ the z score. Although any z score can be either positive or negative, the proportions of area, specified in columns B and C (or columns B′ and C′), are never __(n)__ .

Standard scores are unit-free scores expressed relative to a known __(o)__ and __(p)__ . The most important standard score is a __(q)__ score. Unlike z

scores, transformed standard scores usually lack __(r)__ signs and __(s)__ points. Transformed standard scores accurately reflect the relative standing of the original __(t)__ score.

Answers on page 496.

Finding Proportions

5.11 Scores on the Wechsler Adult Intelligence Scale (WAIS) approximate a normal curve with a mean of 100 and a standard deviation of 15. What proportion of IQ scores are

(a) above 125?

(b) below 82?

(c) within 9 points of the mean?

(d) more than 40 points from the mean?

5.12 Suppose that the burning times of electric light bulbs approximate a normal curve with a mean of 1200 hours and a standard deviation of 120 hours. What proportion of lights burn for

(a) less than 960 hours?

(b) more than 1500 hours?

(c) within 50 hours of the mean?

(d) between 1300 and 1400 hours?

Finding Scores

5.13 IQ scores on the WAIS test approximate a normal curve with a mean of 100 and a standard deviation of 15. What IQ score is identified with

(a) the upper 2 percent, that is, 2 percent to the right (and 98 percent to the left)?

(b) the lower 10 percent?

(c) the upper 60 percent?

(d) the middle 95 percent? [Remember, the middle 95 percent straddles the line perpendicular to the mean (or the 50th percentile), with half of 95 percent, or 47.5 percent, above this line and the remaining 47.5 percent below this line.]

(e) the middle 99 percent?

Finding Proportions and Scores

IMPORTANT NOTE: When doing Questions **5.14** and **5.15,** remember to decide first whether a proportion or a score is to be found.

*5.14 An investigator polls common cold sufferers, asking them to estimate the number of hours of physical discomfort caused by their most recent colds. Assume that their estimates approximate a normal curve with a mean of 83 hours and a standard deviation of 20 hours.

(a) What is the estimated number of hours for the shortest-suffering 5 percent?

(b) What proportion of sufferers estimate that their colds lasted longer than 48 hours?

(c) What proportion suffered for fewer than 61 hours?

(d) What is the estimated number of hours suffered by the extreme 1 percent either above or below the mean?

(e) What proportion suffered for between 1 and 3 days, that is, between 24 and 72 hours?

(f) What is the estimated number of hours suffered by the middle 95 percent? [See the comment about "middle 95 percent" in Question **5.13(d)**.]

(g) What proportion suffered for between 2 and 4 days?

(h) A medical researcher wishes to concentrate on the 20 percent who suffered the most. She will work only with those who estimate that they suffered for more than _____ hours.

(i) Another researcher wishes to compare those who suffered least with those who suffered most. If each group is to consist of only the extreme 3 percent, the mild group will consist of those who suffered for fewer than _____ hours, and the severe group will consist of those who suffered for more than _____ hours.

(j) Another survey found that people with colds who took daily doses of vitamin C suffered, on the average, for 61 hours. What proportion of the original survey (with a mean of 83 hours and a standard deviation of 20 hours) suffered for more than 61 hours?

(k) What proportion of the original survey suffered for *exactly* 61 hours? (Be careful!)

Answers on page 496.

5.15 Admission to a state university depends partially on the applicant's high school GPA. Assume that the applicants' GPAs approximate a normal curve with a mean of 3.20 and a standard deviation of 0.30.

(a) If applicants with GPAs of 3.50 or above are automatically admitted, what proportion of applicants will be in this category?

(b) If applicants with GPAs of 2.50 or below are automatically denied admission, what proportion of applicants will be in this category?

(c) A special honors program is open to all applicants with GPAs of 3.75 or better. What proportion of applicants are eligible?

(d) If the special honors program is limited to students whose GPAs rank in the upper 10 percent, what will Brittany's GPA have to be for admission to this program?

5.16 When describing test results, someone objects to the conversion of raw scores into standard scores, claiming that this constitutes an arbitrary change in the value of the test score. How might you respond to this objection?

CHAPTER 6

Describing Relationships: Correlation

Summary / Important Terms / Key Equations / Review Questions

Preview
....

Is there a relationship between your IQ and the wealth of your parents? Between your computer skills and your GPA? Between your anxiety level and your perceived social attractiveness? Answers to these questions require us to describe the relationship between pairs of variables. The original data must consist of actual pairs of observations, such as, for example, IQ scores and parents' wealth for each member of the freshman class. Two variables are related if pairs of scores show an orderliness that can be depicted graphically with a **scatterplot** *and numerically with a* **correlation coefficient**.

Table 6.1 GREETING CARDS SENT AND RECEIVED BY FIVE FRIENDS		
	NUMBER OF CARDS	
FRIEND	SENT	RECEIVED
Andrea	5	10
Mike	7	12
Doris	13	14
Steve	9	18
John	1	6

Does the familiar saying "You get what you give" accurately describe the exchange of holiday greeting cards? An investigator suspects that a relationship exists between the number of greeting cards *sent* and the number of greeting cards *received* by individuals. Prior to a full-fledged survey—and also prior to any statistical analysis based on variability, as described later in Section 15.9—he obtains the estimates for the most recent holiday season from five friends, as shown in Table 6.1. (The data in Table 6.1 represent a very simple observational study with two dependent variables, as defined in Section 1.6, since numbers of cards sent and received are not under the investigator's control.)

6.1 AN INTUITIVE APPROACH

If the suspected relationship does exist between cards sent and cards received, then an inspection of the data might reveal, as one possibility, a tendency for "big senders" to be "big receivers" and for "small senders" to be "small receivers." More generally, there is a tendency for pairs of scores to occupy similar relative positions in their respective distributions.

Positive Relationship

Trends among pairs of scores can be detected most easily by constructing a list of paired scores in which the scores along one variable are arranged from largest to smallest. In panel A of Table 6.2, the five pairs of scores are arranged from the largest (13) to the smallest (1) number of cards sent. This table reveals a pronounced tendency for pairs of scores to occupy similar *relative* positions in their respective distributions. For example, John sent relatively few cards (1) and received relatively few cards (6), whereas Doris sent relatively many cards (13) and received relatively many cards (14). We can conclude, therefore, that the two variables are related. Furthermore, this relationship implies that "You get what you give." *Insofar as relatively low values are paired with relatively low values, and relatively high values are paired with relatively high values, the relationship is* **positive.**

In panels B and C of Table 6.2, each of the five friends continues to send the same number of cards as in panel A, but new pairs are created to illustrate two other possibilities—a negative relationship and little or no relationship. (In real applications, of course, the pairs are fixed by the data and cannot be changed.)

Negative Relationship

Notice the pattern among the pairs in panel B. Now there is a pronounced tendency for pairs of scores to occupy dissimilar and opposite relative positions in their respective distributions. For example, although John sent relatively few cards (1), he received relatively many (18). From this pattern, we can conclude that the two variables are related. Furthermore, this relationship implies that "You get the opposite of what you give." *Insofar as relatively low values are paired with relatively high values, and relatively high values are paired with relatively low values, the relationship is* **negative.**

Positive Relationship

Occurs insofar as pairs of scores tend to occupy similar relative positions (high with high and low with low) in their respective distributions.

Negative Relationship

Occurs insofar as pairs of scores tend to occupy dissimilar relative positions (high with low and vice versa) in their respective distributions.

Table 6.2 **THREE TYPES OF RELATIONSHIPS**		
A. POSITIVE RELATIONSHIP		
FRIEND	**SENT**	**RE-CEIVED**
Doris	13	14
Steve	9	18
Mike	7	12
Andrea	5	10
John	1	6
B. NEGATIVE RELATIONSHIP		
FRIEND	**SENT**	**RE-CEIVED**
Doris	13	6
Steve	9	10
Mike	7	14
Andrea	5	12
John	1	18
C. LITTLE OR NO RELATIONSHIP		
FRIEND	**SENT**	**RE-CEIVED**
Doris	13	10
Steve	9	18
Mike	7	12
Andrea	5	6
John	1	14

Little or No Relationship

No regularity is apparent among the pairs of scores in panel C. For instance, although both Andrea and John sent relatively few cards (5 and 1, respectively), Andrea received relatively few cards (6) and John received relatively many cards (14). Given this lack of regularity, we can conclude that little, if any, relationship exists between the two variables and that "What you get has no bearing on what you give."

Review

Whether we are concerned about the relationship between cards sent and cards received, years of heavy smoking and life expectancy, educational level and annual income, or scores on a vocational screening test and subsequent ratings as a police officer,

two variables are *positively* related if pairs of scores tend to occupy similar relative positions (*high with high and low with low*) in their respective distributions,
and they are *negatively* related if pairs of scores tend to occupy dissimilar relative positions (*high with low and vice versa*) in their respective distributions.

The remainder of this chapter deals with how best to describe and interpret a relationship between pairs of variables. The intuitive method of searching for regularity among pairs of scores is cumbersome and inexact when the analysis involves more than a few pairs of scores. Although this technique has much appeal, it must be abandoned in favor of several other, more efficient and exact statistical techniques, namely, a special graph known as a *scatterplot* and a measure known as a *correlation coefficient.*

It will become apparent in the next chapter that once a relationship has been identified, it can be used for predictive purposes. Having established that years of heavy smoking is negatively related to length of life (because heavier smokers tend to have shorter lives), we can use this relationship to predict the life expectancy of someone who has smoked heavily for the past 10 years. This type of prediction could serve a variety of purposes, such as calculating a life insurance premium or supplying extra motivation in an antismoking workshop.

Progress Check *6.1 Indicate whether the following statements suggest a positive or negative relationship:

(a) More densely populated areas have higher crime rates.

(b) Schoolchildren who often watch TV perform more poorly on academic achievement tests.

(c) Heavier automobiles yield poorer gas mileage.

(d) Better-educated people have higher incomes.

(e) More anxious people voluntarily spend more time performing a simple repetitive task.

Answers on page 496.

6.2 SCATTERPLOTS

A **scatterplot** *is a graph containing a cluster of dots that represents all pairs of scores.* With a little training, you can use any dot cluster as a preview of a fully measured relationship.

Construction

To construct a scatterplot, as in **Figure 6.1**, scale each of the two variables along the horizontal (X) and vertical (Y) axes, and use each pair of scores to locate a dot within the scatterplot. For example, the pair of numbers for Mike, 7 and 12, define points along the X and Y axes, respectively. Using these points to anchor lines perpendicular (at right angles) to each axis, locate Mike's dot where the two lines intersect. Repeat this process, with imaginary lines, for each of the four remaining pairs of scores to create the scatterplot of Figure 6.1.

Our simple example involving greeting cards has shown the basic idea of correlation and the construction of a scatterplot. Now we'll examine more complex sets of data in order to learn how to interpret scatterplots.

Positive, Negative, or Little or No Relationship?

The first step is to note the tilt or slope, if any, of a dot cluster. *A dot cluster that has a slope from the lower left to the upper right,* as in panel A of **Figure 6.2**, *reflects a positive relationship.* Small values of one variable are paired with small values of the other variable, and large values are paired with large values. In panel A, short people tend to be light, and tall people tend to be heavy.

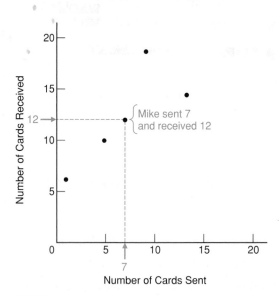

FIGURE 6.1

Scatterplot for greeting card exchange.

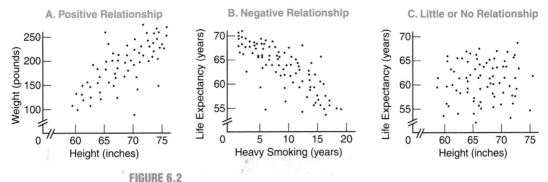

FIGURE 6.2

Three types of relationships.

On the other hand, *a dot cluster that has a slope from the upper left to the lower right,* as in panel B of Figure 6.2, *reflects a negative relationship.* Small values of one variable tend to be paired with large values of the other variable, and vice versa. In panel B, people who have smoked heavily for few years or not at all tend to have longer lives, and people who have smoked heavily for many years tend to have shorter lives.

Finally, *a dot cluster that lacks any apparent slope,* as in panel C of Figure 6.2, *reflects little or no relationship.* Small values of one variable are just as likely to be paired with small, medium, or large values of the other variable. In panel C, notice that the dots are strewn about in an irregular shotgun fashion, suggesting that there is little or no relationship between the height of young adults and their life expectancies.

Strong or Weak Relationship?

Having established that a relationship is either positive or negative, note how closely the dot cluster approximates a straight line. *The more closely the dot cluster approximates a straight line, the stronger (the more regular) the relationship will be.* **Figure 6.3** shows a series of scatterplots, each representing a

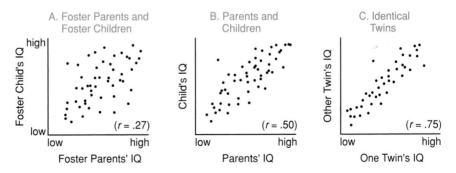

FIGURE 6.3

Three positive relationships. (Scatterplots simulated from a 50-year literature survey.)
Source: L. Erlenmeyer-Kimling and L. F. Jarvik. "Genetics and Intelligence: A Review."
Science, 142, 1477–1479.)

different positive relationship between IQ scores for pairs of people whose backgrounds reflect different degrees of genetic overlap, ranging from minimum overlap between foster parents and foster children to maximum overlap between identical twins. (Ignore the parenthetical expressions involving r, to be discussed later.) Notice that the dot cluster more closely approximates a straight line for people with greater degrees of genetic overlap—for parents and children in panel B of Figure 6.3 and even more so for identical twins in panel C.

Perfect Relationship

A dot cluster that equals (rather than merely approximates) a straight line reflects a perfect relationship between two variables. In practice, perfect relationships are most unlikely.

Curvilinear Relationship

Linear Relationship

A relationship that can be described best with a straight line.

Curvilinear Relationship

A relationship that can be described best with a curved line.

The previous discussion assumes that a dot cluster approximates a *straight* line and, therefore, reflects a **linear relationship.** But this is not always the case. Sometimes a dot cluster approximates a *bent* or *curved* line, as in **Figure 6.4**, and therefore reflects a **curvilinear relationship.** Descriptions of these relationships are more complex than those of linear relationships. For instance, we see in Figure 6.4 that physical strength, as measured by the force of a person's handgrip, is less for children, more for adults, and then less again for older people. Otherwise, the scatterplot can be interpreted as before, that is, the more closely the dot cluster approximates a curved line, the stronger the curvilinear relationship will be.

Look again at the scatterplot in Figure 6.1 for the greeting card data. Although the small number of dots in Figure 6.1 hinders any interpretation, the dot cluster appears to approximate a straight line, stretching from the lower left to the upper right. This suggests a positive relationship between greeting cards sent and received, in agreement with the earlier intuitive analysis of these data.

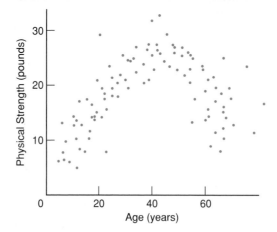

FIGURE 6.4
Curvilinear relationship.

Progress Check *6.2 Critical reading and math scores on the SAT test for students A, B, C, D, E, F, G, and H are shown in the following scatterplot:

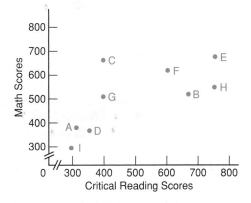

(a) Which student(s) scored about the same on both tests?

(b) Which student(s) scored higher on the critical reading test than on the math test?

(c) Which student(s) will be eligible for an honors program that requires minimum scores of 700 in critical reading and 500 in math?

(d) Is there a negative relationship between the critical reading and math scores?
Answers on page 496.

6.3 A CORRELATION COEFFICIENT FOR QUANTITATIVE DATA: *r*

A *correlation coefficient* is a number between –1 and 1 that describes the relationship between pairs of variables.

The next few sections concentrate on the type of correlation coefficient, designated as *r*, that *describes the linear relationship between pairs of variables for quantitative data*. Many other types of correlation coefficients have been introduced to handle specific types of data, including ranked and qualitative data, and a few of these will be described briefly in Section 6.7.

Key Properties of *r*

Named in honor of the British scientist Karl Pearson, the **Pearson correlation coefficient, *r*,** can equal any value between –1.00 and +1.00 . Furthermore, the following two properties apply:

1. *The sign of* r *indicates the type of linear relationship, whether positive or negative.*

2. *The numerical value of* r, *without regard to sign, indicates the strength of the linear relationship.*

Sign of *r*

A number with a plus sign (or no sign) indicates a positive relationship, and a number with a minus sign indicates a negative relationship. For example, an *r* with a plus sign describes the positive relationship between height and weight shown in panel A of Figure 6.2, and an *r* with a minus sign describes the negative relationship between heavy smoking and life expectancy shown in panel B.

Numerical Value of *r*

The more closely a value of *r* approaches either –1.00 or +1.00, the stronger (more regular) the relationship. Conversely, the more closely the value of *r* approaches 0, the weaker (less regular) the relationship. For example, an *r* of –.90 indicates a stronger relationship than does an *r* of –.70, and an *r* of –.70 indicates a stronger relationship than does an *r* of .50. (Remember, if no sign appears, it is understood to be plus.) In Figure 6.3, notice that the values of *r* shift from .75 to .27 as the analysis for pairs of IQ scores shifts from a relatively strong relationship for identical twins to a relatively weak relationship for foster parents and foster children.

From a slightly different perspective, the value of *r* is a measure of how well a straight line (representing the linear relationship) describes the cluster of dots in the scatterplot. Again referring to Figure 6.3, notice that an imaginary straight line describes the dot cluster less well as the values of *r* shift from .75 to .27.

INTERNET DEMONSTRATION
Go to the Web site for this book (http://www.wiley.com/college/witte). Click on the *Student Companion Site,* then *Internet Demonstrations,* and finally ***Guessing Correlations*** to practice matching values of correlation coefficients with various scatterplots.

Interpretation of *r*

Located along a scale from –1.00 to +1.00, the value of *r* supplies information about the direction of a linear relationship—whether positive or negative—and, generally, information about the relative strength of a linear relationship—whether relatively weak (and a poor describer of the data) because *r* is in the vicinity of 0, or relatively strong (and a good describer of the data) because *r* deviates from 0 in the direction of either +1.00 or –1.00.

If, as usually is the case, we wish to generalize beyond the limited sample of actual paired scores, *r* can't be interpreted at face value. Viewed as the product of chance sampling variability (see Section 15.9), the value of *r* must be evaluated with tools from inferential statistics to establish whether the relationship is real or merely transitory. This evaluation depends not only on the value of *r* but also on the actual number of pairs of scores used to calculate *r*. On the assumption that reasonably large numbers of pairs of scores are involved (preferably hundreds and certainly many more than the five pairs of scores in our purposely simple greeting card example), an *r* of .50 or more, in either the positive or the negative direction, would represent a *very strong* relationship in most areas of behavioral and educational research.* But there are exceptions. An *r* of at least .80 or more would be expected when correlation coefficients measure "test reliability," as determined, for example, from pairs of IQ scores for people who take the same IQ test twice or take two forms of the same test (to establish that any person's two scores tend to be similar and, therefore, that the test scores are reproducible, or "reliable").

Range Restrictions

Except for special circumstances, the value of the correlation coefficient declines whenever the range of possible *X* or *Y* scores is restricted. Range restriction is analogous to magnifying a subset of the original dot cluster and, in the process, losing much of the orderly and predictable pattern in the original dot cluster. For example, **Figure 6.5** shows a dot cluster with an obvious slope, represented by an *r* of .70 for the positive relationship between height and weight for all college students. If, however, the range of heights along *Y* is restricted to students who stand over 6 feet 2 inches (or 74 inches) tall, the abbreviated dot cluster loses its obvious slope because of the more homogeneous weights among tall students. Therefore, as depicted in Figure 6.5, the value of *r* drops to .10.

Sometimes it's impossible to avoid a range restriction. For example, some colleges only admit students with SAT test scores above some minimum value.

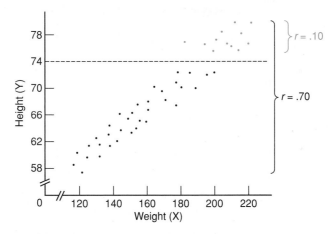

FIGURE 6.5

Effect of range restriction on the value of r.

....

* In his landmark book *Statistical Power Analysis for the Behavioral Sciences,* 2nd ed. (Hillsdale, NJ: Erlbaum, 1988), Jacob Cohen suggests that a value of *r* in the vicinity of .10 or less reflects a small (weak) relationship; a value in the vicinity of .30 reflects a medium (moderate) relationship; and a value in the vicinity of .50 or more reflects a large (strong) relationship.

Subsequently, the value of any correlation between SAT scores and college GPAs for these students will be lower because of the absence of any students with SAT scores below the minimum score required for admission. Always check for any possible restriction on the ranges of X or Y scores—whether by design or accident—that could lower the value of r.

Caution

Be careful when interpreting the actual numerical value of r. An r of .70 for height and weight doesn't signify that the strength of this relationship equals either .70 or 70 percent of the strength of a perfect relationship. *The value of* r *can't be interpreted as a proportion or percentage of some perfect relationship.*

Verbal Descriptions

When interpreting a brand new r, you'll find it helpful to translate the numerical value of r into a verbal description of the relationship. An r of .70 for the height and weight of college students could be translated into "Taller students tend to weigh more" (or some other equally valid statement, such as "Lighter students tend to be shorter"); an r of –.42 for time spent taking an exam and the subsequent exam score could be translated into "Students who take less time tend to make higher scores"; and an r in the neighborhood of 0 for shoe size and IQ could be translated into "Little, if any, relationship exists between shoe size and IQ."

If you have trouble verbalizing the value of r, refer back to the original scatterplot or, if necessary, visualize a rough scatterplot corresponding to the value of r. Use any detectable dot cluster to think your way through the relationship. Does the dot cluster have a slope from the lower left to the upper right—that is, does low go with low and high go with high? Or does the dot cluster have a slope from the upper left to the lower right—that is, does low go with high and vice versa? It is crucial that you translate abstractions such as "Low goes with low and high goes with high" into concrete terms such as "Shorter students tend to weigh less, and taller students tend to weigh more."

Progress Check *6.3 Supply a verbal description for each of the following correlations. (If necessary, visualize a rough scatterplot for r, using the scatterplots in Figure 6.3 as a frame of reference.)

(a) an r of –.84 between total mileage and automobile resale value

(b) an r of –.35 between the number of days absent from school and performance on a math achievement test

(c) an r of .03 between anxiety level and college GPA

(d) an r of .56 between age of schoolchildren and reading comprehension
   Answers on page 496.

Correlation Not Necessarily Cause-Effect

Given a correlation between the prevalence of poverty and crime in U.S. cities, you can *speculate* that poverty causes crime—that is, poverty produces crime with the same degree of inevitability as the flip of a light switch illuminates a room.

According to this view, any widespread reduction in poverty should cause a corresponding decrease in crime. As suggested in Chapter 1, you can also *speculate* that a common cause, such as inadequate education, overpopulation, racial discrimination, etc., or some combination of these factors produces both poverty and crime. According to this view, a widespread reduction in poverty should have no effect on crime. Which speculation is correct? Unfortunately, this issue cannot be resolved merely on the basis of an observed correlation.

> **A correlation coefficient, regardless of size, never provides information about whether an observed relationship reflects a simple cause-effect relationship or some more complex state of affairs.**

In the past, the interpretation of the correlation between cigarette smoking and lung cancer was vigorously disputed. American Cancer Society representatives interpreted the correlation as a causal relationship: Smoking produces lung cancer. On the other hand, tobacco industry representatives interpreted the correlation as, at most, an indication that both the desire to smoke cigarettes and lung cancer are caused by some more basic but yet unidentified factor or factors, such as the body metabolism or personality of some people. According to this reasoning, people with a high body metabolism might be more prone to smoke and, quite independent of their smoking, more vulnerable to lung cancer. Therefore, smoking correlates with lung cancer because both are effects of some common cause or causes.

Role of Experimentation

Sometimes experimentation can resolve this kind of controversy. In the present case, laboratory animals were trained to inhale different amounts of tobacco tars and were then euthanized. Autopsies revealed that the observed incidence of lung cancer (the dependent variable) varied directly with the amount of inhaled tobacco tars (the independent variable), even though possible "contaminating" factors, such as different body metabolisms or personalities, had been neutralized either through experimental control or by random assignment of the subjects to different test conditions. As was noted in Chapter 1, experimental confirmation of a correlation can provide strong evidence in favor of a cause-effect interpretation of the observed relationship; indeed, in the smoking-cancer controversy, cumulative experimental findings overwhelmingly support the conclusion that smoking causes lung cancer.

Progress Check *6.4 Speculate on whether the following correlations reflect simple cause-effect relationships or more complex states of affairs. (**Hint:** A cause-effect relationship implies that, if all else remains the same, any change in the causal variable should always produce a predictable change in the other variable.)

(a) caloric intake and body weight

(b) height and weight

(c) SAT math score and score on a calculus test

(d) poverty and crime

Answers on page 497.

6.4 DETAILS: *z* SCORE FORMULA FOR *r*

The simplest formula for *r* is:

CORRELATION COEFFICIENT (*z* SCORE FORMULA)	
$$r = \frac{\sum z_x z_y}{n-1}$$	(6.1)

where z_x and z_y are the *z* score equivalents for each pair of original scores, *X* and *Y*, and *n* refers to the number of pairs of scores. The term $\sum z_x z_y$ is found by first multiplying each pair of z_x and z_y scores and then adding the products for all pairs. Formula 6.1 directs us to divide $\sum z_x z_y$ by the total number of pairs minus one, $n - 1$. (The $n - 1$ in the denominator reflects the fact that the *z* scores are calculated using sample standard deviations.)

Calculating *r* (*z* Score Formula)

In actual practice, you should *never* use the *z* score formula to calculate the value of *r* because of several complications, including the extra effort of converting original scores to *z* scores. (For example, to obtain Doris's z_x score of 1.34 in panel A of **Table 6.3**, subtract 7, the sample mean $\bar{X}$, from 13, her *X* score, then divide the resulting deviation of 6 by 4.47, the sample standard deviation s_x. Similarly, to obtain her z_y of 0.45, subtract 12, the sample mean $\bar{Y}$, from

Table 6.3
THREE RELATIONSHIPS: *z* SCORE FORMULA FOR *r*

	A POSITIVE RELATIONSHIP			B NEGATIVE RELATIONSHIP			C LITTLE OR NO RELATIONSHIP		
	z_x	z_y	$z_x z_y$	z_x	z_y	$z_x z_y$	z_x	z_y	$z_x z_y$
Doris	1.34	0.45	0.60	1.34	−0.45	−0.60	1.34	−0.45	−0.60
Steve	0.45	1.34	0.60	0.45	−1.34	−0.60	0.45	1.34	0.60
Mike	0.00	0.00	0.00	0.00	0.00	0.00	0.00	0.00	0.00
Andrea	−0.45	−0.45	0.20	−0.45	0.45	−0.20	−0.45	−1.34	0.60
John	−1.34	−1.34	1.80	1.34	−1.34	−1.80	−1.34	0.45	−0.60

$$\sum z_x z_y = 3.20 \qquad\qquad \sum z_x z_y = -3.20 \qquad\qquad \sum z_x z_y = 0.00$$

$$r = \frac{\sum z_x z_y}{n-1} \qquad\qquad r = \frac{\sum z_x z_y}{n-1} \qquad\qquad r = \frac{\sum z_x z_y}{n-1}$$

$$= \frac{3.20}{4} \qquad\qquad = \frac{-3.20}{4} \qquad\qquad = \frac{0}{4}$$

$$r = .80 \qquad\qquad r = -.80 \qquad\qquad r = 0$$

14, her Y score, then divide the resulting deviation of 2 by 4.47, the sample standard deviation s_y.)

In order to clarify some important properties of r, Table 6.3 illustrates how, once z scores replace original scores for the three sets of paired scores in Table 6.2, values of r are calculated for each of the three types of relationships for the greeting card example. Let's look more closely at how Formula 6.1 processes a positive relationship, a negative relationship, and little or no relationship.

Positive Relationship

If there is a positive relationship, as in panel A of Table 6.3, pairs of z scores will tend to have similar relative locations in their respective distributions, and therefore positive z scores will tend to be paired with positive z scores and negative z scores will tend to be paired with negative z scores. Consequently, and this is a crucial point, the products of paired z scores, $z_x z_y$, will tend to be positive because multiplication involves pairs of numbers with like signs, either both plus or both minus. As a result, the numerator term in Formula 6.1, $\Sigma z_x z_y$, becomes a relatively large positive number, which, when divided by $n - 1$, yields a positive r—in the present case, an r of .80.

Perfect Positive Relationship

If pairs of z scores have both the same magnitude and the same sign (for instance, one pair might be 1.34 and 1.34, and another might be 0.45 and 0.45), r would equal 1.00, indicating a perfect positive relationship. Under these circumstances, the relationship would display total regularity, with pairs of z scores occupying *exactly* the same relative locations in their respective distributions. Returning to panel A of Table 6.3, you might verify that if the top two entries in the z_x column had been reversed, causing each pair of z scores to have both the same magnitude and the same sign, then

$$r = \frac{\Sigma z_x z_y}{n-1} = \frac{4.00}{4} = 1.00$$

Negative Relationship

If there is a negative relationship, as in panel B of Table 6.3, pairs of z scores will tend to have relative locations that are reversed in their respective distributions, and therefore positive z scores will tend to be paired with negative scores, and vice versa. Consequently, the products of paired z scores, $z_x z_y$, will tend to be negative because multiplication involves pairs of numbers with unlike signs, one plus and the other minus. As a result, the numerator term in Formula 6.1, $\Sigma z_x z_y$, will tend to be a relatively large negative number, which, when divided by $n - 1$, will be a negative r—in the present case, an r of −.80.

Perfect Negative Relationship

If pairs of z scores have the same magnitude but unlike signs (for instance, one pair might be 1.34 and −1.34, and another pair might be 0.45 and −0.45), r would equal −1.00, indicating a perfect negative correlation. Under these circumstances, the relationship would also display perfect regularity, with pairs of

z scores occupying relative locations that are *exactly reversed* in their respective distributions.

Little or No Relationship

If there is little or no relationship, as in panel C of Table 6.3, no consistent pattern will describe the relative locations of pairs of z scores in their respective distributions. Therefore, a positive z score is equally likely to be paired with either a positive or a negative z score, and vice versa. Consequently, about half of all products of paired z scores, $z_x z_y$, are positive because multiplication involves numbers with like signs, and about half of all products of paired z scores, $z_x z_y$, are negative because multiplication involves numbers with unlike signs. Since positive and negative products tend to cancel each other, the numerator term in Formula 6.1, $\Sigma z_x z_y$, tends toward a small positive or negative number that, when divided by $n - 1$, yields a value of r near 0.

Review

To summarize, an understanding of correlation, as measured by r, can be gained from the z score formula. The pattern among pairs of z scores can be used to anticipate the value of r. If pairs of z scores are similar in both magnitude and sign, the value of r will tend toward 1.00, indicating a strong positive correlation. But if pairs of z scores are similar in magnitude but opposite in sign, the value of r will tend toward -1.00, indicating a strong negative correlation. As the pattern among pairs of z scores becomes less apparent, the value of r tends toward 0, indicating a weak or nonexistent correlation.

r Is Independent of Units of Measurement

The z score formula also pinpoints another important property of r—its independence of the original units of measurement. In fact, the same value of r describes the correlation between height and weight for a group of adults, regardless of whether height is measured in inches or centimeters or whether weight is measured in pounds or grams. In effect, the value of r depends only on the pattern among pairs of z scores, which in turn show no traces of the units of measurement for the original X and Y scores. If you think about it, this is the same as saying that

a positive value of r reflects a tendency for pairs of scores to occupy *similar* relative locations (high with high and low with low) in their respective distributions, while a negative value of r reflects a tendency for pairs of scores to occupy *dissimilar* relative locations (high with low and vice versa) in their respective distributions.

Progress Check *6.5 Pretend that there is a perfect positive (+1.00) relationship between height and weight for adults. (Actually, you might recall, it's in the vicinity of .70 for college students.) In this case, if John stands two standard deviations above the mean height, his weight will be ___**(a)**___ standard deviation units ___**(b)**___ the mean. If Kristen is one and one-half standard deviation units below the mean height, her weight will be ___**(c)**___ standard deviation units ___**(d)**___ the mean. If Carson is one-third of a standard deviation above the mean weight, his height will be ___**(e)**___ of a standard deviation ___**(f)**___ the mean.

Progress Check *6.6 Repeat Question 6.5, assuming a perfect negative (−1.00) relationship between height and weight.

Answers on page 497.

6.5 DETAILS: COMPUTATION FORMULA FOR *r*

Except to provide a more intuitive picture of correlation, *the z score formula should not be used to calculate r.* Converting each *X* and *Y* score into an equivalent *z* score not only is laborious but often produces an appreciable rounding error if means and standard deviations are approximate numbers. It is more efficient and usually more accurate to calculate a value for *r* by using the computation formula:

CORRELATION COEFFICIENT (COMPUTATION FORMULA)

$$r = \frac{SP_{xy}}{\sqrt{SS_x SS_y}}$$ (6.2)

---

where the two sum of squares terms in the denominator are defined as

$$SS_x = \Sigma\left(X - \overline{X}\right)^2 = \Sigma X^2 - \frac{(\Sigma X)^2}{n}$$

$$SS_y = \Sigma\left(Y - \overline{Y}\right)^2 = \Sigma Y^2 - \frac{(\Sigma Y)^2}{n}$$

and the sum of the products term in the numerator, SP_{xy}, is defined in Formula 6.3.

SUM OF PRODUCTS (DEFINITION AND COMPUTATION FORMULAS)

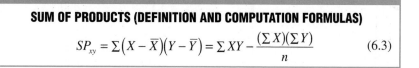

$$SP_{xy} = \Sigma\left(X - \overline{X}\right)\left(Y - \overline{Y}\right) = \Sigma XY - \frac{(\Sigma X)(\Sigma Y)}{n}$$ (6.3)

In the case of SP_{xy}, instead of summing the squared deviation scores for either *X* or *Y*, as with SS_x and SS_y, we find the sum of the products for each pair of deviation score. Notice in Formula 6.2 that, since the terms in the denominator must be positive, only the sum of the products, SP_{xy}, determines whether the value of *r* is positive or negative. Furthermore, the size of SP_{xy} mirrors that of $\Sigma z_x z_y$ discussed in the previous section; stronger relationships are associated with larger positive or negative sums of products. Table 6.4 illustrates the calculation of *r* for the original greeting card data by using the computation formula.

Progress Check *6.7 Couples who attend a clinic for first pregnancies are asked to estimate (independently of each other) the ideal number of children. Given that *X* and *Y* represent the estimates of females and males, respectively, the

Table 6.4
CALCULATION OF *r*: COMPUTATION FORMULA

A. COMPUTATIONAL SEQUENCE

Assign a value to *n* 1, representing the number of pairs of scores.
Sum all scores for *X* 2 and for *Y* 3.
Find the product of each pair of *X* and *Y* scores 4, one at a time, then add all of these products 5.
Square each *X* score 6, one at a time, then add all squared *X* scores 7.
Square each *Y* score 8, one at a time, then add all squared *Y* scores 9.
Substitute numbers into formulas 10 and solve for SP_{xy}, SS_x, and SS_y.
Substitute into formula 11 and solve for *r*.

B. DATA AND COMPUTATIONS

	CARDS		4	6	8
FRIEND	SENT, *X*	RECEIVED, *Y*	*XY*	X^2	Y^2
Doris	13	14	182	169	196
Steve	9	18	162	81	324
Mike	7	12	84	49	144
Andrea	5	10	50	25	100
John	1	6	6	1	36

1 $n = 5$ 2 $\Sigma X = 35$ 3 $\Sigma Y = 60$ 5 $\Sigma XY = 484$ 7 $\Sigma X^2 = 325$ 9 $\Sigma Y^2 = 800$

$$10\quad SP_{xy} = \Sigma XY - \frac{(\Sigma X)(\Sigma Y)}{n} = 484 - \frac{(35)(60)}{5} = 484 - 420 = 64$$

$$SS_x = \Sigma X^2 - \frac{(\Sigma X)^2}{n} = 325 - \frac{(35)^2}{5} = 325 - 245 = 80$$

$$SS_y = \Sigma Y^2 - \frac{(\Sigma Y)^2}{n} = 800 - \frac{(60)^2}{5} = 800 - 720 = 80$$

$$11\quad r = \frac{SP_{xy}}{\sqrt{SS_x SS_y}} = \frac{64}{\sqrt{(80)(80)}} = \frac{64}{80} = .80$$

results are as follows:

COUPLE	X	Y
A	1	2
B	3	4
C	2	3
D	3	2
E	1	0
F	2	3

Calculate a value for *r*, using the computation formula (6.2).

Answer on page 497.

6.6 OUTLIERS AGAIN

In Section 2.3, *outliers* were defined as very extreme scores that require special attention because of their potential impact on a summary of data. This is also true when outliers appear among sets of paired scores. Although quantitative techniques can be used to detect these outliers, we simply focus on dots in scatterplots that deviate conspicuously from the main dot cluster.

Greeting Card Study Revisited

Figure 6.6 shows the effect of each of two possible outliers, substituted one at a time for Doris's dot (13, 14), on the original value of *r* (.80) for the greeting card data. Although both outliers A and B deviate conspicuously from the dot cluster, they have radically different effects on the value of *r*. Outlier A (33, 34) contributes to a new value of .98 for *r* that merely reaffirms the original positive relationship between cards sent and received. On the other hand, outlier B (13, 4) causes a dramatically new value of .04 for *r* that entirely neutralizes the original positive relationship. Neither of the values for outlier B, taken singularly, is extreme. Rather, it is their unusual combination—13 cards sent and only 4 received—that yields the radically different value of .04 for *r*, indicating that the new dot cluster is not remotely approximated by a straight line.

Dealing with Outliers

Of course, serious investigators would use many more than five pairs of scores, and therefore the effect of outliers on the value of *r* would tend not to be as dramatic as the one above. Nevertheless, outliers can have a considerable impact on the value of *r* and, therefore, pose problems of interpretation. Unless there is some reason for discarding an outlier—because of a failed accuracy check or because, for example, you establish that the friend who received only 4 cards had sent 13 cards that failed to include an expected monetary gift—the

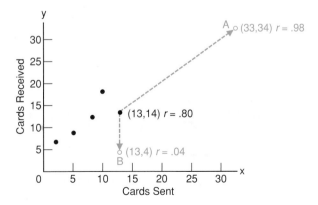

FIGURE 6.6

Effect of each of two outliers on the value of r.

most defensible strategy is to report the values of *r* both with and without any outliers.*

.www.

INTERNET DEMONSTRATION

Go to the Web site for this book (http://www.wiley.com/college/witte). Click on the *Student Companion Site,* then *Internet Demonstrations,* and finally ***Outliers*** to see the effect of outliers on the correlation coefficient.

6.7 OTHER TYPES OF CORRELATION COEFFICIENTS

There are many other types of correlation coefficients, but we will discuss only several that are direct descendants of the Pearson correlation coefficient. Although designed originally for use with quantitative data, the Pearson *r* has been extended, sometimes under the guise of new names and customized versions of Formula 6.2, to other kinds of situations. For example, to describe the correlation between *ranks* assigned independently by two judges to a set of science projects, simply substitute the numerical ranks into Formula 6.2, then solve for a value of the Pearson *r* (also referred to as *Spearman's rho* coefficient for ranked or ordinal data). To describe the correlation between quantitative data (for example, annual income) and *qualitative or nominal data with only two categories* (for example, male and female), assign arbitrary numerical codes, such as 1 and 2, to the two qualitative categories, then solve Formula 6.2 for a value of the Pearson *r* (also referred to as a *point biserial* correlation coefficient). Or to describe the relationship between *two ordered qualitative variables,* such as the attitude toward legal abortion (favorable, neutral, or opposed) and educational level (high school only, some college, college graduate), assign any *ordered* numerical codes to the categories for both qualitative variables, then solve Formula 6.2 for a value of the Pearson *r* (also referred to as *Cramer's phi* coefficient).

Most computer outputs would simply report each of the above correlations as a Pearson *r*. Given the widespread use of computers, the more specialized names for the Pearson *r* will probably survive, if at all, as artifacts of an earlier age, when calculations were manual and some computational relief was obtained by customizing Formula 6.2 for situations involving ranks and qualitative data.

6.8 COMPUTER OUTPUT

Most analyses in this book are performed by hand on small batches of data. When analyses are based on large batches of data, as often happens in practice, it is much more efficient to use a computer. Although we will not show how to enter commands and data into a computer, we will describe the most relevant

---

*For more information about the quantitative detection of outliers among sets of paired scores, see Chapter 15 in D.C. Howell's, *Statistical Methods for Psychology,* 7th ed. (Belmont, CA: Wadsworth, 2010).

portions of some computer outputs. Once you have learned to ignore irrelevant details and references to more advanced statistical procedures, you'll find that statistical results produced by computers are as easy to interpret as those produced by hand.

Three of the most widely used statistical programs, Minitab, SPSS (Statistical Package for the Social Sciences), and SAS (Statistical Analysis System), generate the computer outputs in this book. As interpretive aids, some outputs are cross-referenced with explanatory comments at the bottom of the printout. Since these outputs are based on data already analyzed by hand, computer-produced results can be compared with familiar results. For example, the computer-produced scatterplot, as well as the correlation of .800 in Table 6.5 can be compared with the manually produced scatterplot in Figure 6.1 and the correlation of .80 in Table 6.4.

INTERNET SITES
Go to the Web site for this book (http://www.wiley.com/college/witte). Click on the *Student Companion Site,* then *Internet Sites,* and finally ***Minitab, SPSS, or SAS*** to obtain more information about these statistical packages, as well as demonstration software.

Correlation Matrix

Table showing correlations for all possible pairs of variables.

When every possible pairing of variables is reported, as in lower half of the output in Table 6.5, a **correlation matrix** is produced. The value of .800 occurs twice in the matrix, since the correlation is the same whether the relationship is described as that between cards sent and cards received or vice versa. The value of 1.000, which also occurs twice, reflects the trivial fact that any variable correlates perfectly with itself.

Reading a Larger Correlation Matrix

Since correlation matrices can be expanded to incorporate any number of variables, they are useful devices for showing correlations between all possible pairs of variables when, in fact, many variables are being studied. For example, in Table 6.6, four variables generate a correlation matrix with 4×4, or 16, correlation coefficients. The four perfect (but trivial) correlations of 1.000, produced by pairing each variable with itself, split the remainder of the matrix into two triangular sections, each containing six nontrivial correlations. Since the correlations in these two sectors are mirror images, you can attend to just the values of the six correlations in one sector in order to evaluate all relevant correlations among the four original variables.

Interpreting a Larger Correlation Matrix

Three of the six color-coded correlations in Table 6.6 involve GENDER. GENDER qualifies for a correlation analysis once arbitrary numerical codes (1 for male and 2 for female) have been assigned. Looking across the bottom

Table 6.5
SPSS OUTPUT: SCATTERPLOT AND CORRELATION
FOR GREETING CARD DATA

GRAPH
1

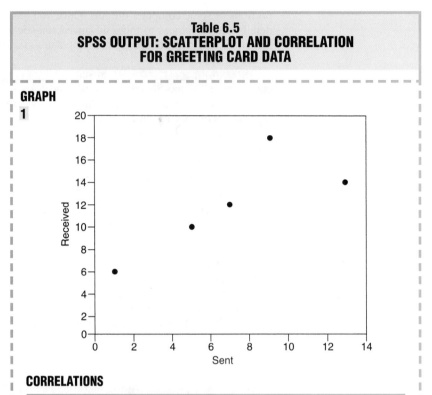

CORRELATIONS

		SENT	**RECEIVED**
Sent	Pearson Correlation	1.000	.800
	Sig. (2-tailed)	–	.104
	N	5	5
Received	Pearson Correlation	2 .800	1.000
	Sig. (2-tailed)	3 .104	–
	N	4 5	5

Comments:

1 Scatterplot for greeting card data (using slightly different scales than in Figure 6.1).
2 The correlation for cards sent and cards received equals .800, in agreement with the calculations in Table 6.4.
3 The value of Sig. helps us interpret the statistical significance of a correlation by evaluating the observed value of r relative to the actual number of pairs of scores used to calculate r. Discussed later in Section 14.6, Sig.-values are referred to as p-values in this book. At this point, perhaps the easiest way to view a Sig.-value is as follows: The smaller the value of Sig. (on a scale from 0 to 1), the more likely that you would observe a correlation with the same sign, either positive or negative, if the study were repeated with new observations. Investigators often focus only on those correlations with Sig.-values smaller than .05.
4 Number of cases or paired scores.

Table 6.6
SPSS OUTPUT: CORRELATION MATRIX FOR FOUR VARIABLES (BASED ON 336 STATISTICS STUDENTS)

CORRELATIONS

		AGE	COLLEGE GPA	HIGH SCHOOL GPA	GENDER
AGE	Pearson Correlation	1.000	.2228	−.0376	.0813
	Sig. (2-tailed)	—	.000	.511	.138
	N	335	333	307	335
COLLEGE GPA	Pearson Correlation	.2228	1.000	.2521	.2069
	Sig. (2-tailed)	.000	—	.000	.000
	N	333	334	306	334
HIGH SCHOOL GPA	Pearson Correlation	−.0376	.2521	1.000	.2981
	Sig. (2-tailed)	.511	.000	—	.000
	N	307	306	307	307
GENDER	Pearson Correlation	.0813	.2069	.2981	1.000
	Sig. (2-tailed)	.138	.000	.000	—
	N	335	334	307	336

row, GENDER is positively correlated with AGE (.0813); with COLLEGE GPA (.2069); and with HIGH SCHOOL GPA (.2981). Looking across the next row, HIGH SCHOOL GPA is negatively correlated with AGE (−.0376) and positively correlated with COLLEGE GPA (.2521). Lastly, COLLEGE GPA is positively correlated with AGE (.2228).

As suggested in Comment 3 at the bottom of Table 6.5, values of *Sig.* help us judge the statistical significance of the various correlations. A smaller value of *Sig.* implies that if the study were repeated, the same positive or negative sign of the corresponding correlation would probably reappear, even though calculations are based on an entirely new group of similarly selected students. Therefore, we can conclude that the four correlations with *Sig.*-values close to zero (.000) probably would reappear as positive relationships. In a new group, female students would tend to have higher high school and college GPAs, and students with higher college GPAs would tend to have higher high school GPAs and to be older. Because of the larger *Sig.*-value of .138 for the correlation between GENDER and AGE we cannot be as confident that female students would be older than male students. Because of the even larger *Sig.*-value of .511 for the small negative correlation between AGE and HIGH SCHOOL GPA, this correlation would be just as likely to reappear as either a positive or negative relationship and should not be taken seriously.

Finally, the numbers in the last row of each cell in Table 6.6 show the total number of cases actually used to calculate the corresponding correlation. Excluded from these totals are those cases in which students failed to supply the requested information.

Progress Check *6.8 Refer to Table 6.6 when answering the following questions.

(a) Would the same positive correlation of .2981 have been obtained between GENDER and HIGH SCHOOL GPA if the assignment of codes had been reversed, with females being coded as 1 and males coded as 2? Explain your answer.

(b) Given the new coding of females as 1 and males as 2, would the results still permit you to conclude that females tend to have higher high school GPAs than do males?

(c) Would the original positive correlation of .2981 have been obtained if, instead of the original coding of males as 1 and females as 2, males were coded as 10 and females as 20? Explain your answer.

(d) Assume that the correlation matrix includes a fifth variable. What would be the total number of relevant correlations in the expanded matrix?
Answers on pages 497.

Summary

The presence of regularity among pairs of X and Y scores indicates that the two variables are related, and the absence of any regularity suggests that the two variables are, at most, only slightly related. When the regularity consists of relatively low X scores being paired with relatively low Y scores and relatively high X scores being paired with relatively high Y scores, the relationship is positive. When it consists of relatively low X scores being paired with relatively high Y scores and vice versa, the relationship is negative.

A scatterplot is a graph with a cluster of dots that represents all pairs of scores. A dot cluster that has a slope from the lower left to the upper right reflects a positive relationship, and a dot cluster that has a slope from the upper left to the lower right reflects a negative relationship. A dot cluster that lacks any apparent slope reflects little or no relationship.

In a positive or negative relationship, the more closely the dot cluster approximates a straight line, the stronger the relationship will be.

When the dot cluster approximates a straight line, the relationship is linear; when it approximates a bent line, the relationship is curvilinear.

Located on a scale from -1.00 to $+1.00$, the value of r indicates both the direction of a linear relationship—whether positive or negative—and, generally, the relative strength of a linear relationship. Values of r in the general vicinity of either -1.00 or $+1.00$ indicate a relatively strong relationship, and values of r in the neighborhood of 0 indicate a relatively weak relationship.

Although the value of r can be used to formulate a verbal description of the relationship, the numerical value of r does not indicate a proportion or percentage of a perfect relationship.

Always check for any possible restriction on the ranges of X and Y scores that could lower the value of r.

The presence of a correlation, by itself, does not resolve the issue of whether it reflects a simple cause-effect relationship or a more complex state of affairs.

The Pearson correlation coefficient, r, describes the linear relationship between pairs of variables for quantitative data. An understanding of correlation, as described by r, can be gained from the z score formula (6.1). In practice, it is both more efficient and more accurate to calculate r by using the computation formula (6.2).

Outliers can have a considerable impact on the value of r and, therefore, pose problems of interpretation.

Although designed originally for use with quantitative data, the Pearson r has been extended to other kinds of situations, including those with ranked and qualitative data.

Whenever there are more than two variables, correlation matrices can be useful devices for showing correlations between all possible pairs of variables.

Important Terms and Symbols

Positive relationship	**Negative relationship**
Scatterplot	**Linear relationship**
Curvilinear relationship	**Correlation coefficient**
Pearson correlation coefficient (r)	**Correlation matrix**

Key Equations

CORRELATION COEFFICIENT

$$r = \frac{SP_{xy}}{\sqrt{SS_x SS_y}}$$

where $SP_{xy} = \Sigma \left(X - \overline{X} \right) \left(Y - \overline{Y} \right) = \Sigma XY - \dfrac{(\Sigma X)(\Sigma Y)}{n}$

REVIEW QUESTIONS

6.9 **(a)** Estimate whether the following pairs of scores for X and Y reflect a positive relationship, a negative relationship, or no relationship. **Hint:** Note any tendency for pairs of X and Y scores to occupy similar or dissimilar relative locations.

X	Y
64	66
40	79
30	98
71	65
55	76
31	83
61	68
42	80
57	72

(b) Construct a scatterplot for X and Y. Verify that the scatterplot does not describe a pronounced curvilinear trend.

(c) Calculate r using the computation formula (6.2).

*6.10 On the basis of an extensive survey, the California Department of Education reported an r of −.32 for the relationship between the amount of time spent watching TV and the achievement test scores of schoolchildren. Each of the following statements represents a possible interpretation of this finding. Indicate whether each is True or False.

(a) *Every* child who watches a lot of TV will perform poorly on the achievement tests.

(b) Extensive TV viewing causes a decline in test scores.

(c) Children who watch little TV will tend to perform well on the tests.

(d) Children who perform well on the tests will tend to watch little TV.

(e) If Gretchen's TV-viewing time is reduced by one-half, we can expect a substantial improvement in her test scores.

(f) TV viewing could not possibly cause a decline in test scores.

Answers on Page 497.

6.11 Assume that an r of .80 describes the relationship between daily food intake, measured in ounces, and body weight, measured in pounds, for a group of adults. Would a shift in the units of measurement from ounces to grams and from pounds to kilograms change the value of r? Justify your answer.

6.12 An extensive correlation study indicates that a longer life is experienced by people who follow the seven "golden rules" of behavior, including moderate drinking, no smoking, regular meals, some exercise, and eight hours of sleep each night. Can we conclude, therefore, that this type of behavior *causes* a longer life?

CHAPTER 7

Regression

Preview

If two variables are correlated, description can lead to prediction. For example, if computer skills and GPAs are related, level of computer skills can be used to predict GPAs. Predictive accuracy increases with the strength of the underlying correlation.

Also discussed is a very prevalent phenomenon known as "regression toward the mean." It often occurs over time to subsets of extreme observations, such as after the superior performance of professional athletes or after the poor performance of learning-challenged children. If misinterpreted as a real effect, regression toward the mean can lead to erroneous conclusions.

A correlation analysis of the exchange of greeting cards by five friends for the most recent holiday season suggests a strong positive relationship between cards sent and cards received. When informed of these results, another friend, Emma, who enjoys receiving greeting cards, asks you to predict how many cards she will receive during the next holiday season, assuming that she plans to send 11 cards.

7.1 TWO ROUGH PREDICTIONS

Predict "Relatively Large Number"

You could offer Emma a very rough prediction by recalling that cards sent and received tend to occupy *similar* relative locations in their respective distributions. Therefore, Emma can expect to receive a *relatively large* number of cards, since she plans to send a *relatively large* number of cards.

Predict "between 14 and 18 Cards"

To obtain a slightly more precise prediction for Emma, refer to the scatterplot for the original five friends shown in **Figure 7.1**. Notice that Emma's plan to send 11 cards locates her along the *X* axis between the 9 cards sent by Steve

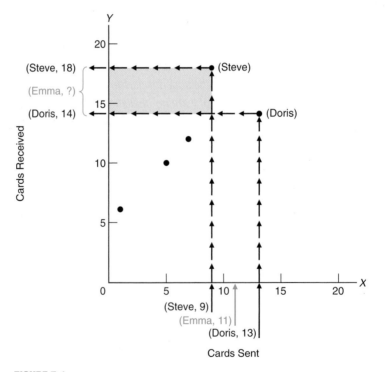

FIGURE 7.1
A rough prediction for Emma (using dots for Steve and Doris).

and the 13 sent by Doris. Using the dots for Steve and Doris as guides, construct two strings of arrows, one beginning at 9 and ending at 18 for Steve and the other beginning at 13 and ending at 14 for Doris. [The direction of the arrows reflects our attempt to predict cards received (*Y*) from cards sent (*X*). Although not required, it is customary to predict from *X* to *Y*.] Focusing on the interval along the *Y* axis between the two strings of arrows, you could predict that Emma's return should be between 14 and 18 cards, the numbers received by Doris and Steve.

The latter prediction might satisfy Emma, but it would not win any statistical awards. Although each of the five dots in Figure 7.1 supplies valuable information about the exchange of greeting cards, our prediction for Emma is based only on the two dots for Steve and Doris.

7.2 A REGRESSION LINE

All five dots contribute to the more precise prediction, illustrated in **Figure 7.2**, that Emma will receive 15.20 cards. Look more closely at the solid line designated as the regression line in Figure 7.2, which guides the string of arrows, beginning at 11, toward the predicted value of 15.20. The regression line is a straight line rather than a curved line because of the linear relationship between cards sent and cards received. As will become apparent, it can be used repeatedly to predict cards received. Regardless of whether Emma decides to send 5, 15, or 25 cards, it will guide a new string of arrows, beginning at 5 or 15 or 25, toward a new predicted value along the *Y* axis.

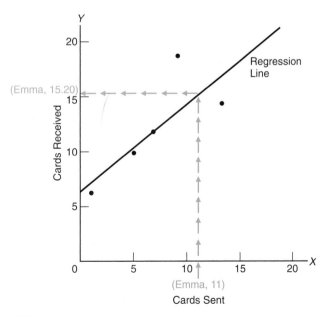

FIGURE 7.2
Prediction of 15.20 for Emma (using the regression line).

Placement of Line

For the time being, forget about any prediction for Emma and concentrate on how the five dots dictate the placement of the regression line. If all five dots had defined a single straight line, placement of the regression line would have been simple; merely let it pass through all dots. When the dots fail to define a single straight line, as in the scatterplot for the five friends, placement of the regression line represents a compromise. It passes through the main cluster, possibly touching some dots but missing others.

Predictive Errors

Figure 7.3 illustrates the predictive errors that would have occurred if the regression line had been used to predict the number of cards received by the five friends. Solid dots reflect the *actual* number of cards received, and open dots, always located along the regression line, reflect the *predicted* number of cards received. (To avoid clutter in Figure 7.3, the strings of arrows have been omitted. However, you might find it helpful to imagine a string of arrows, ending along the *Y* axis, for each dot, whether solid or open.) The largest predictive error, shown as a broken vertical line, occurs for Steve, who sent 9 cards. Although he actually received 18 cards, he should have received slightly fewer than 14 cards, according to the regression line. The smallest predictive error—none whatsoever—occurs for Mike, who sent 7 cards. He actually received the 12 cards that he should have received, according to the regression line.

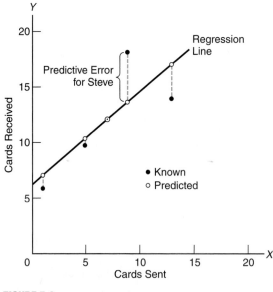

FIGURE 7.3
Predictive errors.

Total Predictive Error

We engage in the seemingly silly activity of predicting what is known already for the five friends to check the adequacy of our predictive effort. The smaller the total for all predictive errors in Figure 7.3, the more favorable will be the prognosis for our predictions. Clearly, it is desirable for the regression line to be placed in a position that *minimizes* the total predictive error, that is, that minimizes the total of the vertical discrepancies between the solid and open dots shown in Figure 7.3.

Progress Check *7.1 To check your understanding of the first part of this chapter, make predictions using the graph below.

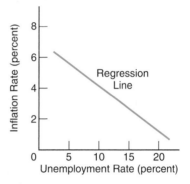

(a) Predict the approximate rate of inflation, given an unemployment rate of 5 percent.

(b) Predict the approximate rate of inflation, given an unemployment rate of 15 percent.

Answers on page 497.

7.3 LEAST SQUARES REGRESSION LINE

To avoid the arithmetic standoff of zero always produced by adding positive and negative predictive errors (associated with errors above and below the regression line, respectively), *the placement of the regression line minimizes* not the total predictive error but *the total squared predictive error*, that is, the total for all squared predictive errors. When located in this fashion, the *regression* line is often referred to as the *least squares regression line*. Although more difficult to visualize, this approach is consistent with the original aim—to minimize the total predictive error or some version of the total predictive error, thereby providing a more favorable prognosis for our predictions.

Need a Mathematical Solution

Without the aid of mathematics, the search for a least squares regression line would be frustrating. Scatterplots would be proving grounds cluttered with tentative regression lines, discarded because of their excessively large totals for squared discrepancies. Even the most time-consuming, conscientious effort would culminate in only a close approximation to the least squares regression line.

> **INTERNET DEMONSTRATION**
> Go to the Web site for this book (http://www.wiley.com/college/witte) and click on **Regression** to try fitting by eye the least squares regression line to a cluster of dots.

Least Squares Regression Equation

Happily, an equation pinpoints the exact least squares regression line for any scatterplot. Most generally, this equation reads:

> **LEAST SQUARES REGRESSION EQUATION**
> $$Y' = bX + a \tag{7.1}$$

where Y' represents the predicted value (the predicted number of cards that will be received by any new friend, such as Emma); X represents the known value (the known number of cards sent by any new friend); and b and a represent numbers calculated from the original correlation analysis, as described below.*

Finding Values of *b* and *a*

To obtain a working regression equation, solve each of the following expressions, first for b and then for a, using data from the original correlation analysis. The expression for b reads:

> **SOLVING FOR *b***
> $$b = \sqrt{\frac{SS_y}{SS_x}}\, r \tag{7.2}$$

where SS_y represents the sum of squares for all Y scores (the cards received by the five friends); SS_x represents the sum of squares for all X scores (the cards sent by the five friends); and r represents the correlation between X and Y (cards sent and received by the five friends).

The expression for a reads:

....

*You might recognize that the least squares equation describes a straight line with a slope of b and a Y-intercept of a.

SOLVING FOR *a*

$$a = \bar{Y} - b\bar{X} \qquad\qquad (7.3)$$

---

where $\bar{Y}$ and $\bar{X}$ refer to the sample means for all Y and X scores, respectively, and b is defined by the preceding expression.

The values of all terms in the expressions for b and a can be obtained from the original correlation analysis either directly, as with the value of r, or indirectly, as with the values of the remaining terms: SS_y, SS_x, $\bar{Y}$, and $\bar{X}$. **Table 7.1** illustrates the computational sequence that produces a least squares regression equation for the greeting card example, namely,

$$Y' = .80\ (X) + 6.40$$

where .80 and 6.40 represent the values computed for b and a, respectively.

Table 7.1
DETERMINING THE LEAST SQUARES REGRESSION EQUATION

A. COMPUTATIONAL SEQUENCE

Determine values of SS_x, SS_y, and r **1** by referring to the original correlation analysis in Table 6.4.

Substitute numbers into the formula **2** and solve for b.

Assign values to $\bar{X}$ and $\bar{Y}$ **3** by referring to the original correlation analysis in Table 6.4.

Substitute numbers into the formula **4** and solve for a.

Substitute numbers for b and a in the least squares regression equation **5**.

B. COMPUTATIONS

1 $SS_x = 80^*$
$SS_y = 80^*$
$r = .80$

2 $b = \sqrt{\dfrac{SS_y}{SS_x}}\ (r) = \sqrt{\dfrac{80}{80}}\ (.80) = .80$

3 $\bar{X} = 7^{**}$
$\bar{Y} = 12^{**}$

4 $a = \bar{Y} - (b)(\bar{X}) = 12 - (.80)(7) = 12 - 5.60 = 6.40$

5 $Y' = (b)(X) + a$
$= (.80)(X) + 6.40$

---

* *Computations not shown. Verify, if you wish, using Formula 4.4.*
** *Computations not shown. Verify, if you wish, using Formula 3.1.*

Least Squares Regression Equation

The equation that minimizes the total of all squared prediction errors for known Y scores in the original correlation analysis.

Key Property

Once numbers have been assigned to b and a, as just described, the **least squares regression equation** emerges as a working equation with a most desirable property: It automatically *minimizes the total of all squared predictive errors for known Y scores in the original correlation analysis.*

Solving for Y'

In its present form, the regression equation can be used to predict the number of cards that Emma will receive, assuming that she plans to send 11 cards. Simply substitute 11 for X and solve for the value of Y' as follows:

$$Y' = .80(11) + 6.40$$
$$= 8.80 + 6.40$$
$$= 15.20$$

Notice that the predicted card return for Emma, 15.20, qualifies as a genuine prediction, that is, a forecast of an unknown event based on information about some known event. This prediction appeared earlier in Figure 7.2.

Our working regression equation provides an inexhaustible supply of predictions for the card exchange. Each prediction emerges simply by substituting some value for X and solving the equation for Y', as described above. Table 7.2 lists the predicted card returns for a number of different card investments. Verify that you can obtain a few of the Y' values shown in Table 7.2 from the regression equation.

Notice that, even when no cards are sent ($X = 0$), we predict a return of 6.40 cards because of the value of a. Also, notice that sending each additional card translates into an increment of only .80 in the predicted return because of the value of b. In other words, whenever b has a value less than 1.00, increments in the predicted return will lag—by an amount equal to the value of b, that is, .80 in the present case—behind increments in cards sent. If the value of b had been greater than 1.00, then increments in the predicted return would have exceeded increments in cards sent. (If the value of b had been negative, because of an underlying negative correlation, then sending additional cards would have triggered decrements, not increments, in the predicted return—and the tradition of sending holiday greeting cards probably would disappear.)

Table 7.2
PREDICTED CARD RETURNS(Y') FOR DIFFERENT CARD INVESTMENTS (X)

X	Y'
0	6.40
4	9.60
8	12.80
10	14.40
12	16.00
20	22.40
30	30.40

A Limitation

Emma might survey these predicted card returns before committing herself to a particular card investment. However, this strategy could backfire because there is no evidence of a simple *cause-effect* relationship between cards sent and cards received. The desired effect might be completely missing if, for instance, Emma expands her usual card distribution to include casual acquaintances and even strangers, as well as her friends and relatives.

Progress Check *7.2 Assume that an r of .30 describes the relationship between educational level (highest grade completed) and estimated number of hours spent reading each week. More specifically:

EDUCATIONAL LEVEL (X)	WEEKLY READING TIME (Y)
$\bar{X} = 13$	$\bar{Y} = 8$
$SS_x = 25$	$SS_y = 50$
$r = .30$	

(a) Determine the least squares equation for predicting weekly reading time from educational level.

(b) Faith's education level is 15. What is her predicted reading time?

(c) Keegan's educational level is 11. What is his predicted reading time?

Answers on page 497.

Graphs or Equations?

Encouraged by Figures 7.2 and 7.3, you might be tempted to generate predictions from graphs rather than equations. However, unless constructed skillfully, graphs yield less accurate predictions than do equations. In the long run, it is more accurate and easier to generate predictions from equations.

7.4 STANDARD ERROR OF ESTIMATE, $s_{y|x}$

Although we predicted that Emma's investment of 11 cards will yield a return of 15.20 cards, we would be surprised if she actually received 15 cards. It is more likely that because of the imperfect relationship between cards sent and cards received, Emma's return will be some number other than 15. Although designed to minimize predictive error, the least squares equation does not eliminate it. Therefore, our next task is to estimate the amount of error associated with our predictions. The smaller the estimated error is, the better the prognosis will be for our predictions.

Finding the Standard Error of Estimate

The estimate of error for new predictions reflects our failure to predict the number of cards received by the original five friends, as depicted by the discrepancies between solid and open dots in Figure 7.3. Known as the *standard error of estimate* and symbolized as $s_{y|x}$, this estimate of predictive error complies with the general format for any sample standard deviation, that is, the square root of some sum of squares term divided by its degrees of freedom. (See Formula 4.10 on page 91.) The formula for $s_{y|x}$ reads:

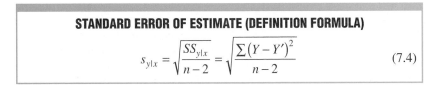

STANDARD ERROR OF ESTIMATE (DEFINITION FORMULA)

$$s_{y|x} = \sqrt{\frac{SS_{y|x}}{n-2}} = \sqrt{\frac{\sum(Y-Y')^2}{n-2}} \qquad (7.4)$$

where the sum of squares term in the numerator, $SS_{y|x}$, represents the sum of the squares for predictive errors, $Y - Y'$, and the degrees of freedom term in the denominator, $n - 2$, reflects the loss of two degrees of freedom because any straight line, including the regression line, can be made to coincide with two data points. The symbol $s_{y|x}$ is read as "s sub y given x."

Although we can estimate the overall predictive error by dealing directly with predictive errors, $Y - Y'$, it is more efficient to use the following computation formula:

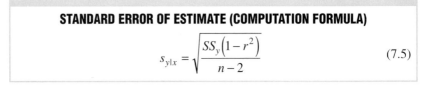

STANDARD ERROR OF ESTIMATE (COMPUTATION FORMULA)

$$s_{y|x} = \sqrt{\frac{SS_y\left(1 - r^2\right)}{n - 2}} \qquad (7.5)$$

where SS_y is the sum of the squares for Y scores (cards received by the five friends), that is,

$$SS_y = \sum\left(Y - \bar{Y}\right) = \sum Y^2 - \frac{\left(\sum Y\right)^2}{n}$$

and r is the correlation coefficient (cards sent and received).

Key Property

Standard Error of Estimate ($s_{y|x}$)

A rough measure of the average amount of predictive error.

The **standard error of estimate** represents a special kind of standard deviation that reflects the magnitude of predictive error.

You might find it helpful to think of the standard error of estimate, $s_{y|x}$, as a rough measure of the average amount of predictive error—that is, as a rough measure of the average amount by which known Y values deviate from their predicted Y' values.

The value of 3.10 for $s_{y|x}$, as calculated in Table 7.3, represents the standard deviation for the discrepancies between known and predicted card returns originally shown in Figure 7.3. In its role as an estimate of predictive error, the value of $s_{y|x}$ can be attached to any new prediction. Thus, a concise prediction statement may read: "The predicted card return for Emma equals 15.20 ± 3.10," in which the latter term serves as a rough estimate of the average amount of predictive error, that is, the average amount by which 15.20 will either overestimate or underestimate Emma's true card return.

---

*Strictly speaking, the standard error of estimate exceeds the average predictive error by 10 to 20 percent. Nevertheless, it is reasonable to describe the standard error in this fashion—as long as you remember that, as with the corresponding definition for the standard deviation in Chapter 4, an approximation is involved.

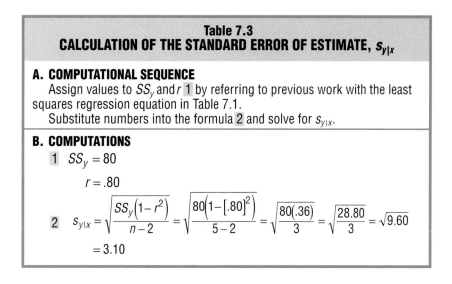

Table 7.3
CALCULATION OF THE STANDARD ERROR OF ESTIMATE, $s_{y|x}$

A. COMPUTATIONAL SEQUENCE
   Assign values to SS_y and r ⟨1⟩ by referring to previous work with the least squares regression equation in Table 7.1.
   Substitute numbers into the formula ⟨2⟩ and solve for $s_{y|x}$.

B. COMPUTATIONS
   ⟨1⟩ $SS_y = 80$

   $r = .80$

   ⟨2⟩ $s_{y|x} = \sqrt{\dfrac{SS_y(1-r^2)}{n-2}} = \sqrt{\dfrac{80\left(1-[.80]^2\right)}{5-2}} = \sqrt{\dfrac{80(.36)}{3}} = \sqrt{\dfrac{28.80}{3}} = \sqrt{9.60}$

   $= 3.10$

Importance of *r*

To appreciate the importance of the correlation coefficient in any predictive effort, let's substitute a few extreme values for *r* in the numerator of Formula 7.5 and note the resulting effect on the sum of squares for predictive errors, $SS_{y|x}$. Substituting a value of 1 for *r*, we obtain

$$SS_{y|x} = SS_y (1 - r^2) = SS_y[1 - (1)^2] = SS_y[1 - 1] = SS_y[0] = 0$$

As expected, when predictions are based on perfect relationships, the sum of squares for predictive errors equals zero, and there is no predictive error. At the other extreme, substituting a value of 0 for *r* in the numerator of Formula 7.5, we obtain

$$SS_{y|x} = SS_y (1 - r^2) = SS_y[1 - (0)^2] = SS_y[1 - 0] = SS_y[1] = SS_y$$

Again, as expected, when predictions are based on a nonexistent relationship, the sum of squares for predictive errors equals SS_y, the sum of squares of Y scores about $\overline{Y}$, and there is no reduction in predictive error. Clearly, the prognosis for a predictive effort is most favorable when predictions are based on strong relationships, as reflected by a sizable positive or negative value of *r*. The prognosis is most dismal—and a predictive effort should not even be attempted—when predictions must be based on a weak or nonexistent relationship, as reflected by a value of *r* near 0.

Progress Check *7.3

(a) Calculate the standard error of estimate for the data in Question 7.2 on page 161, assuming that the correlation of .30 is based on *n* = 35 pairs of observations.

(b) Supply a rough interpretation of the standard error of estimate.

Answers on page 497.

7.5 ASSUMPTIONS

Linearity

Use of the regression equation requires that the underlying relationship be linear. You need to worry about violating this assumption only when the scatterplot for the original correlation analysis reveals an obviously bent or curvilinear dot cluster, such as illustrated in Figure 6.4 on page 132. In the unlikely event that a dot cluster describes a pronounced curvilinear trend, consult more advanced statistics books for appropriate procedures.

Homoscedasticity

Use of the standard error of estimate, $s_{y|x}$, assumes that except for chance, the dots in the original scatterplot will be dispersed equally about all segments of the regression line. You need to worry about violating this assumption, officially known by its tongue-twisting designation as the assumption of *homoscedasticity* (pronounced "ho-mo-skee-das-ti-ci-ty"), only when the scatterplot reveals a dramatically different type of dot cluster, such as that shown in **Figure 7.4**. At the very least, the standard error of estimate for the data in Figure 7.4 should be used cautiously, since its value overestimates the variability of dots about the lower half of the regression line and underestimates the variability of dots about the upper half of the regression line.

7.6 MULTIPLE REGRESSION EQUATIONS

Any serious predictive effort usually culminates in a more complex equation that contains not just one but several *X*, or *predictor variables*. For instance, a serious effort to predict college GPA might culminate in the following equation:

$$Y' = .410(X_1) + .005(X_2) + .001(X_3) + 1.03$$

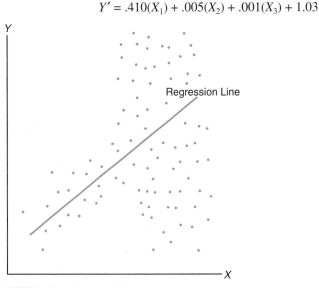

FIGURE 7.4

Violation of homoscedasticity assumption. (Dots lack equal variability about all line segments.)

Multiple Regression Equation

A least squares equation that contains more than one predictor or X variable.

where Y' represents predicted college GPA and X_1, X_2, and X_3 refer to high school GPA, IQ score, and SAT score, respectively. By capitalizing on the combined predictive power of several predictor variables, these **multiple regression equations** supply more accurate predictions for Y' (often referred to as the *criterion variable*) than could be obtained from a simple regression equation.

Common Features

Although more difficult to visualize, multiple regression equations possess many features in common with their simple counterparts. For instance, they still qualify as least squares equations, since they minimize the sum of the squared predictive errors. By the same token, they are accompanied by standard errors of estimate that roughly measure the average amounts of predictive error. Be assured, therefore, that this chapter will serve as a good point of departure if, sometime in the future, you must deal with multiple regression equations.

7.7 REGRESSION TOWARD THE MEAN

Regression Toward the Mean

A tendency for scores, particularly extreme scores, to shrink toward the mean.

Regression toward the mean *refers to a tendency for scores, particularly extreme scores, to shrink toward the mean.* This tendency often appears among subsets of observations whose values are extreme and at least partly due to chance. For example, because of regression toward the mean, we would expect that students who made the top five scores on the first statistics exam would not make the top five scores on the second statistics exam. Although all five students might score above the mean on the second exam, some of their scores would regress back toward the mean. Most likely, the top five scores on the first exam reflect two components. One relatively permanent component reflects the fact that these students are superior because of good study habits, a strong aptitude for quantitative reasoning, and so forth. The other relatively transitory component reflects the fact that, on the day of the exam, at least some of these students were very lucky because all sorts of little chance factors, such as restful sleep, a pleasant commute to campus, etc., worked in their favor. On the second test, even though the scores of these five students continue to reflect an above-average permanent component, some of their scores will suffer because of less good luck or even bad luck. The net effect is that the scores of at least some of the original five top students will drop below the top five scores—that is, regress *back* toward the mean—on the second exam. (When significant regression toward the mean occurs after a spectacular performance by, for example, a rookie athlete or a first-time author, the term *sophomore jinx* often is invoked.)

There is good news for those students who made the five lowest scores on the first exam. Although all five students might score below the mean on the second exam, some of their scores probably will regress *up* toward the mean. On the second exam, some of them will not be as unlucky. The net effect is that the scores of at least some of the original five poorest students will move above the bottom five scores—that is, regress up toward the mean—on the second exam.

Appears in Many Distributions

Regression toward the mean appears among subsets of extreme observations for a wide variety of distributions. For example, it appears for the subset of best (or worst) performing stocks on the New York Stock Exchange across any period, such as a week, month, or year. It also appears for the top (or bottom) major league baseball hitters during consecutive seasons. Table 7.4 lists the top 10 hitters in the major leagues during 2007 and shows how they fared during 2008. Notice that, with the exception of Chipper Jones, each of their batting averages regressed downward, toward .264, the mean for all hitters during 2008. Incidentally, it is not true that, viewed as a group, all major league hitters are headed toward mediocrity. Hitters among the top 10 in 2007, who were not among the top 10 in 2008, were replaced by other mostly above-average hitters, who also were very lucky during 2008. Observed regression toward the mean occurs for individuals or subsets of individuals, not for entire groups.

The Regression Fallacy

Regression Fallacy

Occurs whenever regression toward the mean is interpreted as a real, rather than a chance, effect.

The **regression fallacy** *is committed whenever regression toward the mean is interpreted as a real, rather than a chance, effect.* A classic example of the regression fallacy occurred in an Israeli Air Force study of pilot training reported in a 1974 issue of *Science* by Amos Tversky and Daniel Kahnemann. Some trainees were praised after very good landings, while others were reprimanded after very bad landings. On their next landings, praised trainees did more poorly and reprimanded trainees did better. It was concluded, therefore, that praise hinders but a reprimand helps performance!

A valid conclusion considers regression toward the mean. It's reasonable to assume that, in addition to skill, chance plays a role in landings. Some trainees

---

Table 7.4
REGRESSION EFFECT: BATTING AVERAGES OF
TOP 10 HITTERS IN MAJOR LEAGUE BASEBALL
DURING 2007 AND HOW THEY FARED DURING 2008

| TOP TEN HITTERS (2007) | BATTING AVERAGES* | | REGRESSION EFFECT |
	2007	2008	
1. Ordonez	.363	.317	Yes
2. Suzuki	.351	.310	Yes
3. Polanco	.341	.307	Yes
4. Holliday	.340	.321	Yes
5. Posada	.338	.268	Yes
6. Jones	.337	.364	No
7. H. Ramirez	.332	.301	Yes
8. Ortiz	.332	.264	Yes
9. Renteria	.332	.270	Yes
10. Utley	.332	.292	Yes

* Proportion of hits per official number of times at bat.
Source: http://sports.espn.go.com/mlb/stats/batting.

who made very good landings were lucky, while some who made very bad landings were unlucky. Therefore, there would be a tendency, attributable to chance, that good landings would be followed by less good landings and poor landings would be followed by less poor landings—even if trainees had not been praised after very good landings or reprimanded after very bad landings.

Avoiding the Regression Fallacy

The regression fallacy can be avoided by splitting the subset of extreme observations into two groups. In the above example, one group of trainees would continue to be praised after very good landings and reprimanded after very poor landings. A second group of trainees would receive no feedback whatsoever after very good and very bad landings. In effect, the second group would serve as a control for regression toward the mean, since any shift toward the mean on their second landings would be due to chance. Most important, any observed difference between the two groups (that survives a statistical analysis described in Part 2) would be viewed as a real difference not attributable to the regression effect.

Watch out for the regression fallacy in educational research involving groups of underachievers. For example, a group of fourth graders, selected to attend a special program for underachieving readers, might show an improvement. Whether this improvement can be attributed to the special program or to a regression effect requires information from a control group of similarly underachieving fourth graders who did not attend the special program. It is crucial, therefore, that research with underachievers always includes a control group for regression toward the mean.

Progress Check *7.4 After a group of college students attended a stress-reduction clinic, declines were observed in the anxiety scores of those who, prior to attending the clinic, had scored high on a test for anxiety.

(a) Can this decline be attributed to the stress-reduction clinic? Explain your answer.

(b) What type of study, if any, would permit valid conclusions about the effect of the stress-reduction clinic?

Answers on page 498.

Summary
. . . .

If a linear relationship exists between two variables, then one variable can be predicted from the other by using the least squares regression equation, as described in Formulas 7.1, 7.2, and 7.3.

The least squares equation minimizes the total of all squared predictive errors that would have occurred if the equation had been used to predict known Y scores from the original correlation analysis.

An estimate of predictive error can be obtained from Formula 7.5. Known as the *standard error of estimate,* this estimate is a special kind of standard deviation that roughly reflects the average amount of predictive error. The value of the standard error of estimate depends mainly on the size of the correlation coefficient. The larger the correlation coefficient, in either the positive or negative direction, the smaller the standard error of estimate and the more favorable the prognosis for predictions.

The regression equation assumes a linear relationship between variables, and the standard error of estimate assumes homoscedasticity—approximately equal dispersion of data points about all segments of the regression line.

Serious predictive efforts usually involve multiple regression equations composed of more than one predictor, or X, variable. These multiple regression equations share many common features with the simple regression equations discussed in this chapter.

Regression toward the mean refers to a tendency for scores, particularly extreme scores, to shrink toward the mean. The regression fallacy is committed whenever regression toward the mean is interpreted as a real, rather than a chance effect. To guard against the regression fallacy, control groups should be used to estimate the regression effect.

Important Terms

Least squares regression equation   **Multiple regression equation**

Standard error of estimate ($s_{y|x}$)   **Regression fallacy**

Regression toward the mean

Key Equations

PREDICTION EQUATION

$$Y' = bX + a$$

$$\text{where} \quad b = \sqrt{\frac{SS_y}{SS_x}}\, r$$

$$\text{and} \quad a = \bar{Y} - b\bar{X}$$

REVIEW QUESTIONS

7.5 Assume that an r of $-.80$ describes the strong negative relationship between years of heavy smoking (X) and life expectancy (Y). Assume, furthermore, that the distributions of heavy smoking and life expectancy each have the following means and sums of squares:

$$\bar{X} = 5 \qquad\qquad \bar{Y} = 60$$
$$SS_x = 35 \qquad\qquad SS_y = 70$$

(a) Determine the least squares regression equation for predicting life expectancy from years of heavy smoking.

(b) Determine the standard error of estimate, $s_{y|x}$, assuming that the correlation of $-.80$ was based on $n = 50$ pairs of observations.

(c) Supply a rough interpretation of $s_{y|x}$.

(d) Predict the life expectancy for Sara, who has smoked heavily for eight years.

(e) Predict the life expectancy for Katie, who has never smoked heavily.

7.6 Each of the following pairs represents the number of licensed drivers (X) and the number of cars (Y) for seven houses in my neighborhood:

DRIVERS (X)	CARS (Y)
5	4
5	3
2	2
2	2
3	2
1	1
2	2

(a) Construct a scatterplot to verify a lack of pronounced curvilinearity.

(b) Determine the least squares equation for these data. (Remember, you will first have to calculate r, SS_y, and SS_x.)

(c) Determine the standard error of estimate, $s_{y|x}$, given that $n = 7$.

(d) Predict the number of cars for each of two new families with two and five drivers.

7.7 At a large bank, length of service is the best single predictor of employees' salaries. Can we conclude, therefore, that there is a cause-effect relationship between length of service and salary?

*7.8 In studies dating back over 100 years, it's well established that regression toward the mean occurs between the heights of fathers and the heights of their *adult* sons. Indicate whether the following statements are true or false.

(a) Sons of tall fathers will tend to be shorter than their fathers.

(b) Sons of short fathers will tend to be taller than the mean for all sons.

(c) Every son of a tall father will be shorter than his father.

(d) Taken as a group, adult sons are shorter than their fathers.

(e) Fathers of tall sons will tend to be taller than their sons.

(f) Fathers of short sons will tend to be taller than their sons but shorter than the mean for all fathers.

Answers on page 498.

7.9 Someone suggests that it would be a good investment strategy to buy the five poorest-performing stocks on the New York Stock Exchange and capitalize on regression toward the mean. Comments?

7.10 In the original study of regression toward the mean, Sir Francis Galton noted a tendency for offspring of both tall and short parents to drift toward the mean height for offspring and referred to this tendency as "regression toward mediocrity." What is wrong with the conclusion that eventually all heights will be close to their mean?

PART 2

Inferential Statistics:
Generalizing beyond Data

Preview

The remaining chapters deal with the problem of generalizing beyond sets of actual observations. The next two chapters develop essential concepts and tools for inferential statistics, while subsequent chapters introduce a series of statistical tests or procedures, all of which permit us to generalize beyond an observed result, whether from a survey or an experiment, by considering the effects of chance.

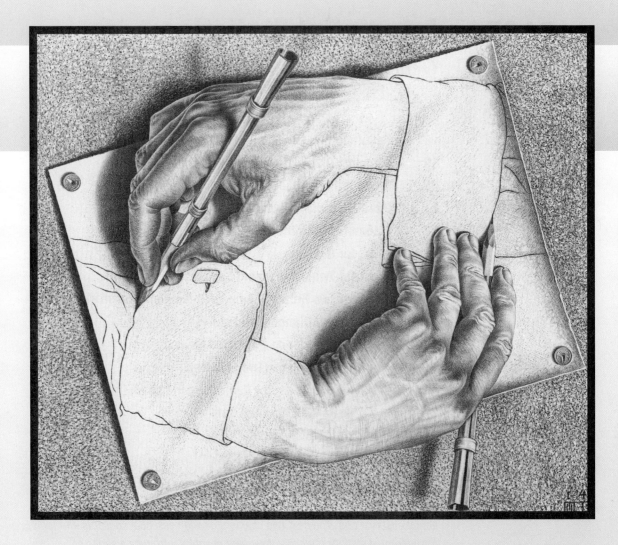

Populations, Samples, and Probability

POPULATIONS AND SAMPLES

PROBABILITY

Summary / Important Terms / Key Equations /Review Questions

Preview

In everyday life, we regularly generalize from limited sets of observations. One sip indicates that the batch of soup is too salty; dipping a toe in the swimming pool reassures us before taking the first plunge; a test drive triggers suspicions that the used car is not what it was advertised to be; and a casual encounter with a stranger stimulates fantasies about a deeper relationship. Valid generalizations in inferential statistics require either random sampling in the case of surveys or random assignment in the case of experiments. Introduced in this chapter, tables of random numbers can be used as aids to random sampling or random assignment.

Conclusions that we'll encounter in inferential statistics, such as "95 percent confident" or "significant at the. 05 level," are statements based on probabilities. We'll define probability for a simple event and then discuss two rules for finding probabilities of more complex outcomes, including (in Review Question 8.14 on page 190) the probability of the catastrophic failure of the Challenger shuttle in 1986, which took the lives of seven astronauts.

POPULATIONS AND SAMPLES

Generalizations can backfire if a sample misrepresents the population. Faced with the possibility of erroneous generalizations, you might prefer to bypass the uncertainties of inferential statistics by surveying an entire population. This is often done if the size of the population is small. For instance, you calculate your GPA from all of your course grades, not just from a sample. If the size of the population is large, however, complete surveys are often prohibitively expensive and sometimes impossible. Under these circumstances, you might have to use samples and risk the possibility of erroneous generalizations. For instance, you might have to use a sample to estimate the mean annual income for parents of all students at a large university.

8.1 POPULATIONS

Reminder:

Population *refers to any complete set of observations (or potential observations).*

Any complete set of observations (or potential observations) may be characterized as a **population.** Accurate descriptions of populations specify the nature of the observations to be taken. For example, a population might be described as "attitudes toward abortion of currently enrolled students at Bucknell University" or as "SAT critical reading scores of currently enrolled students at Rutgers University."

Real Populations

Pollsters, such as the Gallup Organization, deal with real populations. A *real population* is one in which all potential observations are accessible at the time of sampling. Examples of real populations include the two described in the previous paragraph, as well as the ages of all visitors to Disneyland on a given day, the ethnic backgrounds of all current employees of the U.S. Postal Department, and presidential preferences of all currently registered voters in the United States. Incidentally, federal law requires that a complete survey be taken every ten years of the real population of all U.S. households—at considerable expense, involving thousands of data collectors—as a means of revising election districts for the House of Representatives. (An estimated undercount of millions of people in both the 1990 and 2000 censuses has revived a suggestion, long endorsed by statisticians, that the entire U.S. population could be estimated more accurately if a highly trained group of data collectors focused only on a random sample of households.)

WWW

INTERNET SITE

Go to the Web site for this book (http://www.wiley.com\college\witte). Click on the *Student Companion Site,* then *Internet Sites,* and finally *U.S. Census Bureau* to view its Web site, including links to its many reports and to population clocks that show current population estimates for the United States and the world.

Hypothetical Populations

Insofar as research workers concern themselves with populations, they often invoke the notion of a hypothetical population. A *hypothetical* population is one in which all potential observations are not accessible at the time of sampling. In most experiments, subjects are selected from very small, uninspiring real populations: the lab rats housed in the local animal colony or student volunteers from general psychology classes. Experimental subjects often are viewed, nevertheless, as a sample from a much larger hypothetical population, loosely described as "the scores of all similar animal subjects (or student volunteers) who could conceivably undergo the present experiment."

According to the rules of inferential statistics, generalizations should be made only to real populations that, in fact, have been sampled. Generalizations to hypothetical populations should be viewed, therefore, as provisional conclusions based on the wisdom of the researcher rather than on any logical or statistical necessity. In effect, it's an open question—answered only by additional experimentation—whether or not a given experimental finding merits the generality assigned to it by the researcher.

8.2 SAMPLES

Reminder:

Sample *refers to any subset of observations from a population.*

Any subset of observations from a population may be characterized as a **sample.** In typical applications of inferential statistics, the sample size is small relative to the population size. Less than 1 percent of all U.S. households are included in the Bureau of Labor Statistics' monthly survey to estimate the rate of unemployment. Although, at most, only about 4,000 voters have been sampled in recent presidential election polls by Gallup, predictions have been amazingly accurate since 1952—missing the actual percentage of votes for the winning candidate by an average of only 2%, according to the subscription-only service maintained by the Gallup Organization at http://www.gallup.com/poll/topics/ptaccuracy.asp.

Optimal Sample Size

There is no simple rule of thumb for determining the best or optimal sample size for any particular situation. Often sample sizes are in the hundreds or even the thousands for surveys, but they are less than 100 for most experiments. Optimal sample size depends on the answers to a number of questions, including "What is the estimated variability among observations?" and "What is an acceptable amount of error in our conclusion?" Once these types of questions have been answered, with the aid of guidelines such as those discussed in Section 11.11, specific procedures can be followed to determine the optimal sample size for any situation.

Progress Check *8.1 For each of the following pairs, indicate with a Yes or No whether the relationship between the first and second expressions could describe that between a sample and its population, respectively.

(a) students in the last row; students in class

(b) citizens of Wyoming; citizens of New York

(c) 20 lab rats in an experiment; all lab rats, similar to those used, that could undergo the same experiment

(d) all U.S. presidents; all registered Republicans

(e) two tosses of a coin; all possible tosses of a coin

Progress Check *8.2 Identify all of the above expressions that involve a hypothetical population.

Answers on page 498.

8.3 RANDOM SAMPLING

The valid use of techniques from inferential statistics requires that samples be random.

Sampling is random if, at each stage of sampling, the selection process guarantees that all potential observations in the population have an equal chance of being included in the sample.

It's important to note that randomness describes the *selection process,* that is, the conditions under which the sample is taken, and not the particular pattern of observations in the sample. Having established that sampling is random, you still can't predict anything about the unique pattern of observations in that sample. The observations in the sample should be representative of those in the population, but there is no guarantee that they actually will be.

Casual or Haphazard, Not Random

A casual or haphazard sample doesn't qualify as a random sample. Not every student at UC San Diego has an equal chance of being sampled if, for instance, a pollster casually selects only students who enter the main library. Obviously excluded from this sample are all those students (few, we hope) who never enter the main library. Even the final selection of students from among those who do enter the main library might reflect the pollster's various biases, such as an unconscious preference for attractive students who are walking alone.

Progress Check *8.3 Indicate whether each of the following statements is True or False. A random selection of 10 playing cards from a desk of 52 cards implies that

(a) the random sample of 10 cards accurately represents the important features of the whole deck.

(b) each card in the deck has an equal chance of being selected.

(c) it is impossible to get 10 cards from the same suit (for example, 10 hearts).

(d) any outcome, however unlikely, is possible.

Answers on page 498.

8.4 TABLES OF RANDOM NUMBERS

Tables of random numbers can be used to obtain a random sample. These tables are generated by a computer designed to equalize the occurrence of any one of the ten digits: 0, 1, 2, . . . , 8, 9. For convenience, many random number tables are spaced in columns of five-digit numbers. Table H in Appendix C shows a specimen page of random numbers from a book devoted entirely to random digits.

How Many Digits?

The size of the population determines whether you deal with numbers having one, two, three, or more digits. The only requirement is that you have at least as many different numbers as you have potential observations within the population. For example, if you were attempting to take a random sample from a population consisting of 679 students at some college, you could use the 1000 three-digit numbers ranging from 000 to 999. In this case, you could identify each of the potential observations, as represented by a particular student's name, with a single number. For instance, if a student directory were available, the first person, Alice Aakins, might be assigned the three-digit number 001, and so on through to the last person in the directory, Zachary Ziegler, who might be assigned 679.

Using Tables

Enter the random number table at some arbitrarily determined place. Ordinarily this should be determined haphazardly. Open a book of random numbers to any page and begin with the number closest to a blind pencil stab. For illustrative purposes, however, let's use the upper-left-hand corner of the specimen page (Table H, Appendix C) as our entry point. (Ignore the column of numbers that identify the various rows.) Read in a consistent direction—for instance, from left to right. Then as each row is used up, shift down to the start of the next row and repeat the entire process. As a given number between 001 and 679 is encountered, the person identified with that number is included in the random sample.

Since the first number on the specimen page in Table H is 100 (disregard the fourth and fifth digits in each five-digit number), the person identified with that number is included in the sample. The next three-digit number, 325, identifies the second person. Ignore the next number, 765, since none of the numbers between 680 and 999 is identified with any names in the student directory. Also, ignore repeat appearances of any number between 001 and 679. The next three-digit number, 135, identifies the third person. Continue this process until the specified sample size has been achieved.

Efficient Use of Tables

The inefficiency of the previous procedure becomes apparent when a random sample must be obtained from a large population, such as that defined by a city telephone directory. It would be most laborious to assign a different number to each name in the directory prior to consulting the table of random numbers.

Instead, most investigators refer directly to the random number table, using each random number as a guide to a particular name in the directory. For example, a six-digit random number, such as 239421, identifies the name on page 239 (the first three digits) and line 421 (the last three digits). This process is repeated for a series of six-digit random numbers until the required number of names has been sampled.

Progress Check *8.4 Describe how you would use the table of random numbers to take

(a) a random sample of five statistics students in a classroom where each of nine rows consists of nine seats.

(b) a random sample of size 40 from a large city telephone directory consisting of 3041 pages, with 480 lines per page.

Answers on page 498.

A Complication: No Population Directory

Lacking the convenience of an existing population directory, investigators resort to variations on the previous procedure. For instance, the Gallup Organization makes a separate presidential survey in each of the four geographical areas of the United States: Northeast, South, Midwest, and West. Within each of these areas, a series of random selections culminates in the identification of particular election precincts: small geographical districts with a single polling place. Once household directories have been obtained for each of these precincts, households are randomly selected and pre-designated household members are interviewed.

Many pollsters now use *random digit dialing* in an effort to give each telephone number—whether landline or wireless—in the United States an equal chance of being called for an interview. Essentially, the first six digits of a ten-digit phone number, including the area code, are randomly selected from tens of thousands of telephone exchanges, while the final four digits are taken directly from random numbers. This technique ensures that all unlisted telephone numbers will be sampled and called (often to the dismay of those people with unlisted telephone numbers).

Hypothetical Populations

As has been noted, the researcher, unlike the pollster, usually deals with hypothetical populations. Unfortunately, it is impossible to take random samples from hypothetical populations. All potential observations cannot have an equal chance of being included in the sample if, in fact, some observations are not accessible at the time of sampling. It is a common practice, nonetheless, for researchers to treat samples from hypothetical populations *as if* they were random samples and to analyze sample results with techniques from inferential statistics. Our adoption of this practice—to provide a common basis for discussing both surveys and experiments—is less troublesome than you might think inasmuch as random assignment replaces random sampling in well-designed experiments

8.5 RANDOM ASSIGNMENT OF SUBJECTS

Typically, experiments evaluate an independent variable by focusing on a treatment group and a control group. Although subjects in experiments can't be selected randomly from any real population, they can be **assigned randomly,** that is, with equal likelihood, to these two groups. This procedure has a number of desirable consequences:

- Since random assignment or chance determines the membership for each group, all possible configurations of subjects are equally likely. This provides a basis for calculating the chances of observing any specific difference between groups and ultimately deciding whether, for instance, the one observed mean difference between groups is real or merely transitory.
- Random assignment generates groups of subjects that, except for random differences, are similar with respect to any uncontrolled variables at the outset of the experiment.

For instance, to determine whether a study-skill workshop improves academic performance, volunteer subjects should be assigned randomly either to the treatment group (attendance at the workshop) or to the control group. This ensures that, except for random differences, both groups are similar initially with respect to any uncontrolled variables, such as academic preparation, motivation, IQ, etc. At the conclusion of such an experiment, therefore, any observed differences in academic performance between these two groups, *not attributable to random differences,* would provide the most clear-cut evidence of a cause-effect relationship between the independent variable (attendance at the workshop) and the dependent variable (academic performance).

How to Assign Subjects

The random assignment of subjects can be accomplished in a number of ways. For instance, as each new subject arrives to participate in the experiment, a flip of a coin can decide whether that subject should be assigned to the treatment group (if heads turns up) or the control group (if tails turn up). An even better procedure, because it eliminates any biases of a live coin tosser, relies on tables of random numbers. Once the tables have been entered at some arbitrary point, they can be consulted, much like a string of coin tosses, to determine whether each new subject should be assigned to the treatment group (if, for instance, the random number is odd) or to the control group (if the random number is even).

Creating Equal Groups

Equal numbers of subjects should be assigned to the treatment and control groups for a variety of reasons, including the increased likelihood of detecting any difference between the two groups. To achieve this goal, the random assignment should involve pairs of subjects. If the table of random numbers assigns the first volunteer to the treatment group, the second volunteer should be assigned *automatically* to the control group. If the random numbers assign the third volunteer to the control group, the fourth volunteer should be assigned *automatically* to the treatment group, and so forth. This procedure guarantees that at any stage of the random assignment, equal numbers of subjects will be assigned to the two groups.

More Extensive Sets of Random Numbers

Incidentally, the page of random numbers in Table H, Appendix C, serves only as a specimen. For serious applications, refer to a more extensive collection of random numbers, such as that in the book by the Rand Corporation cited on page 542 of Appendix C. If you have access to a computer, you might refer to the list of random numbers that can be generated, almost effortlessly, by computers.

Progress Check *8.5 Assume that twelve subjects arrive, one at a time, to participate in an experiment. Use random numbers to assign these subjects in equal numbers to group A and group B. Specifically, random numbers should be used to identify the first subject as either A or B, the second subject as either A or B, and so forth, until all subjects have been identified. There should be six subjects identified with A and six with B.

(a) Formulate an acceptable rule for single-digit random numbers. Incorporate into this rule a procedure that will ensure equal numbers of subjects in the two groups. *Check your answer in Appendix B before proceeding.*

(b) Reading from left to right in the top row of the random number page (Table H, Appendix C), use the random digits of each random number in conjunction with your assignment rule to determine whether the first subject is A or B, and so forth. List the assignment for each subject.

Answers on page 498.

8.6 SURVEYS OR EXPERIMENTS?

When using random numbers, it's important to have a general perspective. Are you engaged in a *survey* (because subjects have been sampled from a real population) or in an *experiment* (because subjects have been assigned to various groups)? In the case of surveys, the object is to obtain a random sample from some real population. Short-circuit unnecessary clerical work as much as possible, but use random numbers in a fashion that complies with the notion of *random sampling—that all subjects in the population have an equal opportunity of being sampled.* In the case of experiments, the objective is to obtain, at the outset of the experiment, equivalent groups whose membership has been determined by chance. Introduce any restrictions required to generate equal group sizes (for example, the restriction that every other subject be assigned to the smaller group), but use random numbers in a fashion that complies with the notion of *random assignment—that all subjects have an equal opportunity of being assigned to each of the various groups.*

PROBABILITY

Probability considerations are prevalent in everyday life: the *probability* that it will rain this weekend (20 percent, or one in five, according to our morning newspaper), that a projected family of two children will consist of a boy and a girl (one-half, on the assumption that boys and girls are equally likely), or that you'll win a state lottery (one in many millions, unfortunately). Probability considerations also are prevalent in inferential statistics and, therefore, in the remainder of this book.

8.7 DEFINITION

Probability refers to the proportion or fraction of times that a particular event is likely to occur.

Probability

The proportion or fraction of times that a particular event is likely to occur.

The probability of an event can be determined in several ways. We can *speculate* that if a coin is truly fair, heads and tails should be equally likely to occur whenever the coin is tossed, and therefore, the probability of heads should equal .50, or $^1/_2$. By the same token, ignoring the slight differences in the lengths of the months of the year, we can *speculate* that if a couple's wedding is equally likely to occur in each of the months, then the probability of a June wedding should be .08 or $^1/_{12}$.

On the other hand, we might actually *observe* a long string of coin tosses and conclude, on the basis of these observations, that the probability of heads should equal .50, or $^1/_2$. Or we might collect extensive data on wedding months and *observe* that the probability of a June wedding actually is not only much higher than the speculated .08 or $^1/_{12}$, but higher than that for any other month. In this case, assuming that the observed probability is well substantiated, we would use it rather than the erroneous speculative probability.

Probability Distribution of Heights

Sometimes we'll use probabilities that are based on a mixture of observation and speculation, as in Table 8.1. This table shows a probability distribution of heights for all American men (derived from the *observed* distribution of heights for 3091 men by superimposing—and this is the *speculative* component—the idealized normal curve, originally shown in Figure 5.2). These probabilities indicate the proportion of men in the population who attain a particular height. They also indicate the likelihood of observing a particular height when a single man is randomly selected from the population. For example, the probability is .14 that a randomly selected man will stand 68 inches tall. Each of the probabilities in Table 8.1 can vary in value between 0 (impossible) and 1 (certain). Furthermore, an entire set of probabilities always sums to 1.

Probabilities of Complex Events

Often you can find the probabilities of more complex events by using two rules—the addition and multiplication rules—for combining the probabilities of various simple events. Each rule will be introduced, in turn, to solve a problem based on the probabilities from Table 8.1.

Table 8.1
PROBABILITY DISTRIBUTION FOR HEIGHTS OF AMERICAN MEN

HEIGHT (INCHES)	RELATIVE FRE-QUENCY
75 or taller	.02
74	.02
73	.03
72	.05
71	.08
70	.11
69	.12
68	.14
67	.12
66	.11
65	.08
64	.05
63	.03
62	.02
61 or shorter	.02
Total	1.00

Source: See Figure 5.2.

8.8 ADDITION RULE

What's the probability that a randomly selected man will be at least 72 inches tall? That's the same as asking, "What's the probability that a man will stand 72 inches tall *or* taller?" To answer this type of question, which involves a cluster of simple events connected by the word *or,* merely add the respective probabilities. The probability that a man, X, will stand 72 or more inches tall, symbolized as $Pr(X \geq 72)$, equals the sum of the probabilities in Table 8.1 that a man will stand 72 or 73 or 74 or 75 inches or taller, that is,

$$Pr(X \geq 72) = Pr(72) + Pr(73) + Pr(74) + Pr(75 \text{ or taller})$$
$$= .05 + .03 + .02 + .02 = .12$$

Mutually Exclusive Events

Mutually Exclusive Events

Events that cannot occur together.

The addition of probabilities, as just stated, works only when none of the events can occur together. This is true in the present case because, for instance, a single man can't stand both 72 and 73 inches tall. By the same token, a single person's blood type can't be both O and B (or any other type); nor can a single person's birth month be both January and February (or any other month). Whenever events can't occur together—that is, more technically, whenever events are **mutually exclusive**—the probability that any one of these several events will occur is given by the addition rule. Therefore, whenever you must find the probability for two or more sets of mutually exclusive events connected by the word *or,* use the addition rule.

Addition Rule

Add together the separate probabilities of several mutually exclusive events to find the probability that any one of these events will occur.

The **addition rule** *tells us to add together the separate probabilities of several mutually exclusive events in order to find the probability that any one of these events will occur.* Stated generally, the addition rule reads:

ADDITION RULE FOR MUTUALLY EXCLUSIVE EVENTS
$$Pr(A \text{ or } B) = Pr(A) + Pr(B) \tag{8.1}$$

---

where Pr( ) refers to the probability of the event in parentheses and A and B are mutually exclusive events.

When Events Aren't Mutually Exclusive

When events aren't mutually exclusive because they can occur together, the addition rule must be adjusted for the overlap between outcomes. For example, assume that students in your class are seniors with probability .20, psychology majors with probability .70, and both seniors and psychology majors with probability .10. To determine the probability that a student is *either* a senior *or* a psychology major, add the first two probabilities (.20 + .70 = .90), but then subtract the third probability (.90 − .10 = .80), because students who are both seniors and psychology majors are counted twice—once because they are seniors and once because they are psychology majors.

Ordinarily, in this book you will be able to use the addition rule for mutually exclusive outcomes. Before doing so, however, always satisfy yourself that the various events are, in fact, mutually exclusive. Otherwise, the above addition rule yields an inflated answer that must be reduced by subtracting the overlap between events that are not mutually exclusive.

Progress Check *8.6 Assuming that people are equally likely to be born during any one of the months, what is the probability of Jack being born during

(a) June?

(b) any month other than June?

(c) either May or June?

Answers on page 499.

8.9 MULTIPLICATION RULE

Given a probability of .12 that a randomly selected man will be at least 72 inches tall, what is the probability that two randomly selected men will be at least 72 inches tall? That is the same as asking, "What is the probability that the first man will stand at least 72 inches tall *and* that the second man will stand at least 72 inches tall?"

To answer this type of question, which involves clusters of simple events connected by the word *and,* merely multiply the respective probabilities. The probability that both men will stand at least 72 inches tall equals the product of the probabilities in Table 8.1 that the first man, X_1, will stand at least 72 inches tall *and* that the second man, X_2, will stand at least 72 inches tall, that is,

$$\Pr(X_1 \geq 72 \ and \ X_2 \geq 72) = [\Pr(X_1) \geq 72] \ [\Pr(X_2) \geq 72] = (.12)\,(.12) = .0144$$

Notice that the probability of two events occurring together (.0144) is smaller than the probability of either event occurring alone (.12). If you think about it, this should make sense. The combined occurrence of two events is less likely than the solitary occurrence of just one of the two events.

Independent Events

The multiplication of probabilities, as above, works only because the occurrence of one event has no effect on the probability of the other event. This is true in the present case because, when randomly selecting from the population of American men, the initial appearance of a man at least 72 inches tall has no effect, practically speaking, on the probability that the next man also will be at least 72 inches tall. By the same token, the birth of a girl in a family has no effect on the probability of .50 that the next family addition also will be a girl, and the winning lottery number for this week has no effect on the probability that a particular lottery number will be a winner for the next week. Whenever one event has no effect on the other—that is, more technically, whenever events are **independent**—the probability of the combined or joint occurrence of both events is given by the multiplication rule.

Independent Events

The occurrence of one event has no effect on the probability that the other event will occur.

Multiplication Rule

Multiply together the separate probabilities of several independent events to find the probability that these events will occur together.

Whenever you must find the probability for two or more sets of independent events connected by the word *and,* use the multiplication rule. The **multiplication rule** *tells us to multiply together the separate probabilities of several independent events in order to find the probability that these events will occur together.* Stated generally, for the independent events A and B, the multiplication rule reads:

MULTIPLICATION RULE FOR INDEPENDENT EVENTS

$$\Pr(A \text{ and } B) = [\Pr(A)]\,[\Pr(B)] \qquad (8.2)$$

---

where A and B are independent events.

Progress Check *8.7 Assuming that people are equally likely to be born during any of the months, and also assuming (possibly over the objections of astrology fans) that the birthdays of married couples are independent, what's the probability of

(a) the husband being born during January and the wife being born during February?

(b) both husband and wife being born during December?

(c) both husband and wife being born during the spring (April or May)? (**Hint:** First, find the probability of just one person being born during April or May.)

Answers on page 499.

Dependent Events

When the occurrence of one event affects the probability of the other event, these events are dependent. Although the heights of randomly selected pairs of men are independent, the heights of brothers are dependent. Knowing, for instance, that one person is relatively tall increases the probability that his brother also will be relatively tall. Among students in your class, being a senior and a psychology major are dependent if knowing that a student is a senior automatically changes (either increases or decreases) the probability of being a psychology major.

Conditional Probabilities

Conditional Probability

The probability of one event, given the occurrence of another event.

Before multiplying to obtain the probability that two dependent events occur together, the probability of the second event must be adjusted to reflect its dependency on the prior occurrence of the first event. This new probability is the **conditional probability** of the second event, given the first event. Examples of conditional probabilities are the probability that you will earn a grade of A in a course, given that you have already gotten an A on the midterm, or the probability that you'll graduate from college, given that you've already completed the first two years. Notice that, in both examples, these conditional probabilities are different—they happen to be larger—than the regular or unconditional probability of your earning a grade of A in a course (without knowing your grade on the midterm) or of graduating from college (without knowing whether or not you've completed the first two years). Incidentally, a conditional probability also can be smaller than its corresponding unconditional probability. Such is the case for the conditional probability that you'll earn a grade of A in a course, given that you have already gotten (alas) a C on the midterm.

If, as assumed above, being a senior and a psychology major are dependent events among students in your class, then it would be incorrect to use the multiplication rule for two independent outcomes. More specifically, it would be incorrect to simply multiply the observed unconditional probability of being a senior (.20) and the observed unconditional probability of being a psych major (.70), and to find

$$Pr(senior \ and \ psych) \neq (.20)(.70) = .14$$

Instead, you must go beyond knowing merely the proportion of students who are psych majors (the unconditional probability of being a psych major) to find the proportion of psych majors *among the subset of seniors* (the conditional probability of being a psych major, given that a student is a senior). For example, a survey of your class might reveal that, although .70 of *all* students are psych majors (for an observed unconditional probability of .70), only *.50 of all seniors are also psych majors* (for an observed conditional probability of .50 for being a psych major given that a student is a senior). Therefore, it would be correct to multiply the observed unconditional probability of being a senior (.20) and the observed conditional probability of being a psych major, given that a student is a senior (.50), and to find the correct probability, that is,

$$Pr(senior \ and \ psych) = Pr(senior) \ Pr(psych, \ given \ senior) = (.20)(.50) = .10,$$

rather than the erroneous .14, given above, when the dependency between events was ignored.

Ordinarily, in this book, you'll be able to use the multiplication rule for independent events. Before using this rule to calculate the probabilities of complex events, however, satisfy yourself—mustering any information at your disposal, whether speculative or observational—that the various events lack any obvious dependency. That is, satisfy yourself that, just as the last coin toss has no obvious effect on the next toss, the prior occurrence of one event has no obvious effect on the occurrence of the other event. Otherwise, only proceed if one event can be expressed, *most likely on the basis of some data collection,* as a conditional probability of the other.[*]

---

[*]Don't confuse independent and dependent *events* with independent and dependent *variables*. Independent and dependent *events* refer to whether or not the occurrence of one event affects the probability that the other event will occur and dictates the precise form of the multiplication rule. On the other hand, independent and dependent *variables* refer to the manipulated and measured variables in experiments, as described in Chapter 1. Usually, the context—whether calculating the probabilities of complex events or describing the essential features of an experiment—will make the meanings of these terms clear.

Progress Check *8.8 Of 100 couples who had undergone marital counseling, 60 couples described their relationships as improved, and among this latter group, 45 couples had children. The remaining 40 couples described their relationships as unimproved, and among this group, 5 couples had children.

(a) What is the probability of randomly selecting a couple who described their relationship as improved?

(b) What is the probability of randomly selecting a couple with children?

(c) What is the conditional probability of randomly selecting a couple with children, given that their relationship was described as improved?

(d) What is the conditional probability of an improved relationship, given that a couple has children?

Answers on page 499.

8.10 PROBABILITY AND STATISTICS

Probability assumes a key role in inferential statistics including, for instance, the important area known as *hypothesis testing*. Because of the inevitable variability that accompanies any observed result, such as a mean difference between two groups, its value must be viewed within the context of the many possible results that could have occurred just by chance. With the aid of some theoretical curve, such as the normal curve, and a provisional assumption, known as the *null hypothesis,* that chance can reasonably account for the result, probabilities are assigned to the mean difference. If this probability is very small, the result is viewed as a rare outcome, and we conclude that something real—that is, something that can't reasonably be attributed to chance—has occurred. On the other hand, if this probability isn't very small, the result is viewed as a common outcome, and we conclude that something transitory—that is, something that can reasonably be attributed to chance—has occurred.

Common Outcomes

Common outcomes signify, most generally, a lack of evidence that something special has occurred. For instance, they suggest that the observed mean difference—whatever its value—might signify that the true mean difference could equal zero and, therefore, that any comparable study would just as likely produce either a positive or negative mean difference. Therefore, the observed mean difference should not be taken seriously because, in the language of statistics, it lacks *statistical significance.*

Rare Outcomes

On the other hand, rare outcomes signify that something special has occurred. For instance, they suggest that the observed mean difference probably signifies a true mean difference equal to some nonzero value and, therefore, that any comparable study would most likely produce a mean difference with the same sign and a value in the neighborhood of the one originally observed. Therefore, the observed mean difference should be taken seriously because it has statistical significance.

Common or Rare?

As an aid to determining whether observed results should be viewed as common or rare, statisticians interpret different *proportions of area under theoretical curves,* such as the normal curve shown in **Figure 8.1**, *as probabilities of random outcomes.* For instance, the standard normal table indicates that .9500 is the proportion of total area between z scores of -1.96 and $+1.96$. (Verify this proportion by referring to Table A in Appendix C and, if necessary, to the latter part of Section 5.6.) Accordingly, the probability of a randomly selected z score anywhere between ±1.96 equals .95. Because it should happen about 95 times out of 100, this is often designated as a *common* event signifying that, once variability is considered, nothing special is happening. On the other hand, since the standard normal curve indicates that .025 is the proportion of total area above a z score of $+1.96$, and also that .025 is the proportion of total area below a z score of -1.96, then the probability of a randomly selected z score anywhere beyond either $+1.96$ or -1.96 equals .05 (from .025 + .025, thanks to the addition rule). Because it should happen only about 5 times in 100, this is often designated as a *rare* outcome signifying that something special is happening.

At this point, you're not expected to understand the rationale behind the above perspective, but merely that, once identified with a particular result, a specified sector of area under a curve will be interpreted as the probability of that outcome. Furthermore, since the probability of an outcome has important implications for generalizing beyond actual results, probabilities play a key role in inferential statistics.

Progress Check *8.9 Referring to the standard normal table (Table A, Appendix C), find the probability that a randomly selected z score will be

(a) above 1.96

(b) either above 1.96 or below −1.96

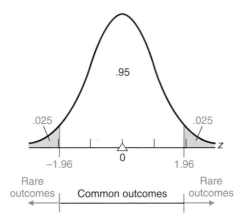

FIGURE 8.1
One possible model for determining common and rare outcomes.

(c) between −1.96 and 1.96

(d) either above 2.58 or below −2.58
Answers on page 499.

Summary

Any set of potential observations may be characterized as a population. Any subset of observations constitutes a sample.

Populations are either real or hypothetical, depending on whether or not all observations are accessible at the time of sampling.

The valid application of techniques from inferential statistics requires that the samples be random or that subjects be randomly assigned. A sample is random if at each stage of sampling the selection process guarantees that all remaining observations in the population have an equal chance of being included in the sample. Random assignment occurs whenever all subjects have an equal opportunity of being assigned to each of the various groups.

Tables of random numbers provide the most effective method both for taking random samples in surveys and for randomly assigning subjects to various groups in experiments. Some type of randomization always should occur during the early stages of any investigation, whether a survey or an experiment.

The probability of an event specifies the proportion of times that this event is likely to occur.

Whenever you must find the probability of sets of mutually exclusive events connected with the word *or,* use the addition rule: Add together the separate probabilities of each of the mutually exclusive events to find the probability that any one of these events will occur. Whenever events aren't mutually exclusive, the addition rule must be adjusted for the overlap between outcomes.

Whenever you must find the probability of sets of independent events connected with the word *and,* use the multiplication rule: Multiply together the separate probabilities of each of the independent events to find the probability that these events will occur together. Whenever events are dependent, the multiplication rule must be adjusted by using the conditional probability of the second outcome, given the occurrence of the first outcome.

In inferential statistics, sectors of area under various theoretical curves are interpreted as probabilities, and these probabilities play a key role in inferential statistics.

Important Terms

Population	**Sample**
Random sampling	**Random assignment**
Probability	**Mutually exclusive events**
Addition rule	**Independent events**
Multiplication rule	**Conditional probability**

Key Equations
....

ADDITION RULE

$$Pr(A \text{ or } B) = Pr(A) + Pr(B)$$

MULTIPLICATION RULE

$$Pr(A \text{ and } B) = [Pr(A)][Pr(B)]$$

REVIEW QUESTIONS

8.10 Television stations sometimes solicit feedback volunteered by viewers about a televised event. Following a televised debate between Barack Obama and John McCain in the 2008 presidential election campaign, a TV station conducted a telephone poll to determine the "winner." Callers were given two phone numbers, one for Obama and the other for McCain, to register their opinions automatically.

(a) Comment on whether or not this was a random sample.

(b) How might this poll have been improved?

8.11 As subjects arrive to participate in an experiment, tables of random numbers are used to make random assignments to either group A or group B. (To ensure equal numbers of subjects in the two groups, alternate subjects are automatically assigned to the other group.) Indicate with a Yes or No whether each of the following rules would work:

(a) Assign the subject to group A if the random number is **even** and to group B if the random number is **odd.**

(b) Assign the subject to group A if the first digit of the random number is between **0 and 4** and to group B if the first digit is between **5 and 9.**

(c) Assign the subject to group A if the first two digits of the random number are between **00 and 40** and to group B if the first two digits are between **41 and 99.**

(d) Assign the subject to group A if the first three digits of the random number are between **000 and 499** and to group B if the first three digits are between **500 and 999.**

*8.12 The probability of a boy being born equals .50, or $1/2$, as does the probability of a girl being born. For a randomly selected family with two children, what's the probability of

(a) two boys, that is, a boy and a boy? (**Reminder:** Before using either the addition or multiplication rule, satisfy yourself that the various events are either mutually exclusive or independent, respectively.)

(b) two girls?

(c) either two boys or two girls?

Answers on page 499.

8.13 Assume the same probabilities as in the previous question. For a randomly selected family with three children, what's the probability of

(a) three boys?

(b) three girls?

(c) either three boys or three girls?

(d) neither three boys nor three girls? (**Hint:** This question can be answered indirectly by first finding the opposite of the specified outcome, then subtracting from 1.)

*8.14 In "Against All Odds," the TV series on statistics (available at http://www.learner.org/resources/series65.html), statistician Bruce Hoadley discusses the catastrophic failure of the *Challenger* space shuttle in 1986. Hoadley estimates that there was a *failure* probability of .02 for each of the six O-rings (designed to prevent the escape of potentially explosive burning gases from the joints of the segmented rocket boosters).

(a) What was the *success* probability of *each* O-ring?

(b) Given that the six O-rings function independently of each other, what was the probability that *all* six O-rings would succeed, that is, perform as designed? In other words, what was the success probability of the first O-ring and the second O-ring and the third O-ring, and so forth?

(c) Given that you know the probability that all six O-rings would succeed (from the previous question), what was the probability that at least one O-ring would fail? (**Hint:** Use your answer to the previous question to solve this problem.)

(d) Given the abysmal failure rate revealed by your answer to the previous question, why, you might wonder, was this space mission even attempted? According to Hoadley, missile engineers thought that a secondary set of O-rings would function independently of the primary set of O-rings. If true and if the failure probability of each of the secondary O-rings was the same as that for each primary O-ring (.02), what would be the probability that *both* the primary and secondary O-rings would fail at any *one* joint? (**Hint:** Concentrate on the present question, ignoring your answers to previous questions.)

(e) In fact, under conditions of low temperature, as on the morning of the *Challenger* catastrophe, both primary and secondary O-rings lost their flexibility, and whenever the primary O-ring failed, its associated secondary O-ring also failed. Under these conditions, what would be the *conditional* probability of a secondary O-ring failure, *given* the failure of its associated primary O-ring? (**Note:** any probability, including a conditional probability, can vary between 0 and 1.)

Answers on page 500.

8.15 A sensor is used to monitor the performance of a nuclear reactor. The sensor accurately reflects the state of the reactor with a probability of .97. But with a probability of .02, it gives a false alarm (by reporting excessive radiation even though the reactor is performing normally), and with a probability of .01, it misses excessive radiation (by failing to report excessive radiation even though the reactor is performing abnormally).

(a) What is the probability that a sensor will give an incorrect report, that is, either a false alarm or a miss?

(b) To reduce costly shutdowns caused by false alarms, management introduces a second completely independent sensor, and the reactor is shut down only when both sensors report excessive radiation. (According to this perspective, solitary reports of excessive radiation should be viewed as false alarms and ignored, since both sensors provide accurate information much of the time.) What is the new probability that the reactor will be shut down because of simultaneous false alarms by both the first and second sensors?

(c) Being more concerned about failures to detect excessive radiation, someone who lives near the nuclear reactor proposes an entirely different strategy: Shut down the reactor whenever either sensor reports excessive radiation. (According to this point of view, even a solitary report of excessive radiation should trigger a shutdown, since a failure to detect excessive radiation is potentially catastrophic.) If this policy were adopted, what is the new probability that excessive radiation will be missed simultaneously by both the first and second sensors?

*8.16 Continue to assume that people are equally likely to be born during any of the months. However, just for the sake of this exercise, assume that there is a tendency for married couples to have been born during the same month. Furthermore, we wish to calculate the probability of a husband and wife both being born during December.

(a) It would be appropriate to use the multiplication rule for independent outcomes? True or False?

(b) The probability of a married couple both being born during December *is smaller than, equal to, or larger than* $(1/12)(1/12) = 1/144$.

(c) With only the above information, it would be possible to calculate the actual probability of a married couple both being born during December? True or False?

Answers on page 500.

CHAPTER 9

Sampling Distribution of the Mean

Preview

This chapter focuses on the single most important concept in inferential statistics—the concept of a sampling distribution. A sampling distribution serves as a frame of reference for every outcome, among all possible outcomes, that could occur just by chance. It reappears in every subsequent chapter as the key to understanding how, once variability has been estimated, we can generalize beyond a limited set of actual observations. In order to use a sampling distribution, we must identify its mean, its standard deviation, and its shape—a seemingly difficult task that, thanks to the theory of statistics, can be performed by invoking the population mean, the population standard deviation, and the normal curve, respectively.

There's a good chance that you've taken the SAT test, and you probably remember your scores. On a nationwide basis, the SAT critical reading scores for all college-bound students during a recent year were distributed around a mean of 500 with a standard deviation of 110. An investigator at a university wishes to test the claim that, on the average, the SAT reading scores for local freshmen equals the national average of 500. His task would be straightforward if, in fact, the reading scores for all local freshmen were readily available. Then, after calculating the mean score for all local freshmen, a direct comparison would indicate whether, on the average, local freshmen score below, at, or above the national average.

Assume that it is not possible to obtain scores for the entire freshman class. Instead, SAT reading scores are obtained for a random sample of 100 students from the local population of freshmen, and the mean score for this sample equals 533. If each sample were an exact replica of the population, generalizations from the sample to the population would be most straightforward. Having observed a mean score of 533 for a sample of 100 freshmen, we could have concluded, without even a pause, that the mean reading score for the entire freshman class also equals 533 and, therefore, exceeds the national average.

9.1 WHAT IS A SAMPLING DISTRIBUTION?

Random samples rarely represent the underlying population exactly. Even a mean reading score of 533 could originate, just by chance, from a population of freshmen whose mean equals the national average of 500. Accordingly, generalizations from a single sample to a population are much more tentative. Indeed, generalizations are based not merely on the single sample mean of 533 but also on its distribution—a distribution of sample means for all possible random samples. Representing the statistician's model of random outcomes,

Sampling Distribution of the Mean

Probability distribution of means for all possible random samples of a given size from some population.

the *sampling distribution of the mean* refers to the probability distribution of means for all possible random samples of a given size from some population.

In effect, this distribution describes the variability among sample means that could occur just by chance and thereby serves as a frame of reference for generalizing from a single sample mean to a population mean.

The sampling distribution of the mean allows us to determine whether, given the variability among all possible sample means, the one observed sample mean can be viewed as a *common* outcome or as a *rare* outcome (from a distribution centered, in this case, about a value of 500). If the sample mean of 533 qualifies as a *common* outcome in this sampling distribution, then the difference between 533 and 500 isn't large enough, relative to the variability of all possible sample means, to signify that anything special is happening in the underlying population. Therefore, we can conclude that the mean reading score for the entire freshman class could be the same as the national average of 500. On the other hand, if the sample mean of 533 qualifies as a *rare* outcome in this sampling distribution, then the difference between 533 and 500 is large enough, relative to the variability of all possible sample means, to signify that something special probably is happening in the underlying population. Therefore, we can conclude that the mean reading score for the entire freshman class probably exceeds the national average of 500.

All Possible Random Samples

When attempting to generalize from a single sample mean to a population mean, we must consult the sampling distribution of the mean. In the present case, this distribution is based on *all possible* random samples, each of size 100 that can be taken from the local population of freshmen. *All possible random samples* refers not to the number of samples of size 100 required to *survey completely* the local population of freshmen but to the number of different ways in which a *single* sample of size 100 can be selected from this population.

"All possible random samples" tends to be a huge number. For instance, if the local population contained at least 1000 freshmen, the total number of possible random samples, each of size 100, would be astronomical in size. The 301 digits in this number would dwarf even the national debt. Even with the aid of a computer, it would be a horrendous task to construct this sampling distribution from scratch, itemizing each mean for all possible random samples.

Fortunately, statistical theory supplies us with considerable information about the sampling distribution of the mean, as will be discussed in the remainder of this chapter. Armed with this information about sampling distributions, we'll return to the current example in the next chapter and test the claim that the mean reading score for the local population of freshmen equals the national average of 500. Only at that point—and not at the end of this chapter—should you expect to understand completely the role of sampling distributions in practical applications.

9.2 CREATING A SAMPLING DISTRIBUTION FROM SCRATCH

Let's establish precisely what constitutes a sampling distribution by creating one from scratch under highly simplified conditions. Imagine some ridiculously small population of four observations with values of 2, 3, 4, and 5, as shown in **Figure 9.1**. Next, itemize all possible random samples, each of size two, that could be taken from this population. There are four possibilities on the first draw from the population and also four possibilities on the second draw from the population, as indicated in **Table 9.1**.* The two sets of possibilities combine to yield a total of sixteen possible samples. At this point, remember, we're clarifying the notion of a sampling distribution of the mean. In practice, only one random sample, not sixteen possible samples, would be taken from the population; the sample size would be very small relative to a much larger population size, and, of course, not all observations in the population would be known.

---

* Ordinarily, a single observation is sampled only once, that is, sampling is *without replacement*. If employed with the present, highly simplified example, however, sampling without replacement would magnify an unimportant technical adjustment.

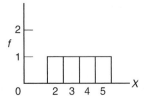

FIGURE 9.1
Graph of a miniature population.

	Table 9.1 ALL POSSIBLE SAMPLES OF SIZE TWO FROM A MINIATURE POPULATION		
	ALL POSSIBLE SAMPLES	**MEAN ($\bar{X}$)**	**PROBABILITY**
(1)	2,2	2.0	$\frac{1}{16}$
(2)	2,3	2.5	$\frac{1}{16}$
(3)	2,4	3.0	$\frac{1}{16}$
(4)	2,5	3.5	$\frac{1}{16}$
(5)	3,2	2.5	$\frac{1}{16}$
(6)	3,3	3.0	$\frac{1}{16}$
(7)	3,4	3.5	$\frac{1}{16}$
(8)	3,5	4.0	$\frac{1}{16}$
(9)	4,2	3.0	$\frac{1}{16}$
(10)	4,3	3.5	$\frac{1}{16}$
(11)	4,4	4.0	$\frac{1}{16}$
(12)	4,5	4.5	$\frac{1}{16}$
(13)	5,2	3.5	$\frac{1}{16}$
(14)	5,3	4.0	$\frac{1}{16}$
(15)	5,4	4.5	$\frac{1}{16}$
(16)	5,5	5.0	$\frac{1}{16}$

For each of the sixteen possible samples, Table 9.1 also lists a sample mean (found by adding the two observations and dividing by 2) and its probability of occurrence (expressed as $\frac{1}{16}$, since each of the sixteen possible samples is equally likely). When cast into a relative frequency or probability distribution, as in **Table 9.2**, the sixteen sample means constitute the sampling distribution of the mean, previously defined as the probability distribution of means for all possible random samples of a given size from some population. Not all probabilities are equal in Table 9.2 since some values of the sample mean occur more than once among the sixteen possible samples. For instance, a sample

Table 9.2 SAMPLING DISTRIBUTION OF THE MEAN (SAMPLES OF SIZE TWO FROM A MINIATURE POPULATION)	
SAMPLE MEAN ($\bar{X}$)	PROBA- BILITY
5.0	$\frac{1}{16}$
4.5	$\frac{2}{16}$
4.0	$\frac{3}{16}$
3.5	$\frac{4}{16}$
3.0	$\frac{3}{16}$
2.5	$\frac{2}{16}$
2.0	$\frac{1}{16}$

mean value of 3.5 appears among four of sixteen possibilities and has a probability of $^4/_{16}$.

Probability of a Particular Sample Mean

The distribution in Table 9.2 can be consulted to determine the probability of obtaining a particular sample mean or set of sample means. For example, the probability of a randomly selected sample mean of 5.0 equals $^1/_{16}$ or .0625. According to the addition rule for mutually exclusive outcomes, described in Chapter 8, the probability of a randomly selected sample mean of either 5.0 or 2.0 equals $^1/_{16} + ^1/_{16} = ^2/_{16} = .1250$. This type of probability statement, based on a sampling distribution, assumes an essential role in inferential statistics and will reappear throughout the remainder of the book.

Review

Figure 9.2 summarizes the previous discussion. It depicts the emergence of the sampling distribution of the mean from the set of all possible (sixteen) samples of size two, based on the miniature population of four observations. Familiarize yourself with this figure, as it will be referred to again.

Progress Check *9.1 Imagine a very simple population consisting of only five observations: 2, 4, 6, 8, 10.

(a) List all possible samples of size two.

(b) Construct a relative frequency table showing the sampling distribution of the mean.

Answers on page 500.

9.3 SOME IMPORTANT SYMBOLS

Having established precisely what constitutes a sampling distribution under highly simplified conditions, we can introduce the special symbols that identify the mean and the standard deviation of the sampling distribution of the mean. Table 9.3 also lists the corresponding symbols for the sample and the population. It would be wise to memorize these symbols.

You are already acquainted with the English letters $\bar{X}$ and s, representing the mean and standard deviation of any sample, and also the Greek letters μ (mu) and σ (sigma), representing the mean and standard deviation of any population. New are the Greek letters $\mu_{\bar{X}}$ (mu sub X-bar) and $\sigma_{\bar{X}}$ (sigma sub X-bar), representing the mean and standard deviation, respectively, of the sampling distribution of the mean. To minimize confusion, the latter term, $\sigma_{\bar{X}}$, is often referred to as the *standard error of the mean* or simply as the *standard error.*

Significance of Greek Letters

Note that Greek letters are used to describe characteristics of both populations and sampling distributions, suggesting a common feature. Both types of distribution deal with all possibilities, that is, with *all possible observations* in

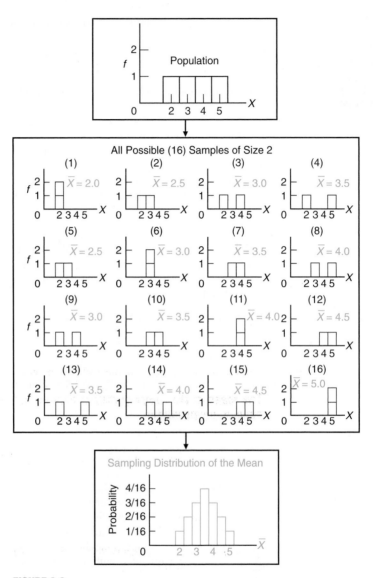

FIGURE 9.2

Emergence of the sampling distribution of the mean from all possible samples.

the population, or with the *means of all possible random samples* in the sampling distribution of the mean.

With this background, let's focus on the three most important characteristics of the sampling distribution of the mean: its mean, its standard deviation, and its shape. In subsequent chapters, these three characteristics will form the basis for applied work in inferential statistics.

Table 9.3		
SYMBOLS FOR THE MEAN AND STANDARD DEVIATION OF THREE TYPES OF DISTRIBUTIONS		
TYPE OF DISTRIBUTION	**MEAN**	**STANDARD DEVIATION**
Sample	$\bar{X}$	s
Population	μ	σ
Sampling distribution of the mean	$\mu_{\bar{X}}$	$\sigma_{\bar{X}}$ (standard error of the mean)

Progress Check *9.2 Without peeking, list the special symbols for the mean of the population __(a)__, mean of the sampling distribution of the mean __(b)__, mean of the sample __(c)__, standard error of the mean __(d)__, standard deviation of the sample __(e)__, and standard deviation of the population __(f)__.

Answers on page 500.

9.4 MEAN OF ALL SAMPLE MEANS ($\mu_{\bar{x}}$)

The distribution of sample means itself has a mean.

The *mean of the sampling distribution* of the mean *always* equals the mean of the population.

Expressed in symbols, we have

MEAN OF THE SAMPLING DISTRIBUTION	
$\mu_{\bar{X}} = \mu$	(9.1)

where $\mu_{\bar{x}}$ represents the mean of the sampling distribution and μ represents the mean of the population.

Interchangeable Means

Since the mean of all sample means ($\mu_{\bar{x}}$) always equals the mean of the population (μ), these two terms are interchangeable in inferential statistics. Any claims about the population mean can be transferred directly to the mean of the sampling distribution, and vice versa. If, as claimed, the mean reading score for the local population of freshmen equals the national average of 500, then the mean of the sampling distribution also automatically will equal 500. For the same reason, it's permissible to view the one observed sample mean of 533 as a deviation either from the mean of the sampling distribution or from the mean of the population. It should be apparent, therefore, that *whether an expression* *involves $\mu_{\bar{X}}$ or μ, it reflects, at most, a difference in emphasis on either the sampling distribution or the population, respectively, rather than any difference in numerical value.*

Explanation

Although important, it's not particularly startling that the mean of all sample means equals the population mean. As can be seen in Figure 9.2, samples are not exact replicas of the population, and most sample means are either larger or smaller than the population mean (equal to 3.5 in Figure 9.2). By taking the mean of all sample means, however, you effectively neutralize chance differences between sample means and retain a value equal to the population mean.

Progress Check *9.3 Indicate whether the following statements are True or False. The mean of all sample means, $\mu_{\bar{X}}$, . . .

(a) always equals the value of a particular sample mean.

(b) equals 100 if, in fact, the population mean equals 100.

(c) usually equals the value of a particular sample mean.

(d) is interchangeable with the population mean.

Answers on page 500.

9.5 STANDARD ERROR OF THE MEAN ($\sigma_{\bar{X}}$)

The distribution of sample means also has a standard deviation, referred to as the standard error of the mean.

Standard Error of the Mean ($\sigma_{\bar{X}}$)

A rough measure of the average amount by which sample means deviate from the mean of the sampling distribution or from the population mean.

> The *standard error of the mean* equals the standard deviation of the population divided by the square root of the sample size.

Expressed in symbols,

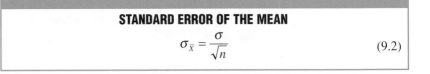

STANDARD ERROR OF THE MEAN

$$\sigma_{\bar{X}} = \frac{\sigma}{\sqrt{n}}$$

(9.2)

where $\sigma_{\bar{X}}$ represents the standard error of the mean; σ represents the standard deviation of the population; and n represents the sample size.

Special Type of Standard Deviation

The standard error of the mean serves as a special type of standard deviation that measures variability in the sampling distribution. It supplies us with a *standard*, much like a yardstick, that describes the amount by which sample means deviate from the mean of the sampling distribution or from the population mean. The *error* in standard error refers not to computational errors, but to errors in generalizations attributable to the fact that, just by chance, most random samples aren't exact replicas of the population.

> **You might find it helpful to think of the standard error of the mean as a rough measure of the average amount by which sample means deviate from the mean of the sampling distribution or from the population mean.**

Insofar as the shape of the distribution sample means approximates a normal curve, as described in the next section, about 68 percent of all sample means deviate less than one standard error from the mean of the sampling distribution, whereas only about 5 percent of all sample means deviate more than two standard errors from the mean of this distribution.

Effect of Sample Size

A most important implication of Formula 9.2 is that whenever the sample size equals two or more, the variability of the sampling distribution is less than that in the population. A modest demonstration of this effect appears in Figure 9.2, where the means of all possible samples cluster closer to the population mean (equal to 3.5) than do the four original observations in the population. A more dramatic demonstration occurs with larger sample sizes. Earlier in this chapter, for instance, 110 was given as the value of σ, the population standard deviation for SAT scores. Much smaller is the variability in the sampling distribution of mean SAT scores, each based on samples of 100 freshmen. According to Formula 9.2, in the present example, there is a

$$\sigma_{\bar{x}} = \frac{\sigma}{\sqrt{n}} = \frac{110}{\sqrt{100}} = \frac{110}{10} = 11$$

tenfold reduction in variability, from 110 to 11, when our focus shifts from the population to the sampling distribution.

According to Formula 9.2, any increase in sample size translates into a smaller standard error and, therefore, into a *new* sampling distribution with less variability. With a larger sample size, sample means cluster more closely about the mean of the sampling distribution and about the mean of the population and, therefore, allow more precise generalizations from samples to populations.

Explanation

It's not surprising that variability should be smaller in sampling distributions than in populations. The population standard deviation reflects variability among *individual observations*, and it is directly affected by any relatively large or small observations within the population. On the other hand, the standard error of the mean reflects variability among *sample means*, each of which represents a collection of individual observations. The appearance of relatively large or small observations within a particular sample tends to affect the sample mean only slightly, because of the stabilizing presence in the same sample of other, more moderate observations or even extreme observations in the opposite direction. This stabilizing effect becomes even more pronounced with larger sample sizes.

Progress Check *9.4 Indicate whether the following statements are True or False. The standard error of the mean, $\sigma_{\bar{x}}$, . . .

(a) roughly measures the average amount by which sample means deviate from the population mean.

(b) measures variability in a particular sample.

(c) increases in value with larger sample sizes.

(d) equals 5, given that $\sigma = 40$ and $n = 64$.
Answers on page 500.

....

9.6 SHAPE OF THE SAMPLING DISTRIBUTION

A product of statistical theory, expressed in its simplest form,

---

Central Limit Theorem

Regardless of the population shape, the shape of the sampling distribution of the mean approximates a normal curve if the sample size is sufficiently large.

> the *central limit theorem* states that, regardless of the shape of the population, the shape of the sampling distribution of the mean approximates a normal curve *if the sample size is sufficiently large.*

According to this theorem, it doesn't matter whether the shape of the parent population is normal, positively skewed, negatively skewed, or some nameless, bizarre shape, as long as the sample size is sufficiently large. What constitutes "sufficiently large" depends on the shape of the parent population. If the shape of the parent population is normal, then any sample size (even a sample size of one) will be sufficiently large. Otherwise, depending on the degree of non-normality in the parent population, a sample size between 25 and 100 is sufficiently large.

Examples

For the population with a non-normal shape in the top panel of Figure 9.2, the shape of the sampling distribution in the bottom panel reveals a preliminary drift toward normality—that is, a shape having a peak in the middle with tapered flanks on either side—even for very small samples of size 2. For the two non-normal populations in the top panel of **Figure 9.3**, the shapes of the sampling distributions in the middle panel show essentially the same preliminary drift toward normality when the sample size equals only 2, while the shapes of the sampling distributions in the bottom panel closely approximate normality when the sample size equals 25.

Earlier in this chapter, 533 was given as the mean SAT critical reading score for a random sample of 100 freshmen. Because this sample size satisfies the requirements of the central limit theorem, we can view the sample mean of 533 as originating from a sampling distribution whose shape approximates a normal curve, even though we lack information about the shape of the population of reading scores for the entire freshman class. It will be possible, therefore, to make precise statements about this sampling distribution, as described in the next chapter, by referring to the table for the standard normal curve.

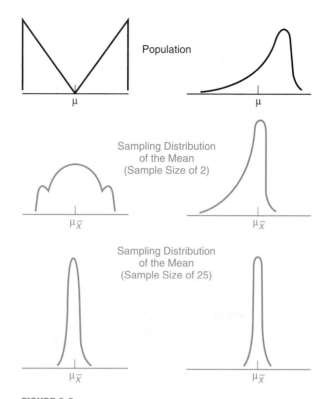

Population

Sampling Distribution
of the Mean
(Sample Size of 2)

Sampling Distribution
of the Mean
(Sample Size of 25)

FIGURE 9.3
Effect of the central limit theorem.

Why the Central Limit Theorem Works

In a normal curve, you will recall, intermediate values are the most prevalent, and extreme values, either larger or smaller, occupy the tapered flanks. Why, when the sample size is large, does the sampling distribution approximate a normal curve, even though the parent population might be non-normal?

Many Sample Means with Intermediate Values

When the sample size is large, it is *most likely* that any single sample will contain the full spectrum of small, intermediate, and large scores from the parent population, *whatever its shape*. The calculation of a mean for this type of sample tends to neutralize or dilute the effects of any extreme scores, and the sample mean emerges with some intermediate value. Accordingly, intermediate values prevail in the sampling distribution, and they cluster around a peak frequency representing the most common or modal value of the sample mean, as suggested at the bottom of Figure 9.3.

Few Sample Means with Extreme Values

To account for the rarer sample mean values in the tails of the sampling distribution, focus on those relatively infrequent samples that, just by chance, contain less than the full spectrum of scores from the parent population. Sometimes, because of the relatively large number of extreme scores in a particular direction, the calculation of a mean only slightly dilutes their effect, and the sample mean emerges with some more extreme value. The likelihood of obtaining extreme sample mean values declines with the extremity of the value, producing the smoothly tapered, slender tails that characterize a normal curve.

Progress Check *9.5 Indicate whether the following statements are True or False. The central limit theorem

(a) states that, with sufficiently large sample sizes, the shape of the population is normal.

(b) states that, regardless of sample size, the shape of the sampling distribution of the mean is normal.

(c) ensures that the shape of the sampling distribution of the mean equals the shape of the population.

(d) applies to the shape of the sampling distribution—not to the shape of the population and not to the shape of the sample.

Answers on page 500.

9.7 OTHER SAMPLING DISTRIBUTIONS

For the Mean

There are many different sampling distributions of means. A new sampling distribution is created by a switch to another population. Furthermore, for any single population, there are as many different sampling distributions as there are possible sample sizes. Although each of these sampling distributions has the same mean, the value of the standard error always differs and depends upon the size of the sample.

For Other Measures

There are sampling distributions for measures other than a single mean. For instance, there are sampling distributions for medians, proportions, standard deviations, variances, and correlations, as well as for differences between pairs of means, pairs of proportions, and so forth. We'll have occasion to work with some of these distributions in later chapters.

`WWW`

INTERNET DEMONSTRATION
Go to the Web site for this book (http://www.wiley.com\college\witte). Click on the *Student Companion Site*, then *Internet Demonstrations*, and finally *Sampling Distributions* to create, from scratch, the sampling distribution of the mean and to observe how this distribution changes with shifts in population shape and sample size.

Summary

The notion of a sampling distribution is the most important concept in inferential statistics. The sampling distribution of the mean is defined as the probability distribution of means for all possible random samples of a given size from some population.

Statistical theory pinpoints three important characteristics of the sampling distribution of the mean:

- The mean of the sampling distribution equals the mean of the population.
- The standard deviation of the sampling distribution, that is, the standard error of the mean, equals the standard deviation of the population divided by the square root of the sample size. An important implication of this formula is that a larger sample size translates into a sampling distribution with a smaller variability, allowing more precise generalizations from samples to populations. The standard error of the mean serves as a rough measure of the average amount by which sample means deviate from the mean of the sampling distribution or from the population mean.
- According to the central limit theorem, regardless of the shape of the population, the shape of the sampling distribution approximates a normal curve if the sample size is sufficiently large. Depending on the degree of non-normality in the parent population, a sample size of between 25 and 100 is sufficiently large.

Any single sample mean can be viewed as originating from a sampling distribution whose (1) mean equals the population mean (whatever its value); whose (2) standard error equals the population standard deviation divided by the square root of the sample size; and whose (3) shape approximates a normal curve (if the sample size satisfies the requirements of the central limit theorem).

Important Terms

Mean of the sampling distribution of the mean ($\mu_{\bar{X}}$)
Sampling distribution of the mean

Standard error of the mean ($\sigma_{\bar{X}}$)
Central limit theorem

Key Equations

SAMPLING DISTRIBUTION MEAN

$$\mu_{\bar{X}} = \mu$$

STANDARD ERROR

$$\sigma_{\bar{X}} = \frac{\sigma}{\sqrt{n}}$$

REVIEW QUESTIONS

9.6 A random sample tends not to be an exact replica of its parent population. This fact has a number of implications. Indicate which are True and which are False.

(a) All possible random samples can include a few samples that are exact replicas of the population, but most samples aren't exact replicas.

(b) A more representative sample can be obtained by handpicking (rather than randomly selecting) observations.

(c) Insofar as it misrepresents the parent population, a random sample can cause an erroneous generalization.

(d) In practice, the mean of a single random sample is evaluated relative to the variability of means for all possible random samples.

9.7 Define the sampling distribution of the mean.

9.8 Indicate whether the following statements are True or False. The sampling distribution of the mean

(a) is always constructed from scratch, even when the population is large.

(b) serves as a bridge to aid generalizations from a sample to a population.

(c) is the same as the sample mean.

(d) always reflects the shape of the underlying population.

(e) has a mean that always coincides with the population mean.

(f) is a device used to determine the effect of variability, that is, what can happen, just by chance, when samples are random.

(g) remains unchanged even with shifts to a new population or sample size.

(h) supplies a spectrum of possibilities against which to evaluate the observed sample mean.

(i) tends to cluster more closely about the population mean with increases in sample size.

9.9 Someone claims that, since the mean of the sampling distribution equals the population mean, any single sample mean must also equal the population mean. Any comment?

9.10 **(a)** A random sample of size 144 is taken from the local population of grade-school children. Each child estimates the number of hours per week spent watching TV. At this point, what can be said about the sampling distribution?

(b) Assume that a standard deviation, σ, of 8 hours describes the TV estimates for the local population of schoolchildren. At this point, what can be said about the sampling distribution?

(c) Assume that a mean, μ, of 21 hours describes the TV estimates for the local population of schoolchildren. Now what can be said about the sampling distribution?

(d) Roughly speaking, the sample means in the sampling distribution should deviate, on average, about ___ hours from the mean of the sampling distribution and from the mean of the population.

(e) About 95 percent of the sample means in this sampling distribution should be between ___ hours and ___ hours.

CHAPTER 10

Introduction to Hypothesis Testing: The *z* Test

Summary / Important Terms / Key Equations / Review Questions

Preview
....

This chapter describes the first in a series of hypothesis tests. Learning the vocabulary of special terms for hypothesis tests will be most helpful throughout the remainder of the book. However, do not become so concerned about either terminology or computational mechanics that you lose sight of the essential role of the sampling distribution—the model of everything that could happen just by chance—in any hypothesis test.

Using the sampling distribution as our frame of reference, the one observed outcome is characterized as either a common outcome or a rare outcome. A common outcome is readily attributable to chance, and therefore, the hypothesis that nothing special is happening—the null hypothesis—is retained. On the other hand, a rare outcome isn't readily attributable to chance, and therefore, the null hypothesis is rejected (usually to the delight of the researcher).

10.1 TESTING A HYPOTHESIS ABOUT SAT SCORES

In the previous chapter, we postponed a test of the hypothesis that the mean SAT reading score for all local freshmen equals the national average of 500. Now, given a mean reading score of 533 for a random sample of 100 freshmen, let's test the hypothesis that, with respect to the national average, nothing special is happening in the local population. Insofar as an investigator usually suspects just the opposite—namely, that something special is happening in the local population—he or she hopes to reject the hypothesis that nothing special is happening, henceforth referred to as the *null* hypothesis and defined more formally in a later section.

Hypothesized Sampling Distribution

If the null hypothesis is true, then the distribution of sample means—that is, the sampling distribution of the mean for all possible random samples, each of size 100, from the local population of freshmen—will be centered about the national average of 500. (Remember, the mean of the sampling distribution always equals the population mean.) In **Figure 10.1**, this sampling distribution is referred to as the *hypothesized* sampling distribution, since its mean equals 500, the hypothesized mean reading score for the local population of freshmen.

Anticipating the key role of the hypothesized sampling distribution in our hypothesis test, let's focus on two more properties of this distribution:

1. In Figure 10.1, vertical lines appear, at intervals of size 11, on either side of the hypothesized population mean of 500. These intervals reflect the size of the standard error of the mean, $\sigma_{\bar{X}}$. To verify this fact, originally demonstrated in Chapter 9, substitute 110 for the population standard deviation, σ, and 100 for the sample size, n, in Formula 9.2 to obtain

$$\sigma_{\bar{X}} = \frac{\sigma}{\sqrt{n}} = \frac{110}{\sqrt{100}} = \frac{110}{10} = 11$$

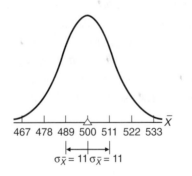

FIGURE 10.1

Hypothesized sampling distribution of the mean centered about a hypothesized population mean of 500.

2. Notice that the shape of the hypothesized sampling distribution in Figure 10.1 approximates a normal curve, since the sample size of 100 is large enough to satisfy the requirements of the central limit theorem. Eventually, with the aid of normal curve tables, we will be able to construct boundaries for common and rare outcomes under the null hypothesis.

The null hypothesis that the population mean for the freshman class equals 500 is *tentatively* assumed to be true. It is tested by determining whether the one observed sample mean qualifies as a common outcome or a rare outcome in the hypothesized sampling distribution of Figure 10.1.

Common Outcomes

An observed sample mean qualifies as a *common* outcome if the difference between its value and that of the hypothesized population mean is small enough to be viewed as a probable outcome under the null hypothesis.

That is, a sample mean qualifies as a common outcome if it doesn't deviate too far from the hypothesized population mean but appears to emerge from the dense concentration of possible sample means in the middle of the sampling distribution. *A common outcome signifies a lack of evidence that, with respect to the null hypothesis, something special is happening in the underlying population.* Because now there is no compelling reason for rejecting the null hypothesis, it is retained.

Key Point:

Does the one observed sample mean qualify as a common or a rare outcome?

Rare Outcomes

An observed sample mean qualifies as a *rare* outcome if the difference between its value and the hypothesized population mean is too large to be reasonably viewed as a probable outcome under the null hypothesis.

That is, a sample mean qualifies as a rare outcome if it deviates too far from the hypothesized mean and appears to emerge from the sparse concentration of possible sample means in either tail of the sampling distribution. *A rare outcome signifies that, with respect to the null hypothesis, something special probably is happening in the underlying population.* Because now there are grounds for suspecting the null hypothesis, it is rejected.

Boundaries for Common and Rare Outcomes

Superimposed on the hypothesized sampling distribution in **Figure 10.2** is one possible set of boundaries for common and rare outcomes, expressed in values of $\bar{X}$. (Techniques for constructing these boundaries are described in Section 10.7.) If the one observed sample mean is located between 478 and 522, it will qualify as a common outcome (readily attributed to variability) under the null hypothesis, and the null hypothesis will be retained. If, however, the one observed sample mean is greater than 522 or less than 478, it will qualify as a rare outcome (not readily attributed to variability) under the null hypothesis, and the null hypothesis will be rejected. Because the observed sample mean of 533 does exceed 522, the null hypothesis is rejected. On the

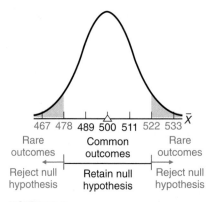

FIGURE 10.2

One possible set of common and rare outcomes (values of $\bar{X}$).

basis of the present test, it is unlikely that the sample of 100 freshmen, with a mean reading score of 533, originates from a population whose mean equals the national average of 500, and, therefore, the investigator can conclude that the mean reading score for the local population of freshmen probably differs from (exceeds) the national average.

10.2 z TEST FOR A POPULATION MEAN

For the hypothesis test with SAT reading scores, it is customary to base the test not on the hypothesized sampling distribution of $\bar{X}$ shown in Figure 10.2, but rather on its standardized counterpart, the hypothesized sampling distribution of z shown in **Figure 10.3**. Now z represents a variation on the familiar standard

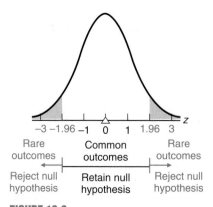

FIGURE 10.3

Common and rare outcomes (values of z).

Sampling Distribution of z

The distribution of z values that would be obtained if a value of z were calculated for each sample mean for all possible random samples of a given size from some population.

score, and it displays all of the properties of standard scores described in Chapter 5. Furthermore, like the sampling distribution of $\overline{X}$, the **sampling distribution of z** *represents the distribution of z values that would be obtained if a value of z were calculated for each sample mean for all possible random samples of a given size from some population.*

The conversion from $\overline{X}$ to z yields a distribution that approximates the standard normal curve in Table A of Appendix C, since, as indicated in Figure 10.3, the original hypothesized population mean (500) emerges as a z score of 0 and the original standard error of the mean (11) emerges as a z score of 1. The shift from $\overline{X}$ to z eliminates the original units of measurement and standardizes the hypothesis test across all situations without, however, affecting the test results.

Reminder: Converting a Raw Score to z

To convert a raw score into a standard score (also described in Chapter 5), express the raw score as a distance from its mean (by subtracting the mean from the raw score), and then split this distance into standard deviation units (by dividing with the standard deviation). Expressing this definition as a word formula, we have

$$Standard\ score = \frac{raw\ score - mean}{standard\ deviation}$$

in which, of course, the standard score indicates the deviation of the raw score in standard deviation units, above or below the mean.

Converting a Sample Mean to z

The z for the present situation emerges as a slight variation of this word formula: Replace the *raw score* with the one observed sample mean $\overline{X}$; replace the *mean* with the mean of the sampling distribution, that is, the hypothesized population mean μ_{hyp}; and replace the *standard deviation* with the standard error of the mean $\sigma_{\overline{X}}$. Now

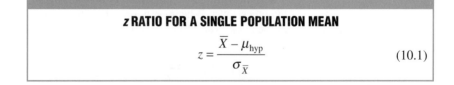

z RATIO FOR A SINGLE POPULATION MEAN

$$z = \frac{\overline{X} - \mu_{hyp}}{\sigma_{\overline{X}}}$$ (10.1)

where z indicates the deviation of the observed sample mean in standard error units, above or below the hypothesized population mean.

To test the hypothesis for SAT scores, we must determine the value of z from Formula 10.1. Given a sample mean of 533, a hypothesized population mean of 500, and a standard error of 11, we find

$$z = \frac{533 - 500}{11} = \frac{33}{11} = 3$$

The observed z of 3 exceeds the value of 1.96 specified in the hypothesized sampling distribution in Figure 10.3. Thus, the observed z qualifies as a rare outcome under the null hypothesis, and the null hypothesis is rejected. The results of this test with z are the same as those for the original hypothesis test with $\bar{X}$.

Assumptions of z Test

---

z Test for a Population Mean

A hypothesis test that evaluates how far the observed sample mean deviates, in standard error units, from the hypothesized population mean.

When a hypothesis test evaluates how far the observed sample mean deviates, in standard error units, from the hypothesized population mean, as in the present example, *it is referred to as a z test* or, more accurately, as a **z test for a population mean.** This z test is accurate only when (1) the population is normally distributed or the sample size is large enough to satisfy the requirements of the central limit theorem and (2) the population standard deviation is known. In the present example, the z test is appropriate because the sample size of 100 is large enough to satisfy the central limit theorem and the population standard deviation is known to be 110.

Progress Check *10.1 Calculate the value of the z test for each of the following situations:

(a) $\bar{X} = 566$; $\sigma = 30$; $n = 36$; $\mu_{hyp} = 560$

(b) $\bar{X} = 24$; $\sigma = 4$; $n = 64$; $\mu_{hyp} = 25$

(c) $\bar{X} = 82$; $\sigma = 14$; $n = 49$; $\mu_{hyp} = 75$

(d) $\bar{X} = 136$; $\sigma = 15$; $n = 25$; $\mu_{hyp} = 146$

Answers on page 501.

10.3 STEP-BY-STEP PROCEDURE

Having been exposed to some of the more important features of hypothesis testing, let's take a detailed look at the test for SAT scores. The test procedure lends itself to a step-by-step description, beginning with a brief statement of the problem that inspired the test and ending with an interpretation of the test results. The following box summarizes the step-by-step procedure for the current hypothesis test. Whenever appropriate, this format will be used in the remainder of the book. Refer to it while reading the remainder of the chapter.

10.4 STATEMENT OF THE RESEARCH PROBLEM

The formulation of a research problem often represents the most crucial and exciting phase of an investigation. Indeed, the mark of a skillful investigator is to focus on an important research problem that can be answered. Do children from broken families score lower on tests of personal adjustment? Do aggressive TV cartoons incite more disruptive behavior in preschool children? Does profit sharing increase the productivity of employees? Because of our emphasis on hypothesis testing, research problems appear in this book as finished products, usually in the first one or two sentences of a new example.

HYPOTHESIS TEST SUMMARY: z TEST FOR A POPULATION MEAN (SAT SCORES)

Research Problem

Does the mean SAT reading score for all local freshmen differ from the national average of 500?

Statistical Hypotheses

$$H_0: \mu = 500$$
$$H_1: \mu \neq 500$$

Decision Rule

Reject H_0 at the .05 level of significance if $z \geq 1.96$ or if $z \leq -1.96$.

Calculations

Given

$$\bar{X} = 533; \quad \mu_{hyp} = 500; \quad \sigma_{\bar{X}} = \frac{\sigma}{\sqrt{n}} = \frac{110}{\sqrt{100}} = 11$$

$$z = \frac{533 - 500}{11} = 3$$

Decision

Reject H_0 at the .05 level of significance because $z = 3$ exceeds 1.96.

Interpretation

The mean SAT reading score for all local freshmen does not equal—it exceeds—the national average of 500.

10.5 NULL HYPOTHESIS (H_0)

Once the problem has been described, it must be translated into a statistical hypothesis regarding some population characteristic. Abbreviated as H_0, the null hypothesis becomes the focal point for the entire test procedure (even though we usually hope to reject it). In the test with SAT scores, the null hypothesis asserts that, with respect to the national average of 500, nothing special is happening to the mean score for the local population of freshmen. An equivalent statement, in symbols, reads:

$$H_0: \mu = 500$$

Null Hypothesis (H₀)

A statistical hypothesis that usually asserts that nothing special is happening with respect to some characteristic of the underlying population.

where H_0 represents the null hypothesis and μ is the population mean for the local freshman class.

Generally speaking, the **null hypothesis, H_0,** *is a statistical hypothesis that usually asserts that nothing special is happening with respect to some characteristic of the underlying population.* Because the hypothesis testing procedure requires that the hypothesized sampling distribution of the mean be centered about a single number (500), the null hypothesis equals a single number ($H_0: \mu = 500$). Furthermore, the null hypothesis always makes a precise statement about a characteristic of the population, never about a sample. Remember, the purpose of a hypothesis test is to determine whether a particular outcome, such as an observed sample mean, could have reasonably originated from a population with the hypothesized characteristic.

Finding the Single Number for H_0

The single number actually used in H_0 varies from problem to problem. Even for a given problem, this number could originate from any of several sources. For instance, it could be based on available information about some relevant population other than the target population, as in the present example in which 500 reflects the mean SAT reading scores for all college-bound students during a recent year. It also could be based on some existing standard or theory—for example, that the mean reading score for the current population of local freshmen should equal 540 because that happens to be the mean score achieved by all local freshmen during recent years.

If, as sometimes happens, it's impossible to identify a meaningful null hypothesis, don't try to salvage the situation with arbitrary numbers. Instead, use another entirely different technique, known as *estimation,* which is described in Chapter 12.

10.6 ALTERNATIVE HYPOTHESIS (H_1)

In the present example, the alternative hypothesis asserts that, with respect to the national average of 500, something special is happening to the mean reading score for the local population of freshmen (because the mean for the local population doesn't equal the national average of 500). An equivalent statement, in symbols, reads:

$$H_1: \mu \neq 500$$

Alternative Hypothesis (H₁)

The opposite of the null hypothesis.

where H_1 represents the alternative hypothesis, μ is the population mean for the local freshman class, and $\neq$ signifies, "is not equal to."

The **alternative hypothesis, H_1,** *asserts the opposite of the null hypothesis.* A decision to retain the null hypothesis implies a lack of support for the alternative hypothesis, and a decision to reject the null hypothesis implies support for the alternative hypothesis.

As will be described in the next chapter, the alternative hypothesis may assume any one of three different forms, depending on the perspective of the investigator. In its present form, H_1 specifies a *range* of possible values about the *single* number (500) that appears in H_0.

Research Hypothesis

Usually identified with the alternative hypothesis, this is the informal hypothesis or hunch that inspires the entire investigation.

Regardless of its form, H_1 usually is identified with the **research hypothesis,** *the informal hypothesis or hunch that, by implying the presence of something special in the underlying population, serves as inspiration for the entire investigation.* "Something special" might be, as in the current example, a deviation from a national average, or it could be, as in later chapters, a deviation from some control condition produced by a new teaching method, a weight-reduction diet, or a self-improvement workshop. In any event, it is this research hypothesis—and certainly not the null hypothesis—that supplies the motive behind an investigation.

Progress Check *10.2 Indicate what's wrong with each of the following statistical hypotheses:

(a) $H_0: \mu = 155$ **(b)** $H_0: \bar{X} = 241$

     $H_1: \mu \neq 160$ $H_1: \bar{X} \neq 241$

Progress Check *10.3 First using words, then symbols, identify the null hypothesis for each of the following situations. (Don't concern yourself about the precise form of the alternative hypothesis at this point.)

(a) A school administrator wishes to determine whether sixth-grade boys in her school district differ, on average, from the national norms of 10.2 pushups for sixth-grade boys.

(b) A consumer group investigates whether, on average, the true weights of packages of ground beef sold by a large supermarket chain differ from the specified 16 ounces.

(c) A marriage counselor wishes to determine whether, during a standard conflict-resolution session, his clients differ, on average, from the 11 verbal interruptions reported for "well-adjusted couples."

Answers on page 501.

10.7 DECISION RULE

Decision Rule

Specifies precisely when H_0 should be rejected (because the observed z qualifies as a rare outcome).

A **decision rule** *specifies precisely when H_0 should be rejected* (because the observed z qualifies as a rare outcome). There are many possible decision rules, as will be seen in Section 11.3. A very common one, already introduced in Figure 10.3, specifies that H_0 should be *rejected* if the observed z equals or is more positive than 1.96 or if the observed z equals or is more negative than −1.96. Conversely, H_0 should be *retained* if the observed z falls between ±1.96.

Critical z Scores

Figure 10.4 indicates that z scores of ±1.96 define the boundaries for the middle .95 of the total area (1.00) under the hypothesized sampling distribution for z. Derived from the normal curve table, as you can verify by checking Table A in Appendix C, these two z scores *separate common from rare outcomes and hence dictate whether H_0 should be retained or rejected.* Because

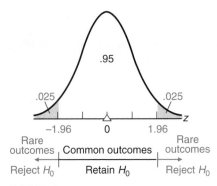

FIGURE 10.4
Proportions of area associated with common and rare outcomes (α = 05).

Critical z Score

A z score that separates common from rare outcomes and hence dictates whether H_0 should be retained or rejected.

Level of Significance (α)

The degree of rarity required of an observed outcome in order to reject the null hypothesis (H_0).

---

of their vital role in the decision about H_0, these scores are referred to as **critical z scores.**

Level of Significance (α)

Figure 10.4 also indicates the proportion (.025 + .025 = .05) of the total area that is identified with rare outcomes. Often referred to as the level of significance of the statistical test, this proportion is symbolized by the Greek letter α (alpha) and discussed more thoroughly in Section 11.4. In the present example, the level of significance, α, equals .05.

The **level of significance** (α) *indicates the degree of rarity required of an observed outcome in order to reject the null hypothesis (H_0).* For instance, the .05 level of significance indicates that H_0 should be rejected if the observed z could have occurred just by chance with a probability of only .05 (one chance out of twenty) *or less.*

10.8 CALCULATIONS

We can use information from the sample to calculate a value for z. As has been noted previously, use Formula 10.1 to convert the observed sample mean of 533 into a z of 3.

10.9 DECISION

Either retain or reject H_0, depending on the location of the observed z value relative to the critical z values specified in the decision rule. According to the present rule, H_0 should be rejected at the .05 level of significance because the observed z of 3 exceeds the critical z of 1.96 and, therefore, qualifies as a rare outcome, that is, an unlikely outcome from a population centered about the null hypothesis.

Retain or Reject H_0?

If you are ever confused about whether to retain or reject H_0, recall the logic behind the hypothesis test. You want to reject H_0 only if the observed value of z qualifies as a rare outcome because it deviates too far into the tails of the sampling distribution. Therefore, you want to reject H_0 only if the observed value of z equals or is more positive than the upper critical z (1.96) or if it equals or is more negative than the lower critical z (−1.96). Before deciding, you might find it helpful to sketch the hypothesized sampling distribution, along with its critical z values and shaded rejection regions, and then use some mark, such as an arrow (↑), to designate the location of the observed value of z (3) along the z scale. If this mark is located in the shaded rejection region—or farther out than this region, as in Figure 10.4—then H_0 should be rejected.

Progress check *10.4 For each of the following situations, indicate whether H_0 should be retained or rejected and justify your answer by specifying the precise relationship between observed and critical z scores. Should H_0 be retained or rejected, given a hypothesis test with critical z scores of ±1.96 and

(a) $z = 1.74$ **(b)** $z = 0.13$ **(c)** $z = -2.51$
     Answers on page 501.

....

10.10 INTERPRETATION

Finally, interpret the decision in terms of the original research problem. In the present example, it can be concluded that, since the null hypothesis was rejected, the mean SAT reading score for the local freshman class probably differs from the national average of 500.

Although not a strict consequence of the present test, a more specific conclusion is possible. Since the sample mean of 533 (or its equivalent z of 3) falls in the *upper* rejection region of the hypothesized sampling distribution, it can be concluded that the population mean SAT reading score for all local freshmen probably *exceeds* the national average of 500. By the same token, if the observed sample mean or its equivalent z had fallen in the *lower* rejection region of the hypothesized sampling distribution, it could have been concluded that the population mean for all local freshmen probably is *below* the national average.

If the observed sample mean or its equivalent z had fallen in the retention region of the hypothesized sampling distribution, it would have been concluded (somewhat weakly, as discussed in Section 11.2) that there is no evidence that the population mean for all local freshmen differs from the national average of 500.

Progress Check *10.5 According to the American Psychological Association, members with a doctorate and a full-time teaching appointment earn, on the average, $82,500 per year, with a standard deviation of $6,000. An investigator wishes to determine whether $82,500 is also the mean salary for all female members with a doctorate and a full-time teaching appointment. Salaries are obtained for a random sample of 100 women from this population, and the mean salary equals $80,100.

(a) Someone claims that the observed difference between $80,100 and $82,500 is large enough by itself to support the conclusion that female members earn less than male members. Explain why it is important to conduct a hypothesis test.

(b) The investigator wishes to conduct a hypothesis test for what population?

(c) What is the null hypothesis, H_0?

(d) What is the alternative hypothesis, H_1?

(e) Specify the decision rule, using the .05 level of significance.

(f) Calculate the value of z. (Remember to convert the standard deviation to a standard error.)

(g) What is your decision about H_0?

(h) Using words, interpret this decision in terms of the original problem.
Answers on page 501.

Summary

To test a hypothesis about the population mean, a single observed sample mean is viewed within the context of a hypothesized sampling distribution, itself centered about the null-hypothesized population mean. If the sample mean appears to emerge from the dense concentration of possible sample means in the middle of the sampling distribution, it qualifies as a common outcome, and the null hypothesis is retained. On the other hand, if the sample mean appears to emerge from the sparse concentration of possible sample means in the extremities of the sampling distribution, it qualifies as a rare outcome, and the null hypothesis is rejected.

Hypothesis tests are based not on the sampling distribution of $\bar{X}$ expressed in original units of measurement, but on its standardized counterpart, the sampling distribution of z. Referred to as the z test for a single population mean, this test is appropriate only when (1) the population is normally distributed or the sample size is large enough to satisfy the central limit theorem and (2) the population standard deviation is known.

When testing a hypothesis, adopt the following step-by-step procedure:

- **State the research problem.** Using words, state the problem to be resolved by the investigation.
- **Identify the statistical hypotheses.** The statistical hypotheses consist of a null hypothesis (H_0) and an alternative (or research) hypothesis (H_1). The null hypothesis supplies the value about which the hypothesized sampling distribution is centered. Depending on the outcome of the hypothesis test, H_0 will either be retained or rejected. Insofar as H_0 implies that nothing special is happening in the underlying population, the investigator usually hopes to reject it in favor of H_1, the research hypothesis. In the present chapter, the statistical hypotheses take the form

$$H_0: \mu = \text{some number}$$
$$H_1: \mu \neq \text{some number}$$

(Two other possible forms for statistical hypotheses will be described in Chapter 11.)

- **Specify a decision rule.** This rule indicates precisely when H_0 should be rejected. The exact form of the decision rule depends on a number of factors, to be discussed in Chapter 11. In any event, H_0 is rejected whenever the observed z deviates from 0 as far as, or farther than, the critical z does.
  The level of significance indicates how rare an observed z must be (assuming that H_0 is true) before H_0 can be rejected.
- **Calculate the value of the observed z.** Express the one observed sample mean as an observed z, using Formula 10.1.
- **Make a decision.** Either retain or reject H_0 at the specified level of significance, justifying this decision by noting the relationship between observed and critical z scores.
- **Interpret the decision.** Using words, interpret the decision in terms of the original research problem. Rejection of the null hypothesis supports the research hypothesis, while retention of the null hypothesis fails to support the research hypothesis.

Important Terms
. . . .

Sampling distribution of z	**z Test for a population mean**
Null hypothesis (H_0)	**Alternative hypothesis (H_1)**
Research hypothesis	**Decision rule**
Critical z score	**Level of significance (α)**

Key Equations
. . . .

z RATIO

$$z = \frac{\overline{X} - \mu_{\text{hyp}}}{\sigma_{\overline{X}}}$$

$$\text{where} \quad \sigma_{\overline{X}} = \frac{\sigma}{\sqrt{n}}$$

REVIEW QUESTIONS

*10.6 For the population at large, the Wechsler Adult Intelligence Scale is designed to yield a normal distribution of test scores with a mean of 100 and a standard deviation of 15. School district officials wonder whether, on the average, an IQ score of 100 describes the intellectual aptitudes of all students in their district. Wechsler IQ scores are obtained for a random sample of 25 of their students, and the mean IQ is found to equal 105.

Using the step-by-step procedure described in this chapter, test the null hypothesis at the .05 level of significance.

Answer on page 502.

10.7 According to a U.S. Census Bureau survey during 2005–2007, the daily one-way commute time of U.S. workers averages 25 minutes with, we'll assume, a standard deviation of 13 minutes. An investigator wishes to determine whether the national average describes the mean commute time for all workers in the Chicago area. Commute times are obtained for a random sample of 169 workers from this area, and the mean time is found to be 22.5 minutes. Test the null hypothesis at the .05 level of significance.

10.8 Supply the missing word(s) in the following statements:

If the one observed sample mean can be viewed as a __(a)__ outcome under the hypothesis, H_0 will be __(b)__ . Otherwise, if the one observed sample mean can be viewed as a __(c)__ outcome under the hypothesis, H_0 will be __(d)__ .

The pair of z scores that separates common and rare outcomes is referred to as __(e)__ z scores. Within the hypothesized sampling distribution, the proportion of area allocated to rare outcomes is referred to as the __(f)__ and is symbolized by the Greek letter __(g)__ .

When based on the sampling distribution of z, the hypothesis test is referred to as a __(h)__ test. This test is appropriate if the sample size is sufficiently large to satisfy the __(i)__ and if the __(j)__ is known.

CHAPTER

11

More about Hypothesis Testing

Preview

Based on the notion of everything that could possibly happen just by chance—in other words, based on the concept of a sampling distribution—hypothesis tests permit us to draw conclusions that go beyond a limited set of actual observations. This chapter describes why rejecting the null hypothesis is stronger than retaining the null hypothesis and why a one-tailed test is more likely than a two-tailed test to detect a false null hypothesis.

We speculate about how the hypothesis test fares if we assume, in turn, that the null hypothesis is true and then that it is false. The two types of incorrect decisions—rejecting a true null hypothesis (a false alarm) or retaining a false null hypothesis (a miss)—can be controlled by our selection of the level of significance and of the sample size.

11.1 WHY HYPOTHESIS TESTS?

There is a crucial link between hypothesis tests and the need of investigators, whether pollsters or researchers, to generalize beyond existing data. If the 100 freshmen in the SAT example of the previous chapter had been not a sample but a *census* of the entire freshman class, there wouldn't have been any need to generalize beyond existing data, and it would have been inappropriate to conduct a hypothesis test. Now, the observed difference between the newly observed population mean of 533 and the national average of 500, by itself, would have been sufficient grounds for concluding that the mean SAT reading score for all local freshmen exceeds the national average. Indeed, *any* observed difference in favor of the local freshmen, regardless of the size of the difference, would have supported this conclusion.

If we must generalize beyond the 100 freshmen to a larger local population, as was actually the case, the observed difference between 533 and 500 cannot be interpreted at face value. The basic problem is that the sample mean for a second random sample of 100 freshmen probably would differ, just by chance, from the sample mean of 533 for the first sample. Accordingly, the variability among sample means must be considered when we attempt to decide whether the observed difference between 533 and 500 is real or merely transitory.

Importance of the Standard Error

To evaluate the effect of chance, we use the concept of a sampling distribution, that is, the concept of the sample means for all possible random outcomes. A key element in this concept is the standard error of the mean, a measure of the average amount by which sample means differ, just by chance, from the population mean. Dividing the observed difference (533 − 500) by the standard error (11) to obtain a value of z (3) locates the original observed difference along a z scale of either common outcomes (reasonably attributable to chance) or rare outcomes (not reasonably attributable to chance). If, when expressed as z, the ratio of the observed difference to the standard error is small enough to be reasonably attributed to chance, we retain H_0. Otherwise, if the ratio of the observed difference to the standard error is too large to be reasonably attributed to chance, as in the SAT example, we reject H_0.

Before generalizing beyond the existing data, we must always measure the effect of chance; that is, we must obtain a value for the standard error. To appreciate the vital role of the standard error in the SAT example, increase its value from 11 to 33 and note that even though the observed difference remains the same (533 − 500), we would retain, not reject, H_0 because now z would equal 1 (rather than 3) and be less than the critical z of 1.96.

Possibility of Incorrect Decisions

Having made a decision about the null hypothesis, we never know absolutely whether that decision is correct or incorrect, unless, of course, we survey the entire population. Even if H_0 is true (and, therefore, the hypothesized distribution of z about H_0 also is true), there is a *slight* possibility that, just by chance, the one observed z actually originates from one of the shaded rejection regions of the hypothesized distribution of z, thus causing the true H_0 to be rejected. This type of incorrect decision—rejecting a true H_0—is referred to as a *type I error* or a *false alarm.*

On first impulse, it might seem desirable to abolish the shaded rejection regions in the hypothesized sampling distribution to ensure that a true H_0 never is rejected. A most unfortunate consequence of this strategy, however, is that no H_0, not even a radically false H_0, ever would be rejected. This second type of incorrect decision—retaining a false H_0—is referred to as a *type II error* or a *miss.* Both type I and type II errors are described in more detail later in this chapter.

Minimizing Incorrect Decisions

Traditional hypothesis-testing procedures, such as the one illustrated in **Figure 11.1**, tend to minimize both types of incorrect decisions. *If H_0 is true,* there is a high probability that the observed z will qualify as a common outcome under the hypothesized sampling distribution and that the true H_0 will be retained. (In Figure 11.1, this probability equals the proportion of white area (.95) in the hypothesized sampling distribution.) On the other hand, *if H_0 is seriously false,* because the hypothesized population mean differs considerably from the true population mean, there is also a high probability that the observed z will qualify as a rare outcome under the hypothesized distribution and that the false H_0 will be rejected. (In Figure 11.1, this probability can't be determined since, in this case, the hypothesized sampling distribution does not actually reflect the true sampling distribution. More about this later in the chapter.)

> **Even though we never really know whether a particular decision is correct or incorrect, it is reassuring that in the long run, *most* decisions will be correct—assuming the null hypotheses are *either true or seriously false.***

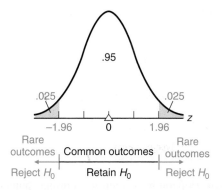

FIGURE 11.1

Proportions of area associated with common and rare outcomes ($\alpha = .05$).

11.2 STRONG OR WEAK DECISIONS

Retaining H_0 Is a *Weak* Decision

There are subtle but important differences in the interpretation of decisions to retain H_0 and to reject H_0. H_0 is retained whenever the observed z qualifies as a common outcome on the assumption that H_0 is true. Therefore, H_0 *could* be true. However, the same observed result also would qualify as a common outcome when the original value in H_0 (500) is replaced with a slightly different value. Thus, the retention of H_0 must be viewed as a relatively weak decision. Because of this weakness, many statisticians prefer to describe this decision as simply a *failure to reject H_0* rather than as the retention of H_0. In any event, the retention of H_0 can't be interpreted as proving H_0 to be true. If H_0 had been retained in the present example, it would have been appropriate to conclude not that the mean SAT reading score for all local freshmen equals the national average, but that the mean SAT reading score *could* equal the national average, as well as many other possible values in the general vicinity of the national average.

Rejecting H_0 Is a *Strong* Decision

On the other hand, H_0 is rejected whenever the observed z qualifies as a rare outcome—one that could have occurred just by chance with a probability of .05 or less—on the assumption that H_0 is true. This suspiciously rare outcome implies that H_0 is probably false (and conversely, that H_1 is probably true). Therefore, the rejection of H_0 can be viewed as a strong decision. When H_0 was rejected in the present example, it was appropriate to report a definitive conclusion that the mean SAT reading score for all local freshmen probably exceeds the national average.

To summarize,

> the decision to retain H_0 implies not that H_0 is probably true, but only that H_0 *could* be true, whereas the decision to reject H_0 implies that H_0 is *probably* false (and that H_1 is *probably* true).

Since most investigators hope to reject H_0 in favor of H_1, the relative weakness of the decision to retain H_0 usually does not pose a serious problem.

Why the Research Hypothesis Isn't Tested Directly

Even though H_0, the null hypothesis, is the focus of a statistical test, it is usually of secondary concern to the investigator. Nevertheless, there are several reasons why, although of primary concern, the research hypothesis is identified with H_1 and tested indirectly.

Lacks Necessary Precision

> The research hypothesis, but not the null hypothesis, lacks the necessary precision to be tested directly.

To be tested, a hypothesis must specify a single number about which the hypothesized sampling distribution can be constructed. *Because it specifies a single number, the null hypothesis, rather than the research hypothesis, is tested directly.* In the SAT example, the null hypothesis specifies that a precise value (the national average of 500) describes the mean for the current population of interest (all local freshmen). Typically, the research hypothesis lacks the required precision. It merely specifies that some inequality exists between the hypothesized value (500) and the mean for the current population of interest (all local freshmen).

Supported by a Strong Decision to Reject

Logical considerations also argue for the indirect testing of the research hypothesis and the direct testing of the null hypothesis.

Because the research hypothesis is identified with the alternative hypothesis, the decision to reject the null hypothesis, should it be made, will provide *strong* support for the research hypothesis, while the decision to retain the null hypothesis, should it be made, will provide, at most, *weak* support for the null hypothesis.

As mentioned previously, the decision to reject the null hypothesis is stronger than the decision to retain it. Logically, a statement such as "All cows have four legs" can never be proven in spite of a steady stream of positive instances. It only takes one negative instance—one cow with three legs—to disprove the statement. By the same token, one positive instance (common outcome) doesn't prove the null hypothesis, but one negative instance (rare outcome) disproves the null hypothesis. (Strictly speaking, however, since a rare outcome implies that the null hypothesis is probably *but not definitely* false, remember that there always is a very small possibility that the rare outcome reflects a true null hypothesis.)

Logically, therefore, it makes sense to identify the research hypothesis with the alternative hypothesis. If, as hoped, the data favor the research hypothesis, the test will generate strong support for your hunch: It's *probably* true. If the data do not favor the research hypothesis, the hypothesis test will generate, at most, weak support for the null hypothesis: It *could* be true. *Weak support for the null hypothesis is of little consequence, as this hypothesis—that nothing special is happening in the population—usually serves only as a convenient testing device.*

Reminder:

Rejecting H_0 implies that it probably is false, while retaining H_0 implies only that it could *be true.*

11.3 ONE-TAILED AND TWO-TAILED TESTS

Let's consider some techniques that make the hypothesis test more responsive to special conditions.

Two-Tailed Test

Generally, the alternative hypothesis, H_1, is the complement of the null hypothesis, H_0. Under typical conditions, the form of H_1 resembles that shown for the SAT example, namely,

$$H_1: \mu \neq 500$$

This alternative hypothesis says that the null hypothesis should be rejected if the mean reading score for the population of local freshmen differs in either direction from the national average of 500. An observed z will qualify as a rare outcome if it deviates too far either below or above the national average. Panel A of **Figure 11.2** shows rejection regions that are associated with both tails of the hypothesized sampling distribution. The corresponding decision rule, with its pair of critical z scores of ± 1.96, is referred to as a **two-tailed** or **nondirectional test.**

One-Tailed Test (Lower Tail Critical)

Now let's assume that the research hypothesis for the investigation of SAT reading scores was based on complaints from instructors about the poor preparation of local freshmen. Assume also that if the investigation supports these complaints, a remedial program will be instituted. Under these circumstances, the investigator might prefer a hypothesis test that is specially designed to detect only whether the population mean reading score for all local freshmen is *less* than the national average.

This alternative hypothesis reads:

$$H_1: \mu < 500$$

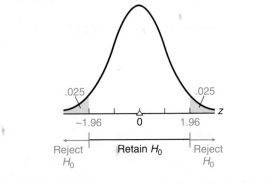

A. Two-Tailed or Nondirectional Test

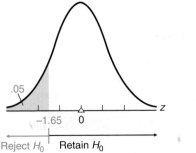

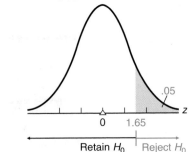

B. One-Tailed or Directional Test (Lower Tail Critical)

C. One-Tailed or Directional Test (Upper Tail Critical)

FIGURE 11.2
Three different types of tests ($\alpha = .05$).

It reflects a concern that the null hypothesis should be rejected only if the population mean reading score for all local freshmen is less than the national average of 500. Accordingly, an observed z triggers the decision to reject H_0 only if z deviates too far below the national average. Panel B of Figure 11.2 illustrates a rejection region that is associated with only the lower tail of the hypothesized sampling distribution. The corresponding decision rule, with its critical z of -1.65, is referred to as a **one-tailed** or **directional test** *with the lower tail critical.* Use Table A in Appendix C to verify that if the critical z equals -1.65; then .05 of the total area under the distribution of z has been allocated to the lower rejection region. Notice that the level of significance, α, equals .05 for this one-tailed test and also for the original two-tailed test.

One-Tailed or Directional Test

Rejection region is located in just one tail of the sampling distribution.

Extra Sensitivity of One-Tailed Tests

This new one-tailed test is extra sensitive to any drop in the population mean for the local freshmen below the national average. If H_0 is false because a drop has occurred, then the observed z will be more likely to deviate below the national average. As can be seen in panels A and B of Figure 11.2, an observed deviation in the direction of concern—below the national average—is more likely to penetrate the broader rejection region for the one-tailed test than that for the two-tailed test. Therefore, the decision to reject a *false H_0* (in favor of the research hypothesis) is more likely to occur in the one-tailed test than in the two-tailed test.

One-Tailed Test (Upper Tail Critical)

Panel C of Figure 11.2 illustrates a **one-tailed** or **directional test** *with the upper tail critical.* This one-tailed test is the mirror image of the previous test. Now the alternative hypothesis reads:

$$H_1: \mu > 500$$

and its critical z equals 1.65. This test is specially designed to detect only whether the population mean reading score for all local freshmen *exceeds* the national average. For example, the research hypothesis for this investigation might have been inspired by the possibility of eliminating an existing remedial reading program if it can be demonstrated that, on the average, the SAT reading scores of all local freshmen exceed the national average.

One or Two Tails?

Before a hypothesis test, if there is a concern that the true population mean differs from the hypothesized population mean *only* in a particular direction, use the appropriate one-tailed or directional test for extra sensitivity. Otherwise, use the more customary two-tailed or nondirectional test.

Having committed yourself to a one-tailed test with its single rejection region, you must retain H_0, regardless of how far the observed z deviates from the hypothesized population mean in the direction of "no concern." For instance, if a one-tailed test with the lower tail critical had been used with the data for 100 freshmen from the SAT example, H_0 would have been retained because, even though the observed z equals an impressive value of 3, it deviates in the direction of no concern—in this case, above the national average. Clearly, a one-tailed test should be adopted only when there is absolutely no concern about deviations, even very large deviations, in one direction. If there is the slightest concern about these deviations, use a two-tailed test.

The selection of a one- or two-tailed test should be made before the data are collected. Never "peek" at the value of the observed z to determine whether to locate the rejection region for a one-tailed test in the upper or the lower tail of the distribution of z. To qualify as a one-tailed test, the location of the rejection region must reflect the investigator's concern only about deviations in a particular direction *before any inspection of the data*. Indeed, the investigator should be able to muster a compelling reason, based on an understanding of the research hypothesis, to support the direction of the one-tailed test.

New Null Hypothesis for One-Tailed Tests

When tests are one-tailed, a complete statement of the null hypothesis also should include all possible values of the population mean in the direction of no concern. For example, given a one-tailed test with the lower tail critical, such as H_1: $\mu < 500$, the complete null hypothesis should be stated as H_0: $\mu \geq 500$ instead of H_0: $\mu = 500$. By the same token, given a one-tailed test with the upper tail critical, such as H_1: $\mu > 500$, the complete null hypothesis should be stated as H_0: $\mu \leq 500$.

If you think about it, the complete H_0 describes all of the population means that could be true if a one-tailed test results in the retention of the null hypothesis. For instance, if a one-tailed test with the lower tail critical results in the retention of H_0: $\mu \geq 500$, the complete H_0 accurately reflects the fact that not only $\mu = 500$ could be true, but also that any other value of the population mean in the direction of no concern, that is, $\mu > 500$, could be true. (Remember, when the test is one-tailed, even a very deviant result in the direction of no concern—possibly reflecting a μ much larger than 500—still would trigger the decision to retain H_0.) Henceforth, whenever a one-tailed test is employed, write H_0 to include values of the population mean in the direction of no concern—*even though the single number in the complete H_0 identified by the equality sign is the one value about which the hypothesized sampling distribution is centered and, therefore, the one value actually used in the hypothesis test.*

Reminder:
In the absence of compelling reasons for a one-tailed test, use a two-tailed test.

Progress Check *11.1 Each of the following statements could represent the point of departure for a hypothesis test. Given only the information in each statement, would you use a two-tailed (or nondirectional) test, a one-tailed (or directional) test with the lower tail critical, or a one-tailed (or directional) test with the upper tail critical? Indicate your decision by specifying the appropriate H_0 and H_1. Furthermore, whenever you conclude that the test is one-tailed, indicate the precise word (or words) in the statement that justifies the one-tailed test.

(a) An investigator wishes to determine whether, for a sample of drug addicts, the mean score on the depression scale of a personality test differs from a score of 60, which, according to the test documentation, represents the mean score for the general population.

(b) To increase rainfall, extensive cloud-seeding experiments are to be conducted, and the results are to be compared with a baseline figure of 0.54 inch of rainfall (for comparable periods when cloud seeding was not done).

(c) Public health statistics indicate, we will assume, that American males gain an average of 23 lbs during the 20-year period after age 40. An ambitious weight-reduction program, spanning 20 years, is being tested with a sample of 40-year-old men.

(d) When untreated during their lifetimes, cancer-susceptible mice have an average life span of 134 days. To determine the effects of a potentially life-prolonging (and cancer-retarding) drug, the average life span is determined for a group of mice that receives this drug.

Progress Check *11.2 For each of the following situations, indicate whether H_0 should be retained or rejected.

Given a one-tailed test, lower tail critical with $\alpha = .01$, and

(a) $z = -2.34$ **(b)** $z = -5.13$ **(c)** $z = 4.04$

Given a one-tailed test, upper tail critical with $\alpha = .05$, and

(d) $z = 2.00$ **(e)** $z = -1.80$ **(f)** $z = 1.61$
     Answers on page 502.

11.4 CHOOSING A LEVEL OF SIGNIFICANCE (α)

The level of significance indicates how rare an observed z must be before H_0 can be rejected. To reject H_0 at the .05 level of significance implies that the observed z would have occurred, just by chance, with a probability of only .05 (one chance out of twenty) *or less.*

The level of significance also spotlights an inherent risk in hypothesis testing, that is, the risk of rejecting a true H_0. When the level of significance equals .05, there is a probability of .05 that, even though H_0 is true, the observed z will stray into the rejection region and cause the true H_0 to be rejected.

Which Level of Significance?

When the rejection of a true H_0 is particularly serious, a smaller level of significance can be selected. For example, the .01 level of significance implies that before H_0 can be rejected, the observed z must achieve a degree of rarity equal to .01 (one chance out of 100) *or less;* it also limits, to a probability of .01, the risk of rejecting a true H_0. The .01 level might be used in a hypothesis test in which the rejection of a true H_0 would cause the introduction of a costly new remedial education program, even though the population mean reading score for all local freshmen really equals the national average. An even smaller level of significance, such as the .001 level, might be used when the rejection of a true H_0 would have horrendous consequences—for instance, the treatment of serious illnesses, such as AIDS, exclusively with a new, very expensive drug that not only is worthless but also has severe side effects.

Although many different levels of significance are possible, most tables for hypothesis tests are geared to the .05 and .01 levels. In this book, the level of significance will be specified for you. However, in real-life applications, you, as an investigator, might have to select a level of significance. *Unless there are obvious reasons for selecting either a larger or a smaller level of significance, use the customary .05 level*—the largest level of significance reported in most professional journals.

When testing hypotheses with the z test, you may find it helpful to refer to **Table 11.1**, which lists the critical z values for one- and two-tailed tests at the .05 and .01 levels of significance. These z values were obtained from Table A in Appendix C.

Progress Check *11.3 Specify the decision rule for each of the following situations (referring to Table 11.1 to find critical z values):

(a) a two-tailed test with $\alpha = .05$

(b) a one-tailed test, upper tail critical, with $\alpha = .01$

(c) a one-tailed test, lower tail critical, with $\alpha = .05$

(d) a two-tailed test with $\alpha = .01$

Answers on page 502.

INTERNET DEMONSTRATION
Go to the Web site for this book, http://www.wiley.com\college\witte. Click on the *Student Companion Site,* then *Internet Demonstrations* and finally **Hypothesis Test** to explore how decisions about the null hypothesis vary with the form of the alternative hypothesis and the level of significance.

Table 11.1
CRITICAL z VALUES

TYPE OF TEST	LEVEL OF SIGNIFICANCE (α)	
	.05	.01
Two-tailed or nondirectional test ($H_0: \mu =$ some number) ($H_1: \mu \neq$ some number)	± 1.96	± 2.58
One-tailed or directional test, lower tail critical ($H_0: \mu \geq$ some number) ($H_1: \mu <$ some number)	-1.65	-2.33
One-tailed or directional test, upper tail critical ($H_0: \mu \leq$ some number) ($H_1: \mu >$ some number)	$+1.65$	$+2.33$

11.5 TESTING A HYPOTHESIS ABOUT VITAMIN C

Let's look more closely at the four possible outcomes of a hypothesis test by focusing on a study to determine whether vitamin C increases the intellectual aptitude of high school students. After being randomly selected from some large school district, each of 36 students takes a daily dose of 60 milligrams of vitamin C (the commonly recommended dosage) for a period of two months before being tested for IQ.

Ordinarily, IQ scores for all students in this school district approximate a normal distribution with a mean of 100 and a standard deviation of 15. According to the null hypothesis, a mean of 100 still would describe the distribution of IQ scores even if all of the students in the district were to receive the vitamin C treatment. Furthermore, given our exclusive concern about detecting only any deviation of the population mean *above* 100, the null hypothesis takes the form appropriate for a one-tailed test with the upper tail critical, namely:

$$H_0: \mu \leq 100$$

The rejection of H_0 would support H_1, the research hypothesis that something special is happening in the underlying population (because vitamin C increases intellectual aptitude), namely:

$$H_1: \mu > 100$$

z Test Is Appropriate

To determine whether the sample mean IQ for the 36 students qualifies as a common or a rare outcome under the null hypothesis, a z test will be used. The z test for a population mean is appropriate since, for IQ scores, the population standard deviation is known to be 15 and the shape of the population is known to be normal.

Two Groups Would Have Been Better

Although poorly designed, the present experiment supplies a perspective that will be most useful in later chapters. A better-designed experiment would contrast the IQ scores for the group of subjects who receive vitamin C with the IQ scores for a *placebo control group* of subjects who receive fake vitamin C—thereby controlling for the "*placebo effect,*" *a self-induced improvement in performance caused by the subject's awareness of being treated in a special way.* Hypothesis tests for experiments with two groups are described in Chapters 14 and 15.

The box on page 236 summarizes those features of the hypothesis test that can be identified before the collection of any data.

11.6 FOUR POSSIBLE OUTCOMES

Table 11.2 summarizes the four possible outcomes of any hypothesis test. Before testing a hypothesis, we must be concerned about all four possible outcomes because we don't know whether H_0 is true or false—that's why we're

---

HYPOTHESIS TEST SUMMARY:
z TEST FOR A POPULATION MEAN (*PRIOR* TO THE VITAMIN C EXPERIMENT)

Research Problem

Does the daily ingestion of vitamin C cause an increase, on average, in IQ scores among all students in the school district?

Statistical Hypotheses

$$H_0: \mu \le 100$$
$$H_1: \mu > 100$$

Decision Rule

Reject H_0 at the .05 level of significance if $z \ge 1.65$.

Calculations

$$\sigma_{\bar{X}} = \frac{\sigma}{\sqrt{n}} = \frac{15}{\sqrt{36}} = \frac{15}{6} = 2.5$$

---

testing the hypothesis. If, unknown to us, H_0 really is true, a well-designed hypothesis test will tend to confirm this fact; that is, it will cause us to retain H_0 and conclude that H_0 could be true. To conclude otherwise, as is always a slight possibility, reflects a type I error. On the other hand, if, unknown to us, H_0 really is *seriously* false, a well-designed hypothesis test also will tend to confirm this fact; that is, it will cause us to reject H_0 and conclude that H_0 is false. To conclude otherwise, as is always a slight possibility, reflects a type II error.

Four Possible Outcomes of the Vitamin C Experiment

It's instructive to describe the four possible outcomes in Table 11.2 in terms of the vitamin C experiment.

Table 11.2
POSSIBLE OUTCOMES OF A HYPOTHESIS TEST

DECISION	STATUS OF H_0 TRUE H_0	FALSE H_0
Retain H_0	(1) Correct decision	(3) Type II error (miss)
Reject H_0	(2) Type I error (false alarm)	(4) Correct decision

1. If H_0 really is true (because vitamin C does not cause an increase in the population mean IQ), then *it is a correct decision to retain the true H_0.* In this case, we would conclude correctly that there is no evidence that vitamin C increases IQ.

2. If H_0 really is true, then *it is a* **type I error** *to reject the true H_0* and conclude that vitamin C increases IQ when, in fact, it doesn't. Type I errors are sometimes called *false alarms* because, as with their firehouse counterparts, they trigger wild goose chases after something that does not exist. For instance, a type I error might encourage a batch of worthless experimental efforts to discover precisely what dosage of vitamin C maximizes the nonexistent "increase" in IQ.

3. If H_0 really is false (because vitamin C really causes an increase in the population mean IQ), then *it is a* **type II error** *to retain the false H_0* and conclude that there is no evidence that vitamin C increases IQ when, in fact, it does. Type II errors are sometimes called *misses* because they fail to detect a potentially important relationship, such as that between vitamin C and IQ.

4. If H_0 really is false, then *it is a correct decision to reject the false H_0* and conclude that vitamin C increases IQ.

Type I Error

Rejecting a true null hypothesis.

Type II Error

Retaining a false null hypothesis.

Importance of Null Hypothesis

Refer to Table 11.2 when, as in the following exercise, you must describe the four possible outcomes for a particular hypothesis test. To avoid confusing the type I and II errors, first identify the null hypothesis, H_0. Typically, *the null hypothesis asserts that there is no effect, thereby contradicting the research hypothesis.* In the present case, contrary to the research hypothesis, the null hypothesis (H_0: $\mu \leq 100$) assumes that vitamin C has no positive effect on IQ.

Decisions Usually Are Correct

When generalizing beyond existing observations, there is always the possibility of a type I or type II error, and we never can be absolutely certain of having made the correct decision. At best, we can use a test procedure that *usually* produces a correct decision when H_0 is either true or seriously false. This claim will be examined in the context of the vitamin C experiment, assuming first that H_0 really is true and then that H_0 really is false. Although you might view this approach as hopelessly theoretical, *since we never know whether H_0 really is true or false,* read the next few sections carefully, for they have important implications for any hypothesis test.

Progress Check *11.4

(a) List the four possible outcomes for any hypothesis test.

(b) Under the U.S. Criminal Code, a defendant is presumed innocent until proven guilty. Viewing a criminal trial as a hypothesis test (with H_0 specifying that the defendant is innocent), describe each of the four possible outcomes.

Answers on page 503.

11.7 IF H_0 REALLY IS TRUE

Assume that H_0 really is true because vitamin C doesn't increase the population mean IQ. In this case, we need be concerned only about either retaining or rejecting a true H_0 (the two leftmost outcomes in Table 11.2). It's instructive to view these two possible outcomes in terms of the sampling distribution in **Figure 11.3**. Centered about a value of 100, the hypothesized sampling distribution in Figure 11.3 reflects the properties of the projected one-tailed test for vitamin C. If H_0 really is true—and this is a crucial point—the hypothesized sampling distribution also can be viewed as the *true* sampling distribution (from which the one observed sample mean actually originates). Therefore, the one observed sample mean (or z) in the experiment can be viewed as being randomly selected from the hypothesized distribution.

Probability of a Type I Error

Alpha (α)

The probability of a type I error, that is, the probability of rejecting a true null hypothesis.

When, just by chance, a randomly selected sample mean originates from the small, shaded portion of the sampling distribution in Figure 11.3, its z value equals or exceeds 1.65, and hence H_0 is rejected. Because H_0 really is true, this is an incorrect decision or type I error—a false alarm, announced as evidence that vitamin C increases IQ, even though it really does not. *The probability of a type I error equals* **alpha (α),** *the level of significance.* (The level of significance, remember, indicates the proportion of the total area of the sampling distribution in the rejection region for H_0.) In the present case, the probability of a type I error equals .05, as indicated in Figure 11.3.

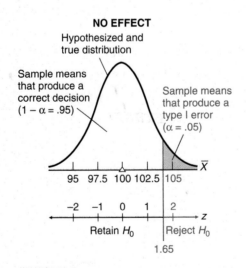

FIGURE 11.3

Hypothesized and true sampling distribution when H_0 is true (because vitamin C causes no increase in IQ).

Probability of a Correct Decision

When, just by chance, a randomly selected sample mean originates from the large white portion of the sampling distribution in Figure 11.3, its z value is less than 1.65 and H_0 is retained. Because H_0 really is true, this is a correct decision—announced as a lack of evidence that vitamin C increases IQ. The probability of a correct decision equals $1 - \alpha$, that is, .95.

Reducing the Probability of a Type I Error

If H_0 really is true, the present test will produce a correct decision with a probability of .95 and a type I error with a probability of .05.* If a false alarm has serious consequences, the probability of a type I error can be reduced to .01 or even to .001 simply by using the .01 or .001 level of significance, respectively. One of these levels of significance might be preferred for the vitamin C test if, for instance, a false alarm could cause the adoption of an expensive program to supply worthless vitamin C to all students in the district and, perhaps, the creation of an accelerated curriculum to accommodate the fictitious increase in intellectual aptitude.

True *H₀* Usually Retained

Reminder:

If H_0 is true and an error is committed, it must be a type I error.

If H_0 really is true, the probability of a type I error, α, equals the level of significance, and the probability of a correct decision equals $1 - \alpha$.

Because values of .05 or less are usually selected for α, we can conclude that if H_0 really is true, correct decisions will occur much more frequently than will type I errors.

Progress Check *11.5 In order to eliminate the type I error, someone decides to use the .00 level of significance. What's wrong with this procedure?

Answer on page 503.

11.8 IF *H₀* REALLY IS FALSE BECAUSE OF A *LARGE* EFFECT

Next, assume that H_0 really is false because vitamin C increases the population mean by not just a few points, but *by many points*—for example, by ten points. Using the vocabulary of most investigators, we also could describe this increase as a "ten-point effect," since *any difference between a true and a hypothesized*

---

*Strictly speaking, if H_0: $\mu \leq 100$ really is true, the true sampling distribution also could be centered about some value less than 100, in the direction of no concern. In this case, the consequences of the hypothesis test would be even more favorable than suggested above. Essentially, because the true sampling distribution would be shifted to the left of the one shown in Figure 11.3, while everything else remains the same, the type I error would have a smaller probability than .05, and a correct decision would have a larger probability than .95.

Effect

Any difference between a true and a hypothesized population mean.

Hypothesized Sampling Distribution

Centered about the hypothesized population mean, this distribution is used to generate the decision rule.

True Sampling Distribution

Centered about the true population mean, this distribution produces the one observed mean (or z).

population mean is referred to as an **effect.** If H_0 really is false, because of the relatively large ten-point effect of vitamin C on IQ, we need be concerned only about either retaining or rejecting a false H_0 (the two rightmost outcomes in Table 11.2). Let's view each of these two possible outcomes in terms of the sampling distributions in **Figure 11.4**.

Hypothesized Sampling Distribution

It is essential to distinguish between the *hypothesized* sampling distribution and the *true* sampling distribution shown in Figure 11.4. Centered about the hypothesized population mean of 100, the **hypothesized sampling distribution** serves as the parent distribution for the familiar decision rule with a critical z of 1.65 for the projected one-tailed test. Once the decision rule has been identified, attention shifts from the hypothesized sampling distribution to the true sampling distribution.

True Sampling Distribution

Centered about the true population mean of 110 (which reflects the ten-point effect, that is, $100 + 10 = 110$), the **true sampling distribution** serves as the parent distribution for the one randomly selected sample mean (or z) that will be observed in the experiment. Viewed relative to the decision rule (based on the hypothesized sampling distribution), the one randomly selected sample mean (originating from the true sampling distribution) dictates whether we retain or reject the false H_0.

Low Probability of a Type II Error for a *Large* Effect

When, just by chance, a randomly selected sample mean originates from the very small black portion of the true sampling distribution of the mean, its z value

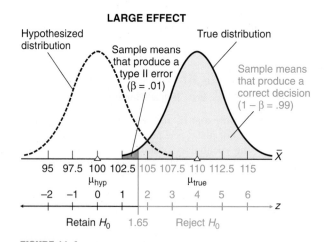

FIGURE 11.4
Hypothesized and true sampling distribution when H_0 is false because of a large effect.

is less than 1.65, and therefore, in compliance with the decision rule, H_0 is retained. Because H_0 really is false, this is an incorrect decision or type II error—a miss, announced as a lack of evidence that vitamin C increases IQ, even though, in fact, it does. With the aid of tables for the normal curve, it can be demonstrated that in the present case, *the probability of a type II error,* symbolized by the Greek letter **beta (β),** equals .01.

Beta (β)

The probability of a type II error, that is, the probability of retaining a false null hypothesis.

(The present argument does not require that you know how to calculate this probability of .01 or those given in the remainder of the chapter. In brief, these probabilities represent areas under the *true* sampling distribution found by re-expressing the critical z as a deviation from the true population mean [110] rather than from the hypothesized population mean [100] and referring to Table A in Appendix C, the normal curve table. As will become apparent in Section 11.11, where these probabilities—or more accurately, the complements $(1 - \beta)$ of these probabilities—aid the selection of sample size, they can be calculated most efficiently by using a computerized statistical program, such as Minitab, which incorporates the normal curve table.)

High Probability of a Correct Decision for a *Large* Effect

When, just by chance, a sample mean originates from the large shaded portion of the true sampling distribution, its z value equals or exceeds 1.65, and H_0 is rejected. Because H_0 really is false, this is a correct decision—announced as evidence that vitamin C increases IQ. In the present case, the probability of a correct decision, symbolized as $1 - \beta$, equals .99.

Review

Reminder:

If H_0 is false and an error is committed, it must be a type II error.

If H_0 really is false, because vitamin C has a large ten-point effect on the population mean IQ, the projected one-tailed test will do quite well. There is a high probability of .99 that a correct decision will be made and a probability of only .01 that a type II error will be committed. This conclusion, when combined with that for the previous section, justifies the earlier claim that hypothesis tests tend to produce correct decisions when either H_0 really is true or H_0 really is false because of a large effect.

Progress Check *11.6 Indicate whether the following statements, *all referring to Figure 11.4,* are True or False:

(a) The assumption that H_0 really is false is depicted by the separation of the hypothesized and true distributions.

(b) In practice, when actually testing a hypothesis, we would not know that the true population mean equals 110.

(c) The one observed sample mean is viewed as originating from the hypothesized sampling distribution.

(d) A correct decision would be made if the one observed sample mean has a value of 103.

Answers on page 503.

11.9 IF H_0 REALLY IS FALSE BECAUSE OF A *SMALL* EFFECT

The projected hypothesis test does not fare nearly as well if H_0 really is false because vitamin C increases the population mean IQ by *only a few points*—for example, by only three points. Once again, as indicated in **Figure 11.5**, there are two different distributions of sample means: the *hypothesized* sampling distribution centered about the hypothesized population mean of 100 and the *true* sampling distribution centered about the true population mean of 103 (which reflects the three-point effect, that is, $100 + 3 = 103$). After the decision rule has been constructed with the aid of the hypothesized sampling distribution, attention shifts to the true sampling distribution from which the one randomly selected sample mean actually will originate.

Low Probability of a Correct Decision for a *Small* Effect

Viewed relative to the decision rule, the true sampling distribution supplies two types of randomly selected sample means: those that produce a type II error because they originate from the black sector and those that produce a correct decision because they originate from the shaded sector. Because of the small three-point effect, the true and hypothesized population means are much closer in Figure 11.5 than in Figure 11.4. As a result, the entire true sampling distribution in Figure 11.5 is shifted toward the retention region for the false H_0, and proportionately more of this distribution is black. Now the projected one-tailed test performs more poorly; there is a fairly high probability of .67 that a type II error will be committed and a low probability of .33 that the correct decision

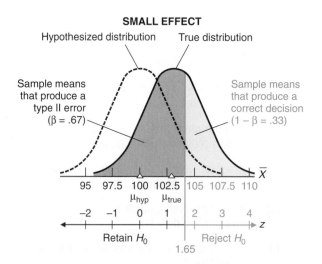

FIGURE 11.5

Hypothesized and true sampling distribution when H_0 is false because of a small effect.

will be made. (Remember, you need not determine these normal curve probabilities to understand the argument.)

Rejection of False H_0 Depends on Size of Effect

If H_0 really is false, the probability of a type II error, β, and the probability of a correct decision, $1 - \beta$, depend on the size of the effect, that is, the difference between the true and the hypothesized population means. The smaller the effect, the higher the probability of a type II error and the lower the probability of a correct decision.

If you think about it, this conclusion is not particularly surprising. If H_0 really is false, there must be some effect. The smaller this effect is, the less likely that it will be detected (by correctly rejecting the false H_0) and the more likely that it will be missed (by erroneously retaining the false H_0). As will be described in the next section, if it's important to detect even a relatively small effect, the probability of a correct decision can be raised to any desired value by increasing the sample size.

Progress Check *11.7 Indicate whether the following statements, *all referring to Figure 11.5,* are True or False:

(a) The value of the true population mean (103) dictates the location of the true sampling distribution.

(b) The critical value of z (1.65) is based on the true sampling distribution.

(c) Since the hypothesized population mean of 100 really is false, it would be impossible to observe a sample mean value less than or equal to 100.

(d) A correct decision would be made if the one observed sample mean has a value of 105.

Answers on page 503.

11.10 INFLUENCE OF SAMPLE SIZE

Ordinarily, the investigator might not be too concerned about the low detection rate of .33 for the relatively small three-point effect of vitamin C on IQ. Under special circumstances, however, this low detection rate might be unacceptable. For example, previous experimentation might have established that vitamin C has many positive effects, including the reduction of common colds, and no apparent negative side effects. Furthermore, huge quantities of vitamin C might be available at no cost to the school district. The establishment of one more positive effect, even a fairly mild one such as a small increase in the population mean IQ, might clinch the case for supplying vitamin C to all students in the district. The investigator, therefore, might wish to use a test procedure for which, when H_0 really is false because of a small effect, the detection rate is appreciably higher than .33.

To increase the probability of detecting a false H_0, increase the sample size.

Assuming that vitamin C still has only a small three-point effect on IQ, we can check the properties of the projected one-tailed test when the sample size is increased from 36 to 100 students. Recall the formula for the standard error of the mean, $\sigma_{\bar{X}}$, namely,

$$\sigma_{\bar{X}} = \frac{\sigma}{\sqrt{n}}$$

For the original experiment with its sample size of 36,

$$\sigma_{\bar{X}} = \frac{15}{\sqrt{36}} = \frac{15}{6} = 2.5$$

whereas for the new experiment with its sample size of 100,

$$\sigma_{\bar{X}} = \frac{15}{\sqrt{100}} = \frac{15}{10} = 1.5$$

Clearly, any increase in sample size causes a reduction in the standard error of the mean.

Consequences of Reducing Standard Error

As can be seen by comparing Figures 11.5 and **11.6**, the reduction of the standard error from 2.5 to 1.5 has two important consequences:

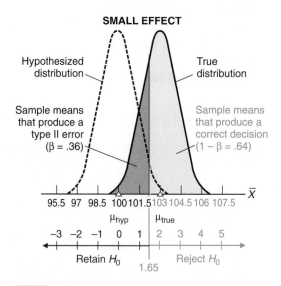

SMALL EFFECT

Hypothesized distribution

True distribution

Sample means that produce a type II error ($\beta = .36$)

Sample means that produce a correct decision ($1 - \beta = .64$)

$\bar{X}$

95.5 97 98.5 100 101.5 103 104.5 106 107.5

μ_{hyp} μ_{true}

−3 −2 −1   0   1   2   3   4   5

Retain H_0 Reject H_0

1.65

FIGURE 11.6

Hypothesized and true sampling distribution when H_0 is false because of a small effect but sample size is relatively large.

1. It shrinks the upper retention region back toward the hypothesized population mean of 100.

2. It shrinks the entire true sampling distribution toward the true population mean of 103.

The net result is that, among randomly selected sample means for 100 students, fewer sample means (.36) produce a type II error because they originate from the black sector, and more sample means (.64) produce a correct decision—that is, more lead to the detection of a false H_0—because they originate from the shaded sector.

An obvious implication is that the standard error can be reduced to any desired value merely by increasing the sample size. To cite an extreme case, when the sample size equals 10,000 students (!), the standard error drops to 0.15. In this case, the upper retention region shrinks to the immediate vicinity of the hypothesized population mean of 100, and the entire true sampling distribution of the mean shrinks to the immediate vicinity of the true population mean of 103. The net result is that a type II error hardly ever is committed, and the small three-point effect virtually always is detected.

Samples Can Be Too Large

At this point, you might think that the sample size always should be as large as possible in order to maximize the detection of a false H_0. Not so. An excessively large sample size produces an extra-sensitive hypothesis test that detects even a very small effect that, from almost any perspective, lacks importance. For example, an excessively large sample size could cause H_0 to be rejected, even though vitamin C actually increases the population mean IQ by only $1/2$ point. Since from almost any perspective this very small effect lacks importance, most investigators would just as soon miss it; that is, most would just as soon retain this false H_0. Thus, before an experiment, a wise investigator attempts to select a sample size that, because it is not excessively large, minimizes the detection of a small, unimportant effect.

Samples Can Be Too Small

On the other hand, the sample size can be too small. An unduly small sample size will produce an insensitive hypothesis test (with a large standard error) that will miss even a very large, important effect. For example, an unduly small sample size can cause H_0 to be retained, even though vitamin C actually increases the population mean IQ by 15 points. Before an experiment, a wise investigator also attempts to select a sample size that, because it is not unduly small, maximizes the detection of a large, important effect.

Neither Too Large Nor Too Small

For the purposes of most investigators, a sample size of hundreds is excessively large and one of less than about five is unduly small. There remains, of course, considerable latitude for sample size selection between these rough extremities. Statistics supplies investigators with charts, often referred to as *power curves*, to help select the appropriate sample size for a particular experiment.

Progress Check *11.8 Comment critically on the following experimental reports:

(a) Using a group of 4 subjects, an investigator announces that H_0 was retained at the .05 level of significance.

(b) Using a group of 600 subjects, an investigator reports that H_0 was rejected at the .05 level of significance.

Answers on page 503.

11.11 POWER AND SAMPLE SIZE

Power ($1 - \beta$)

The probability of detecting a particular effect.

The **power** of a hypothesis test *equals the probability* $(1 - \beta)$ *of detecting a particular effect* when the null hypothesis (H_0) is false. Power is simply the complement $(1 - \beta)$ of the probability (β) of failing to detect the effect, that is, the complement of the probability of a type II error. The color-shaded sectors in Figures 11.4, 11.5, and 11.6 illustrate varying degrees of power.

In Figures 11.5 and 11.6, sample sizes of 36 and 100 were selected, with computational convenience in mind, to dramatize different degrees of power for a small three-point effect of vitamin C on IQ. Preferably, the selection of sample size should reflect—as much as circumstances permit—your considered judgment about what constitutes (1) the smallest important effect and (2) a reasonable degree of power for detecting that effect. For example, the following considerations might influence the selection of a new sample size for the vitamin C study.

1. The smallest effect that merits detection, we might conclude, equals seven points. This might reflect our judgment, possibly supported by educational consultants, that only a mean IQ of at least 107 for all students in the school district justifies the effort and expense of upgrading the entire curriculum. Another possible reason for focusing on a seven-point effect—in the absence of any compelling reason to the contrary—might be that, since 7 is about one-half the size of the standard deviation of 15, it avoids extreme effect sizes by qualifying as a "medium" effect size, according to Jacob Cohen's widely adopted guidelines described in Section 14.9.

2. A reasonable degree of power for this seven-point effect, we might conclude, equals .80. This degree of power will detect the specified effect with a tolerable rate of eighty times out of one hundred. In the absence of special concerns about the type II error, many investigators would choose .80 as a default value for power—along with .05 as the default value for the level of significance—to avoid the large sample sizes required by high degrees of power, such as .95 or .99.

Power Curve

Shows how the likelihood of detecting any possible effect varies for a fixed sample size.

Power Curves

Basically, a **power curve** *shows how the likelihood of detecting any possible effect*—ranging from very small to very large—*varies for a fixed sample size.**

....

*For more information about power curves, see J. Cohen, A power primer. *Psychological Bulletin*, 1992, vol. 112, 155–159.

With just a few key strokes, Minitab's *Power and Sample Size* software calculates that a sample size of 29 will satisfy the original specifications to detect a seven-point effect with power .80. The upper (solid line) power curve in **Figure 11.7** is based on a sample size of 29, and it features a colored dot whose coordinates are a seven-point effect (difference) and a power of .80.

The S-shaped power curve for a sample of 29 also shows the growth in power with increases in effect size. Verify that power equals only about .40 for a smaller four-point effect and about .95 for a larger ten-point effect. A four-point effect will be detected only about forty times in one hundred, while a ten-point effect will be detected about ninety-five times in one hundred.

Practical considerations, such as limitations in money or facilities, might force a reduction (always painful) in the prescribed sample size of 29. Although the original specifications represent our best judgment about an appropriate sample size, there usually is latitude for compromise. For example, referring to Figure 11.7, we could consider the properties of the lower (broken line) power curve for a smaller sample size of 13. (Ordinarily, to minimize the loss of power, we probably would have considered power curves for more modest reductions in the original sample size, such as 28, 27, etc., but we selected the power curve for 13 to accentuate the graphic differences between the curves in Figure 11.7.) The colored dot on the power curve for a sample of 13 indicates that a seven-point effect will be detected with power of approximately .50. Most investigators would be reluctant to reduce sample size to 13 since a seven-point effect would be missed about as often as it is detected, that is, about fifty times in one hundred.

The sample size of 29 also could be reduced indirectly by compromising other properties of the original specifications. We could reduce the prescribed sample size by *enlarging* the smallest important effect (preferably by small increments above the seven-point effect); by *lowering* the degree of power

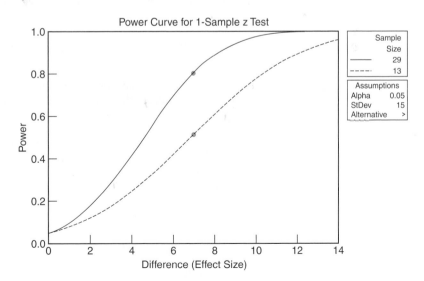

FIGURE 11.7

Power Curve by Minitab for Vitamin C experiment, given n = 29 (solid line) and n = 13 (broken line).

(preferably not much below .80); by *increasing* the level of significance (preferably not above .10); by *selecting,* if appropriate, a one-tailed rather than a two-tailed test (if this had not been done already in the vitamin C investigation); or by taking some combination of these actions. For instance, we could enlarge the smallest important effect from seven to eight points. Although not shown in Figure 11.7, Minitab calculates that a smaller sample of 22 detects the larger eight-point effect with power equal to .80.

Since a power analysis depends on a number factors, including the investigator's subjective judgment about what constitutes a *reasonable* detection rate for the *smallest* important effect—as well as the availability of local resources and any subsequent compromises—two equally competent investigators might select different sample sizes for the same study. Nonetheless, in the hands of a judicious investigator,

> **the use of power curves represents a distinct improvement over the arbitrary selection of sample size, for power curves help identify a sample size that, being neither unduly small nor excessively large, produces a hypothesis test with the proper sensitivity.**

Power Analysis of Studies by Others

If you suspect that another investigator's reported *failure to reject H_0* might have been caused by an unduly small sample size, power curves can be consulted retroactively to evaluate the adequacy of the publicized results. For example, if the sample size reported for a vitamin C study had been only 13, you could have consulted the lower curve in Figure 11.7 to establish that your smallest important effect of seven points would have been detected with a very low power of approximately .50. You could have endorsed, therefore, the need for a *replication* or duplication of the original study with a more powerful, larger sample size.

Need Not Predict True Effect Size

The use of power curves does not require that you predict the *true* effect size—an impossible task—but merely that you specify the smallest effect that, *if present,* merits detection. If the true effect size actually is larger than the specified effect, the true power actually will exceed the specified power—since more of the true sampling distribution overlaps the rejection region for the false H_0 than does the sampling distribution for the specified effect. (If this is not obvious, compare Figures 11.4 and 11.5.) Thus, a more important effect is even more likely to be detected. On the other hand, if the true effect size actually is smaller than the specified effect, the entire process works in reverse but still to your advantage, since an unimportant effect, which you would just as soon miss, is even less likely to be detected.

Initiating a Power Analysis

It is beyond the scope of this book to provide detailed information about either manual or electronic calculations for a power analysis. Manual calculations are described in Chapter 8 of D. C. Howell, *Statistical Methods for*

Psychology, 7th ed. (Belmont, CA: Wadsworth, 2010). Electronic calculations are made by each of the three statistical packages—Minitab, SPSS, and SAS—featured in this book, as well a number of free Internet Web sites, such as G*Power at http://www.psycho.uni-duesseldorf.de/abteilungen/aap/gpower3/. Once you have decided what constitutes the smallest important effect that merits detection with a certain power, the step-by-step details of a power analysis, whether manual or electronic, usually are straightforward and amenable to any power analysis that you yourself might initiate.

Progress Check *11.9 Consult the power curves in Figure 11.7 to estimate the approximate detection rates, rounded to the nearest tenth, for the following situations:

(a) a three-point effect, with a sample size of 29

(b) a six-point effect, with a sample size of 13

(c) a twelve-point effect, with a sample size of 13

Progress Check *11.10 An investigator consults a chart to determine the sample size required to detect an eight-point effect with a probability of .80. What happens to this detection rate of .80—will it actually be *smaller*, the *same*, or *larger*—if, unknown to the investigator, the true effect actually equals

(a) twelve points?

(b) five points?

Answers on page 503.

INTERNET DEMONSTRATION
Go to the Web site for this book (http://www.wiley.com\college\witte).
Click on the *Student Companion Site,* then *Internet Demonstrations,* and finally ***Power*** to determine how power—the probability of detecting a false null hypothesis—varies with the size of the effect and also with the size of the sample.

Summary

Chance must be considered when we make a decision about the null hypothesis (H_0) by determining whether an observed difference qualifies as a common or rare outcome. Even though we never know whether or not a particular decision about the null hypothesis is correct, it is reassuring that, in the long run, most decisions will be correct, assuming that the null hypotheses are either true or seriously false.

The decision to retain H_0 is weak; it implies only that H_0 *could* be true, whereas the decision to reject H_0 is strong; it implies that H_0 is *probably* false (and conversely that H_1 is *probably* true).

Although the research hypothesis, rather than the null hypothesis, is of primary concern, the research hypothesis is usually identified with the alternative hypothesis and tested indirectly for two reasons: (1) it lacks the necessary precision, and (2) logical considerations, based on the fact that rejecting the null hypothesis (on the basis of one negative instance or a rare outcome) is a stronger decision than retaining the null hypothesis.

Use a more sensitive one-tailed test only when, before an investigation, there's an exclusive concern about deviations in a particular direction. Otherwise, use a two-tailed test.

Select the statistical hypotheses from among the following three possibilities: For a two-tailed, nondirectional test,

$$H_0: \mu = \text{some number}$$
$$H_1: \mu \neq \text{some number}$$

For a one-tailed or directional test with the lower tail critical,

$$H_0: \mu \geq \text{some number}$$
$$H_1: \mu < \text{some number}$$

For a one-tailed or directional test with the upper tail critical,

$$H_0: \mu \leq \text{some number}$$
$$H_1: \mu > \text{some number}$$

Unless there are obvious reasons for selecting either a larger or a smaller level of significance, use the customary .05 level.

There are four possible outcomes for any hypothesis test:

- If H_0 really is true, it is a correct decision to retain the true H_0.
- If H_0 really is true, it is a type I error to reject the true H_0.
- If H_0 really is false, it is a type II error to retain the false H_0.
- If H_0 really is false, it is a correct decision to reject the false H_0.

When generalizing beyond the existing data, there is always the possibility of a type I or type II error. At best, a hypothesis test tends to produce a correct decision when either H_0 really is true or H_0 really is false because of a large effect.

If H_0 really is true, the probability of a type I error, α, equals the level of significance, and the probability of a correct decision equals $1 - \alpha$.

If H_0 really is false, the probability of a type II error, β, and the probability of a correct decision, $1 - \beta$, depend on the size of the effect—that is, the difference between the true and the hypothesized population means. The larger the effect, the lower the probability of a type II error and the higher the probability of a correct decision.

To increase the probability of detecting a false H_0, even a false H_0 that reflects a very small effect, use a larger sample size.

It is desirable to select a sample size that, being neither unduly small nor excessively large, produces a hypothesis test with the proper sensitivity.

Power curves help the investigator select a sample size that ensures a reasonable detection rate for the smallest important effect. If the originally specified sample size is too large, it can be reduced by *enlarging* the smallest important effect; by *lowering* the degree of power; by *increasing* the level of significance; by *selecting,* if appropriate, a one-tailed test; or by taking some combination of these actions.

Important Terms

Two-tailed or nondirectional test	**Hypothesized sampling distribution**
One-tailed or directional test	**True sampling distribution**
Type I error	**Beta (β)**
Type II error	**Power ($1 - \beta$)**
Alpha (α)	**Power curve**
Effect	

REVIEW QUESTIONS

11.11 A production line at a candy plant is designed to yield two-pound boxes of assorted candies whose weights in fact follow a normal distribution with a mean of 33 ounces and a standard deviation of .30 ounce. A random sample of 36 boxes from the production of the most recent shift reveals a mean weight of 33.09 ounces. (Incidentally, if you think about it, this is an exception to the usual situation where the investigator hopes to reject the null hypothesis.)

(a) Describe the population being tested.

(b) Using the customary procedure, test the null hypothesis at the .05 level of significance.

(c) Someone uses a one-tailed test, upper tail critical, because the sample mean of 33.09 exceeds the hypothesized population mean of 33. Any comment?

11.12 Re-read the problem described in Question 10.5 on page 219.

(a) What form should H_0 and H_1 take if the investigator is concerned only about salary discrimination against female members?

(b) If this hypothesis test supports the conclusion of salary discrimination against female members, a costly class-action suit will be initiated against American colleges and universities. Under these circumstances, do you recommend using the .05 or the .01 level of significance? Why?

*11.13 Recalling the vitamin C experiment described in this chapter, you could describe the null hypothesis in both symbols and words as follows:

H_0: $\mu \leq 100$, that is, vitamin C does not increase IQ

Following the format of Table 11.2 and being as specific as possible, you could describe the four possible outcomes of the vitamin C experiment as follows:

	STATUS OF H_0	
DECISION	**TRUE H_0**	**FALSE H_0**
Retain H_0	*Correct Decision:* Conclude that there is no evidence that vitamin C increases IQ when in fact it doesn't.	*Type II Error:* Conclude that there is no evidence that vitamin C increases IQ when in fact it does.
Reject H_0	*Type I Error:* Conclude that vitamin C increases IQ when in fact it doesn't.	*Correct Decision:* Conclude that vitamin C increases IQ when in fact it does.

Using the answer for the vitamin C experiment as a model, specify the null hypothesis and the four possible outcomes for each of the following exercises:

*(a) Question 11.1(b) on page 233.
Answer on page 503.

(b) Question 11.1(c).

11.14 We must be concerned about four possible outcomes *before* conducting a hypothesis test.

(a) Assuming that the test already has been conducted and the *null hypothesis has been retained*, about which of the four possible outcomes must we still be concerned?

(b) Assuming that the test already has been conducted and the *null hypothesis has been rejected*, about which of the four possible outcomes must we still be concerned?

11.15 Using the .05 level of significance, an investigator retains H_0. There is, he concludes, a probability of .95 that H_0 is true. Comments?

11.16 In another study, an investigator rejects H_0 at the .01 level of significance. There is, she concludes, a probability of .99 that H_0 is false. Comments?

11.17 For a projected one-tailed test, lower tail critical, at the .05 level of significance, construct two rough graphs. Each graph should show the sector in the true sampling distribution that produces a type II error and the sector that produces a correct decision. One graph should reflect the case when H_0 really is false because the true population mean is *slightly less* than the hypothesized population mean, and the other graph should reflect the case when H_0 really is false because the true population mean is *appreciably less* than the hypothesized population mean. (**Hint:** First, identify the decision rule for the hypothesized population mean, and then draw the true sampling distribution for each case.)

11.18 How should a projected hypothesis test be modified if you're particularly concerned about

(a) the type I error?

(b) the type II error?

CHAPTER 12

Estimation
(Confidence Intervals)

Summary / Important Terms / Key Equation / Review Questions

Preview

As a research area matures, the use of confidence intervals becomes more prevalent. A hypothesis test merely indicates whether an effect is present. A confidence interval is more informative since it indicates, with a known degree of confidence, the range of possible effects. A confidence interval can appear either in isolation or in the aftermath of a test that has rejected the null hypothesis.

In Chapter 10, an investigator was concerned about detecting any difference between the mean SAT reading score for all local freshmen and the national average. This concern led to a z test and the conclusion that the mean for the local population exceeds the national average. Given a concern about the national average, this conclusion is most informative; it might even create some joy among local university officials. However, the same SAT investigation could have been prompted by a wish merely to *estimate* the value of the local population mean rather than to test *a hypothesis* based on the national average. This new concern translates into an estimation problem, and with the aid of point estimates and confidence intervals, information in a sample can be used to estimate the unknown population mean for all local freshmen.

12.1 POINT ESTIMATE FOR μ

Point Estimate

A single value that represents some unknown population characteristic, such as the population mean.

A *point estimate* for μ uses a single value to represent the unknown population mean.

This is the most straightforward type of estimate. If a random sample of 100 local freshmen reveals a sample mean SAT score of 533, then 533 will be the point estimate of the unknown population mean for all local freshmen. The best single point estimate for the unknown population mean is simply the observed value of the sample mean.

A Basic Deficiency

Although straightforward, simple, and precise, point estimates suffer from a basic deficiency. They tend to be inaccurate. Because of sampling variability, it's unlikely that a single sample mean, such as 533, will coincide with the population mean. Since point estimates convey no information about the degree of inaccuracy due to sampling variability, statisticians supplement point estimates with another, more realistic type of estimate, known as *interval estimates* or *confidence intervals*.

Progress Check *12.1 A random sample of 200 graduates of U.S. colleges reveals a mean annual income of $62,600. What is the best estimate of the unknown mean annual income for all graduates of U.S. colleges?

Answer on page 504.

12.2 CONFIDENCE INTERVAL (CI) FOR μ

Confidence Interval (CI)

A range of values that, with a known degree of certainty, includes an unknown population characteristic, such as a population mean.

A *confidence interval* for μ uses a range of values that, with a known degree of certainty, includes the unknown population mean.

For instance, the SAT investigator might use a confidence interval to claim, *with 95 percent confidence,* that the interval between 511.44 and 554.56 includes the population mean reading score for all local freshmen. To be 95 percent confident signifies that if many of these intervals were constructed for a long series of samples, approximately 95 percent would include the population mean for all local freshmen. In the long run, 95 percent of these confidence intervals are true because they include the unknown population mean. The remaining 5 percent are false because they fail to include the unknown population mean.

Why Confidence Intervals Work

To understand confidence intervals, you must view them in the context of three important properties of the sampling distribution of the mean described in Chapter 10. For the sampling distribution from which the sample mean of 533 originates, as shown in **Figure 12.1**, the three important properties are as follows:

- The mean of the sampling distribution equals the unknown population mean for all local freshmen, whatever its value, because the mean of this sampling distribution always equals the population mean.
- The standard error of the sampling distribution equals the value (11) obtained from dividing the population standard deviation (110) by the square root of the sample size ($\sqrt{100}$).
- The shape of the sampling distribution approximates a normal distribution because the sample size of 100 satisfies the requirements of the central limit theorem.

A Series of Confidence Intervals

In practice, only one sample mean is actually taken from this sampling distribution and used to construct a single 95 percent confidence interval. However, imagine taking not just one but a series of randomly selected sample means from this sampling distribution. Because of sampling variability, these sample means tend to differ among themselves. For each sample mean, construct a 95 percent confidence interval by adding 1.96 standard errors to the sample mean and subtracting 1.96 standard errors from the sample mean; that is, use the expression

$$\bar{X} \pm 1.96\,\sigma_{\bar{X}},$$

to obtain a 95 percent confidence interval for each sample mean.

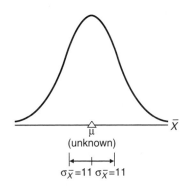

FIGURE 12.1
*Sampling distribution of the mean
(SAT scores).*

True Confidence Intervals

Why, according to statistical theory, do 95 percent of these confidence intervals include the unknown population mean? As indicated in **Figure 12.2**, because the sampling distribution is normal, 95 percent of all sample means are within 1.96 standard errors of the unknown population mean, that is, 95 percent of all sample means deviate less than *1.96 standard errors from the unknown*

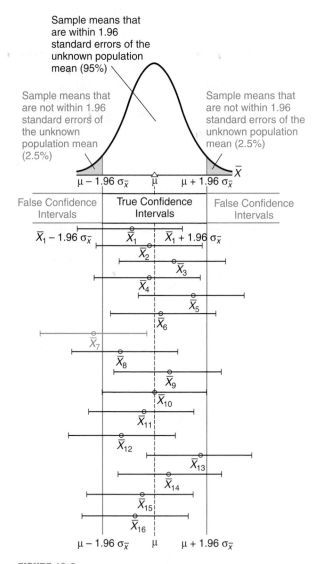

FIGURE 12.2

A series of 95 percent confidence intervals (emerging from a sampling distribution).

population mean. Therefore, and this is the key point, when sample means are expanded into confidence intervals—by adding and subtracting 1.96 standard errors—95 percent of all possible confidence intervals are true because they include the unknown population mean. To illustrate this point, fifteen of the sixteen sample means shown in Figure 12.2 are within 1.96 standard errors of the unknown population mean. The corresponding fifteen confidence intervals, shown in black, have ranges that span the broken line for the population mean, thereby qualifying as true intervals because they include the value of the unknown population mean.

False Confidence Intervals

Five percent of all confidence intervals fail to include the unknown population mean. As indicated in Figure 12.2, 5 percent of all sample means (2.5 percent in each tail) deviate more than 1.96 standard errors from the unknown population mean. Therefore, when sample means are expanded into confidence intervals— by adding and subtracting 1.96 standard errors—5 percent of all possible confidence intervals are false because they fail to include the unknown population mean. To illustrate this point, only one of the sixteen sample means shown in Figure 12.2 is not within 1.96 standard errors of the unknown population mean. The resulting confidence interval, shown in color, has a range that does not span the broken line for the population mean, thereby being designated as a false interval because it fails to include the value of the unknown population mean.

Confidence Interval for μ Based on z

To determine the previously reported confidence interval of 511.44 to 554.56 for the unknown mean reading score of all local freshmen, use the following general expression:

CONFIDENCE INTERVAL FOR μ (BASED ON z)

$$\bar{X} \pm (z_{conf})(\sigma_{\bar{X}}) \qquad (12.1)$$

---

where $\bar{X}$ represents the sample mean; z_{conf} represents a number from the standard normal table that satisfies the confidence specifications for the confidence interval; and $\sigma_{\bar{X}}$ represents the standard error of the mean.

Given that $\bar{X}$, the sample mean SAT reading score, equals 533, that z_{conf} equals 1.96 (from the standard normal tables, where z scores of ± 1.96 define the middle 95 percent of the area under the normal curve), and that the standard error, $\sigma_{\bar{X}}$, equals 11, Formula 12.1 becomes

$$533 \pm (1.96)(11) = 533 \pm 21.56 = \begin{cases} 554.56 \\ 511.44 \end{cases}$$

where 554.56 and 511.44 represent the upper and lower limits of the confidence interval. Now it can be claimed, with 95 percent confidence, that the interval between 511.44 and 554.56 includes the value of the unknown mean reading score for all local freshmen.

Two Assumptions

The use of Formula 12.1 to construct confidence intervals assumes that the population standard deviation is known and that the population is normal or that the sample size is sufficiently large—at least 25—to satisfy the requirements of the central limit theorem.

Progress Check *12.2 Reading achievement scores are obtained for a group of fourth graders. A score of 4.0 indicates a level of achievement appropriate for fourth grade, a score below 4.0 indicates underachievement, and a score above 4.0 indicates overachievement. Assume that the population standard deviation equals 0.4. A random sample of 64 fourth graders reveals a mean achievement score of 3.82.

(a) Construct a 95 percent confidence interval for the unknown population mean. (Remember to convert the standard deviation to a standard error.)

(b) Interpret this confidence interval; that is, do you find any consistent evidence either of overachievement or of underachievement?

Answers on page 504.

12.3 INTERPRETATION OF A CONFIDENCE INTERVAL

A 95 percent confidence claim reflects a long-term performance rating for an extended series of confidence intervals. If a series of confidence intervals is constructed to estimate the same population mean, as in Figure 12.2, approximately 95 percent of these intervals should include the population mean. In practice, only one confidence interval, not a series of intervals, is constructed, and that one interval is either true or false, because it either includes the population mean or fails to include the population mean. Of course, *we never really know whether a particular confidence interval is true or false* unless the entire population is surveyed. However,

> when the level of confidence equals 95 percent or more, we can be *reasonably confident* that the one observed confidence interval includes the true population mean.

For instance, we can be *reasonably confident* that the true population mean reading score for all local freshmen is neither less than 511.44 nor more than 554.56. That's the same as being *reasonably confident* that the true population mean for all local freshmen is between 511.44 and 554.56.

Progress Check *12.3 Before taking the GRE, a random sample of college seniors received special training on how to take the test. After analyzing their scores on the GRE, the investigator reported a dramatic gain, relative to the national average of 500, as indicated by a 95 percent confidence interval of 507 to 527. Are the following interpretations True or False?

(a) About 95 percent of all subjects scored between 507 and 527.

(b) The interval from 507 to 527 refers to possible values of the population mean for all students who undergo special training.

(c) The true population mean definitely is between 507 and 527.

(d) This *particular* interval describes the population mean about 95 percent of the time.

(e) In practice, we never really know whether the interval from 507 to 527 is true or false.

(f) We can be reasonably confident that the population mean is between 507 and 527.

Answers on page 504.

12.4 LEVEL OF CONFIDENCE

Level of Confidence

The percent of time that a series of confidence intervals includes the unknown population characteristic, such as the population mean.

The **level of confidence** *indicates the percent of time that a series of confidence intervals includes the unknown population characteristic, such as the population mean.* Any level of confidence may be assigned to a confidence interval merely by substituting an appropriate value for z_{conf} in Formula 12.1. For instance, to construct a 99 percent confidence interval from the data for SAT reading scores, first consult Table A in Appendix C to verify that z_{conf} values of ± 2.58 define the middle 99 percent of the total area under the normal curve. Then substitute numbers for symbols in Formula 12.1 to obtain

$$533 \pm (2.58)(11) = 533 \pm 28.38 = \begin{cases} 561.38 \\ 504.62 \end{cases}$$

It can be claimed, *with 99 percent confidence,* that the interval between 504.62 and 561.38 includes the value of the unknown mean reading score for all local freshmen. This implies that, in the long run, 99 percent of these confidence intervals will include the unknown population mean.

Effect on Width of Interval

Notice that the 99 percent confidence interval of 504.62 to 561.38 is wider and, therefore, less precise than the corresponding 95 percent confidence interval of 511.44 to 554.56. The shift from a 95 percent to a 99 percent level of confidence requires an increase in the value of z_{conf} from 1.96 to 2.58. This increase, in turn, causes a wider, less precise confidence interval. Any shift to a higher level of confidence always produces a wider, less precise confidence interval unless offset by an increase in sample size, as mentioned in the next section.

Choosing a Level of Confidence

Although many different levels of confidence have been used, 95 percent and 99 percent are the most prevalent. Generally, a larger level of confidence, such as 99 percent, should be reserved for situations in which a false interval might have particularly serious consequences, such as the failure of a national opinion pollster to predict the winner of a presidential election.

12.5 EFFECT OF SAMPLE SIZE

The larger the sample size, the smaller the standard error and, hence, the more precise (narrower) the confidence interval will be. Indeed, as the sample size grows larger, the standard error will approach zero and the confidence interval will shrink to a point estimate. Given this perspective, the sample size for a confidence interval, unlike that for a hypothesis test, never can be too large.

Selection of Sample Size

As with hypothesis tests, sample size can be selected according to specifications established before the investigation. To generate a confidence interval that possesses the desired precision (width), yet complies with the desired level of confidence, refer to formulas for sample size in other statistics books.* Valid use of these formulas requires that before the investigation, the population standard deviation be either known or estimated.

Progress Check *12.4 On the basis of a random sample of 120 adults, a pollster reports, with 95 percent confidence, that between 58 and 72 percent of all Americans believe in life after death.

(a) If this interval is too wide, what, if anything, can be done with the existing data to obtain a narrower confidence interval?

(b) What can be done to obtain a narrower 95 percent confidence interval if another similar investigation is being planned?

Answers on page 504.

INTERNET DEMONSTRATION
Go to the Web site for this book (http://www.wiley.com\college\witte).
Click on the *Student Companion Site,* then *Internet Demonstration,* and finally *Confidence Intervals* to determine whether an extended series of 95 percent and 99 percent confidence intervals cover a known population mean the specified percent of times.

*For instance, see Section 17.8 in B. M. King and E. W. Minium, *Statistical Reasoning in the Behavioral Sciences,* 5th ed. (Hoboken, NJ: Wiley, 2008).

12.6 HYPOTHESIS TESTS
OR CONFIDENCE INTERVALS?

Ordinarily, data are used either to test a hypothesis or to construct a confidence interval, but not both. Hypothesis tests usually have been preferred to confidence intervals in the behavioral sciences, and that emphasis is reflected in this book. As a matter of fact, however, *confidence intervals tend to be more informative than hypothesis tests.*

Hypothesis tests merely indicate whether or not an effect is present, whereas confidence intervals indicate the possible size of the effect.

For the vitamin C experiment described in Chapter 11, a hypothesis test merely indicates whether or not vitamin C has an effect on IQ scores, whereas a 95 percent confidence interval indicates the possible size of the effect of vitamin C on IQ scores; for instance, we could claim, with 95 percent confidence, that the interval between 102 and 112 includes the true population mean IQ for students who receive vitamin C. In other words, the true effect of vitamin C is probably somewhere between 2 and 12 IQ points (above the null hypothesized value of 100).

When to Use Confidence Intervals

If the primary concern is whether or not an effect is present—as is often the case in relatively new research areas—use a hypothesis test. For example, given that a social psychologist is uncertain whether the consumption of alcohol by witnesses increases the number of inaccuracies in their recall of a simulated robbery, it would be appropriate to use a hypothesis test. Otherwise, given that previous research clearly demonstrates alcohol-induced inaccuracies in witnesses' testimonies, a new investigator might use a confidence interval to estimate the possible mean number of these inaccuracies.

Indeed, you should consider using a confidence interval whenever a hypothesis test results in the rejection of the null hypothesis. For example, referring again to the vitamin C experiment proposed in Chapter 11, after it's been established (by rejecting the null hypothesis) that vitamin C has an effect on IQ scores, it makes sense to estimate, with a 95 percent confidence interval, that the interval between 102 and 112 describes the possible size of that effect, namely, an increase (above 100) of between 2 and 12 IQ points.

12.7 CONFIDENCE INTERVAL
FOR POPULATION PERCENT

Margin of Error
That which is added to and subtracted from some sample value, such as the sample proportion or sample mean, to obtain the limits of a confidence interval.

Let's describe briefly a type of confidence interval—that for population percents or proportions—often encountered in the media. For example, a recent news release reported that among a random or "scientific" sample of 1500 adult Americans, 64 percent favor some form of capital punishment. Furthermore, the **margin of error** equals ±3 percent, given that we wish to be 95 percent confident of our results. Rephrased slightly, this is the same as claiming, with 95 percent confidence, that the interval between 61 and 67 percent (from 64 ± 3) includes the true percent of Americans who favor some form of capital punishment.

Essentially, this 95 percent confidence interval originates from the following expression:

$$sample\ percent \pm (1.96)(standard\ error\ of\ the\ percent)$$

where 1.96 comes from the standard normal curve and the standard error of the percent is analogous to the standard error of the mean.* Otherwise, all of the previous comments about confidence intervals for population means apply to confidence intervals for population percents or proportions. Thus, in the present case, we can be reasonably certain that the true population percent is between 61 and 67 percent.

Sample Size and Margin of Error

Often encountered in national polls, the huge sample of 1500 Americans reduces the size of the standard error and thereby guarantees a relatively small margin of error of ±3 percent. If, in the pollster's judgment, a larger margin of error would have been tolerable, smaller samples could have been used. For instance, if a larger margin of error of ±5 percent would have been tolerable, a random sample of about 500 adults could have been used, while if a still larger margin of error of ±10 percent would have been tolerable, a random sample of about only 100 adults could have been used.

Pollsters Use Larger Samples

In any event, pollsters often use samples in the hundreds, or even the thousands, to produce narrower, more precise confidence intervals. When contrasted with the much smaller samples of most researchers, these larger samples reflect a number of factors, including the relative cheapness of pollsters' observations, often just a randomly dialed phone call away, as well as the notion that samples can never be too large in surveys—although they can be too large in experiments, as discussed in Section 11.10.

A Final Caution

When based on randomly selected respondents, confidence intervals reflect only one kind of error—the *statistical* error due to random sampling variability. There are other kinds of *nonstatistical* errors that could compromise the value of a confidence interval. For example, the previous estimate that 61 to 67 percent of all Americans favor capital punishment might have been inflated by adding to a neutral question such as "Do you favor capital punishment?" a biased phrase, "in

----

*A proportion (or a percent, which is merely 100 times a proportion) is a special type of mean where, after all observations have been coded as either 0 or 1, the 1s are added and divided by the total number of observations. Therefore, although not emphasized in this book, the standard error of the proportion (or percent) could be obtained from the formula for the standard error of the mean.

view of the recent epidemic of murders of innocent children?" Or the previous interval might fail to reflect the targeted population of all adult Americans because the random sample actually reflects a severely limited population. For example, there might be a substantial number of nonrespondents (often as high as 30 percent) whose attitudes toward capital punishment differ appreciably from the attitudes of those who responded. In the absence of this kind of background information, reports of confidence intervals should be interpreted cautiously.

Progress Check *12.5 In a recent scientific sample of about 900 adult Americans, 70 percent favor some form of stricter gun control, with a margin of error of ±4 percent for a 95 percent confidence interval. Therefore, the 95 percent confidence interval equals 66 to 74 percent. Indicate whether the following interpretations are True or False:

(a) The interval from 66 to 74 percent refers to possible values of the sample percent.

(b) The true population percent is between 66 and 74 percent.

(c) In the long run, a series of intervals similar to this one would fail to include the population percent about 5 percent of the time.

(d) We can be reasonably confident that the population percent is between 66 and 74 percent.

Answers on page 504.

Other Types of Confidence Intervals

Confidence intervals can be constructed not only for population means and percents but also for differences between two population means, as discussed in subsequent chapters. Although not discussed in this book, confidence intervals also can be constructed for other characteristics of populations, including variances and correlation coefficients.

Summary

Rather than test a hypothesis about a single population mean, you might choose to estimate this population characteristic, using a point estimate or a confidence interval.

In point estimation, a single sample characteristic, such as a sample mean, estimates the corresponding population characteristic. Point estimates ignore sampling variability and, therefore, tend to be inaccurate.

Confidence intervals specify ranges of values that, in the long run, include the unknown population characteristic, such as the mean, a certain percent of the time. For instance, given a 95 percent confidence interval, then, in the long run, approximately 95 percent of all of these confidence intervals are true because they include the unknown population characteristic. Confidence intervals work because they are products of sampling distributions.

Any level of confidence can be assigned to a confidence interval, but the 95 percent and 99 percent levels are the most prevalent. Given one of these levels of confidence, then, even though we can never know whether a particular confidence interval is true or false, we can be reasonably confident that a particular interval actually includes the unknown population characteristic.

Narrower, more precise confidence intervals are produced by lower levels of confidence (for example, 95 percent rather than 99 percent) and by larger sample sizes.

Confidence intervals tend to be more informative than hypothesis tests. Hypothesis tests merely indicate whether or not an effect is present, whereas confidence intervals indicate the possible size of the effect. Whenever appropriate—including whenever the null hypothesis has been rejected—consider using confidence intervals.

Confidence intervals for population percents or proportions are similar, both in origin and interpretation, to confidence intervals for population means.

Important Terms
. . . .

Point estimate   **Confidence interval (CI)**

Level of confidence   **Margin of error**

Key Equation
. . . .

CONFIDENCE INTERVAL

$$\text{CI} = \bar{X} \pm (z_{conf})(\sigma_{\bar{X}})$$

REVIEW QUESTIONS

*12.6 In Question 10.5 on page 219, it was concluded that, the mean salary among the population of female members of the American Psychological Association is less than that ($82,500) for all comparable members who have a doctorate and teach full time.

(a) Given a population standard deviation of $6000 and a sample mean salary of $80,100 for a random sample of 100 female members, construct a 99 percent confidence interval for the mean salary for all female members.

(b) Given this confidence interval, is there any consistent evidence that the mean salary for all female members falls below $82,500, the mean salary for all members?

Answers on page 504.

12.7 In Review Question 11.11 on page 251, instead of testing a hypothesis, you might prefer to construct a confidence interval for the mean weight of all two-pound boxes of candy during a recent production shift.

(a) Given a population standard deviation of .30 ounce and a sample mean weight of 33.09 ounces for a random sample of 36 candy boxes, construct a 95 percent confidence interval.

(b) Interpret this interval, given the manufacturer's desire to produce boxes of candy that, on the average, exceed 32 ounces.

12.8 It's tempting to claim that, once a particular 95 percent confidence interval has been constructed, it includes the unknown population characteristic with a probability of .95. What is wrong with this claim?

*12.9 Imagine that one of the following 95 percent confidence intervals estimates the effect of vitamin C on IQ scores:

95% CONFIDENCE INTERVAL	LOWER LIMIT	UPPER LIMIT
1	102	108
2	95	104
3	112	115
4	90	111
5	91	98

(a) Which one most strongly supports the conclusion that vitamin C *increases* IQ scores?

(b) Which one implies the largest sample size?

(c) Which one most strongly supports the conclusion that vitamin C *decreases* IQ scores?

(d) Which one would most likely stimulate the investigator to conduct an additional experiment using larger sample sizes?

Answers on page 505.

12.10 Unlike confidence intervals, hypothesis tests require that some predetermined population value be used to evaluate sample values. Can you think of any other differences between hypothesis tests and confidence intervals?

CHAPTER 13

t Test for One Sample

Summary / Important Terms / Key Equations / Review Questions

Preview

The next three chapters describe various t tests. Whenever, as usually is the case, the population standard deviation is unknown, it must be estimated with the sample standard deviation. Estimating the unknown population standard deviation has important implications that require both the use of degrees of freedom and the replacement of the z test with the t test. (You might wish to review the discussion of degrees of freedom in Section 4.6.)

13.1 GAS MILEAGE INVESTIGATION

Federal law might eventually specify that new automobiles must average, for example, 45 miles per gallon (mpg) of gasoline. Because it's impossible to test all new cars, compliance tests would be based on random samples from the entire production of each car model. If a hypothesis test indicates substandard performance, the manufacturer would be penalized, we'll assume, $50 per car for the entire production.

In these tests, the null hypothesis states that, with respect to the mandated mean of 45 mpg, nothing special is happening in the population for some car model—that is, there is no substandard performance and the population mean equals or exceeds 45 mpg. The alternative hypothesis reflects a concern that the population mean is less than 45 mpg. Symbolically, the two statistical hypotheses read:

$$H_0: \mu \geq 45$$
$$H_1: \mu < 45$$

From the manufacturer's perspective, a type I error (a stiff penalty, even though the car complies with the standard) is very serious. Accordingly, to control the type I error, let's use the .01 instead of the customary .05 level of significance. From the federal regulator's perspective, a type II error (not penalizing the manufacturer even though the car fails to comply with the standard) also is serious. In practice, a sample size should be selected, as described in Section 11.11, to control the type II error, that is, to ensure a reasonable detection rate for the smallest decline (judged to be important) of the true population mean below the mandated 45 mpg. To simplify computations in the present example, however, the projected one-tailed test is based on data from a very small sample of only six randomly selected cars.

For reasons that will become apparent, the z test must be replaced by a new hypothesis test, the *t* test. Spend a few minutes familiarizing yourself with the boxed summary for the gas mileage investigation, noting the considerable similarities between it and summaries of previous hypothesis tests with the z test.

13.2 SAMPLING DISTRIBUTION OF *t*

Sampling Distribution of t

The distribution that would be obtained if a value of t were calculated for each sample mean for all possible random samples of a given size from some population.

Like the sampling distribution of z, the **sampling distribution of** *t represents the distribution that would be obtained if a value of* t *were calculated for each sample mean for all possible random samples of a given size from some population.* In the early 1900s, William Gosset discovered the sampling distribution of *t* and subsequently reported his achievement under the pen name of "Student." Actually, Gosset discovered not just one but an entire family of *t* sampling distributions (or "Student's" distributions). Each *t* distribution is associated with a special number referred to as *degrees of freedom*, first discussed in Section 4.6. The concept of degrees of freedom is introduced because we're using variability in a sample to estimate the unknown variability in the population. Recall that when the *n deviations about the sample mean* are used to estimate variability in the population, only $n - 1$ are free to vary because of the restriction that the sum

HYPOTHESIS TEST SUMMARY: *t* TEST FOR A POPULATION MEAN (GAS MILEAGE INVESTIGATION)

Research Problem

Does the mean gas mileage for some population of cars drop below the legally required minimum of 45 mpg?

Statistical Hypotheses

$$H_0: \mu \geq 45$$
$$H_1: \mu < 45$$

Decision Rule

Reject H_0 at the .01 level of significance if $t \leq -3.365$ (from Table B, Appendix C, given $df = n - 1 = 6 - 1 = 5$).

Calculations

Given $\overline{X} = 43$, $s_{\overline{X}} = 0.89$
(See Table 13.1 on page 277 for computations.)

$$t = \frac{43 - 45}{0.89} = -2.25$$

Decision

Retain H_0 at the .01 level of significance because $t = -2.25$ is less negative than -3.365.

Interpretation

The population mean gas mileage *could* equal the required 45 mpg or more. The manufacturer shouldn't be penalized.

Reminder:

Degrees of freedom (df) refers to the number of values free to vary when, for example, sample variability is used to estimate the unknown population variability.

---

of these deviations must always equal zero. Since one degree of freedom is lost because of the zero-sum restriction, there are only $n - 1$ degrees of freedom, that is, symbolically,

DEGREES OF FREEDOM (ONE SAMPLE)

$$df = n - 1 \qquad (13.1)$$

where *df* represents degrees of freedom and *n* equals the sample size.

Since the gas mileage investigation involves six cars, the corresponding *t* test is based on a sampling distribution with five degrees of freedom (from $df = 6 - 1$).

Compared to the Standard Normal Distribution

Figure 13.1 shows three *t* distributions. When there is an infinite (∞) number of degrees of freedom (and the sample standard deviation becomes the same as the population standard deviation), the distribution of *t* is the same as the standard normal distribution of *z*. Notice that even with only four or ten degrees of freedom, a *t* distribution shares a number of properties with the normal distribution. All *t* distributions are symmetrical, unimodal, and bell-shaped, with a dense concentration that peaks in the middle (when *t* equals 0) and tapers off both to the right and left of the middle (as *t* becomes more positive or negative, respectively). *The inflated tails of the* t *distribution, particularly apparent with small values of* df, *constitute the most important difference between* t *and* z *distributions.*

Table for *t* Distributions

To save space, tables for *t* distributions concentrate only on the critical values of *t* that correspond to the more common levels of significance. Table B of Appendix C lists the critical *t* values for either one- or two-tailed hypothesis tests at the .05, .01, and .001 levels of significance. All listed critical *t* values are positive and originate from the upper half of each distribution. Because of the symmetry of the *t* distribution, you can obtain the corresponding critical *t* values for the lower half of each distribution merely by placing a negative sign in front of any entry in the table.

Finding Critical *t* Values

To find a critical *t* in Table B, read the entry in the cell intersected by the row for the correct number of degrees of freedom and the column for the test specifications. For example, to find the critical *t* for the gas mileage investigation, first go to the right-hand panel for a one-tailed test, then locate both the row corresponding to five degrees of freedom and the column for a one-tailed test at the .01 level of significance. The intersected cell specifies 3.365. A negative sign

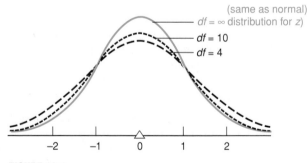

FIGURE 13.1
Various t *distributions.*

must be placed in front of 3.365, since the hypothesis test requires the lower tail to be critical. Thus, −3.365 is the critical *t* for the gas mileage investigation, and the corresponding decision rule is illustrated in **Figure 13.2**, where the distribution of *t* is centered about zero (the equivalent value of *t* for the original null hypothesized value of 45 mpg).

If the gas mileage investigation had involved a two-tailed test (still at the .01 level with five degrees of freedom), then the left-hand panel for a two-tailed test would have been appropriate, and the intersected cell would have specified 4.032. Both positive and negative signs would have to be placed in front of 4.032, since both tails are critical. In this case, ±4.032 would have been the pair of critical *t* values.

Missing *df* in Table B of Appendix C

If the desired number of degrees of freedom doesn't appear in the *df* column of Table B, use the row in the table with the next smallest number of degrees of freedom. For example, if 36 degrees of freedom are specified, use the information from the row for 30 degrees of freedom. Always rounding off to the next smallest *df* produces a slightly larger critical *t*, making the null hypothesis slightly more difficult to reject. This procedure defuses potential disputes about borderline decisions by investigators with a stake in rejecting the null hypothesis.

Progress Check *13.1 Find the critical *t* values for the following hypothesis tests:

(a) two-tailed test, $\alpha = .05$, $df = 12$

(b) one-tailed test, lower tail critical, $\alpha = .01$, $df = 19$

(c) one-tailed test, upper tail critical, $\alpha = .05$, $df = 38$

(d) two-tailed test, $\alpha = .01$, $df = 48$

 Answers on page 505.

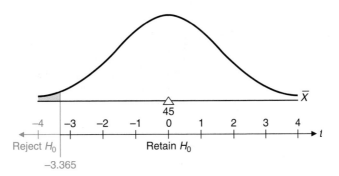

FIGURE 13.2
Hypothesized sampling distribution of t *(gas mileage investigation).*

13.3 *t* TEST

Usually, as in the gas mileage investigation, *the population standard deviation is unknown and must be estimated from the sample.* The subsequent shift from the standard error of the mean, $\sigma_{\bar{X}}$, to its estimate, $s_{\bar{X}}$, has an important effect on the entire hypothesis test for a population mean. The familiar *z* test,

$$z = \frac{sample\ mean - hypothesized\ population\ mean}{standard\ error} = \frac{\bar{X} - \mu_{hyp}}{\sigma_{\bar{X}}}$$

with its normal distribution, must be replaced by a new *t* test,

---

t Ratio

A replacement for the z ratio whenever the unknown population standard deviation must be estimated.

---

t RATIO FOR A SINGLE POPULATION MEAN
$$t = \frac{sample\ mean - hypothesized\ population\ mean}{estimated\ standard\ error} = \frac{\bar{X} - \mu_{hyp}}{s_{\bar{X}}} \quad (13.2)$$

with its *t* sampling distribution and $n-1$ degrees of freedom.

For the gas mileage investigation, given that the sample mean gas mileage, $\bar{X}$, equals 43; that the hypothesized population mean, μ_{hyp}, equals 45; and that the estimated standard error, $s_{\bar{X}}$, equals 0.89 (from Table 13.1), Formula 13.2 becomes

$$t = \frac{43 - 45}{0.89} = -2.25$$

with $df = 5$. Since the observed value of t (−2.25) is less negative than the critical value of t (−3.365), the null hypothesis is retained, and we can conclude that the auto manufacturer shouldn't be penalized since the mean gas mileage for the population cars could equal the mandated 45 mpg.

Greater Variability of *t* Ratio

As has been noted, the tails of the sampling distribution for *t* are more inflated than those for *z*, particularly when the sample size is small.* Consequently, to accommodate the greater variability of *t*, the critical *t* value must be larger than the corresponding critical *z* value. For example, given the one-tailed test at the .01 level of significance for the gas mileage investigation, the critical value for t (−3.365) is larger than that for z (−2.33).

---

*Essentially, the inflated tails are caused by the extra variability of the estimated standard error in the denominator of *t*. For a complete explanation, see Chapter 7 in D. C. Howell, *Statistical Methods for Psychology,* 7th ed. (Belmont, CA: Wadsworth, 2010).

13.4 COMMON THEME OF HYPOTHESIS TESTS

The remainder of this book discusses an alphabet variety of tests—*z, t, F, U, T,* and *H*—for an assortment of situations. Notwithstanding the new formulas with their special symbols,

> **all of these hypothesis tests represent variations on the same theme: If some observed characteristic, such as the mean for a random sample, qualifies as a rare outcome under the null hypothesis, the hypothesis will be rejected. Otherwise, the hypothesis will be retained.**

To determine whether an outcome is rare, the observed characteristic is converted to some new value, such as *t*, and compared with critical values from the appropriate sampling distribution. Generally, if the observed value equals or exceeds a positive critical value (or if it equals or is more negative than a negative critical value), the outcome will be viewed as rare and the null hypothesis will be rejected.

13.5 REMINDER ABOUT DEGREES OF FREEDOM

The notion of degrees of freedom is used throughout the remainder of this book. Typically, when it is used to estimate some unknown population characteristic, not all observed values within the sample are free to vary. For example, the gas mileage data consist of six values: 40, 44, 46, 41, 43, and 44. Nevertheless, the *t* test for these data has only five degrees of freedom because of the zero-sum restriction. Only five of these six observed values are free to vary about their mean of 43 and, therefore, provide valid information for purposes of estimation. The *concept of degrees of freedom is introduced only because we are using observations in a sample to estimate some unknown characteristic of the population.*

In subsequent sections, we'll encounter other mathematical restrictions, and sometimes several degrees of freedom will be lost. In any event, however, the degrees of freedom always indicate the number of values free to vary, given one or more mathematical restrictions on a set of values used to *estimate* some unknown population characteristic.

13.6 DETAILS: ESTIMATING THE STANDARD ERROR (s$_{\bar{x}}$)

If the population standard deviation is unknown, it must be estimated from the sample. This seemingly minor complication has important implications for hypothesis testing—indeed, it is the reason why the *z* test must be replaced by the *t* test. Now *s* replaces σ in the formula for the standard error of the mean. Instead of

$$\sigma_{\bar{X}} = \frac{\sigma}{\sqrt{n}}$$

we have

ESTIMATED STANDARD ERROR OF THE MEAN	
$$s_{\overline{X}} = \frac{s}{\sqrt{n}}$$	(13.3)

where $s_{\overline{x}}$ represents the estimated standard error of the mean; n equals the sample size; and s has been defined as

$$s = \sqrt{\frac{SS}{n-1}} = \sqrt{\frac{SS}{df}}$$

where s is the sample standard deviation; df refers to the degrees of freedom; and SS has been defined as

$$SS = \sum\left(X - \overline{X}\right)^2 = \sum X^2 - \frac{\left(\sum X\right)^2}{n}$$

This new version of the standard error, the **estimated standard error of the mean,** *is used whenever the unknown population standard deviation must be estimated.*

Progress Check *13.2 A consumers' group randomly samples 10 "one-pound" packages of ground beef sold by a supermarket. Calculate **(a)** the mean and **(b)** the estimated standard error of the mean for this sample, given the following weights in ounces: 16, 15, 14, 15, 14, 15, 16, 14, 14, 14.

(NOTE: Refer to Panels I and II of Table 13.1 for detailed guidance when calculating the mean and estimated standard error for this new set of data.)

    Answers on page 505.

13.7 DETAILS: CALCULATIONS FOR THE *t* TEST

The three panels in **Table 13.1** show the computational steps that produce a *t* of −2.25 for the gas mileage investigation.

Panel I

    This panel involves most of the computational labor, and it generates values for the sample mean, $\overline{X}$, and the sample standard deviation, s. The sample standard deviation is obtained by first using Formula 4.4 (on page 85) to calculate the sum of squares,

$$SS = \sum X^2 - \frac{\left(\sum X\right)^2}{n}$$

and after dividing the sum of squares, SS, by its degrees of freedom, $n - 1$, extracting the square root.

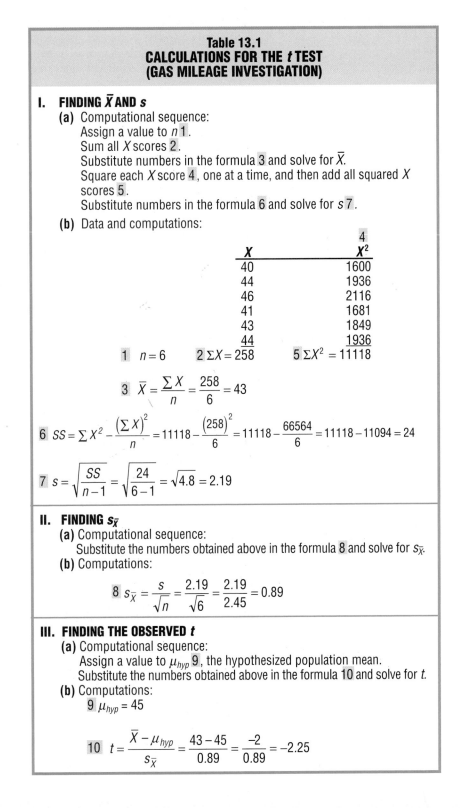

Table 13.1
CALCULATIONS FOR THE *t* TEST
(GAS MILEAGE INVESTIGATION)

I. FINDING $\bar{X}$ AND s

   (a) Computational sequence:
   Assign a value to *n* **1**.
   Sum all *X* scores **2**.
   Substitute numbers in the formula **3** and solve for $\bar{X}$.
   Square each *X* score **4**, one at a time, and then add all squared *X* scores **5**.
   Substitute numbers in the formula **6** and solve for *s* **7**.

   (b) Data and computations:

	X	**4** X^2
	40	1600
	44	1936
	46	2116
	41	1681
	43	1849
	44	1936
1 $n = 6$	**2** $\Sigma X = 258$	**5** $\Sigma X^2 = 11118$

   $$\text{3} \quad \bar{X} = \frac{\Sigma X}{n} = \frac{258}{6} = 43$$

   $$\text{6} \quad SS = \Sigma X^2 - \frac{(\Sigma X)^2}{n} = 11118 - \frac{(258)^2}{6} = 11118 - \frac{66564}{6} = 11118 - 11094 = 24$$

   $$\text{7} \quad s = \sqrt{\frac{SS}{n-1}} = \sqrt{\frac{24}{6-1}} = \sqrt{4.8} = 2.19$$

II. FINDING $s_{\bar{X}}$

   (a) Computational sequence:
   Substitute the numbers obtained above in the formula **8** and solve for $s_{\bar{X}}$.
   (b) Computations:

   $$\text{8} \quad s_{\bar{X}} = \frac{s}{\sqrt{n}} = \frac{2.19}{\sqrt{6}} = \frac{2.19}{2.45} = 0.89$$

III. FINDING THE OBSERVED *t*

   (a) Computational sequence:
   Assign a value to μ_{hyp} **9**, the hypothesized population mean.
   Substitute the numbers obtained above in the formula **10** and solve for *t*.
   (b) Computations:
   9 $\mu_{hyp} = 45$

   $$\text{10} \quad t = \frac{\bar{X} - \mu_{hyp}}{s_{\bar{X}}} = \frac{43 - 45}{0.89} = \frac{-2}{0.89} = -2.25$$

Panel II

Dividing the sample standard deviation, s, by the square root of the sample size, n, gives the value for the estimated standard error, $s_{\bar{X}}$.

Panel III

Finally, dividing the difference between the sample mean, $\bar{X}$, and the null hypothesized value, μ_{hyp}, by the estimated standard error, $s_{\bar{X}}$, yields the value of the t ratio.

Progress Check *13.3 The consumers' group in Question 13.2 suspects that a supermarket makes extra money by supplying less than the specified weight of 16 ounces in its "one-pound" packages of ground beef. Given that a random sample of 10 packages yields a mean of 14.7 ounces and an estimated standard error of the mean of 0.26 ounce, use the customary step-by-step procedure to test the null hypothesis at the .05 level of significance with t.

Answer on page 505.

13.8 CONFIDENCE INTERVALS FOR μ BASED ON t

Under slightly different circumstances, you might wish to estimate the unknown mean gas mileage for the population of cars, rather than test a hypothesis based on 45 mpg. For example, there might be no legally required minimum of 45 mpg, but merely a desire on the part of the manufacturer to estimate the mean gas mileage for a population of cars—possibly as a first step toward the design of a new, improved version of the current model.

When the population standard deviation is unknown and, therefore, must be estimated, as in the present case, t replaces z in the new formula for a confidence interval:

CONFIDENCE INTERVAL FOR μ BASED ON t

$$\bar{X} \pm (t_{conf})(s_{\bar{X}}) \tag{13.4}$$

---

where $\bar{X}$ represents the sample mean; t_{conf} represents a number (distributed with $n − 1$ degrees of freedom) from the t tables, which satisfies the confidence specifications for the confidence interval; and $s_{\bar{X}}$ represents the estimated standard error of the mean, defined in Formula 13.3.

Finding t_{conf}

To find the appropriate value for t_{conf} in Formula 13.4, refer to Table B in Appendix C. Read the entry from the cell intersected by the row for the correct number of degrees of freedom and the column for the confidence specifications. In the present case, if a 95 percent confidence interval is desired, first locate the row corresponding to 5 degrees of freedom (from $df = n − 1 = 6 − 1 = 5$), and then locate the column for the 95 percent level of confidence, that is, the column heading identified with a single asterisk. (A double asterisk identifies the column for the 99 percent level of confidence.) The intersected cell specifies that a value of 2.571 should be entered in Formula 13.4.*

Given this value for t_{conf}, as well as the values of 43 for $\bar{X}$ (from Table 13.1), the sample mean gas mileage, and 0.89 for $s_{\bar{X}}$, the estimated standard error, Formula 13.3 becomes

$$43 \pm (2.571)(0.89) = 43 \pm 2.29 = \begin{cases} 45.29 \\ 40.71 \end{cases}$$

It can be claimed, with 95 percent confidence, that the interval between 40.71 and 45.29 includes the true mean gas mileage for all of the cars in the population.

Interpretation

The interpretation of this confidence interval is the same as that based on z. In the long run, 95 percent of all confidence intervals, similar to the one just discussed, will include the unknown population mean. Although we never really know whether this particular confidence interval is true or false, we can be *reasonably confident* that the true mean for the entire population of cars is neither less than 40.71 mpg nor more than 45.29 mpg.

Progress Check *13.4 The consumers' group (in Question 13.3) concludes that, in spite of the claims of the supermarket, the mean weight of its "one-pound" packages of ground beef drops below the specified 16 ounces even when chance sampling variability is taken into account.

(a) Construct a 95 percent confidence interval for the true weight of all "one-pound" packages of ground beef.

(b) Interpret this confidence interval.
Answers on page 505.

13.9 ASSUMPTIONS

Whether testing hypotheses or constructing confidence intervals for population means, use t rather than z whenever, *as almost always is the case,* the population standard deviation is unknown. Strictly speaking, when using t, you must assume that the underlying population is normally distributed. Even if this normality assumption is violated, t retains much of its accuracy as long as the sample size isn't too small. If a very small sample (less than about 10) is being used

....

*Specifications for confidence intervals are taken from the left-hand panel of Table B because the symmetrical limits of a confidence interval are analogous to a two-tailed hypothesis test. Essentially, both procedures require that a specified number of standard errors be added and subtracted relative to either the value of the null hypothesis (to obtain the upper and lower critical values for a two-tailed hypothesis test) or the value of the sample mean (to obtain the upper and lower limits of a confidence interval).

and you believe that the sample originates from a non-normal population—possibly because of a pronounced positive or negative skew among the observations in the sample—it would be wise to increase the size of the sample before testing a hypothesis or constructing a confidence interval.

Summary

When the population standard deviation, σ, is unknown, it must be estimated with the sample standard deviation, s. By the same token, the standard error of the mean, $\sigma_{\bar{X}}$, then must be estimated with $s_{\bar{X}}$. Under these circumstances, t rather than z should be used to test a hypothesis or to construct a confidence interval for the population mean.

The t ratio is distributed with $n-1$ degrees of freedom, and the critical t values are obtained from Table B in Appendix C. Because of the inflated tails of t sampling distributions, particularly when the sample size is small, critical t values are larger (either positive or negative) than the corresponding critical z values.

Degrees of freedom (df) refer to the number of values free to vary, given one or more mathematical restrictions on a set of values used to estimate some population characteristic.

The use of t assumes that the underlying population is normally distributed. Violations of this assumption are important only when the observations in small samples appear to originate from non-normal populations.

Important Terms

Sampling distribution of t

t ratio

Degrees of freedom (df)

Estimated standard error of the mean ($s_{\bar{X}}$)

Key Equations

t RATIO

$$t = \frac{\bar{X} - \mu_{hyp}}{s_{\bar{X}}}$$

where $\quad s_{\bar{X}} = \frac{s}{\sqrt{n}}$

REVIEW QUESTIONS

*13.5 A library system lends books for periods of 21 days. This policy is being reevaluated in view of a possible new loan period that could be either longer or shorter than 21 days. To aid in making this decision, book-lending records were consulted to determine the loan periods actually used by the patrons. A random sample of eight records revealed the following loan periods in days: 21, 15, 12, 24, 20, 21, 13, and 16. Test the null hypothesis with t, using the .05 level of significance.

Answer on page 505.

13.6 It's well established, we'll assume, that lab rats require an average of 32 trials in a complex water maze before reaching a learning criterion of three consecutive errorless trials. To determine whether a mildly adverse stimulus has any effect on performance, a sample of seven lab rats were given a mild electrical shock just before each trial.

(a) Given that $\bar{X} = 34.89$ and $s = 3.02$, test the null hypothesis with t, using the .05 level of significance.

(b) Construct a 95 percent confidence interval for the true number of trials required to learn the water maze.

(c) Interpret this confidence interval.

*13.7 Is the temperature of the earth getting warmer because heat is trapped by so-called greenhouse gas emissions, such as carbon dioxide, in the earth's atmosphere? The National Climatic Data Center reports on its Web site at http://www.ncdc.noaa.gov/oa/climate/research/anomalies/anomalies.html that the average global temperatures for recent years have deviated above the long-term mean temperature for the entire twentieth century. Expressed in Fahrenheit degrees, the annual *deviations above* the long-term mean temperature for each of ten recent years, listed in chronological order up to 2007, were 1.0, 0.7, 0.7, 0.9, 1.0, 1.0, 1.0, 1.1, 1.0, and 1.0.

(a) Given that $\bar{X} = 0.94$ and $s = 0.14$ for these ten years, use t at the .01 level of significance to test the null hypothesis that the temperature of earth is not getting warmer. In other words, could the sample mean deviation for these ten years have originated from a population of annual deviations for the entire twentieth century having a mean deviation *equal to zero?*

(b) If appropriate (because the null hypothesis has been rejected), construct a 99 percent confidence interval and interpret this interval.

Answers on page 506.

13.8 Assume that, on average, healthy young adults dream 90 minutes each night, as inferred from a number of measures, including rapid eye movement (REM) sleep. An investigator wishes to determine whether drinking coffee just before going to sleep affects the amount of dream time. After drinking a standard amount of coffee, dream time is monitored for each of 28 healthy young adults in a random sample. Results show a sample mean, $\bar{X}$, of 88 minutes and a sample standard deviation, s, of 9 minutes.

(a) Use t to test the null hypothesis at the .05 level of significance.

(b) If appropriate (because the null hypothesis has been rejected), construct a 95 percent confidence interval and interpret this interval.

13.9 In the gas mileage test described in this chapter, would you prefer a smaller or a larger sample size if you were

(a) the car manufacturer? Why?

(b) a vigorous prosecutor for the federal regulatory agency? Why?

13.10 Even though the population standard deviation is unknown, an investigator uses z rather than the more appropriate t to test a hypothesis at the .05 level of significance.

(a) Is the true level of significance larger or smaller than .05?

(b) Is the true critical value larger or smaller than that for the critical z?

t Test for Two Independent Samples

Summary / Important Terms / Key Equations / Review Questions

Preview

This chapter describes the t test for studies that compare a treatment group with a control group and that, if designed properly, permit unambiguous conclusions about cause-effect relationships. If the null hypothesis for this test is rejected, the result often is described as "statistically significant." Statistically significant results can be evaluated further by estimating the size of the underlying effect (difference between population means).

A variation on the hypothesis testing approach, known as "p-values," better reflects the perspective of many investigators. p-values concentrate solely on the degree of rarity of the observed result without regard to an arbitrary pre-determined level of significance.

14.1 EPO EXPERIMENT

During recent Tours de France, the world's best-known bicycle race, some cyclists have been expelled for attempting to enhance their performance by "blood doping" with a synthetic hormone, erythropoietin (EPO), that stimulates the production of oxygen-bearing (and fatigue-inhibiting) red blood cells. Assume that a mental health investigator at a large clinic wants to determine whether EPO—viewed as a potential therapeutic tool—might increase the endurance of severely depressed patients. Volunteer patients are randomly assigned to one of two groups: a treatment group (X_1) that receives a prescribed amount of EPO and a control group (X_2) that receives a harmless neutral substance. Subsequent endurance scores are based on the total time, in minutes, that each patient remains on a rapidly moving treadmill. The statistical analysis focuses on the difference between mean endurance scores for the treatment and control groups.

For computational convenience, the results for the current experiment are based on very small samples of only six endurance scores per group (rather than on larger sample sizes selected with the aid of power curves described in Section 11.11). Also for computational convenience, endurance scores have been rounded to the nearest minute even though, in practice, they surely would reflect measurement that is more precise. A glance at **Figure 14.1** suggests considerable overlap in the scores for the two groups. The treatment scores tend to be slightly larger than the control scores, and this tendency is supported by the mean difference of $11 - 6 = 5$ minutes in favor of the treatment group. How do we interpret this tendency? Is it real and, therefore, likely to reappear in a repeat experiment as a difference favoring the treatment group? Or, given the obvious overlap in scores for the two groups, combined with the inevitable variability among scores, is this tendency transitory and, therefore (to the dismay of the investigator), just as likely to appear in a repeat experiment as either no difference or even a difference favoring the control group? A *t* test for two independent samples, which evaluates the mean difference of 5 minutes relative to its variability, helps us answer this question.

Two Independent Samples

Two Independent Samples

Observations in each sample are based on different (and unmatched) subjects.

In the current experiment, the two samples are **independent** because each of the two groups consists of different patients. When samples are independent,

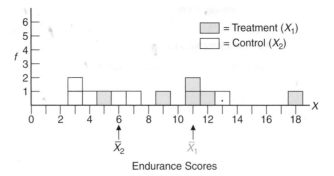

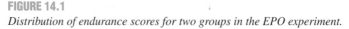

FIGURE 14.1

Distribution of endurance scores for two groups in the EPO experiment.

observations in one sample are not paired, on a one-to-one basis, with observations in the other sample. The current discussion for two independent samples can be compared with that in the next chapter for two related samples, when the investigator creates pairs of observations either by using the same patients or by matching patients in the treatment and control conditions.

Two Populations

The subjects in the current experiment are from a very limited real population: all volunteers from the pool of severely depressed patients at some clinic. This is hardly an inspiring target for statistical inference. A standard remedy is to characterize the sample of patients *as if* it were a random sample from a much larger hypothetical population, loosely defined as "all similar volunteer patients who could conceivably participate in the experiment." Strictly speaking, there are two hypothetical populations: a treatment population defined for the endurance scores of patients who receive EPO and a control population defined for the endurance scores of patients who don't receive EPO. These two populations are cited in the null hypothesis, and as has been noted, any generalizations must be viewed as provisional conclusions based on the wisdom of the investigator rather than on any logical or statistical necessity. Only additional experimentation can determine whether a given experimental finding merits the generality assigned to it by the investigator.

Difference between Population Means

Reminder:

Effect *refers to any difference between two population means.*

The difference between population means reflects the **effect** of EPO on endurance. If EPO has little or no effect on endurance, then the endurance scores would tend to be about the same for both populations of patients, and the difference between population means would be close to zero. But if EPO facilitates endurance, the scores for the treatment population would tend to exceed those for the control population, and the difference between population means would be positive. The stronger the facilitative effect of EPO on endurance, the larger the positive difference between population means. On the other hand, if EPO hinders endurance, the endurance scores for the treatment population would tend to be exceeded by those for the control population, and the difference between population means would be negative.

14.2 STATISTICAL HYPOTHESES

Null Hypothesis

According to the null hypothesis, nothing special is happening because EPO does not facilitate endurance. In other words, either there is no difference between the means for the two populations (because EPO has no effect on endurance) or the difference between population means is negative (because EPO hinders endurance). An equivalent statement in symbols reads:

$$H_0: \mu_1 - \mu_2 \leq 0$$

where H_0 represents the null hypothesis and μ_1 and μ_2 represent the mean endurance scores for the treatment and control populations, respectively.

Alternative (or Research) Hypothesis

The investigator wants to reject the null hypothesis only if the treatment increases endurance scores. Given this perspective, the alternative (or research) hypothesis should specify that the difference between population means is positive because EPO facilitates endurance. An equivalent statement in symbols reads:

$$H_1: \mu_1 - \mu_2 > 0$$

where H_1 represents the alternative hypothesis and, as above, μ_1 and, μ_2 represent the mean endurance scores for the treatment and control populations, respectively. This directional alternative hypothesis translates into a one-tailed test with the upper tail critical. As emphasized in Section 11.3, a directional alternative hypothesis should be used when there's a concern *only* about differences in a particular direction.

Two Other Possible Alternative Hypotheses

Although not appropriate for the current experiment, there are two other possible alternative hypotheses:

1. Another directional hypothesis, expressed as

$$H_1: \mu_1 - \mu_2 < 0$$

   translates into a one-tailed test with the lower tail critical.
2. A nondirectional hypothesis, expressed as

$$H_1: \mu_1 - \mu_2 \neq 0$$

translates into a two-tailed test.

Progress Check *14.1 Identifying the treatment group with μ_1, specify both the null and alternative hypotheses for each of the following studies. Select a directional alternative hypothesis only when a word or phrase justifies an exclusive concern about population mean differences in a particular direction.

(a) After randomly assigning migrant children to two groups, a school psychologist determines whether there is a difference in the mean reading scores between groups exposed to either a special bilingual or a traditional reading program.

(b) On further reflection, the school psychologist decides that, because of the extra expense of the special bilingual program, the null hypothesis should be rejected only if there is evidence that reading scores are improved, on average, for the group exposed to the special bilingual program.

(c) An investigator wishes to determine whether, on average, cigarette consumption is reduced for smokers who chew caffeine gum. Smokers in attendance at an anti-smoking workshop are randomly assigned to two groups—one that chews caffeine gum and one that does not—and their daily cigarette consumption is monitored for six months after the workshop.

(d) A political scientist determines whether males and females differ, on average, about the amount of money that, in their opinion, should be spent by the U.S. government on homeland security. After being informed about the size of the current budget for homeland security, in billions of dollars, randomly selected males and females are asked to indicate the percent by which they would alter this amount—for example, –8 percent for an 8 percent reduction, 0 percent for no change, 4 percent for a 4 percent increase.

Answers on page 506.

14.3 SAMPLING DISTRIBUTION OF $\bar{X}_1 - \bar{X}_2$

Sampling Distribution of
$\bar{X}_1 - \bar{X}_2$

Differences between sample means based on all possible pairs of random samples from two underlying populations.

Because of the inevitable variability associated with any difference between the sample mean endurance scores for the treatment and control groups, $\bar{X}_1 - \bar{X}_2$, we can't interpret a single observed mean difference at face value. The new mean difference for a repeat experiment would most likely differ from that for the original experiment. The **sampling distribution of** $\bar{X}_1 - \bar{X}_2$ is a concept introduced to account for the variability associated with differences between sample means. *It represents the entire spectrum of differences between sample means based on all possible pairs of random samples from the two underlying populations.* Once the sampling distribution has been centered about the value of the null hypothesis, we can determine whether the one observed sample mean difference qualifies as a common or a rare outcome. (A common outcome signifies that the observed sample mean difference could be due to variability or chance and, therefore, shouldn't be taken seriously. On the other hand, a rare outcome signifies that the observed sample mean difference probably reflects a real difference and, therefore, should be taken seriously.) Since all the possible pairs of random samples usually translate into a huge number of possibilities—often of astronomical proportions—the sampling distribution of $\bar{X}_1 - \bar{X}_2$ isn't constructed from scratch. As with the sampling distribution of $\bar{X}$ described in Chapter 9, statistical theory must be relied on for information about the mean and standard error for this new sampling distribution.

Mean of the Sampling Distribution, $\mu_{\bar{X}_1 - \bar{X}_2}$

Recall from Chapter 9 that the mean of the sampling distribution of $\bar{X}$ equals the population mean, that is,

$$\mu_{\bar{X}} = \mu$$

where $\mu_{\bar{X}}$ is the mean of the sampling distribution and μ is the population mean. Similarly, the mean of the new sampling distribution of $\bar{X}_1 - \bar{X}_2$ equals the difference between population means, that is,

$$\mu_{\bar{X}_1 - \bar{X}_2} = \mu_1 - \mu_2$$

where $\mu_{\bar{X}_1 - \bar{X}_2}$ is the mean of the new sampling distribution and $\mu_1 - \mu_2$ is the difference between population means. This conclusion is not particularly startling. Because of sampling variability, it's unlikely that the one observed difference between sample means equals the difference between population means.

Instead, it's likely that, just by chance, the one observed difference is either larger or smaller than the difference between population means. However, because not just one but all possible differences between sample means contribute to the mean of the sampling distribution, $\mu_{\bar{X}_1 - \bar{X}_2}$, the effects of sampling variability are neutralized, and the mean of the sampling distribution equals the difference between population means. Accordingly, these two terms are used interchangeably. Any claims about the difference between population means, including the null hypothesized claim that this difference equals zero, can be transferred directly to the mean of the sampling distribution.

Standard Error of the Sampling Distribution, $\sigma_{\bar{X}_1 - \bar{X}_2}$

Also recall from Chapter 9 that the standard deviation of the sampling distribution (or standard error) of $\bar{X}$ equals

$$\sigma_{\bar{X}} = \frac{\sigma}{\sqrt{n}} = \sqrt{\frac{\sigma^2}{n}}$$

where $\sigma_{\bar{X}}$ is the standard error, σ is the population standard deviation, and n is the sample size. To highlight the similarity between this expression and that for the new sampling distribution, the population variance, σ^2, is introduced in the above equation by placing both the numerator and denominator under a common square root sign.

The standard deviation of the new sampling distribution of $\bar{X}_1 - \bar{X}_2$ equals

$$\sigma_{\bar{X}_1 - \bar{X}_2} = \sqrt{\frac{\sigma_1^2}{n_1} + \frac{\sigma_2^2}{n_2}}$$

where $\sigma_{\bar{X}_1 - \bar{X}_2}$ is the new standard error, σ_1^2 and σ_2^2 are the two population variances, and n_1 and n_2 are the two sample sizes.

The new standard error emerges directly from the original standard error with the addition of a second term, σ_2^2 divided by n_2, reflecting extra variability due to the shift from a single sample mean to differences between two sample means. Therefore, the value of the new standard error always will be larger than that of the original one. The original standard error reflects only the variability of single sample means about the mean of their sampling distribution. But the new standard error reflects extra variability when, as a result of random pairings, large differences between pairs of sample means occur, just by chance, because they happen to deviate in opposite directions.

Standard Error of the Difference Between Means, $\sigma_{\bar{X}_1 - \bar{X}_2}$
A rough measure of the average amount by which any sample mean difference deviates from the difference between population means.

You might find it helpful to view the **standard error of the difference between means**, $\sigma_{\bar{X}_1 - \bar{X}_2}$, as a rough measure of the average amount by which any sample mean difference deviates from the difference between population means. Viewed in this fashion, if the observed difference between sample means is smaller than the standard error, it qualifies as a common outcome—well within the average expected by chance, and the null hypothesis, H_0, is retained. On the other hand, if the observed difference is sufficiently larger than the standard error, it qualifies as a rare outcome—well beyond the average expected by chance, and H_0 is rejected.

The size of the standard error for two samples, $\sigma_{\bar{X}_1 - \bar{X}_2}$—much like that of the standard error for one sample described earlier—becomes smaller with increases in sample sizes. With larger sample sizes, the values of $\bar{X}_1 - \bar{X}_2$ tend to cluster closer to the difference between population means, $\mu_1 - \mu_2$, allowing more precise generalizations.

14.4 *t* TEST

The hypothesis test for the current experiment will be based not on the sampling distribution of $\bar{X}_1 - \bar{X}_2$ but on its standardized counterpart, the sampling distribution of *t*. Although there also is a sampling distribution of *z*, its use requires that both population standard deviations be known. Since, in practice, this information is rarely available, the *z* test is hardly ever appropriate, and only the *t* test will be described.

t Ratio

The null hypothesis can be tested using a *t* ratio. Expressed in words,

$$t = \frac{(\textit{difference between sample means}) - (\textit{hypothesized difference between population means})}{\textit{estimated standard error}}$$

Expressed in symbols,

---

t RATIO FOR TWO POPULATION MEANS (TWO INDEPENDENT SAMPLES)

$$t = \frac{\left(\bar{X}_1 - \bar{X}_2\right) - \left(\mu_1 - \mu_2\right)_{hyp}}{s_{\bar{X}_1 - \bar{X}_2}} \qquad (14.1)$$

---

which complies with a *t* sampling distribution having degrees of freedom equal to the sum of the two sample sizes minus two, that is, $df = n_1 + n_2 - 2$, for reasons discussed in Section 14.5. In Formula 14.1, $\bar{X}_1 - \bar{X}_2$ represents the one observed difference between sample means; $(\mu_1 - \mu_2)_{hyp}$ represents the hypothesized difference of zero between population means; and $s_{\bar{X}_1 - \bar{X}_2}$ represents the estimated standard error, as defined later in Formula 14.3.

Finding Critical *t* Values

Once again, we must consult Table B in Appendix C to determine critical values that distinguish between common and rare values of *t* on the assumption that the null hypothesis is true. To find a critical *t* in Table B, follow the same procedure described previously. Read the entry in the cell intersected by the row for the correct number of degrees of freedom, adjusted for two independent samples, and the column for the test specifications. To find the critical *t* for the current experiment, first go to the right-hand panel for a one-tailed test; next,

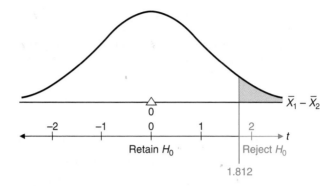

FIGURE 14.2
Hypothesized sampling distribution of t *(EPO experiment).*

locate the row corresponding to 10 degrees of freedom (from $df = n_1 + n_2 - 2 = 6 + 6 - 2 = 10$); and then locate the column for a one-tailed test at the .05 level of significance. The intersected cell specifies 1.812. The corresponding decision rule is illustrated in **Figure 14.2**, where the sampling distribution of t is centered about the null hypothesized value of zero.

Progress Check *14.2 Using Table B in Appendix C, find the critical t values for each of the following hypothesis tests:

(a) two-tailed test; $\alpha = .05$; $n_1 = 12$; $n_2 = 11$

(b) one-tailed test, upper tail critical; $\alpha = .05$; $n_1 = 15$; $n_2 = 13$

(c) one-tailed test, lower tail critical; $\alpha = .01$; $n_1 = n_2 = 25$

(d) two-tailed test; $\alpha = .01$; $n_1 = 8$; $n_2 = 10$
    Answers on page 507.

Summary for EPO Experiment

Spend a few minutes familiarizing yourself with the boxed hypothesis test summary for the EPO experiment. Note the considerable similarities between it and previous summaries of hypothesis tests. Given the apparent separation between the two groups depicted in Figure 14.1, you might have anticipated that the calculated t of 2.16 would exceed the critical t of 1.812. Therefore, we can reject H_0 and conclude that, on average, EPO increases the endurance scores of treatment patients.

14.5 DETAILS: CALCULATIONS FOR THE *t* TEST

Four panels in **Table 14.1** represent the steps required to produce a t of 2.16 for the EPO experiment.

HYPOTHESIS TEST SUMMARY
t Test for Two Population Means: Independent Samples
(EPO Experiment)

Research Problem

Does the population mean endurance score for treatment (EPO) patients exceed that for control patients?

Statistical Hypotheses

$$H_0: \mu_1 - \mu_2 \leq 0$$
$$H_1: \mu_1 - \mu_2 > 0$$

Decision Rule

Reject H_0 at the .05 level of significance if $t \geq 1.812$ (from Table B in Appendix C, given $df = n_1 + n_2 - 2 = 6 + 6 - 2 = 10$).

Calculations

$$t = \frac{(11-6)-0}{2.32} = 2.16 \text{ (See Table 14.1 for all computations.)}$$

Decision

Reject H_0 at the .05 level of significance because $t = 2.16$ exceeds 1.812.

Interpretation

The difference between population means is greater than zero. There is evidence that EPO increases the mean endurance scores of treatment patients.

Panel I

Requiring the most computational effort, this panel produces values for the two sample means, $\bar{X}_1$ and $\bar{X}_2$, and for the two sample sums of squares, SS_1 and SS_2, where

$$SS_1 = \sum X_1^2 - \frac{\left(\sum X_1\right)^2}{n_1}$$

and

$$SS_2 = \sum X_2^2 - \frac{\left(\sum X_2\right)^2}{n_2}$$

Table 14.1
CALCULATIONS FOR THE *t* TEST: TWO INDEPENDENT SAMPLES
(EPO EXPERIMENT)

I. FINDING SAMPLE MEANS AND SUMS OF SQUARES, $\bar{X}_1, \bar{X}_2, SS_1,$ AND SS_2

(a) Computational sequence:

Assign a value to n_1 **1**.

Sum all X_1 scores **2**.

Substitute numbers in the formula **3** and solve for $\bar{X}_1$.

Square each X_1 score **4**, one at a time, and then add all squared X_1 scores **5**.

Substitute numbers in the formula **6** and solve for SS_1.

Repeat this entire computational sequence for n_2 and X_2 and solve for $\bar{X}_2$ and SS_2.

(b) Data and computations:

ENDURANCE SCORES (MINUTES)

EPO **4**		CONTROL	
X_1	X_1^2	X_2	X_2^2
12	144	7	49
5	25	3	9
11	121	4	16
11	121	6	36
9	81	3	9
18	324	13	169
1 $n_1 = 6$ **2** $\Sigma X_1 = 66$	**5** $\Sigma X_1^2 = 816$	$n_2 = 6$ $\Sigma X_2 = 36$	$\Sigma X_2^2 = 288$

3 $\bar{X}_1 = \dfrac{\Sigma X_1}{n_1} = \dfrac{66}{6} = 11$ $\qquad\qquad$ $\bar{X}_2 = \dfrac{\Sigma X_2}{n_2} = \dfrac{36}{6} = 6$

6 $SS_1 = \Sigma X_1^2 - \dfrac{\left(\Sigma X_1\right)^2}{n_1}$ $\qquad\qquad$ $SS_2 = \Sigma X_2^2 - \dfrac{\left(\Sigma X_2\right)^2}{n_2}$

$\quad = 816 - \dfrac{(66)^2}{6}$ $\qquad\qquad\qquad\quad = 288 - \dfrac{(36)^2}{6}$

$\quad = 816 - 726$ $\qquad\qquad\qquad\qquad\quad = 288 - 216$

$\quad = 90$ $\qquad\qquad\qquad\qquad\qquad\quad = 72$

II. FINDING THE POOLED VARIANCE, s_p^2

(a) Computational sequence:

Substitute numbers obtained above in the formula **7** and solve for s_p^2.

(b) Computations:

7 $\qquad\qquad s_p^2 = \dfrac{SS_1 + SS_2}{n_1 + n_2 - 2} = \dfrac{90 + 72}{6 + 6 - 2} = \dfrac{162}{10} = 16.2$

III. FINDING THE STANDARD ERROR, $s_{\bar{X}_1 - \bar{X}_2}$
(a) Computational sequence:
   Substitute numbers obtained above in the formula **8** and solve for $s_{\bar{X}_1 - \bar{X}_2}$.
(b) Computations:

8 $\quad s_{\bar{X}_1 - \bar{X}_2} = \sqrt{\dfrac{s_p^2}{n_1} + \dfrac{s_p^2}{n_2}} = \sqrt{\dfrac{16.2}{6} + \dfrac{16.2}{6}} = \sqrt{\dfrac{32.4}{6}} = \sqrt{5.4} = 2.32$

IV. FINDING THE OBSERVED t RATIO
(a) Computational sequence:
   Substitute numbers obtained above in the formula **9**, as well as a value of 0 for the expression $(\mu_2 - \mu_2)_{hyp}$ and solve for t.
(b) Computations:

9 $\quad t = \dfrac{\left(\bar{X}_1 - \bar{X}_2\right) - \left(\mu_1 - \mu_2\right)_{hyp}}{s_{\bar{X}_1 - \bar{X}_2}} = \dfrac{(11 - 6) - 0}{2.32} = \dfrac{5}{2.32} = 2.16$

Panel II

The present t test assumes that the two population variances are equal. Given that $\sigma_1^2 = \sigma_2^2 = \sigma^2$, the variance common to both populations can be estimated most accurately by combining the two sample variances to obtain the pooled variance estimate, s_p^2. This is accomplished by simply adding the two sample sums of squares, SS_1 and SS_2, and dividing this sum by their degrees of freedom, $df = n_1 + n_2 - 2$, that is,

---

Pooled Variance Estimate (s_p^2)

The most accurate estimate of the population variance (assumed to be the same for both populations) based on a combination of two sample sums of squares and their degrees of freedom.

POOLED VARIANCE ESTIMATE, s_p^2

$$s_p^2 = \frac{SS_1 + SS_2}{df} = \frac{SS_1 + SS_2}{n_1 + n_2 - 2} \qquad (14.2)$$

The degrees of freedom for s_p^2 equal the sum of the degrees of freedom for the two samples minus two. Two degrees of freedom are lost, one for each sample, because of the zero-sum restriction for the deviations of observations about their respective means. Although not obvious from Formula 14.2, the pooled variance, s_p^2, represents the mean of the variances, s_1^2 and s_2^2, for the two samples once these estimates have been adjusted for their degrees of freedom. Accordingly, if the values of s_1^2 and s_2^2 are different, s_p^2 will always assume some intermediate value. If sample sizes (and, therefore, degrees of freedom) are equal, the value of s_p^2 will be exactly midway between those of s_1^2 and s_2^2. Otherwise, the value of s_p^2 will be shifted proportionately toward the sample variance with the larger number of degrees of freedom.

Panel III

The estimated standard error, $s_{\bar{X}_1 - \bar{X}_2}$, is calculated by substituting the pooled variance, s_p^2, twice, once as an estimate for σ_1^2 and once as an estimate for σ_2^2; then dividing each term by its sample size, either n_1 or n_2; and finally, taking the square root of the entire expression, that is,

---

ESTIMATED STANDARD ERROR, $s_{\bar{X}_1 - \bar{X}_2}$

$$s_{\bar{X}_1 - \bar{X}_2} = \sqrt{\frac{s_p^2}{n_1} + \frac{s_p^2}{n_2}} \qquad (14.3)$$

Panel IV

Finally, dividing the difference between the two sample means, $\bar{X}_1 - \bar{X}_2$, and the null hypothesized population mean difference, $(\mu_1 - \mu_2)_{hyp}$, (of zero) by the estimated standard error, $s_{\bar{X}_1 - \bar{X}_2}$, generates a value for the t ratio, as defined in Formula 14. 1.

Progress Check *14.3 A psychologist investigates the effect of instructions on the time required to solve a puzzle. Each of 20 volunteers is given the same puzzle to be solved as rapidly as possible. Subjects are randomly assigned, in equal numbers, to receive two different sets of instructions prior to the task. One group is told that the task is difficult (X_1), and the other group is told that the task is easy (X_2). The score for each subject reflects the time in minutes required to solve the puzzle. Use a t to test the null hypothesis at the .05 level of significance.

SOLUTION TIMES	
"DIFFICULT" TASK	**"EASY" TASK**
5	13
20	6
7	6
23	5
30	3
24	6
9	10
8	20
20	9
12	12

Answers on page 507.

14.6 *p*-VALUES

Most investigators adopt a less structured approach to hypothesis testing than that described in this book. The null hypothesis is neither retained nor rejected, but viewed with *degrees of suspicion*, depending on the degree of rarity of the observed value of t or, more generally, the test result. Instead of subscribing to a single *predetermined* level of significance, the investigator waits until *after* the test result has been observed and then assigns a probability, known as a *p*-value, representing the degree of rarity attained by the test result.

p-value

The degree of rarity of a test result, given that the null hypothesis is true.

The *p-value* for a test result represents the degree of rarity of that result, given that the null hypothesis is true. Smaller *p*-values tend to discredit the null hypothesis and to support the research hypothesis.

Strictly speaking, the *p*-value indicates the degree of rarity of the observed test result when combined with all potentially *more deviant* test results. In other words, the *p*-value represents the proportion of area, beyond the observed result, in the tail of the sampling distribution, as shown in **Figure 14.3** by the shaded sectors for two different test results. In the left panel of Figure 14.3, a relatively deviant (from zero) observed t is associated with a small *p*-value that makes the null hypothesis suspect, while in the right panel, a relatively nondeviant observed t is associated with a large *p*-value that does not make the null hypothesis suspect.

Figure 14.3 illustrates *one-tailed p*-values that are appropriate whenever the investigator has an interest only in deviations in a particular direction, as with a one-tailed hypothesis test. Otherwise, *two-tailed p*-values are appropriate. Although not shown in Figure 14.3, two-tailed *p*-values would require equivalent shaded areas to be located in *both* tails of the sampling distribution, and the resulting two-tailed *p*-value would be twice as large as its corresponding one-tailed *p*-value.

Finding Approximate *p*-Values

Table B in Appendix C can be used to find *approximate p*-values, that is, *p*-values involving an inequality, such as $p < .05$ or $p > .05$. To aid in the identification of these approximate *p*-values, a color-coded outline has been superimposed over the entries for t in Table B. Once you've located the observed t relative to the tabular entries, simply follow the vertical line upward to identify the correct approximate *p*-value.

To find the approximate *p*-value for the t of 2.16 for the EPO experiment, first, identify the row in Table B for a one-tailed test with 10 degrees of freedom. The

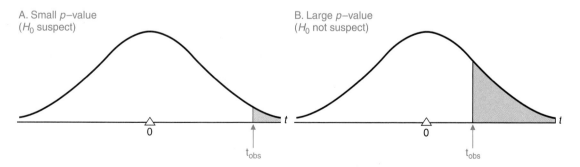

A. Small *p*–value
(H_0 suspect)

B. Large *p*–value
(H_0 not suspect)

t_{obs}

t_{obs}

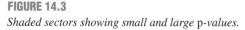

FIGURE 14.3
Shaded sectors showing small and large p-*values.*

three entries in this row, 1.812, 2.764, and 4.144, serve as benchmarks for degrees of rarity corresponding to p-values of .05, .01, and .001, respectively. Since the observed t of 2.16 is located between the first entry of 1.812 and the second entry of 2.764, follow the vertical line between the two entries upward to $p < .05$. From most perspectives, this is a small p-value: The test result is rare—it could have occurred just by chance with a probability less than .05, given that H_0 is true. Therefore, support has been mustered for the research hypothesis. This conclusion is consistent with the decision to reject H_0 when a more structured hypothesis test at the .05 level of significance was conducted for the same data.

Progress Check *14.4 Find the approximate p-value for each of the following test results:

(a) one-tailed test, upper tail critical; $df = 12$; $t = 4.61$

(b) one-tailed test, lower tail critical; $df = 19$; $t = -2.41$

(c) two-tailed test; $df = 15$; $t = 3.76$

(d) two-tailed test; $df = 42$; $t = 1.305$

(e) one-tailed test, upper tail critical; $df = 11$; $t = -4.23$ (Be careful!)
   Answers on page 507.

Reading *p*-Values Reported by Others

A single research report might describe a batch of tests with a variety of approximate p-values, such as $p < .05$, $p < .01$, and $p < .001$, and, if the test failed to support the research hypothesis, $p > .05$. You must attend carefully to the direction of the inequality symbol. For example, the test result supports the research hypothesis when $p < .05$ but not when $p > .05$.

As illustrated in many of the computer outputs in this book, when statistical tests are performed by computers, with their capacity to obtain *exact* p-values (or values of *Sig.* in the case of SPSS), reports contain many different p-values, such as $p = .03$, $p = .27$, and $p = .009$. Even though more precise equalities replace inequalities, exact p-values listed on computer printouts are interpreted the same way as approximate p-values read from tables. For example, it's still true that $p = .03$ describes a rare test result, while $p = .27$ describes a result that is not particularly rare. Sometimes you'll see even a very rare $p = .000$, which, however, does not signify that p actually equals zero—an impossibility, since the t sampling distribution extends outward to infinity—but merely that rounding off causes the disappearance of non-zero digits from the reported p-value.

Evaluation of the *p*-Value Approach

This less structured approach does have merit. Having eliminated the requirement that the null hypothesis be either retained or rejected, you can postpone a decision until sufficient evidence has been mustered, possibly from a series of investigations. This perspective is very attractive when test results are borderline. For instance, imagine a hypothesis test in which the null hypothesis is retained, even though an observed t of 1.70 is only slightly less deviant than the critical t of 1.812 for the .05 level of significance. Given the less structured approach, an investigator might, with the aid of a computer, establish that $p = .06$ for the observed t. Reporting the borderline result, with $p = .06$, implies at least some support for the research hypothesis.

One weakness of this less structured approach is that, in the absence of a firm commitment to either retain or reject the null hypothesis according to some predetermined level of significance, it's difficult to deal with the important notions of type I and type II errors. For this reason, a more structured approach to hypothesis testing will continue to be featured in this book, although not to the exclusion of the important approach involving p-values.

Level of Significance or p-Value?

A final word of caution. Do not confuse the level of significance with a p-value, even though both originate from the same column headings of Table B in Appendix C. Specified *before* the test result has been observed, the level of significance describes a degree of rarity that, if attained subsequently by the test result, triggers the decision to reject H_0. Specified *after* the test result has been observed, a p-value describes the most impressive degree of rarity actually attained by the test result.

You need not drop a personal preference for a more structured hypothesis test, with a predetermined level of significance, just because a research report contains only p-values. For instance, any p-value less than .05, such as $p < .05$, $p = .03$, $p < .01$, or $p < .001$, implies that, with the same data, H_0 would have been rejected at the .05 level of significance. By the same token, any p-value greater than .05, such as $p > .05$, $p < .10$, $p < .20$, or $p = .18$ implies that, with the same data, H_0 would have been retained at the .05 level of significance.

Progress Check *14.5 Indicate which member of each of the following pairs of p-values describes the *more rare* test result:

(a_1) $p > .05$ (a_2) $p < .05$

(b_1) $p < .001$ (b_2) $p < .01$

(c_1) $p < .05$ (c_2) $p < .01$

(d_1) $p < .10$ (d_2) $p < .20$

(e_1) $p = .04$ (e_2) $p = .02$

Progress Check *14.6 Treating each of the p-values in the previous exercise separately, indicate those that would cause you to reject the null hypothesis at the .05 level of significance.

Answers on page 507.

14.7 STATISTICALLY SIGNIFICANT RESULTS

It's important that you accurately interpret the findings of others—often reported as "having statistical significance." Tests of hypotheses often are referred to as *tests of significance*, and test results are described as being *statistically significant* (if the null hypothesis has been rejected) or as not being statistically significant (if the null hypothesis has been retained). *Rejecting the null hypothesis* and *statistically significant* both signify that the test result can't be attributed to chance. However, correct usage dictates that *rejecting the null hypothesis* always refers to the population, such as rejecting the hypothesized zero difference between two population means, while *statistically significant* always refers to the sample, such as assigning statistical significance to the observed difference between two sample means. Either phrase can be used. However, assigning *statistical significance* to a population mean difference would be misleading, since a population mean difference equals a fixed value controlled by "nature," not something controlled by the results of a statistical test. *Rejecting* a sample mean difference also would be misleading, since a sample mean difference is an observed result that serves as the basis for statistical tests, not something to be rejected.

Statistical significance doesn't imply that the underlying effect is important. **Statistical significance** between pairs of sample means *implies only that the null hypothesis is probably false, and not whether it's false because of a large or small difference between population means.*

Beware of Excessively Large Sample Sizes

Using excessively large sample sizes can produce statistically significant results that lack importance. For instance, assume a new EPO experiment with the same amount of variability among endurance scores as in the original experiment, that is, with a pooled variance, s_p^2, equal to 16.2 (from Table 14.1). But assume that the new experiment has a *much smaller* mean difference, $\bar{X}_1 - \bar{X}_2$, equal to only 0.50 minutes (instead of 5 minutes in the original experiment) and much *larger* sample sizes each equal to 500 patients (instead of 6). Because of these much larger sample sizes, the new standard error would equal only 0.25 (instead of 2.32) and the new *t* would equal 2.00. Now we would have rejected the null hypothesis at the .05 level, even though the new difference between sample means is only one-tenth the size of the original difference. With large sample sizes and, therefore, with a small standard error, even a very small and unimportant *effect* (*difference between population means*) will be detected, and the test will be reported as statistically significant.

Statistical significance merely indicates that an observed effect, such as an observed difference between the sample means, is sufficiently large, relative to the standard error, to be viewed as a rare outcome. (Statistical significance also implies that the observed outcome is *reliable*, that is, it would reappear as a similarly rare outcome in a repeat experiment.) It's very desirable, therefore, that we go beyond reports of statistical significance by estimating the size of the effect and, if possible, judging its importance.

14.8 ESTIMATING EFFECT SIZE: POINT ESTIMATES AND CONFIDENCE INTERVALS

It would make sense to estimate the effect for the EPO experiment featured in this chapter since the results are statistically significant. (But, strictly speaking, *only* if the results are statistically significant. Otherwise, we would be estimating an "effect" that could be merely transitory and attributed to chance.)

Statistical Significance

Implies only that the null hypothesis is probably false, and not whether it's false because of a large or small difference between population means.

Point Estimate ($\bar{X}_1 - \bar{X}_2$)

As you probably recall from Chapter 12, a point estimate is the most straightforward type of estimate. It identifies the observed difference for $\bar{X}_1 - \bar{X}_2$, in this case, 5 minutes, as an estimate of the unknown effect, that is, the unknown difference between population means, $\mu_1 - \mu_2$. On average, the treatment patients stay on the treadmill for 11 minutes, which is almost twice as long as the 6 minutes for the control patients. If you think about it, this impressive estimate of effect size isn't surprising. With the very small groups of only 6 patients, we had to create a large, fictitious mean difference of 5 minutes in order to claim a statistically significant result. If this result had occurred in a real experiment, it would have signified a powerful effect of EPO on endurance that could be detected even with very small samples.

Confidence Interval

Although simple, straightforward, and precise, point estimates tend to be inaccurate because they ignore sampling variability. Confidence intervals do not because, as noted in Chapter 12, they are based on the variability in the sampling distribution of $\bar{X}_1 - \bar{X}_2$. To estimate the range of possible effects of EPO on endurance, a confidence interval can be constructed for the difference between population means, $\mu_1 - \mu_2$.

Confidence Intervals
for $\mu_1 - \mu_2$
Ranges of values that, in the long run, include the unknown effect a certain percent of the time.

Confidence intervals for $\mu_1 - \mu_2$ specify ranges of values that, in the long run, include the unknown effect (difference between population means) a certain percent of the time.

Given two independent samples, a confidence interval for $\mu_1 - \mu_2$ can be constructed from the following expression:

CONFIDENCE INTERVAL (CI) FOR $\mu_1 - \mu_2$ (TWO INDEPENDENT SAMPLES)
$$\bar{X}_1 - \bar{X}_2 \pm (t_{conf})(s_{\bar{X}_1 - \bar{X}_2}) \qquad (14.4)$$

---

where $\bar{X}_1 - \bar{X}_2$ represents the difference between sample means; t_{conf} represents a number, distributed with $n_1 + n_2 - 2$ degrees of freedom, from the t tables, which satisfies the confidence specifications; and $s_{\bar{X}_1 - \bar{X}_2}$ represents the estimated standard error defined in Formula 14.3.

To find the appropriate value of t_{conf} in Formula 14.4, refer to Table B in Appendix C and follow essentially the same procedure described earlier. For example, if a 95 percent confidence interval is desired for the EPO experiment, first locate the row corresponding to 10 degrees of freedom (from $df = n_1 + n_2 - 2 = 6 + 6 - 2 = 10$) and then locate the column for the 95 percent level of confidence, that is, the column heading identified with a single asterisk. The intersected cell specifies a value of 2.228 to be entered for t_{conf} in Formula 14.4. Given this value for t_{conf}, and values of 5 for the difference between sample means, $\bar{X}_1 - \bar{X}_2$, and of 2.32 for the estimated standard error, $s_{\bar{X}_1 - \bar{X}_2}$ (from Table 14.1), Formula 14.4 becomes

$$5 \pm (2.228)(2.32) = 5 \pm 5.17 = \left\{ \begin{array}{l} 10.17 \\ -0.17 \end{array} \right.$$

Now it can be claimed, with 95 percent confidence, that the interval between −0.17 minutes and 10.17 minutes includes the true effect size, that is, the true difference between population means for endurance scores.

Interpreting Confidence Intervals for $\mu_1 - \mu_2$

The numbers in this confidence interval refer to *differences* between population means, and the signs are particularly important since they indicate the *direction* of these differences. Otherwise, the interpretation of a confidence interval for $\mu_1 - \mu_2$ is the same as that for μ. In the long run, 95 percent of all confidence intervals, similar to the one just stated, will include the unknown difference between population means. Although we never really know whether this particular confidence interval is true or false, we can be *reasonably confident* that the true effect (or true difference between population means) is neither less than −0.17 minutes nor more than 10.17 minutes If only positive differences had appeared in this confidence interval, a single interpretation would have been possible. However, the appearance of a negative difference in the lower limit indicates that EPO might hinder endurance, and therefore, no single interpretation is possible. Furthermore, the automatic inclusion of a zero difference in an interval with dissimilar signs indicates that EPO may have had no effect whatsoever on endurance.*

The range of possible differences (from a low of −0.17 minutes to a high of 10.17 minutes) is very large and imprecise—as you would expect, given the very small sample sizes and, therefore, the relatively large standard error. A repeat experiment should use larger sample sizes in order to produce a narrower, more precise confidence interval that would reduce the range of possible population mean differences and effect sizes.

Progress Check *14.7 Imagine that one of the following 95 percent confidence intervals is based on an EPO experiment. (Because of the appearance of pairs of limits with dissimilar signs, a statistically significant result wasn't required as a preliminary screen for constructing the confidence interval—possibly because, in

Key Point:

A single interpretation is possible only if the two limits of the confidence interval for $\mu_1 - \mu_2$ share the same signs, either both positive or both negative.

---

* Because of the common statistical origins of confidence intervals and hypothesis tests, the appearance of only positive limits (and the automatic absence of a zero difference) in the 95 percent confidence interval signifies that the null hypothesis would have been rejected if the *same data* were used to conduct a comparable hypothesis test—that is, in this case, a *two-tailed* test at the .05 level of significance. The seemingly contradictory conclusions between the previous hypothesis test and the current confidence interval for the EPO data indicate that a new hypothesis test would *not* have rejected the null hypothesis if a two-tailed rather than a one-tailed test had been used.

the early stages of research, the investigator simply wanted to know the range of estimates, whether positive or negative, for any possible effect of EPO.)

95% CONFIDENCE INTERVAL	LOWER LIMIT	UPPER LIMIT
1	−3.45	4.25
2	1.89	2.21
3	−1.54	−0.32
4	0.21	1.53
5	−2.53	1.78

(a) Which confidence interval is most precise?

(b) Which confidence interval most strongly supports the conclusion that EPO *facilitates* endurance?

(c) Which confidence interval most strongly supports the conclusion that EPO *hinders* endurance?

(d) Which confidence interval would most likely stimulate the investigator to conduct an additional experiment using larger sample sizes?

Answers on page 507.

14.9 ESTIMATING EFFECT SIZE: COHEN'S *d*

Standardized Effect Estimate, Cohen's d

Describes effect size by expressing the observed mean difference in standard deviation units.

Using a variation of the *z* score formula in Chapter 5, **Cohen's *d*** describes effect size by expressing *the observed mean difference in standard deviation units.* To calculate *d*, divide the observed mean difference by the standard deviation, that is,

---

STANDARDIZED EFFECT SIZE, COHEN'S *d* (TWO INDEPENDENT SAMPLES)

$$d = \frac{mean\ difference}{standard\ deviation} = \frac{\overline{X}_1 - \overline{X}_2}{\sqrt{s_p^2}} \qquad (14.5)$$

---

where, according to current usage, *d* refers to a standardized *estimate* of the effect size; $\overline{X}_1$ and $\overline{X}_2$ are the two sample means; and $\sqrt{s_p^2}$ is the sample standard deviation obtained from the square root of the pooled variance estimate.

Division of the mean difference by the standard deviation has several desirable consequences:

- The standard deviation supplies a *stable* frame of reference not influenced by increases in sample size. Unlike the standard error, whose value decreases as sample size increases, the value of the standard deviation remains the same, except for chance, as sample size increases. Therefore, straightforward comparisons can be made between *d* values based on studies with appreciably different sample sizes.

Table 14.2 COHEN'S GUIDELINES FOR *d*	
d	**EFFECT SIZE**
.20	Small
.50	Medium
.80	Large

■ The original units of measurement cancel out because of their appearance in both the numerator and denominator. Subsequently, *d* always emerges as an estimate in standard deviation units, regardless of whether the original mean difference is based on, for example, reaction times in *milliseconds* of pilots to two different cockpit alarms or weight losses in *pounds* of overweight subjects to two types of dietary restrictions. Except for chance, comparisons are straightforward between values of *d*—with larger values of *d* reflecting larger effect sizes—even though the original mean differences are based on very different units of measurement, such as milliseconds and pounds.

Cohen's Guidelines for *d*

After surveying the research literature, Jacob Cohen suggested a number of general guidelines for interpreting values of *d*:

■ Effect size is *small if d* is less than or in the vicinity of 0.20, that is, one-fifth of a standard deviation.

■ Effect size is *medium* if *d* is in the vicinity of 0.50, that is, one-half of a standard deviation.

■ Effect size is *large* if *d* is more than or in the vicinity of 0.80, that is, four-fifths of a standard deviation. *

Although widely adopted, Cohen's abstract guidelines for small, medium, and large effects can be difficult to interpret. You might find these guidelines more comprehensible by referring to Table 14.3, where Cohen's guidelines for *d* are converted into more concrete mean differences involving GPAs, IQs, and SAT scores. Notice that Cohen's medium effect, a *d* value of .50, translates into mean differences of .25 for GPAs, 7.5 for IQs, and 50 for SAT scores. To qualify as medium effects, the average GPA would have to increase, for example,

Table 14.3
COHEN'S GUIDELINES FOR *d* AND MEAN DIFFERENCES FOR GPA, IQ, AND SAT SCORES

		MEAN DIFFERENCE		
		GPA	**IQ**	**SAT**
d	**EFFECT SIZE**	$s_P = 0.50$	$s_P = 15$	$s_P = 100$
.20	Small	0.10	3	20
.50	Medium	0.25	7.5	50
.80	Large	0.40	12	80

* J. Cohen, *Statistical Power Analysis for the Behavioral Sciences,* 2nd ed. (Hillsdale, NJ: Erlbaum, 1988).

from 3.00 to 3.25; the average IQ from 100 to 107.5; and the average SAT score from 500 to 550.

Furthermore, for a particular measure, such as SAT scores, a 20-point mean difference corresponds to Cohen's small effect, while an 80-point mean difference corresponds to his large effect. However, *do not interpret Cohen's guidelines without regard to special circumstances*. A "small" 20-point increase in SAT scores might be viewed as virtually worthless if it occurred after a lengthy series of workshops on taking SAT tests, but viewed as worthwhile if it occurred after a brief study session.

You might also find it helpful to visualize the impact of each of Cohen's guidelines on the degree of separation between pairs of normal curves. Although, of course, not every distribution is normal, these curves serve as a convenient frame of reference to render values of *d* more meaningful. As shown in Figure 14.4, separation between pairs of normal curves is non-existent (and overlap is complete) when *d* = 0. Separation becomes progressively more conspicuous as the values of *d*, corresponding to Cohen's small, medium, and large effects, increase from .20 to .50 and then to .80. Separation becomes very conspicuous, with relatively little overlap, given a *d* value of 3.00, equivalent to three standard deviations, for a very large effect.

To dramatize further the differences between selected *d* values, the percents (and shaded sectors) in Figure 14.4 reflect scores in the higher curve that exceed the mean of the lower curve. When *d* = 0, the two curves coincide, and it's a tossup, 50%, whether or not the scores in one curve exceed the mean of the other curve. As values of *d* increase, the percent of scores in the higher curve that exceed the mean of the lower curve varies from a modest 59% (six out of ten)

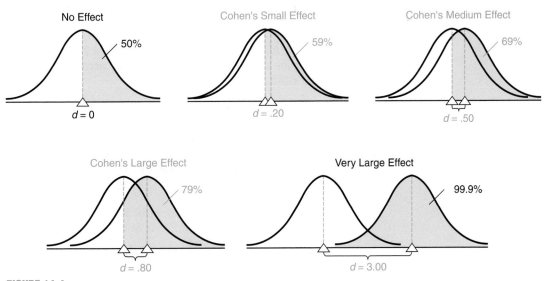

FIGURE 14.4

Separation between pairs of normal curves for selected values of d. Colored sectors reflect the percent of scores in one curve that exceed the mean of the other curve.

when $d = .20$ to a more impressive 79% (eight out of ten) when $d = .80$ to a most impressive 99.9% (ten out of ten) when $d = 3.00$.

We can use d to estimate the standardized effect size for the statistically significant results in the EPO experiment described in this chapter. When the mean difference of 5 is divided by the standard deviation of 4.02 (from the square root of the pooled variance estimate of 16.2 in Table 14.1), the value of d equals a large 1.24, that is, a mean difference equivalent to one and one-quarter standard deviations. (Being itself a product of chance sampling variability, this value of d—even if based on real data—would be highly speculative because of the instability of d when sample sizes are small.)

The most recent *Publication Manual of the American Psychological Association* recommends that reports of statistical significance tests include some estimate of effect size. Beginning in the next section, we'll adopt this recommendation by including the standardized estimate of effect size, d, in reports of statistically significant mean differences. (A slightly more complicated estimate will be used in later chapters when effect size can't be conceptualized as a simple mean difference.) The routine reporting of effect sizes will greatly facilitate more advanced quantitative techniques, known as *meta-analysis*, designed to summarize research findings for entire sets of related studies.*

14.10 REPORTS IN THE LITERATURE

It's become common practice to report means and standard deviations, as well as the results of statistical tests. Reports of statistical tests usually are brief, often consisting only of a parenthetical statement that summarizes the statistical analysis and usually includes a p-value and some estimate of effect size, such as Cohen's d. A published report of the EPO experiment might read as follows:

> *Endurance scores for the EPO group ($\bar{X} = 11$, s = 4.24) significantly exceed those for the control group ($\bar{X} = 6$, s = 3.79), according to a t test [t(10) = 2.16, p < .05 and d = 1.24].*

Or expressed in a format prevalent in the current psychological literature, where the mean and standard deviation are symbolized as M and SD, respectively:

> *The endurance scores for the EPO group (M = 11, SD = 4.24) and control group (M = 6, SD = 3.79) differed significantly [t(10) = 2.16, p < .05 and d = 1.24].*

In both examples, the parenthetical statement indicates that a t based on 10 degrees of freedom was found to equal 2.16. Since the p-value of less than .05 reflects a rare test result, given that the null hypothesis is true, this result

---

* For an excellent introduction to meta-analysis, see Chapter 1 in M. W. Lipsey and D. B. Wilson, *Practical Meta-Analysis* (Thousand Oaks, CA: Sage, 2000).

supports the research hypothesis, as implied in the interpretative statements. The d of 1.24 suggests that the observed mean difference of 5 is equivalent to one and one-quarter standard deviations and qualifies as a large effect size. Values for the two standard deviations were obtained by converting $SS_1 = 90$ and $SS_2 = 72$ in Table 14.1 into their respective sample variances and standard deviations, using Formulas 4.9 and 4.10. (For your convenience, values of standard deviations will be supplied in subsequent questions requiring a literature report.)

It's also become common practice to describe results with data graphs. In data graphs, such as that shown in **Figure 14.5**, the dependent variable, mean endurance, is identified with the vertical axis, while values of the independent variable, EPO and control, are located as points along the horizontal axis. Dots identify the mean endurance score for EPO and control groups, while error bars reflect the standard error associated with each dot. (Since error bars could reflect other measures of variability, such as standard deviations or 95 percent confidence intervals, it's important to identify which measure is being used.) Generally speaking, non-overlapping error bars (for standard errors) imply that differences between means *might* be statistically significant, as, in fact, is the case for the mean differences shown in Figure 14.5. Incidentally, data graphs also can appear as bar charts, where error bars are centered on bar tops and extend vertically above and below bar tops.

Progress Check *14.8 Recall that in Question 14.3, a psychologist determined the effect of instructions on the time required by subjects to solve the same puzzle. For two independent samples of ten subjects per group, mean solution times, in minutes, were longer for subjects given "difficult" instructions ($\overline{X} = 15.8$, $s = 8.64$) than for subjects given "easy" instructions ($\overline{X} = 9.0$, $s = 5.01$). A t ratio of 2.15 led to the rejection of the null hypothesis.

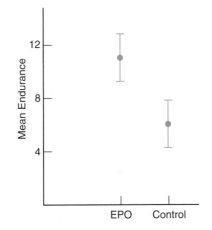

FIGURE 14.5
Data graph where dots identify the mean endurance scores for EPO and control groups. Error bars show deviations equal to one standard error above and below each mean.

(a) Given a standard deviation, s_p, of 7.06, calculate the value of the standardized effect size, d.

(b) Indicate how these results might be described in the literature.

Answers on page 507.

14.11 ASSUMPTIONS

Whether testing a hypothesis or constructing a confidence interval, t assumes that both underlying populations are normally distributed with equal variances. You need not be too concerned about violations of these assumptions, particularly if both sample sizes are equal and each is fairly large (greater than about 10). Otherwise, in the *unlikely* event that you observe conspicuous departures from normality or equality of variances in the data for the two groups, consider the following possibilities:

1. Increase sample sizes to minimize the effect of any non-normality.
2. Equate sample sizes to minimize the effect of unequal population variances.
3. Use a slightly less sensitive, more complex version of t designed for unequal variances, alluded to in the next section and described more fully in Chapter 7 of D. C. Howell's *Statistical Methods for Psychology,* 7th ed. (Belmont, CA: Wadsworth, 2010).
4. Use a less sensitive but more assumption-free test, such as the Mann-Whitney U test described in Chapter 20.

14.12 COMPUTER OUTPUT

Table 14.4 shows an SAS output for the t test for EPO, as summarized in the box on page 293. Spend a few moments reviewing this material.

Progress Check *14.9 The following questions refer to the SAS output in Table 14.4.

(a) Although, in this case, the results are the same for the t test for equal variances and for the t test for unequal variances, which test should be reported? Why?

(b) The exact p-value equals .0569 for a two-tailed test, the default test for SAS. What is the more appropriate (exact) one-tailed p-value?

(c) SAS gives the upper and lower confidence limits (CL) for each of six different 95 percent confidence intervals, three for means and three for standard deviations. Is the single set of CLs for the difference between population means, that is, Diff (1-2), consistent with the two-tailed p-values for the t test?

Answers on page 508.

Table 14.4
SAS OUTPUT: *t* TEST FOR ENDURANCE SCORES

The SAS System
17:20 Friday, June 5, 2009
t test Procedure

Variable	group	N	Lower CL Mean	Mean	Upper CL Mean	Lower CL Std Dev	Std Dev	Upper CL Std Dev	Std Err
endure	EPO	6	6.5476	11	15.452	2.6483	4.2426	10.406	1.7321
endure	control	6	2.0177	6	9.9823	2.3687	3.7947	9.307	1.5492
endure	Diff (1–2)		–0.178	5	10.1777	2.8123	4.0249	7.0635	2.3238

t Tests

Variable	Method	Variances	df	*t* Value	Pr > |t|
endure	Pooled	Equal	10	1 2.16	0.0569
endure	Satterthwaite	Unequal	9.88	2.16	0.0572

Equality of Variances

Variable	Method	Num *df*	Den *df*	*F* Value	Pr > *F*
endure	2 Folded *F*	5	5	1.25	0.8125

Comments:

1 Compare the value of t *with that given in Table 14.1. Report the results for the customary* t *test (discussed in this book) that assumes equal variances rather than the more generalized* t *test (not discussed in this book) that accommodates unequal variances unless, as explained in comment 2 below, the assumption of equal population variances has been rejected.*

2 The folded F *(or two-tailed* F*) test for equal population variances or, as it is often called, the "F test for homogeneity of variance." The folded* F *value of 1.25 is found by dividing the square of the larger standard deviation (4.24)(4.24) by the square of the smaller standard deviation (3.79)(3.79). When the p-value for* F*, shown as Pr >* F *in the SAS output, is too small—say, less than .10—there is a possibility that the population variances are not equal. In this case, the more accurate results for the* t *test for unequal variances should be reported. (Because the* F *test responds to any non-normality. as well as to unequal population variances, some practitioners prefer other tests, such as Levene's test for equal population variances as a screening device for reporting* t *test results based on unequal variances. For more information about both the* t *test that accommodates unequal population variances and Levene's test, see* Chapter 7 in *D. C. Howell, Statistical Methods for Psychology, 7th ed. (Belmont, CA: Wadsworth, 2010).*

Summary

Statistical hypotheses for the difference between two population means must be selected from among the following three possibilities:

Nondirectional: $H_0: \mu_1 - \mu_2 = 0$
$H_1: \mu_1 - \mu_2 \neq 0$

Directional, lower tail critical: $H_0: \mu_1 - \mu_2 \geq 0$
$H_1: \mu_1 - \mu_2 < 0$

Directional, upper tail critical: $H_0: \mu_1 - \mu_2 \leq 0$
$H_1: \mu_1 - \mu_2 > 0$

Tests of this null hypothesis are based on the sampling distribution of the difference between sample means, $\bar{X}_1 - \bar{X}_2$. The mean of this sampling distribution equals the difference between population means, and its standard error roughly measures the average amount by which any difference between sample means deviates from the difference between population means.

Because the standard error must be estimated, hypothesis tests use the *t* ratio for two independent samples.

The *p*-value for a test result indicates its degree of rarity, given that the null hypothesis is true. Smaller *p*-values tend to discredit the null hypothesis.

A confidence interval also can be constructed to estimate differences between population means. A single interpretation is possible only if the two limits of the confidence interval share the same sign, either both positive or both negative.

The importance of a statistically significant result can be evaluated with Cohen's *d*, the unit-free, standardized estimate of effect size. Cohen's guidelines identify *d* values in the vicinity of .20, .50, and .80 with small, medium, and large effects, respectively.

The *t* test assumes that both underlying populations are normally distributed with equal variances. Except under rare circumstances, you need not be concerned about violations of these assumptions.

Important Terms
. . . .

Two independent samples   **Effect**

Sampling distribution of $\bar{X}_1 - \bar{X}_2$ **Estimated standard error ($s_{\bar{X}_1 - \bar{X}_2}$)**

Pooled variance estimate (s_p^2)   **Statistical significance**

p-value   **Standardized effect estimate,**

Confidence intervals for $\mu_1 - \mu_2$ **Cohen's d**

Key Equations
. . . .

t RATIO

$$t = \frac{(\bar{X}_1 - \bar{X}_2) - (\mu_1 - \mu_2)_{hyp}}{s_{\bar{X}_1 - \bar{X}_2}}$$

where $$s_{\bar{X}_1 - \bar{X}_2} = \sqrt{\frac{s_p^2}{n_1} + \frac{s_p^2}{n_2}}$$

and $$s_p^2 = \frac{SS_1 + SS_2}{n_1 + n_2 - 2}$$

STANDARDIZED EFFECT

$$d = \frac{\overline{X}_1 - \overline{X}_2}{\sqrt{s_p^2}}$$

REVIEW QUESTIONS

*14.10 Figure 4.2 on page 75 describes the results for two fictitious experiments, each with the same mean difference of 2 but with noticeably different variabilities. Unresolved was the question "Once variability has been considered, should the difference between each pair of means be viewed as real or merely transitory?" A t test for two independent samples permits us to answer this question for each experimental result.

(a) Referring to Figure 4.2, again decide which of the two identical differences between pairs of means—that for Experiment B or for Experiment C—is more likely to be viewed as real.

(b) Given that $s_p^2 = .33$ for Experiment B, test the null hypothesis at the .05 level of significance.

(c) Given that $s_p^2 = 3.67$ for Experiment C, test the null hypothesis at the .05 level of significance. You needn't repeat the usual step-by-step hypothesis test procedure, but specify the observed value of t and the decision about the null hypothesis.

(d) Specify the approximate p-values for both t tests.

(e) Answer the original question about whether the difference between each pair of means is real or merely transitory.

Answers on page 508.

14.11 To test compliance with authority, a classical experiment in social psychology requires subjects to administer increasingly painful electric shocks to seemingly helpless victims who agonize in an adjacent room.* Each subject earns a score between 0 and 30, depending on the point at which the subject refuses to comply with authority—an investigator, dressed in a white lab coat, who orders the administration of increasingly intense shocks. A score of 0 signifies the subject's unwillingness to comply at the very outset, and a score of 30 signifies the subject's willingness to comply completely with the experimenter's orders.

Ignore the very real ethical issues raised by this type of experiment, and assume that you want to study the effect of a "committee atmosphere" on compliance with authority. In one condition, shocks are administered only after an affirmative decision by the committee, consisting of one

....

* See S. Milgram, *Obedience to Authority: An Experimental View* (New York: HarperPerennial, 1975).

real subject and two associates of the investigator, who act as subjects but, in fact, merely go along with the decision of the real subject. In the other condition, shocks are administered only after an affirmative decision by a solitary real subject.

A total of twelve subjects are randomly assigned, in equal numbers, to the committee condition (X_1) and to the solitary condition (X_2). A compliance score is obtained for each subject. Use t to test the null hypothesis at the .05 level of significance.

COMPLIANCE SCORES	
COMMITTEE	SOLITARY
2	3
5	8
20	7
15	10
4	14
10	0

14.12 To determine whether training in a series of workshops on creative thinking increases IQ scores, a total of 70 students are randomly divided into treatment and control groups of 35 each. After two months of training, the sample mean IQ ($\bar{X}_1$) for the treatment group equals 110, and the sample mean IQ ($\bar{X}_2$) for the control group equals 108. The estimated standard error equals 1.80.

(a) Using t, test the null hypothesis at the .01 level of significance.

(b) If appropriate (because the null hypothesis has been rejected), estimate the standardized effect size, construct a 99 percent confidence interval for the true population mean difference, and interpret these estimates.

*14.13 Is the performance of college students affected by the grading policy? In an introductory biology class, a total of 40 student volunteers are randomly assigned, in equal numbers, to take the course for either letter grades or a simple pass/fail. At the end of the academic term, the mean achievement score for the letter grade students ($\bar{X}_1$) equals 86.2, and the mean achievement score for pass/fail students ($\bar{X}_2$) equals 81.6. The estimated standard error is 1.50.

(a) Use t to test the null hypothesis at the .05 level of significance.

(b) How would the above hypothesis test change if the roles of X_1 and X_2 were reversed—that is, if X_1 were identified with pass/fail students and X_2 were identified with letter grade students?

(c) Most students would doubtless prefer to select their favorite grading policy rather than be randomly assigned to a particular grading policy. Therefore, why not replace random assignment with self-selection?

(d) Specify the p-value for this test result.

(e) If the test result is statistically significant, estimate the standardized effect size, given that the standard deviation, s_p, equals 5.

(f) State how the test results might be reported in the literature, given that $s_1 = 5.39$ and $s_2 = 4.58$.

Answers on page 508.

*14.14 An investigator wishes to determine whether alcohol consumption causes a deterioration in the performance of automobile drivers. Before the driving test, subjects drink a glass of orange juice, which, in the case of the treatment group, is laced with two ounces of vodka. Performance is measured by the number of errors made on a driving simulator. A total of one hundred and twenty volunteer subjects are randomly assigned, in equal numbers, to the two groups. For subjects in the treatment group, the mean number of errors ($\bar{X}_1$) equals 26.4, and for subjects in the control group, the mean number of errors ($\bar{X}_2$) equals 18.6. The estimated standard error equals 2.4.

(a) Use t to test the null hypothesis at the .05 level of significance.

(b) Specify the p-value for this test result.

(c) If appropriate, construct a 95 percent confidence interval for the true population mean difference and interpret this interval.

(d) If the test result is statistically significant, use Cohen's d to estimate the effect size, given that the standard deviation, s_p, equals 13.15.

(e) State how these test results might be reported in the literature, given $s_1 = 13.99$ and $s_2 = 12.15$.

Answers on page 509.

14.15 Review Question 2.14 on page 53 lists the GPAs for groups of 27 meditators and 27 non-meditators.

(a) Given that the mean GPA equals 3.19 for the meditators and 2.90 for the non-meditators, and that s_p^2 equals .20, specify the observed value of t and its approximate p-value.

(b) Answer the original question about whether these two groups tend to differ.

(c) If the p-value is less than .05, use Cohen's d to estimate the effect size.

14.16 After testing several thousand high school seniors, a state department of education reported a statistically significant difference between the mean GPAs for female and male students. Comments?

CHAPTER 15

t Test for Two Related Samples (Repeated Measures)

Preview

Although differences among individuals make life interesting, they also can blunt the precision of a statistical analysis because of their considerable impact on the overall variability among scores. You can control for individual differences by measuring each subject twice and using a t *test for repeated measures. This* t *test can be extra sensitive to detecting a false null hypothesis. However, several potential problems must be addressed before adopting a repeated-measures design.*

15.1 EPO EXPERIMENT WITH REPEATED MEASURES

In the EPO experiment of Chapter 14, the endurance scores of patients reflect not only the effect of EPO, *if it exists,* but also the random effects of many uncontrolled factors. One very important type of uncontrolled factor, referred to as *individual differences,* reflects the array of characteristics, such as differences in attitude, physical fitness, personality, etc., that distinguishes one person from another. If uncontrolled, individual differences can cause appreciable random variations among endurance scores and, therefore, make it more difficult to detect any treatment effect. When each subject is measured twice, as in the experiment described in this chapter, the *t* test for repeated measures can be extra sensitive to detecting a treatment effect by eliminating the distorting effect of variability due to individual differences.

Difference (*D*) Scores

Computations can be simplified by working directly with the difference between pairs of endurance scores, that is, by working directly with

---

DIFFERENCE SCORE (*D*)

$$D = X_1 - X_2 \qquad (15.1)$$

Difference Score (D)

The arithmetic difference between each pair of scores in repeated measures or, more generally, in two related samples.

where D is the **difference score** and X_1 and X_2 are the paired endurance scores for each patient measured twice, once under the treatment condition and once under the control condition, respectively. Essentially, the use of difference scores converts a two-sample problem with X_1 and X_2 scores into a one-sample problem with D scores.

Mean Difference Score (*D̄*)

To obtain the mean for a set of difference scores, add all difference scores and divide by the number of scores, that is,

---

MEAN DIFFERENCE SCORE (*D̄*)

$$\bar{D} = \frac{\Sigma D}{n} \qquad (15.2)$$

---

where $\bar{D}$ is the mean difference score, ΣD is the sum of all positive difference scores *minus* the sum of all negative difference scores, and n is the number of difference scores. The sign of $\bar{D}$ is crucial. For example, in the current experiment, a positive value of $\bar{D}$ would signify that EPO facilitates endurance, while a negative value of $\bar{D}$ would signify that EPO hinders endurance.

Comparing the Two Experiments

To simplify comparisons, exactly the same six X_1 scores and six X_2 scores in the original EPO experiment with two independent samples are used to generate

Table 15.1 SCORES FOR TWO EPO EXPERIMENTS		
ORIGINAL		**NEW**
X_1	X_2	D
12	7	5
5	3	2
11	4	7
11	6	5
9	3	6
18	13	5

the six D scores in the new EPO experiment with repeated measures, as indicated in Table 15.1. Therefore, the sample mean difference also is the same, both for the original experiment, where $\bar{X}_1 - \bar{X}_2 = 11 - 6 = 5$, and for the new experiment, where $\bar{D} = 5$. To dramatize the beneficial effects of repeated measures, highly similar pairs of X_1 and X_2 scores appear in the new experiment. For example, high endurance scores of 18 and 13 minutes are paired, presumably for a very physically fit patient, while low scores of only 5 and 3 minutes are paired, presumably for another patient in terrible shape. Since in real applications there is no guarantee that individual differences will be this large, the net effect of a repeated-measures experiment might not be as beneficial as that described in the current analysis.

Figure 15.1 shows the much smaller variability among paired differences in endurance scores, D, for the new experiment. The range of scores in the top histogram for X_1 and X_2 equals 15 (from $18 - 3$), while that in the bottom histogram for D equals only 5 (from $7 - 2$). This suggests that once the new data have been analyzed with a t test for repeated measures, it should be possible not only to reject the null hypothesis again, but also to claim a much smaller p-value than that ($p < .05$) for the t test for the original experiment with two independent samples.

Repeated Measures

Repeated Measures

Whenever the same subject is measured more than once.

A favorite technique for controlling individual differences is referred to as **repeated measures,** *because each subject is measured more than once.* By

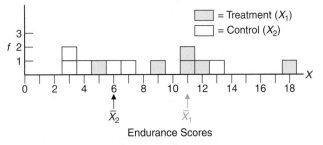

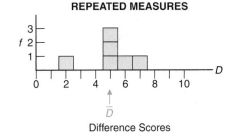

FIGURE 15.1

Different variabilities (with identical mean differences of 5) in EPO experiments with two independent samples and with repeated measures.

focusing on the *differences* between pairs of scores for each subject, the investigator effectively eliminates, by the simple act of subtraction, each individual's unique impact on both endurance scores. Accordingly, an analysis of the resulting difference scores reflects only any effects due to EPO, *if it exists,* and random variations of other uncontrolled factors or *experimental errors* not attributable to individual differences. (Experimental errors refer to random variations in endurance scores due to the combined impact of numerous uncontrolled changes, such as slight changes in temperature, treadmill speed, etc., as well as any changes in a particular subject's motivation, health, etc., between the two experimental sessions.) Because of the smaller standard error term, the result is a test with an increased likelihood of detecting any effect due to EPO.

Two Related Samples

Two Related Samples

Each observation in one sample is paired, on a one-to-one basis, with a single observation in the other sample.

Favored by investigators who wish to control for individual differences, repeated measures represent the most important special case of two related samples. **Two related samples** occur whenever *each observation in one sample is paired, on a one-to-one basis, with a single observation in the other sample.*

Repeated measures might not always be feasible since, as discussed below, several potential complications must be resolved before measuring subjects twice. An investigator still might choose to use two related samples by matching pairs of different subjects in terms of some uncontrolled variable that appears to have a considerable impact on the dependent variable. For example, patients might be matched for their body weight because preliminary studies revealed that, regardless of whether or not they received EPO, lightweight patients have better endurance scores than heavyweight patients. Before collecting data, patients could be matched, beginning with the two lightest and ending with the two heaviest. Now, as with repeated measures, the endurance scores for pairs of matched patients tend to be more similar (than those of unmatched subjects in two independent samples), and so the statistical test must be altered to reflect this new dependency between pairs of matched endurance scores.

Progress Check *15.1 Indicate whether each of the following studies involves two independent samples or two related samples, and in the latter case, indicate whether the study involves repeated measures for the same subjects or matched pairs of different subjects.

(a) Estimates of weekly TV-viewing time of third-grade girls compared with those of third-grade boys.

(b) Number of cigarettes smoked by participants before and after an anti-smoking workshop.

(c) Annual incomes of husbands compared with those of their wives.

(d) Problem-solving skills of recognized scientists compared with those of recognized artists, given that scientists and artists have been matched for IQ.

Answers on page 510.

Some Complications with Repeated Measurements

Unfortunately, the attractiveness of repeated measures sometimes fades upon closer inspection. For instance, since each patient is measured twice, once in the treatment condition and once in the control condition, sufficient time must elapse between these two conditions to eliminate any lingering effects due to the treatment. If there is any concern that these effects cannot be eliminated, use each subject in only one condition.

Counterbalancing

Otherwise, when subjects do perform double duty in both conditions, *it is customary to randomly assign half of the subjects to experience the two conditions in a particular order*—say, first the treatment and then the control condition—*while the other half of the subjects experience the two conditions in the reverse order.* Known as **counterbalancing,** this adjustment controls for any sequence effect, that is, any potential bias in favor of one condition merely because subjects happen to experience it first (or second).*

Counterbalancing

Reversing the order of conditions for equal numbers of all subjects.

Presumably, the investigator considered these potential complications before beginning the EPO experiment with repeated measures. The two sessions should have been separated by a sufficiently long period of time—possibly several weeks—in order to dissipate any lingering effects of EPO. In addition, a randomly selected half of the six patients should have experienced the two conditions in one order, while the remaining patients should have experienced the two conditions in the reverse order.

15.2 STATISTICAL HYPOTHESES

Null Hypothesis

Converting to difference scores generates a single population of difference scores, and the null hypothesis is expressed in terms of this new population. If EPO has either no consistent effect or a negative effect on endurance scores when patients are measured twice, the population mean of all difference scores, μ_D, should equal zero or less. In symbols, an equivalent statement reads:

$$H_0 : \mu_D \leq 0$$

Alternative (or Research) Hypothesis

As before, the investigator wants to reject the null hypothesis only if EPO actually increases endurance scores. An equivalent statement in symbols reads:

$$H_1 : \mu_D > 0$$

---

*Counterbalancing would be inappropriate for repeated-measure experiments that focus on any changes in the dependent variable *before* and *after* some special event, such as the anti-smoking workshop described in Questions 15.1(b) and 15.8.

This directional alternative hypothesis translates into a one-tailed test with the upper tail critical.

Two Other Possible Alternative Hypotheses

Although not appropriate for the current experiment, there are two other possible alternative hypotheses. Another directional hypothesis, expressed as

$$H_1 : \mu_D < 0$$

translates into a one-tailed test with the lower tail critical, and a nondirectional hypothesis, expressed as

$$H_1 : \mu_D \neq 0$$

translates into a two-tailed test.

15.3 SAMPLING DISTRIBUTION OF $\bar{D}$

The sample mean of the difference scores, $\bar{D}$, varies from sample to sample, and it has a sampling distribution with its own mean, $\mu_{\bar{D}}$, and standard error, $\sigma_{\bar{D}}$. When $\bar{D}$ is viewed as the mean for a single sample of difference scores, its sampling distribution can be depicted as a straightforward extension of the sampling distribution of $\bar{X}$, the mean for a single sample of original scores, as described in Chapter 9. Therefore, the mean, $\mu_{\bar{D}}$, and standard error, $\sigma_{\bar{D}}$, of the sampling distribution of $\bar{D}$ have essentially the same properties as the mean, $\mu_{\bar{X}}$, and standard error, $\sigma_{\bar{X}}$, respectively, of the sampling distribution of of $\bar{X}$.

Since the mean of the sampling distribution of $\bar{X}$ equals the population mean, that is, since $\mu_{\bar{X}} = \mu$, the mean of the sampling distribution of $\bar{D}$ equals the corresponding population mean (for difference scores), that is,

$$\mu_{\bar{D}} = \mu_D$$

Likewise, since the standard error of $\bar{X}$ equals the population standard deviation divided by the square root of the sample size, that is, since $\sigma_{\bar{X}} = \sigma/\sqrt{n}$, the standard error of $\bar{D}$ equals the corresponding population standard deviation (for difference scores) divided by the square root of the sample size, that is,

$$\sigma_{\bar{D}} = \frac{\sigma_D}{\sqrt{n}}$$

15.4 t TEST

The null hypothesis for two related samples can be tested with a t ratio. Expressed in words,

$$t = \frac{(sample\ mean\ difference) - (hypothesized\ population\ mean\ difference)}{estimated\ standard\ error}$$

Expressed in symbols,

---

t RATIO FOR TWO POPULATION MEANS (TWO RELATED SAMPLES)

$$t = \frac{\overline{D} - \mu_{D_{hyp}}}{s_{\overline{D}}}$$

(15.3)

---

which has a t sampling distribution with $n - 1$ degrees of freedom. In Formula 15.3, $\overline{D}$ represents the sample mean of the difference scores; $\mu_{D_{hyp}}$ represents the hypothesized population mean (of zero) for the difference scores; and $s_{\overline{D}}$ represents the estimated standard error of $\overline{D}$, as defined later in Formula 15.5.

Finding Critical *t* Values

To find a critical t in Table B in Appendix C, follow the usual procedure. Read the entry in the cell intersected by the row for the correct number of degrees of freedom and the column for the test specifications. To find the critical t for the current EPO experiment, go to the right-hand panel for a one-tailed test in Table B, then locate the row corresponding to 5 degrees of freedom (from $df = n - 1 = 6 - 1 = 5$), and locate the column for a one-tailed test at the .05 level of significance. The intersected cell specifies 2.015.

Summary for EPO Experiment

The boxed hypothesis test summary for the current EPO experiment indicates that since the calculated t of 7.35 exceeds the critical t of 2.015, we're able to reject H_0.

It's important to mention the use of repeated measures (or any matching) in the conclusion of the report. Repeated measures eliminates one important source of variability among endurance scores—the variability due to individual differences—that otherwise inflates the standard error term and causes an increase in β, the probability of a type II error.

Because of the smaller standard error for repeated measures, the calculated t of 7.35, with $df = 5$, permits us to claim a much smaller p-value ($p < .001$) than that ($p < .05$) for a t test based on the same data in the original EPO experiment with two independent samples.

15.5 DETAILS: CALCULATIONS FOR THE *t* TEST

The three panels in Table 15.2 show the computational steps that produce a t of 7.35 in the current experiment.

Panel I

Panel I involves most of the computational labor, and it generates values for the sample mean difference, $\overline{D}$, and the sample standard deviation for the difference scores, s_D. To obtain the sample standard deviation, first use a variation on

HYPOTHESIS TEST SUMMARY
t Test for Two Population Means:
Repeated Measures (EPO Experiment)

Research Problem

When patients are measured twice, once with and once without EPO, does the population mean difference score show greater endurance due to EPO?

Statistical Hypotheses

$$H_0: \mu_D \leq 0$$
$$H_1: \mu_D > 0$$

Decision Rule

Reject H_0 at the .05 level of significance if $t \geq 2.015$ (from Table B in Appendix C, given that $df = n - 1 = 6 - 1 = 5$).

Calculations

$$t = \frac{5 - 0}{0.68} = 7.35 \qquad \text{(See Table 15.1 for all computations.)}$$

Decision

Reject H_0 at the .05 level of significance because the calculated t of 7.35 exceeds 2.015.

Interpretation

There is evidence that when patients are measured twice, EPO is found to increase the mean endurance score.

the computation formula for the sum of squares (Formula 4.4 on page 85), where X has been replaced with D, that is,

$$SS_D = \sum D^2 - \frac{(\sum D)^2}{n}$$

and then, after dividing the sum of squares, SS_D, by its degrees of freedom, $n - 1$, extract the square root, that is,

SAMPLE STANDARD DEVIATION, s_D

$$s_D = \sqrt{\frac{SS_D}{n - 1}} \qquad (15.4)$$

Table 15.2
CALCULATIONS FOR THE *t* TEST: REPEATED MEASURES
(EPO EXPERIMENT)

I. FINDING THE MEAN AND STANDARD DEVIATION, $\bar{D}$ AND s_D

(a) Computational sequence:

Assign a value to n, the number of difference scores 1
Subtract X_2 from X_1 to obtain D 2
Sum all D scores 3
Substitute numbers in the formula 4 and solve for $\bar{D}$
Square each D score 5, one at a time, and then add all squared D scores 6
Substitute numbers in the formula 7 for SS_D, and then solve for s_D 8

(b) Data and computations:

ENDURANCE SCORES (MINUTES)

PATIENT	EPO X_1	CONTROL X_2	DIFFERENCE SCORES 2 D	5 D^2
1	12	7	5	25
2	5	3	2	4
3	11	4	7	49
4	11	6	5	25
5	9	3	6	36
6	18	13	5	25
1 $n = 6$			3 $\Sigma D = 30$	6 $\Sigma D^2 = 164$

$$4 \quad \bar{D} = \frac{\Sigma D}{n} = \frac{30}{6} = 5$$

$$7 \quad SS_D = \Sigma D^2 - \frac{(\Sigma D)^2}{n} = 164 - \frac{(30)^2}{6} = 164 - 150 = 14$$

$$8 \quad s_D = \sqrt{\frac{SS_D}{n-1}} = \sqrt{\frac{14}{6-1}} = \sqrt{2.8} = 1.67$$

II. FINDING THE STANDARD ERROR, $s_{\bar{D}}$

(a) Computational sequence:

Substitute numbers obtained above in the formula 9 and solve for $s_{\bar{D}}$

(b) Computations:

$$9 \quad s_{\bar{D}} = \frac{s_D}{\sqrt{n}} = \frac{1.67}{\sqrt{6}} = \frac{1.67}{2.45} = 0.68$$

III. FINDING THE OBSERVED *t* RATIO

(a) Computational sequence:

Substitute numbers obtained above in the formula 10, as well as a value of 0 for $\mu_{D_{hyp}}$, and solve for t.

(b) Computations:

$$10 \quad t = \frac{\bar{D} - \mu_{D_{hyp}}}{s_{\bar{D}}} = \frac{5 - 0}{0.68} = 7.35$$

Panel II

Dividing the sample standard deviation, s_D, by the square root of its sample size, n, gives the estimated standard error, $s_{\bar{D}}$, that is,

---

ESTIMATED STANDARD ERROR, $s_{\bar{D}}$

$$s_{\bar{D}} = \frac{s_D}{\sqrt{n}}$$ (15.5)

Panel III

Finally, as defined in Formula 15.3, dividing the difference between the sample mean, $\bar{D}$, and the null hypothesized value, $\mu_{D_{hyp}}$ (of zero), by the estimated standard error, $s_{\bar{D}}$, culminates in the value for the t ratio.

Progress Check *15.2 An investigator tests a claim that vitamin C reduces the frequency of common colds. To eliminate the variability due to different family environments, pairs of children from the same family are randomly assigned to either a treatment group that receives vitamin C or a control group that receives fake vitamin C. Each child has a score that reflects the total number of days ill because of colds during the school year. The following scores are obtained for ten pairs of children:

PAIR NUMBER	DAYS ILL DUE TO COLDS	
	VITAMIN C (X_1)	FAKE VITAMIN C (X_2)
1	2	3
2	5	4
3	7	9
4	0	3
5	3	5
6	7	7
7	4	6
8	5	8
9	1	2
10	3	5

Using t, test the null hypothesis at the .05 level of significance.
Answer on page 510.

....

15.6 ESTIMATING EFFECT SIZE

Confidence Interval for μ_D

Given that two samples are related, as when patients were measured twice in the EPO experiment, a confidence interval for μ_D can be constructed from the following expression:

> ## CONFIDENCE INTERVAL FOR μ_D (TWO RELATED SAMPLES)
>
> $$\bar{D} \pm (t_{conf})(s_{\bar{D}}) \tag{15.6}$$

where $\bar{D}$ represents the sample mean of the difference scores; t_{conf} represents a number (distributed with $n - 1$ degrees of freedom) from the t tables, which satisfies the confidence specifications; and $s_{\bar{D}}$ represents the estimated standard error defined in Formula 15.5.

Finding t_{conf}

To find the appropriate value of t_{conf} in Formula 15.6, refer to Table B in Appendix C and follow the usual procedure for obtaining confidence intervals. If a 95 percent confidence interval is desired for the EPO experiment with repeated measures, first locate the row corresponding to 5 degrees of freedom, and then locate the column for the 95 percent level of confidence, that is, the column heading identified with a single asterisk. The intersected cell specifies a value of 2.571 for t_{conf}.

Given a value of 2.571 for t_{conf}, and (from Table 15.1) values of 5 for $\bar{D}$, the sample mean of the difference scores, and 0.68 for $s_{\bar{D}}$, the estimated standard error, Formula 15.6 becomes

$$5 \pm (2.571)(0.68) = 5 \pm 1.75 = \begin{cases} 6.75 \\ 3.25 \end{cases}$$

It can be claimed, with 95 percent confidence, that the interval between 3.25 minutes and 6.75 minutes includes the true mean for the population of difference endurance scores.

Interpreting Confidence Intervals for μ_D

Because both limits have similar (positive) signs, a single interpretation describes all of the possibilities included in this confidence interval. The appearance of only positive differences indicates that when patients are measured twice, EPO facilitates endurance. Furthermore, we can be *reasonably confident* that, on average, the true facilitative effect is neither less than 3.25 minutes nor more than 6.75 minutes.

Compare the confidence limits of the current interval for two related samples, 3.25 to 6.75, to those of the previous interval for two independent samples, –0.17 to 10.17. Although both intervals are based on the same data with identical mean differences of 2, the more precise interval for repeated measures, with both limits positive, reflects a reduction in the standard error caused by the elimination of variability due to individual differences.

Progress Check 15.3 Referring to the vitamin C experiment in Question 15.2, construct and interpret a 95 percent confidence interval for the population mean difference score.

Answer on page 510.

Standardized Effect Size, Cohen's *d*

Having rejected the null hypothesis for the EPO experiment with repeated measures, we can claim that the sample mean difference of 5 minutes is statistically significant. As has been noted in Chapter 14, one way to gauge the importance of a statistically significant result is to calculate Cohen's *d*. When the two samples are related, the formula for Cohen's *d* is:

STANDARDIZED EFFECT SIZE, COHEN'S *d* (TWO RELATED SAMPLES)

$$d = \frac{\bar{D}}{s_D} \qquad (15.7)$$

---

where *d* refers to the standardized estimate of effect size, while $\bar{D}$ and s_D represent the sample mean and standard deviation, respectively, of the difference scores.

When the mean difference of 5 is divided by the standard deviation of 1.67 (from Table 15.1), Cohen's *d* equals 2.99, a very large value equivalent to three standard deviations. (According to Cohen's guidelines, mentioned previously, the estimated effect size is small, medium, or large, depending on whether *d* is .20 or less, .50, or .80 or more, respectively.)

Progress Check *15.4 For the vitamin C experiment in Question 15.2, estimate and interpret the standardized effect size, *d*, given a mean, $\bar{D}$, of −1.50 days and a standard deviation, s_D, of 1.27 days.

Answer on page 510.

15.7 ASSUMPTIONS

Whether testing a hypothesis or constructing a confidence interval, *t* assumes that the population of difference scores is normally distributed. You need not be too concerned about violations of this assumption as long as the sample size is fairly large (greater than about ten pairs). Otherwise, in the *unlikely* event that you encounter conspicuous departures from normality, consider either increasing the sample size or using the less sensitive but more assumption-free Wilcoxon *T* test described in Chapter 20.

15.8 OVERVIEW: THREE *t* TESTS FOR POPULATION MEANS

In Chapters 13, 14, and 15, three *t* tests for population means have been described, and their more distinctive features are summarized in **Table 15.3**. Given a hypothesis test for one or two population means, a *t* test is appropriate if, as almost always is the case, the population standard deviation must be estimated. You must decide whether to use a *t* test for one sample, two independent samples, or two related samples. This decision is fairly straightforward if you proceed, step by step, as follows:

Table 15.3
SUMMARY OF *t* TESTS FOR POPULATION MEANS

TYPE OF SAMPLE	SAMPLE MEAN	NULL HYPOTHESIS*	STANDARD ERROR	*t* RATIO	DEGREES OF FREEDOM
One sample	$\bar{X}$	$H_0: \mu = $ some number	$s_{\bar{X}}$ (Formula 13.3)	$\dfrac{\bar{X} - \mu_{hyp}}{s_{\bar{X}}}$	$n - 1$
Two independent samples (no pairing)	$\bar{X}_1 - \bar{X}_2$	$H_0: \mu_1 - \mu_2 = 0$	$s_{\bar{X}_1 - \bar{X}_2}$ (Formula 14.3)	$\dfrac{(\bar{X}_1 - \bar{X}_2) - (\mu_1 - \mu_2)_{hyp}}{s_{\bar{X}_1 - \bar{X}_2}}$	$n_1 + n_2 - 2$
Two related samples	$\bar{D}$	$H_0: \mu_D = 0$	$s_{\bar{D}}$ (Formula 15.5)	$\dfrac{\bar{D} - \mu_{D_{hyp}}}{s_{\bar{D}}}$	$n - 1$ (where n refers to pairs of observations)

* For a two-tailed test.

One or Two Samples?

First, decide whether there are one or two samples. If there is only one sample, because the study deals with a single set of observations, then, of course, you need not search any further: The appropriate *t* is that for one sample.

Are the Two Samples Paired?

Second, if there are two samples, decide whether or not there is any pairing. If each observation is paired, on a one-to-one basis, with a single observation in the other sample (because of either repeated measures or matched pairs of different subjects), then the appropriate *t* is that for two related samples.

Finally, if there is no evidence of pairing between individual observations, then the appropriate *t* is that for two independent samples.

Examples

Let's identify the appropriate *t* test for each of several similar studies where, with the aid of radar guns, investigators clock the speeds of randomly selected motorists on a dangerous section of a state highway. Follow the recommended decision procedure to arrive at your own answer before checking the answer in the book.

Study A

Research Problem: Clocked speeds of randomly selected trucks are compared with clocked speeds of randomly selected cars.

Answer: Because there are two sets of observations (speeds for trucks and speeds for cars), there are two samples. Furthermore, since there is no indication of pairing among individual observations, the appropriate *t* test is that for two independent samples.

Study B

Research Problem: Clocked speeds of randomly selected motorists are compared with the posted speed limit of 50 miles per hour.

Answer: Because there is a single set of observations, the appropriate *t* test is that for one sample (where the null hypothesis equals 50 miles per hour).

Study C

Research Problem: Clocked speeds of randomly selected motorists are compared at two different locations: one mile before and one mile after a large sign listing the number of fatalities on that stretch of highway during the previous year.

Answer: Because there are two sets of observations (speeds before and speeds after the sign), there are two samples. Furthermore, since each observation in one sample (the speed of a particular motorist one mile before the sign) is paired with a single observation in the other sample (the speed of the *same* motorist one mile after the sign), the appropriate *t* test is that for two related samples, with repeated measures.

Beginning with the next set of exercises, you will be exposed to a variety of studies for which you must identify the appropriate statistical test. By following a step-by-step procedure, such as the one described here, you will be able to make this identification not only for textbook studies, but also for those encountered in everyday practice.

Progress Check *15.5 Each of the following studies requires a *t* test for one or more population means. Specify whether the appropriate *t* test is for one sample, two independent samples, or two related samples, and in the last case, whether it involves repeated measures or matched pairs of different subjects.

(a) College students are randomly assigned to receive either behavioral or cognitive therapy. After twenty therapeutic sessions, each student earns a score on a mental health questionnaire.

(b) A researcher wishes to determine whether attendance at a day-care center increases the scores of three-year-old children on a motor skill test. Random assignment dictates which twin from each pair of twenty twins attends the day-care center and which twin stays at home. (Such a draconian experiment doubtless would incur great resistance from the parents, not to mention the twins!)

(c) One hundred college freshmen are randomly assigned to sophomore roommates who have either similar or dissimilar vocational goals. At the end of their first year, the mean GPAs of these two groups are to be analyzed.

(d) According to the U.S. Department of Health, the average 16-year-old male can do 23 pushups. A physical education instructor finds that in his school district, 30 randomly selected 16-year-old males can do an average of 28 pushups.

(e) A child psychologist assigns aggression scores to each of ten children during two 60-minute observation periods separated by an intervening exposure to a series of violent TV cartoons.

Answers on page 510.

WWW

INTERNET DEMONSTRATION
Go to the Web site for this book (http://www.wiley.com\college\witte).
Click on the *Student Companion Site,* then *Internet Demonstrations,* and
finally ***Experiments*** to simulate the outcomes for either two independent
or two related samples, given specified differences between population
means and varying sample sizes.

15.9 *t* TEST FOR THE POPULATION CORRELATION COEFFICIENT, ρ

In Chapter 6, .80 describes the sample correlation coefficient, *r*, between the number of cards sent and the number of cards received by five friends. Any conclusions about the correlation coefficient in the underlying population—for instance, the population of all friends—must consider chance sampling variability as described by the sampling distribution of *r*.

Null Hypothesis

Let's view the greeting card data for the five friends as if they were a random sample of pairs of observations from the population of all friends. Then it's possible to test the null hypothesis that the population correlation coefficient, symbolized by the Greek letter ρ (rho), equals zero. In other words, it is possible to test the hypothesis that in the population of all friends, there is no correlation between the number of cards sent and the number of cards received.

Focus on Relationships Instead of Mean Differences

These five pairs of observations also can be viewed as two related samples, since each observation in one sample is paired with a single observation in the other sample. Now, however, we wish to determine whether there is a *relationship* between the number of cards sent and received, not whether there is a *mean difference* between the number of cards sent and received. Accordingly, the appropriate measure is the correlation coefficient, not the sample mean difference, and the appropriate *t* test is for the population correlation coefficient, not for the population mean of difference scores.

t Test

A new *t* test must be used to determine whether the observed *r* of .80 qualifies as a common or a rare outcome under the null hypothesis that ρ equals zero. To obtain a value for the *t* ratio, use the following formula:

---

t RATIO FOR A SINGLE POPULATION CORRELATION COEFFICIENT

$$t = \frac{r - \rho_{hyp}}{\sqrt{\dfrac{1 - r^2}{n - 2}}} \tag{15.8}$$

HYPOTHESIS TEST SUMMARY
t TEST FOR A POPULATION CORRELATION COEFFICIENT
(Greeting Card Exchange)

Problem

Could there be a correlation between the number of cards sent and the number of cards received for the population of all friends?

Statistical Hypotheses

$$H_0: \rho = 0$$
$$H_1: \rho \neq 0$$

Decision Rule

Reject H_0 at the .05 level of significance if $t \geq 3.182$ or if $t \leq -3.182$ (from Table B in Appendix C, given that $df = n - 2 = 5 - 2 = 3$).

Calculations

Given that $r = 0.80$ and $n = 5$:

$$t = \frac{.80 - 0}{\sqrt{\dfrac{1 - (.80)^2}{5 - 2}}} = \frac{.80}{\sqrt{\dfrac{1 - .64}{3}}} = \frac{.80}{\sqrt{\dfrac{.36}{3}}} = \frac{.80}{\sqrt{.12}} = \frac{.80}{.35} = 2.29$$

Decision

Retain H_0 at the .05 level of significance because $t = 2.29$ is less positive than 3.182.

Interpretation

The population correlation coefficient *could* equal zero. There is no evidence of a relationship between the number of cards sent and the number of cards received in the population of friends.

where r refers to the sample correlation coefficient (Formula 6.2); ρ_{hyp} refers to the hypothesized population correlation coefficient (which always must equal zero); and n refers to the number of pairs of observations. The expression in the denominator represents the estimated standard error of the sample correlation coefficient. As implied by the term at the bottom of this expression, the sampling distribution of t has $n - 2$ degrees of freedom. When pairs of observations are represented as points in a scatterplot, r assumes that the cluster of points approximates a straight line. Two degrees of freedom are lost because only $n - 2$ points are free to vary about some straight line that, itself, always depends on two points.

Importance of Sample Size

According to the present hypothesis test, the population correlation coefficient *could* equal zero.* This conclusion might seem surprising, given that an *r* of .80 was observed for the greeting card exchange. When the value of *r* is based on only five pairs of observations, as in the present example, its sampling variability is huge, and in fact, an *r* of .88 would have been required to reject the null hypothesis at the .05 level. Ordinarily, a serious investigation would use a larger sample size, preferably one that, with the aid of power curves similar to those described in Section 11.11, reflects the investigator's judgment about what would be the smallest important correlation.

If, in fact, a larger sample size had permitted the rejection of the null hypothesis, an *r* of .80 would have indicated a strong relationship. As mentioned in Chapter 6, values of *r* in the general vicinity of .10, .30, and .50 indicate weak, moderate, or strong relationships, respectively, according to Cohen's guidelines.

Progress Check *15.6 A random sample of 27 California taxpayers reveals an *r* of .43 between years of education and annual income. Use *t* to test the null hypothesis at the .05 level of significance that there is no relationship between educational level and annual income for the population of California taxpayers.

Answer on page 511.

Assumptions

When using the *t* test for the population correlation coefficient, you must assume that the relationship between the two variables, *X* and *Y*, can be described with a straight line and that the sample originates from a *normal bivariate population*. The latter term means that the separate population distributions for each variable (*X* and *Y*) should be normal. When these assumptions are suspect—for instance, if the observed distribution for one variable appears to be extremely non-normal—the test results are only approximate and should be interpreted accordingly.

Summary

Variability due to individual differences can be eliminated by using repeated measures, that is, measuring the same subject twice. Whether because of repeated measures for the same subject or matched pairs of different subjects, two samples are related whenever each observation in one sample is paired, on a one-to-one basis, with a single observation in the other sample.

When using repeated measures, be aware of potential complications due to inadvertent interactions between conditions or to a lack of counterbalancing.

The statistical hypotheses must be selected from among the following three possibilities, where μ_D represents the population mean for all difference scores:

---

* Strictly speaking, since it could have originated from a population with a zero correlation, the current *r* of .80 should have been ignored in Chapters 6 and 7, where it was featured, nonetheless, because of its computational simplicity.

Nondirectional:

$$H_0: \mu_D = 0$$
$$H_1: \mu_D \neq 0$$

Directional, lower tail critical:

$$H_0: \mu_D \geq 0$$
$$H_1: \mu_D < 0$$

Directional, upper tail critical:

$$H_0: \mu_D \leq 0$$
$$H_1: \mu_D > 0$$

The t ratio for two related samples has a sampling distribution with $n - 1$ degrees of freedom, given that n equals the number of paired observations.

A confidence interval can be constructed for estimating μ_D. A single interpretation is possible only if the limits of the interval have the same sign, either both positive or both negative.

If the t test is statistically significant, Cohen's d can be used as a standardized estimate of effect size.

When using t for two related samples, you must assume that the population of difference scores is normally distributed. You need not be too concerned about violations of this assumption as long as sample sizes are relatively large.

To test the hypothesis that the population correlation coefficient equals zero, use a new t ratio with $n - 2$ degrees of freedom.

Important Terms

Difference score (D)

Related samples

Sample mean of difference scores ($\bar{D}$)

Sample standard error ($s_{\bar{D}}$)

Population correlation coefficient (ρ)

Repeated measures

Counterbalancing

Key Equations

t RATIO

$$t = \frac{\bar{D} - \mu_{D_{hyp}}}{s_{\bar{D}}}$$

where $s_{\bar{D}} = \frac{s_D}{\sqrt{n}}$

REVIEW QUESTIONS

*15.7 An educational psychologist wants to check the claim that regular physical exercise improves academic achievement. To control for academic aptitude, pairs of college students with similar GPAs are randomly assigned to either a treatment group that attends daily exercise classes or a control group. At the end of the experiment, the following GPAs are reported for the seven pairs of participants:

PAIR NUMBER	GPAs	
	PHYSICAL EXERCISE (X_1)	**NO PHYSICAL EXERCISE** (X_2)
1	4.00	3.75
2	2.67	2.74
3	3.65	3.42
4	2.11	1.67
5	3.21	3.00
6	3.60	3.25
7	2.80	2.65

(a) Using t, test the null hypothesis at the .01 level of significance.

(b) Specify the p-value for this test result.

(c) If appropriate (because the test result is statistically significant), use Cohen's d to estimate the effect size.

(d) How might this test result be reported in the literature?

Answers on page 511.

15.8 A school psychologist wishes to determine whether a new anti-smoking film actually reduces the daily consumption of cigarettes by teenage smokers. The mean daily cigarette consumption is calculated for each of eight teenage smokers during the month *before* and the month *after* the film presentation, with the following results:

SMOKER NUMBER	MEAN DAILY CIGARETTE CONSUMPTION	
	BEFORE FILM (X_1)	**AFTER FILM** (X_2)
1	28	26
2	29	27
3	31	32
4	44	44
5	35	35
6	20	16
7	50	47
8	25	23

(**Note**: When deciding on the form of the alternative hypothesis, H_1, remember that a positive difference score $(D = X_1 - X_2)$ reflects a *decline* in cigarette consumption.)

(a) Using t, test the null hypothesis at the .05 level of significance.

(b) Specify the p-value for this test result.

(c) If appropriate (because the null hypothesis was rejected), construct a 95 percent confidence interval for the true population mean for all difference scores and use Cohen's d to obtain a standardized estimate of the effect size. Interpret these results.

(d) What might be done to improve the design of this experiment?

15.9 A manufacturer of a gas additive claims that it improves gas mileage. A random sample of 30 drivers tests this claim by determining their gas mileage for a full tank of gas that contains the additive (X_1) and for a full tank of gas that does not contain the additive (X_2). The sample mean difference, $\bar{D}$, equals 2.12 miles (in favor of the additive), and the estimated standard error equals 1.50 miles.

(a) Using t, test the null hypothesis at the .05 level of significance.

(b) Specify the p-value for this result.

(c) Are there any special precautions that should be taken with the present experimental design?

*15.10 In a classic study, which predates the existence of the EPO drug, Melvin Williams of Old Dominion University actually injected extra oxygen-bearing red cells into the subjects' bloodstream just prior to a treadmill test. Twelve long-distance runners were tested in five-mile runs on treadmills. Essentially, two running times were obtained for each athlete, once in the treatment or blood-doped condition after the injection of two pints of blood and once in the placebo control or non-blood-doped condition after the injection of a comparable amount of a harmless red saline solution. The presentation of the treatment and control conditions was counterbalanced, with half of the subjects unknowingly receiving the treatment first, then the control, and the other half receiving the conditions in reverse order.

Since the difference scores, as reported in the *New York Times*, on May 4, 1980, are calculated by subtracting blood-doped running times from control running times, a positive mean difference signifies that the treatment has a facilitative effect, that is, the athletes' running times are shorter when blood doped. The twelve athletes had a mean running time, $\bar{D}$, of 51.33 seconds with a standard deviation, s_D, of 66.33 seconds.

(a) Test the null hypothesis at the .05 level of significance.

(b) Specify the p-value for this result.

(c) Would you have arrived at the same decision about the null hypothesis if the difference scores had been reversed by subtracting the control times from the blood-doped times?

(d) If appropriate, construct and interpret a 95 percent confidence interval for the true effect of blood doping.

(e) Why is it important to counterbalance the presentation of blood-doped and control conditions?

(f) Comment on the wisdom of testing each subject twice—once under the blood-doped condition and once under the control condition—during a single 24-hour period. (Williams actually used much longer intervals in his study.)

Answers on page 512.

15.11 A researcher randomly assigns college freshmen to either of two experimental conditions. Because both groups consist of college freshmen, someone claims that it is appropriate to use a *t* test for the two related samples. Comments?

15.12 Although the samples are actually related, an investigator ignores this fact in the statistical analysis and uses a *t* test for two independent samples. How will this mistake affect the probability of a type II error?

15.13 A random sample of 38 statistics students from a large statistics class reveals an *r* of –.24 between their test scores on a statistics exam and the time they spent taking the exam. Test the null hypothesis with *t*, using the .01 level of significance.

CHAPTER
16

Analysis of Variance (One Factor)

Preview

The next three chapters describe a type of statistical analysis known as "analysis of variance." It is designed to detect differences between two or more groups defined for a single factor or independent variable with measures on different subjects (Chapter 16); for a single factor with repeated measures on the same subjects (Chapter 17); and for two factors (Chapter 18). As its name implies, variability or variance among observations is identified with various sources that, when tested appropriately, indicate whether observed differences between group means are probably real or merely due to chance.

A significant F test often is a prelude to additional analyses, including an estimate of the size of any detected effect, as well as multiple comparison tests that are designed to pinpoint precisely which pairs of mean differences contribute to the overall significant result.

16.1 TESTING A HYPOTHESIS ABOUT SLEEP DEPRIVATION AND AGGRESSION

Does sleep deprivation cause us to be either more or less aggressive? To test this assumption, a psychologist randomly assigns volunteer subjects to sleep-deprivation periods of either 0, 24, or 48 hours (the independent variable or factor). Subsequently, subjects are tested for aggressive behavior in a controlled social situation. Aggression scores (the dependent variable) indicate the total number of different aggressive behaviors, such as put-downs, arguments, or verbal interruptions, demonstrated by subjects during the test period.

Statistical Hypotheses

The current null hypothesis states that, on average, the three populations of subjects, who are deprived of sleep for either 0, 24, or 48 hours, will have similar aggression scores. Expressed symbolically, the null hypothesis reads:

$$H_0: \mu_0 = \mu_{24} = \mu_{48}$$

where μ_0, μ_{24}, and μ_{48} represent the mean aggression scores for the populations of subjects who are deprived of sleep for 0, 24, and 48 hours, respectively. Rejection of the null hypothesis implies, most generally, that sleep deprivation influences aggressive behavior, since the alternative or research hypothesis, H_1, simply states that the null hypothesis is false. Ordinarily, the alternative or research hypothesis reads:

$$H_1: H_0 \text{ is false.}$$

New Test for More Than Two Population Means

Resist any urge to test this null hypothesis with t, since, as will be discussed in Section 16.10, the regular t test usually can't handle null hypotheses for more than two population means. *When data are quantitative, an overall test of the null hypothesis for more than two population means requires a new statistical procedure known as **analysis of variance**,* which is often abbreviated as **ANOVA** (from ANalysis Of VARiance and pronounced an-OH'-vuh).

Analysis of Variance (ANOVA)
An overall test of the null hypothesis for more than two population means.

One-Factor ANOVA

One-Factor ANOVA
The simplest type of ANOVA that tests for differences among population means categorized by only one independent variable.

This chapter describes the simplest type of analysis of variance. Often referred to as a **one-factor (or one-way) ANOVA,** *it tests whether differences exist among population means categorized by only one factor or independent variable,* such as hours of sleep deprivation, *with measures on different subjects.* The ANOVA techniques described in this chapter presume that all scores are independent. In other words, each subject contributes just one score to the overall analysis. Special ANOVA techniques, described in Chapter 17, must be used when scores lack independence because each subject contributes more than one score (or because subjects are matched across groups). Later sections in the current chapter treat the computational procedures for ANOVA; the next few sections emphasize the intuitive basis for ANOVA.

Two Possible Outcomes

To simplify computations, unrealistically small, numerically friendly samples are used in this and the next two chapters. In practice, samples that are either unduly small or excessively large should be avoided, as suggested in Section 11.11.* Let's assume that the psychologist randomly assigns only three subjects to each of the three levels of sleep deprivation. Subsequently, subjects' aggression scores reflect their behavior in a controlled social situation.

Table 16.1 shows two fictitious experimental outcomes that, when analyzed with ANOVA, produce different decisions about the null hypothesis: it is retained for one outcome but rejected for the other. Before reading on, predict which outcome would cause the null hypothesis to be retained and which would cause it to be rejected.

You are correct if you predicted that Outcome A would cause the null hypothesis to be retained, while Outcome B would cause the null hypothesis to be rejected.

Mean Differences Still Important

Your predictions for Outcomes A and B most likely were based on the relatively small differences between group means for Outcome A and the relatively large differences between group means for Outcome B. Observed mean differences

Table 16.1
TWO POSSIBLE OUTCOMES OF A SLEEP-DEPRIVATION EXPERIMENT: AGGRESSION SCORES

	OUTCOME A	HOURS OF SLEEP DEPRIVATION	
	ZERO	**TWENTY-FOUR**	**FORTY-EIGHT**
	3	4	2
	5	8	4
	7	6	6
Group mean:	5	6	4	Grand mean = 5

	OUTCOME B	HOURS OF SLEEP DEPRIVATION	
	ZERO	**TWENTY-FOUR**	**FORTY-EIGHT**
	0	3	6
	4	6	8
	2	6	10
Group mean:	2	5	8	Grand mean = 5

----

* A power analysis could be used—with the aid of software, such as Minitab's *Power and Sample Size* or G*Power at http://www.psycho.uni-duesseldorf.de/aap/projects/gpower/—to identify sample sizes that will reasonably detect the smallest important effect, as defined for the multiple population means in one-factor and two-factor ANOVA.

have been a major ingredient in previous *t* tests, and these differences are just as important in ANOVA. It is easy to lose sight of this fact because observed mean differences appear, somewhat disguised, as one type of variability in ANOVA. It takes extra effort to view ANOVA—with its emphasis on the analysis of several sources of variability—as related to previous *t* tests. Reminders of this fact occur throughout the current chapter.

16.2 TWO SOURCES OF VARIABILITY

Differences between Group Means

First, without worrying about computational details, look more closely at one source of variability in Outcomes A and B: the differences between group means. Differences of 5, 6, and 4 appear between group means in Outcome A, and these relatively small differences might reflect only chance. Even though the null hypothesis is true (because sleep deprivation does not affect the subjects' aggression scores), group means tend to differ merely because of chance sampling variability. It's reasonable to expect, therefore, that the null hypothesis for Outcome A should not be rejected. There appears to be a lack of evidence that sleep deprivation affects the subjects' aggression scores in Outcome A.

On the other hand, differences of 2, 5, and 8 appear between the group means for Outcome B, and these relatively large differences might not be attributable to chance. Instead, they indicate that the null hypothesis probably is false (because sleep deprivation affects the subjects' aggression scores). It's reasonable to expect, therefore, that the null hypothesis for Outcome B should be rejected. There appears to be evidence of a **treatment effect,** that is, *the existence of at least one difference between the population means defined by the independent variable* (sleep deprivation).

Variability within Groups

A more definitive decision about the null hypothesis views differences between group means as one source of variability to be compared with a second source of variability. An estimate of **variability between groups,** that is, *the variation among scores of subjects who, being in different groups, receive different experimental treatments,* must be compared with another, completely independent estimate of **variability within groups,** that is, *the variation among scores of subjects who, being in the same group, receive the same experimental treatment.* As will be seen,

the more that the variability between groups exceeds the variability within groups, the more suspect will be the null hypothesis.

Let's focus on the second source of variability—the variability within groups for subjects treated similarly. Referring to Table 16.1, focus on the differences among the scores of 3, 5, and 7 for the three subjects who are treated similarly in the first group. Continue this procedure, one group at a time, to obtain an overall impression of variability within groups for all three groups in Outcome A and for all three groups in Outcome B. Notice the relative stability of the differences among the three scores within each of the various groups, regardless of whether the group happens to be in Outcome A or Outcome B. For instance, one crude

---

Treatment Effect

The existence of at least one difference between the population means.

Variability between Groups

Variability among scores of subjects who, being in different groups, receive different experimental treatments.

Variability within Groups

Variability among scores of subjects who, being in the same group, receive the same experimental treatment.

measure of variability, the range, equals either 3 or 4 for each group shown in Table 16.1.

A key point is that the variability within each group depends entirely on the scores of subjects treated similarly (exposed to the same sleep deprivation period), and it never involves the scores of subjects treated differently (exposed to different sleep deprivation periods). In contrast to the variability between groups, the variability within groups never reflects the presence of a treatment effect. Regardless of whether the null hypothesis is true or false, the variability within groups reflects only **random error,** that is, *the combined effects on the scores of individual subjects of all uncontrolled factors,* such as individual differences among subjects, slight variations in experimental conditions, and errors in measurement. In ANOVA, the within-group estimate often is referred to simply as the *error term,* and it is analogous to the pooled variance estimate (s_p^2) in the *t* test for two independent samples.

Random Error

The combined effects of all uncontrolled factors on the scores of individual subjects.

Progress Check *16.1 Imagine a simple experiment with three groups, each containing four observations. For each of the following outcomes, indicate whether there is variability between groups and also whether there is variability within groups.

NOTE: You need not do any calculations, with the possible exception of an occasional group mean, in order to answer this question.

(a)	GROUP 1	GROUP 2	GROUP 3
	8	8	8
	8	8	8
	8	8	8
	8	8	8
(b)	**GROUP 1**	**GROUP 2**	**GROUP 3**
	8	4	12
	8	4	12
	8	4	12
	8	4	12
(c)	**GROUP 1**	**GROUP 2**	**GROUP 3**
	4	6	5
	6	6	7
	8	10	9
	14	10	11
(d)	**GROUP 1**	**GROUP 2**	**GROUP 3**
	6	11	20
	8	12	18
	8	14	23
	10	15	25

Answers on page 512.

16.3 *F* TEST

In previous chapters, the null hypothesis has been tested with a t ratio. In the two-sample case, t reflects the ratio between the observed difference between the two sample means in the numerator and the estimated standard error in the denominator. For three or more samples, the null hypothesis is tested with a new ratio, the F ratio. Essentially, F reflects the ratio of the observed differences between all sample means (measured as variability between groups) in the numerator and the estimated error term or pooled variance estimate (measured as variability within groups) in the denominator term, that is,

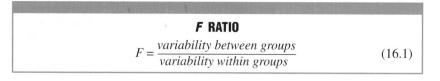

F RATIO

$$F = \frac{variability\ between\ groups}{variability\ within\ groups} \tag{16.1}$$

Like t, F has its own family of sampling distributions that can be consulted, as described in Section 16.6, to test the null hypothesis. The resulting test is known as an F test.

An *F* test of the null hypothesis is based on the notion that if the null hypothesis is true, both the numerator and the denominator of the *F* ratio would tend to be about the same, but if the null hypothesis is false, the numerator would tend to be larger than the denominator.

If Null Hypothesis Is True

If the null hypothesis is true (because there is no treatment effect due to different sleep deprivation periods), the two estimates of variability (between and within groups) would reflect only random error. In this case,

$$F = \frac{random\ error}{random\ error}$$

Except for chance, estimates in both the numerator and the denominator are similar, and generally, F varies about a value of 1.

If Null Hypothesis Is False

If the null hypothesis is false (because there is a treatment effect due to different sleep deprivation periods), both estimates still would reflect random error, but the estimate for between groups would also reflect the treatment effect. In this case,

$$F = \frac{random\ error + treatment\ effect}{random\ error}$$

When the null hypothesis is false, the presence of a treatment effect tends to cause a chain reaction: The observed differences between group means tend to be large, as also does the variability between groups. Accordingly, the numerator term tends to exceed the denominator term, producing an F whose value is larger than 1. When the null hypothesis is false because of a *large* treatment effect, there is an even more pronounced chain reaction, beginning with very large observed differences between group means and ending with an F whose value tends to be *considerably* larger than 1.

Progress Check *16.2 If the null hypothesis is true, both the numerator and denominator of the F ratio would reflect only ___(a)___ . If the null hypothesis is false, the numerator of the F ratio would also reflect the ___(b)___ . If the null hypothesis is false because of a large treatment effect, the value of F would tend to be considerably larger than ___(c)___ .

Answers on page 513.

When Status of Null Hypothesis Is Unknown

In practice, of course, we never really know whether the null hypothesis is true or false. Following the usual procedure, we assume the null hypothesis to be true and view the observed F within the context of its hypothesized sampling distribution, as shown in **Figure 16.1**. If, because the differences between group means are relatively small, the observed F appears to emerge from the dense concentration of possible F ratios smaller than the critical F, the experimental outcome will be viewed as a common occurrence. Therefore, the null hypothesis would be retained. On the other hand, if, because the differences between group means are relatively large, the observed F appears to emerge from the sparse concentration of possible F ratios equal to or greater than the critical F, the experimental outcome would be viewed as a rare occurrence, and the null hypothesis would be rejected. In the latter case, the value of the observed F is presumed to be inflated by a treatment effect.

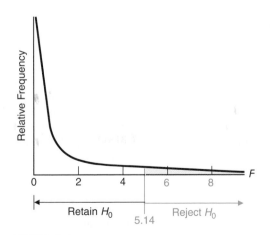

FIGURE 16.1
Hypothesized sampling distribution of F *(for 2 and 6 degrees of freedom).*

HYPOTHESIS TEST SUMMARY

One-Factor *F* Test (Sleep Deprivation Experiment, Outcome B)

Research Problem

On average, are subjects' aggression scores in a controlled social situation affected by sleep deprivation periods of 0, 24, or 48 hours?

Statistical Hypotheses

$$H_0: \mu_0 = \mu_{24} = \mu_{48}$$
$$H_1: H_0 \text{ is false.}$$

Decision Rule

Reject H_0 at the .05 level of significance if $F \geq 5.14$ (from Table C, Appendix C, given $df_{between} = 2$ and $df_{within} = 6$).

Calculations

$F = 7.36$ (See Tables 16.3 and 16.6 for additional details.)

Decision

Reject H_0 at the .05 level of significance because $F = 7.36$ exceeds 5.14.

Interpretation

Hours of sleep deprivation affect the subjects' mean aggression scores in a controlled social situation.

Test Results for Outcomes A and B

Full-fledged *F* tests for Outcomes A and B agree with the earlier intuitive decisions. Given the .05 level of significance, the null hypothesis should be retained for Outcome A, since the observed *F* of 0.75 is smaller than the critical *F* of 5.14. However, the null hypothesis should be rejected for Outcome B, since the observed *F* of 7.36 exceeds the critical *F*. The hypothesis test for Outcome B, as summarized in the accompanying box, will be discussed later in more detail.

16.4 DETAILS: VARIANCE ESTIMATES

The analysis of variance uses sample variance estimates to measure variability between groups and within groups. Introduced in Chapter 4, the *sample variance* measures variability among any set of observations by first finding the sum of squares, *SS*, that is, the sum of the squared deviations about their mean:

$$SS = \sum \left(X - \bar{X} \right)^2$$

and then dividing the sum of squares, SS, by its degrees of freedom, that is,

$$s^2 = \frac{SS}{n-1} = \frac{SS}{df}$$

where s^2 is the sample variance. This estimate can be used to identify two general features for each of the several variance estimates in ANOVA:

1. Sum of Squares, SS, in the Numerator: The numerator term for s^2 represents the sum of the squared deviations about the sample mean, $\bar{X}$. More generally, the numerator term for any variance estimate in ANOVA always is the *sum of squares,* that is, *the sum of squared deviations for some set of scores about their mean.*

2. Degrees of Freedom, df, in the Denominator: The denominator for s^2 represents the number of degrees of freedom for these deviations. (Remember, as discussed in Section 4.6, only $n - 1$ of these deviations are free to vary. One degree of freedom is lost because the sum of n deviations about their own mean always must equal 0.) More generally, the denominator term for any variance estimate in ANOVA always is the number of *degrees of freedom*, that is, *the number of deviations in the numerator that are free to vary and, therefore, supply valid information for the purpose of estimation.*

Mean Square

A variance estimate in ANOVA, referred to as a *mean square,* consists of some sum of squares divided by its degrees of freedom.

***Mean Square* (MS)**

A variance estimate obtained by dividing a sum of squares by its degrees of freedom.

This operation always produces a number equal to the mean of the squared deviations, hence the designation *mean square,* abbreviated as *MS*. In ANOVA, the latter term is the most common, and it will be used in subsequent discussions. A general expression for any variance estimate reads:

MEAN SQUARE: GENERAL EXPRESSION

$$MS = \frac{SS}{df} \tag{16.2}$$

---

where MS represents the mean square; SS denotes the sum of squared deviations about their mean; and df equals the corresponding number of degrees of freedom. Formula 16.2 should be read as "the mean square equals the sum of squares divided by its degrees of freedom."

The F test of the null hypothesis for the sleep deprivation experiment reflects the ratio of two variance estimates: the mean square for variability between the three sleep deprivation groups in the numerator and the mean square for variability within these three groups, often referred to as the *error term*, in the denominator. To obtain values for these mean squares, first we must calculate their respective sums of squares and degrees of freedom, as described next.

Sum of Squares (*SS*): Definitional Formulas

Most of the computational effort in ANOVA is directed toward the various sum of squares terms: the sum of squares for variability between groups, $SS_{between}$; the sum of squares for variability within groups, SS_{within}; and the sum of squares for the total of these two, SS_{total}. Remember, *any* **sum of squares** *always equals the sum of the squared deviations of some set of scores about their mean*. Let's begin with the definitional formula for SS_{total} because it's the most straightforward extension of the sample sum of squares, *SS*, first encountered in Chapter 4.

Sum of Squares (SS)

The sum of squared deviations of some set of scores about their mean.

- SS_{total} equals the sum of the squared deviations of all scores about the grand mean. Expressed symbolically, $SS_{total} = \Sigma(X - \bar{X}_{grand})^2$, where X represents each score and $\bar{X}_{grand}$ represents the one overall mean for all scores. Although SS_{total} isn't directly involved in the calculation of the F ratio, it serves as a valuable computational check.

- $SS_{between}$ equals the sum of the squared deviations of group means about the grand mean, the overall mean based on all groups (or all scores). Expressed symbolically, $SS_{between} = n\Sigma(\bar{X}_{group} - \bar{X}_{grand})^2$, where n represents the number of scores in each group, $\bar{X}_{group}$ is the mean for each group, and $\bar{X}_{grand}$ is the overall mean for all groups. This term contributes to the numerator of the F ratio. The sample size for each group, n, in the expression for $SS_{between}$ reflects the fact that the deviation $\bar{X}_{group} - \bar{X}_{grand}$ is the same for every score, n, in that group.

- SS_{within} equals the sum of the squared deviations of all scores about their respective group means. Expressed symbolically, $SS_{within} = \Sigma(X - \bar{X}_{group})^2$, where X represents each score and $\bar{X}_{group}$ is the mean for each group. This term contributes to the denominator of the F ratio. Essentially, it requires that we calculate the sum of squares, *SS*, within each group and then add these terms across all groups—in a procedure similar to that used with the two *SS* terms in the numerator of Formula 14.2 (page 295) for the polled variance estimate, s_p^2. Since SS_{within} always reflects only the pooled variability among subjects treated similarly, it can be referred to, more generally, as the *sum of squares for random error* and symbolized as SS_{error}.

Sum of Squares (*SS*): Computation Formulas

Sums of squares can be calculated by using either definition formulas with means or computation formulas with totals. Calculating the various *SS* terms with means is not only cumbersome but also inaccurate if, because of rounding off, the means are approximate numbers. It is both more efficient and more accurate to use the equivalent computation formulas, as we first did in Chapter 4 (page 85), when the definition formula for the sample sum of squares was transformed into its corresponding computation formula, that is,

$$SS = \Sigma \left(X - \bar{X} \right)^2 = \Sigma X^2 - \frac{\left(\Sigma X \right)^2}{n}$$

where the total, ΣX, represents a key component in the conversion from means in the definition formulas to totals in the computation formulas.

The color-coded computation formulas for the three new *SS* terms in Table 16.2 can be viewed as variations on the original computation formula for the sum of squares. Note the following features common to both the original computation formula and the three new computation formulas:

1. Each formula consists of two components separated by a minus sign.

2. Means are replaced by their corresponding totals. The grand mean, $\bar{X}_{grand}$, is replaced by the grand total, G, and any group mean, $\bar{X}_{group}$, is replaced by its group total, T.

3. Whether a score or a total, each entry in the numerator is squared and, in the case of a total, divided by its sample size, either N for the grand total or n for any group total.

Table 16.2
WORD, DEFINITION, AND COMPUTATION FORMULAS FOR *SS* TERMS

For the total sums of squares,

SS_{total} = the sum of squared deviations for scores about the grand mean

$$= \Sigma(X - \bar{X}_{grand})^2$$

$SS_{total} = \Sigma X^2 - \dfrac{G^2}{N}$, where G is the grand total and N is its sample size

---

For the between sum of squares,

$SS_{between}$ = the sum of squared deviations for group means about the grand mean

$$= n\Sigma(\bar{X}_{group} - \bar{X}_{grand})^2$$

$SS_{between} = \Sigma \dfrac{T^2}{n} - \dfrac{G^2}{N}$, where T is the group total and n is its sample size

---

For the within sum of squares,

SS_{within} = the sum of squared deviations of scores about their respective group means

$$= \Sigma(X - \bar{X}_{group})^2$$

$SS_{within} = \Sigma X^2 - \Sigma \dfrac{T^2}{n}$

REMINDER:
X = raw score
T = group total
n = group sample size
G = grand total
N = grand (combined) sample size

Table 16.3 indicates how to use these computation formulas for the nine aggression scores from Outcome B of the sleep deprivation experiment. Note that the expression $\sum \frac{T^2}{n}$ requires the following computation sequence: first,

---

Table 16.3
CALCULATION OF *SS* TERMS

A. COMPUTATION SEQUENCE

Find each group total, *T*, and the grand total, *G*, for all combined groups 1.
Substitute numbers into computation formula 2 and solve for $SS_{between}$.
Substitute numbers into computation formula 3 and solve for SS_{within}.
Substitute numbers into computation formula 4 and solve for SS_{total}.
Do accuracy check 5.

B. DATA AND COMPUTATIONS

HOURS OF SLEEP DEPRIVATION

0	24	48
0	3	6
4	6	8
2	6	10

1 Group Totals $(T) = 6$ 15   24   Grand Total $(G) = 45$

2   $SS_{between} = \sum \dfrac{T^2}{n} - \dfrac{G^2}{N}$

$$= \left[\frac{(6)^2}{3} + \frac{(15)^2}{3} + \frac{(24)^2}{3} \right] - \frac{(45)^2}{9} = \left[\frac{36}{3} + \frac{225}{3} + \frac{576}{3} \right] - \frac{2025}{9}$$

$$= \left[12 + 75 + 192 \right] - 225 = 279 - 225 = 54$$

3   $SS_{within} = \sum X^2 - \sum \dfrac{T^2}{n}$

$$= (0)^2 + (4)^2 + (2)^2 + (3)^2 + (6)^2 + (6)^2 + (6)^2 + (8)^2 + (10)^2 - \left[\frac{(6)^2}{3} + \frac{(15)^2}{3} + \frac{(24)^2}{3} \right]$$

$$= 0 + 16 + 4 + 9 + 36 + 36 + 36 + 64 + 100 - \left[\frac{36}{3} + \frac{225}{3} + \frac{576}{3} \right] = 301 - 279 = 22$$

4   $SS_{total} = \sum X^2 - \dfrac{G^2}{N}$

$$= (0)^2 + (4)^2 + (2)^2 + (3)^2 + (6)^2 + (6)^2 + (6)^2 + (8)^2 + (10)^2 - \frac{(45)^2}{9}$$

$$= 0 + 16 + 4 + 9 + 36 + 36 + 36 + 64 + 100 - \frac{2025}{9} = 301 - 225 = 76$$

5   $SS_{total} = SS_{between} + SS_{within}$

$$76 = 54 + 22$$

$$76 = 76$$

square each group total, T; then divide by its sample size, n; and finally, sum across all groups.

Checking Computational Accuracy

To minimize computational errors, calculate from scratch each of the three SS terms, even though this entails some duplication of effort.* Then, as an almost foolproof check of computational accuracy, as shown at the bottom of Table 16.3, substitute numerical results to verify that SS_{total} equals the sum of the various SS terms, that is,

---

SUMS OF SQUARES (ONE FACTOR)

$$SS_{total} = SS_{between} + SS_{within} \qquad (16.3)$$

Degrees of Freedom (*df*)

Formulas for the number of degrees of freedom differ for each SS term, and for convenience, the various df formulas are listed in **Table 16.4**. Remember, the **degrees of freedom** *reflect the number of deviations free to vary in any sum of squares term, given one or more restrictions.* In the present case, the restriction always entails the loss of one degree of freedom because the sum must equal zero for each set of deviations about its respective mean. The $N - 1$ degrees of freedom for df_{total} reflect the loss of one degree of freedom when all N scores are expressed as deviations about their grand mean. The $k - 1$ degrees of freedom for $df_{between}$ reflect the loss of one degree of freedom when the k group means are expressed as deviations about the one grand mean. Finally, the $N - k$ degrees of freedom for df_{within} reflect the loss of one degree of freedom (for each of the k groups) when each subset of the N scores is expressed as deviations about their respective (k) group means.

To determine the df for any SS, simply substitute the appropriate numbers and subtract. For the present experiment, which involves a total of nine scores ($N = 9$) and three groups ($k = 3$):

Table 16.4
FORMULAS FOR *df* TERMS

df_{total} = $N - 1$, that is, the number of all scores − 1

$df_{between}$ = $k - 1$, that is, the number of groups − 1

df_{within} = $N - k$, that is, the number of all scores − number of groups

---

....

* You may have noticed in Table 16.2 that three components, namely, ΣX^2, $\Sigma \frac{T^2}{n}$, and $\frac{G^2}{N}$, each appear twice in the various SS terms. Some practitioners prefer to simply calculate each of these components and then solve for the SS terms. Although more efficient, this shortcut compromises the use of Formula 16.3 as a check for computational accuracy.

$$df_{total} = N - 1 = 9 - 1 = 8$$
$$df_{between} = k - 1 = 3 - 1 = 2$$
$$df_{within} = N - k = 9 - 3 = 6$$

Checking for Accuracy

In ANOVA, the degrees of freedom for df_{total} always equal the combined degrees of freedom for the remaining df terms, that is,

---

Reminder:

Degrees of freedom *refers to the number of deviations free to vary in any sum of squares term, given one or more restrictions.*

DEGREES OF FREEDOM (ONE FACTOR)
$$df_{total} = df_{between} + df_{within}$$ (16.4)

This formula can be used to verify that the correct number of degrees of freedom has been assigned to each of the SS terms in the present experiment.

16.5 DETAILS: MEAN SQUARES (*MS*) AND THE *F* RATIO

Having found the values of the various SS terms and their degrees of freedom, we can determine the values of the two mean squares for variability between and within groups and then calculate the value of F, as suggested in **Figure 16.2**.

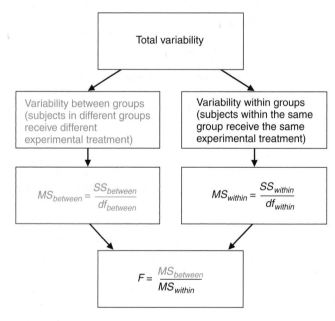

FIGURE 16.2
Sources of variability for ANOVA and the F ratio.

The value of the mean square for variability between groups, $MS_{between}$, is given by the following expression:

MEAN SQUARE BETWEEN GROUPS

$$MS_{between} = \frac{SS_{between}}{df_{between}}$$

(16.5)

---

where $MS_{between}$ reflects the variability between means for groups of subjects who are treated differently. Relatively large values of $MS_{between}$ suggest the presence of a treatment effect.

For the sleep deprivation experiment,

$$MS_{between} = \frac{SS_{between}}{df_{between}} = \frac{54}{2} = 27$$

The value of the mean square for variability within groups, MS_{within}, is given by the following expression:

MEAN SQUARE WITHIN GROUPS

$$MS_{within} = \frac{SS_{within}}{df_{within}}$$

(16.6)

Reminder:

SS_{within} and MS_{within} also are symbolized as SS_{error} and MS_{error}, respectively.

where MS_{within} reflects the variability among scores for subjects who are treated similarly within each group, pooled across all groups. (MS_{within}, which also is symbolized as MS_{error}, is a generalized version of the pooled sample variance, s_p^2, used with the t test for two independent samples in Chapter 14). Even if there is a treatment effect, MS_{within} measures only random error.

For the sleep deprivation experiment,

$$MS_{within} = \frac{SS_{within}}{df_{within}} = \frac{22}{6} = 3.67$$

Finally, Formula 16.1 for F can be rewritten as

F RATIO (ONE FACTOR)

$$F = \frac{MS_{between}}{MS_{within}}$$

(16.7)

As mentioned previously, if the null hypothesis is true (because aggression scores are not affected by hours of sleep deprivation), the value of F will vary

F Ratio

Ratio of the between-group mean square (for subjects treated differently) to the within-group mean square (for subjects treated similarly).

about a value of approximately 1, but if the null hypothesis is false, the value of F will tend to be larger than 1.

The null hypothesis is suspect for the sleep deprivation experiment since

$$F = \frac{MS_{between}}{MS_{within}} = \frac{27}{3.67} = 7.36$$

16.6 TABLE FOR THE F DISTRIBUTION

A decision about the null hypothesis requires that the observed F be compared with a critical F. The critical F is identified through the pair of degrees of freedom for the mean squares in the numerator and denominator of the F ratio. Critical F values for hypothesis tests at the .05 level (light numbers) and the .01 level (dark numbers) are listed in Table 16.5 (for a few F sampling distributions) and in Table C, Appendix C (for the full range of F sampling distributions). To read either table, simply find the cell intersected by the column with the degrees of freedom equal to $df_{between}$ and by the row with the degrees of freedom equal to

Reminder:

To use the F table, you must know the df in the numerator and denominator of the F ratio.

Table 16.5
SPECIMEN TABLE FROM TABLE C OF APPENDIX C
CRITICAL VALUES OF F
.05 LEVEL OF SIGNIFICANCE (LIGHT NUMBERS)
.01 LEVEL OF SIGNIFICANCE (DARK NUMBERS)

DEGREES OF FREEDOM IN DENOMINATOR	DEGREES OF FREEDOM IN NUMERATOR			
	1	2	3	4**
1	161	200	216	
	4052	**4999**	**5403**	
2	18.51	19.00	19.16	
	98.49	**99.01**	**99.17**	
3	10.13	9.55	9.28	
	34.12	**30.81**	**29.46**	
4	7.17	6.94	6.59	
	21.20	**18.00**	**16.69**	
5	6.61	5.79	5.41	
	16.26	**13.27**	**12.06**	
6	5.99	5.14	4.76	
	13.74	**10.92**	**9.78**	
7	5.59	4.47	4.35	
	12.25	**9.55**	**8.45**	
8				
*				
*				
*				

df_{within}. Table 16.5 illustrates this procedure when, as in the present experiment, 2 and 6 degrees of freedom are associated with the numerator and denominator of F, respectively. In this case, the column with 2 degrees of freedom and the row with 6 degrees of freedom intersect a cell (shaded in color) that lists a critical F value of 5.14 for a hypothesis test at the .05 level of significance. Because the observed F of 7.36 exceeds this critical F, the overall null hypothesis can be rejected. There is evidence that, on average, sleep deprivation affects the subjects' aggression scores.

Progress Check *16.3 Find the critical values for the following F tests:

(a) $\alpha = .05$, $df_{between} = 1$, $df_{within} = 18$

(b) $\alpha = .01$, $df_{between} = 3$, $df_{within} = 56$

(c) $\alpha = .05$, $df_{between} = 2$, $df_{within} = 36$

(d) $\alpha = .05$, $df_{between} = 4$, $df_{within} = 95$

Answers on page 513.

Finding Approximate p-Values

To find its approximate p-value, locate an observed F relative to the .05 level (light numbers) and the .01 level (dark numbers) listed in Table C in Appendix C. As noted in the upper corner of Table C, if the observed F is smaller than the light numbers, $p > .05$. If the observed F is between light and dark numbers, $p < .05$. If the observed F is larger than the dark numbers, $p < .01$.

Progress Check *16.4 Find the approximate p-value for the following observed F ratios, where the numbers in parentheses refer to the degrees of freedom in the numerator and denominator, respectively.

(a) $F(2, 11) = 4.56$

(b) $F(1, 13) = 11.25$

(c) $F(3, 20) = 2.92$

(d) $F(2, 29) = 3.66$

Answers on page 513.

16.7 ANOVA SUMMARY TABLES

Traditionally, both in statistics textbooks and the literature, ANOVA results have been summarized as shown in Table 16.6. "Source" refers to the source of variability, that is, between groups, within groups, and total. Notice the arrangement of column headings from SS and df to MS and F. Also, notice that the bottom row for total variability contains entries only for SS and df. Ordinarily, the shaded numbers in parentheses don't appear in ANOVA tables, but in Table 16.6 they show the origin of each MS and of F. The asterisk in Table 16.6 emphasizes that the observed F of 7.36 exceeds the critical F of 5.14 and therefore causes the null hypothesis to be rejected at the .05 level of significance.

Table 16.6
ANOVA TABLE (SLEEP DEPRIVATION EXPERIMENT)

SOURCE	SS	df	MS	F
Between	54	2	$\left(\frac{54}{2}=\right)27$	$\left(\frac{27}{3.67}=\right)7.36^*$
Within	22	6	$\left(\frac{22}{6}=\right)3.67$	
Total	76	8		

* Significant at the .05 level.

Other Labels

Some ANOVA summary tables use labels other than those shown in Table 16.6. For instance, "Between" might be replaced with "Treatment," since the variability between groups reflects any treatment effect. Or "Between" might be replaced by a description of the actual experimental treatment, such as "Hours of Sleep Deprivation" or "Sleep Deprivation." Likewise, "Within" might be replaced with "Error," since variability within groups reflects only the presence of random error.

Progress Check *16.5 A psychologist tests whether a series of workshops on assertive training increases eye contacts initiated by shy college students in controlled interactions with strangers. A total of 32 subjects are randomly assigned, 8 to a group, to attend either zero, one, two, or three workshop sessions. The results, expressed as the number of eye contacts during a standard observation period, are shown in the following chart. (Also shown for your computational convenience are the values for the sum of squares, group totals, and the grand total.)

EYE CONTACTS AS A FUNCTION OF NUMBER OF SESSIONS			
ZERO	ONE	TWO	THREE
1	2	4	7
0	1	2	1
0	2	3	6
2	4	6	9
3	4	7	10
4	6	8	12
2	3	5	8
1	3	5	7

T   13   25   40   60 $\Sigma X = G = 138$

$\Sigma X^2 = 882$

(a) Test the null hypothesis at the .05 level of significance. (Use computation formulas for various sums of squares.)

(b) Summarize the results with an ANOVA table. Save these results for subsequent questions.

Answers on page 513.

16.8 *F* TEST IS NONDIRECTIONAL

It might seem strange that even though the entire rejection region for the null hypothesis appears only in the upper tail of the *F* sampling distribution, as in Figure 16.1, *the F test in ANOVA is the equivalent of a nondirectional test.* Recall that all variations in ANOVA are squared. When squared, all values become positive, regardless of whether the original differences between groups (or group means) are positive or negative. All squared differences between groups have a cumulative positive effect on the observed *F* and thereby ensure that *F* is a nondirectional test, even though only the upper tail of its sampling distribution contains the rejection region.

F and t^2

Squaring the *t* test would produce a similar effect. When squared, all values of t^2 become positive, regardless of whether the original value for the observed *t* was positive or negative. Hence, the t^2 test also qualifies as a nondirectional test, even though the entire rejection region appears only in the upper tail of the t^2 sampling distribution. In fact, the values of t^2 and *F* are identical when both tests are applied to the same data for two independent groups. When only two groups are involved, the t^2 test can be viewed as a special case of the more general *F* test in ANOVA for two or more groups.

16.9 ESTIMATING EFFECT SIZE

As discussed in Chapter 14, a statistically significant *t* test indicates that the null hypothesis is probably false but nothing about the size of the effect. Cohen's *d* supplies a standardized estimate of effect size, which has the desirable property of being *independent of sample sizes.*

Like the *t* test, a statistically significant *F* indicates merely that the null hypothesis is probably false; otherwise, it fails to provide an accurate estimate of effect size. A new estimate of effect size must both reflect the overall effect associated with the null hypothesis in ANOVA and also be independent of sample sizes.* A most straightforward estimate, denoted as η^2, capitalizes on existing

---

*Independence of sample size is an important property of estimates of effect size. Essentially, large sample sizes in ANOVA automatically inflate the numerator term, $MS_{between}$, *relative* to the denominator term, MS_{within}, of the *F* test. For instance, the *F* of 0.75 for Outcome A in Table 16.1, was not significant at the .05 level. If, however, the sample size for each of the three groups were increased from $n = 3$ to $n = 30$, the new *F* of 7.50 would have been significant at the .01 level *even though the differences between group means remain the same.*

information in the ANOVA summary table by specifying that $SS_{between}$ be divided by SS_{total}, that is,

---

PROPORTION OF EXPLAINED VARIANCE, η^2 (ONE-FACTOR ANOVA)

$$\eta^2 = \frac{SS_{between}}{SS_{total}} \qquad (16.8)$$

---

where η^2 represents the proportion of explained variance and $SS_{between}$ and SS_{total} represent the between group and total sum of squares, respectively. This ratio estimates not population mean differences, but the proportion (from 0 to 1) of the total variance for all scores, as reflected in SS_{total}, that can be explained by or attributed to the variance of treatment groups, as reflected in $SS_{between}$. Speaking very generally, η^2 indicates the proportion of differences among all scores attributable to differences among treatment groups. The larger this proportion, the larger the estimated size of the overall effect of the treatment on the dependent variable.

The Greek symbol η^2, pronounced eta-squared, is often referred to as the *squared curvilinear correlation coefficient.* This terminology reinforces the notion that η^2 is just a square root away from a number describing the nonlinear correlation between values of the independent and dependent variables.

Refer to **Figure 16.3** to gain some appreciation of how the **squared curvilinear correlation,** η^2, *reflects the proportion of variance explained by the independent variable.* This figure shows values of η^2 for three different outcomes, reflecting no effect, a maximum effect, and a partial effect, for the sleep deprivation experiment.

Squared Curvilinear Correlation (η^2)

The proportion of variance in the dependent variable that can be explained by or attributed to the independent variable.

Panel I

There is no apparent visual separation between the scores for each of the three groups, since each group mean, $\bar{X}_{group}$, equals the grand mean, $\bar{X}_{grand}$. Therefore, there is no variability between groups, $SS_{between} = 0$, and

$$\eta^2 = \frac{SS_{between}}{SS_{total}} = \frac{SS_{between}}{SS_{between} + SS_{within}} = \frac{0}{0 + SS_{within}} = \frac{0}{SS_{within}} = 0$$

The value of 0 for η^2 implies that *none* of the variance among scores can be attributed to variance between treatment groups. The treatment variable has no effect whatsoever on the dependent variable.

Panel II

There is complete visual separation between the scores for each of the three groups, since each score, X, coincides with its own distinctive group mean, $\bar{X}_{group}$. Therefore, there is no variability within groups, $SS_{within} = 0$, and

$$\eta^2 = \frac{SS_{between}}{SS_{total}} = \frac{SS_{between}}{SS_{between} + SS_{within}} = \frac{SS_{between}}{SS_{between} + 0} = \frac{SS_{between}}{SS_{between}} = 1$$

The value of 1 for η^2 implies that *all* of the variance among scores can be attributed to the variance between treatment groups. The treatment variable has a maximum (perfect) effect on the dependent variable.

I *NO* VARIABILITY BETWEEN GROUPS
$$(\eta^2 = 0)$$

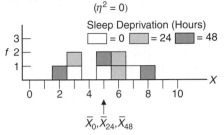

II *ALL* VARIABILITY BETWEEN GROUPS
$$(\eta^2 = 1)$$

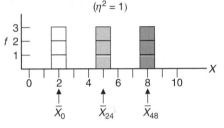

III *SOME* VARIABILITY BETWEEN GROUPS
$$(\eta^2 = .71)$$

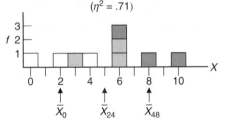

FIGURE 16.3
Values of η^2 for three possible outcomes of the sleep deprivation experiment.

Panel III

In spite of some overlap, there is an apparent visual separation between scores for the three groups. Now there is variability both within and between groups, as for Outcome B of the sleep deprivation experiment (Table 16.6), $SS_{between} = 54$ and $SS_{within} = 22$, and

$$\eta^2 = \frac{SS_{between}}{SS_{total}} = \frac{SS_{between}}{SS_{between} + SS_{within}} = \frac{54}{54 + 22} = \frac{54}{76} = .71$$

The value of .71 for η^2 implies that .71 (or 71 percent) of the variance among scores can be attributed to variance between treatment groups, as reflected in $SS_{between}$. More specifically, this large value of .71 suggests that 71 percent of the variance in aggression scores is attributable to whether subjects are deprived of sleep for 0, 24, or 48 hours, while the remaining 29 percent of variance in

Table 16.7 GUIDELINES FOR η^2	
η^2	**EFFECT**
.01	Small
.09	Medium
.25	Large

aggression scores is not attributable to hours of sleep deprivation. (Notice that, although the same differences appear between the group means in the two bottom panels, the value of η^2 drops from 1 in Panel II to .71 in Panel III. This is a reminder that our estimate of effect size, η^2, depends not only on the variability between group means but also on the error variability within groups.)

Guidelines for η^2 can be derived from Cohen's recommendations for a similar measure, the correlation coefficient, r, that, when squared, also uses the proportion of explained variance to estimate the effect size. As indicated in Table 16.7, estimated effect size is small, medium, or large, depending on whether the value η^2 is in the general vicinity of .01; .09; or .25, respectively.* The estimated effect size of .71 for Outcome B of the sleep deprivation experiment would be considered spectacularly large, and it reflects the fact that these data were created to dramatize the differences due to sleep deprivation with small, computationally friendly sample sizes. (However, even if the data were real, this estimate of effect size—itself a product of sampling variability—would be considered highly speculative because of the instability of η^2 when sample sizes are small.)

A Recommendation

Consider calculating η^2 (or its less straightforward but more accurate competitor, omega-squared, symbolized as ω^2 and cited in more advanced statistics books) whenever F is statistically significant. As mentioned in Section 14.9, don't apply Cohen's guidelines without regard to special circumstances that could give considerable importance to even a very small estimated effect.

Progress Check *16.6 Given the rejection of the null hypothesis in Question 16.5, estimate the effect size with η^2.

Answer on page 513.

16.10 MULTIPLE COMPARISONS

Rejection of the overall null hypothesis indicates only that all population means are not equal. In the case of the original sleep deprivation experiment, the rejection of H_0 signals the presence of one or more inequalities between the mean aggression scores for populations of subjects exposed to 0, 24, or 48 hours of sleep deprivation, that is, between μ_0, μ_{24}, and μ_{48}. To pinpoint the one or more differences between pairs of population means that contribute to the rejection of the overall H_0, we must use a test of multiple comparisons. A test of **multiple comparisons** is designed to evaluate not just one but a series of differences between population means, such as those for each of the three possible differences between pairs of population means for the present experiment, namely, $\mu_0 - \mu_{24}$, $\mu_0 - \mu_{48}$, and $\mu_{24} - \mu_{48}$.

Multiple Comparisons

The possible comparisons whenever more than two population means are involved.

t Test Not Appropriate

These differences can't be evaluated with a series of regular t tests, except under special circumstances alluded to later in this section. The regular t test is

---

* J. Cohen, *Statistical Power Analysis in the Behavioral Sciences,* 2nd ed. (Hillsdale, NJ: Erlbaum, 1988).

designed to evaluate a *single* comparison for a pair of observed means, not *multiple* comparisons for all possible pairs of observed means. Among other complications, the use of multiple *t* tests increases the probability of a type I error (rejecting a true null hypothesis) beyond the value specified by the level of significance.

Coin-Tossing Example

A coin-tossing example might clarify this problem. When a fair coin is tossed only once, the probability of heads equals .50—just as, when a single *t* test is to be conducted at the .05 level of significance, the probability of a type I error equals .05. When a fair coin is tossed three times, however, heads can appear not only on the first toss but also on the second or third toss, and hence the probability of heads on *at least one* of the three tosses exceeds .50. By the same token, for a series of three *t* tests, each conducted at the .05 level of significance, a type I error can be committed not only on the first test but also on the second or third test, and hence the probability of committing a type I error on *at least one* of the three tests exceeds .05. In fact, the cumulative probability of at least one type I error can be as large as .15 for a series of three *t* tests and even larger for a more extended series of *t* tests.

Tukey's *HSD* Test

Tukey's HSD Test

A multiple comparison test for which the cumulative probability of at least one type I error never exceeds the specified level of significance.

The above shortcoming does not apply to a number of specially designed multiple comparison tests, including Tukey's *HSD* or "honestly significant difference" test. Once the overall null hypothesis has been rejected in ANOVA, **Tukey's *HSD* test** *can be used to test all possible differences between pairs of means, and yet the cumulative probability of at least one type I error never exceeds the specified level of significance.*

Finding the Critical Value

Given a significant *F* for the overall null hypothesis, as in the sleep deprivation experiment, Tukey's test supplies a single critical value, *HSD*, for evaluating the significance of each difference for every possible pair of means, that is, $\bar{X}_0 - \bar{X}_{24}$, $\bar{X}_0 - \bar{X}_{48}$, and $\bar{X}_{24} - \bar{X}_{48}$. Essentially, the critical value for *HSD* is adjusted upward for the number of group means, *k*, being compared to compensate for the increased cumulative probability of at least one type I error. The net effect of this upward adjustment is to make it more difficult to reject the null hypothesis for any particular pair of population means—and to increase the likelihood of detecting only honestly significant (or real) differences.

If the *absolute* difference between any pair of means equals or exceeds the critical value for *HSD*, the null hypothesis for that particular pair of population means can be rejected. To determine *HSD*, use the following expression:

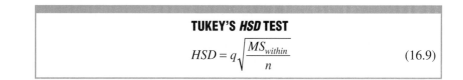

TUKEY'S *HSD* TEST

$$HSD = q\sqrt{\frac{MS_{within}}{n}}$$
(16.9)

where *HSD* is the positive critical value for any difference between two means; q is a value, technically referred to as the *Studentized Range Statistic,* obtained from Table G in Appendix C; MS_{within} is the customary mean square for within-group variability for the overall ANOVA; and n is the sample size in each group.[*]

To obtain a value for q at the .05 level (light numbers) or the .01 level (dark numbers) in Table G, find the cell intersected by k, the number of groups, and df_{within}, the degrees of freedom for within-group (or error) variability in the original ANOVA. Given values of $k = 3$ and $df_{within} = 6$ for the sleep deprivation experiment, the intersected cell shows a value of 4.34 for q at the .05 level. Substituting $q = 4.34$, $MS_{within} = 3.67$, and $n = 3$ in Equation 16.9, we can solve for *HSD* as follows:

$$HSD = q\sqrt{\frac{MS_{within}}{n}} = 4.34\sqrt{\frac{3.67}{3}} = 4.34\,(1.10) = 4.77$$

Interpretation for Sleep Deprivation Experiment

Table 16.8 shows absolute differences of either 3, 6, or 3 for the three pairs of means in the current experiment. (This table serves as a good model for evaluating the significance of differences between all possible pairs of sample means.) Since only the difference of 6 for the comparison involving $\bar{X}_0$ and $\bar{X}_{48}$ exceeds the critical *HSD* value of 4.77, only the null hypothesis for $\mu_0 - \mu_{48}$ can be rejected at the .05 level. We can conclude that, when compared with 0 hours of sleep deprivation, 48 hours of sleep deprivation tends to produce, on average, more aggressive behavior in a controlled social situation. There is no evidence, however, that subjects deprived of sleep for 24 hours are either more aggressive than those deprived for 0 hours or less aggressive than those deprived for 48 hours.

Table 16.8
ALL POSSIBLE ABSOLUTE DIFFERENCES BETWEEN PAIRS OF MEANS (FOR THE SLEEP DEPRIVATION EXPERIMENT)

	$\bar{X}_0 = 2$	$\bar{X}_{24} = 5$	$\bar{X}_{48} = 8$
$\bar{X}_0 = 2$	—	3	6*
$\bar{X}_{24} = 5$		—	3
$\bar{X}_{48} = 8$			—

* Significant at the .05 level.

....
[*] Equation 16.9 assumes equal sample sizes. Otherwise, if samples sizes are not equal and you lack access to an automatically adjusting computer program, such as Minitab, SAS, or SPSS, replace n in Equation 16.9 with the mean of all sample sizes, $\bar{n}$.

Estimating Effect Size

The effect size for any significant difference between pairs of means can be estimated with Cohen's d, as adapted from Equation 14.5 on page 303, that is,

---

STANDARDIZED EFFECT SIZE, COHEN'S d (ADAPTED FOR ANOVA)

$$d = \frac{\overline{X}_1 - \overline{X}_2}{\sqrt{s_p^2}} = \frac{\overline{X}_1 - \overline{X}_2}{\sqrt{MS_{within}}} \qquad (16.10)$$

---

where d is an estimate of the standardized effect size, $\overline{X}_1$ and $\overline{X}_2$ are the pair of significantly different means, and $\sqrt{MS_{within}}$, the square root of the within-group mean square for the one-factor ANOVA, represents the sample standard deviation.

To estimate the standardized effect size for the one significant difference between means for 0 and 48 hours of sleep deprivation, enter $\overline{X}_{48} - \overline{X}_0 = 6$ and $MS_{within} = 3.67$ in Equation 16.10 and solve for d:

$$d\left(\overline{X}_{48}, \overline{X}_0\right) = \frac{6}{\sqrt{3.67}} = \frac{6}{1.92} = 3.13$$

which is a very large effect, equivalent to more than three standard deviations. (According to Cohen's guidelines for d, described on page 304, the effect size is large if d is more than 0.8.) This result isn't surprising given the very large effect size of $\eta^2 = .71$ for the proportion of explained variance attributable to the differences between all three groups in the sleep deprivation experiment.

Progress Check *16.7 Given the rejection of the null hypothesis in Question 16.5, Tukey's *HSD* test can be used to identify pairs of population means that differ. Using the .05 level of significance, calculate the critical value for *HSD* and use it to evaluate the statistical significance of each possible mean difference. Use the matrix shown in Table 16.8 as a model. The various sample means are $\overline{X}_0 = 1.63$, $\overline{X}_1 = 3.13$, $\overline{X}_2 = 5.00$, and $\overline{X}_3 = 7.50$.

(a) Estimate the standardized effect size for any significant pair of mean differences with Cohen's d.

(b) Interpret the results of your analysis.

Answers on page 513.

Other Multiple Comparison Tests

That only Tukey's *HSD* test, sometimes referred to as *Tukey's a test,* has been discussed should not be interpreted as an unqualified endorsement. At least a half dozen other multiple comparison tests are available, and depending on a number of considerations, any of these could be the most appropriate test for a particular set of comparisons. For example, a very conservative multiple comparison test, *Scheffe's test,* provides better protection against false alarms or type I errors, but at the price of being more vulnerable to misses or type II errors. (Unlike Tukey's *HSD* test, Scheffe's test also can be used to evaluate more complex comparisons, such as, for example, the difference between the mean for 0 hours and the *combined* mean for both 24 and 48 hours.) On the other hand, other, more liberal multiple comparison tests, including even an extension of the *regular t* test for two independent samples, variously referred to as the *protected t test* or as the *LSD (least significant difference) test,* provide better protection against misses or type II errors, but at the price of being more vulnerable to false alarms or type I errors. Depending on the relative seriousness of the type I and II errors, therefore, you might choose to use some other multiple comparison test—possibly one that reverses the strength and weakness of Tukey's *HSD* test.

Selecting a Multiple Comparison Test

We will not deal with the relatively complex, controversial issue of when, depending on circumstances, a specific multiple comparison test is most appropriate.* Indeed, sometimes it isn't even necessary to resolve this issue. With a computer program, such as Minitab, SPSS, or SAS, a few keystrokes can initiate not just one, but an entire series of multiple comparison tests. Insofar as the pattern of significant and nonsignificant comparisons remains about the same for all tests—as has often happened, in our experience—you simply can report this finding without concerning yourself about *the* most appropriate multiple comparison test for that particular set of comparisons. In those cases where the status of a particular comparison is ambiguous, being designated as significant by some of the multiple comparison tests and as nonsignificant by the remaining tests, this comparison could be reported as having "borderline" significance.

16.11 OVERVIEW: FLOW CHART FOR ANOVA

Figure 16.4 serves as a reminder about the steps that should be taken whenever you're using an *F* test in ANOVA. Only if the *F* test is significant should you proceed to estimate the overall effect size with η^2 and to test for significant mean differences with Tukey's *HSD* test. Finally, the effect size for any significant difference between pairs of means can be estimated with Cohen's *d*.

16.12 REPORTS IN THE LITERATURE

For the sake of brevity, reports of hypothesis tests in the current literature usually don't reproduce an ANOVA summary table, such as Table 16.6, but are limited to a review of relevant descriptive statistics, such as the group means and standard deviations, and one or more general conclusions. A parenthetical statement summarizes the statistical test and estimates the effect size. Also reported are the results of any multiple comparison tests, as well as estimates of effect

---

*For more information about tests of multiple comparisons, including tests of special "planned" comparisons that can replace the overall *F* test in ANOVA, see Chapter 12 in D. C. Howell, *Statistical Methods for Psychology*, 7th ed. (Belmont, CA-Wadsworth, 2010).

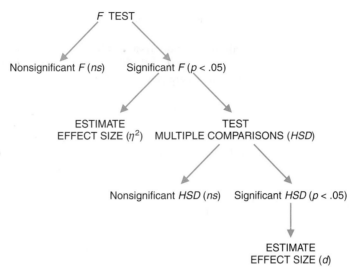

FIGURE 16.4

Overview: Flow chart for one-factor ANOVA.

sizes for any significant multiple comparisons. For example, an investigator might report the sleep deprivation experiment as follows:

> **Aggression scores for subjects deprived of sleep for 0 hours ($\bar{X}$ = 2, s = 2.00), those deprived for 24 hours ($\bar{X}$ = 5, s = 1.73), and those deprived for 48 hours ($\bar{X}$ = 8, s = 2.00) differ significantly [F (2, 6) = 7.36; *MSE* = 3.67; p < .05; η^2 = .71]. According to Tukey's *HSD* test, however, only the difference of 6 between mean aggression scores for the 0 and 48 hour groups is significant (*HSD* = 4.77, p < .05, d = 3.13).**

The first sentence identifies the means and standard deviations for the various groups. Otherwise, if references were limited to results of the statistical analysis, there would be no information about the actual pattern of group differences, along with the variabilities of individual scores for the three groups. The parenthetical statement indicates that an F based on 2 and 6 degrees of freedom equals 7.36. *MSE* represents MS_{error}, the within-group or error mean square used in the denominator of F.

The F test has an approximate p-value of less than .05 because, as can be seen in Table 16.5, the observed F of 7.36 is larger than the critical F of 5.14 for the .05 level of significance (but smaller than the critical F of 10.92 at the .01 level of significance). Furthermore, since the p-value of less than .05 reflects a rare outcome, given that the null hypothesis is true, it supports the research hypothesis, as implied in the interpretative statement. The entry, η^2 = .71, is the estimated effect size, and it signifies that .71 or 71 percent—over two-thirds—of the total variance in aggression scores can be attributed to the three differences in hours of sleep deprivation. Finally, Tukey's *HSD* test, with a critical value of 4.77, reveals that the only significant difference occurs between groups deprived of sleep for 0 and 48 hours, and this difference has a very large standardized effect size, d, estimated to be 3.13.

16.13 ASSUMPTIONS

The assumptions for F tests in ANOVA are the same as those for t tests for two independent samples. All underlying populations are assumed to be normally distributed, with equal variances. You need not be too concerned about violations of these assumptions, particularly if all sample sizes are equal and each sample is fairly large (greater than about 10). Otherwise, in the *unlikely* event that you encounter conspicuous departures from normality or equality of variances, consider various alternatives similar to those discussed in Chapter 14 for the t test. More specifically, you might (1) increase sample sizes (to minimize the effect of non-normality); (2) equalize sample sizes (to minimize the effect of unequal population variances); (3) use a more complex version of F (designed for unequal population variances); or (4) use a less sensitive but more assumption-free test, such as the Kruskal-Wallis H test described in Chapter 20.*

16.14 COMPUTER OUTPUT

Table 16.9 shows the Minitab output for a one-factor ANOVA for the original sleep deprivation experiment. Compare this output with the results described in Table 16.6.

Progress Check *16.8 The following questions refer to the Minitab printout.

(a) Calculate the value of eta squared (η^2).

(b) Determine the value that best estimates the unknown population standard deviation assumed to be common to the three sleep deprivation conditions.

(c) Indicate whether the results for Tukey's pairwise comparisons, expressed as intervals in the output, can be interpreted as confirming the results for Tukey's *HSD*, expressed as mean differences in Table 16.8.

Answers on page 514.

Summary

Analysis of variance (ANOVA), tests the null hypothesis for two or more population means by classifying total variability into two independent components: variability between groups and variability within groups. Both components reflect only random error if the null hypothesis is true, and the resulting F ratio (variability between groups divided by variability within groups) tends toward a value of approximately 1. If the null hypothesis is false, variability between groups reflects both random error and a treatment effect, whereas variability within groups still reflects only random error, and the resulting F ratio tends toward a value greater than 1.

---

*For more information about the version of F designed for unequal variances, see Chapter 11 in D. C. Howell, *Statistical Methods for Psychology,* 7th ed. (Belmont, CA-Wadsworth, 2010).

Table 16.9
MINITAB OUTPUT: ONE-FACTOR ANALYSIS OF VARIANCE FOR AGGRESSION SCORES AS A FUNCTION OF SLEEP DEPRIVATION

ONE-WAY ANALYSIS OF VARIANCE
ANALYSIS OF VARIANCE FOR AGGRESS

Source	df	SS	MS	F	p
DEPRIV	2	54.00	27.00	7.36	0.024
Error	6	22.00	3.67		
Total	8	76.00			

INDIVIDUAL 95% CIs FOR MEAN BASED ON POOLED STDEV

```
Level   N    Mean    StDev     ---+---------+---------+---------
--+---
0       3    2.000   2.000     (-------*--------)
24      3    5.000   1.732              (--------*-------)
48      3    8.000   2.000                       (-------*-------)
                               ---+---------+----------+---------+
--+---
Pooled StDev =   1.915                  0.0    3.5    7.0   10.5
```

TUKEY'S PAIRWISE COMPARISONS

1 Family error rate = 0.0500
Individual error rate = 0.0220
Critical value = 4.34
Intervals for (column level mean) – (row level mean)

2

	0	24
24	−7.798	
	1.798	
48	−10.798	−7.798
	−1.202	1.798

Comments:
1 The family error rate refers to the probability of at least one type I error for the entire set (3) of pairwise comparisons.
2 Although the Minitab format for Tukey's HSD test differs from that shown in Table 16.8, the results are the same. Now each comparison is described with a 95 percent confidence interval for the population mean difference, adjusted for multiple comparisons. As implied in the discussion of confidence intervals in Section 14.8, intervals whose limits have the same sign, either both positive or both negative, are associated with statistically significant differences.

Each variance estimate or mean square (MS) is found by dividing the appropriate sum of squares (SS) term by its degrees of freedom (df). Once a value of F has been obtained, it's compared with a critical F from the table for the F distribution. If the observed F equals or is larger than the critical F, the null hypothesis is rejected. Otherwise, for all smaller observed values of F, the null hypothesis is retained.

Whenever F is statistically significant, use η^2 to estimate effect size.

Rejection of the overall null hypothesis indicates only that not all population means are equal. To pinpoint differences between specific pairs of population means that contribute to the rejection of the overall null hypothesis, use Tukey's *HSD* test. This test ensures that the cumulative probability of a type I error never exceeds the specified level of significance. When the *HSD* test identifies a significant difference, use Cohen's *d* to estimate effect size.

F tests in ANOVA assume that all underlying populations are normally distributed, with equal variances. Ordinarily, you need not be too concerned about violations of these assumptions.

Important Terms

Analysis of variance (ANOVA)
Treatment effect
Variability within groups
Mean square (*MS*)
Degrees of freedom (*df*)
Squared curvilinear correlation (η^2)
Tukey's *HSD* test

One-factor ANOVA
Variability between groups
Random error
Sum of squares (*SS*)
F ratio
Multiple comparisons

Key Equations

F RATIO

$$F = \frac{MS_{between}}{MS_{within}}$$

$$\text{where } MS_{between} = \frac{SS_{between}}{df_{between}}$$

$$\text{and } MS_{within} = \frac{SS_{within}}{df_{within}}$$

$$SS_{total} = SS_{between} + SS_{within}$$

$$df_{total} = df_{between} + df_{within}$$

PROPORTION OF EXPLAINED VARIANCE

$$\eta^2 = \frac{SS_{between}}{SS_{total}}$$

REVIEW QUESTIONS

Note: When answering review questions in this chapter and the next two ANOVA chapters, you can bypass the customary step-by-step hypothesis testing procedure and summarize your results with an ANOVA table, as in Table 16.6.

16.9 Given the aggression scores below for Outcome A of the sleep deprivation experiment, verify that, as suggested earlier, these mean differences shouldn't be taken seriously by testing the null hypothesis at the .05 level of significance. Use the computation formulas for the various sums of squares and summarize results with an ANOVA table.

	HOURS OF SLEEP DEPRIVATION		
	ZERO	TWENTY-FOUR	FORTY-EIGHT
	3	4	2
	5	8	4
	7	6	6
Group mean:	5	6	4	Grand mean = 5

*16.10 Another psychologist conducts a sleep deprivation experiment. For reasons beyond his control, unequal numbers of subjects occupy the different groups. (Therefore, when calculating $\Sigma \frac{T^2}{n}$ in $SS_{between}$ and SS_{within}, you must adjust the denominator term, n, to reflect the unequal numbers of subjects in the group totals.)

(a) Summarize the results with an ANOVA table. You need not do a step-by-step hypothesis test procedure.

HOURS OF SLEEP DEPRIVATION		
ZERO	TWENTY-FOUR	FORTY-EIGHT
1	4	7
3	7	12
6	5	10
2		9
1		

(b) If appropriate, estimate the effect size with η^2.

(c) If appropriate, use Tukey's *HSD* test (with $\bar{n} = 4$ for the sample size, n) to identify pairs of means that contribute to the significant F, given that $\bar{X}_0$ = 2.60, $\bar{X}_{24}$ = 5.33, *and* $\bar{X}_{48}$ = 9.50.

(d) If appropriate, estimate effect sizes with Cohen's *d*.

(e) Indicate how all of the above results would be reported in the literature, given sample standard deviations of $s_0 = 2.07$, $s_{24} = 1.53$, *and* $s_{48} = 2.08$.

Answers on page 000.

16.11 The investigator mentioned in Review Question 14.14 wishes to conduct a more extensive test of the effect of alcohol consumption on the performance of automobile drivers, possibly to gain more information about the legal maximum for DUI arrests. Before the driving test, subjects drink a glass of orange juice laced with controlled amounts of vodka. Their performance is measured by the number of errors on a driving simulator. Five subjects are randomly assigned to each of five groups receiving different amounts of vodka (either 0, 1, 2, 4, or 6 ounces), and the following results were obtained:

	DRIVING ERRORS AS A FUNCTION OF ALCOHOL CONSUMPTION (OUNCES)				
	ZERO	**ONE**	**TWO**	**FOUR**	**SIX**
	1	4	6	15	20
	1	3	1	6	25
	3	1	2	9	10
	6	7	10	17	10
	4	5	7	9	9
T	15	20	26	56	74

$$\Sigma X = G = 191 \quad \Sigma X^2 = 2371$$

(a) Summarize the results with an ANOVA table. (**Note:** Save these results for use with Review Question 17.7.)

(b) If appropriate, estimate the effect size with η^2.

(c) If appropriate, use Tukey's *HSD* test to pinpoint pairs of means that contribute to the significant *F*, given that $\bar{X}_0 = 3$, $\bar{X}_1 = 4$, $\bar{X}_2 = 5.2$, $\bar{X}_4 = 11.2$, and $\bar{X}_6 = 14.8$. Furthermore, if appropriate, estimate effect sizes with Cohen's *d*.

*16.12 For some experiment, imagine four possible outcomes, as described in the following ANOVA table.

A.	**SOURCE**	**SS**	**df**	**MS**	**F**
	Between	900	3	300	3
	Within	8000	80	100	
	Total	8900	83		

B.	**SOURCE**	**SS**	**df**	**MS**	**F**
	Between	1500	3	500	5
	Within	8000	80	100	
	Total	9500	83		

C.	**SOURCE**	**SS**	**df**	**MS**	**F**
	Between	300	3	100	1
	Within	8000	80	100	
	Total	8300	83		

D.	**SOURCE**	**SS**	**df**	**MS**	**F**
	Between	300	3	100	1
	Within	400	4	100	
	Total	700	7		

(a) How many groups are in Outcome D?

(b) Assuming groups of equal size, what's the size of each group in Outcome C?

(c) Which outcome(s) would cause the null hypothesis to be rejected at the .05 level of significance?

(d) Which outcome provides the least information about a possible treatment effect?

(e) Which outcome would be the least likely to stimulate additional research?

(f) Specify the approximate p-values for each of these outcomes.
Answers on page 515

16.13 Twenty-three overweight male volunteers are randomly assigned to three different treatment programs designed to produce a weight loss by focusing on either diet, exercise, or the modification of eating behavior. Weight changes were recorded, to the nearest pound, for all participants who completed the two-month experiment. Positive scores signify a weight drop; negative scores, a weight gain.

Note: See the comment in Review Question 16.10 about calculations when sample sizes are unequal.

WEIGHT CHANGES		
DIET	**EXERCISE**	**BEHAVIOR MODIFICATION**
3	−1	7
4	8	1
0	4	10
−3	2	0
5	2	18
10	−3	12
3		4
0		6
		5
T 22	12	63
n 8	6	9

$$\Sigma X = G = 97; \; N = 23 \quad \Sigma X^2 = 961$$

(a) Summarize the results with an ANOVA table.

(b) Whenever appropriate, use Tukey's *HSD* test and estimate all effect sizes, given that the means for diet, exercise, and behavior modification equal 2.75, 2.00, and 7.00, respectively.

16.14 The F test describes the ratio of two sources of variability: that for subjects treated differently and that for subjects treated similarly. Is there any sense in which the t test for two independent groups can be viewed likewise?

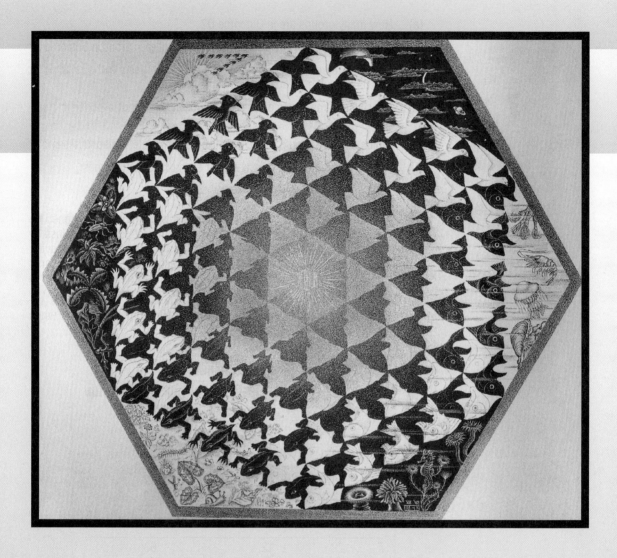

CHAPTER 17

Analysis of Variance (Repeated Measures)

Summary / Important Terms / Key Equations / Review Questions

Preview

This chapter is an extension of the t test for two related samples (Chapter 15) to the F test for more than two related samples. As before, when differences between two or more groups are based on repeated measures for the same subjects, an important source of variability caused by individual differences can be eliminated from the main analysis. This can yield a more powerful analysis, that is, one more likely to detect a false null hypothesis. Also as before, several potential problems must be addressed before adopting a repeated-measures design.

17.1 SLEEP DEPRIVATION EXPERIMENT WITH REPEATED MEASURES

Recall the sleep deprivation experiment featured in the previous chapter. Three subjects in each of three groups were deprived of sleep for either 0, 24, or 48 hours and then were assigned aggression scores based on their behavior in a controlled social situation. The F test was significant $[F(2, 6) = 7.36, MSE = 3.67, p < .05, \eta^2 = .71]$, and according to Tukey's *HSD* test, there was a significant difference between the means for the 0- and 48-hour deprivation groups *(p < .05, d = 3.13)*.

This chapter describes an important alternative design for the sleep deprivation experiment, where each subject serves under not just one but all three levels of sleep deprivation. Referred to as **repeated-measures ANOVA,** *this type of analysis tests whether differences exist among population means with measures on the same subjects.* To facilitate comparisons between the original experiment with single measures on different subjects and the new experiment with repeated measures on the same subjects, exactly the same set of nine scores originally shown as Outcome B in Table 16.1 will be used to illustrate repeated-measures ANOVA. Table 17.1 shows these nine scores, but now the three scores in each row are viewed as repeated measures across the three levels of sleep deprivation for single subjects, coded as either A, B, or C.

Since the same subject serves in all three levels of sleep deprivation, differences in aggression scores between 0, 24, and 48 hours are based on identical sets of subjects and, therefore, key estimates of variability no longer are inflated by a most important type of random error—the variability due to differences between individuals. If the null hypothesis is false, the net effect is a more powerful F test. In the absence of individual differences, both numerator and denominator terms of the F ratio become smaller, but the error term in the denominator of the F ratio, MS_{error}, becomes disproportionately smaller, as demonstrated later in Section 17.7. This translates into a most desirable outcome: an increased likelihood of rejecting the false null hypothesis with a significant F test.

Repeated-Measures ANOVA

A type of analysis that tests whether differences exist among population means with measures on the same subjects.

Table 17.1
SLEEP DEPRIVATION EXPERIMENT WITH REPEATED MEASURES: AGGRESSION SCORES

| | HOURS OF SLEEP DEPRIVATION | | | $\bar{X}_{subject}$ |
SUBJECT	ZERO	TWENTY-FOUR	FORTY-EIGHT	(SUBJECT MEAN)
A	0	3	6	3
B	4	6	8	6
C	2	6	10	6
$\bar{X}_{group} =$ (Group mean)	2	5	8	$\bar{X}_{grand} = 5$ (Grand mean)

Progress Check *17.1 Imagine a simple experiment with repeated measures for four subjects, coded as W, X, Y, and Z, across three levels or values of the independent variable. For each of the following outcomes, indicate the presence or absence of variability due to individual differences (by inspecting the totals for each subject). Among those outcomes where this variability is present, identify the outcome having the greatest amount of variability due to individual differences.

(a)	LEVEL 1	LEVEL 2	LEVEL 3
W	6	3	10
X	6	3	10
Y	6	3	10
Z	6	3	10

(b)	LEVEL 1	LEVEL 2	LEVEL 3
W	4	3	5
X	6	6	7
Y	18	20	19
Z	24	20	21

(c)	LEVEL 1	LEVEL 2	LEVEL 3
W	5	13	20
X	7	14	18
Y	8	15	21
Z	11	14	23

Answers on page 515.

....
17.2 *F* TEST

Except for the fact that measures are repeated, the new *F* test is essentially the same as that described in Chapter 16. The statistical hypotheses still are:

$$H_0: \mu_0 = \mu_{24} = \mu_{48}$$
$$H_1: H_0 \text{ is false}$$

where μ_0, μ_{24}, and μ_{48} represent the mean aggression scores for the *single* population of subjects who are deprived of sleep for 0, 24, and 48 hours. Once again, rejection of the null hypothesis implies that sleep deprivation influences aggressive behavior.

As before, the *F* test of the null hypothesis is based on the notion that if the null hypothesis really is true, both the numerator and denominator of the *F* ratio will tend to be about the same, but if the null hypothesis is false, the numerator (still $MS_{between}$) will tend to be larger than the denominator (now MS_{error}). As

HYPOTHESIS TEST SUMMARY
Repeated-Measures F Test (Sleep Deprivation Experiment)

Research Problem

On average, are subjects' aggression scores in a controlled social situation affected by sleep deprivation periods of 0, 24, and 48 hours, where each subject experiences all three periods?

Statistical Hypotheses

$$H_0: \mu_0 = \mu_{24} = \mu_{48}$$
$$H_1: H_0 \text{ is false}$$

Decision Rule

Reject H_0 at the .05 level of significance if $F \geq 6.94$ (from Table C in Appendix C, given $df_{between} = 2$ and $df_{error} = 4$).

Calculations

$$F = 27 \text{ (See Tables 17.3 and 17.5 for more details.)}$$

Decision

Reject H_0 at the .05 level of significance because $F = 27$ exceeds 6.94.

Interpretation

Mean aggression scores in a controlled social situation are affected by sleep deprivation when subjects experience all three levels of deprivation.

---

implied above, the new denominator term, MS_{error}, tends to be smaller than that for the original one-factor ANOVA because of the elimination of variability due to individual differences in repeated-measures ANOVA.

The hypothesis test for the sleep deprivation experiment with repeated measures, as summarized in the accompanying box, will be discussed later in more detail. Notice the huge increase in the value of F from 7.36 (for the original one-factor ANOVA) to 27 (for the repeated-measures ANOVA), even though both F ratios are based on the same set of nine scores (and the same differences between the three deprivation conditions). The relatively large individual differences in the current example illustrate the beneficial effects of repeated-measures ANOVA. In practice, the net effect of a repeated-measures experiment might not be as dramatic.

17.3 TWO COMPLICATIONS

The same two complications exist for repeated-measures ANOVA as for the repeated-measures *t* test (see Section 15.1). Presumably, in the sleep deprivation experiment, sufficient time elapses between successive sessions to eliminate any lingering effects due to earlier deprivation periods. If there is any concern that earlier effects of the independent variable linger during subsequent sessions, do not use repeated measures.

An extension of counterbalancing can be used to eliminate any potential bias in favor of one condition merely because of the order in which it was experienced. Presumably, in the sleep deprivation experiment, each of the three subjects has been randomly assigned to undergo a different one of three possible orders of deprivation sequences—either 0, 24, and 48 hours; or 48, 0, and 24 hours; or 24, 48, and 0 hours—that, taken together over all three subjects, equalizes the number of times a particular deprivation level was experienced first, second, or third.

17.4 DETAILS: VARIANCE ESTIMATES

Sum of Squares (*SS*): Definitional Formulas

As a point of departure, the total sum of squares still equals the sum of the between-group and within-group components, namely,

$$SS_{total} = SS_{between} + SS_{within}$$

and as indicated in Table 17.2, these three sum of squares terms have the same definitional formulas as in one-factor ANOVA. In repeated-measures ANOVA, however, the total sum of squares is expanded to include a new component for subjects, namely,

---

SUM OF SQUARES (REPEATED MEASURES)

$$SS_{total} = SS_{between} + SS_{subject} + SS_{error} \tag{17.1}$$

---

where the original sum of squares for variability within groups, SS_{within}, is partitioned into two new sum of squares terms, $SS_{subject}$ and SS_{error}, since

$$SS_{within} = SS_{subject} + SS_{error}$$

- $SS_{subject}$ equals the sum of squared deviations of the means for each subject about the grand mean. Its definition formula is $SS_{subject} = k\Sigma(\bar{X}_{subjects} - \bar{X}_{grand})^2$, where k represents the number of repeated measures for each subject, $\bar{X}_{subject}$ is the mean for each subject, and $\bar{X}_{grand}$ is the overall mean for all scores of all subjects. This term reflects variability due to individual differences. The number k in the expression for $SS_{subject}$ reflects the fact that the deviation $\bar{X}_{subject} - \bar{X}_{grand}$ is the same for all repeated measures, k, for any given subject.

■ SS_{error} equals the remaining variability after variability due to individual differences, $SS_{subject}$, has been subtracted from variability within groups, SS_{within}. After being divided by its degrees of freedom, this reduced error term is used in the denominator of the F ratio.

Sum of Squares (SS): Computation Formulas

Totals replace means in the more efficient color-coded computation formulas shown in **Table 17.2**. Notice the highly predictable computational pattern first described in Section 16.4. Each entry in the numerator is squared, and each total, whether for a group, a subject, or the grand total, is then divided by its respective sample size. Among the two new formulas for repeated measures ANOVA, the first term in the formula for $SS_{subject}$, $\Sigma \frac{T^2_{subject}}{k}$, requires that, after squaring the total score for each subject and dividing by the number of repeated measures (or levels of the independent variable), k, these quantities are summed across all subjects. The formula for SS_{error} specifies that $SS_{subject}$ be subtracted from SS_{within}. Although SS_{error} could be calculated directly, the current formula serves as a reminder about the link between a smaller error term and the removal of variability due to differences between subjects.

Table 17.3 indicates how to use the computation formulas for the data from the sleep deprivation experiment with repeated measures.

Degrees of Freedom (df)

The various formulas for degrees of freedom for repeated-measures ANOVA are listed in **Table 17.4**. The degrees of freedom for subjects, $df_{subject} = n - 1$, reflect the loss of one degree of freedom when the means for the n subjects are expressed as deviations about the grand mean. The degrees of freedom for the error term, $df_{error} = df_{within} - df_{subject}$, are found by subtracting the degrees of freedom for subjects from the degrees of freedom for within groups. For the present repeated-measures experiment, which involves a total of nine scores ($N = 9$), with three repeated measures ($k = 3$) for each of three subjects ($n = 3$):

$$df_{total} = N - 1 = 9 - 1 = 8$$
$$df_{between} = k - 1 = 3 - 1 = 2$$
$$df_{within} = N - k = 9 - 3 = 6$$
$$df_{subject} = n - 1 = 3 - 1 = 2$$
$$df_{error} = df_{within} - df_{subject} = 6 - 2 = 4$$

Check for Accuracy

To establish that degrees of freedom have been assigned correctly to each of the above SS terms, substitute numbers into the following formula:

DEGREES OF FREEDOM (REPEATED MEASURES)

$$df_{total} = df_{between} + df_{subject} + df_{error} \qquad (17.2)$$

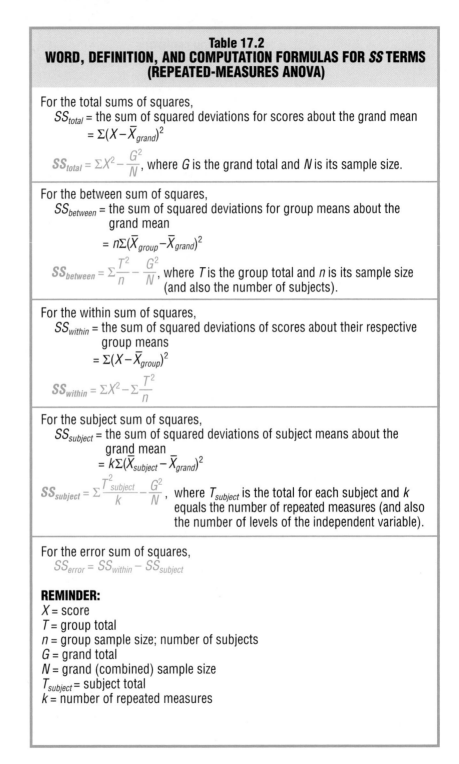

Table 17.2
WORD, DEFINITION, AND COMPUTATION FORMULAS FOR *SS* TERMS (REPEATED-MEASURES ANOVA)

For the total sums of squares,
SS_{total} = the sum of squared deviations for scores about the grand mean
$$= \Sigma(X - \bar{X}_{grand})^2$$

$SS_{total} = \Sigma X^2 - \dfrac{G^2}{N}$, where G is the grand total and N is its sample size.

For the between sum of squares,
$SS_{between}$ = the sum of squared deviations for group means about the grand mean
$$= n\Sigma(\bar{X}_{group} - \bar{X}_{grand})^2$$

$SS_{between} = \Sigma \dfrac{T^2}{n} - \dfrac{G^2}{N}$, where T is the group total and n is its sample size (and also the number of subjects).

For the within sum of squares,
SS_{within} = the sum of squared deviations of scores about their respective group means
$$= \Sigma(X - \bar{X}_{group})^2$$

$SS_{within} = \Sigma X^2 - \Sigma \dfrac{T^2}{n}$

For the subject sum of squares,
$SS_{subject}$ = the sum of squared deviations of subject means about the grand mean
$$= k\Sigma(\bar{X}_{subject} - \bar{X}_{grand})^2$$

$SS_{subject} = \Sigma \dfrac{T^2_{subject}}{k} - \dfrac{G^2}{N}$, where $T_{subject}$ is the total for each subject and k equals the number of repeated measures (and also the number of levels of the independent variable).

For the error sum of squares,
$SS_{error} = SS_{within} - SS_{subject}$

REMINDER:
X = score
T = group total
n = group sample size; number of subjects
G = grand total
N = grand (combined) sample size
$T_{subject}$ = subject total
k = number of repeated measures

Table 17.3
CALCULATION OF *SS* TERMS (REPEATED-MEASURES ANOVA)

A. COMPUTATION SEQUENCE

Find each group total, T, each subject total, $T_{subject}$, and the grand total, G, for all combined groups **1**

Substitute numbers into computation formula **2** and solve for $SS_{between}$.

Substitute numbers into computation formula **3** and solve for SS_{within}.

Substitute numbers into computation formula **4** and solve for $SS_{subject}$.

Substitute numbers into computation formula **5** and solve for SS_{error}.

Substitute numbers into computation formula **6** and solve for SS_{total}.

B. DATA AND COMPUTATIONS

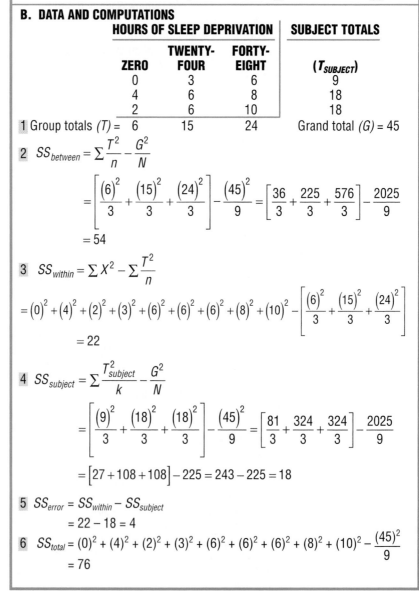

	HOURS OF SLEEP DEPRIVATION			SUBJECT TOTALS
	ZERO	TWENTY-FOUR	FORTY-EIGHT	$(T_{SUBJECT})$
	0	3	6	9
	4	6	8	18
	2	6	10	18
1 Group totals $(T) =$	6	15	24	Grand total $(G) = 45$

2 $SS_{between} = \Sigma \dfrac{T^2}{n} - \dfrac{G^2}{N}$

$$= \left[\frac{(6)^2}{3} + \frac{(15)^2}{3} + \frac{(24)^2}{3} \right] - \frac{(45)^2}{9} = \left[\frac{36}{3} + \frac{225}{3} + \frac{576}{3} \right] - \frac{2025}{9}$$

$$= 54$$

3 $SS_{within} = \Sigma X^2 - \Sigma \dfrac{T^2}{n}$

$$= (0)^2 + (4)^2 + (2)^2 + (3)^2 + (6)^2 + (6)^2 + (6)^2 + (8)^2 + (10)^2 - \left[\frac{(6)^2}{3} + \frac{(15)^2}{3} + \frac{(24)^2}{3} \right]$$

$$= 22$$

4 $SS_{subject} = \Sigma \dfrac{T_{subject}^2}{k} - \dfrac{G^2}{N}$

$$= \left[\frac{(9)^2}{3} + \frac{(18)^2}{3} + \frac{(18)^2}{3} \right] - \frac{(45)^2}{9} = \left[\frac{81}{3} + \frac{324}{3} + \frac{324}{3} \right] - \frac{2025}{9}$$

$$= \left[27 + 108 + 108 \right] - 225 = 243 - 225 = 18$$

5 $SS_{error} = SS_{within} - SS_{subject}$

$$= 22 - 18 = 4$$

6 $SS_{total} = (0)^2 + (4)^2 + (2)^2 + (3)^2 + (6)^2 + (6)^2 + (6)^2 + (8)^2 + (10)^2 - \dfrac{(45)^2}{9}$

$$= 76$$

Table 17.4
FORMULAS FOR *df* TERMS: REPEATED-MEASURES ANOVA

$df_{total} = N - 1$, the number of all scores $- 1$
$df_{between} = k - 1$, the number of repeated measures (or levels of the independent variable) $- 1$
$df_{within} = N - k$, the number of all scores $-$ number of levels
$df_{subject} = n - 1$, the number of subjects $- 1$
$df_{error} = df_{within} - df_{subject} = (N - k) - (n - 1)$

17.5 DETAILS: MEAN SQUARE (*MS*) AND THE *F* RATIO

Having calculated values for the various *SS* terms and their degrees of freedom, we can determine the mean squares for between groups and for error, and calculate the value of *F* as shown in **Figure 17.1**. The top part of Figure 17.1 shows the partitioning of SS_{total} into $SS_{between}$ and SS_{within} for a one-factor ANOVA. The bottom part shows the partitioning of SS_{within} into $SS_{subject}$ and SS_{error} for repeated-measures ANOVA. Among the latter two *SS* terms, only SS_{error} is converted into a mean square, MS_{error}, to be entered into the denominator of the *F* ratio. Calculating $MS_{subject}$ serves no useful purpose, since it usually would culminate in the trivial rejection of the null hypothesis for individual differences.

As suggested in Figure 17.1, the mean square for variability between groups, $MS_{between}$, is given by the following expression:

MEAN SQUARE BETWEEN GROUPS (REPEATED MEASURES)

$$MS_{between} = \frac{SS_{between}}{df_{between}} \qquad (17.3)$$

$MS_{between}$ reflects the variability between treatment means, each of which is based on the repeated measures for all subjects.

For the sleep deprivation experiment with repeated measures,

$$MS_{between} = \frac{SS_{between}}{df_{between}} = \frac{54}{2} = 27$$

which has the same numerical value as $MS_{between}$ for the independent-measures experiment in Chapter 16—as it should, since identical sets of numbers are being used to calculate these equivalent expressions in both examples.

The value of the mean square for error, MS_{error}, is given by the following expression:

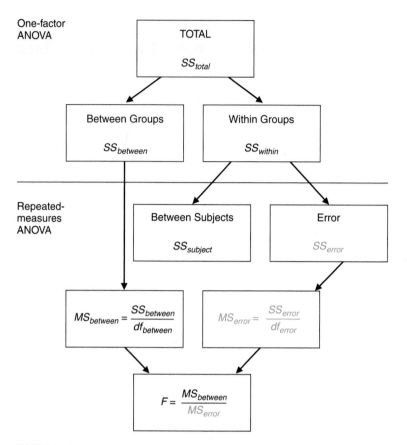

One-factor
ANOVA

Repeated-
measures
ANOVA

FIGURE 17.1

Sources of variability for one-factor and repeated-measures ANOVA.

MEAN SQUARE FOR ERROR (REPEATED MEASURES)

$$MS_{error} = \frac{SS_{error}}{df_{error}} \qquad (17.4)$$

where MS_{error} reflects the variability among scores of subjects within each treatment group, pooled across all treatments, after the removal of variability attributable to individual differences.

For the sleep deprivation experiment with repeated measures,

$$MS_{error} = \frac{SS_{error}}{df_{error}} = \frac{4}{4} = 1$$

which, because of the removal of variability due to individual differences, is much smaller than the corresponding error term, MS_{within}, of 3.67 for the independent-measures experiment in Chapter 16.

Finally, the F ratio is as follows:

> **F RATIO (REPEATED MEASURES)**
>
> $$F = \frac{MS_{between}}{MS_{error}}$$ (17.5)

For the sleep deprivation experiment with repeated measures, the null hypothesis is very suspect because

$$F = \frac{MS_{between}}{MS_{error}} = \frac{27}{1} = 27$$

17.6 TABLE FOR F DISTRIBUTION

As usual, a decision about the null hypothesis requires that the observed F be compared with a critical F. Critical F values for hypothesis tests at the .05 level (light numbers) and the .01 level (dark numbers) are listed in Table C in Appendix C. To read the F table, find the cell intersected by the column with degrees of freedom equal to those in the numerator of F, $df_{between}$, and by the row with degrees of freedom equal to those in the denominator of F, df_{error}. In the present case, the column with 2 degrees of freedom and the row with 4 degrees of freedom intersect a critical F of 6.94 (for the .05 level) and 18.00 (for the .01 level). Given an observed F of 27, we can reject the null hypothesis at the .05 (or the .01) level of significance. There is dramatic evidence that, when subjects are measured repeatedly, the three levels of sleep deprivation affect aggression scores.

17.7 ANOVA SUMMARY TABLES

ANOVA results can be summarized as shown in **Table 17.5**. Ordinarily, the shaded numbers in parentheses do not appear in ANOVA tables, but they show the origin of the two relevant MS terms and the F ratio.

Table 17.5
ANOVA TABLE: SLEEP DEPRIVATION EXPERIMENT (REPEATED MEASURES)

SOURCE	SS	df	MS	F
Between	54	2	$\left(\frac{54}{2}=\right)27$	$\left(\frac{27}{1}=\right)27*$
Within	22	6		
Subject	18	2		
Error	4	4	$\left(\frac{4}{4}=\right)1$	
Total	76	8		

* Significant at the .01 level.

Table 17.6
COMPARISON OF SUMMARY TABLES FOR ONE-FACTOR ANOVA AND REPEATED-MEASURE ANOVA

ANOVA TABLE: ORIGINAL SLEEP DEPRIVATION EXPERIMENT (ONE FACTOR)					ANOVA TABLE: SLEEP DEPRIVATION EXPERIMENT (REPEATED MEASURES)				
SOURCE	SS	df	MS	F	SOURCE	SS	df	MS	F
Between	54	2	27	7.36*	Between	54	2	27	27**
Within	22	6	3.67		Within	22	6		
					Subject	18	2		
					Error	4	4	1	
Total	76	8			Total	76	8		

Significant at the .05 level.   **Significant at the .01 level.*

Table 17.6 compares the ANOVA summary tables for the two sleep deprivation experiments. Since, to facilitate comparisons, exactly the same nine scores were used for both experiments, the two summary tables possess many similarities. Sums of squares and degrees of freedom are the same for between and total variability. The main difference appears in the denominator terms for the F ratios. The MS_{error} for the repeated-measures ANOVA is about one-third as small as the MS_{within} for the one-factor ANOVA.

Why More Powerful?

In applications with real data, $MS_{between}$ also would tend to be smaller in repeated-measures ANOVA than in one-factor ANOVA because of the absence of individual differences from variability between treatment groups. But then why can it be claimed that, if the null hypothesis is false, the repeated-measures F will tend to be larger? If the null hypothesis is false, the F ratio will tend to be greater than 1. Therefore, the subtraction of essentially the same amount of variability due to individual differences from both the numerator and denominator of the F ratio causes *relatively* more shrinkage in the smaller denominator term. To illustrate with a simple numerical example: Given any F greater than 1, say a one-factor $F = \frac{8}{4} = 2$, then, subtract from both numerator and denominator any constant (representing individual differences), say 2, to obtain a larger repeated-measures

$$F = \frac{8-2}{4-2} = \frac{6}{2} = 3 \; .$$

Progress Check *17.2 A school psychologist tests the effects of environmental noises on the reading comprehension scores of high school students who rotate, with the customary controls, through three different conditions: silence, white noise, and rock music. The reading comprehension scores for six subjects are as follows:

SUBJECT	SILENCE	WHITE NOISE	ROCK	$T_{SUBJECT}$
A	6	4	2	12
B	11	3	0	14
C	5	4	1	10
D	7	6	2	15
E	4	6	4	14
F	10	7	5	22
T	43	30	14 $\Sigma X = G = 87$	$\Sigma X^2 = 559$

Summarize the results in an ANOVA table.

Answers on page 515.

17.8 ESTIMATING EFFECT SIZE

Whenever F is statistically significant in a repeated-measures ANOVA, a variation on the squared curvilinear correlation coefficient, η^2, can be used to estimate effect size. The formula for a repeated-measures η^2 differs from that for an independent-measures η^2 (Formula 16.8 on page 356) because $SS_{total} - SS_{subject}$ replaces SS_{total} in the denominator.

Partial Squared Curvilinear Correlation (η_p^2)

The proportion of explained variance in the dependent variable after one or more sources have been eliminated from the total variance.

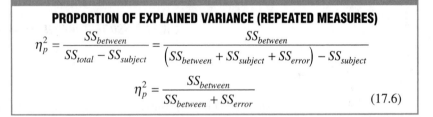

PROPORTION OF EXPLAINED VARIANCE (REPEATED MEASURES)

$$\eta_p^2 = \frac{SS_{between}}{SS_{total} - SS_{subject}} = \frac{SS_{between}}{\left(SS_{between} + SS_{subject} + SS_{error}\right) - SS_{subject}}$$

$$\eta_p^2 = \frac{SS_{between}}{SS_{between} + SS_{error}} \qquad (17.6)$$

where η_p^2 is referred to as a *partial* η^2, or more technically as a **partial squared curvilinear correlation,** *because the effects of individual differences have been eliminated from the reduced or partial total variance.* This adjustment reflects the fact that, when measures are repeated, the value of η^2 for the treatment variable can't possibly account for that portion of total variability attributable to individual differences, that is, $SS_{subject}$.

Substituting of values for the SS terms from the ANOVA summary in Table 17.5, we have

$$\eta_p^2 = \frac{54}{76 - 18} = \frac{54}{58} = .93$$

When compared with guidelines for effect sizes in **Table 17.7**, this estimated effect size of .93 would be spectacularly large, indicating that .93, or 93 percent, of total variance in aggression scores (excluding variance due to individual

Table 17.7
GUIDELINES FOR
η_p^2

η_p^2	EFFECT
.01	Small
.09	Medium
.25	Large

differences) is explained by differences between 0, 24, and 48 hours of sleep deprivation, while the remaining 7 percent of the variance in aggression scores is not explained by hours of sleep deprivation. This very large value for η_p^2 reflects a number of factors. Identical sets of fictitious data (used for both the independent-measures and the repeated-measures experiments) were selected to dramatize the effects of sleep deprivation. Furthermore, although based on the same data, the value of.93 for the repeated-measures estimate, η_p^2, exceeds that of .71 for the independent-measures estimate, η^2, essentially because of the smaller denominator term in η_p^2.

Progress Check *17.3 Since the null hypothesis was rejected in Question 17.2, estimate effect size with η_p^2.

Answer on page 515.

17.9 MULTIPLE COMPARISONS

Rejection of the overall null hypothesis indicates only that not all population means are equal. To pinpoint the one or more differences between pairs of population means that contribute to the rejection of the overall null hypothesis, use a multiple comparison test, such as Tukey's *HSD* test. *Tukey's test supplies a single critical value, HSD, for evaluating the significance of each difference for every possible pair of means.* The value of *HSD* can be calculated using the following formula:

TUKEY'S *HSD* TEST (REPEATED MEASURES)

$$HSD = q\sqrt{\frac{MS_{error}}{n}} \qquad\qquad (17.7)$$

---

where *HSD* is the positive critical value for any difference between two means; q is a value obtained from Table G in Appendix C; MS_{error} is the error term for the repeated-measures ANOVA; and n is the sample size in each treatment group (which in repeated-measures ANOVA is simply the number of subjects).

To obtain a value for q at the .05 level (light numbers) in Table G, find the cell intersected by k, the number of repeated measures or treatment levels, and df_{error}, the degrees of freedom for the error term in the repeated-measures ANOVA. Given values of $k = 3$ and $df_{error} = 4$ for the sleep deprivation experiment, the intersected cell shows a value of 5.04 for q at the .05 level. Substituting $q = 5.04$, $MS_{error} = 1$, and $n = 3$ in Equation 17.7, we can solve for *HSD* as follows:

$$HSD = q\sqrt{\frac{MS_{error}}{n}} = 5.04\sqrt{\frac{1}{3}} = 5.04\,(.57) = 2.87$$

Interpretation

Table 17.8 shows absolute differences of either 3, 6, or 3 for the three pairs of means in the repeated-measures experiment. (These absolute differences are the

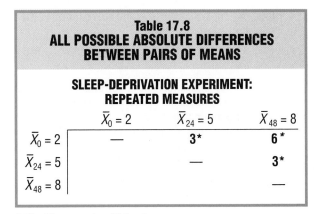

Table 17.8
ALL POSSIBLE ABSOLUTE DIFFERENCES
BETWEEN PAIRS OF MEANS

SLEEP-DEPRIVATION EXPERIMENT:
REPEATED MEASURES

	$\bar{X}_0 = 2$	$\bar{X}_{24} = 5$	$\bar{X}_{48} = 8$
$\bar{X}_0 = 2$	—	3*	6*
$\bar{X}_{24} = 5$		—	3*
$\bar{X}_{48} = 8$			—

* Significant at the .05 level.

same as those for the three pairs of means for the one-factor ANOVA shown in Table 16.8 on page 360.) In the case of the repeated-measures experiment, however, all three of the observed differences exceed the critical *HSD* value of 2.87. We can conclude, therefore, that the population mean aggression scores become progressively higher as the sleep deprivation period increases from 0 to 24 and then to 48 hours. Because of its smaller error term, the repeated-measures ANOVA resulted in significant differences for all three comparisons, while the one-factor ANOVA resulted in a significant difference for only the one most extreme comparison (between 0 and 48 hours of deprivation). In practice, of course, there is no guarantee that the beneficial effects of repeated measures will always be as dramatic.

Estimating Effect Size

The effect size for any significant difference between pairs of means can be estimated with Cohen's *d*, as adapted from Equation 14.5 on page 303, that is,

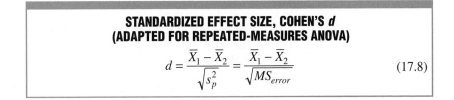

STANDARDIZED EFFECT SIZE, COHEN'S *d*
(ADAPTED FOR REPEATED-MEASURES ANOVA)

$$d = \frac{\bar{X}_1 - \bar{X}_2}{\sqrt{s_p^2}} = \frac{\bar{X}_1 - \bar{X}_2}{\sqrt{MS_{error}}} \qquad (17.8)$$

where *d* is an estimate of the standardized effect size; $\bar{X}_1$ and $\bar{X}_2$ is the pair of significantly different means; and $\sqrt{MS_{error}}$, the square root of the error mean square for the repeated-measures ANOVA, represents the sample standard deviation.

To estimate the standardized effect size for the one significant difference of 6 between means for 0 and 48 hours of sleep deprivation, enter $\bar{X}_{48} - \bar{X}_0 = 6$ and

$MS_{error} = 1$ in Equation 17.8 and solve for d:

$$d\left(\overline{X}_{48}, \overline{X}_0\right) = \frac{6}{\sqrt{1}} = 6$$

which is an extremely large effect, equivalent to six standard deviations. (According to Cohen's guidelines for d, described on page 304, effect size is large if d is more than 0.8.)

To estimate the standardized effect size for the two significant differences of 3 between means for 0 and 24 hours, and between means for 24 and 48 hours of sleep deprivation, enter 3 and $MS_{error} = 1$ in Equation 17.8 and solve for d:

$$d\left(\overline{X}_{24}, \overline{X}_0\right) = d\left(\overline{X}_{48}, \overline{X}_{24}\right) = \frac{3}{\sqrt{1}} = 3$$

which is a very large effect, equivalent to three standard deviations.

These three large values for d aren't surprising, given the spectacularly large effect size of $\eta^2 = .93$ for the proportion of explained variance attributable to differences between all three groups in the sleep deprivation experiment with repeated measures.

Progress Check *17.4 **(a)** Since the null hypothesis was rejected in Question 17.2, use Tukey's *HSD* test to identify which pairs of population means differ significantly at the .05 level, given that the means for silence, white noise, and rock equal 7.17, 5.00, and 2.33, respectively.

(b) Use Cohen's *d* to estimate the effect size for any statistically significant pairs of observed means.

(c) Interpret the results.
Answers on page 515.

17.10 REPORTS IN THE LITERATURE

Literature reports are usually limited to a review of relevant descriptive statistics, such as the group means, and one or more general conclusions. A parenthetical statement summarizes the statistical test and estimates effect size. Also reported are the results of any multiple comparison tests. An investigator might report the sleep deprivation experiment as follows:

> **Mean aggression scores of 2, 5, and 8 were obtained when the same subjects were exposed to 0, 24, and 48 hours of sleep deprivation, respectively. There is evidence that, on average, aggression scores increase with hours of sleep deprivation [$F(2, 4) = 27$, $MSE = 1.0$, $p < .01$, $\eta_p^2 = .93$]. According to Tukey's *HSD* test, all pairs of differences were significant ($HSD = 2.87$, $p < .05$ with $3 \leq d \leq 6$).**

The test result has an approximate p-value of less than .01, since the observed F of 27 is larger than the critical F of 18.00 for the .01 level of significance in Table C in Appendix C. The η_p^2 value of .93 is the estimated effect size expressed as a proportion of total variance with individual differences excluded. All three pairs of means differ significantly, and the standardized estimate of effect size, *d*, equals between three and six standard deviations.

....

17.11 ASSUMPTIONS

In addition to the usual ANOVA assumptions about normality and equal variances, repeated-measures ANOVA also assumes *sphericity,* the assumption of equality among all possible population correlation coefficients. For example, in the sleep deprivation experiment, it assumes equality among the three correlations for aggression scores between 0 and 24, between 0 and 48, and between 24 and 48 hours. Fortunately, the accuracy of the *F* test is not greatly affected unless this assumption is seriously violated. If you think it might be seriously violated—possibly because one or more levels of the independent variable appear to *radically* alter the typical ranking among the scores of individual subjects—refer to more advanced stat books.*

Summary
....

Repeated-measures ANOVA tests for differences between population means when measures for all populations are based on the same subjects. Because measures are repeated, an important source of variability caused by individual differences can be eliminated from the main analysis.

Two potential complications are associated with repeated measures. First, if performance in one condition might be contaminated by the subject's prior experience with other conditions, do not use repeated measures. Second, use an extension of counterbalancing to eliminate any potential bias in favor of one condition merely because of the order in which it was experienced.

Whenever *F* is statistically significant, estimate effect size by calculating η_p^2, where variability due to individual differences has been excluded from the total variance.

To pinpoint differences between specific pairs of population means that contribute to the rejection of the overall null hypothesis, use Tukey's *HSD* test for multiple comparisons.

Whenever the *HSD* test is significant, use Cohen's *d* to estimate effect size.

In addition to the customary ANOVA assumptions about normality and equal variances, repeated-measures ANOVA assumes sphericity, the assumption of equality among all possible correlations between populations. You need be concerned about these assumptions only in the unlikely event of serious violations.

....

*For more information about alternative methods when the sphericity assumption is suspect, see Chapter 14 in D. C. Howell, *Statistical Methods for Psychology,* 7th ed. (Belmont, CA: Wadsworth, 2010).

Important Terms

Repeated-measures ANOVA

Partial squared curvilinear correlation (η_p^2)

Key Equations

F RATIO

$$F = \frac{MS_{between}}{MS_{error}}$$

$$\text{where } MS_{error} = \frac{SS_{error}}{df_{error}}$$

$$SS_{total} = SS_{between} + SS_{subject} + SS_{error}$$

$$df_{total} = df_{between} + df_{subject} + df_{error}$$

REVIEW QUESTIONS

*17.5 Capitalizing on the additivity of *SS* and *df* terms, complete the following ANOVA summary table, assuming repeated measures for 12 subjects across four levels of the independent variable and the .05 level of significance.

SOURCE	SS	df	MS	F
Between	—	—	—	—
Within	8800	—		
Subject	5500	—		
Error	—	—	—	
Total	10000	—		

Answers on page 516.

*17.6 Return to the study first described in Question 16.5 on page 354, where a psychologist tests whether shy college students initiate more eye contacts with strangers because of training sessions in assertive behavior. Use the same data, but now assume that eight subjects, coded as A, B, . . . G, H, are tested *repeatedly* after zero, one, two, and three training sessions. (Incidentally, since the psychologist is interested in any learning or sequential effect, it would not make sense—indeed, it's impossible, given the sequential nature of the independent variable—to counterbalance the four sessions.) The results are expressed as the observed number of eye contacts:

		WORKSHOP SESSIONS			
SUBJECT	**ZERO**	**ONE**	**TWO**	**THREE**	$T_{SUBJECT}$
A	1	2	4	7	14
B	0	1	2	6	9
C	0	2	3	6	11
D	2	4	6	7	19
E	3	4	7	9	23
F	4	6	8	10	28
G	2	3	5	8	18
H	1	3	5	7	16
					$G = 138$

(a) Summarize the results with an ANOVA table. Short-circuit computational work by using the results in Question 16.5 for the SS terms, that is, $SS_{between} = 154.12$, $SS_{within} = 132.75$, and $SS_{total} = 286.87$.

(b) Whenever appropriate, estimate effect sizes with η_p^2 and with d, and conduct Tukey's *HSD* test.

(c) Compare these results with repeated measures with those in Question 16.5 for independent samples.

Answers on page 516.

17.7 Recall the experiment described in Review Question 16.11 on page 367, where errors on a driving simulator were obtained for subjects whose orange juice had been laced with controlled amounts of vodka. Now assume that repeated measures are taken across all five conditions for each of five subjects. (Assume that no lingering effects occur because sufficient time elapses between successive tests, and no order bias appears because the orders of the five conditions are equalized across the five subjects.)

DRIVING ERRORS AS A FUNCTION OF ALCOHOL CONSUMPTION						
			(OUNCES)			
SUBJECT	**ZERO**	**ONE**	**TWO**	**FOUR**	**SIX**	$T_{SUBJECT}$
A	1	4	6	15	20	46
B	1	3	1	6	25	36
C	3	1	2	9	10	25
D	6	7	10	17	10	50
E	4	5	7	9	9	34
T	15	20	26	56	74	

$$\Sigma X = G = 191 \qquad \Sigma X^2 = 2371$$

(a) Summarize the results in an ANOVA table. If you did Review Question 16.11 and saved your results, you can use the known values for $SS_{between}$, SS_{within}, and SS_{total} to short-circuit computations.

(b) If appropriate, estimate the effect sizes and use Tukey's *HSD* test.

17.8 While analyzing data, an investigator treats each score as if it were contributed by a different subject even though, in fact, scores were repeated measures. What effect, if any, would this mistake probably have on the F test if the null hypothesis were

(a) true?

(b) false?

17.9 Typically, variability due to individual differences is appreciable. If the opposite were true, that is, if there were little or no variability due to individual differences, would it make sense to use repeated measures? Explain your answer.

CHAPTER 18

Analysis of Variance (Two Factors)

Summary / Important Terms / Key Equations / Review Questions

Preview

Two-factor ANOVA is a most efficient design where you not only can analyze two factors, but also an important new source of variability caused by the interaction between the two factors. Interaction implies that two factors combine in an unexpected fashion, and if present, it can dominate the interpretation of the analysis. Everyday examples of interaction are the potentially fatal combination of tranquilizers and alcohol and, in a lighter vein, the taste clash between certain wines and cheeses.

18.1 A TWO-FACTOR EXPERIMENT: RESPONSIBILITY IN CROWDS

Do crowds affect our willingness, either positively or negatively, to assume responsibility for the welfare of others and ourselves? For instance, does the presence of other people either facilitate or inhibit our reaction to potentially dangerous smoke seeping from a wall vent? Hoping to answer this question, a social psychologist measures any delay in a subject's alarm reaction (the dependent variable) as smoke gradually fills a waiting room occupied only by the subject, plus "crowds" of either zero, two, or four associates of the experimenter (the first independent variable or factor) who act as regular subjects but, in fact, ignore the smoke.

If gender were viewed as important, possibly because of the noticeably different reactions of males and females during a pilot study, the social psychologist might cross-classify subjects as either female or male (the second independent variable or factor). Using this **two-factor ANOVA** design, the psychologist can test not just two but three null hypotheses, namely, the effect on subjects' reaction times of (1) crowd size, (2) gender, and, as a bonus, (3) the combination or interaction of crowd size and gender.

For computational simplicity, assume that the social psychologist randomly assigns two female subjects to be tested (one at a time) with crowds of either zero, two, or four people and then repeats the random assignment for an equal number of male subjects. The resulting six groups, each consisting of two subjects, represent all possible combinations of the two factors.

Tables for Main Effects and Interaction

Table 18.1 shows one set of possible outcomes for the two-factor study. Although, as indicated in Chapter 16, the actual computations in ANOVA usually are based on totals, preliminary interpretations can be based on either totals or means. In Table 18.1, the numbers in color represent four different types of means:

Two-Factor ANOVA

A more complex type of analysis that tests whether differences exist among population means categorized by two factors or independent variables.

Table 18.1
OUTCOME OF TWO-FACTOR EXPERIMENT
(REACTION TIMES IN MINUTES)

GENDER	CROWD SIZE						ROW MEAN
	ZERO		TWO		FOUR		
Female	8 8	8	8 6	7	10 8	9	8
Male	9 11	10	15 19	17	24 18	21	16
Column mean		9		12		15	Grand mean = 12

Note: Numbers in color are means.

1. The three column means (9, 12, 15) represent the mean reaction times for each crowd size *when gender is ignored.* Any differences among these column means not attributable to chance are referred to as the main effect of crowd size on reaction time. In ANOVA, **main effect** *always refers to the effect of a single factor,* such as crowd size, when any other factor, such as gender, is ignored.

2. The two row means (8, 16) represent the mean reaction times for gender when crowd size is ignored. Any difference between these row means not attributable to chance is referred to as the *main effect of gender on reaction time.*

3. The mean of the reaction times for each group of two subjects yields the six means (8, 7, 9, 10, 17, 21) for each combination of the two factors. Often referred to as *cell means* or *treatment-combination means,* these means reflect not only the main effects for crowd size and gender described earlier but, more importantly, any effect due to the interaction between crowd size and gender, as described below.

4. Finally, the one mean for all three column means—or for both row means—yields the overall or grand mean (12) for all subjects in the study.

Graphs for Main Effects

To preview the experimental outcomes, let's look for obvious trends in a series of graphs based on Table 18.1. The slanted line in panel A of **Figure 18.1** depicts the large differences between column means, that is, between mean reaction times for subjects, regardless of gender, with crowds of zero, two, and four people. The relatively steep slant of this line suggests that the null hypothesis for crowd size might be rejected. The steeper the slant is, the larger the observed differences between column means and the greater the suspected main effect of crowd size will be. On the other hand, a fairly level line in panel A of Figure 18.1 would have reflected the relative absence of any main effect due to crowd size.

The slanted line in panel B of Figure 18.1 depicts the large difference between row means, that is, between mean reaction times for females and males, regardless of crowd size. The relatively steep slope of this line suggests that the null hypothesis for gender also might be rejected; that is, there might be a main effect due to gender.

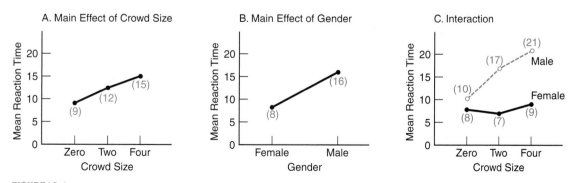

FIGURE18.1

Graphs of outcomes of the two-factor experiment.

Graph for Interaction

These preliminary conclusions about main effects must be qualified because of a complication due to the combined effect or interaction of crowd size and gender on reaction time.

Interaction occurs whenever the effects of one factor on the dependent variable are not consistent for all values (or levels) of the second factor.

Panel C of Figure 18.1 depicts the interaction between crowd size and gender. The two nonparallel lines in panel C depict differences between the three cell means in the first row and the three cell means in the second row, that is, between the mean reaction times of females for different crowd sizes and the mean reaction times of males for different crowd sizes. Although the line for female subjects remains fairly level, that for male subjects is slanted, suggesting that the reaction times of male subjects, but not those of female subjects, are influenced by crowd size. Because the effect of crowd size is not consistent for female and male subjects—portrayed by the apparent nonparallelism between the two lines in panel C of Figure 18.1—the null hypothesis (that there is no interaction between the two factors) might be rejected. Section 18.3 contains additional comments about interaction, as well as a more preferred definition of interaction.

Summary of Preliminary Interpretations

To summarize, a nonstatistical evaluation of the graphs of data for the two-factor experiment suggests a number of preliminary interpretations. Each of the three null hypotheses regarding the effects of crowd size, gender, and the interaction of these factors might be rejected. Because of the suspected interaction, however, any generalizations about the main effects of one factor must be qualified in terms of specific levels of the second factor. Pending the outcome of the statistical analysis, you can speculate that the crowd size probably influences the reaction times of male subjects but not those of female subjects.

Progress Check *18.1 A college dietitian wishes to determine whether students prefer a particular pizza topping (either plain, vegetarian, salami, or everything) and one type of crust (either thick or thin). A total of 160 volunteers are randomly assigned to one of the eight cells in this two-factor experiment. After eating their assigned pizza, the 20 subjects in each cell rate their preference on a scale ranging from 0 (inedible) to 10 (the best). The results, in the form of means for cells, rows, and columns, are as follows:

MEAN PREFERENCE SCORES FOR PIZZA AS A FUNCTION OF TOPPING AND CRUST

	TOPPING				
CRUST	**PLAIN**	**VEGETARIAN**	**SALAMI**	**EVERYTHING**	**ROW**
Thick	7.2	5.7	4.8	6.1	6.0
Thin	8.9	4.8	8.4	1.3	5.9
Column	8.1	5.3	6.6	3.7	

Construct graphs for each of the three possible effects, and use this information to make preliminary interpretations about pizza preferences. Ordinarily, of course, you would verify these speculations by performing an ANOVA—a task that cannot be performed for these data, since only means are supplied.

Answers on page 517.

18.2 THREE *F* TESTS

As suggested in **Figure 18.2**, *F* ratios in both a one- and a two-factor ANOVA always consist of a numerator, shown in color, that measures some aspect of variability between groups or cells and a denominator, shown in black, that measures variability within groups or cells. In a one-factor ANOVA, a single null hypothesis is tested with one *F* ratio.

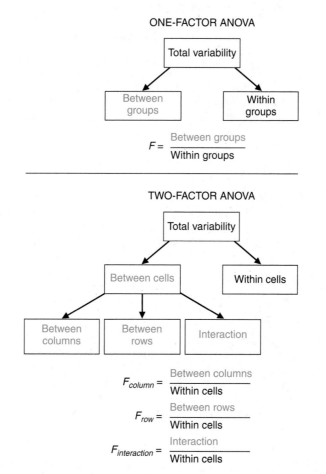

FIGURE 18.2

Sources of variability and F *ratios in one- and two-factor ANOVAs.*

In two-factor ANOVA, three different null hypotheses are tested, one at a time, with three F ratios: F_{column}, F_{row}, and $F_{interaction}$.

The numerator of each of these three F ratios reflects a different aspect of variability between cells: variability between columns (crowd size), variability between rows (gender), and interaction—any *remaining* variability between cells not attributable to either variability between columns (crowd size) or rows (gender).

The numerator terms for the three F ratios in the bottom panel of Figure 18.2 estimate random error and, if present, a treatment effect (for subjects treated differently by the investigator, in the case of crowd size, and by "nature," in the case of gender).[*] The black denominator term always estimates only random error (for subjects treated similarly in the same cell).

In practice, a sufficiently large F value is viewed as rare, given that the null hypothesis is true, and therefore, it leads to the rejection of the null hypothesis. Otherwise, the null hypothesis is retained.

Test Results for Two-Factor Experiment

As indicated in the boxed summary for the hypothesis test for a smoke alarm experiment, test results agree with our preliminary interpretations based on graphs. Each of the three null hypotheses is rejected at the .05 level of significance. The significant main effects indicate that crowd size and gender, in turn, influence the reaction times of subjects to smoke. The significant interaction, however, indicates that the effect of crowd size on reaction times differs for male and female subjects.

18.3 INTERACTION

Interaction emerges as the most striking feature of a two-factor ANOVA. As noted previously, two factors interact if the effects of one factor on the dependent variable are not consistent for all of the levels of a second factor. More generally, when two factors are combined, something happens that represents more than a mere composite of their separate effects.

Supplies Valuable Information

Rather than being a complication to be avoided, an interaction often highlights pertinent issues for future research. For example, the interaction between crowd size and gender suggests that subsequent studies might attempt to identify those factors that cause the reaction times of male subjects, but not female subjects, to be relatively sensitive to crowd size. In the process, much might be learned about why some people in groups assume or fail to assume social responsibility.

---

[*] Strictly speaking, since gender cannot be manipulated by the investigator, it fails to qualify as a true independent variable and, therefore, any conclusion about the causal effect of gender on reaction times is open to discussion.

HYPOTHESIS TEST SUMMARY
Two-Factor Anova (Smoke Alarm Experiment)

Research Problem

Do crowd size and gender, as well as the interaction of these two factors, influence the subjects' mean reaction times to potentially dangerous smoke?

Statistical Hypotheses

H_0: no main effect due to columns or crowd size
  (or $\mu_0 = \mu_2 = \mu_4$).
H_0: no main effect due to rows or gender
  (or $\mu_{female} = \mu_{male}$).
H_0: no interaction.
H_1: H_0 is not true.
  (Same H_1 accommodates each H_0.)

Decision Rule

Reject H_0 at the .05 level of significance if F_{column} or $F_{interaction}$ ≥ 5.14 (from Table C in Appendix C, given 2 and 6 degrees of freedom) and if $F_{row} \geq 5.99$ (given 1 and 6 degrees of freedom).

Calculations

$$F_{column} = 6.75$$
$$F_{row} = 36.02$$
$$F_{interaction} = 5.25$$

(See Tables 18.3 and 18.6 for more details.)

Decision

Reject all three null hypotheses at the .05 level of significance because $F_{column} = 6.75$ exceeds 5.14; $F_{row} = 36.02$ exceeds 5.99; and $F_{interaction} = 5.25$ exceeds 5.14.

Interpretation

Both crowd size and gender influence the subjects' mean reaction times to smoke. The interaction indicates that the influence of crowd size depends on whether subjects are males or females. It appears that the mean reaction times of males, but not those of females, increase with crowd size.

Other Examples

The combined effect of crowd size and gender could have differed from that described in panel C of Figure 18.1. Examples of some other possible effects are shown in **Figure 18.3**. The two top panels in Figure 18.3 describe outcomes that, because of their consistency, would cause the retention of the null hypothesis for interaction. The two bottom panels in Figure 18.3 describe outcomes that, because of their inconsistency, probably would cause the rejection of the null hypothesis for interaction.

Simple Effects

Simple Effect

The effect of one factor on the dependent variable at a single level of another factor.

The notion of interaction can be clarified further by viewing each line in Figure 18.3 as a simple effect. A **simple effect** *represents the effect of one factor on the dependent variable at a single level of the second factor.* Thus, in panel A, there are two simple effects of crowd size, one for males and one for females, and both simple effects are consistent, showing an increase in mean reaction times with larger crowd sizes. Accordingly, the main effect of crowd size can be interpreted without referring to its two simple effects.

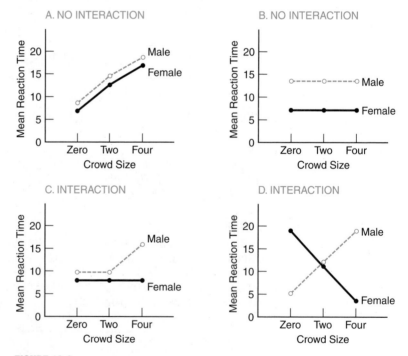

FIGURE 18.3

Some possible outcomes (two-factor experiment).

Inconsistent Simple Effects

In panel D, on the other hand, the two simple effects of crowd size, one for males and one for females, clearly are inconsistent; the simple effect of crowd size for females shows a decrease in mean reaction times with larger crowd sizes, while the simple effect of crowd size for males shows just the opposite—an increase in mean reaction times with larger crowd sizes. Accordingly, the main effect of crowd size—assuming one exists—cannot be interpreted without referring to its radically different simple effects.

Simple Effects and Interaction

In Figure 18.3, no interaction is present in panels A and B because their respective simple effects are consistent, as suggested by the parallel lines. Interactions could be present in panels C and D because their respective simple effects are inconsistent, as suggested by the diverging or crossed lines. Given the present perspective, **interaction** *can be viewed as the product of inconsistent simple effects.*

Interaction

The product of inconsistent simple effects.

Progress Check *18.2 A recent example of interaction from the psychological literature is the tendency of college students, when assigning prison sentences on the basis of photos of "convicted defendants," to judge attractive swindlers more harshly than unattractive swindlers but to judge attractive robbers less harshly than unattractive robbers.

(a) Construct a data (or line) graph showing this interaction. As is customary, identify the vertical axis with the dependent variable, the mean prison sentence assigned by students. For the sake of uniformity, identify the two points along the horizontal axis with swindlers and robbers, and identify the two lines inside the graph with attractive and unattractive defendants.

(b) Assume that, in fact, there is no interaction. Instead, independently of their degree of attractiveness, swindlers are judged more harshly than robbers, and, independently of their crime, unattractive defendants are judged more harshly than attractive defendants. Using the same identifications as in the previous question, construct a data graph that depicts this result.

Answers on page 517.

Describing Interactions

The original interaction between crowd size and gender could have been described in two different ways. First, we could have portrayed the inconsistent simple effects of crowd size for females and males by showing panel A of **Figure 18.4** (originally shown in panel C of Figure 18.1). Alternately, we could have portrayed the inconsistent simple effects of gender for crowds of zero, two, and four people by showing panel B of Figure 18.4. Although different, the configurations in both panels A and B suggest essentially the same interpretation: Crowd size influences the reaction times of male subjects but not those of female subjects. In cases where one perspective seems to make as much sense as another, it's customary to plot along the horizontal axis the factor with the larger number of levels, as in panel A.

TWO VERSIONS OF THE SAME INTERACTION

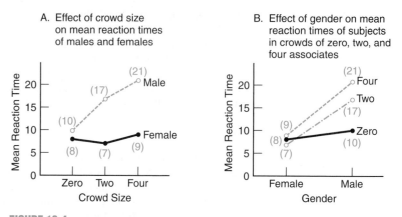

FIGURE 18.4

Two versions of the same interaction. Note: *Colored numbers represent group means from Table 18.1.*

18.4 DETAILS: VARIANCE ESTIMATES

Each of the three F ratios in a two-factor ANOVA is based on a ratio involving two variance estimates: a mean square in the numerator that reflects random error plus, if present, any specific treatment effect and a mean square in the denominator that reflects only random error. Before using these mean squares (or variance estimates), we must calculate their sums of squares and their degrees of freedom.

Sums of Squares (Definition Formulas)

Ultimately, the total sum of squares, SS_{total}, will be divided among its various component sums of squares, that is,

---

SUMS OF SQUARES (TWO FACTOR)

$$SS_{total} = SS_{column} + SS_{row} + SS_{interaction} + SS_{within} \qquad (18.1)$$

The computation of the various SS terms can be viewed as a two-step effort.

1. The two factors and their interaction are ignored, and we calculate the first three sum of squares terms as if the data originated from a one-factor ANOVA where total variability is partitioned into two components: variability between cells and variability within cells, since

$$SS_{total} = SS_{between} + SS_{within}$$

Variability within cells, SS_{within}, which is often referred to as SS_{error}, will serve as the sum of squares portion of the error mean square in the denominator of each of the three F ratios.

- As always, the total sum of squares, SS_{total}, equals the sum of squared deviations of all scores, X, about the grand mean for all scores, $\bar{X}_{grand}$, that is, $SS_{total} = \Sigma(X - \bar{X}_{grand})^2$.

- The between-cells (or treatment) sum of squares, $SS_{between}$, equals the sum of squared deviations of all cell (or treatment) means, $\bar{X}_{cell}$, about the grand mean, $\bar{X}_{grand}$. Expressed symbolically, $SS_{between} = n\Sigma(\bar{X}_{cell} - \bar{X}_{grand})^2$, where n, the sample size in each cell, adjusts for the fact that the deviation $\bar{X}_{cell} - \bar{X}_{grand}$ is the same for every score in its cell.

- The within-cells (or error) sum of squares, SS_{within}, equals the sum of squared deviations of all scores, X, about their respective cell means, $\bar{X}_{cell}$, that is, $SS_{within} = \Sigma(X - \bar{X}_{cell})^2$. Essentially, this expression requires that the sum of squares within each cell be added across all cells as the first step toward a pooled variance estimate of random error.

2. Variability between cells, $SS_{between}$, is partitioned into three additional sums of squares—SS_{column}, SS_{row}, and $SS_{interaction}$—that reflect identifiable sources of treatment variability in the two-factor ANOVA, since

$$SS_{between} = SS_{column} + SS_{row} + SS_{interaction}$$

- The between-columns sum of square, SS_{column}, equals the sum of squared deviations of column means, $\bar{X}_{column}$, about the grand mean, $\bar{X}_{grand}$. Expressed symbolically, $SS_{column} = rn\Sigma(\bar{X}_{column} - \bar{X}_{grand})^2$, where r equals the number of rows, n equals the sample size in each cell, and rn equals the total sample size for each column. The product rn adjusts for the fact that the mean deviation, $\bar{X}_{column} - \bar{X}_{grand}$, is the same for every score in its column.

- The between-rows sum of squares, SS_{row}, equals the sum of squared deviations of row means, $\bar{X}_{row}$, about the grand mean, $\bar{X}_{grand}$. Expressed symbolically, $SS_{row} = cn\Sigma(\bar{X}_{row} - \bar{X}_{grand})^2$, where c equals the number of columns and cn equals the total sample size in each row. The product cn adjusts for the fact that the mean deviation, $\bar{X}_{row} - \bar{X}_{grand}$, is the same for every score in its row.

- The interaction sum of squares, $SS_{interaction}$, equals the variability between cells, $SS_{between}$, after the removal of variability between columns, SS_{column}, and variability between rows, SS_{row}, that is,

$$SS_{interaction} = SS_{between} - (SS_{column} + SS_{row})$$

Although $SS_{interaction}$ could be expressed more directly by expanding these three SS terms, the result tends to be more cumbersome than enlightening.

Sums of Squares (Computation Formulas)

Table 18.2 shows the more efficient, color-coded computation formulas, where totals replace means. Notice the highly predictable computational pattern

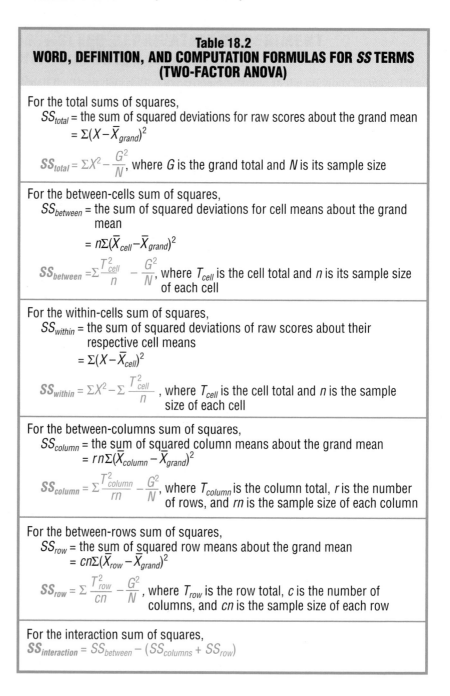

Table 18.2
WORD, DEFINITION, AND COMPUTATION FORMULAS FOR *SS* TERMS
(TWO-FACTOR ANOVA)

For the total sums of squares,

SS_{total} = the sum of squared deviations for raw scores about the grand mean

$$= \Sigma(X - \bar{X}_{grand})^2$$

$SS_{total} = \Sigma X^2 - \dfrac{G^2}{N}$, where G is the grand total and N is its sample size

---

For the between-cells sum of squares,

$SS_{between}$ = the sum of squared deviations for cell means about the grand mean

$$= n\Sigma(\bar{X}_{cell} - \bar{X}_{grand})^2$$

$SS_{between} = \Sigma \dfrac{T_{cell}^2}{n} - \dfrac{G^2}{N}$, where T_{cell} is the cell total and n is its sample size of each cell

---

For the within-cells sum of squares,

SS_{within} = the sum of squared deviations of raw scores about their respective cell means

$$= \Sigma(X - \bar{X}_{cell})^2$$

$SS_{within} = \Sigma X^2 - \Sigma \dfrac{T_{cell}^2}{n}$, where T_{cell} is the cell total and n is the sample size of each cell

---

For the between-columns sum of squares,

SS_{column} = the sum of squared column means about the grand mean

$$= rn\Sigma(\bar{X}_{column} - \bar{X}_{grand})^2$$

$SS_{column} = \Sigma \dfrac{T_{column}^2}{rn} - \dfrac{G^2}{N}$, where T_{column} is the column total, r is the number of rows, and rn is the sample size of each column

---

For the between-rows sum of squares,

SS_{row} = the sum of squared row means about the grand mean

$$= cn\Sigma(\bar{X}_{row} - \bar{X}_{grand})^2$$

$SS_{row} = \Sigma \dfrac{T_{row}^2}{cn} - \dfrac{G^2}{N}$, where T_{row} is the row total, c is the number of columns, and cn is the sample size of each row

---

For the interaction sum of squares,

$SS_{interaction} = SS_{between} - (SS_{columns} + SS_{row})$

first described in Section 16.4. Each entry is squared, and each total, whether for a column, a row, a cell, or the grand total, is then divided by its respective sample size. **Table 18.3** illustrates the application of these formulas to the data for the two-factor experiment.

Table 18.3

CALCULATION OF *SS* TERMS (TWO-FACTOR ANOVA)

A. COMPUTATIONAL SEQUENCE

Find (and circle) each cell total **1**.
Find each column and row total and also the grand total **2**.
Substitute numbers into computational formula **3** and solve for SS_{total}.
Substitute numbers into computational formula **4** and solve for $SS_{between}$.
Substitute numbers into computational formula **5** and solve for SS_{within}.
Substitute numbers into computational formula **6** and solve for SS_{column}.
Substitute numbers into computational formula **7** and solve for SS_{row}.
Substitute numbers into formula **8** and solve for $SS_{interaction}$.

B. DATA AND COMPUTATIONS

Crowd Size

Gender	ZERO	TWO	FOUR	**2** Row Totals
Female	8 (16) 8	8 (14) 6	10 (18) 8	48
Male	9 (20) 11	15 (34) 19	24 (42) 18	96

2 Column Totals ⟶ 36   48   60 | **2** Grand Total = 144

3 $SS_{total} = \sum X^2 - \dfrac{G^2}{N}$

$$= (8)^2 + (8)^2 + \ldots + (24)^2 + (18)^2 - \frac{(144)^2}{(12)} = 2080 - 1728 = 352$$

4 $SS_{between} = \sum \dfrac{T_{cell}^2}{n} - \dfrac{G^2}{N}$

$$= \frac{(16)^2}{2} + \frac{(20)^2}{2} + \frac{(14)^2}{2} + \frac{(34)^2}{2} + \frac{(18)^2}{2} + \frac{(42)^2}{2} - \frac{(144)^2}{12} = 2048 - 1728 = 320$$

5 $SS_{within} = \sum X^2 - \sum \dfrac{T_{cell}^2}{n}$

$$= (8)^2 + (8)^2 + \ldots + (24)^2 + (18)^2 - \left[\frac{(16)^2}{2} + \frac{(20)^2}{2} + \frac{(14)^2}{2} + \frac{(34)^2}{2} + \frac{(18)^2}{2} + \frac{(42)^2}{2} \right] = 2080 - 2048 = 32$$

6 $SS_{column} = \sum \dfrac{T_{column}^2}{rn} - \dfrac{G^2}{N}$

$$= \left[\frac{(36)^2}{4} + \frac{(48)^2}{4} + \frac{(60)^2}{4} \right] - \frac{(144)^2}{12} = 1800 - 1728 = 72$$

7 $SS_{row} = \sum \dfrac{T_{row}^2}{cn} - \dfrac{G^2}{N}$

$$= \left[\frac{(48)^2}{6} + \frac{(96)^2}{6} \right] - \frac{(144)^2}{12} = 1920 - 1728 = 192$$

8 $SS_{interaction} = SS_{between} - (SS_{column} + SS_{row})$

$$= 320 - (72 + 192) = 56$$

Table 18.4
FORMULAS FOR *df* TERMS: TWO-FACTOR ANOVA

$df_{total} = N - 1$, that is, the number of all scores $- 1$

$df_{column} = c - 1$, that is, the number of columns $- 1$

$df_{row} = r - 1$, that is, the number of rows $- 1$

$df_{interaction} = (c - 1)(r - 1)$, that is, the product of df_{row} and df_{column}

$df_{within} = N - (c)(r)$, that is, the number of all scores $-$ the number of cells

---

Degrees of Freedom (*df*)

The number of degrees of freedom must be determined for each *SS* term in a two-factor ANOVA, and for convenience, the various *df* formulas are listed in Table 18.4. The $(c - 1)(r - 1)$ degrees of freedom for $df_{interaction}$ reflect the fact that, from the perspective of degrees of freedom, the original matrix with $c \times r$ cells shrinks to $(c - 1)(r - 1)$ cells for $df_{interaction}$. One row and one column of cell totals in the original matrix are not free to vary because of the restriction that all cell totals in each column and all cell totals in each row must sum to fixed totals in the margins (associated with column and row factors.) The $N - (c)(r)$ *degrees of freedom for* df_{within} reflect the fact that the *N* scores within all cells must sum to the fixed totals in their respective cells, causing one degree of freedom to be lost in each of the $(c)(r)$ cells.

The *df* values for the present study are:

$$df_{total} = N - 1 = 12 - 1 = 11$$
$$df_{column} = c - 1 = 3 - 1 = 2$$
$$df_{row} = r - 1 = 2 - 1 = 1$$
$$df_{interaction} = (c - 1)(r - 1) = (3 - 1)(2 - 1) = 2$$
$$df_{within} = N - (c)(r) = 12 - (3)(2) = 6$$

Check for Accuracy

Recall the general rule that the degrees of freedom for SS_{total} equal the combined degrees of freedom for all remaining *SS* terms, that is,

---

DEGREES OF FREEDOM (TWO FACTOR)

$$df_{total} = df_{column} + df_{row} + df_{interaction} + df_{within} \qquad (18.2)$$

This formula can be used to verify that the correct number of degrees of freedom has been assigned to each *SS* term.

18.5 DETAILS: MEAN SQUARES (*MS*) AND *F* RATIOS

Having found values for the various *SS* terms and their *df*, we can determine values for the corresponding *MS* terms and then calculate the three *F* ratios using the formulas in Table 18.5. Notice that MS_{within} appears in the denominator of

Table 18.5
FORMULAS FOR MEAN SQUARES (*MS*) AND *F* RATIOS

SOURCE	MS	F
Column	$MS_{column} = \dfrac{SS_{column}}{df_{column}}$	$F_{column} = \dfrac{MS_{column}}{MS_{within}}$
Row	$MS_{row} = \dfrac{SS_{row}}{df_{row}}$	$F_{row} = \dfrac{MS_{row}}{MS_{within}}$
Interaction	$MS_{interaction} = \dfrac{SS_{interaction}}{df_{interaction}}$	$F_{interaction} = \dfrac{MS_{interaction}}{MS_{within}}$
Within	$MS_{within} = \dfrac{SS_{within}}{df_{within}}$	

each of these three F ratios. MS_{within} is based on the variability among scores of subjects who are treated similarly within each cell, pooled across all cells. Regardless of whether any treatment effect is present, it measures only random error.

The ANOVA results for the two-factor study are summarized in **Table 18.6**. The numbers in color (which ordinarily don't appear in ANOVA summary tables) indicate the origin of each *MS* term and of each *F*.

Other Labels

Other labels also might have appeared in Table 18.6. For instance, "Column" and "Row" might have been replaced by descriptions of the treatment variables,

Table 18.6
ANOVA TABLE (TWO-FACTOR EXPERIMENT)

SOURCE	SS	df	MS	F
Column	72	2	$\left(\frac{72}{2}=\right)$ 36	$\left(\frac{36}{5.33}=\right)$ 6.75*
Row	192	1	$\left(\frac{192}{1}=\right)$ 192	$\left(\frac{192}{5.33}=\right)$ 36.02*
Interaction	56	2	$\left(\frac{56}{2}=\right)$ 28	$\left(\frac{28}{5.33}=\right)$ 5.25*
Within	32	6	$\left(\frac{32}{6}=\right)$ 5.33	
Total	352	11		

* Significant at the .05 level.

in this case, "Crowd Size" and "Gender." Similarly, "Interaction" might have been replaced by "Crowd Size × Gender," by "Crowd Size * Gender," or by some abbreviation, such as "CS × G" (for Crowd Size × Gender), and "Within" might have been replaced by "Error."

18.6 TABLE FOR THE *F* DISTRIBUTION

Each of the three *F* ratios in Table 18.6 exceeds its respective critical *F* ratio. To obtain critical *F* ratios from the *F* sampling distribution, refer to Table C in Appendix C. Follow the usual procedure, described in Section 16.6, to verify that when 2 and 6 degrees of freedom are associated with F_{column} and $F_{interaction}$, the critical *F* equals 5.14, and that when 1 and 6 degrees of freedom are associated with F_{row}, the critical *F* equals 5.99.

Progress Check *18.3 A school psychologist wishes to determine the effect of TV violence on disruptive behavior of first graders in the classroom. Two first graders are randomly assigned to each of the various combinations of the two factors: the type of violent TV program (either cartoon or real life) and the amount of viewing time (either 0, 1, 2, or 3 hours). The subjects are then observed in a controlled classroom setting and assigned a score, reflecting the total number of disruptive class behaviors displayed during the test period.

AGGRESSION SCORES OF FIRST GRADERS				
	VIEWING TIME (HOURS)			
TYPE OF PROGRAM	**0**	**1**	**2**	**3**
Cartoon	0,1	1,0	3,5	6,9
Real life	0,0	1,1	6,2	6,10

(a) Test the various null hypotheses at the .05 level of significance.

(b) Summarize the results with an ANOVA table. Save the ANOVA summary table for use in subsequent questions.

Answers on page 518.

18.7 ESTIMATING EFFECT SIZE

In the previous chapter, a version of the squared curvilinear correlation, η_p^2, was used to estimate effect size after variance due to individual differences had been removed. Essentially the same type of analysis can be conducted for *each* significant *F* in a two-factor ANOVA. Each η_p^2 estimates the proportion of the total variance attributable to either one of the two factors or to the interaction—after excluding from the total known amounts of variance attributable to the remaining treatment components.

In each case, η_p^2 is calculated by dividing the appropriate sum of squares (either SS_{column}, SS_{row}, or $SS_{interaction}$) by the appropriately reduced total sum of squares, that is,

---

PROPORTION OF EXPLAINED VARIANCE (TWO-FACTOR ANOVA)

$$\eta_p^2(\text{column}) = \frac{SS_{column}}{SS_{total} - \left(SS_{row} + SS_{interaction}\right)} = \frac{SS_{column}}{SS_{column} + SS_{within}}$$

$$\eta_p^2(\text{row}) = \frac{SS_{row}}{SS_{row} + SS_{within}} \tag{18.3}$$

$$\eta_p^2(\text{interaction}) = \frac{SS_{interaction}}{SS_{interaction} + SS_{within}}$$

---

where each η_p^2 is referred to as a *partial* η^2 for that component because the effects of the other two treatment components have been eliminated from the reduced or partial total variance.

Substituting values for the SS terms from Table 18.6, we have

$$\eta_p^2(\text{column}) = \frac{72}{72 + 32} = .69$$

$$\eta_p^2(\text{row}) = \frac{192}{192 + 32} = .86$$

$$\eta_p^2(\text{interaction}) = \frac{56}{56 + 32} = .64$$

All three of these estimates would be considered spectacularly large since, according to guidelines derived from Cohen, the estimated effect for any factor or interaction is small if η_p^2 approximates .01; medium if η_p^2 approximates .09; and large if η_p^2 approximates .25 or more. For instance, the value of .86 for $\eta_p^2(\text{row})$ indicates that .86, or 86 percent, of total variance in reaction times (excluding variance due to crowd size and the interaction) is explained by differences between males and females, while only the remaining 14 percent of the variance in reaction times is not explained by gender.

Progress Check *18.4 Referring to the ANOVA summary table in your answer to Question 18.3, estimate the effect size for any significant F with η_p^2.

Answer on page 518.

18.8 MULTIPLE COMPARISONS

Tukey's *HSD* test for multiple comparisons can be used to pinpoint important differences between pairs of column or row means whenever the corresponding main effects are statistically significant and *interpretations of these main effects are not compromised by any inconsistencies associated with a statistically significant interaction.*

To determine *HSD*, use the following expression:

TUKEY'S *HSD* TEST (TWO-FACTOR ANOVA)

$$HSD = q\sqrt{\frac{MS_{within}}{n}} \qquad\qquad (18.4)$$

---

where *HSD* is the positive critical value for any difference between two column or row means; q is a value obtained from Table G in Appendix C; MS_{within} is the mean square for within-cells variability in the two-factor ANOVA; and, *if pairs of column means are being compared, n is rn, the sample size for the entire column, or if pairs of row means are being compared, n is cn, the sample size for an entire row.* To find the value of q at the .05 level (light numbers) or the .01 level (dark numbers) in Table G, find the cell intersected by c (if column means are being compared) or by r (if row means are being compared), and by df_{within}, the number of degrees of freedom for within-group variability, $N - (c)(r)$, the total number of scores in the two-factor ANOVA, N, minus the total number of cells, $(c)(r)$.

In the smoke alarm experiment, Tukey's *HSD* test isn't conducted for the one significant main effect, crowd size, with more than two group means because of the presence of a significant interaction that compromises any interpretation of the main effect.

Progress Check *18.5 In Question 18.3, the *F* for the interaction isn't significant, but *F* for one of the main effects, Viewing Time, is significant. Using the .05 level, calculate the critical value for Tukey's *HSD*; evaluate the significance of each possible mean difference for Viewing Time; and interpret the results.

Answers on page 518.

18.9 SIMPLE EFFECTS

Whenever the interaction is statistically significant, as in the two-factor smoke alarm experiment, we can conduct new F_{se} tests, where the *se* subscript stands for "simple effect," to identify the inconsistencies among simple effects that produce the interaction. These new tests require that, by ignoring the second factor, the original two-factor ANOVA be transformed into several one-factor or simple-effect ANOVAs. Essentially, the F_{se} **test for simple effects** *tests the effect of one factor on the dependent variable at a single level of another factor.* Table 18.7 shows how the totals for the original two-factor experiment can be viewed as two simple effects for crowd size (corresponding to each one of the two rows in the original two-factor matrix) and three simple effects for gender (corresponding to each of the three columns). Inconsistencies among a set of simple effects usually are associated with a mixture of both significant and nonsignificant F_{se} tests for that set of simple effects. Among the two simple (row) effects for crowd size, the F_{se} test is nonsignificant (*ns*) at females but

---

F_{se} Test for Simple Effects

A test of the effect of one factor on the dependent variable at a single level of another factor.

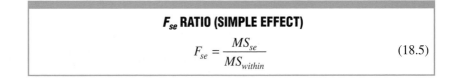

Table 18.7
SIMPLE EFFECTS FOR SMOKE ALARM EXPERIMENT (TOTALS)

TWO-FACTOR EXPERIMENT

GENDER	CROWD SIZE ZERO	TWO	FOUR	ROW TOTAL		SIMPLE EFFECT OF CROWD SIZE AT
						FEMALE
Female	16	14	18	48	→	16 14 18 48 *(ns)*
						MALE
Male	20	34	42	96	→	20 34 42 96 *(p < .01)*
Column Total	36	48	60			

Simple Effect of Gender at

Zero	Two	Four
16	14	18
20	34	42
36	48	60
(ns)	*(p < .01)*	*(p < .01)*

significant ($p < .01$) at males, suggesting that reaction times of males, but not those of females, increase with larger crowd sizes. Essentially the same conclusion is suggested by the other set of three simple effects. Among these simple (column) effects for gender, the F_{se} test for crowd sizes of zero is nonsignificant (*ns*), but it is significant ($p < .01$) for crowd sizes of two and four, suggesting that the reaction times of males exceed those of females for crowd sizes of two and four but not for crowd sizes of zero. Ordinarily, you needn't test both sets of simple effects, as was done above for the sake of completeness. Instead, test only one set, preferably the one that seems to describe best the significant interaction.

F_{se} Test for Simple Effects

The new F_{se} test for any simple effect is very similar to the F test for the corresponding main effect in a two-factor ANOVA. The degrees of freedom is the same, as is the term in the denominator, MS_{within}. Only the term in the numerator, MS_{se}, must be adjusted to estimate the variability associated with just one row or one column. The ratio for any simple effect, F_{se} reads:

F_{se} RATIO (SIMPLE EFFECT)

$$F_{se} = \frac{MS_{se}}{MS_{within}}$$

(18.5)

where MS_{se} represents the mean square for the variation of every cell mean in a single row (or a single column) about the overall or grand mean for that entire row (or column) and MS_{within} represents the mean square for the variation of all scores about their cell means for the entire two-factor matrix. (Being based on all scores, MS_{within} serves in the denominator term as the best estimate of random error.)

The degrees of freedom for the numerator of the simple-effect F_{se} ratio is the same as that for the corresponding main-effect F ratio, namely, $df_{between}$, which equals either $c - 1$ *or* $r - 1$, the number of groups (that is, the number of columns or of rows) in the simple effect minus one. The degrees of freedom for the denominator of the simple-effect F_{se} ratio is the same as that for any two-factor F ratio, namely, df_{within}, which equals $N - (c)(r)$, the total number of scores, N, minus the total number of cells, $(c)(r)$, in the two-factor ANOVA.

Calculating F_{se}

Let's calculate F_{se} for the simple effect of crowd size at male (that is, for the second row in Table 18.7). Since MS_{within} already has been calculated and, as shown in Table 18.6, equals 5.33, we can concentrate on calculating SS_{se}, which, when divided by its degrees of freedom, gives a value for MS_{se}. The computational formula for SS_{se} reads:

SUM OF SQUARES (SIMPLE EFFECT)

$$SS_{se} = \sum \frac{T_{se}^2}{n} - \frac{G_{se}^2}{N_{se}} \qquad (18.6)$$

---

where SS_{se} now signifies the sum of squares for the simple effect; T_{se}^2 represents the squared total for each cell in a single row (or a single column); G_{se}^2 represents the grand total for all cells in the entire row (or column); n equals the sample size for each cell; and N_{se} equals the total sample size for the entire row (or column).

When totals from the second row in Table 18.7 are substituted into Equation 18.6, it reads:

$$SS_{se}(crowd\ size\ at\ male) = \frac{(20)^2}{2} + \frac{(34)^2}{2} + \frac{(42)^2}{2} - \frac{(96)^2}{6} = 124$$

Given that the degrees of freedom for MS_{se} (*crowd size at male*) equals the number of columns minus one, that is, $c - 1 = 3 - 1 = 2$, then

$$MS_{se}(crowd\ size\ at\ male) = \frac{SS_{se}(crowd\ size\ at\ male)}{df_{column}} = \frac{124}{2} = 62$$

and

$$F_{se}(crowd\ size\ at\ male) = \frac{MS_{se}(crowd\ size\ at\ male)}{MS_{within}} = \frac{62}{5.33} = 11.63$$

which is significant ($p < .01$) since 11.63 exceeds the value of 10.92 in Table C in Appendix C for the .01 level of significance, given 2 and 6 degrees of freedom. Using essentially the same procedure, we also can establish that the simple effect of crowd size at female (that is, the first row in Table 18.7), is nonsignificant (*ns*) since F_{se} (*crowd size at female*) = 0.38, again with 2 and 6 degrees of freedom. The different test results—one significant, the other nonsignificant—provide statistical support for an important result of the smoke alarm study, namely, that the reaction times of males, but not those of females, tend to increase with crowd size.

Tukey's *HSD* Test for Multiple Comparisons

If a simple effect is significant and involves more than two groups, Tukey's *HSD* test, as defined in Equation 18.4, can be used to identify pairs of cell means that differ significantly. When using Equation 18.4, the *n* in the denominator always refers to the sample size of the means being compared, that is, in the case of a simple effect, the sample size for each cell mean. Otherwise, all substitutions are the same whether you're testing a simple effect or a main effect.

Since the simple effect for crowd size at males is significant and involves more than two groups, Tukey's *HSD* test can be used. Consult Table G in Appendix C, given c (or k) = 3 for the three cells in the simple effect and df_{within} = 6, to find the value of q for the .01 level. Substituting values for $q = 6.33$, $MS_{within} = 5.33$, and $n = 2$ into Equation 18.4:

$$HSD = q\sqrt{\frac{MS_{within}}{n}} = 6.33\sqrt{\frac{5.33}{2}} = 6.33(1.63) = 10.32$$

Given values of 10, 17, and 21 for the mean reaction times of males with crowds of zero, two, and four people, respectively, a significant difference ($p < .01$) occurs between the mean reaction times of males for crowds of zero and four people because the observed mean difference, $21 - 10 = 11$, exceeds the *HSD* value of 10.32. A "borderline" significant difference (within a rounding margin of $p < .05$) occurs between the mean reaction times of males for crowds of zero and two people because the observed mean difference, $17 - 10 = 7$, is only slightly less than the *HSD* value of 7.07. (This value is obtained from the *HSD* equation above, given $q = 4.34$ from the .05 level of Table G.)

Estimating Effect Size

As we have seen, a significant simple effect with more than two groups can be analyzed further with Tukey's *HSD* test. A significant difference between pairs of means can, in turn, have its effect size estimated with Cohen's *d*, as defined in Equation 16.10 on page 361, that is,

$$d = \frac{\bar{X}_1 - \bar{X}_2}{\sqrt{MS_{within}}}$$

where *d* is an estimate of the standardized effect size; $\bar{X}_1$ and $\bar{X}_2$ are the pair of significantly different means; and $\sqrt{MS_{within}}$, the square root of the within-group mean square for the two-factor ANOVA, represents the sample standard deviation.

To estimate the standardized effect size for the significant difference between means for males with zero and four confederates, enter $\bar{X}_4 - \bar{X}_0 = 11$ and $MS_{within} = 5.33$ in the above equation and solve for d:

$$d(\bar{X}_4, \bar{X}_0) = \frac{11}{\sqrt{5.33}} = \frac{11}{2.31} = 4.76$$

which is a very large effect, equivalent to almost five standard deviations. To estimate the standardized effect size for the significant difference between means for males with crowds of zero and two people, enter $\bar{X}_2 - \bar{X}_0 = 7$ and $MS_{within} = 5.33$ in the above equation and solve for d:

$$d(\bar{X}_2, \bar{X}_0) = \frac{7}{\sqrt{5.33}} = \frac{7}{2.31} = 3.03$$

which also is a very large effect, equivalent to three standard deviations. Ordinarily, such large values of d, as well as the large values for η_p^2 in the current example, wouldn't be obtained with real data. The fictitious data for the sleep deprivation experiment were selected to dramatize various effects in two-factor ANOVA, including an interaction with a significant simple effect, using very small sample sizes.

Progress Check *18.6 Using the data in Table 18.7 for the smoke alarm experiment, conduct F_{se} tests for the three simple effects of gender at crowd sizes of zero, two, or four. Whenever appropriate, estimate effect sizes using Cohen's d. (Tukey's *HSD* test can be ignored since each simple effect involves only a difference between a single pair of means.) Interpret your findings.

Answers on page 519.

18.10 OVERVIEW: FLOW CHART FOR TWO-FACTOR ANOVA

Figure 18.5 shows the steps to be taken when you are analyzing data for a two-factor ANOVA. Once an ANOVA summary table has been obtained, focus on the left-hand panel of Figure 18.5 for the interaction. If the interaction is significant, estimate its effect size with η_p^2 and conduct F_{se} tests for at least one set of simple effects. Ordinarily, the significant interaction will translate into a mix of significant and nonsignificant simple effects. Further, analyze any significant simple effect with *HSD* tests and any significant *HSD* test with an estimate of its effect size, d.

Next, focus on the right-hand panel for the main effects. Proceed with additional estimates for η_p^2 and d, and with the *HSD* test, only if the interpretation of the significant main effect isn't compromised by a significant interaction.

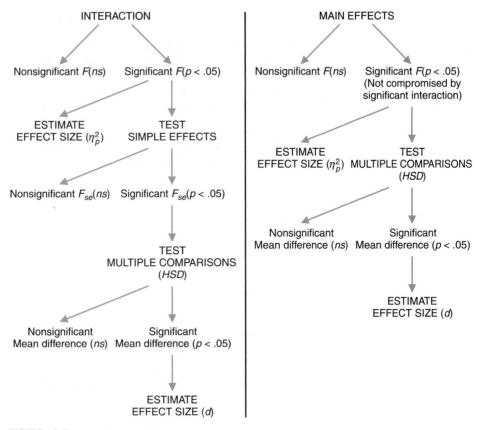

FIGURE 18.5
Flow chart for two-factor ANOVA.

18.11 REPORTS IN THE LITERATURE

Test results for the smoke alarm experiment might be reported as follows:

The following table shows the mean reaction times to smoke for subjects as a function of crowd size (zero, two, and four people) and gender (female and male):

	ZERO	TWO	FOUR	GENDER
Females	8	7	9	8
Males	10	17	21	16
Crowd Size	9	12	15	12

Mean reaction times increase with crowd size [$F(2, 6) = 6.75$, *MSE* = 5.33, $p < .05$, $\eta_p^2 = .69$]; they are larger for males than females [$F(1, 6) =$

36.02, $p < .01$, $\eta_p^2 = .86$]; but these findings must be qualified because of the significant interaction [$F(2, 6) = 5.25$, $p < .05$, $\eta_p^2 = .64$]. An analysis of simple effects for crowd size confirms that reaction times increase with crowd size for males [$F_{se}(2, 6) = 11.63$, $p < .01$] but not for females [$F_{se}(2, 6) = 0.38$, ns]. Furthermore, compared with the mean reaction time of 10 for males with zero people, the mean reaction time of 17 for males with two people is significantly longer ($HSD = 7.07$, $p = .05$, $d = 3.03$), and the mean reaction time of 21 for males with four people also is significantly longer ($HSD = 10.32$, $p < .01$, $d = 4.76$). To summarize, the mean reaction times of males, but not those of females, increase in the presence of crowds of two or four people.

This report reflects the very prevalent use of approximate *p*-values rather than a fixed level of significance. The error (or within-group) mean square, $MSE = 5.33$, appears only for the initial F test since it's the same for all remaining F tests. The expression $p = .05$ (rather than $p < .05$) reflects the previously mentioned borderline significance of $\bar{X}_2 - \bar{X}_0 = 7$, given a critical value of $HSD = 7.07$.

18.12 ASSUMPTIONS

The assumptions for F tests in a two-factor ANOVA are similar to those for a one-factor ANOVA. All underlying populations (for each treatment combination or cell) are assumed to be normally distributed, with equal variances. As with the one-factor ANOVA, you need not be too concerned about violations of these assumptions, *particularly if all cell sizes are equal* and each cell is fairly large (greater than about 10). Otherwise, in the unlikely event that you encounter conspicuous departures from normality or equality of variances, consult a more advanced statistics book.*

Importance of Equal Sample Sizes

As far as possible, *all cells in two-factor studies should have equal sample sizes.* Otherwise, to the degree that sample sizes are unequal and the resulting design lacks balance, not only are any violations of assumptions more serious, but problems of interpretation can occur. If you must analyze data based on unequal sample sizes—possibly because of missing subjects, equipment breakdowns, or recording errors—consult a more advanced statistics book.*

18.13 OTHER TYPES OF ANOVA

One- and two-factor studies do not exhaust the possibilities for ANOVA. For instance, you could use ANOVA to analyze the results of a three-factor study with three independent variables, three 2-way interactions, and one 3-way interaction. Furthermore, regardless of the number of factors, each subject might be measured repeatedly along all levels of one or more factors. Although the basic concepts described in this book transfer almost intact to a wide assortment of more intricate research designs, computational procedures grow more

*See G. Keppel and T. Wickens, *Design and Analysis: A Researcher's Handbook,* 4th ed. (Upper Saddle River, NJ: Prentice-Hall, 2004); or D. C. Howell, *Statistical Methods for Psychology,* 7th ed. (Belmont, CA: Wadsworth, 2010).

complex, and the interpretation of results often is more difficult. Intricate research designs, requiring the use of complex types of ANOVA, provide the skilled investigator with powerful tools for evaluating complicated situations. Under no circumstances, however, should a study be valued simply because of the complexity of its design and statistical analysis. Use the least complex design and analysis that will answer your research questions.

Summary

Before any statistical analysis, and particularly before complex analyses such as a two-factor ANOVA, it is often helpful to form preliminary impressions by constructing graphs of the various possible effects.

In a two-factor ANOVA, three null hypotheses are tested with three different F ratios. The numerator of each F ratio measures a different aspect of variability between cells: variability between columns, variability between rows, and any remaining variability between cells due to interaction. The numerator of each F ratio measures some component of between variability and reflects random error plus any associated treatment effect. The denominator of each F ratio measures the variability within cells and always reflects only random error.

Two factors interact if their simple effects are inconsistent. Interaction emerges as the most striking feature of a two-factor ANOVA.

Whenever F is statistically significant, calculate the partial eta-squared, η_p^2, to estimate the effect size.

Given a significant main effect—not compromised by a significant interaction—Tukey's *HSD* test can be used to pinpoint differences between specific pairs of column means or pairs of row means.

Given a significant interaction, F_{se} tests can be used to identify significant and nonsignificant simple effects. Significant simple effects can be analyzed further with Tukey's *HSD* test for multiple comparisons.

The effect size for any significant comparison involving two means can be estimated with Cohen's *d*.

The assumptions for F tests in a two-factor ANOVA are the same as those for one-factor ANOVA. As far as possible, all cells in two-factor studies should have equal sample sizes.

Important Terms

Two-factor ANOVA	**Main effect**
Interaction	**Simple effect**

Key Equations

F RATIOS

$$F_{column} = \frac{MS_{column}}{MS_{within}}$$

$$F_{row} = \frac{MS_{row}}{MS_{within}}$$

$$F_{interaction} = \frac{MS_{interaction}}{MS_{within}}$$

$$SS_{total} = SS_{column} + SS_{row} + SS_{interaction} + SS_{within}$$

$$df_{total} = df_{column} + df_{row} + df_{interaction} + df_{within}$$

REVIEW QUESTIONS

*18.7 A psychologist randomly assigns ten lab rats to each cell in a two-factor experiment designed to determine the effect of food deprivation (either 0 or 24 hours) and reward amount (either 1 or 2 food pellets) on their rate of bar pressing under a schedule of intermittent rewards.

(a) Construct an ANOVA summary table, specifying the various sources of variability and degrees of freedom.

(b) One possible outcome is that there is a main effect for food deprivation, no main effect for reward amount, and no interaction. Viewed in this fashion, there are seven other possible outcomes for this experiment. Counting the stated outcome as one possibility, list all eight possibilities by indicating with a Y(es) or N(o) whether or not a given effect is present.

(c) Among the eight possible outcomes specified in (b), which outcome would by least preferred by the psychologist?

Answers on page 519.

*18.8 For the two-factor experiment described in the previous question, assume that, as shown, mean bar press rates of either 4 or 8 are identified with three of the four cells in the 2 × 2 table of outcomes.

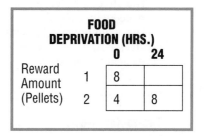

Furthermore, just for the sake of this question, ignore sampling variability and assume that effects occur whenever any numerical differences correspond to either food deprivation, reward amount, or the interaction. Indicate whether or not effects occur for each of these three components if the empty cell in the 2 × 2 table is occupied by a mean of

(a) 12

(b) 8

(c) 4

Answers on page 520.

18.9 Each of the following (incomplete) ANOVA tables represents some experiment. Determine the number of levels for each factor; the total number of groups; and, on the assumption that all groups have equal numbers of subjects, the number of subjects in each group. Then, using the .05 level of significance for all hypothesis tests, complete the ANOVA summary table.

(a)	SOURCE	SS	df	MS	F
	Column	790	1		
	Row	326	2		
	Interaction	1887			
	Within	14702	60		
	Total				

(b)	SOURCE	SS	df	MS	F
	Treatment A	142	2		
	Treatment B	480	2		
	$A \times B$	209			
	Error	5030	81		
	Total				

(c) For each significant F in (**a**) or (**b**), estimate the effect size.

*18.10 A health educator suspects that the "days of discomfort" caused by common colds can be reduced by ingesting large doses of vitamin C and visiting a sauna every day. Using a two-factor design, subjects with new colds are randomly assigned to one of four different daily dosages of vitamin C (either 0, 500, 1000, or 1500 milligrams) and to one of three different daily exposures to a sauna (either 0, $\frac{1}{2}$ or 1 hour).

NUMBER OF DAYS OF DISCOMFORT DUE TO COLDS

SAUNA EXPOSURE (HOURS)	VITAMIN C DOSAGE (MILLIGRAMS)				T_{row}	T^2_{row}
	0	500	1000	1500		
0	6	5	4	2		
	4	3	2	3	42	1764
	5	3	3	2		
$\frac{1}{2}$	5	4	3	2		
	4	3	2	1	36	1296
	5	2	3	2		
1	4	4	3	1		
	3	2	2	2	31	961
	4	3	2	1		
$\Sigma X^2 = 385$ T_{column}	40	29	24	16		$G = 109$
T^2_{column}	1600	841	576	256		$G^2 = 11881$

(a) After converting individual scores to cell means and margin totals to margin means, use appropriate sets of means to graph the various possible effects and tentatively interpret the experimental outcomes.

(b) Summarize the results with an ANOVA table.

(c) Whenever appropriate, estimate effect sizes with η_p^2 and d and use the *HSD* test.

(d) Interpret these results.
Answers on page 520.

18.11 In what sense does a two-factor ANOVA use observations more efficiently than a one-factor ANOVA does?

18.12 A psychologist employs a two-factor experiment to study the combined effect of sleep deprivation and alcohol consumption on the performance of automobile drivers. Before the driving test, the subjects go without sleep for various time periods and then drink a glass of orange juice laced with controlled amounts of vodka. Their performance is measured by the number of errors made on a driving simulator. Two subjects are randomly assigned to each cell, that is, each possible combination of sleep deprivation (either 0, 24, 48, or 72 hours) and alcohol consumption (either 0, 1, 2, or 3 ounces), yielding the following results:

NUMBER OF DRIVING ERRORS

ALCOHOL CONSUMPTION (OUNCES)	SLEEP DEPRIVATION (HOURS) 0	24	48	72	T_{row}	T_{row}^2
0	0	2	5	5	29	841
	3	4	4	6		
1	1	3	6	5	36	1296
	3	3	7	8		
2	3	2	8	7	53	2809
	5	5	11	12		
3	4	4	10	9	68	4624
	6	7	13	15		
$\Sigma X^2 = 1466$ T_{column}	25	30	64	67	$G = 186$	
T_{column}^2	625	900	4096	4489	$G^2 = 34596$	

(a) Summarize the results with an ANOVA table.

(b) If appropriate, conduct additional *F* tests, estimate effect sizes, and use Tukey's *HSD* test.

18.13 Does the type of instruction in a college sociology class (either lecture or self-paced) and its grading policy (either letter or pass/fail) influence the performance of students, as measured by the number of quizzes successfully completed during the semester? Six students are randomly assigned to each of the four possible cells, yielding the following results:

NUMBER OF QUIZZES SUCCESSFULLY COMPLETED

GRADING POLICY	TYPE OF INSTRUCTION LECTURE	SELF-PACED	T_{row}	T_{row}^2
Letter grades	4	7		
	3	8		
	5	6	72	5184
	2	4		
	6	10		
	5	12		
Pass/fail	8	4		
	9	1		
	4	3	68	4624
	5	2		
	8	6		
	10	8		
$\Sigma X^2 = 1004$ T_{column}	69	71	$G = 140$	
T_{column}^2	4761	5041	$G^2 = 19600$	

(a) Summarize the results with an ANOVA table.

(b) If appropriate, conduct additional F tests, estimate effect sizes, and use Tukey's *HSD* test.

18.14 In this chapter, all examples of two-factor studies involve at least two observations per cell. Would it be possible to perform an ANOVA for a two-factor study having only one observation per cell?

Chi-Square (χ^2) Test for Qualitative (Nominal) Data

Preview

When data are qualitative with nominal measurement, statistical analyses are based on observed frequencies. The chi-square (χ^2) test focuses on any discrepancies between these observed frequencies and the corresponding set of expected frequencies, which are derived from the null hypothesis. Each of two χ^2 tests is described. When data are distributed along a single qualitative variable, the one-variable χ^2 test evaluates these discrepancies as a test for "goodness of fit." When data are cross-classified along two qualitative variables, the two-variable χ^2 test evaluates these discrepancies as a "test of independence" or a lack of predictability between the two qualitative variables.

ONE-VARIABLE χ^2 TEST

19.1 SURVEY OF BLOOD TYPES

Your blood belongs to one of four genetically determined types: O, A, B, or AB. A bulletin issued by a large blood bank claims that these four blood types are distributed in the U.S. population according to the following proportions: .44 are type 0, .41 are type A, .10 are type B, and .05 are type AB. Let's treat this claim as a null hypothesis to be tested with a random sample of 100 students from a large university.

A Test for Qualitative (Nominal) Data

When observations are merely classified into various categories—for example, as blood types: O, A, B, and AB; as political affiliations: Republican, Democrat, and independent; as ethnic backgrounds: African-American, Asian-American, European-American, etc., the data are qualitative and measurement is nominal, as discussed in Chapter 1. Hypothesis tests for qualitative data require the use of a new test known as the *chi-square test* (symbolized as χ^2 and pronounced "ki square").

One-Variable versus Two-variable

When observations are classified in only one way, that is, classified along a single qualitative variable, as with the four blood types, the test is a **one-variable χ^2 test.** Designed to evaluate the adequacy with which observed frequencies are described by hypothesized or expected frequencies, a one-variable χ^2 test is also referred to as a *goodness-of-fit* test. Later, when observations are classified in two ways, that is, cross-classified according to two qualitative variables, the test is a two-variable χ^2.

One-Variable χ^2 Test

Evaluates whether observed frequencies for a single qualitative variable are adequately described by hypothesized or expected frequencies.

19.2 STATISTICAL HYPOTHESES

Null Hypothesis

For the one-variable χ^2 test, the null hypothesis makes a statement about two or more population proportions whose values, in turn, generate the hypothesized or expected frequencies for the statistical test. Sometimes these population proportions are specified directly, as in the survey of blood types:

$$H_0: P_O = .44; P_A = .41; P_B = .10; P_{AB} = .05$$

where P_O refers to the hypothesized proportion of students with type O blood in the population from which the sample was taken, and so forth. Notice that the values of population proportions always must sum to 1.00.

Other Examples

At other times, you will have to infer the values of population proportions from verbal statements. For example, the null hypothesis that artists are equally likely to be left-handed or right-handed translates into

$$H_0: P_{left} = P_{right} = .50 \text{ (or } 1/2)$$

where P_{left} represents the hypothesized proportion of left-handers in the population of artists.

The hypothesis that voters are equally likely to prefer any one of four different candidates (coded 1, 2, 3, and 4) translates into

$$H_0: P_1 = P_2 = P_3 = P_4 = .25 \text{ (or } 1/4)$$

where P_1 represents the hypothesized proportion of voters who prefer candidate 1 in the population of voters, and so forth.

Alternative Hypothesis

Because the null hypothesis will be false if population proportions deviate in *any* direction from that hypothesized, the alternative or research hypothesis can be described simply as

$$H_1: H_0 \text{ is false}$$

As usual, the alternative hypothesis indicates that, relative to the null hypothesis, something special is happening in the underlying population, such as, for instance, a tendency for artists to be left-handed or for voters to prefer one or two candidates.

Progress Check *19.1 Specify the null hypothesis for each of the following situations. (Remember, the null hypothesis usually represents a negation of the researcher's hunch or hypothesis.)

(a) A political scientist wants to determine whether voters prefer candidate A more than candidate B for president.

(b) A biologist suspects that, upon being released 10 miles south of their home roost, migratory birds are more likely to fly toward home (north) rather than in any of the three remaining directions (east, south, or west).

(c) A sociologist believes that crimes are not committed with equal likelihood on each of the seven days of the week.

(d) Another sociologist suspects that *proportionately* more crimes are committed during the two days of the weekend (Saturday and Sunday) than during the five other days of the week. **Hint:** There are just two (unequal) proportions: one representing the two weekend days and the other representing the five week days.

Answers on page 522.

....

19.3 DETAILS: CALCULATING χ^2

If the null hypothesis is true, then, except for chance, hypothetical or expected frequencies (generated from the hypothetical proportions) should describe the observed frequencies in the sample. For example, when testing the blood bank's claim with a sample of 100 students, 44 students should have type O (from the

Table 19.1					
OBSERVED AND EXPECTED FREQUENCIES:					
BLOOD TYPES OF 100 STUDENTS					
		BLOOD TYPE			
FREQUENCY	**O**	**A**	**B**	**AB**	**TOTAL**
Observed (f_o)	38	38	20	4	100
Expected (f_e)	44	41	10	5	100

Expected Frequency (f_e)

The hypothesized frequency for each category, given that the null hypothesis is true.

Observed Frequency (f_o)

The obtained frequency for each category.

product of .44 and 100); 41 should have type A; 10 should have type B; and only 5 should have type AB. In **Table 19.1**, each of these numbers is referred to as an **expected frequency, f_e,** that is, *the hypothesized frequency for each category of the qualitative variable if, in fact, the null hypothesis is true.* An expected frequency is compared with its **observed frequency, f_o,** that is, *the frequency actually obtained in the sample for each category.*

To find the expected frequency for any category, multiply the hypothesized or expected proportion for that category by the total sample size, namely,

---

EXPECTED FREQUENCY (ONE-VARIABLE χ^2 TEST)

$$f_e = (expected\ proportion)(total\ sample\ size) \qquad (19.1)$$

---

where f_e represents the expected frequency.

Evaluating Discrepancies

It's most unlikely that a random sample—because of its inevitable variability—will exactly reflect the characteristics of its population. Even though the null hypothesis is true, discrepancies will appear between observed and expected frequencies, as in Table 19.1.

The crucial question is whether the discrepancies between observed and expected frequencies are small enough to be regarded as a common outcome, given that the null hypothesis is true. If so, the null hypothesis is retained. Otherwise, if the discrepancies are large enough to qualify as a rare outcome, the null hypothesis is rejected.

Computing χ^2

To determine whether discrepancies between observed and expected frequencies qualify as a common or rare outcome, a value is calculated for χ^2 and compared with its hypothesized sampling distribution. To calculate χ^2, use the following expression:

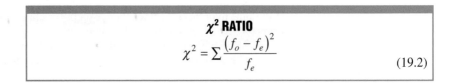

χ^2 RATIO

$$\chi^2 = \Sigma \frac{(f_o - f_e)^2}{f_e} \qquad (19.2)$$

where f_o denotes the observed frequency and f_e denotes the expected frequency for each category of the qualitative variable. Table 19.2 illustrates how to use Formula 19.2 to calculate χ^2 for the present example.

Some Properties of χ^2

Notice several features of Formula 19.2. The larger the discrepancies are between the observed and expected frequencies, $f_o - f_e$, the larger the value of χ^2 and, therefore, as will be seen, the more suspect the null hypothesis will be. Because of the squaring of each discrepancy, negative discrepancies become positive, and the value of χ^2 never can be negative. Division by f_e indicates that discrepancies must be evaluated not in isolation, but relative to the size of expected frequencies. For example, a discrepancy of 5 looms more importantly (and translates into a larger value of χ^2) relative to an expected frequency of 10 than relative to an expected frequency of 100.

Table 19.2
CALCULATION OF χ^2 (ONE-VARIABLE TEST)

A. COMPUTATIONAL SEQUENCE
Find an expected frequency for each expected proportion **1**.
List observed and expected frequencies **2**.
Substitute numbers in formula **3** and solve for χ^2.

B. DATA AND COMPUTATIONS

1 $\quad f_e = $ (expected proportion)(sample size)
$f_e(O) = (.44)(100) = 44$
$f_e(A) = (.41)(100) = 41$
$f_e(B) = (.10)(100) = 10$
$f_e(AB) = (.05)(100) = 5$

2 Frequency	O	A	B	AB	Total
f_o	38	38	20	4	100
f_e	44	41	10	5	100

3 $\quad \chi^2 = \Sigma \dfrac{(f_o - f_e)^2}{f_e}$

$$= \frac{(38-44)^2}{44} + \frac{(38-41)^2}{41} + \frac{(20-10)^2}{10} + \frac{(4-5)^2}{5}$$

$$= \frac{(-6)^2}{44} + \frac{(-3)^2}{41} + \frac{(10)^2}{10} + \frac{(-1)^2}{5}$$

$$= \frac{36}{44} + \frac{9}{41} + \frac{100}{10} + \frac{1}{5}$$

$$= .82 + .22 + 10.00 + .20$$

$$= 11.24$$

19.4 TABLE FOR THE χ^2 DISTRIBUTION

Like t and F, χ^2 has not one but a family of distributions. Table D in Appendix C supplies critical values from various χ^2 distributions for hypothesis tests at the .10, .05, .01, and .001 levels of significance.

To locate the appropriate row in Table D, first identify the correct number of degrees of freedom. For the one-variable test, the degrees of freedom for χ^2 can be obtained from the following expression:

DEGREES OF FREEDOM (ONE-VARIABLE χ^2 TEST)

$$df = c - 1 \qquad\qquad (19.3)$$

---

where c refers to the total number of categories of the qualitative variable.

Lose One Degree of Freedom

To understand Formula 19.3, focus on the set of observed frequencies for 100 students in Table 19.1. In practice, of course, the observed frequencies for the four (c) categories have equal status, and any combination of four frequencies that sums to 100 is possible. From the more abstract perspective of degrees of freedom, however, only three ($c - 1$) of these frequencies are free to vary because of the mathematical restriction that, when calculating χ^2 for the present data, all observed (or expected) frequencies must sum to 100. Although the observed frequencies of any three of the four categories are free to vary, the frequency of the fourth category must be some number that, when combined with the other three frequencies, will yield a sum of 100. Similarly, if there had been five categories, the frequencies of any four categories would have been free to vary, but not that of the fifth category. For the one-variable test, the number of degrees of freedom always equals one less than the total number of categories (c), as indicated in Formula 19.3.

In the present example, in which the categories consist of the four blood types,

$$df = 4 - 1 = 3$$

To find the critical χ^2 for a hypothesis test at the .05 level of significance, locate the cell in Table D, Appendix C, intersected by the row for 3 degrees of freedom and the column for the .05 level of significance. This cell lists a value of 7.81 for the critical χ^2.

19.5 χ^2 TEST

Following the usual procedure, assume the null hypothesis to be true and view the observed χ^2 within the context of its hypothesized distribution shown in **Figure 19.1**. If, because the discrepancies between observed and expected frequencies are relatively small, the observed χ^2 appears to emerge from the dense

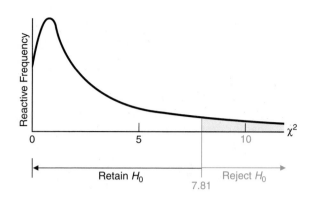

FIGURE 19.1
Hypothesized sampling distribution of χ^2 (3 degrees of freedom).

concentration of possible χ^2 values smaller than the critical χ^2, the observed outcome would be viewed as a common occurrence, on the assumption that the null hypothesis is true. Therefore, the null hypothesis would be retained. On the other hand, if, because the discrepancies between observed and expected frequencies are relatively large, the observed χ^2 appears to emerge from the sparse concentration of possible χ^2 values equal to or greater than the critical χ^2, the observed outcome would be viewed as a rare occurrence, and the null hypothesis would be rejected.

In fact, because the observed χ^2 of 11.24 is larger than the critical χ^2 of 7.81, the null hypothesis should be rejected: There is evidence that the distribution of blood types in the student population differs from that claimed for the U.S. population.

Speculations about Particular Discrepancies

Because all discrepancies contribute to the rejection of the null hypothesis, there are no statistical grounds for identifying the largest discrepancy as *the* discrepancy that causes the null hypothesis to be rejected. However, it is sometimes helpful to speculate about one or more of the most obvious discrepancies between observed and expected frequencies. As can be seen in Table 19.1, the present survey contains an unexpectedly large number of students with type B blood. A subsequent investigation revealed that the sample included a large number of Asian-American students, a group that has an established high incidence of type B blood. This might explain why the hypothesized distribution of blood types fails to describe that for the population of students from which the random sample was taken. Certainly, a random sample should be taken from a much broader spectrum of the general population before questioning the blood bank's claim about the distribution of blood types in the U.S. population.

Progress Check *19.2 A random sample of 90 college students indicates whether they most desire love, wealth, power, health, fame, or family happiness.

(a) Using the .05 level of significance and the following results, test the null hypothesis that, in the underlying population, the various desires are equally popular.

HYPOTHESIS TEST SUMMARY
One-Variable χ^2 Test (Survey of Blood Types)

Research Problem
Does the distribution of blood types in a population of college students comply with that described in a blood bank bulletin for the U.S. population?

Statistical Hypotheses

$$H_0: P_O = .44; \ P_A = .41; \ P_B = .10; \ P_{AB} = .05$$

(where P_O is the proportion of type O blood in the population, etc.)

$$H_1: H_0 \text{ is false.}$$

Decision Rule
Reject H_0 at the .05 level of significance if $\chi^2 \geq 7.81$ (from Table D in Appendix C, given $df = c - 1 = 4 - 1 = 3$).

Calculations

$$\chi^2 = 11.24 \text{ (See Table 19.2.)}$$

Decision
Reject H_0 at the .05 level of significance because $\chi^2 = 11.24$ exceeds 7.81.

Interpretation
The distribution of blood types in a student population differs from that claimed for the U.S. population.

(b) Specify the approximate *p*-value for this test result.

DESIRES OF COLLEGE STUDENTS						
FREQUENCY	LOVE	WEALTH	POWER	HEALTH	FAME	FAMILY HAP.	TOTAL
Observed (f_0)	25	10	5	25	10	15	90

Answers on page 522.

χ^2 Test Is Nondirectional

The χ^2 test is nondirectional, as all discrepancies between observed and expected frequencies are squared. All squared discrepancies have a cumulative positive effect on the value of the observed χ^2 and thereby ensure that χ^2 is a nondirectional test, even though, as illustrated in Figure 19.1, only the upper tail of its distribution contains the rejection region.

> **INTERNET DEMONSTRATION**
> Go to the Web site for this book (http://www.wiley.com/college/witte). Click on the *Student Companion Site*, then *Internet Demonstration,* and finally, **One-variable Chi-square** to simulate outcomes for each of two sets of expected frequencies that either reflect or fail to reflect the known shape of the underlying population.

TWO-VARIABLE χ^2 TEST

So far, we have considered the case where observations are classified in terms of only one qualitative variable. Now let's deal with the case where observations are cross-classified in terms of two qualitative (nominal) variables.

19.6 LOST LETTER STUDY

Viewing the return rate of lost letters as a measure of social responsibility in neighborhoods, a social psychologist intentionally "loses" self-addressed, stamped envelopes near mailboxes. Furthermore, to determine whether *social responsibility,* as inferred from the mailed return rates, varies with the *type of neighborhood,* lost letters are scattered throughout three different neighborhoods: downtown, suburbia, and a college campus.

Letters are "lost" in *each* of the three types of neighborhoods according to procedures that control for possible contaminating factors, such as the density of pedestrian traffic and mailbox accessibility. (Ordinarily, the social psychologist would probably scatter equal numbers of letters among the three neighborhoods, but to maximize the generality of the current example, we will assume that a total of 200 letters were scattered as follows: 60 downtown, 70 in suburbia, and 70 on campus.) Each letter is cross-classified on the basis of the type of neighborhood where it was lost and whether or not it was returned, as shown in **Table 19.3**. For instance, of the 60 letters lost downtown, 39 were returned,

Table 19.3
OBSERVED FREQUENCIES OF RETURNED LETTERS

RETURNED LETTERS	NEIGHBORHOOD			TOTAL
	DOWNTOWN	SUBURBIA	CAMPUS	
Yes	39	30	51	120
No	21	40	19	80
Total	60	70	70	200

while of the 70 letters lost in suburbia, 40 were not returned. When observations are cross-classified according to two qualitative variables, as with the lost letter study, the test is a **two-variable χ^2 test.**

Two-Variable χ^2 Test

Evaluates whether observed frequencies reflect the independence of two qualitative variables.

19.7 STATISTICAL HYPOTHESES

Null Hypothesis

For the two-variable χ^2 test, the null hypothesis always makes a statement about the lack of relationship between two qualitative variables in the underlying population. In the present case, it states that there is no relationship—that is, no predictability—between type of neighborhood and whether or not letters are returned. This is the same as claiming that the proportions of returned letters are the same for all three types of neighborhoods. Accordingly, the two-variable χ^2 test often is referred to as a *test of independence* for the two qualitative variables.

Although symbolic statements of the null hypothesis are possible, it is much easier to use word descriptions such as

H_0: Type of neighborhood and return rate of lost letters are independent.

or as another example,

H_0: Gender and political preference are independent.

If these null hypotheses are true, then among the population of lost letters, the type of neighborhood should not change the probability that a randomly selected lost letter is returned, and among the population of voters, gender should not change the probability that a randomly selected voter prefers the Democrats. Otherwise, if these null hypotheses are false, type of neighborhood should change the probability that a randomly selected lost letter is returned, and gender should change the probability that a randomly selected voter prefers the Democrats.

Alternative Hypothesis

The alternative or research hypothesis always takes the form

H_1: H_0 is false.

Progress Check *19.3 Specify the null hypothesis for each of the following situations.

(a) A political scientist suspects that there is a relationship between the educational level of adults (grade school, high school, college) and whether or not they favor right-to-abortion legislation.

(b) A marital therapist believes that groups of clients and nonclients are distinguishable on the basis of whether or not their parents are divorced.

(c) An organizational psychologist wonders whether employees' annual evaluations, as either satisfactory or unsatisfactory, tend to reflect whether they have fixed or flexible work schedules.

Answers on page 522.

19.8 DETAILS: CALCULATING χ^2

As in the one-variable χ^2 test, expected frequencies are calculated on the assumption that the null hypothesis is true, and, depending on the size of the discrepancies between observed and expected frequencies, the null hypothesis is either retained or rejected.

Finding Expected Frequencies from Proportions

According to the present null hypothesis, type of neighborhood and return rates are independent. Except for chance, the same proportion of returned letters should be observed for each of the three neighborhoods. Referring to the totals in Table 19.3, you will notice that when all three types of neighborhoods are considered together, 120 of the 200 lost letters were returned. Therefore, if the null hypothesis is true, 120/200, or .60, should describe the proportion of returned letters from *each* of the three neighborhoods. More specifically, among the total of 60 letters lost downtown, .60 of this total, that is (.60)(60), or 36 letters, should be returned, and 36 is the expected frequency of returned letters from downtown, as indicated in **Table 19.4**. By the same token, among the total of 70 letters lost in suburbia (or on campus), .60 of this total, that is, (.60)(70), or 42, is the expected frequency of returned letters from suburbia (or from the campus).

As can be verified in Table 19.4, the expected frequencies for nonreturned letters can be calculated in the same way, after establishing that when all three neighborhoods are considered together, only 80 of the 200 lost letters were not returned. Now, if the null hypothesis is true, 80/200, or .40, should describe the proportion of letters not returned from *each* of the three neighborhoods. For example, among the total of 60 letters lost downtown, .40 of this total, or 24, will be the expected frequency of letters not returned from downtown.

Table 19.4
OBSERVED AND EXPECTED FREQUENCIES OF RETURNED LETTERS

RETURNED LETTERS		DOWNTOWN	SUBURBIA	CAMPUS	TOTAL
		NEIGHBORHOOD			
Yes	f_o	39	30	51	120
	f_e	36	42	42	
No	f_o	21	40	19	80
	f_e	24	28	28	
Total		60	70	70	200

Finding Expected Frequencies from Totals

Expected frequencies have been derived from expected proportions in order to spotlight the reasoning behind the test. In the long run, *it is more efficient to calculate the expected frequencies directly from the various marginal totals*, according to the following formula:

EXPECTED FREQUENCY (TWO-VARIABLE χ^2 TEST)

$$f_e = \frac{(column\ total)(row\ total)}{grand\ total} \qquad (19.4)$$

---

where f_e refers to the expected frequency for any cell in the cross-classification table; *column total* refers to the total frequency for the column occupied by that cell; *row total* refers to the total frequency for the row occupied by that cell; and *grand total* refers to the total for all columns (or all rows).

Using the marginal totals in Table 19.4, we may verify that Formula 19.4 yields the expected frequencies shown in that table. For example, the expected frequency of returned letters from downtown is

$$f_e = \frac{(60)(120)}{200} = \frac{7200}{200} = 36$$

and the expected frequency of returned letters from suburbia is

$$f_e = \frac{(70)(120)}{200} = \frac{8400}{200} = 42$$

Having determined the set of expected frequencies, you may use Formula 19.2 to calculate the value of χ^2, as described in **Table 19.5**. Incidentally, for computational convenience, all of the fictitious totals in the margins of Table 19.5 were selected to be multiples of 10. In actual practice, the marginal totals are unlikely to be multiples of 10, and consequently, expected frequencies will not always be whole numbers.

19.9 TABLE FOR THE χ^2 DISTRIBUTION

Locating a critical χ^2 value in Table D, Appendix C, requires that you know the correct number of degrees of freedom. For the two-variable test, degrees of freedom for χ^2 can be obtained from the following expression:

DEGREES OF FREEDOM (TWO-VARIABLE χ^2 TEST)

$$df = (c - 1)(r - 1) \qquad (19.5)$$

Table 19.5
CALCULATION OF χ^2 (TWO-VARIABLE TEST)

A. COMPUTATIONAL SEQUENCE

Use formula **1** to obtain all expected frequencies from table of observed frequencies
Construct a table of observed and expected frequencies **2**
Substitute numbers in formula **3** and solve for χ^2

B. DATA AND COMPUTATIONS

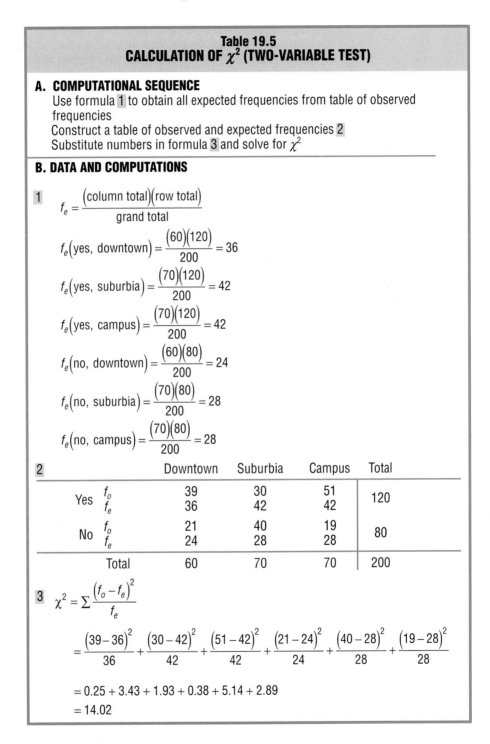

1
$$f_e = \frac{(\text{column total})(\text{row total})}{\text{grand total}}$$

$$f_e(\text{yes, downtown}) = \frac{(60)(120)}{200} = 36$$

$$f_e(\text{yes, suburbia}) = \frac{(70)(120)}{200} = 42$$

$$f_e(\text{yes, campus}) = \frac{(70)(120)}{200} = 42$$

$$f_e(\text{no, downtown}) = \frac{(60)(80)}{200} = 24$$

$$f_e(\text{no, suburbia}) = \frac{(70)(80)}{200} = 28$$

$$f_e(\text{no, campus}) = \frac{(70)(80)}{200} = 28$$

2

		Downtown	Suburbia	Campus	Total
Yes	f_o	39	30	51	120
	f_e	36	42	42	
No	f_o	21	40	19	80
	f_e	24	28	28	
	Total	60	70	70	200

3
$$\chi^2 = \Sigma \frac{(f_o - f_e)^2}{f_e}$$

$$= \frac{(39-36)^2}{36} + \frac{(30-42)^2}{42} + \frac{(51-42)^2}{42} + \frac{(21-24)^2}{24} + \frac{(40-28)^2}{28} + \frac{(19-28)^2}{28}$$

$$= 0.25 + 3.43 + 1.93 + 0.38 + 5.14 + 2.89$$

$$= 14.02$$

where c equals the number of categories for the column variable and r equals the number of categories for the row variable. In the present example, which has three columns (downtown, suburbia, and campus) and two rows (returned and not returned),

$$df = (3 - 1)(2 - 1) = (2)(1) = 2$$

To find the critical χ^2 for a test at the .05 level of significance, locate the cell in Table D intersected by the row for 2 degrees of freedom and the column for the .05 level. In this case, the value of the critical χ^2 equals 5.99.

Explanation for Degrees of Freedom

To understand Formula 19.5, focus on the set of observed frequencies in Table 19.3. In practice, of course, the observed frequencies for the six cells (within the table) have equal status, and any combination of six frequencies that sum to the various marginal totals is possible. However, only two of these frequencies are free to vary. One row and one column of cell frequencies in the original matrix are not free to vary because of the restriction that all cell frequencies in each column and in each row must sum to fixed totals in the margins. From the more abstract perspective of degrees of freedom, the original matrix with $c \times r$ or 3×2 cells shrinks to $(c - 1)(r - 1)$ or $(3 - 1)(2 - 1)$ cells and $df = 2$.

19.10 χ^2 TEST

Because the calculated χ^2 of 14.02 exceeds the critical χ^2 of 5.99, the null hypothesis should be rejected: There is evidence that the type of neighborhood is not independent of the return rate of lost letters. Knowledge about the type of neighborhood supplies extra information about the likelihood that lost letters will be returned. A comparison of observed and expected frequencies in Table 19.5 suggests that lost letters are more likely to be returned from either downtown or the campus than from suburbia.

Progress Check *19.4 An investigator suspects that there might be a relationship, possibly based on genetic factors, between hair color and susceptibility to poison oak. Three hundred volunteer subjects are exposed to a small amount of poison oak and then classified according to their susceptibility (rash or no rash) and their hair color (red, blond, brown, or black), yielding the following frequencies:

HAIR COLOR AND SUSCEPTIBILITY TO POISON OAK

	HAIR COLOR				
SUSCEPTIBILITY	RED	BLOND	BROWN	BLACK	TOTAL
Rash	10	30	60	80	180
No rash	20	30	30	40	120
Total	30	60	90	120	300

HYPOTHESIS TEST SUMMARY
Two-Variable χ^2 Test (Lost Letter Study)

Research Problem
Is there a relationship between the type of neighborhood and the return rate of lost letters?

Statistical Hypotheses
H_0: Type of neighborhood and return rates of lost letters are independent.
H_1: H_0 is false.

Decision Rule
Reject H_0 at the .05 level of significance if $\chi^2 \geq 5.99$ [from Table D, Appendix C, given that $df = (c-1)(r-1) = (3-1)(2-1) = 2$].

Calculations
$$\chi^2 = 14.02 \text{ (See Table 19.5.)}$$

Decision
Reject H_0 at the .05 level of significance because $\chi^2 = 14.02$ exceeds 5.99.

Interpretation
Type of neighborhood and return rate of lost letters are not independent.

(a) Test the null hypothesis at the .01 level of significance.

(b) Specify the approximate p-value for this test result.
Answers on page 522.

19.11 ESTIMATING EFFECT SIZE

Squared Cramer's Phi Coefficient (ϕ_c^2)

A very rough estimate of the proportion of explained variance (or predictability) between two qualitative variables.

One way to check the importance of a statistically significant two-variable χ^2 is to use a measure analogous to the squared curvilinear correlation coefficient, η^2, known as the **squared Cramer's phi coefficient** and symbolized as ϕ_c^2. Being independent of sample size (unlike χ^2), ϕ_c^2 *very roughly estimates the proportion of explained variance (or predictability) between two qualitative variables.*

Squared Cramer's Phi Coefficient (ϕ_c^2)

Solve for the squared Cramer's phi coefficient using the following formula:

PROPORTION OF EXPLAINED VARIANCE (TWO-VARIABLE χ^2)

$$\phi_c^2 = \frac{\chi^2}{n(k-1)} \qquad (19.6)$$

---

where χ^2 is the obtained value of the statistically significant two-variable χ^2, n is the sample size (total observed frequency), and k is the smaller of either the c columns or the r rows (or the value of either if they are the same).

For the lost letter study, given a significant χ^2 of 14.02, $n = 200$, and $k = 2$ (from $r = 2$), we can calculate

$$\phi_c^2 = \frac{14.02}{200(2-1)} = .07$$

Table 19.6 GUIDELINES FOR ϕ_c^2	
ϕ_c^2	EFFECT
.01	Small
.09	Medium
.25	Large

See footnote at the bottom of this page.

One guideline, suggested by Cohen for correlations and listed in **Table 19.6**, is that the strength of the relationship between the two variables is small if ϕ_c^2 approximates .01, medium if ϕ_c^2 approximates .09, and large if ϕ_c^2 approximates or exceeds .25.* Using these guidelines, the estimated strength of the relationship between type of neighborhood and return rate is medium, since $\phi_c^2 = .07$.

Consider calculating ϕ_c^2 whenever a statistically significant two-variable χ^2 has been obtained. However, do not apply these guidelines about the strength of a relationship without regard to special circumstances that could give considerable importance to even a very weak relationship, as suggested in the next section.

Progress Check *19.5 Given the significant χ^2 in Exercise 19.4, use Formula 19.6 to estimate whether the strength of the relationship between hair color and susceptibility to poison oak is small, medium, or large.

Answer on page 523.

19.12 ODDS RATIOS

A widely publicized report in *The New England Journal of Medicine* (January 28, 1988) described the incidence of heart attacks (the dependent variable) among over 22,000 physicians who took either an aspirin or a placebo (the independent variable) every other day for the duration of the study. Although a statistical analysis of the results, shown in panel B of **Table 19.7**, yields a highly significant chi square [$\chi^2(1, n = 22,071) = 25.01$, $p < .001$, $\phi_c^2 = .001$], the strength of the relationship between these two qualitative variables is very weak, as indicated by the minuscule value of only .001 for Cramer's phi coefficient, ϕ_c^2. (Verify, if you wish, using Formula 19.6.) Sometimes the importance of a

---

*This is the recommended rule of thumb if χ^2 is based on tables with either two columns or two rows (or both), as often is the case. Otherwise, the values for small, medium, and large (.01, .09, and .25) probably should be adjusted downward. See pp. 224–227 in J. Cohen, *Statistical Power Analysis for the Behavioral Sciences,* 2nd ed. (Hillsdale, NJ: Erlbaum, 1988).

Table 19.7
CALCULATING THE ODDS RATIO

A. COMPUTATIONAL SEQUENCE
Enter data in 2×3 table. 1
Calculate odds for each group by dividing the frequency of occurrence by the frequency of nonoccurrence. 2
Calculate the odds ratio by dividing odds for the two groups. 3
Interpret the odds ratio. 4

B. DATA AND COMPUTATIONS
1
Effect of Aspirin on Heart Attacks

	Heart Attack	No Heart Attack	2 Odds	3 Odds Ratio
Placebo	189	10,845	189/10,845 = .0174 (to 1)	$\frac{.0174}{.0095} = 1.83$
Aspirin	104	10,933	104/10,933 = .0095 (to 1)	

4 A physician in the placebo group is 1.83 times more likely to have a heart attack than one in the aspirin group.

Source: Rosenthal, American Psychologist, 45, 63–73 (1990).

Odds Ratio (OR)

Indicates the relative occurrence of one value of the dependent variable across the two categories of the independent variable.

---

seemingly weak relationship can be appreciated more fully by calculating an odds ratio. An **odds ratio (OR)** *indicates the relative occurrence of one value of the dependent variable* (occurrence of heart attacks) *across the two categories of the independent variable* (aspirin or a placebo).

Calculating the Odds Ratio

First, find the ***odds*** (*defined as the ratio of frequencies of occurrence to non-occurrence*) of the dependent variable for each value of the independent variable. Referring to the data in Table 19.7, find the odds of a heart attack among physicians in the placebo group by dividing frequencies of their occurrence (189) by their non-occurrence (10,845) to obtain odds of .0174 to 1 (or, after multiplying by one thousand, 17.4 to 1,000.) Likewise, find the odds of a heart attack among physicians in the aspirin group by dividing frequencies of their occurrence (104) by their non-occurrence (10,933) to obtain odds of .0095 to 1.

Next, *calculate the ratio of these two odds.* Divide .0174 by .0095 to obtain an odds ratio of 1.83. A physician in the placebo group is 1.83 times more likely, or almost twice as likely(!), to have a heart attack as a physician in the aspirin group. (Conversely, if the division of odds is reversed, the odds ratio of .55 signifies that a physician in the aspirin group is .55 times less likely, or about only half as likely, to have a heart attack as a physician in the placebo group.) Given the seriousness of even one heart attack, especially if it happens to you or to someone you know, odds ratios reaffirm the importance of these findings in spite of the very small value of .001 for ϕ_c^2. Subsequently, the investigators discontinued this study and recommended aspirin therapy for all high-risk individuals in the population.

Consider calculating an odds ratio to clarify further the importance of a significant χ^2. A 95 percent confidence interval for an odds ratio also can be constructed by using procedures, such as Minitab's *Binary Logistic Regression,* not discussed in this book.

Progress Check *19.6 Odds ratios can be calculated for larger cross-classification tables, and one way of doing this is by reconfiguring into a smaller 2 × 2 table. The 2 × 3 table for the lost letter study, Table 19.4, could be reconfigured into a 2 × 2 table if, for example, the investigator is primarily interested in comparing return rates of lost letters only for campus and off-campus locations (both suburbia and downtown), that is,

RETURNED LETTERS	OFF-CAMPUS	NEIGHBORHOOD CAMPUS	TOTAL
YES	69	51	120
NO	61	19	80
TOTAL	130	70	200

(a) Given $\chi^2(1, n = 200) = 7.42$, $p < .01$, $\phi_c^2 = .037$ for these data, calculate and interpret the odds ratio for a returned letter from campus.

(b) Calculate and interpret the odds ratio for a returned letter from off-campus.

Answers on page 523.

19.13 REPORTS IN THE LITERATURE

A report of the original lost letter study might be limited to an interpretative comment, plus a parenthetical statement that summarizes the statistical analysis and includes a *p*-value and an estimate of effect size. For example, an investigator might report the following:

There is evidence that the return rate of lost letters is related to the type of neighborhood [$\chi^2(2, n = 200) = 14.02$, $p < .001$, $\phi_c^2 = .07$].

The parenthetical statement indicates that a χ^2 based on 2 degrees of freedom and a sample size, n, of 200 was found to equal 14.02. The test result has an approximate *p*-value less than .001 because, as can be seen in Table D, Appendix C, the observed χ^2 of 14.02 is larger than the critical χ^2 of 13.82 for the .001 level of significance. Furthermore, since a *p*-value of less than .001 is a very rare event, given that the null hypothesis is true, it supports the research hypothesis, as implied in the interpretative statement. Finally, a value of .07 for ϕ_c^2 indicates that approximately 7 percent of the variance in returned letters is attributable to differences among the three neighborhoods.

Progress Check *19.7 How might the results of the hair color/poison oak study be reported in the literature?

Answer on page 523.

19.14 SOME PRECAUTIONS

Avoid Dependent Observations

The valid use of χ^2 requires that *observations be independent of one another*. One observation should have no influence on another. For instance, when tossing a pair of dice, the appearance of a six spot on one die has no influence on the number of spots displayed on the other die. A violation of independence occurs whenever a single subject contributes more than one observation (or in the two-variable case, more than one pair of observations). For example, it would have occurred in a preference test for four brands of soda if each subject's preference had been counted more than once, possibly because of a series of taste trials. When considering the use of χ^2, *the total for all observed frequencies never should exceed the total number of subjects.*

Avoid Small Expected Frequencies

The valid use of χ^2 also requires that expected frequencies not be too small. A conservative rule specifies that *all expected frequencies be 5 or more*. Small expected frequencies need not necessarily lead to a statistical dead end; sometimes it is possible to create a larger expected frequency from the combination of smaller expected frequencies (see Review Question 19.15). Otherwise, avoid small expected frequencies by using a larger sample size.

Avoid Extreme Sample Sizes

As discussed in previous chapters, avoid either very small or very large samples. An unduly small sample size produces a test that tends to miss even a seriously false null hypothesis. (By avoiding small expected frequencies, you will automatically protect the χ^2 test from the more severe cases of small sample size.) An excessively large sample size produces a test that tends to detect small, unimportant departures from null hypothesized values. A power analysis, similar to that described in Section 11.11, could be used—with the aid of software, such as G*Power at http://www.psycho.uni-duesseldorf.de/aap/projects/gpower/—to identify a sample size with a reasonable detection rate for the smallest important departure from the null hypothesis.

WWW

INTERNET DEMONSTRATION
Go to the Web site for this book (http://www.wiley.com/college/witte). Click on the *Student Companion Site*, then *Internet Demonstration,* and finally, **Two-variable Chi-square** to simulate outcomes by manipulating the degree of dependency between two qualitative variables and by manipulating sample sizes.

....

19.15 COMPUTER OUTPUT

Table 19.8 shows an SAS output for the return rates of lost letters in the three neighborhoods. Compare these results—both observed frequencies and the value of χ^2—with those shown in Table 19.5.

Progress Check *19.8 Referring to the SAS output, identify

(a) the observed frequency of returned letters in suburbia.

Table 19.8
SAS OUTPUT: TWO-VARIABLE χ^2 TEST FOR LOST LETTER DATA

```
                    THE SAS SYSTEM
            12:45 FRIDAY, OCTOBER 24, 2008
            TABLE OF RETURNED BY NEIGHBORHOOD
```

RETURNED Frequency Percent Row Pct Col Pct	NEIGHBORHOOD			
	Downtown	Suburbia	Campus	Total
Yes	39	30	51	120
	19.50	15.00	25.50	60.00
	32.50	25.00	42.50	
	65.00	42.86	72.86	
No	21	40	19	80
	10.50	20.00	9.50	40.00
	26.25	50.00	23.75	
	35.00	57.14	27.14	
Total	60	70	70	200
	30.00	35.00	35.00	100.00

STATISTICS FOR TABLE OF RETURNED BY NGHBRHD

Statistic	DF	Value	Prob
Chi-Square	2	14.018	0.0009
Likelihood Ratio Chi-Square	2	14.049	0.0009
Mantel-Haenszel Chi-Square	1	13.059	0.0003
Phi Coefficient		0.265	
Contingency Coefficient		0.256	
1 Cramer's V		0.265	

Comment:
1 This is Cramer's phi coefficient, ϕ_c, which, when squared, serves as an estimate of effect size.

(b) the set of three percents (inside the 2×3 box) that can be most meaningfully compared with the three *total* percents of 30.00, 35.00, and 35.00, for downtown, suburbia, and campus, respectively.

(c) the value of Cramer's squared phi, ϕ_p^2. (Be careful!)
Answers on page 523.

Summary

The χ^2 test is designed to test the null hypothesis for qualitative or nominal data, expressed as frequencies. For the one-variable χ^2 test, the null hypothesis claims that the population distribution complies with a set of hypothesized proportions. For the two-variable χ^2 test, the null hypothesis claims that the two qualitative variables are independent. In either case, the null hypothesis is used to generate a set of expected frequencies that is compared to a corresponding set of observed frequencies.

Essentially, χ^2 reflects the size of the discrepancies between observed and expected frequencies, expressed relative to their expected frequencies, and the larger the value of χ^2 is, the more suspect the null hypothesis will be.

To obtain critical values for χ^2, Table D, Appendix C, must be consulted, with the appropriate number of degrees of freedom for the one- and two-variable tests.

Whenever χ^2 is statistically significant, use Cramer's phi coefficient, ϕ_c^2, to estimate the strength of the relationship.

Sometimes the importance of a relationship, even a weak relationship, can be appreciated more fully by calculating an odds ratio.

Use of the χ^2 test requires that observations be independent and that expected frequencies be sufficiently large. Unduly small or excessively large sample sizes should be avoided.

Important Terms

One-variable χ^2 test
Observed frequency (f_o)
Squared Cramer's phi coefficient (ϕ_c^2)

Expected frequency (f_e)
Two-variable χ^2 test
Odds ratio

Key Equations

χ^2 RATIO

$$\chi^2 = \Sigma \frac{\left(f_o - f_e\right)^2}{f_e}$$

where $f_e = (expected\ proportion)(total\ sample\ size)$ for the one-variable χ^2

and $f_e = \dfrac{(column\ total)(row\ total)}{grand\ total}$ for the two-variable χ^2

REVIEW QUESTIONS

19.9 Randomly selected records of 140 convicted criminals reveal that their crimes were committed on the following days of the week:

FREQUENCY	DAYS WHEN CRIMES WERE COMMITTED							
	MON.	TUE.	WED.	THU.	FRI.	SAT.	SUN.	TOTAL
Observed (f_o)	17	21	22	18	23	24	15	140

(a) Using the .01 level of significance, test the null hypothesis that in the underlying population, crimes are equally likely to be committed on any day of the week.

(b) Specify the approximate *p*-value for this test result.

(c) How might this result be reported in the literature?

*19.10 A number of investigators have reported a tendency for more people to die (from natural causes, such as cancer and strokes) *after*, rather than *before*, a major holiday. This post-holiday death peak has been attributed to a number of factors, including the willful postponement of death until after the holiday, as well as holiday stress and post-holiday depression. Writing in the *Journal of the American Medical Association* (April 11, 1990), Phillips and Smith report that, among a total of 103 elderly California women of Chinese descent who died of natural causes within one week of the Harvest Moon Festival, only 33 died the week before, while 70 died the week after.

(a) Using the .05 level of significance, test the null hypothesis that, in the underlying population, people are equally likely to die either the week before or the week after this holiday.

(b) Specify the approximate *p*-value for this test result.

(c) How might this result be reported in the literature?

Answers on page 523.

19.11 While playing a coin-tossing game in which you are to guess whether heads or tails will appear, you observe 30 heads in a string of 50 coin tosses.

(a) Test the null hypothesis that this coin is unbiased, that is, that heads and tails are equally likely to appear in the long run.

(b) Specify the approximate *p*-value for this test result.

19.12 In Chapter 1, Table 1.1 lists the weights of 53 male statistics students. Although students were asked to report their weights to the nearest pound, inspection of Table 1.1 reveals that a disproportionately large number (27) reported weights ending in either a 0 or a 5. This suggests that many students probably reported their weights rounded to the nearest 5 or 10 pounds rather than to the nearest pound. Using the .05 level of significance, test the null hypothesis that in the underlying population, weights are rounded to the nearest pound. (**Hint:** If the null hypothesis is true, only two-tenths of all weights should end in either a 0 or a 5, and the remaining eight-tenths of all weights should end in a 1, 2, 3, 4, 6, 7, 8, or 9. Therefore, the situation requires a one-variable test with only two categories, and $df = 1$.)

*19.13 Students are classified according to religious preference (Buddhist, Jewish, Protestant, Roman Catholic, or Other) and political affiliation (Democrat, Republican, Independent, or Other).

RELIGIOUS PREFERENCE AND POLITICAL AFFILIATION

POLITICAL AFFILIATION	RELIGIOUS PREFERENCE					
	BUDDHIST	JEWISH	PROTESTANT	ROM. CATH.	OTHER	TOTAL
Democrat	30	30	40	60	40	200
Republican	10	10	40	20	20	100
Independent	10	10	20	20	40	100
Other	0	0	0	0	100	100
Total	50	50	100	100	200	500

(a) Is anything suspicious about these observed frequencies?

(b) Using the .05 level of significance, test the null hypothesis that these two variables are independent.

(c) If appropriate, estimate the effect size.
Answers on page 524.

*19.14 In 1912 over 800 passengers perished after the ocean liner *Titanic* collided with an iceberg and sank. The table below compares the survival frequencies of cabin and steerage passengers.

ACCOMMODATIONS ON THE *TITANIC*

SURVIVED	CABIN	STEERAGE	TOTAL
Yes	299	186	485
No	280	526	806
Total	579	712	1291

Source: Dawson, Journal of Statistical Education (1995) vol. 3, no. 3.

(a) Using the .05 level of significance, test the null hypothesis that survival rates are independent of the passengers' accommodations (cabin or steerage).

(b) Assuming a significant χ^2, estimate the strength of the relationship.

(c) To more fully appreciate the importance of this relationship, calculate an odds ratio to determine how much more likely a cabin passenger is to have survived than a steerage passenger.

Answers on page 524.

19.15 Test the null hypothesis at the .01 level of significance that the distribution of blood types for college students complies with the proportions described in the blood bank bulletin, namely, .44 for O, .41 for A, .10 for B, and .05 for AB. Now, however, assume that the results are available for a random sample of only 60 students. The results are as follows: 27 for O, 26 for A, 4 for B, and 3 for AB.

NOTE: The expected frequency for AB, (.05)(60) = 3, is less than 5, the smallest permissible expected frequency. Create a sufficiently large expected frequency by combining B and AB blood types.

19.16 A social scientist cross-classifies the responses of 100 randomly selected people on the basis of gender and whether or not they favor strong gun control laws to obtain the following:

GENDER AND ATTITUDE TOWARD STRONG GUN CONTROL			
	ATTITUDE TOWARD GUN CONTROL		
GENDER	FAVOR	OPPOSE	TOTAL
Male	40	20	60
Female	30	10	40
Total	70	30	100

(a) Using the .05 level of significance, test the null hypothesis for gender and attitude toward gun control.

(b) Specify the approximate *p*-value for the test result.

(c) How might these results be reported in the literature?

19.17 To appreciate the impact of large sample size on the value of χ^2, multiply each of the observed frequencies in the previous question by 10 to obtain the following:

GENDER AND ATTITUDE TOWARD STRONG GUN CONTROL			
	ATTITUDE TOWARD GUN CONTROL		
GENDER	FAVOR	OPPOSE	TOTAL
Male	400	200	600
Female	300	100	400
Total	700	300	1000

Note: Even though the sample size has increased by a factor of 10, the proportion of males (and females) who favor gun control remains the same as in the previous question. In both questions, gun control is favored by .67 of all males (from 40/60 = 400/600 = .67) and by .75 of all females (from 30/40 = 300/400 = .75).

(a) Using the .05 level of significance, again test the null hypothesis for gender and attitude toward gun control.

(b) Specify the approximate p-value for this test result.

(c) Given a significant χ^2 for the current analysis, estimate the effect size.

CHAPTER 20

Tests for Ranked (Ordinal) Data

Preview

If data are ranked with ordinal measurement or if quantitative data seem to violate the assumptions of the t *and* F *tests, use the more assumption-free tests described in this chapter. However, do not adopt one of these tests merely as a matter of computational convenience since they are less likely to detect a false null hypothesis than do the corresponding* t *or* F *tests.*

20.1 USE ONLY WHEN APPROPRIATE

Use the Mann-Whitney *U*, Wilcoxon *T*, and Kruskal-Wallis *H* tests described in this chapter only under appropriate circumstances, that is, (1) when the original data are ranked (ordinal) or (2) when the original data are quantitative but do not appear to originate from normally distributed populations with equal variances.

In the latter case, beware of *non-normality* when the sample sizes are small (less than about 10), and beware of *unequal variances* when the sample sizes are small and unequal.

When the original data are quantitative and the populations appear to be normally distributed, with equal variances, use the *t* and *F* tests.

Under these circumstances, the *t* and *F* tests are more powerful, that is, they are more likely to detect a false null hypothesis because they minimize the probability of a type II error.

20.2 A NOTE ON TERMINOLOGY
Nonparametric Tests

Nonparametric Tests

Tests, such as U, T, *and* H, *that evaluate* entire *population distributions rather than specific population characteristics.*

The *U*, *T*, and *H* tests for ranked data described in this chapter, as well as the χ^2 test for qualitative (nominal) data discussed in the previous chapter, are often referred to as **nonparametric tests.** Parameter refers to any descriptive measure of a population, such as the population mean. Nonparametric tests, such as *U*, *T*, and *H*, evaluate hypotheses for *entire* population distributions, whereas parametric tests, such as the *t* and *F* tests discussed in Chapters 13 through 18, evaluate hypotheses for a specific parameter, usually the population mean.

Distribution-Free Tests

Distribution-Free Tests

Tests, such as U, T, *and* H, *that make no assumptions about the form of the population distribution.*

Nonparametric tests also are referred to as **distribution-free tests.** This name highlights the fact that these tests require no assumptions about the precise form of the population distribution. As will be noted, the *U*, *T*, and *H* tests can be conducted without assumptions about the underlying population distributions. In contrast, the *t* and *F* tests require populations to be normally distributed, with equal variances.

Labels Can Be Misleading

Although widely used, these labels can be misleading. If the two population distributions are assumed to have roughly similar variabilities and shapes, as in the examples for the *U* and *T* tests in the next two sections, we sacrifice the distribution-free status of these tests to gain a more precise parametric test of any differences in central tendency. Consequently, depending on the perspective of the investigator, the *U*, *T*, or *H* tests might qualify as neither nonparametric nor distribution-free.

Table 20.1 ESTIMATES OF WEEKLY TV-VIEWING TIME (HOURS)	
TV FAVOR-ABLE	TV UNFAVOR-ABLE
12	43
4	14
5	42
20	1
5	2
5	0
10	0
49	

20.3 MANN-WHITNEY *U* TEST (TWO INDEPENDENT SAMPLES)

If high school students are asked to estimate the number of hours they spend watching TV each week, are their anonymous replies influenced by whether TV viewing is depicted favorably or unfavorably? More specifically, one-half of the members of a social studies class are selected at random to receive questionnaires that depict TV viewing favorably (as the preferred activity of better students), and the other half of the class receive questionnaires that depict TV viewing unfavorably (as the preferred activity of poorer students). After discarding the replies of several students who responded not with numbers but with words such as "a lot" and "hardly at all," the results were listed in **Table 20.1**.

Why Not a *t* Test?

When taken at face value, it might appear that the estimates in Table 20.1 could be tested with the customary *t* test for two independent samples. However, closer inspection reveals a complication. Each group of estimates includes one or two very large values, suggesting that the underlying populations are positively skewed rather than normal. When the sample sizes are small, as in the present experiment, violations of the normality assumption could seriously impair the accuracy of the *t* test by causing the probability of a type I error to differ considerably from that specified in the level of significance.

One remedy is to convert all of the estimates in Table 20.1 into ranks and to analyze the newly ranked data with the Mann-Whitney *U* test for two independent samples. As is true of all tests for ranked data, the *U* test is immune to violations of assumptions about normality and equal variances.

Statistical Hypotheses for *U*

For the TV-viewing study, the statistical hypotheses take the form

H_0: population distribution 1 = population distribution 2
H_1: population distribution 1 ≠ population distribution 2

in which TV viewing is depicted as the preferred activity of better students in population 1 and of poorer students in population 2.

Unspecified Differences

Notice that the null hypothesis equates two *entire* population distributions. Any type of inequality between population distributions, whether caused by differences in central tendency, variability, or shape, could contribute to the rejection of H_0. Strictly speaking, the *rejection of H_0 signifies only that the two populations differ because of some unspecified inequality, or combination of inequalities,* between the original population distributions.

Specified Differences

More precise conclusions are possible if both population distributions are assumed to have about equal variabilities and roughly similar shapes, that is, for instance, if both population distributions are symmetrical or if both are similarly skewed. Under these circumstances, the rejection of H_0 signifies that the two population distributions occupy different locations and, therefore, possess different central tendencies that can be interpreted as a difference between population medians.

Calculation of U

Table 20.2 indicates how to convert the estimates in Table 20.1 into ranks. Before assigning numerical ranks to the two groups, coded as groups 1 and 2, list all observations from smallest to largest for the combined groups. Beginning with the smallest estimate, assign the consecutive numerical ranks 1, 2, 3, and so forth, until all the estimates have been converted to ranks. When two or more estimates are the same, assign the median of the numerical ranks that would have been assigned if the estimates had been different. For example, each of the two estimates of 0 hours receives a rank of 1.5, the median of ranks 1 and 2, and each of the three estimates of 5 hours receives a rank of 7, the median of ranks 6, 7, and 8.

Progress Check *20.1 Beginning with a rank of 1 for the smallest observation, rank each of the following sets of observations:

(a) 4, 6, 9, 10, 10, 12, 15, 23, 23, 23, 31

(b) 103, 104, 104, 105, 105, 109, 112, 118, 119, 124

(c) 51, 54, 54, 54, 54, 59, 60, 71, 71, 79

Answers on page 525.

Preliminary Interpretation

Differences in ranks between groups 1 and 2 are not mentioned in Table 20.2, but it is wise to pause at this point and to form a preliminary impression of any of these differences. The more one group tends to outrank the other, the larger the difference between the median ranks for the two groups and the more suspect will be the null hypothesis. Since, in Table 20.2, the median rank for group 1 equals 8 (midway between 7 and 9) and the median rank for group 2 equals 4, there is a tendency for group 1 to outrank group 2, that is, there is a tendency for the TV-favorable group to rank higher in their estimates of hours spent viewing TV. It remains to be seen whether, once variability is estimated, this result will cause the null hypothesis to be rejected.

After all of the observations have been ranked, find the sum of ranks for group 1, R_1, and the sum of the ranks for group 2, R_2. To verify that ranks have been assigned and added correctly, perform the computational check shown in Table 20.2. Finally, calculate values for both U_1 and U_2 and set the smaller of these two values equal to U, that is,

Mann-Whitney U *Test*
A test for ranked data when there are two independent groups.

MANN-WHITNEY *U* TEST (TWO INDEPENDENT SAMPLES)

$$U_1 = n_1 n_2 + \frac{n_1(n_1 + 1)}{2} - R_1$$

$$U_2 = n_1 n_2 + \frac{n_2(n_2 + 1)}{2} - R_2 \qquad (20.1)$$

$$U = \text{the smaller of } U_1 \text{ or } U_2$$

Table 20.2
CALCULATION OF U

A. COMPUTATIONAL SEQUENCE

Identify the sample sizes of group 1, n_1, group 2, n_2, and the combined groups, n **1**.

List observations from smallest to largest for the combined groups **2**.

Assign numerical ranks to the ordered observations for the combined groups **3**.

Sum the ranks for group 1 **4** and for group 2 **5**.

Substitute numbers in formula **6** and verify that ranks have been assigned and added correctly.

Substitute numbers in formula **7** and solve for U_1.

Substitute numbers in formula **8** and solve for U_2.

Set U equal to whichever is smaller—U_1 or U_2 **9**.

B. DATA AND COMPUTATIONS

1 $n_1 = 8$; $n_2 = 7$; $n = 8 + 7 = 15$

2 Observations / **3** Ranks

(1) TV Favorable	(2) TV Unfavorable	(1) TV Favorable	(2) TV Unfavorable
	0		1.5
	0		1.5
	1		3
	2		4
4		5	
5		7	
5		7	
5		7	
10		9	
12		10	
	14		11
20		12	
	42		13
	43		14
49		15	
		4 $R_1 = 72$	**5** $R_2 = 48$

6 Computational Check:

$$R_1 + R_2 = \frac{n(n+1)}{2}$$

$$72 + 48 = \frac{15(15+1)}{2}$$

$$120 = 120$$

7

$$U_1 = n_1 n_2 + \frac{n_1(n_1+1)}{2} - R_1$$

$$= (8)(7) + \frac{8(8+1)}{2} - 72$$

$$= 56 + 36 - 72$$

$$= 20$$

8

$$U_2 = n_1 n_2 + \frac{n_2(n_2+1)}{2} - R_2$$

$$= (8)(7) + \frac{7(7+1)}{2} - 48$$

$$= 56 + 28 - 48$$

$$= 36$$

9 U = whichever is smaller—U_1 or U_2

$$= 20$$

in which n_1 and n_2 represent the sample sizes of groups 1 and 2 and R_1 and R_2 represent the sum of ranks for groups 1 and 2. The value of U equals 20 for the present study.

Table for *U* Distribution

Critical values of U are supplied for values of n_1 and n_2 (no larger than 20 each) in Table E, Appendix C.* Notice that there are two sets of tables, one for nondirectional tests and one for directional tests. Both tables supply critical values of U for hypothesis tests at the .05 level (light numbers) and the .01 level (dark numbers).

To find the correct critical U, identify the entry in the cell intersected by n_1 and n_2, the sample sizes of groups 1 and 2. For the present study, given a nondirectional test at the .05 level of significance with an n_1 of 8 and an n_2 of 7, the value of the critical U equals 10.

Decision Rule

An unusual feature of hypothesis tests involving U (and T, described later) is that the null hypothesis will be rejected only if the observed U is *less* than or equal to the critical U. Otherwise, if the observed U exceeds the critical U, the null hypothesis will be retained.

Explanation of Topsy-Turvy Rule

To appreciate this topsy-turvy decision rule for the U test, look more closely at U. Although not apparent in Formula 20.1, *U represents the number of times that individual ranks in the lower-ranking group exceed individual ranks in the higher-ranking group.* When a maximum difference separates two groups—because no rank in the lower-ranking group exceeds any rank in the higher-ranking group—U equals 0. At the other extreme, when a minimum difference separates two groups—because, as often as not, individual ranks in the lower-ranking group exceed individual ranks in the higher-ranking group—U equals a large number given by the expression

$$\frac{n_1 n_2}{2}$$

which is 28 for the present study.

Ordinarily, the difference in ranks between groups is neither maximum nor minimum, and U equals some intermediate value that, to be interpreted, must be compared with the appropriate critical U value. In the present study, since the observed U of 20 exceeds the critical U of 10, only a moderate difference separates the two groups, and the null hypothesis is retained.

Progress Check *20.2 Does it matter whether leaders of therapy groups adopt either a directive or nondirective role to facilitate growth among group members? Six randomly selected graduate trainees are taught to be directive, and six other

---

* In the unlikely event that you will be using this test with sample sizes larger than 20 each, use the large sample approximation discussed in, for example, W. Conover, *Practical Nonparametric Statistics* (New York: Wiley, 1999).

HYPOTHESIS TEST SUMMARY

Mann-Whitney *U* Test (Two Independent Samples)
(Estimates Of TV Viewing)

Research Problem

Are high school students' estimates of their weekly TV-viewing time influenced by depicting TV viewing as the preferred activity of either better (1) or poorer (2) students?

Statistical Hypotheses

H_0: population distribution 1 = population distribution 2

H_1: population distribution 1 $\neq$ population distribution 2

Decision Rule

Reject H_0 at the .05 level of significance if $U \leq 10$ (from Table E in Appendix C, given $n_1 = 8$ and $n_2 = 7$).

Calculations

$U = 20$ (See Table 20.2 for computations.)

Decision

Retain H_0 at the .05 level of significance because $U = 20$ exceeds 10.

Interpretation

There is no evidence that depicting TV viewing as the preferred activity of either better or poorer students influences high school students' estimates of their weekly TV-viewing times.

---

trainees are taught to be nondirective. Subsequently, each trainee is randomly assigned to lead a small therapy group. Without being aware of the nature of the experiment, an experienced group leader ranks each of the twelve groups from least (1) to most (12) growth promoting, based on anonymous diaries submitted by all members of each group. The results are as follows:

GROWTH-PROMOTING RANKS FOR PATIENTS WITH DIFFERENT LEADERS	
DIRECTIVE LEADER	**NONDIRECTIVE LEADER**
1	9
2	6
4.5	12
11	10
3	7
4.5	8

(a) Use U to test the null hypothesis at the .05 level of significance.

(b) Specify the approximate p-value for this test result.
Answers on page 525.

....
20.4 WILCOXON T TEST (TWO RELATED SAMPLES)

The previous experiment failed to support the investigator's hunch that estimates of TV-viewing time could be influenced by depicting it as a preferred activity of either better or poorer students. Noting the large differences among the estimates of students *within* the same group, the investigator might attempt to reduce this variability—and improve the precision of the analysis—by matching students with the aid of some relevant variable (see Section 15.1). For instance, some of the variability among estimates might be due to differences in home environment. The investigator could match for home environment by using pairs of students who are siblings. One member of each pair is randomly assigned to one group, and the other sibling is assigned automatically to the second group. As in the previous experiment, the questionnaires depict TV viewing as the preferred activity of either better or poorer students. The results for the eight pairs of students are listed in the middle portion of **Table 20.3**.

Why Not a t Test?

It might appear that the eight difference scores in Table 20.3 could be tested with the t test for two matched samples. But once again, there is a complication. The set of difference scores appears to be symmetrical but somewhat nonnormal, with no obvious cluster of scores in the middle range. When sample sizes are small, as in the present experiment, violations of the normality assumption can seriously impair the accuracy of the t test for two related samples. One remedy is to rank all difference scores and to analyze the resulting ranked data with the Wilcoxon T test.

Statistical Hypotheses for T

For the present study, the statistical hypotheses take the form

H_0: population distribution 1 = population distribution 2
H_1: population distribution 1 ≠ population distribution 2

where TV viewing is depicted as the preferred activity of better students in population 1 and of poorer students in population 2.

As with the null hypothesis for U, that for T equates two entire population distributions. Strictly speaking, the rejection of H_0 signifies only that the two populations differ because of some unspecified inequality, or combination of inequalities, between the original population distributions. More precise conclusions about central tendencies are possible only if it can be assumed that both population distributions have roughly similar variabilities and shapes.

Table 20.3
CALCULATION OF T

A. COMPUTATIONAL SEQUENCE

For each pair of observations, subtract the second observation from the first observation to obtain a difference score **1**.

Ignore difference scores of zero, and without regard to sign, list the remaining difference scores from smallest to largest **2**.

Assign numerical ranks to the ordered difference scores (still without regard to sign) **3**.

List the ranks for positive difference scores in the plus ranks column **4** and list the ranks for negative difference scores in the minus ranks column **5**.

Sum the ranks for positive differences, R_+ **6**, and sum the ranks for negative differences, R_- **7**.

Determine *n*, the number of nonzero difference scores **8**.

Substitute numbers in formula **9** to verify that ranks have been assigned and added correctly.

Set *T* equal to whichever is smaller—R_+ or R_- **10**.

B. DATA AND COMPUTATIONS

| | Observations | | | | Ranks | | |
| | (1) TV Favorable | (2) TV Unfavorable | **1** Difference Scores | **2** Ordered Scores | **3** Ranks | **4** Plus Ranks | **5** Minus Ranks |
Pairs of Students							
A	2	0	2	2	1.5	1.5	
B	11	5	6	−2	1.5		1.5
C	10	12	−2	3	3	3	
D	6	6	0	5	4	4	
E	7	2	5	6	5	5	
F	43	33	10	8	6	6	
G	33	25	8	10	7	7	
H	5	2	3				

6 $R_+ = 26.5$ **7** $R_- = 1.5$

8 $n = 7$

9 Computational check:

$$R_+ + R_- = \frac{n(n+1)}{2}$$

$$26.5 + 1.5 = \frac{7(7+1)}{2}$$

$$28 = 28$$

10 *T* = whichever is smaller—R_+ or R_-
  $T = 1.5$

Calculation of T

Table 20.3 shows how to calculate *T*. When ordering difference scores from smallest to largest, ignore all difference scores of zero and *temporarily treat all negative difference scores as though they were positive.* Beginning with the smallest difference score, assign the consecutive numerical ranks, 1, 2, 3, and so forth, until all nonzero difference scores have been ranked. When two or more difference scores are the same (regardless of sign), assign them the median of the numerical ranks that would have been assigned if the scores had been different. For example, each of the two difference scores 2 and –2 receives a rank of 1.5, the median of ranks 1 and 2.

Once numerical ranks have been assigned, those ranks associated with positive difference scores should be listed in the plus ranks column, and those associated with negative difference scores should be listed in the minus ranks column. Next, find the sum of all ranks for positive difference scores, R_+, and the sum of all ranks for negative difference scores, R_-. (Notice that the more one group of difference scores outranks the other, the larger the discrepancy between the two sums of ranks, R_+ and R_-, and the more suspect the null hypothesis will be.) To verify that the ranks have been assigned and added correctly, perform the computational check in Table 20.3. Finally, the value of T equals the smaller value, either R_+ or R_-, that is,

---

WILCOXON *T* TEST (TWO RELATED SAMPLES)

$$T = \text{the smaller of } R_+ \text{ or } R_- \tag{20.2}$$

---

where R_+ and R_- represent the sum of the ranks for positive and negative difference scores. The value of T equals 1.5 for the present study.

Table for the *T* Distribution

Critical values of T are supplied for values of n up to 50 in Table F, Appendix C. There are two sets of tables, one for nondirectional tests and one for directional tests. Both tables supply critical values of T for hypothesis tests at the .05 and .01 levels of significance.

To find the correct critical T value, locate the cell intersected by n, the number of nonzero difference scores, and the desired level of significance, given either a nondirectional or a directional test. In the present example, in which n equals 7, the critical T equals 2 for a nondirectional test at the .05 level of significance.

Decision Rule

As with U, the null hypothesis will be rejected only if the observed T is *less* than or equal to the critical T. Otherwise, if the observed T exceeds the critical T, the null hypothesis will be retained. The properties of T are similar to those of U. The greater the discrepancy is in ranks between positive and negative difference scores, the smaller the value of T will be. In effect, T represents the sum of the ranks for the lower-ranking set of difference scores. For example, when the lower-ranking set of difference scores fails to appear in the rankings, because all difference scores have the same sign, the value of T equals zero, and the null hypothesis is suspect. In the present study, as the calculated T of 1.5 is less positive than the critical T of 2, the null hypothesis is rejected.

HYPOTHESIS TEST SUMMARY
Wilcoxon *t* Test (Two Related Samples)
(Estimate of TV Viewing)

Research Problem
If high school students are matched for home environment, will depicting TV viewing as the preferred activity of better students (1) or poorer students (2) influence their estimates of weekly TV-viewing time?

Statistical Hypotheses
H_0: population distribution 1 = population distribution 2
H_1: population distribution 1 ≠ population distribution 2

Decision Rule
Reject H_0 at the .05 level if $T \leq 2$ (from Table F in Appendix C, given $n = 7$).

Calculation

$$T = 1.5 \text{ (See Table 20.3 for computations.)}$$

Decision
Reject H_0 at the .05 level of significance because $T = 1.5$ is less than 2.

Interpretation
If high school students are matched for home environment, depicting TV viewing as the preferred activity of either better or poorer students will influence their estimates of TV-viewing time. Their estimates of TV-viewing time tend to be larger when TV viewing is depicted as the preferred activity of better students.

Reports in the Literature

For the current study, a report might read as follows:

Given that students have been matched for home environment, estimates of TV-viewing time tend to be larger when TV viewing is depicted as the preferred activity of better rather than poorer students [$T (n = 7) = 1.5$, $p < .05$].

Progress Check *20.3 Does a quit-smoking workshop cause a decline in cigarette smoking? The daily consumption of cigarettes is estimated for a random sample of nine smokers during each month before (1) and after (2) their attendance at a quit-smoking workshop consisting of several hours of films, lectures, and testimonials. The results are as follows:

DAILY CIGARETTE CONSUMPTION		
SMOKER	**BEFORE (1)**	**AFTER (2)**
A	22	14
B	15	7
C	10	0
D	21	22
E	14	10
F	3	3
G	11	10
H	8	7
I	15	12

(a) Why might the Wilcoxon T test be preferred to the customary t test for these data?

(b) Use T to test the null hypothesis at the .05 level of significance.

(c) Specify the approximate p-value for this test result.

(d) How might this result be reported in the literature?

Answers on page 525.

20.5 KRUSKAL-WALLIS *H* TEST (THREE OR MORE INDEPENDENT SAMPLES)

Some parents are concerned about the amount of violence in children's TV cartoons. During five consecutive Saturday mornings, 10-minute cartoon sequences were randomly selected and videotaped from the offerings of each of three TV cartoon channels, coded as A, B, and C. A child psychologist, who cannot identify the source of each cartoon, ranked the 15 videotapes from least violent (1) to most violent (15). Based on these ranks, as shown in Table 20.4, can it be concluded that the underlying populations of cartoons for the three TV channels rank differently in terms of violence?

Why Not an *F* Test?

An inspection of the numerical ranks in Table 20.4 might suggest an F test for three independent samples within the context of a one-way ANOVA. However, when original observations are numerical ranks, as in the present example, there is no basis for speculating about whether the underlying populations are normally distributed with equal variances, as assumed in ANOVA. It is advisable to use a test, such as the Kruskal-Wallis H test, that retains its accuracy, even though these assumptions might be violated.

Table 20.4
CALCULATION OF H

A. COMPUTATIONAL SEQUENCE

Find the sum of ranks for each group ▢1 .

Identify the sizes of group 1, n_1, group 2, n_2, group 3, n_3, and the combined groups, n ▢2 .

Substitute numbers in formula ▢3 and verify that ranks have been added correctly.

Substitute numbers in formula ▢4 and solve for H.

B. DATA AND COMPUTATIONS

Ranks

(1) A	(2) B	(3) C
8	4.5	10
4.5	14	15
2	12	6
13	7	1
10	3	10

▢1 $R_1 = 37.5$ $R_2 = 40.5$ $R_3 = 42$

▢2 $n_1 = 5$ $n_2 = 5$ $n_3 = 5$ $n = 5 + 5 + 5 = 15$

▢3   Computational check:

$$R_1 + R_2 + R_3 = \frac{n(n+1)}{2}$$

$$37.5 + 40.5 + 42 = \frac{15(15+1)}{2}$$

$$120 = 120$$

▢4 $$H = \frac{12}{n(n+1)}\left[\frac{R_1^2}{n_1} + \frac{R_2^2}{n_2} + \frac{R_3^2}{n_3}\right] - 3(n+1)$$

$$= \frac{12}{15(15+1)}\left[\frac{(37.5)^2}{5} + \frac{(40.5)^2}{5} + \frac{(42)^2}{5}\right] - 3(15+1)$$

$$= \frac{12}{240}\left[\frac{4810.5}{5}\right] - 48$$

$$= .05\left[962.1\right] - 48$$

$$= 48.11 - 48 = 0.11$$

Statistical Hypotheses for H

For the TV cartoon study, the statistical hypotheses take the form

H_0: population A = population B = population C
H_1: H_0 is false.

where A, B, and C represent the three TV cartoon channels.

This null hypothesis equates three entire population distributions. Unless the population distributions can be assumed to have roughly similar variabilities and shapes, the rejection of H_0 will signify only that two or more of the populations differ in some unspecified manner because of differences in central tendency, variability, shape, or some combination of these factors. When the original observations consist of numerical ranks, as in the present example, there is no obvious basis for speculating that the population distributions have similar shapes. Therefore, if H_0 is rejected, it will be impossible to pinpoint the precise differences among populations.

Calculating of H

Table 20.4 shows how to calculate H. (If the original data had been quantitative rather than ranked, then the first step would have been to assign numerical ranks—beginning with 1 for the smallest, and so forth—for the *combined* three groups. Essentially the same ranking procedure is followed for H as for U in Section 20.3.) When ties occur between ranks, assign a median rank. In Table 20.4, two cartoons are assigned ranks of 4.5, the median of ranks 4 and 5.

Find the sums of ranks for groups 1, 2, and 3, that is, R_1, R_2, and R_3. (Notice that when the sample sizes are equal, the larger the differences are between these three sums, the more the three groups differ from each other, and the more suspect is the null hypothesis. Otherwise, to gain a preliminary impression when the sample sizes are unequal, compare the median ranks of the various groups.) Use the computational check in Table 20.4 to verify that the ranks have been added correctly. Finally, the value of H can be determined from the following formula:

---

*Kruskal-Wallis **H** Test*

A test for ranked data when there are more than two independent groups.

KRUSKAL-WALLIS H TEST (THREE OR MORE INDEPENDENT SAMPLES)

$$H = \frac{12}{n(n+1)}\left[\sum \frac{R_i^2}{n_i} \right] - 3(n+1) \qquad (20.3)$$

where n equals the combined sample size of all groups; R_i represents the sum of ranks of the ith group; and n_i represents the sample size of the ith group. Each sum of ranks, R_i, is squared and divided by its sample size. The value of H equals 0.11 for the present study.

Table for the χ^2 Distribution

When the sample sizes are very small, the critical values of H must be obtained from special tables. When each sample consists of at least four observations, as is ordinarily the case, relatively accurate critical values can be obtained from the χ^2 distribution (Table D in Appendix C). As usual, the value of the critical χ^2 appears in the cell intersected by the desired level of significance and the number of degrees of freedom. The number of degrees of freedom, *df*, can be determined from

---

DEGREES OF FREEDOM *H* TEST

$$df = number\ of\ groups - 1 \qquad (20.4)$$

Decision Rule

In contrast with the decision rules for *U* and *T*, *the null hypothesis will be rejected only if the observed* H *is equal to or more positive than the critical* χ^2. The larger the differences are in ranks among groups, the larger the value of *H* and the more suspect will be the null hypothesis. In the present study, since the observed *H* of 0.11 is less positive than the critical χ^2 of 5.99, the null hypothesis is retained.

HYPOTHESIS TEST SUMMARY

Kruskal-Wallis *H* Test (Three Independent Samples) (Violence in TV Cartoons)

Research Problem

Does violence in cartoon programming, as judged by a child psychologist, differ for three TV cartoon channels, coded as A, B, and C?

Statistical Hypotheses

H_0: population A = population B = population C
H_1: H_0 is false.

Decision Rule

Reject H_0 at the .05 level of significance if $H \geq 5.99$ (from Table D in Appendix C, given $df = 2$).

Calculations

$H = 0.11$ (See Table 20.4 for calculations.)

Decision

Retain H_0 at the .05 level of significance because $H = 0.11$ is less than 5.99.

Interpretation

There is no evidence that violence in cartoon programming differs for the three TV cartoon channels.

H Test Is Nondirectional

Because the sum of ranks for the ith group, R_i, is squared in Formula 20.3, the H test—like the F test and χ^2 test—is always nondirectional.

Progress Check *20.4 A consumers' group wishes to determine whether motion picture ratings are, in any sense, associated with the number of violent or sexually explicit scenes in films. Five films are randomly selected from among each of the five ratings (NC-17: No One 17 and Under Admitted; R: Restricted; PG-13: Parents Strongly Cautioned; PG: Parental Guidance Suggested; and G: General Audiences), and a trained observer counts the number of violent or sexually explicit incidents in each film to obtain the following results:

NUMBER OF VIOLENT OR SEXUALLY EXPLICIT INCIDENTS				
NC-17	**R**	**PG-13**	**PG**	**G**
15	8	12	7	6
20	16	7	11	0
19	14	13	6	4
17	10	8	4	0
23	7	9	9	2

(a) Why might the H test be preferred to the F test for these data?

(b) Use H to test the null hypothesis at the .05 level of significance.

(c) Specify the approximate p-value for this test result.

Answers on page 526.

....

20.6 GENERAL COMMENT: TIES

In addition to the customary assumption about random sampling, all tests in this chapter assume that the underlying distributions are continuous, as discussed in Section 1.6. Therefore, since no two observations or ranks should be exactly the same, there should not be any ties in ranks. Refer to more advanced statistics books for a corrected version of the test if (1) the observed value of U, T, or H is in the vicinity of its critical value but is *not* statistically significant *and* (2) there are more than a few ties.[*]

Summary
....

This chapter describes three different tests of the null hypothesis, using ranked data for two independent samples (Mann-Whitney U test), two related samples (Wilcoxon T test), and three or more independent samples (Kruskal-Wallis H test). Being relatively free of assumptions, these tests can replace the t and F tests whenever populations cannot be assumed to be normally distributed, with equal variances.

....

[*] W. Conover, *Practical Nonparametric Statistics* (New York: Wiley, 1999).

Once observations have been expressed as ranks, each test prescribes its own special measure of the difference in ranks between groups, as well as tables of critical values for evaluating significance.

Strictly speaking, U, T, and H test the null hypothesis that entire population distributions are equal. The rejection of H_0 signifies merely that populations differ in some unspecified manner. If populations are assumed to have roughly similar variabilities and shapes, then the rejection of H_0 will signify that the populations differ in their central tendencies.

Although the U, T, and H tests assume that there are no ties in ranks, the occurrence of ties can be ignored except in those cases where a test just fails to reach statistical significance and more than a few ties occur.

Important Terms
. . . .

Nonparametric tests

Mann-Whitney *U* test

Kruskal-Wallis *H* test

Distribution-free tests

Wilcoxon *T* test

REVIEW QUESTIONS

20.5 A group of high-risk automobile drivers (with three moving violations in one year) are required, according to random assignment, either to attend a traffic school or to perform supervised volunteer work. During the subsequent five-year period, these same drivers were cited for the following number of moving violations:

| NUMBER OF MOVING VIOLATIONS | |
TRAFFIC SCHOOL	VOLUNTEER WORK
0	26
0	7
15	4
9	1
7	1
0	14
2	6
23	10
7	
8	

(a) Why might the Mann-Whitney *U* test be preferred to the *t* test for these data?

(b) Use *U* to test the null hypothesis at the .05 level of significance.

(c) Specify the approximate *p*-value for this test result.

20.6 A social psychologist wishes to test the assertion that our attitude toward other people tends to reflect our perception of their attitude toward us. A randomly selected member of each of 12 couples who live together is told (in private) that his or her partner has rated that person at the high end of a 0 to 100 scale of trustworthiness. The other member is told (also in private) that his or her partner has rated that person at the low end of the trustworthiness scale. Each person is then asked to estimate, in turn, the trustworthiness of his or her partner, yielding the following results. (According to the original assertion, the people in the trustworthy condition should give higher ratings than should their partners in the untrustworthy condition.)

COUPLE	TRUSTWORTHINESS RATINGS TRUSTWORTHY (1)	UNTRUSTWORTHY (2)
A	75	60
B	35	30
C	50	55
D	93	20
E	74	12
F	47	34
G	95	22
H	63	63
I	44	43
J	88	79
K	56	33
L	86	72

(a) Use T to test the null hypothesis at the .01 level.

(b) Specify the approximate p-value for this test result.

20.7 Does background music influence the scores of college students on a reading comprehension test? Sets of 10 randomly selected students take a reading comprehension test with rock, country-and-western, or classical music in the background. The results are as follows (higher scores reflect better comprehension):

READING COMPREHENSION SCORES ROCK (1)	COUNTRY-WESTERN (2)	CLASSICAL (3)
90	99	52
11	94	75
82	95	91
67	23	94
98	72	97
93	81	31
73	79	83
90	28	85
87	94	100
84	77	69

(a) Why might the *H* test be preferred to the *F* test for these data?

(b) Use *H* to test the null hypothesis at the .05 level of significance.

20.8 Use *U* rather than *t* to test the results in Review Question 14.11 on page 311.

20.9 Use *T* rather than *t* to test the effects of physical exercise described in Review Question 15.7 on page 333.

20.10 Use *H* rather than *F* to test the weight change data recorded in Review Question 16.13 on page 369.

20.11 Noting that the calculations for the *H* test tend to be much easier than those for the *F* test, one person always uses the *H* test. Any objection?

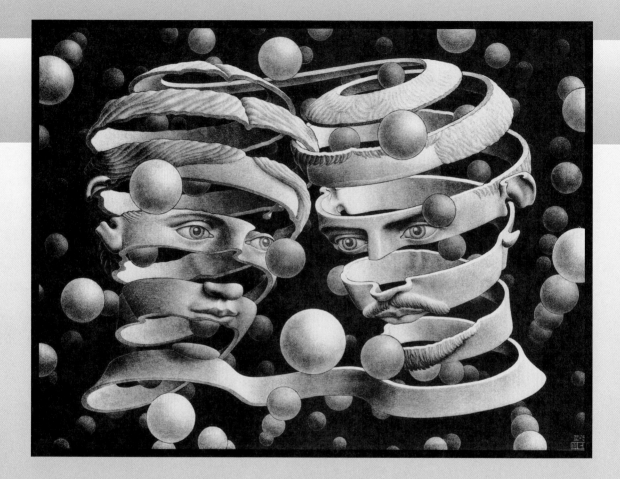

CHAPTER

21

Postscript: Which Test?

Preview

Congratulations! You have reached the final chapter. This chapter summarizes when it is appropriate to use the various statistical tests described in the book, and it should serve you well whenever you are doing simple statistical analyses. Furthermore, it can be a point of departure for more complex types of statistical analysis—if you consult someone more knowledgeable in statistics, or refer to a more advanced statistics book, or surf the many statistics Web sites on the Internet.

Although by no means exhaustive, the statistical tests in this book represent those most frequently encountered in straightforward investigations, including many reported in the research literature. If you initiate a test, there is a good chance that it also will be selected from among these tests. It is worthwhile, therefore, to review briefly the main themes of this book, particularly from the standpoint of selecting the appropriate statistical test for a given problem.

21.1 DESCRIPTIVE OR INFERENTIAL STATISTICS?

Descriptive Statistics

Is your intent descriptive because you wish merely to *summarize* existing data, or is your intent inferential because you wish to *generalize* beyond existing data? For instance, a data-oriented marriage counselor, who works with clients in groups, might suspect that some of the marital stress of current clients is attributable to the length, in years, of their marital relationships. Accordingly, during an orientation session for the group, the marriage counselor describes the mean number of years—or if there are outliers, the median number of years—of the marital relationships. Wishing merely to summarize this information for current clients, the counselor's intent is descriptive, and it is appropriate to use any tools—tables, graphs, means, standard deviations, correlations—that enhance communication.

Inferential Statistics

On the other hand, assuming that the current group is representative of a much broader spectrum of clients, the counselor might use the same mean to estimate, possibly with a confidence interval, the mean years of marital relationships among *all* couples who seek professional help. Wishing to generalize beyond current clients, the counselor's intent is inferential, and it is appropriate to use confidence intervals and hypothesis tests as aids to generalizations.

21.2 HYPOTHESIS TESTS OR CONFIDENCE INTERVALS?

Traditionally, in the behavioral sciences, hypothesis tests have been preferred to confidence intervals, and that preference probably would be expressed by the counselor if he or she chooses to conduct an investigation rather than a survey. For example, suspecting that the early years of marriage are both more stressful and more likely to produce clients for marital therapy, the counselor might use a *t* test to determine whether the mean number of years of marital relationships for a randomly selected group of clients is significantly less than that for a randomly selected group of nonclients.

The present review, as summarized in **Figure 21.1**, also reflects this preference for hypothesis tests, even though, if the null hypothesis is rejected, you should consider estimating the possible size of an effect or true difference with a confidence interval or other estimates of effect size, such as d, η^2, or ϕ_c^2.

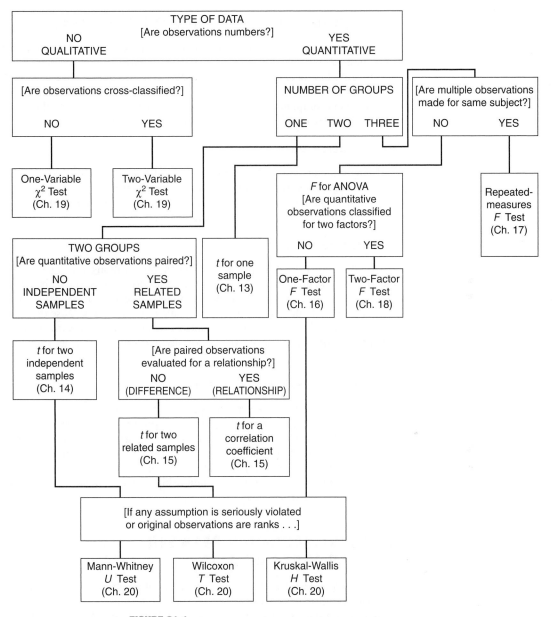

FIGURE 21.1

Guidelines for selecting the appropriate hypothesis test.

21.3 QUANTITATIVE OR QUALITATIVE DATA?

When attempting to identify the appropriate hypothesis test for a given situation, first decide whether observations are quantitative or qualitative. More specifically, first decide whether the observations are quantitative because they are numbers that reflect an amount or a count (with an interval/ratio level of measurement) or qualitative because they are words or codes that reflect classes or categories (with a nominal or ordinal level of measurement).

Quantitative Data

Being numbers that reflect a count, years of marital relationships are quantitative observations with interval/ratio measurement. *When observations are quantitative, the appropriate statistical test should be selected from the various t or F tests or from their nonparametric counterparts,* as described later.

Qualitative Data

To illustrate the other possibility, when observations are qualitative and measurement is nominal, assume that the counselor wishes to test the prevalent notion that females are more likely than males to seek professional help. Now, clients are merely designated as either female or male, and because these observations reflect classes, they are qualitative. *When observations are qualitative, the appropriate test is either a one- or two-variable χ^2 test,* as suggested in Figure 21.1.

One- or Two-Variable χ^2 Test?

If qualitative observations are categorized in terms of only one variable, as in the present case, the one-variable χ^2 test is appropriate. If, however, qualitative observations are cross-classified in terms of two variables, the two-variable χ^2 test is appropriate. For example, clients could be cross-classified in terms of both gender (female or male) and the marital status of their parents (married or separated) in order to test for any relationship between clients' gender and the marital status of their parents.

21.4 DISTINGUISHING BETWEEN THE TWO TYPES OF DATA

The distinction between quantitative and qualitative observations is crucial, and it is usually fairly easy, as suggested earlier. *First, always make the distinction between quantitative and qualitative data.* In those cases where you feel uncomfortable about making this distinction, consider the following guidelines:

Focusing on a Single Observation

When you have access to the original observations, focus on any *single* observation. If an observation represents an amount or a count, expressed numerically, it is quantitative; if it represents a class or category, described by a word or a code, it is qualitative.

Focusing on Numerical Summaries

When you do not have access to the original observations, focus on any numerical summaries specified for the data. If means and standard deviations are specified, the data are quantitative; if only frequencies are specified, the data are qualitative.

Focusing on Key Words

When, as in the case of the questions at the end of this chapter, you have neither access to the original observations nor numerical summaries of data, read the description of the study very carefully, attending to key words, such as *scores* or *means,* which, if present, typify quantitative data or, if absent, typify qualitative data.

If All Else Fails

If all else fails, try *visualizing* the value of a single observation, whether a meaningful number (quantitative) or a word or numerical code (qualitative), based on any information given. A careful evaluation, combined with an occasional speculation, usually reveals whether data are quantitative or qualitative.

21.5 ONE, TWO, OR MORE GROUPS?

Given that observations such as the years of marital relationships are quantitative, either *t* or *F* tests are appropriate, assuming that no assumption is seriously violated. Now, the key issue is whether there are one, two, or more groups.

One Group

If only one group is involved, then a *t* test for a single population mean is appropriate. For example, the counselor determines whether, among the population of clients, the mean number of years of their marital relationships differs from a specific number, such as seven years, to evaluate the popularly acclaimed "seven-year itch" as a source of marital stress.

Two Groups

If, as suggested previously, the counselor wishes to determine whether the mean number of years of marital relationships for clients is significantly less than that for a group of nonclients, two groups are involved and a *t* test is appropriate. In the absence of any pairing, the two samples are independent, and the appropriate *t* test is for two population means (with independent samples).

Mean Difference or Correlation?

If observations are paired, the appropriate *t* test depends on the intent of the investigator—whether there is a concern about a mean difference or a correlation. If the paired observations are evaluated for a significant mean difference, the appropriate *t* test is for two population means (with related samples). This would be the case if, for example, each client is paired or matched with a particular nonclient, possibly based on their chronological age and income, and then a *t* test is based on the mean difference in marital years between clients and nonclients.

If, on the other hand, the paired observations are being evaluated for a significant correlation, the appropriate *t* test is for a population correlation coefficient. This would be the case if the correlation between years of courtship and years of marriage for clients were tested, possibly to determine whether, for instance, there's a tendency for short courtships to be associated with early marital difficulties.

More Than Two Groups with Repeated Measures

If the counselor wishes to determine whether scores on an anxiety test change for the *same* group of clients at three different times (the initial group meeting, the final group meeting, and six months after the final group meeting), the *F* test for repeated-measures ANOVA would be appropriate.

More Than Two Groups with One or Two Factors

If the counselor wishes to determine whether significant differences exist among the mean years of marital relationships for three randomly selected groups of clients with different ethnic backgrounds—African-American, Asian-American, and Hispanic—three population means along a single factor are involved, and the *F* test for one-factor ANOVA is appropriate. If, however, the mean years of marital relationships are evaluated according to the levels of two factors—for instance, according to both ethnic background and gender—then the *F* test for two-factor ANOVA is appropriate.

21.6 CONCLUDING COMMENTS

Nonparametric Tests

Figure 21.1 also includes the various nonparametric counterparts for selected *t* and *F* tests. Since these nonparametric tests are less likely to detect any effect, they are to be used only in those rare instances when some assumption is seriously violated or when the original observations are ranked.

Use Figure 21.1

This chapter concludes with a series of questions that require you to identify the appropriate statistical test from among those discussed in this book. Figure 21.1 should serve as a helpful guide when you're answering these questions. For ease of reference, Figure 21.1 also appears inside the back book cover.

REVIEW QUESTIONS

Note: Decide first whether data are quantitative or qualitative. Unless mentioned otherwise, no assumption has been seriously violated, and, therefore, the appropriate test should be selected from among *t*, *F*, or χ^2 tests. Specify the precise form of the test. For example, specify that the *t* test is for two population means with related samples, or that the χ^2 test is for two variables, or that the F test is for repeated measures.

*21.1   A political scientist wishes to determine whether males and females differ with respect to their attitudes toward the funding of energy conservation programs by the federal government. She randomly selects equal numbers of males and females and asks each person if he or she thinks that the current level of federal funding of energy conservation should be increased, remain the same, or be decreased.

*21.2   Another political scientist also wishes to determine, in more detail, whether males or females differ with respect to their attitudes toward the funding of energy conservation programs by the federal government. He randomly selects equal numbers of males and females. After being informed about the current budget for these programs, each person is asked to estimate, to the nearest one hundred million dollars, an appropriate level of spending.

*21.3   To determine whether speed reading influences reading comprehension, a researcher obtains two reading comprehension scores for each student in a group of high school students, once before and once after training in speed reading.

Answers on page 527.

21.4   Another investigator criticizes the design of the previous study, saying that high school students should have been randomly assigned to either the special training condition or a control condition and tested just once at the end of the study. Subsequently, she conducts this study.

*21.5   An educator wishes to determine whether chance can reasonably account for the fact that 40 of the top 100 students come from the northern district (rather than the eastern, southern, or western districts) of a large metropolitan school district.

*21.6   To determine whether a new sleeping pill has an effect that varies with dosage, a researcher randomly assigns adult insomniacs, in equal numbers, to receive either 0, 4, or 8 grams of the sleeping pill. The amount of sleeping time is measured for each subject during an eight-hour period after the administration of the dosage.

Answers on page 527.

21.7   An investigator wishes to test whether creative artists are equally likely to be born under each of the 12 astrological signs.

21.8   To determine whether there is a relationship between the sexual codes of primitive tribes and their behavior toward neighboring tribes, an anthropologist consults available records, classifying each tribe on the basis of its sexual codes (permissive or repressive) and its behavior toward neighboring tribes (friendly or hostile).

*21.9   In a study of group problem solving, a researcher randomly assigns college students either to unstructured groups of 2, 3, or 4 students (without a designated leader) or to structured groups of 2, 3, or 4 students (with a designated leader) and measures the amount of time required to solve a complex puzzle.

*21.10   A school psychologist compares the reading comprehension scores of migrant children who, as a result of random assignment, are enrolled in either a special bilingual reading program or a traditional reading program.

*21.11   Another school psychologist wishes to determine whether reading comprehension scores are associated with the number of months of formal education, as reported on school transcripts, for a group of 12-year-old migrant children.

Answers on page 527.

21.12   Over a century ago, the British surgeon Joseph Lister investigated the relationship between the operating room environment (presence or absence of disinfectant) and the fate of about 100 emergency amputees (survived or failed to survive).

21.13   A comparative psychologist suspects that chemicals in the urine of male rats trigger an increase in the activity of other rats. To check this hunch, she randomly assigns rats, in equal numbers, to either a sterile cage, a cage sprayed with a trace of the chemicals, or a cage sprayed thoroughly with the chemicals. Furthermore, to check out the possibility that reactions might be sex-linked, equal numbers of female and male rats are assigned to the three cage conditions. An activity score is recorded for each rat during a five-minute observation period in the specified cage.

21.14   A psychologist wishes to evaluate the effectiveness of relaxation training on the subsequent performance of college students in a public speaking class. After being matched on the basis of the quality of their initial speeches, students are randomly assigned either to receive relaxation training or to serve in a control group. Evaluation is based on scores awarded to students for their speeches at the end of the class.

21.15   An investigator wishes to determine whether, for a random sample of drug addicts, the mean score on the depression scale of a personality test differs from that which, according to the test documentation, represents the mean score for the general population.

21.16   Another investigator wishes to determine whether, for a random sample of drug addicts, the mean score on the depression scale of a personality test differs from the corresponding mean score for a random sample of nonaddicted people.

21.17   To determine whether cramming can increase GRE scores, a researcher randomly assigns college students to either a specialized GRE test-taking workshop, a general test-taking workshop, or a control (non-test-taking) workshop. Furthermore, to check the effect of scheduling, students are randomly assigned, in equal numbers, to attend their workshop either during a marathon weekend or during a series of weekly sessions.

21.18   A criminologist suspects that there is a relationship between the degree of structure provided for paroled ex-convicts (a supervised or unsupervised "rehab" house) and whether or not there is a violation of parole during the first six months of freedom.

21.19   A psychologist uses chimpanzees to test the notion that more crowded living conditions cause aggressive behavior. The same chimps live in a succession of cages containing either one, several, or many other chimps. After several days in each cage, chimps are assigned scores on the basis of their aggressive behavior toward a chimplike stuffed doll in an observation cage.

21.20   In an extrasensory perception experiment involving a deck of special playing cards, each of 30 subjects attempts to predict the one correct pattern (on each playing card) from among five possible patterns during each of 100 trials. The mean number of correct predictions for all 30 subjects is compared with 20, the number of correct predictions per 100 trials on the assumption that subjects lack extrasensory perception.

21.21   A social scientist wishes to determine whether there is a relationship between the attractiveness scores (on a 100-point scale) assigned to college students by a panel of peers and their scores on a paper-and-pencil test of anxiety.

APPENDIX A

Math Review

This appendix summarizes many of the basic math symbols and operations used in this book. Little, if any, of this material will be entirely new, but—possibly because of years of little or no use—much may seem only slightly familiar. In any event, it's important that you master this material.

First, take the pretest in Section A.1, comparing your answers with those in Section A.9. Whenever errors occur, study the review section indicated for that set of answers. Then, after browsing through all review sections, take the posttest in Section A.8, again checking your answers with those in Section A.9. If you're still making lots of errors, repeat the entire process, spending even more time studying the various review sections. If errors persist, consult your instructor for additional guidance.

A.1 PRETEST

Questions 1–6 Are the following statements true or false?

1. $(5)(4) = 20$ **2.** $4 > 6$ **3.** $7 \leq 10$ **4.** $|-5| = 5$

5. $(8)^2 = 56$ **6.** $\sqrt{9} = 3$

Questions 7–30 Find the answers.

7. $\dfrac{5-3}{2-1} =$ **8.** $\sqrt{5+4+7} =$ **9.** $3(4+3) =$

10. $16 - \dfrac{10}{\sqrt{25}} =$ **11.** $(3)^2(10) - 4 =$ **12.** $[3^2 + 2^2]^2 =$

13. $\sqrt{\dfrac{2(3) - 2^2}{5 - 3}} =$ **14.** $\sqrt{\dfrac{(8-6)^2 + (5-3)^2}{2}} =$

15. $2 + 4 + (-1) =$ **16.** $5 - (3) =$ **17.** $2 + 7 + (-8) + (-3) =$

18. $5 - (-1) =$ **19.** $(-4)(-3) =$ **20.** $(-5)(6) =$

21. $\dfrac{-10}{2} =$ **22.** $\dfrac{4}{5} - \dfrac{1}{5} =$ **23.** $\dfrac{1}{4} + \dfrac{2}{5} =$

24. $\dfrac{2^2}{4} + \dfrac{3^2}{3} - \dfrac{2^2}{8} =$ **25.** $\left(\dfrac{2}{3}\right)\left(\dfrac{6}{7}\right) =$ **26.** $\sqrt{16 + 9} =$

27. $\sqrt{(4)(9)} =$ **28.** $\sqrt{4}\sqrt{9} =$ **29.** $\dfrac{\sqrt{25}}{\sqrt{100}} =$ **30.** $\sqrt{\dfrac{25}{100}} =$

Questions 31–35 Round to the nearest hundredth.

31. 98.769   **32.** 3.274   **33.** 23.765   **34.** 5476.375003

35. 54.1499

A.2 COMMON SYMBOLS

SYMBOL	MEANING	EXAMPLE
$\neq$	doesn't equal	$4 \neq 2$
$\pm$	plus and minus	$4 \pm 2 = 4 + 2$ and $4 - 2$
( )( )	times (multiplication)*	$(3)(2) = 3(2) = 6$
/, ( )/( )	divided by (division)	$6/2 = 3$, $(8)/(2) = 4$
>	greater than	$4 > 3$
<	less than	$5 < 8$
$\geq$	equal or greater than	$z \geq 2$
$\leq$	equal or less than	$t \leq 4$
$\sqrt{}$	the square root of**	$\sqrt{9} = 3$
$(\ )^2$	the square of	$(4)^2 = (4)(4) = 16$
| |	the absolute (positive) value of	$\|4\| = 4$, $\|-4\| = 4$
…	continuing the pattern	$1, 2, 3, …, 8$
		translates as: 1, 2, 3, 4, 5, 6, 7, 8

*When multiplication involves symbols, parentheses can be dropped. For instance, $(X)(Y) = X(Y) = XY$.
**The square root of a number is that number which, when multiplied by itself, yields the original number.

A.3 ORDER OF OPERATIONS

Expressions should be treated as single numbers when they appear in parentheses, square root signs, or in the top (or bottom) of fractions.

EXAMPLES

$$2(4 - 1) = 2(3) = 6$$

$$\sqrt{12 - 8} = \sqrt{4} = 2$$

$$\frac{8 - 4}{2 + 2} = \frac{4}{4} = 1$$

If all expressions contain single numbers, the order for performing operations is as follows:

1. square or square root
2. multiplication or division
3. addition or subtraction

EXAMPLES

$$10 + \frac{6}{\sqrt{4}} = 10 + \frac{6}{2} = 10 + 3 = 13$$

$$(3)(2)^2 - 1 = (3)(4) - 1 = 12 - 1 = 11$$

When expressions are nested, one within the other, work outward from the inside.

EXAMPLES

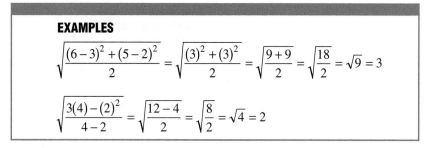

$$\sqrt{\frac{(6-3)^2 + (5-2)^2}{2}} = \sqrt{\frac{(3)^2 + (3)^2}{2}} = \sqrt{\frac{9+9}{2}} = \sqrt{\frac{18}{2}} = \sqrt{9} = 3$$

$$\sqrt{\frac{3(4) - (2)^2}{4-2}} = \sqrt{\frac{12-4}{2}} = \sqrt{\frac{8}{2}} = \sqrt{4} = 2$$

A.4 POSITIVE AND NEGATIVE NUMBERS

In the absence of any sign, a number is understood to be positive.

EXAMPLE

$8 = +8$

To *add* numbers with unlike signs,

1. find two separate sums, one for all positive numbers and the other for all negative numbers
2. find the difference between these two sums
3. attach the sign of the larger sum

EXAMPLE

$2 + 3 + (-4) + (-3) = 5 + (-7) = -2$

To *subtract* one number from another,

1. change the sign of the number to be subtracted
2. proceed as in addition

EXAMPLES

$4 - (3) = 4 + (-3) = 1$

$4 - (-3) = 4 + 3 = 7$

To *multiply* (or *divide*) two signed numbers,

1. obtain the numerical result
2. attach a positive sign if the two original numbers have like signs or a negative sign if the two original numbers have unlike signs

EXAMPLES

$(-4)(-2) = 8;\ (4)(-2) = -8$

$\dfrac{4}{2} = 2;\ \dfrac{-4}{2} = -2$

A.5 FRACTIONS

A fraction consists of an upper part, the numerator, and a lower part, the denominator.

To *add* (or *subtract*) fractions, their denominators must be the same.

1. If denominators are the same, merely add (or subtract) numbers in the numerators and leave the number in the denominator unchanged.

EXAMPLES

$\dfrac{3}{5} + \dfrac{1}{5} = \dfrac{3+1}{5} = \dfrac{4}{5}$

$\dfrac{7}{10} - \dfrac{3}{10} = \dfrac{7+(-3)}{10} = \dfrac{4}{10}$

2. If denominators are different, first find a common denominator. To obtain a common denominator, multiply both parts of each fraction by the denominators of all remaining fractions. Then proceed as in (1) above.

EXAMPLES

$\dfrac{2}{3} + \dfrac{1}{4} = \dfrac{(4)2}{(4)3} + \dfrac{(3)1}{(3)4} = \dfrac{8}{12} + \dfrac{3}{12} = \dfrac{11}{12}$

$\dfrac{4}{6} + \dfrac{2}{5} = \dfrac{(5)4}{(5)6} + \dfrac{(6)2}{(6)5} = \dfrac{20}{30} + \dfrac{12}{30} = \dfrac{32}{30}$

To *add* (or *subtract*) fractions, sometimes it's more efficient to follow a different procedure. First, express each fraction as a decimal number—by dividing the denominator into the numerator—and then merely add (or subtract) the resulting decimal numbers.

EXAMPLES

$$\frac{3}{4} - \frac{1}{4} = .75 - .25 = .50$$

$$\frac{3}{10} + \frac{2}{6} + \frac{1}{5} = .30 + .33 + .20 = .83$$

To multiply fractions, multiply all numerators to obtain the new numerator, and multiply all denominators to obtain the new denominator.

EXAMPLES

$$\left(\frac{2}{3}\right)\left(\frac{3}{5}\right) = \frac{6}{15}$$

$$\left(\frac{2}{4}\right)\left(\frac{3}{4}\right) = \frac{6}{16}$$

A.6 SQUARE ROOT RADICALS ($\sqrt{\ }$)

The square root of a sum *doesn't* equal the sum of the square roots.

EXAMPLES

$$\sqrt{16 + 9} \neq \sqrt{16} + \sqrt{9}$$
$$5 \neq 4 + 3$$

The square root of a product equals the product of the square roots.

EXAMPLE

$$\sqrt{(4)(9)} = \left(\sqrt{4}\right)\left(\sqrt{9}\right) = (2)(3) = 6$$

The square root of a fraction equals the square root of the numerator divided by the square root of the denominator.

EXAMPLE

$$\sqrt{\frac{4}{16}} = \frac{\sqrt{4}}{\sqrt{16}} = \frac{2}{4}$$

A.7 ROUNDING NUMBERS

When the first term of the number to be dropped is 5 or more, increase the remaining number by one unit. Otherwise, leave the remaining number unchanged. In this book, for purposes of standardization, numbers are usually rounded to the nearest hundredth.

> **EXAMPLES**
> When rounding to the nearest hundredth:
>   21.86<u>6</u> rounds to 21.87
>   37.36<u>4</u> rounds to 37.36
>   102.64<u>5</u>332 rounds to 102.65
>   87.98<u>4</u>97 rounds to 87.98
>   52.10<u>5</u>000 rounds to 52.11

A.8 POSTTEST

Questions 101–112 Find the answers.

101. $\sqrt{36} =$ **102.** $|24| =$ **103.** $(7)^2 =$ **104.** $5 \pm 3 =$

105. $3\sqrt{8 - (2)^2} =$ **106.** $\dfrac{1^2 + 4^2 + 5^2}{4^2 - 3^2} =$ **107.** $18 - (-3) =$

108. $(-10)(-8)$ **109.** $\dfrac{3}{5} + \dfrac{2}{8} =$ **110.** $\dfrac{(2-3)^2}{2} + \dfrac{(6-4)^2}{3} =$

111. $\sqrt{9 + 9 + 9 + 9} =$ **112.** $\sqrt{25}\sqrt{4} =$

Questions 113–114 Round to the nearest hundredth.

113. 107.455   **114.** 3.2499

A.9 ANSWERS (WITH RELEVANT REVIEW SECTIONS)

Pretest

1. True
2. False
3. True   } Review Section A.2
4. True
5. False
6. True

7. 2
8. $\sqrt{16} = 4$ } Review Section A.3
9. 21
10. 14

11. 86
12. $(13)^2 = 169$
13. $\sqrt{1} = 1$
14. $\sqrt{4} = 2$
} Review Section A.3

15. 5
16. 2
17. −2
18. 6
19. 12
20. −30
21. −5
} Review Section A.4

22. $\dfrac{3}{5}$ or .60

23. $\dfrac{13}{20}$ or .65

24. $\dfrac{84}{24}$ or 3.5

25. $\dfrac{12}{21}$
} Review Section A.5

26. 5
27. 6
28. 6
29. $\dfrac{1}{2}$

30. $\dfrac{1}{2}$
} Review Section A.6

31. 98.77
32. 3.27
33. 23.77
34. 5476.38
35. 54.15
} Review Section A.7

Posttest

101. 6
102. 24
103. 49
104. 8 and 2
} Review Section A.2

105. 6
106. 6
} Review Section A.3

107. 21
108. 80
} Review Section A.4

109. $\dfrac{34}{40}$ or .85

110. $\dfrac{11}{6}$ or 1.83
} Review Section A.5

111. 6
112. 10
} Review Section A.6

113. 107.46
114. 3.25
} Review Section A.7

B

Answers to Selected Questions

ANSWERS TO SELECTED QUESTIONS

Chapter 1

1.1 **(a)** descriptive statistics   **(c)** descriptive statistics
     (b) inferential statistics   **(d)** inferential statistics

1.2 **(a)** E   **(e)** E
     (b) S   **(f)** S
     (c) S   **(g)** E
     (d) E   **(h)** E

1.3 **(a)** qualitative   **(f)** quantitative
     (b) quantitative   **(g)** quantitative
     (c) quantitative   **(h)** ranked
     (d) qualitative   **(i)** qualitative
     (e) qualitative   **(j)** quantitative

1.4 **(a)** interval/ratio   **(e)** ordinal
     (b) nominal   **(f)** nominal
     (c) approximately interval   **(g)** approximately interval
     (d) interval/ratio   **(h)** nominal

1.5 **(a)** discrete   **(e)** continuous
     (b) continuous   **(f)** discrete
     (c) discrete   **(g)** continuous
     (d) continuous

1.6 **(a)** observational study
     (b) experiment (independent variable: prescribed hours of sleep deprivation)
     (c) experiment (independent variable: two programs; possible confounding variable: self-selection of program)
     (d) observational study
     (e) experiment (independent variable: different rehabilitation programs)
     (f) experiment (independent variable: on campus or off campus)

Chapter 2

2.1

RATING	TALLY*	f
10	/	1
9	//	2
8	///	3
7	⊬⊬	5
6	//	2
5	//	2
4	/	1
3	⊬⊬ /	6
2	//	2
1	/	1
	Total	25

* Tally column usually is omitted from the finished table.

2.2 (a) Calculating the class width,

$$\frac{123 - 69}{10} = \frac{54}{10} = 5.4$$

Round off to a convenient number, such as 5.

IQ	TALLY*	f
120–124	/	1
115–119		0
110–114	//	2
105–109	///	3
100–104	₦//	4
95–99	₦// /	6
90–94	//// //	7
85–89	////	4
80–84	///	3
75–79	///	3
70–74	/	1
65–69	/	1
	Total	35

* Tally column usually is omitted from the
finished table.

(b) 64.5–69.5

2.3 Not all observations can be assigned to one and only one class (because of gap between 20–22 and 25–30 and overlap between 25–30 and 30–34). All classes are not equal in width (25–30 versus 30–34). All classes do not have both boundaries (35–above).

2.4 Outliers are a summer income of $25,700; an age of 61; and a family size of 18. No outliers for GPA.

2.5

GRE	RELATIVE f
725–749	.01
700–724	.02
675–699	.07
650–674	.15
625–649	.17
600–624	.21
575–599	.15
550–574	.14
525–549	.07*
500–524	.02
475–499	.01
	Totals 1.02

* From 13/200 = .065, which rounds to .07.

2.6

GRE	(a) CUMULATIVE f	(b) CUMULATIVE PERCENT(%)
725–749	200	100
700–724	199	100
675–699	196	98
650–674	182	91
625–649	152	76
600–624	118	59
575–599	76	38
550–574	46	23
525–549	19	10
500–524	6	3
475–499	2	1

2.7 The approximate percentile rank for weights between 200 and 209 lbs is 92 (because 92 is the cumulative percent for this interval).

2.8

MOVIE RATINGS	(a) f	(b) RELATIVE f (%)	(c) CUMULATIVE f
NC-17	2	10	20
R	4	20	18
PG-13	3	15	14
PG	8	40	11
G	3	15	3
Totals	20	100%	

(d) Percentile rank for films with a PG rating is 55 (from $\frac{11}{20}$ multiplied by 100).

2.9

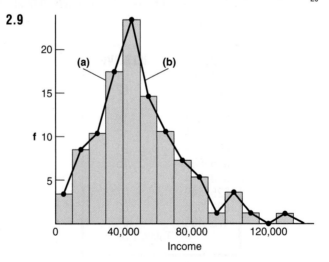

NOTE: Ordinarily, only either **(a)** a histogram, or **(b)** a frequency polygon would be shown. When closing the left flank of **(b)**, imagine extending a line to the midpoint of the first unoccupied class (−10,000 to −1) on the left, but stop the line at the vertical axis, as shown.

(c) Lopsided.

2.10

7	8				
8	5	8			
9	8	9	6		
10	8	2	9	6	4
11	8	7	1	3	
12	0	6	3	4	
13	2	7			
14	1	3			

NOTE: The *order* of the leaves within each stem depends on whether you entered IQ scores column by column (as above) or row by row.

2.11 (a) Positively skewed   **(d)** Bimodal
(b) Normal   **(e)** Negatively skewed
(c) Positively skewed

2.12

2.13 (a) Widths of two rightmost bars aren't the same as those of two leftmost bars.
(b) Histogram is more appropriate, assuming numbers are for a continuous quantitative variable.
(c) Height of the vertical axis is too small relative to the width of the horizontal axis, causing the histogram to be squashed.
(d) Poorly selected frequency scale along the vertical axis, causing the histogram to be squashed.

(e) Bars have unequal widths. There are no wiggly lines along vertical axis indicating a break between 0 and 50.

(f) Height of the vertical axis is too large relative to the horizontal axis, causing the differences between the bars to be exaggerated.

2.15 (a)

AGE	SMALL TOWN RELATIVE f (%)	U.S. POPULATION RELATIVE f (%)
65–above	21	12
60–64	11	4
55–59	9	5
50–54	8	7
45–49	9	7
40–44	8	8
35–39	6	7
30–34	5	7
25–29	5	7
20–24	4	7
15–19	4	7
10–14	4	7
5–9	3	7
0–4	3	7
Totals	100%	99%

(b) Among small-town residents, there are relatively more older people and relatively fewer younger people.

(c)

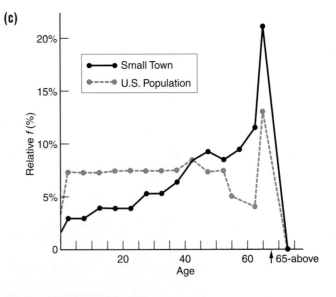

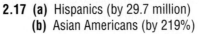

2.17 (a) Hispanics (by 29.7 million)

(b) Asian Americans (by 219%)

(c) Whites increased by 10% while the general population increased by 31%.

(d) Asian American and Hispanic populations are growing most rapidly. (Or some variation on this conclusion, such as that the non-white population is growing more rapidly than the white population.)

Chapter 3

3.1 mode = 63

3.2 mode = 27.4

3.3 median = 63

3.4 median = 27.15 (halfway between 26.9 and 27.4)

3.5 mean = $\frac{672}{11}$ = 61.09

3.6 mean = $\frac{163.3}{6}$ = 27.22

3.7 (a) negatively skewed because the median exceeds the mean
(b) positively skewed because the mean exceeds the median
(c) positively skewed
(d) negatively skewed

3.8 mode = DB (Daytona Beach)
Impossible to find the median when qualitative data are unordered, with only nominal measurement.

3.9 mode = 3
median = 3
mean = 3.28

3.12 Two different averages are being used to describe the central tendency in a skewed distribution of pilots' salaries. Management is probably using the mean (because of its concern about total expenditures), while the pilots' union is probably using the median (because of its concern about the actual salaries of typical, middle-ranked pilots).

Chapter 4

4.1 (a) $80,000 to $100,000
(b) $70,000
(c) $110,000
(d) $88,000 to $92,000; $86,000; $94,000

4.2 (a) False. Relatively few students will score exactly one standard deviation from the mean.
(b) False. Students will score both *within* and *beyond* one standard deviation from the mean.
(c) True
(d) True
(e) False. See (b).
(f) True

4.3 $s = \sqrt{\dfrac{(1-3)^2 - (3-3)^2 + (4-3)^2 + (4-3)^2}{4-1}} = \sqrt{\dfrac{6}{3}} = 1.41$

4.4 (a) $\sigma = \sqrt{\dfrac{137 - \dfrac{729}{8}}{8}} = \sqrt{5.73} = 2.39$

(b) $s = \sqrt{\dfrac{325 - \dfrac{1849}{9}}{9-1}} = \sqrt{14.95} = 3.87$

4.5 (a) 18 hours
(b) 23 hours
(c) $df = 1$ in **(a)** and $df = 3$ in **(b)**
(d) When all observations are expressed as deviations from their mean, the sum of all deviations must equal zero.

4.6 (a) range = 25; $IQR = 65 - 60 = 5$
(b) range = 11; $IQR = 4 - 1 = 3$

4.7 (a) a_1 larger than a_2. Graduating high school seniors with very low SAT scores tend not to become college freshmen.
(b) b_1 larger than b_2
(c) c_2 larger than c_1
(d) about the same
(e) e_1 larger than e_2
(f) f_2 larger than f_1

4.11 (a) A $70 per month raise would increase the original mean (by $70) but would not change the original standard deviation. Raising everyone's pay by a constant amount has no effect on variability.
(b) A 5 percent per month increase would increase both the original mean and the standard deviation (by 5 percent). Raising everyone's pay by 5 percent generates a larger raise in actual dollars for higher-paid employees and thus increases variability among monthly wages.

4.16 (a) False. Degrees of freedom refer to the number of values free to vary in the sample, not in the population.
(b) True
(c) True
(d) False. All observations are assumed to be equal in quality. Degrees of freedom are introduced because of mathematical restrictions when sample observations are used to estimate a population characteristic.

Chapter 5

NOTE: Answers reflect the complete tabular entry—for instance, .0571, rather than the usual procedure of rounding answers to two digits to the right of the decimal point.

5.1 **(a)** 2.33 **(d)** 0.00
(b) −0.30 **(e)** −1.50
(c) −1.60

5.2 **(a)** .0359 **(d)** .4505
(b) .1664 **(e)** .4750
(c) .0013

5.3 (a_1) **(b_1)** C′ **(c_1)** $z = -1.00$
answer = .1587

(a_2) **(b_2)** C **(c_2)** $z = 1.50$
answer = .0668

(a_3) **(b_3)** .5000 + B **(c_3)** $z = 2.00$
answer = .5000 + .4772
= .9772

5.5

(a_1) **(b_1)** C **(c_1)** $z = 0.70$
.2420

(a_2) **(b_2)** .5000 + B **(c_2)** $z = 0.15$
.5000 + .0596 = .5596

(a_3) **(b_3)** larger B − **(c_3)** $z = 0.20$; $z = 0.40$
smaller B .1554 − .0793 = .0761
or larger C − or .4207 − .3446 = .0761
smaller C

(a_4) **(b_4)** B′ + B **(c_4)** $z = -0.30$; $z = 0.20$
.1179 + .0793 = .1972

(a_5) **(b_5)** C **(c_5)** $z = 0.50$
.3085

(a_6) **(b_6)** C′ + C **(c_6)** $z = -1.00$; $z = 1.00$
or 2(C) .1587 + .1587 = .3174

(a_7) **(b_7)** B′ + B **(c_7)** $z = -0.50$; $z = 0.50$
or 2(B) .1915 + .1915 = .3830

5.6 **(a)** 1200 + (−2.33)(120) = 920.40
(b) 1200 + (0.00)(120) = 1200
(c) 1200 + (1.65)(120) = 1398
or 1200 + (1.64)(120) = 1396.80
(d) 1200 + (−1.41)(120) = 1030.80

5.7 **(a)** 0.33 **(c)** 0.75
(b) −0.20 **(d)** 0.40

5.8 **(a)** A test score of 45 from distribution **c** because it converts to the largest
z score (0.75).
(b) Distribution **b**, because it yields a larger z score (2.40) than any other
distribution.

5.9

	$\mu = 0;$ $\sigma = 1$	$\mu = 50;$ $\sigma = 10$	$\mu = 100;$ $\sigma = 15$	$\mu = 500;$ $\sigma = 100$
(a)	0.80	58	112	580
(b)	−1.67	33.3	74.95	333

5.10 (a) mean   **(h)** mean   **(o)** mean
      (b) standard deviation   **(i)** standard deviation   **(p)** standard deviation
      (c) z **(j)** one   **(q)** z
      (d) standard deviations   **(k)** .5000 or $\frac{1}{2}$ **(r)** negative
      (e) above   **(l)** mean   **(s)** decimal
      (f) below   **(m)** beyond   **(t)** z (or standard)
      (g) one   **(n)** negative

5.14 (a) $83 + (-1.64)(20) = 50.2$
           or $83 + (-1.65)(20) = 50$
      (b) .9599
      (c) .1357
      (d) $83 + (\pm 2.33)(20) = \begin{cases} 129.6 \\ 36.4 \end{cases}$
      (e) .2896
      (f) $83 + (\pm 1.96)(20) = \begin{cases} 122.2 \\ 43.8 \end{cases}$
      (g) .7021
      (h) $83 + (0.84)(20) = 99.8$
      (i) $83 + (\pm 1.88)(20) = \begin{cases} 120.6 \\ 45.4 \end{cases}$
      (j) .8643
      (k) 0 since *exactly* 61 equals 61.000 etc. to infinity, a point along the base of the normal curve that is associated with no area under the normal curve.

Chapter 6

6.1 (a) Positive. The crime rate is higher, square mile by square mile, in densely populated cities than in sparsely populated rural areas.
      (b) Negative. As TV viewing increases, performance on academic achievement tests tends to decline.
      (c) Negative. Increases in car weight are accompanied by decreases in miles per gallon.
      (d) Positive. Increases in educational level—grade school, high school, college—tend to be associated with increases in income.
      (e) Positive. Highly anxious people willingly spend more time performing a simple repetitive task than do less anxious people.

6.2 (a) I, D, F   **(c)** E, H
      (b) B, H, E   **(d)** No. The relationship is positive.

6.3 (a) Cars with more total miles tend to have lower resale values.
      (b) Students with more absences from school tend to score lower on math achievement tests.

(c) Little or no relationship between anxiety level and college GPA.

(d) Older schoolchildren tend to have better reading comprehension.

6.4 (a) simple cause-effect (c) complex

  (b) complex (d) complex

6.5 (a) 2 (b) above (c) $1\frac{1}{2}$ (d) below (e) $\frac{1}{3}$ (f) above

6.6 (a) 2 (b) below (c) $1\frac{1}{2}$ (d) above (e) $\frac{1}{3}$ (f) below

6.7 $r = \dfrac{4}{\sqrt{(4)(9.33)}} = .65$

6.8 (a) No. The new correlation would have the same numerical value but the opposite sign, that is, it would equal $-.2981$. The change from positive to negative reflects the original tendency for males, the group now with the larger code of 2, to have lower high school GPAs.

  (b) Yes. The new negative correlation still reflects the original tendency of females, now coded as 1, to have higher high school GPAs than males, now coded as 2.

  (c) Yes. The actual numerical value of the correlation, .2981, reflects only the pattern of predictability across pairs of z scores which, in turn, show no traces of the arbitrary codes assigned to females and males. The positive value of r reflects only the relatively higher coding of females (20) than males (10).

  (d) Ten. The fifth variable would add four new correlations to the original six.

6.10 (a) False. This statement would be true only if a perfect negative relationship (-1.00) described the relationship between TV viewing time and test scores.

  (b) False. Correlation does not necessarily signify cause-effect.

  (c) True

  (d) True

  (e) False. See (b).

  (f) False. Although correlation does not necessarily signify cause-effect, it opens the *possibility* of cause-effect.

Chapter 7

7.1 (a) approximately 5–6 percent

  (b) approximately 2–3 percent

7.2 (a) $b = \sqrt{\dfrac{50}{25}}(.30) = .42;\ a = 8 - (.42)(13) = 2.54$

  (b) $Y' = (.42)(15) + 2.54 = 8.84$

  (c) $Y' = (.42)(11) + 2.54 = 7.16$

7.3 (a) $s_{Y|X} = \sqrt{\dfrac{50\left(1-[.30]^2\right)}{35-2}} = \sqrt{\dfrac{50(.91)}{33}} = \sqrt{1.38} = 1.17$

  (b) Roughly indicates the average amount by which the prediction is in error.

7.4 **(a)** No, because the observed decline could be due to regression toward the mean, given that the students scored high on the anxiety test prior to attending the clinic.

(b) An experiment where students who score high on the anxiety test are randomly assigned either to attend the stress-reduction clinic or to be in a control group.

7.8 **(a)** True

(b) False. Sons of short fathers will tend to be taller than their fathers but still shorter than the mean for all sons.

(c) False. Regression toward the mean is only a tendency, so there will be exceptions.

(d) False. Taken as an entire group, adult sons will be as tall as their fathers. (In fact, a comparison of entire groups might reveal that sons tend to be slightly taller because of an improvement in nutrition across generations.)

(e) False. *Given the subset of tall sons,* their fathers will tend to be shorter because of regression toward the mean.

(f) True

Chapter 8

8.1 **(a)** Yes

(b) No. Citizens of Wyoming aren't a subset of citizens of New York.

(c) Yes

(d) No. All U.S. presidents aren't a subset of all registered Republicans.

(e) Yes

8.2 Expressions in **8.1(c)** and **8.1(e)** involve hypothetical populations.

8.3 **(a)** False. Sometimes, just by chance, a random sample of 10 cards fails to represent the important features of the whole deck. More about this problem in Chapter 11.

(b) True

(c) False. Although unlikely, 10 hearts could appear in a random sample of 10 cards.

(d) True

8.4 **(a)** There are many ways. For instance, consult the tables of random numbers, using the first digit of each 5-digit random number to identify the row (previously labeled 1, 2, 3, and so on), and the second digit of the same random number to locate a particular student's seat within that row. Repeat this process until five students have been identified. (If the classroom is larger, use additional digits so that every student can be sampled.)

(b) Once again, there are many ways. For instance, use the initial 4 digits of each random number (between 0001 and 3041) to identify the page number of the telephone directory and the next 3 digits (between 001 and 480) to identify the particular line on that page. Repeat this process, using 7-digit numbers, until 40 telephone numbers have been identified.

8.5 **(a)** For instance, if the first digit is odd (1, 3, 5, 7, or 9), the first subject is assigned to group A, and if the first digit is even (0, 2, 4, 6, or 8), the first subject is assigned to group B. To ensure equal groups, the second subject is assigned automatically to the group opposite that for the first subject. Repeat this procedure for the remaining five pairs of subjects.

There are other acceptable rules, all involving pairs of subjects (to ensure equal group sizes). For instance, if the first digit equals 0, 1, 2, 3, or 4, the first subject is assigned to group A; otherwise, the first subject is assigned to group B, and so on.

(b) Answer shows two possible assignment rules. In practice only one assignment rule actually would be used.

SUBJECT#	RANDOM NUMBER (TOP ROW, TABLE H)	ASSIGNMENT RULE 1*	OR	ASSIGNMENT RULE 2**
1	1	A		A
2	–	automatically B		automatically B
3	0	B		A
4	–	automatically A		automatically B
5	0	B		A
6	–	automatically A		automatically B
7	9	A		B
8	–	automatically B		automatically A
9	7	A		B
10	–	automatically B		automatically A
11	3	A		A
12	–	automatically B		automatically B

Odd digits = group A; even digits = group B.
**Digits 0, 1, 2, 3, 4 = group A; digits 5, 6, 7, 8, 9 = group B.*

8.6 (a) $\frac{1}{12}$ (b) $\frac{11}{12}$ (c) $\frac{2}{12}$

8.7 (a) $\left(\frac{1}{12}\right)\left(\frac{1}{12}\right) = \frac{1}{144}$

     (b) $\left(\frac{1}{12}\right)\left(\frac{1}{12}\right) = \frac{1}{144}$

     (c) $\left(\frac{2}{12}\right)\left(\frac{2}{12}\right) = \frac{4}{144}$

8.8 (a) $\frac{60}{100} = .60$ (c) $\frac{45}{60} = .75$

     (b) $\frac{45+5}{100} = \frac{50}{100} = .50$ (d) $\frac{45}{45+5} = \frac{45}{50} = .90$

8.9 (a) .0250
     (b) .0250 + .0250 = .0500
     (c) .4750 + .4750 = .9500
     (d) .0049 + .0049 = .0098

8.12 (a) $\left(\frac{1}{2}\right)\left(\frac{1}{2}\right) = \frac{1}{4}$

     (b) $\left(\frac{1}{2}\right)\left(\frac{1}{2}\right) = \frac{1}{4}$

     (c) $\left(\frac{1}{4}\right) + \left(\frac{1}{4}\right) = \frac{2}{4}$

8.14 (a) .98
   (b) (.98)(.98)(.98)(.98)(.98)(.98) = .89
   (c) 1 – .89 = .11
   (d) (.02)(.02) = .0004
   (e) 1.00 (According to Hoadley, the *Challenger* catastrophe has led to several improvements, including the addition of a third set of truly independent O-rings.)

8.16 (a) False. The multiplication rule is not valid when events are dependent.
   (b) is larger than 1/144.
   (c) False. The value of the conditional probability is not known.

Chapter 9

9.1 (a)

(1) 2,2	(6) 4,2	(11) 6,2	(16) 8,2	(21) 10,2
(2) 2,4	(7) 4,4	(12) 6,4	(17) 8,4	(22) 10,4
(3) 2,6	(8) 4,6	(13) 6,6	(18) 8,6	(23) 10,6
(4) 2,8	(9) 4,8	(14) 6,8	(19) 8,8	(24) 10,8
(5) 2,10	(10) 4,10	(15) 6,10	(20) 8,10	(25) 10,10

(b)

$\bar{X}$	PROBABILITY
10	1/25
9	2/25
8	3/25
7	4/25
6	5/25
5	4/25
4	3/25
3	2/25
2	1/25

9.2 (a) μ **(b)** $\mu_{\bar{x}}$ **(c)** $\bar{X}$ **(d)** $\sigma_{\bar{x}}$ **(e)** s **(f)** σ

9.3 (a) False. It always equals the value of the population mean.
   (b) True
   (c) False. Because of chance, most sample means tend to be either larger or smaller than the mean of all sample means.
   (d) True

9.4 (a) True
   (b) False. It measures variability among sample means.
   (c) False. It decreases in value with larger sample sizes.
   (d) True

9.5 (a) False. The shape of the population remains the same regardless of sample size.
   (b) False. It requires that the sample size be sufficiently large—usually between 25 and 100.
   (c) False. It ensures that the shape of the sampling distribution approximates a normal curve, regardless of the shape of the population (which remains intact).
   (d) True

Chapter 10

10.1 (a) $z = \dfrac{566 - 560}{30 / \sqrt{36}} = \dfrac{6}{5} = 1.20$

(b) $z = \dfrac{24 - 25}{4 / \sqrt{64}} = \dfrac{-1}{.5} = -2.00$

(c) $z = \dfrac{82 - 75}{14 / \sqrt{49}} = \dfrac{7}{2} = 3.50$

(d) $z = \dfrac{136 - 146}{15 / \sqrt{25}} = \dfrac{-10}{3} = -3.33$

10.2 (a) Different numbers appear in H_0 and H_1.
(b) Sample means (rather than population means) appear in H_0 and H_1.

10.3 (a) Sixth-grade boys in her school district average 10.2 pushups. H_0: $\mu = 10.2$
(b) On average, weights of packages of ground beef sold by a large supermarket chain equal 16 ounces. H_0: $\mu = 16$
(c) The marriage counselor's clients average 11 interruptions per session. H_0: $\mu = 11$

10.4 (a) Retain H_0 at the .05 level of significance because $z = 1.74$ is less positive than 1.96.
(b) Retain H_0 at the .05 level of significance because $z = 0.13$ is less positive than 1.96.
(c) Reject H_0 at the .05 level of significance because $z = -2.51$ is more negative than -1.96.

10.5 (a) The observed difference between $80,100 and $82,500 cannot be interpreted at face value, as it could have happened just by chance. A hypothesis test permits us to evaluate the effect of chance by measuring the observed difference relative to the standard error of the mean.
(b) All female members of the APA with a Ph.D. degree and a full-time teaching appointment.
(c) H_0: $\mu = 82,500$
(d) H_1: $\mu \neq 82,500$
(e) Reject H_0 at the .05 level of significance if $z \geq 1.96$ *or* $z \leq -1.96$

(f) $z = \dfrac{80,100 - 82,500}{\dfrac{6000}{\sqrt{100}}} = \dfrac{-2,400}{600} = -4.00$

(g) Reject H_0 at the .05 level of significance because $z = -4.00$ is more negative than -1.96.
(h) The average salary of all female APA members (with a Ph.D. and a full-time teaching appointment) is less than $82,500.

10.6 *Research Problem*

Does the mean IQ of all students in the district differ from 100?

Statistical Hypotheses

H_0: $\mu = 100$
H_1: $\mu \neq 100$

Decision Rule

Reject H_0 at the .05 level of significance if z equals or is more positive than 1.96 or if z equals or is more negative than −1.96.

Calculations

Given that $\bar{X} = 105$; $\sigma_{\bar{x}} = \dfrac{15}{\sqrt{25}} = \dfrac{15}{5} = 3$

$$z = \frac{105 - 100}{3} = \frac{5}{3} = 1.67$$

Decision

Retain H_0 at the .05 level of significance because $z = 1.67$ is less positive than 1.96.

Interpretation

There is no evidence that the mean IQ of all students differs from 100.

Chapter 11

11.1 (a) H_0: $\mu = 60$
H_1: $\mu \neq 60$

(b) H_0: $\mu \leq 0.54$
H_1: $\mu > 0.54$
Justification: to increase rainfall

(c) H_0: $\mu \geq 23$
H_1: $\mu < 23$
Justification: weight-reduction program

(d) H_0: $\mu \leq 134$
H_1: $\mu > 134$
Justification: life-prolonging drug

11.2 (a) Reject H_0 at the .01 level of significance because $z = -2.34$ is more negative than −2.33.

(b) Reject H_0 at the .01 level of significance because $z = -5.13$ is more negative than −2.33.

(c) Retain H_0 at the .01 level of significance because $z = 4.04$ is *less negative* than −2.33. (The value of the observed z is in the direction of no concern.)

(d) Reject H_0 at the .05 level of significance because $z = 2.00$ is more positive than 1.65.

(e) Retain H_0 at the .05 level of significance because $z = -1.80$ is *less positive* than 1.65. (The value of the observed z is in the direction of no concern.)

(f) Retain H_0 at the .05 level of significance because $z = 1.61$ is less positive than 1.65.

11.3 (a) Reject H_0 at the .05 level of significance if z equals or is more positive than 1.96 of if z equals or is more negative than −1.96.

(b) Reject H_0 at the .01 level of significance if z equals or is more positive than 2.33.

(c) Reject H_0 at the .05 level of significance if z equals or is more negative than -1.65.

(d) Reject H_0 at the .01 level of significance if z equals or is more positive than 2.58 or if z equals or is more negative than -2.58.

11.4 (a) Correct decision (True H_0 is retained)
Type I error
Correct decision (False H_0 is rejected)
Type II error

(b)

	STATUS OF H_0	
DECISION	**TRUE H_0 (INNOCENT)**	**FALSE H_0 (GUILTY)**
Retain H_0 (Release)	*Correct Decision:* Innocent defendant is released.	*Type II Error:* Guilty defendant is released (Miss).
Reject H_0 (Sentence)	*Type I Error:* Innocent defendant is sentenced (False Alarm).	*Correct Decision:* Guilty defendant is sentenced.

11.5 A false H_0 will never be rejected.

11.6 (a) True
(b) True
(c) False. The one observed sample mean originates from the true sampling distribution.
(d) False. If the one observed sample mean has a value of 103, an incorrect decision would be made because the false H_0 would be retained.

11.7 (a) True
(b) False. The critical value of z (1.65) is based on the hypothesized sampling distribution.
(c) False. Since the true sampling distribution goes below 100, a sample mean less than or equal to 100 is possible, although not highly likely.
(d) True

11.8 (a) Because of the small sample size, only very large effects will be detected.
(b) Because of the large sample size, even small, unimportant effects will be detected.

11.9 (a) .3
(b) .4
(c) .9

11.10 (a) The power for the 12-point effect is larger than .80 because the true sampling distribution is shifted further into the rejection region for the false H_0.
(b) The power for the 5-point effect is smaller than .80 because the true sampling distribution is shifted further into the retention region for the false H_0.

11.13 (a) H_0: $\mu \le 0.54$, that is, cloud seeding has no effect on rainfall.

	STATUS OF H_0	
DECISION	**TRUE H_0**	**FALSE H_0**
Retain H_0	*Correct Decision:* Conclude that there is no evidence that cloud seeding increases rainfall when in fact it does not.	*Type II Error:* Conclude that there is no evidence that cloud seeding increases rainfall when in fact it does.
Reject H_0	*Type I Error:* Conclude that cloud seeding increases rainfall when in fact it does not.	*Correct Decision:* Conclude that cloud seeding increases rainfall when in fact it does.

Chapter 12

12.1 $62,600

12.2 **(a)** $3.82 \pm 1.96 \left(\dfrac{.4}{\sqrt{64}} \right) = \begin{cases} 3.92 \\ 3.72 \end{cases}$

(b) We can claim, with 95 percent confidence, that the interval between 3.72 and 3.92 includes the *true population mean* reading score for the fourth graders. All of these values suggest that, on average, the fourth graders are underachieving.

12.3 **(a)** False. We can be 95 percent confident that the mean for all subjects will be between 507 and 527.
(b) True
(c) False. We can be reasonably confident—but not absolutely confident—that the true population mean lies between 507 and 527.
(d) False. This particular interval either describes the one true population mean or fails to describe the one true population mean.
(e) True
(f) True

12.4 **(a)** Switch to an interval having a lesser degree of confidence, such as 90 percent or 75 percent.
(b) Increase the sample size.

12.5 **(a)** False. The interval from 66 to 74 percent refers to possible values of the population proportion.
(b) False. We can be reasonably confident—but not absolutely confident—that the true population proportion is between 66 and 74 percent.
(c) True
(d) True

12.6 **(a)** $80,100 \pm 2.58 \left(\dfrac{6,000}{\sqrt{100}} \right) = \begin{cases} 81,648 \\ 78,552 \end{cases}$

(b) We can claim, with 99 percent confidence, that the interval between $78,552 and $81,648 includes the *true population mean* salary for all female members of the American Psychological Association. All of these values suggest that, on average, females' salaries are less than males' salaries.

12.9 (a) 3   (b) 3   (c) 5   (d) 4

Chapter 13

13.1 (a) ± 2.179 (c) 1.697
  (b) -2.539 (d) ± 2.704

13.2 (a) $\bar{X} = \dfrac{147}{10} = 14.7$

  (b) $s = \sqrt{\dfrac{2167 - \dfrac{21609}{10}}{10-1}} = \sqrt{\dfrac{6.10}{9}} = \sqrt{.68} = .82$

  $s_{\bar{x}} = \dfrac{.82}{\sqrt{10}} = \dfrac{.82}{3.16} = .26$

13.3 *Research Problem*
  Does the mean weight for all packages of ground beef drop below the specified weight of 16 ounces?
  Statistical Hypothesis
  H_0: $\mu \geq 16$
  H_1: $\mu < 16$
  Decision Rule
  Reject H_0 at the .05 level of significance if $t \leq -1.833$ given $df = 10 - 1 = 9$.
  Calculations
  $t = \dfrac{14.7 - 16}{.26} = -5.00$
  Decision
  Reject H_0.
  Interpretation
  The mean weight for all packages drops below the specified weight of 16 ounces.

13.4 (a) $14.7 \pm (2.26)(.26) = \begin{cases} 15.29 \\ 14.11 \end{cases}$

  (b) We can be 95 percent confident that the interval between 14.11 and 15.29 ounces includes the true population mean weight for all packages.

13.5 *Research Problem*
  On average, do library patrons borrow books for longer or shorter periods than the currently specified loan period of 21 days?
  Statistical Hypotheses
  H_0: $\mu = 21$
  H_1: $\mu \neq 21$

Decision Rule
   Reject H_0 at the .05 level of significance if $t \geq 2.365$ or $t \leq -2.365$ given $df = 8 - 1 = 7$.
Calculations

$$\bar{X} = \frac{142}{8} = 17.75 \quad s = \sqrt{\frac{2652 - \frac{20164}{8}}{8 - 1}} = 4.33$$

$$s_{\bar{X}} = \frac{4.33}{\sqrt{8}} = 1.53 \quad t = \frac{17.75 - 21}{1.53} = -2.12$$

Decision
   Retain H_0 at the .05 level of significance because $t = -2.12$ is less negative than -2.365.
Interpretation
   No evidence that, on average, library patrons borrow books for longer or shorter periods than 21 days.

13.7 **(a)** *Research Problem*
   Is the temperature of the earth getting warmer?
Statistical Hypotheses
   H_0: $\mu \leq 0.0$ (where 0.0 is the mean deviation from the twentieth-century average)
   H_1: $\mu > 0.0$
Decision Rule
   Reject H_0 at the .01 level of significance if $t \geq 2.821$, given $df = 10 - 1 = 9$.
Calculations

$$\bar{X} = \frac{9.4}{10} = 0.94 \quad s = \sqrt{\frac{9.00 - \frac{88.36}{10}}{10 - 1}} = .14$$

$$s_{\bar{X}} = \frac{.14}{\sqrt{10}} = .04 \quad t = \frac{0.94 - 0.00}{.04} = 23.50$$

Decision
   Reject H_0 at the .01 level of significance because the t of 23.50 exceeds the critical t of 2.821.
Interpretation
   The temperature of the earth is getting warmer.
(b) Since H_0 was rejected, a confidence interval is appropriate.

$$0.94 \pm (3.25)(.04) = \begin{cases} 1.07 \\ 0.81 \end{cases}$$

   We can be 99 percent confident that the interval between 0.81 and 1.07 degrees Fahrenheit includes the true mean increase in global temperature above the average temperature for the twentieth century.

Chapter 14

14.1 **(a)** H_0: $\mu_1 - \mu_2 = 0$ **(c)** H_0: $\mu_1 - \mu_2 \geq 0$
   H_1: $\mu_1 - \mu_2 \neq 0$ H_1: $\mu_1 - \mu_2 < 0$

(b) $H_0: \mu_1 - \mu_2 \leq 0$ **(d)** $H_0: \mu_1 - \mu_2 = 0$
        $H_1: \mu_1 - \mu_2 > 0$ $H_1: \mu_1 - \mu_2 \neq 0$

14.2   **(a)** ± 2.080 **(c)** -2.423
        (b) 1.706 **(d)** ± 2.921

14.3   *Research Problem*
          Is there a difference, on average, between the puzzle-solving times required by subjects who are told that the puzzle is difficult and those required by subjects who are told that the puzzle is easy?
        Statistical Hypotheses
$$H_0: \mu_1 - \mu_2 = 0$$
$$H_1: \mu_1 - \mu_2 \neq 0$$
        Decision Rule
          Reject H_0 at the .05 level of significance if $t \geq 2.101$ or $t \leq -2.101$, given $df = 10 + 10 - 2 = 18$.
        Calculations

$$\bar{X}_1 = \frac{158}{10} = 15.8 \quad \bar{X}_2 = \frac{90}{10} = 9.0$$

$$SS_1 = 3168 - \frac{(158)^2}{10} = 671.6 \quad SS_2 = 1036 - \frac{(90)^2}{10} = 226$$

$$s_p^2 = \frac{671.6 + 226}{10 + 10 - 2} = 49.87 \quad s_{\bar{X}_1 - \bar{X}_2} = \sqrt{\frac{49.87}{10} + \frac{49.87}{10}} = 3.16$$

$$t = \frac{(15.8 - 9.0) - 0}{3.16} = 2.15$$

        Decision
          Reject H_0 at the .05 level of significance because $t = 2.15$ exceeds 2.101.
        Interpretation
          Puzzle-solving times are longer, on average, for subjects who are told that the puzzle is difficult than for those who are told that the puzzle is easy.

14.4   **(a)** $p < .001$ **(d)** $p > .05$
        (b) $p < .05$ **(e)** $p > .05$
        (c) $p < .01$

14.5 a_2, b_1, c_2, d_1, e_2

14.6 $a_2, b_1, b_2, c_1, c_2, e_1, e_2$

14.7   **(a)** 2   **(c)** 3
        (b) 2   **(d)** 1

14.8   **(a)** $d = \dfrac{15.8 - 9.0}{7.06} = .96$
        (b) Puzzle-solving times are longer, on average, for subjects who are told that the puzzle is difficult ($\bar{X} = 15.8$, $s = 8.64$) than for those who are told that the puzzle is easy ($\bar{X} = 9.0$, $s = 5.01$), according to the t test $[t(18) = 2.15, p < .05, d = .96]$.

14.9 **(a)** The t test for equal variances should be reported. This test is appropriate because the F test for equal variances has a large p-value of 0.8125.

(b) The more appropriate (exact) one-tailed $p = .0285$ (from .0569 divided by 2).

(c) The confidence limits (CLs) for this interval are −0.178 to 10.1777. The dissimilar signs (and inclusion of zero) is consistent with the two-tailed p-value of .0569 which, in turn, would have resulted in the retention of the null hypothesis.

14.10 **(a)** The difference between means for experiment B is more likely to be viewed as real because of its smaller variability.

(b) *Research Problem*

Do the population means differ from zero for experiment B?

Statistical Hypotheses

$H_0: \mu_{B^*} - \mu_B = 0$
$H_1: \mu_{B^*} - \mu_B \neq 0$

Decision Rule

Reject H_0 at the .05 level if $t \geq 2.179$ or if $t \leq -2.179$, given $df = 7 + 7 - 2 = 12$.

Calculations

$$t = \frac{2-0}{.30} = 6.67$$

Decision

Reject H_0 at the .05 level since $t = 6.67$ exceeds 2.179.

Conclusion

Population means differ for experiment B.

(c) For experiment C, $t = \dfrac{2-0}{1.02} = 1.96$. Therefore, since $t = 1.96$ doesn't exceed 2.179, retain H_0.

(d) For experiment B, $p < .001$, while for experiment C, $p > .05$.

(e) The difference between the means for experiment B is probably real, while that for experiment C is merely transitory.

14.13 **(a)** *Research Problem*

Is the mean performance of college students in an introductory biology course affected by the grading policy?

Statistical Hypotheses

$H_0: \mu_1 - \mu_2 = 0$
$H_1: \mu_1 - \mu_2 \neq 0$

Decision Rule

Reject H_0 at the .05 level of significance if $t \geq 2.042$ or $t \leq -2.042$, given $df = 20 + 20 - 2 = 38$ (read as 30 in Table B).

Calculations

$$t = \frac{(86.2 - 81.6) - 0}{1.50} = 3.07$$

Decision

Reject H_0 at the .05 level of significance because $t = 3.07$ exceeds 2.042.

Interpretation

Introductory biology students have higher achievement scores, on average, when awarded letter grades rather than a simple pass/fail.

(b) The calculated t ratio would have been equal to -3.07 rather than 3.07. Most important, however, the same interpretation would have been appropriate: Introductory biology students have higher achievement scores, on average, when awarded letter grades rather than a simple pass/fail.

(c) Because of self-selection, groups might differ with respect to any one or several uncontrolled variables, such as motivation, aptitude, and so on, in addition to the difference in grading policy. Hence, any observed difference between the mean achievement scores for these two groups could not be attributed solely to the difference in grading policy.

(d) $p < .01$

(e) $d = \dfrac{86.2 - 81.6}{5} = .92$

(f) Introductory biology students have higher mean achievement scores when awarded letter grades ($\bar{X} = 86.2$, $s = 5.39$) rather than a simple pass/fail ($\bar{X} = 81.6$, $s = 4.58$), according to the t test [$t(38) = 3.07$, $p < .01$, $d = .92$].

14.14 (a) *Research Problem*

Does alcohol consumption cause an increase in mean performance errors on a driving simulator?

Statistical Hypotheses

$H_0: \mu_1 - \mu_2 \leq 0$
$H_1: \mu_1 - \mu_2 > 0$

Decision Rule

Reject H_0 at the .05 level of significance if $t \geq 1.671$, given $df = 60 + 60 - 2 = 118$ (read as 60 in Table B).

Calculations

$$t = \frac{26.4 - 18.6}{2.4} = 3.25$$

Decision

Reject H_0 at the .05 level of significance because $t = 3.25$ exceeds 1.671.

Interpretation

Alcohol consumption causes an increase in mean performance errors on a driving simulator.

(b) $p < .001$

(c) $7.8 \pm (2.00)(2.4) = \begin{cases} 12.6 \\ 3.0 \end{cases}$

We are 95 percent confident that the interval from 3.0 to 12.6 describes the increase in population mean performance errors attributable to alcohol.

(d) $d = \dfrac{26.4 - 18.6}{13.15} = .59$

(e) Mean errors on a driving simulator are significantly greater when alcohol is consumed ($\bar{X} = 26.4$, $s = 13.99$) than when no alcohol is consumed ($\bar{X} = 18.6$, $s = 12.15$), according to a t test [$t(118) = 3.25$, $p < .001$, $d = .59$].

(Incidentally, compared to the very rare value of $p < .001$ for the t ratio, the comparatively modest standardized estimate of .59 for effect size illustrates the immunity of d to the large sample size of 60 subjects per group.)

Chapter 15

15.1 **(a)** two independent samples
(b) two related samples, repeated measures
(c) two related samples, matched pairs
(d) two related samples, matched pairs

15.2 *Research Problem*
When schoolchildren are matched for home environment, does vitamin C consumption reduce the mean frequency of common colds?
Statistical Hypotheses
H_0: $\mu_D \geq 0$
H_1: $\mu_D < 0$
Decision Rule
Reject H_0 at the .05 level of significance if $t \leq -1.833$, given $df = 10 - 1 = 9$.
Calculations

$$\bar{D} = \frac{-15}{10} = -1.5 \quad SS_D = 37 - \frac{(15)^2}{10} = 14.5$$

$$s_D = \sqrt{\frac{14.5}{10-1}} = \sqrt{1.61} = 1.27 \quad s_{\bar{D}} = \frac{1.27}{\sqrt{10}} = 0.40$$

$$t = \frac{-1.5 - 0}{.40} = -3.75$$

Decision
Reject H_0 at the .05 level of significance because $t = -3.75$ is more negative than -1.833.
Interpretation
When schoolchildren are matched for home environment, vitamin C consumption reduces the mean frequency of common colds.

15.3 $-1.50 \pm (2.262)(0.40) = -1.50 \pm 0.90 = \begin{cases} -0.60 \\ -2.40 \end{cases}$

We are 95 percent confident that the interval between -0.60 and -2.40 days covers the population mean difference (reduction attributable to vitamin C) in days on which matched schoolchildren suffered from the common cold.

15.4 $d = \frac{-1.50}{1.27} = 1.18$.
According to Cohen's guidelines, this is a large effect, equivalent to more than one standard deviation.

15.5 **(a)** t test for two independent samples
(b) t test for two related samples, matched pairs
(c) t test for two independent samples

(d) t test for one sample

(e) t test for two related samples, repeated measures

15.6 *Research Problem*

For the population of California taxpayers, is there a relationship between educational level and annual income?

Statistical Hypotheses

H_0: $\rho = 0$

H_1: $\rho \neq 0$

Decision Rule

Reject H_0 at the .05 level of significance if $t \geq 2.060$ or $t \leq -2.060$, given $df = 27 - 2 = 25$.

Calculations

$$t = \frac{.43 - 0}{\sqrt{\dfrac{1 - (.43)^2}{27 - 2}}} = \frac{.43}{.18} = 2.39$$

Decision

Reject H_0 at the .05 level of significance because $t = 2.39$ exceeds 2.060.

Interpretation

For the population of California taxpayers, there is a relationship (positive) between educational level and annual income.

15.7 **(a)** *Research Problem:*

Does physical exercise cause an increase in the mean GPAs of students, given that pairs of students are originally matched for their GPAs?

Statistical Hypotheses

H_0: $\mu_D \leq 0$

H_1: $\mu_D > 0$

Decision Rule

Reject H_0 at the .01 level of significance if $t \geq 3.143$, given $df = 7 - 1 = 6$.

Calculations

$$\overline{D} = \frac{1.56}{7} = .22 \quad SS_D = .48 - \frac{(1.56)^2}{7} = .48 - .35 = .13$$

$$s_D = \sqrt{\frac{.13}{7-1}} = \sqrt{.02} = .14 \quad s_{\overline{D}} = \frac{.14}{\sqrt{7}} = \frac{.14}{2.65} = .05$$

$$t = \frac{.22 - 0}{.05} = 4.40$$

Decision

Reject H_0 at the .01 level of significance because $t = 4.40$ exceeds 3.143.

Conclusion

Physical exercise causes an increase in mean GPAs when pairs of students are matched for their original GPAs.

(b) $p < .01$

(c) $d = \dfrac{.22}{.14} = 1.57$

(d) Physical exercise causes an increase in mean GPAs ($\bar{D} = .22$, $s_D = .14$), according to a t test [$t(6) = 4.40$, $p < .01$, $d = 1.57$], when pairs of students are matched for their original GPAs.

15.10 (a) *Research Problem*

Is there a decline in the mean running time of blood-doped athletes?

Statistical Hypotheses

H_0: $\mu_D \leq 0$

H_1: $\mu_D > 0$

Decision Rule

Reject H_0 at the .05 level of significance if $t \geq 1.796$, given $df = 12 - 1 = 11$.

Calculations

Given that $\bar{D} = 51.33$ and $s_D = 66.33$,

$$s_{\bar{D}} = \frac{66.33}{\sqrt{12}} = 19.17 \quad t = \frac{51.33 - 0}{19.17} = 2.68$$

Decision

Reject H_0 at the .05 level of significance because $t = 2.68$ exceeds 1.796.

Interpretation

Blood doping causes a decline in the mean running time (for athletes who serve as their own controls).

(b) $p < .05$

(c) Yes. Although the appearance of the test results would change (since now negative rather than positive difference scores would support the research hypothesis), H_0 still would have been rejected, and the interpretation would have been the same.

(d) $51.33 \pm (2.20)(19.17) = \begin{cases} 93.50 \\ 9.16 \end{cases}$

We can claim, with 95 percent confidence, that the interval between 9.16 and 93.50 seconds includes the true effect of blood doping. Being positive, all of these differences suggest that blood doping has the desired effect.

(e) Counterbalancing eliminates any possible bias due to the order of testing.

(f) The interval between tests would have been too short to eliminate the lingering effects of blood doping on those subjects who were tested first with real blood. Consequently, any effect due to blood doping would tend to be obscured.

Chapter 16

16.1

		TYPE OF VARIABILITY	
		BETWEEN GROUPS	**WITHIN GROUPS**
(a)		No	No
(b)		Yes	No
(c)		No	Yes
(d)		Yes	Yes

16.2 **(a)** random error
  (b) treatment effect
  (c) one

16.3 **(a)** 4.41   **(c)** 3.26
  (b) 4.16   **(d)** 2.48

16.4 **(a)** $p < .05$ **(c)** $p > .05$
  (b) $p < .01$ **(d)** $p < .05$

16.5 **(a)** *Research Problem*
  On average, are the number of eye contacts initiated by shy students affected when they attend either zero, one, two, or three workshop sessions on assertive training?
  Statistical Hypotheses
  H_0: $\mu_0 = \mu_1 = \mu_2 = \mu_3$
  H_1: H_0 is false.
  Decision Rule
  Reject H_0 at the .05 level of significance if $F \geq 2.95$ (from Table C), given $df_{between} = 3$ and $df_{within} = 28$.
  Calculations
  $F = 10.84$. See **(b)** for more information.
  Decision
  Reject H_0 at the .05 level of significance because $F = 10.84$ is larger than 2.95.
  Interpretation
  Average number of eye contacts is affected by attendance at either zero, one, two, or three sessions of an assertiveness training workshop.

(b)

SOURCE	SS	df	MS	F
Between	154.12	3	51.37	10.84*
Within	132.75	28	4.74	
Total	286.87	31		

* Significant at the .05 level.

16.6 $\eta^2 = \dfrac{154.12}{286.87} = .54$, a large effect, according to the guidelines.

16.7 **(a)** $HSD(k = 4,\ df_{within} = 24) = (3.90)\sqrt{\dfrac{4.74}{8}} = 3.00$

ALL POSSIBLE ABSOLUTE DIFFERENCES BETWEEN PAIRS OF MEANS

	$\bar{X}_0 = 1.63$	$\bar{X}_1 = 3.13$	$\bar{X}_2 = 5.00$	$\bar{X}_3 = 7.50$
$\bar{X}_0 = 1.63$	—	1.50	3.37*	5.87*
$\bar{X}_1 = 3.13$		—	1.87	4.37*
$\bar{X}_2 = 5.00$			—	2.50
$\bar{X}_3 = 7.50$				—

* Significant at the .05 level.

$$d\left(\bar{X}_3, \bar{X}_0\right) = \frac{5.87}{\sqrt{4.74}} = \frac{5.87}{2.18} = 2.69$$

$$d\left(\bar{X}_2, \bar{X}_0\right) = \frac{3.37}{\sqrt{4.74}} = \frac{3.37}{2.18} = 1.55$$

$$d\left(\bar{X}_3, \bar{X}_1\right) = \frac{4.37}{\sqrt{4.74}} = \frac{4.37}{2.18} = 2.00$$

(b) Students who attend either two or three workshop sessions initiate, on average, more eye contacts than those who attend zero sessions. Furthermore, those who attend three sessions initiate, on average, more eye contacts than those who attend one session. All three significant differences had large effect sizes, with d values ranging from 1.55 to 2.69.

16.8 **(a)** $\eta^2 = \dfrac{54.00}{76.00} = .71$

(b) $\sqrt{MS_{error}} = \sqrt{3.67} = 1.915$

(which also is listed as the pooled standard deviation).

(c) Only the limits for CI between 0 and 48 hours have the same signs (both negative) in agreement with the one significant difference between 0 and 48 hours described in Table 16.8.

16.10 **(a)**

SOURCE	SS	df	MS	F
Between	106.05	2	53.03	13.70*
Within	34.87	9	3.87	
Total	140.92	11		

* Significant at the .05 level.

(b) $\eta^2 = \dfrac{106.05}{140.92} = .75$, a large effect, according to the guidelines.

(c) $HSD(k = 3,\ df_{within} = 9) = (3.95)\sqrt{\dfrac{3.87}{4}} = (3.95)(0.98) = 3.87$

ALL POSSIBLE ABSOLUTE DIFFERENCES BETWEEN PAIRS OF MEANS			
	$\bar{X}_0 = 2.60$	$\bar{X}_{24} = 5.33$	$\bar{X}_{48} = 9.50$
$\bar{X}_0 = 2.60$	—	2.73	6.90*
$\bar{X}_{24} = 5.33$		—	4.17*
$\bar{X}_{48} = 9.50$			—

* Significant at the .05 level.

(d) $d(\bar{X}_{48}, \bar{X}_0) = \dfrac{6.90}{\sqrt{3.87}} = 3.50$

$$d(\bar{X}_{48}, \bar{X}_{24}) = \frac{4.17}{\sqrt{3.87}} = 2.12$$

(e) Aggression scores for subjects deprived of sleep for 0 hours ($\bar{X} = 2.60$, $s = 2.07$), for 24 hours ($\bar{X} = 5.33$, $s = 1.53$), and for 48 hours ($\bar{X} = 9.50$, $s = 2.08$) differ significantly [$F(2,9) = 13.70$, $MSE = 3.87$, $p < .05$, $\eta^2 = .75$]. According to Tukey's HSD test, the mean differences between the 24- and 48-hour groups (4.17) and between the 0- and 48-hour groups (6.90) are significant ($HSD = 3.87$, $p < .05$, $d = 2.12, 3.50$).

16.12 (a) 4
     (b) 21
     (c) A and B
     (d) D. Because of the small number of subjects, only a larger treatment effect would have been detected.
     (e) C. Because of the relatively large number of subjects, even a fairly small treatment effect would have been detected.
     (f) For A, $p < .05$ For C, $p > .05$
        For B, $p < .01$ For D, $p > .05$

Chapter 17

17.1 Variability due to individual differences is present in outcomes b and c but not in outcome a. It is greater in outcome b.

17.2

SOURCE	SS	df	MS	F
Between	70.33	2	35.17	8.73*
Within	68.17	15		
Subject	27.83	5		
Error	40.34	10	4.03	
Total	138.50	17		

Significant at the .05 level, since F(2,10) = 8.73 exceeds the critical F of 4.10.

17.3 $\eta_p^2 = \dfrac{70.33}{70.33 + 40.34} = .64$

17.4 (a) $HSD(k = 3, df_{error} = 10) = (3.88)\sqrt{\dfrac{4.03}{6}} = (3.88)(.82) = 3.18$

ALL POSSIBLE ABSOLUTE DIFFERENCES BETWEEN PAIRS OF MEANS			
	$\bar{X}_{silence} = 7.17$	$\bar{X}_{white\ noise} = 5.00$	$\bar{X}_{rock} = 2.33$
$\bar{X}_{silence} = 7.17$	—	2.17	4.84*
$\bar{X}_{white\ noise} = 5.00$		—	2.67
$\bar{X}_{rock} = 2.33$			—

Significant at the .05 level.

(b) $d(silence, rock) = \dfrac{7.17 - 2.33}{\sqrt{4.03}} = 2.41$

(c) The partial eta-squared, η_p^2, equals .64, a large effect. Mean reading comprehension is significantly higher when silence is compared with rock, with a standardized effect size. d, equivalent to almost two and one-half standard deviations.

17.5

SOURCE	SS	df	MS	F
Between	1,200	3	400	4.00*
Within	8,800	44		
Subject	5,500	11		
Error	3,300	33	100	
Total	10,000	47		

Significant at the .05 level.

17.6 (a)

SOURCE	SS	df	MS	F
Between	154.12	3	51.37	16.62*
Within	132.75	28		
Subject	67.87	7		
Error	64.88	21	3.09	
Total	286.87	31		

Significant at the .05 level.

NOTE: $SS_{error} = 64.88$ was obtained from $SS_{within} - SS_{subject} = 132.75 - 67.87$

(b) $\eta_p^2 = \dfrac{154.12}{154.12 + 64.88} = .70$

$HSD(k = 4, df_{error} = 20) = (3.96)\sqrt{\dfrac{3.09}{8}} = 2.46$

ALL POSSIBLE ABSOLUTE DIFFERENCES BETWEEN PAIRS OF MEANS

	$\bar{X}_0 = 1.63$	$\bar{X}_1 = 3.13$	$\bar{X}_2 = 5.00$	$\bar{X}_3 = 7.50$
$\bar{X}_0 = 1.63$	—	1.50	3.37*	5.87*
$\bar{X}_1 = 3.13$		—	1.87	4.37*
$\bar{X}_2 = 5.00$			—	2.50*
$\bar{X}_3 = 7.50$				—

Significant at the .05 level.

$d(\bar{X}_3, \bar{X}_0) = \dfrac{5.87}{\sqrt{3.09}} = 3.34$

$$d\left(\bar{X}_3, \bar{X}_1\right) = \frac{4.37}{\sqrt{3.09}} = 2.48$$

$$d\left(\bar{X}_3, \bar{X}_2\right) = \frac{2.50}{\sqrt{3.09}} = 1.42$$

$$d\left(\bar{X}_2, \bar{X}_0\right) = \frac{3.37}{\sqrt{3.09}} = 1.91$$

(c) Because of the smaller error term for repeated measures (compared to that in Question 16.5 for independent samples with exactly the same data), results for repeated measures are more dramatic: The value of F is 16.62 compared to 10.84; an additional pair of means, $\bar{X}_2$ and $\bar{X}_0$, is significantly different; and all comparable standardized effect estimates, d, are increased by about 25 percent.

Chapter 18

18.1

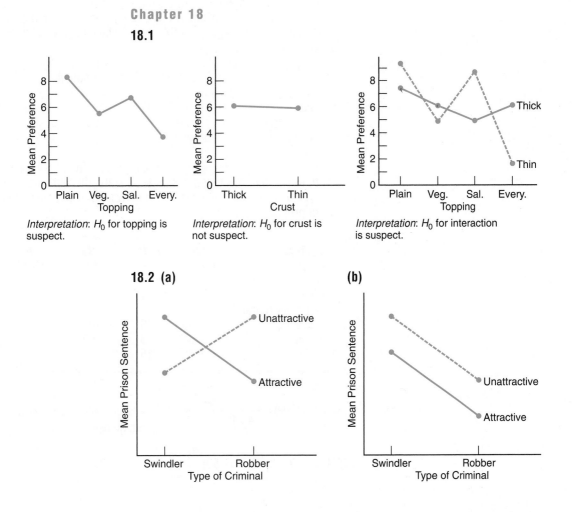

Interpretation: H_0 for topping is suspect.

Interpretation: H_0 for crust is not suspect.

Interpretation: H_0 for interaction is suspect.

18.2 (a)   **(b)**

The two lines in **(a)** should cross (in any manner). Note that the solid line represents the simple effect of type of criminal for attractive defendants, whereas the broken line represents the simple effect of type of criminal for unattractive defendants.

The two lines in **(b)** should be parallel and sloped from upper left to lower right.

18.3 **(a)** *Research Problem*

Do viewing time and type of program, as well as the interaction of these two factors, affect mean aggression scores?

Statistical Hypotheses

H_0: no main effect for columns or viewing time (or $\mu_0 = \mu_1 = \mu_2 = \mu_3$).
H_0: no main effect for rows or type of program (or $\mu_{cartoon} = \mu_{real\ life}$).
H_0: no interaction effect.
H_1: H_0 is false.

Decision Rule

Reject H_0 at the .05 level of significance if $F_{column} \geq 4.07$, given 3 and 8 degrees of freedom; if $F_{row} \geq 5.32$, given 1 and 8 degrees of freedom; and if $F_{interaction} \geq 4.07$, given 3 and 8 degrees of freedom.

Calculations

$$
\left.
\begin{aligned}
F_{column} &= 16.35 \\
F_{row} &= 0.02 \\
F_{interaction} &= 0.08
\end{aligned}
\right\} \text{See (b) for more information.}
$$

Decision

Reject H_0 for column (viewing time) at the .05 level of significance because $F = 16.35$ exceeds 4.07.

Interpretation

Viewing time affects mean aggression scores. There is no evidence, however, that mean aggression scores are affected either by the type of program or the interaction between viewing time and type of program.

(b)

SOURCE	SS	df	MS	F
Column (Viewing Time)	144.19	3	48.06	16.35*
Row (Type of Program)	0.07	1	0.07	0.02
Interaction	0.68	3	0.23	0.08
Within	23.50	8	2.94	
Total	168.44	15		

* *Significant at the .05 level.*

18.4 $\eta_p^2 (viewing\ time) = \dfrac{144.19}{144.19 + 23.50} = .86$, a large effect size, according to the guidelines.

18.5 $HSD(k = 4,\ df_{within} = 8) = (4.53)\sqrt{\dfrac{2.94}{4}} = (4.53)(0.86) = 3.90$

ALL POSSIBLE ABSOLUTE DIFFERENCES BETWEEN PAIRS OF COLUMN MEANS

	$\bar{X}_0 = 0.25$	$\bar{X}_1 = 0.75$	$\bar{X}_2 = 4.00$	$\bar{X}_3 = 7.75$
$\bar{X}_0 = 0.25$	—	0.50	3.75	7.50*
$\bar{X}_1 = 0.75$		—	3.25	7.00*
$\bar{X}_2 = 4.00$			—	3.75
$\bar{X}_3 = 7.75$				—

* Significant at the .05 level.

On average, aggression scores are higher for a viewing time of 3 hours compared to a viewing time of either 0 hours or 1 hour.

18.6 SS_{se} *(gender at zero)* $= \dfrac{(16)^2}{2} + \dfrac{(20)^2}{2} - \dfrac{(36)^2}{4} = 4$

(where the 2 in the denominator refers to the sample size in each cell, n)

MS_{se} *(gender at zero)* $= \dfrac{4}{1} = 4$

(where the 1 in the denominator refers to the number of degrees of freedom for the simple effect, $df_{se} = r - 1$)

F_{se} *(gender at zero)* $= \dfrac{4}{5.33} = 0.75$, nonsignificant, given 1 and 6 degrees of freedom

F_{se} *(gender at two)* $= \dfrac{100}{5.33} = 18.76 \ (p < .01)$

F_{se} *(gender at four)* $= \dfrac{144}{5.33} = 27.02 \ (p < .01)$

d*(gender at two)* $= \dfrac{17-7}{\sqrt{5.33}} = 4.33$; d *(gender at four)* $= \dfrac{21-9}{\sqrt{5.33}} = 5.19$

As expected, given the significant interaction, simple effects are inconsistent. Both simple effects for gender at two and at four are significant, while that for gender at zero is nonsignificant. Standardized effect size estimates at two and four are very large, each being equivalent to more than four standard deviations. This analysis suggests that crowds of two or four people cause the mean reaction times of males to exceed those for females.

18.7 (a)

SOURCE	df
Food deprivation *(F)*	1
Reward amount *(R)*	1
$F \times R$	1
Within	36
Total	39

(b) Effects

	FOOD DEPRIVATION	REWARD AMOUNT	INTERACTION
(1)	Yes	Yes	Yes
(2)	Yes	Yes	No
(3)	Yes	No	Yes
(4)	No	Yes	Yes
(5)	Yes	No	No
(6)	No	Yes	No
(7)	No	No	Yes
(8)	No	No	No

(c) Outcome (8) probably would be least preferred, since it contains no effects.

18.8 (a) Effects for food deprivation and reward amount but not interaction.
(b) Effects for food deprivation, reward amount, and interaction.
(c) Effect for interaction, but not for food deprivation or reward amount.

18.10 (a)

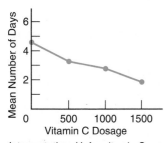

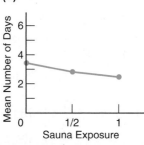

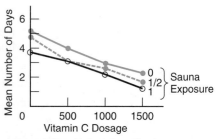

Interpretation: H_0 for vitamin C dosage is suspect.

Interpretation: H_0 for sauna exposure is suspect (although not as much as H_0 for vitamin C dosage).

Interpretation: H_0 for interaction is *not* suspect.

(b)

SOURCE	SS	df	MS	F
Column (Vitamin C)	33.64	3	11.21	17.52*
Row (Sauna)	5.05	2	2.53	3.95*
Interaction	0.95	6	0.16	0.25
Within	15.33	24	0.64	
Total	54.97	35		

Significant at the .05 level.

(c) Since the interaction is nonsignificant, F_{se} tests for simple effects are inappropriate. Given a significant main effect for vitamin C,

$$\eta_p^2 (vitamin\ C) = \frac{33.64}{33.64 + 15.33} = .69, \text{ a large effect.}$$

$$HSD\ (k = 4,\ df_{within} = 24) = (3.90)\sqrt{\frac{0.64}{9}} = 1.01$$

ALL POSSIBLE ABSOLUTE DIFFERENCES BETWEEN PAIRS OF COLUMN MEANS

	$\bar{X}_0 = 4.44$	$\bar{X}_{500} = 3.22$	$\bar{X}_{1000} = 2.67$	$\bar{X}_{1500} = 1.78$
$\bar{X}_0 = 4.44$	—	1.22*	1.77*	2.66*
$\bar{X}_{500} = 3.22$		—	0.55	1.44*
$\bar{X}_{1000} = 2.67$			—	0.89
$\bar{X}_{1500} = 1.78$				—

---

* Significant at the .05 level.

$$d\left(\bar{X}_{500}, \bar{X}_0\right) = \frac{1.22}{\sqrt{0.64}} = \frac{1.22}{0.80} = 1.53 \quad d\left(\bar{X}_{1000}, \bar{X}_0\right) = \frac{1.77}{0.80} = 2.21$$

$$d\left(\bar{X}_{1500}, \bar{X}_0\right) = \frac{2.66}{0.80} = 3.33 \quad d\left(\bar{X}_{1500}, \bar{X}_{500}\right) = \frac{1.44}{0.80} = 1.80$$

All standardized estimates of effect sizes are large.

Given a significant main effect for sauna,

$$\eta_p^2\ (sauna) = \frac{5.05}{5.05 + 15.33} = .25, \text{ a large effect.}$$

$$HSD(k = 3,\ df_{within} = 24) = (3.53)\sqrt{\frac{0.64}{12}} = (3.53)(0.22) = 0.78$$

ALL POSSIBLE ABSOLUTE DIFFERENCES BETWEEN PAIRS OF ROW MEANS

	$\bar{X}_0 = 3.50$	$\bar{X}_{1/2} = 3.00$	$\bar{X}_1 = 2.58$
$\bar{X}_0 = 3.50$	—	0.50	0.92*
$\bar{X}_{1/2} = 3.00$		—	0.42
$\bar{X}_1 = 2.58$			—

---

* Significant at the .05 level.

$$d(\bar{X}_1, \bar{X}_0) = \frac{0.92}{0.80} = 1.15, \text{ a large standardized effect}$$

(d) The main effect for vitamin C was significant [$F(3, 24) = 17.52$; $MSE = 0.64$, $p < .01$, $\eta_p^2 = .69$], as was the main effect for sauna [$F(2, 24) = 3.95$; $p < .05$, $\eta_p^2 = .25$], but not the interaction [$F(6, 24) = 0.25$, *ns*]. On average, fewer days of discomfort occur for subjects who receive vitamin C dosages of 500 mg ($\bar{X}_{500} = 3.22$, $d = 1.53$), 1000 mg ($\bar{X}_{1000} = 2.67$, $d = 2.21$), and 1500 mg ($\bar{X}_{1500} = 1.78$, $d = 3.33$) compared to those control subjects who receive no vitamin C ($\bar{X}_0 = 4.44$). Furthermore, on average, fewer days of discomfort occur for subjects who receive vitamin C dosages of 1500 mg compared to those who receive only 500 mg ($d = 1.80$). Finally on average, fewer days of discomfort occur for subjects with daily sauna exposures of

1 hour ($\bar{X}_1 = 2.58$, $d = 1.15$) compared to those with no daily sauna exposure ($\bar{X}_0 = 3.50$).

Chapter 19

19.1 **(a)** $H_0: P_A = P_B = \frac{1}{2}$
(b) $H_0: P_{north} = P_{east} = P_{south} = P_{west} = \frac{1}{4}$
(c) $H_0: P_{Mon} = P_{Tue} = P_{Wed} = P_{Thu} = P_{Fri} = P_{Sat} = P_{Sun} = \frac{1}{7}$
(d) $H_0: P_{weekday} = \frac{5}{7}; P_{weekend} = \frac{2}{7}$

19.2 **(a)** *Research Problem*
The attribute most desired by a population of college students is equally distributed among various possibilities.
Statistical Hypotheses
$H_0: P_{love} = P_{wealth} = P_{power} = P_{health} = P_{fame} = P_{family\ happiness} = \frac{1}{6}$
$H_1: H_0$ is false.
Decision Rule
Reject H_0 at the .05 level of significance if $\chi^2 \geq 11.07$, given $df = 5$.
Calculations

$$\chi^2 = \frac{(25-15)^2}{15} + \frac{(10-15)^2}{15} + \frac{(5-15)^2}{15} + \frac{(25-15)^2}{15} + \frac{(10-15)^2}{15} + \frac{(15-15)^2}{15} = 23.33$$

Decision
Reject H_0 at the .05 level of significance because $\chi^2 = 23.33$ exceeds 11.07.
Interpretation
The attribute most desired by a population of college students is not equally distributed among various possibilities.
(b) $p < .001$

19.3 **(a)** Educational level and attitude toward right-to-abortion legislation are independent.
(b) Clients and nonclients are not distinguishable on the basis of—or are independent of—whether or not their parents are divorced.
(c) Employees' annual evaluations are independent of whether they have fixed or flexible work schedules.

19.4 **(a)** *Research Problem*
Is hair color related to susceptibility to poison oak?
Statistical Hypotheses
H_0: Hair color and susceptibility to poison oak are independent.
$H_1: H_0$ is false.
Decision Rule
Reject H_0 at the .01 level if $\chi^2 \geq 11.34$ given $df = (2-1)(4-1) = 3$.
Calculations

$$\chi^2 = \frac{(10-18)^2}{18} + \frac{(30-36)^2}{36} + \frac{(60-54)^2}{54} + \frac{(80-72)^2}{72} + \frac{(20-12)^2}{12}$$

$$+ \frac{(30-24)^2}{24} + \frac{(30-36)^2}{36} + \frac{(40-48)^2}{48} = 15.28$$

Decision

Reject H_0 at the .01 level of significance because $\chi^2 = 15.28$ exceeds 11.34.

Interpretation

There is a relationship between hair color and susceptibility to poison oak.

(b) $p < .01$

19.5 $\phi_c^2 = \dfrac{15.28}{300(2-1)} = .05$ (between a small and a medium effect, according to Cohen's guidelines)

19.6 **(a)** Odds ratio for returned letters from campus

$$OR = \frac{51/19}{69/61} = \frac{2.68}{1.13} = 2.37$$

A returned letter is 2.37 times more likely to come from campus than from off-campus.

(b) $OR = \dfrac{69/61}{51/19} = \dfrac{1.13}{2.68} = .42$

A returned letter is .42 times less likely to come from off-campus than from campus.

19.7 There is a relationship between hair color and susceptibility to poison oak $[\chi^2 (3, n = 300) = 15.28, p < .01, \phi_c^2 = .05]$

19.8 **(a)** 30

(b) Either the next-to-last set of percents (designated as Row Pct because they sum to 100 percent in each row) for Yes or returned letters, that is, 32.50, 25.00, and 42.50, or the same set of percents for the No or unreturned letters, that is, 26.25, 50.00, and 23.75. When compared with the total percents, that is, 30.00, 35.00, and 35.00, either set of percents spotlights the relatively low rate of returns in suburbia and the relatively high rates on campus.

(c) Square "Cramer's V (phi)," that is, (.265)(.265) = .07.

19.10 **(a)** *Research Problem*

Are people more likely to die after rather than before a major holiday?

Statistical Hypotheses

$H_0: P_{before} = P_{after} = \dfrac{1}{2}$

$H_1: H_0$ is false.

Decision Rule

Reject H_0 at the .05 level of significance if $\chi^2 \geq 3.84$, given $df = 1$.

Calculations

$$\chi^2 = \frac{(33 - 51.5)^2}{51.5} + \frac{(70 - 51.5)^2}{51.5} = 13.29$$

Decision
Reject H_0 at the .05 level of significance because $\chi^2 = 13.29$ exceeds 3.84.
Interpretation
People are more likely to die after rather than before a major holiday.
(b) $p < .001$
(c) More elderly California women of Chinese descent died of natural causes during a 1-week period after rather than before the Harvest Moon Festival [$\chi^2(1, n = 103) = 13.29$, $p < .001$, $\phi_c^2 = .13$].

19.13 (a) Yes. All frequencies end in multiplies of 10, suggesting that the observed frequencies might be fictitious, as is actually the case (both for this exercise and for some others in this chapter) in order to simplify computations.
(b) *Research Problem*
Is the religious preference of students related to their political affiliation?
Statistical Hypotheses
H_0: Religious preference and political affiliation are independent.
H_1: H_0 is false.
Decision Rule
Reject H_0 at the .05 level of significance if $\chi^2 \geq 21.03$, given $df = (5 - 1)(4 - 1) = 12$.
Calculations
$$\chi^2 = \frac{(30 - 20)^2}{20} + \frac{(30 - 20)^2}{20} + \ldots + \frac{(100 - 40)^2}{40} = 220$$
Decision
Reject H_0 at the .05 level of significance because $\chi^2 = 220$ exceeds 21.03.
Interpretation
There is a relationship between the religious preference of students and their political affiliation.
(c) $\phi_c^2 = \dfrac{220}{500(4 - 1)} = .15$, a medium effect size, according to the (unadjusted) guidelines. (See footnote on page 438.)

19.14 (a) *Research Problem*
Is there a relationship between the type of accommodation and survival rate?
Statistical Hypotheses
H_0: Type of accommodation and survival rate are independent.
H_1: H_0 is false.
Decision Rule
Reject H_0 at the .05 level of significance if $\chi^2 \geq 3.84$, given that $df = (c - 1)(r - 1) = (2 - 1)(2 - 1) = 1$.
Calculations
$$\chi^2 = \frac{(299 - 217.52)^2}{217.52} + \frac{(186 - 267.48)^2}{267.48} + \frac{(280 - 361.48)^2}{361.48} + \frac{(526 - 444.52)^2}{444.52}$$
$$= 30.52 + 24.82 + 18.37 + 14.94 = 88.65$$

Decision

Reject H_0 at the .05 level of significance because χ^2 = 88.65 exceeds 3.84.

Interpretation

Type of accommodation and survival rate are not independent. (Survival rate was lower in steerage.)

(b) $\phi_c^2 = \dfrac{88.65}{1291\,(2-1)} = .07$ (The strength of the relationship is medium, according to Cohen's guidelines.)

NOTE: The relatively modest value of .07 for ϕ_c^2 compensates for the role of the very large sample size of 1291 in generating the highly significant χ^2 value of 88.65 and a minuscule exact p-value of .000.

(c) $OR = \dfrac{299/280}{186/526} = \dfrac{1.07}{.35} = 3.06$

A cabin passenger is 3.06 times more likely to have survived than a steerage passenger.

Chapter 20

20.1 **(a)** 1, 2, 3, 4.5, 4.5, 6, 7, 9, 9, 9, 11
(b) 1, 2.5, 2.5, 4.5, 4.5, 6, 7, 8, 9, 10
(c) 1, 3.5, 3.5, 3.5, 3.5, 6, 7, 8.5, 8.5, 10

20.2 **(a)** *Research Problem*

Do therapy groups with directive leaders (1) produce more or less growth (in members) than therapy groups with nondirective leaders (2)?

Statistical Hypotheses

H_0: Population distribution 1 = Population distribution 2
H_1: Population distribution 1 $\neq$ Population distribution 2

Decision Rule

Reject H_0 at the .05 level of significance if $U \leq 5$, given $n_1 = 6$ and $n_2 = 6$.

Calculations

$U_1 = 31$
$U_2 = 5$
$U = 5$

Decision

Reject H_0 at the .05 level of significance because $U = 5$ equals 5.

Interpretation

Therapy groups with directive leaders produce less growth than those with nondirective leaders.

(b) $p = .05$ (since the calculated U equals the critical U for $p = .05$)

20.3 **(a)** Each distribution of difference scores tends to be non-normal, with "heavy" tails and a "light" middle.

(b) *Research Problem*

Does a quit-smoking workshop cause a decline in cigarette smoking?

Statistical Hypotheses

H_0: Population distribution 1 ≤ Population distribution 2
H_1: Population distribution 1 > Population distribution 2
NOTE: The directional H_1 assumes that both population distributions have roughly similar shapes.

Decision Rule

Reject H_0 at the .05 level (directional test) if T equals or is less than 5 given $n = 8$.

Calculations

$R_+ = 34$
$R_- = 2$
$T = 2$

Decision

Reject H_0 at the .05 level of significance because $T = 2$ is less than 5.

Interpretation

A quit-smoking workshop causes a decline in smoking.

(c) $p < .05$

(d) Smoking is significantly less after a quit-smoking workshop [$T (n = 8) = 2, p < .05$].

20.4 **(a)** Observed scores tend not to be normally distributed. There is no obvious cluster of scores in the middle range of each of the five groups.

(b) *Research Problem*

Are motion picture ratings associated with the number of violent or sexually explicit scenes in films?

Statistical Hypotheses

H_0: Population dist. NC-17 = Population dist. R = Population dist. PG-13 = Population dist. PG = Population dist. G
H_1: H_0 is false.

Decision Rule

Reject H_0 at the .05 level if $H \geq 9.49$, given $df = 4$.

Calculations

$$H = \frac{12}{25(25+1)} \left[\frac{(114)^2}{5} + \frac{(75.5)^2}{5} + \frac{(69)^2}{5} + \frac{(49.5)^2}{5} + \frac{(17)^2}{5} \right] - 3(25+1)$$

$$= .02[5239.30] - 78.00$$

$$= 26.79$$

Decision

Reject H_0 at the .05 level of significance because $H = 26.79$ exceeds 9.49.

Interpretation

Motion picture ratings are associated with the number of violent or sexually explicit scenes in films.

(c) $p < .001$

Chapter 21

21.1 Two-variable χ^2

21.2 t for two independent samples

21.3 t for two related samples (repeated measures)

21.5 One-variable χ^2

21.6 One-factor F

21.9 Two-factor F

21.10 t for two independent samples

21.11 t for correlation coefficient

APPENDIX C

Tables

Table A entries were computed by the second author.

Table B is taken from Table 12 of E. Pearson and H. Hartley (Eds.), *Biometrika Tables for Statisticians*, Vol. 1, 3rd ed. Cambridge: University Press, 1966, with permission of the Biometrika Trustees.

Table C is taken from *Statistical Methods,* by George W. Snedecor and William G. Cochran, 8th ed. Ames: Iowa State University Press, 1989, with permission of Wiley-Blackwell, Inc., a subsidiary of John Wiley & Sons, Inc.

Table D is taken from Table 8 of E. Pearson and H. Hartley (Eds.), *Biometrika Tables For Statisticians,* Vol. 1, 3rd. ed. Cambridge: University Press, 1966, with permission of the Biometrika Trustees.

Table E is taken from the Bulletin of the Institute of Educational Research, 1953, Vol. No. 2, Indiana University, with permission of the publishers.

Table F is taken from F. Wilcoxon and R. A. Wilcox. *Some Rapid Approximate Statistical Procedures,* 2nd edition. Pearl River, New York: Lederle Laboratories. 1964, with permission of the American Cyanamid Company.

Table G is taken from Table 29 of E. Pearson and H. Hartley (Eds.), *Biometrika Tables for Statisticians*, Vol. 1, 3rd ed. Cambridge: University Press, 1966, with permission of the Biometrika Trustees.

Table H reprinted from page 1 of *A. Million Random Digits with 100,000 Normal Deviates*, Rand, 1994. RP-295, 200 pp. Used by permission.

Table A[a]
PROPORTIONS (OF AREA) UNDER THE STANDARD NORMAL CURVE FOR VALUES OF z

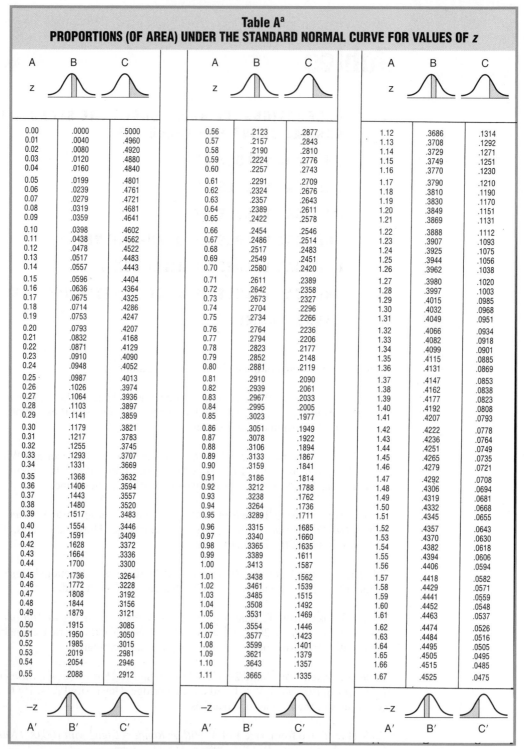

A — z	B	C	A — z	B	C	A — z	B	C
0.00	.0000	.5000	0.56	.2123	.2877	1.12	.3686	.1314
0.01	.0040	.4960	0.57	.2157	.2843	1.13	.3708	.1292
0.02	.0080	.4920	0.58	.2190	.2810	1.14	.3729	.1271
0.03	.0120	.4880	0.59	.2224	.2776	1.15	.3749	.1251
0.04	.0160	.4840	0.60	.2257	.2743	1.16	.3770	.1230
0.05	.0199	.4801	0.61	.2291	.2709	1.17	.3790	.1210
0.06	.0239	.4761	0.62	.2324	.2676	1.18	.3810	.1190
0.07	.0279	.4721	0.63	.2357	.2643	1.19	.3830	.1170
0.08	.0319	.4681	0.64	.2389	.2611	1.20	.3849	.1151
0.09	.0359	.4641	0.65	.2422	.2578	1.21	.3869	.1131
0.10	.0398	.4602	0.66	.2454	.2546	1.22	.3888	.1112
0.11	.0438	.4562	0.67	.2486	.2514	1.23	.3907	.1093
0.12	.0478	.4522	0.68	.2517	.2483	1.24	.3925	.1075
0.13	.0517	.4483	0.69	.2549	.2451	1.25	.3944	.1056
0.14	.0557	.4443	0.70	.2580	.2420	1.26	.3962	.1038
0.15	.0596	.4404	0.71	.2611	.2389	1.27	.3980	.1020
0.16	.0636	.4364	0.72	.2642	.2358	1.28	.3997	.1003
0.17	.0675	.4325	0.73	.2673	.2327	1.29	.4015	.0985
0.18	.0714	.4286	0.74	.2704	.2296	1.30	.4032	.0968
0.19	.0753	.4247	0.75	.2734	.2266	1.31	.4049	.0951
0.20	.0793	.4207	0.76	.2764	.2236	1.32	.4066	.0934
0.21	.0832	.4168	0.77	.2794	.2206	1.33	.4082	.0918
0.22	.0871	.4129	0.78	.2823	.2177	1.34	.4099	.0901
0.23	.0910	.4090	0.79	.2852	.2148	1.35	.4115	.0885
0.24	.0948	.4052	0.80	.2881	.2119	1.36	.4131	.0869
0.25	.0987	.4013	0.81	.2910	.2090	1.37	.4147	.0853
0.26	.1026	.3974	0.82	.2939	.2061	1.38	.4162	.0838
0.27	.1064	.3936	0.83	.2967	.2033	1.39	.4177	.0823
0.28	.1103	.3897	0.84	.2995	.2005	1.40	.4192	.0808
0.29	.1141	.3859	0.85	.3023	.1977	1.41	.4207	.0793
0.30	.1179	.3821	0.86	.3051	.1949	1.42	.4222	.0778
0.31	.1217	.3783	0.87	.3078	.1922	1.43	.4236	.0764
0.32	.1255	.3745	0.88	.3106	.1894	1.44	.4251	.0749
0.33	.1293	.3707	0.89	.3133	.1867	1.45	.4265	.0735
0.34	.1331	.3669	0.90	.3159	.1841	1.46	.4279	.0721
0.35	.1368	.3632	0.91	.3186	.1814	1.47	.4292	.0708
0.36	.1406	.3594	0.92	.3212	.1788	1.48	.4306	.0694
0.37	.1443	.3557	0.93	.3238	.1762	1.49	.4319	.0681
0.38	.1480	.3520	0.94	.3264	.1736	1.50	.4332	.0668
0.39	.1517	.3483	0.95	.3289	.1711	1.51	.4345	.0655
0.40	.1554	.3446	0.96	.3315	.1685	1.52	.4357	.0643
0.41	.1591	.3409	0.97	.3340	.1660	1.53	.4370	.0630
0.42	.1628	.3372	0.98	.3365	.1635	1.54	.4382	.0618
0.43	.1664	.3336	0.99	.3389	.1611	1.55	.4394	.0606
0.44	.1700	.3300	1.00	.3413	.1587	1.56	.4406	.0594
0.45	.1736	.3264	1.01	.3438	.1562	1.57	.4418	.0582
0.46	.1772	.3228	1.02	.3461	.1539	1.58	.4429	.0571
0.47	.1808	.3192	1.03	.3485	.1515	1.59	.4441	.0559
0.48	.1844	.3156	1.04	.3508	.1492	1.60	.4452	.0548
0.49	.1879	.3121	1.05	.3531	.1469	1.61	.4463	.0537
0.50	.1915	.3085	1.06	.3554	.1446	1.62	.4474	.0526
0.51	.1950	.3050	1.07	.3577	.1423	1.63	.4484	.0516
0.52	.1985	.3015	1.08	.3599	.1401	1.64	.4495	.0505
0.53	.2019	.2981	1.09	.3621	.1379	1.65	.4505	.0495
0.54	.2054	.2946	1.10	.3643	.1357	1.66	.4515	.0485
0.55	.2088	.2912	1.11	.3665	.1335	1.67	.4525	.0475

[a] Discussed in Section 5.3.

Table A[a] (Continued)
PROPORTIONS (OF AREA) UNDER THE STANDARD NORMAL CURVE FOR VALUES OF z

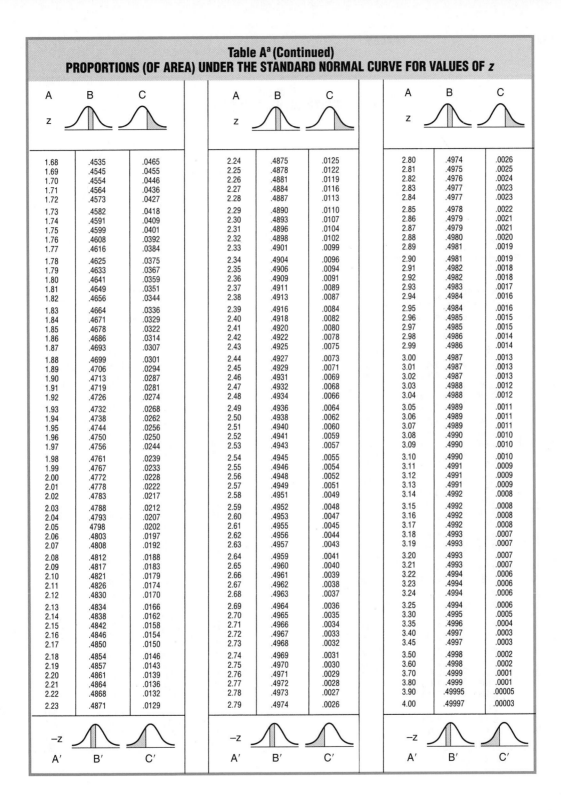

A z	B	C	A z	B	C	A z	B	C
1.68	.4535	.0465	2.24	.4875	.0125	2.80	.4974	.0026
1.69	.4545	.0455	2.25	.4878	.0122	2.81	.4975	.0025
1.70	.4554	.0446	2.26	.4881	.0119	2.82	.4976	.0024
1.71	.4564	.0436	2.27	.4884	.0116	2.83	.4977	.0023
1.72	.4573	.0427	2.28	.4887	.0113	2.84	.4977	.0023
1.73	.4582	.0418	2.29	.4890	.0110	2.85	.4978	.0022
1.74	.4591	.0409	2.30	.4893	.0107	2.86	.4979	.0021
1.75	.4599	.0401	2.31	.4896	.0104	2.87	.4979	.0021
1.76	.4608	.0392	2.32	.4898	.0102	2.88	.4980	.0020
1.77	.4616	.0384	2.33	.4901	.0099	2.89	.4981	.0019
1.78	.4625	.0375	2.34	.4904	.0096	2.90	.4981	.0019
1.79	.4633	.0367	2.35	.4906	.0094	2.91	.4982	.0018
1.80	.4641	.0359	2.36	.4909	.0091	2.92	.4982	.0018
1.81	.4649	.0351	2.37	.4911	.0089	2.93	.4983	.0017
1.82	.4656	.0344	2.38	.4913	.0087	2.94	.4984	.0016
1.83	.4664	.0336	2.39	.4916	.0084	2.95	.4984	.0016
1.84	.4671	.0329	2.40	.4918	.0082	2.96	.4985	.0015
1.85	.4678	.0322	2.41	.4920	.0080	2.97	.4985	.0015
1.86	.4686	.0314	2.42	.4922	.0078	2.98	.4986	.0014
1.87	.4693	.0307	2.43	.4925	.0075	2.99	.4986	.0014
1.88	.4699	.0301	2.44	.4927	.0073	3.00	.4987	.0013
1.89	.4706	.0294	2.45	.4929	.0071	3.01	.4987	.0013
1.90	.4713	.0287	2.46	.4931	.0069	3.02	.4987	.0013
1.91	.4719	.0281	2.47	.4932	.0068	3.03	.4988	.0012
1.92	.4726	.0274	2.48	.4934	.0066	3.04	.4988	.0012
1.93	.4732	.0268	2.49	.4936	.0064	3.05	.4989	.0011
1.94	.4738	.0262	2.50	.4938	.0062	3.06	.4989	.0011
1.95	.4744	.0256	2.51	.4940	.0060	3.07	.4989	.0011
1.96	.4750	.0250	2.52	.4941	.0059	3.08	.4990	.0010
1.97	.4756	.0244	2.53	.4943	.0057	3.09	.4990	.0010
1.98	.4761	.0239	2.54	.4945	.0055	3.10	.4990	.0010
1.99	.4767	.0233	2.55	.4946	.0054	3.11	.4991	.0009
2.00	.4772	.0228	2.56	.4948	.0052	3.12	.4991	.0009
2.01	.4778	.0222	2.57	.4949	.0051	3.13	.4991	.0009
2.02	.4783	.0217	2.58	.4951	.0049	3.14	.4992	.0008
2.03	.4788	.0212	2.59	.4952	.0048	3.15	.4992	.0008
2.04	.4793	.0207	2.60	.4953	.0047	3.16	.4992	.0008
2.05	4798	.0202	2.61	.4955	.0045	3.17	.4992	.0008
2.06	.4803	.0197	2.62	.4956	.0044	3.18	.4993	.0007
2.07	.4808	.0192	2.63	.4957	.0043	3.19	.4993	.0007
2.08	.4812	.0188	2.64	.4959	.0041	3.20	.4993	.0007
2.09	.4817	.0183	2.65	.4960	.0040	3.21	.4993	.0007
2.10	.4821	.0179	2.66	.4961	.0039	3.22	.4994	.0006
2.11	.4826	.0174	2.67	.4962	.0038	3.23	.4994	.0006
2.12	.4830	.0170	2.68	.4963	.0037	3.24	.4994	.0006
2.13	.4834	.0166	2.69	.4964	.0036	3.25	.4994	.0006
2.14	.4838	.0162	2.70	.4965	.0035	3.30	.4995	.0005
2.15	.4842	.0158	2.71	.4966	.0034	3.35	.4996	.0004
2.16	.4846	.0154	2.72	.4967	.0033	3.40	.4997	.0003
2.17	.4850	.0150	2.73	.4968	.0032	3.45	.4997	.0003
2.18	.4854	.0146	2.74	.4969	.0031	3.50	.4998	.0002
2.19	.4857	.0143	2.75	.4970	.0030	3.60	.4998	.0002
2.20	.4861	.0139	2.76	.4971	.0029	3.70	.4999	.0001
2.21	.4864	.0136	2.77	.4972	.0028	3.80	.4999	.0001
2.22	.4868	.0132	2.78	.4973	.0027	3.90	.49995	.00005
2.23	.4871	.0129	2.79	.4974	.0026	4.00	.49997	.00003

−z			−z			−z		
A′	B′	C′	A′	B′	C′	A′	B′	C′

Table B[a]
CRITICAL VALUES OF *t*

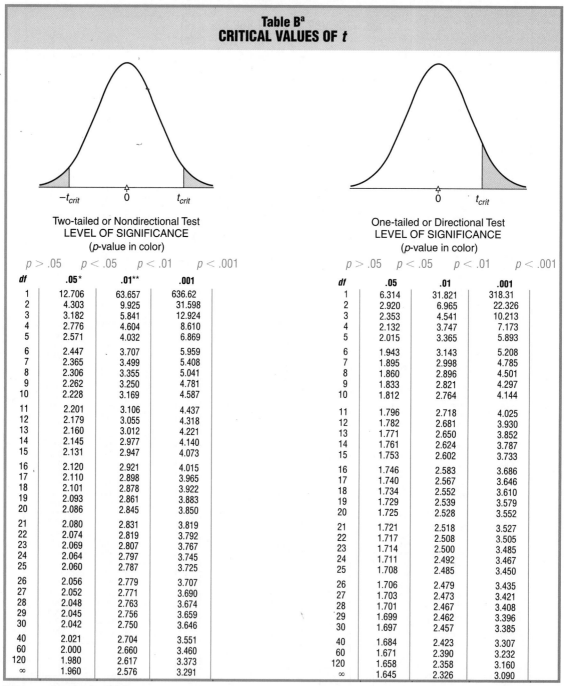

Two-tailed or Nondirectional Test
LEVEL OF SIGNIFICANCE
(*p*-value in color)

$p > .05$ $p < .05$ $p < .01$ $p < .001$

df	.05*	.01**	.001
1	12.706	63.657	636.62
2	4.303	9.925	31.598
3	3.182	5.841	12.924
4	2.776	4.604	8.610
5	2.571	4.032	6.869
6	2.447	3.707	5.959
7	2.365	3.499	5.408
8	2.306	3.355	5.041
9	2.262	3.250	4.781
10	2.228	3.169	4.587
11	2.201	3.106	4.437
12	2.179	3.055	4.318
13	2.160	3.012	4.221
14	2.145	2.977	4.140
15	2.131	2.947	4.073
16	2.120	2.921	4.015
17	2.110	2.898	3.965
18	2.101	2.878	3.922
19	2.093	2.861	3.883
20	2.086	2.845	3.850
21	2.080	2.831	3.819
22	2.074	2.819	3.792
23	2.069	2.807	3.767
24	2.064	2.797	3.745
25	2.060	2.787	3.725
26	2.056	2.779	3.707
27	2.052	2.771	3.690
28	2.048	2.763	3.674
29	2.045	2.756	3.659
30	2.042	2.750	3.646
40	2.021	2.704	3.551
60	2.000	2.660	3.460
120	1.980	2.617	3.373
∞	1.960	2.576	3.291

One-tailed or Directional Test
LEVEL OF SIGNIFICANCE
(*p*-value in color)

$p > .05$ $p < .05$ $p < .01$ $p < .001$

df	.05	.01	.001
1	6.314	31.821	318.31
2	2.920	6.965	22.326
3	2.353	4.541	10.213
4	2.132	3.747	7.173
5	2.015	3.365	5.893
6	1.943	3.143	5.208
7	1.895	2.998	4.785
8	1.860	2.896	4.501
9	1.833	2.821	4.297
10	1.812	2.764	4.144
11	1.796	2.718	4.025
12	1.782	2.681	3.930
13	1.771	2.650	3.852
14	1.761	2.624	3.787
15	1.753	2.602	3.733
16	1.746	2.583	3.686
17	1.740	2.567	3.646
18	1.734	2.552	3.610
19	1.729	2.539	3.579
20	1.725	2.528	3.552
21	1.721	2.518	3.527
22	1.717	2.508	3.505
23	1.714	2.500	3.485
24	1.711	2.492	3.467
25	1.708	2.485	3.450
26	1.706	2.479	3.435
27	1.703	2.473	3.421
28	1.701	2.467	3.408
29	1.699	2.462	3.396
30	1.697	2.457	3.385
40	1.684	2.423	3.307
60	1.671	2.390	3.232
120	1.658	2.358	3.160
∞	1.645	2.326	3.090

[a] Discussed in Section 13.2.
*95% level of confidence.
**99% level of confidence.

Table C[a]
CRITICAL VALUES OF F

.05 level of significance (light numbers)
.01 level of significance (dark numbers)

FINDING p-VALUE
If observed F is
. . . smaller than light number, p > .05
. . . between light and dark numbers, p < .05
. . . larger than dark number, p < .01

DEGREES OF FREEDOM IN NUMERATOR

Each cell shows: .05 value (light) / .01 value (dark).

DF denom.	1	2	3	4	5	6	7	8	9	10	11	12	14	16	20	24	30	40	50	75	100	200	500	∞
1	161 / 4,052	200 / 4,999	216 / 5,403	225 / 5,625	230 / 5,764	234 / 5,859	237 / 5,928	239 / 5,981	241 / 6,022	242 / 6,056	243 / 6,082	244 / 6,106	245 / 6,142	246 / 6,169	248 / 6,208	249 / 6,234	250 / 6,258	251 / 6,286	252 / 6,302	253 / 6,323	253 / 6,334	254 / 6,352	254 / 6,361	254 / 6,366
2	18.51 / 98.49	19.00 / 99.00	19.16 / 99.17	19.25 / 99.25	19.30 / 99.30	19.33 / 99.33	19.36 / 99.34	19.37 / 99.36	19.38 / 99.38	19.39 / 99.40	19.40 / 99.41	19.41 / 99.42	19.42 / 99.43	19.43 / 99.44	19.44 / 99.45	19.45 / 99.46	19.46 / 99.47	19.47 / 99.48	19.47 / 99.48	19.48 / 99.49	19.49 / 99.49	19.49 / 99.49	19.50 / 99.50	19.50 / 99.50
3	10.13 / 34.12	9.55 / 30.82	9.28 / 29.46	9.12 / 28.71	9.01 / 28.24	8.94 / 27.91	8.88 / 27.67	8.84 / 27.49	8.81 / 27.34	8.78 / 27.23	8.76 / 27.13	8.74 / 27.05	8.71 / 26.92	8.69 / 26.83	8.66 / 26.69	8.64 / 26.60	8.62 / 26.50	8.60 / 26.41	8.58 / 26.35	8.57 / 26.27	8.56 / 26.23	8.54 / 26.18	8.54 / 26.14	8.53 / 26.12
4	7.71 / 21.20	6.94 / 18.00	6.59 / 16.69	6.39 / 15.98	6.26 / 15.52	6.16 / 15.21	6.09 / 14.98	6.04 / 14.80	6.00 / 14.66	5.96 / 14.54	5.93 / 14.45	5.91 / 14.37	5.87 / 14.24	5.84 / 14.15	5.80 / 14.02	5.77 / 13.93	5.74 / 13.83	5.71 / 13.74	5.70 / 13.69	5.68 / 13.61	5.66 / 13.57	5.65 / 13.52	5.64 / 13.48	5.63 / 13.46
5	6.61 / 16.26	5.79 / 13.27	5.41 / 12.06	5.19 / 11.39	5.05 / 10.97	4.95 / 10.67	4.88 / 10.45	4.82 / 10.27	4.78 / 10.15	4.74 / 10.05	4.70 / 9.96	4.68 / 9.89	4.64 / 9.77	4.60 / 9.68	4.56 / 9.55	4.53 / 9.47	4.50 / 9.38	4.46 / 9.29	4.44 / 9.24	4.42 / 9.17	4.40 / 9.13	4.38 / 9.07	4.37 / 9.04	4.36 / 9.02
6	5.99 / 13.74	5.14 / 10.92	4.76 / 9.78	4.53 / 9.15	4.39 / 8.75	4.28 / 8.47	4.21 / 8.26	4.15 / 8.10	4.10 / 7.98	4.06 / 7.87	4.03 / 7.79	4.00 / 7.72	3.96 / 7.60	3.92 / 7.52	3.87 / 7.39	3.84 / 7.31	3.81 / 7.23	3.77 / 7.14	3.75 / 7.09	3.72 / 7.02	3.71 / 6.99	3.69 / 6.94	3.68 / 6.90	3.67 / 6.88
7	5.59 / 12.25	4.47 / 9.55	4.35 / 8.45	4.12 / 7.85	3.97 / 7.46	3.87 / 7.19	3.79 / 7.00	3.73 / 6.84	3.68 / 6.71	3.63 / 6.62	3.60 / 6.54	3.57 / 6.47	3.52 / 6.35	3.49 / 6.27	3.44 / 6.15	3.41 / 6.07	3.38 / 5.98	3.34 / 5.90	3.32 / 5.85	3.29 / 5.78	3.28 / 5.75	3.25 / 5.70	3.24 / 5.67	3.23 / 5.65
8	5.32 / 11.26	4.46 / 8.65	4.07 / 7.59	3.84 / 7.01	3.69 / 6.63	3.58 / 6.37	3.50 / 6.19	3.44 / 6.03	3.39 / 5.91	3.34 / 5.82	3.31 / 5.74	3.28 / 5.67	3.23 / 5.56	3.20 / 5.48	3.15 / 5.36	3.12 / 5.28	3.08 / 5.20	3.05 / 5.11	3.03 / 5.06	3.0 / 5.00	2.98 / 4.96	2.96 / 4.91	2.94 / 4.88	2.93 / 4.86
9	5.12 / 10.56	4.26 / 8.02	3.86 / 6.99	3.63 / 6.42	3.48 / 6.06	3.37 / 5.80	3.29 / 5.62	3.23 / 5.47	3.18 / 5.35	3.13 / 5.26	3.10 / 5.18	3.07 / 5.11	3.02 / 5.00	2.98 / 4.92	2.93 / 4.80	2.90 / 4.73	2.86 / 4.64	2.82 / 4.56	2.80 / 4.51	2.77 / 4.45	2.76 / 4.41	2.73 / 4.36	2.72 / 4.33	2.71 / 4.31
10	4.96 / 10.04	4.10 / 7.56	3.71 / 6.55	3.48 / 5.99	3.33 / 5.64	3.22 / 5.39	3.14 / 5.21	3.07 / 5.06	3.02 / 4.95	2.97 / 4.85	2.94 / 4.78	2.91 / 4.71	2.86 / 4.60	2.82 / 4.52	2.77 / 4.41	2.74 / 4.33	2.70 / 4.25	2.67 / 4.17	2.64 / 4.12	2.61 / 4.05	2.59 / 4.01	2.56 / 3.96	2.55 / 3.93	2.54 / 3.91
11	4.84 / 9.65	3.98 / 7.20	3.59 / 6.22	3.36 / 5.67	3.20 / 5.32	3.09 / 5.07	3.01 / 4.88	2.95 / 4.74	2.90 / 4.63	2.86 / 4.54	2.82 / 4.46	2.79 / 4.40	2.74 / 4.29	2.70 / 4.21	2.65 / 4.10	2.61 / 4.02	2.57 / 3.94	2.53 / 3.86	2.50 / 3.80	2.47 / 3.74	2.45 / 3.70	2.42 / 3.66	2.41 / 3.62	2.40 / 3.60
12	4.75 / 9.33	3.88 / 6.93	3.49 / 5.95	3.26 / 5.41	3.11 / 5.06	3.00 / 4.82	2.92 / 4.65	2.85 / 4.50	2.80 / 4.39	2.76 / 4.30	2.72 / 4.22	2.69 / 4.16	2.64 / 4.05	2.60 / 3.98	2.54 / 3.86	2.50 / 3.78	2.46 / 3.70	2.42 / 3.61	2.40 / 3.56	2.36 / 3.49	2.35 / 3.46	2.32 / 3.41	2.31 / 3.38	2.30 / 3.36
13	4.67 / 9.07	3.80 / 6.70	3.41 / 5.74	3.18 / 5.20	3.02 / 4.86	2.92 / 4.62	2.84 / 4.44	2.77 / 4.30	2.72 / 4.19	2.67 / 4.10	2.63 / 4.02	2.60 / 3.96	2.55 / 3.85	2.51 / 3.78	2.46 / 3.67	2.42 / 3.59	2.38 / 3.51	2.34 / 3.42	2.32 / 3.37	2.28 / 3.30	2.26 / 3.27	2.24 / 3.21	2.22 / 3.18	2.21 / 3.16

DEGREES OF FREEDOM IN DENOMINATOR

[a] Discussed in Section 16.6.

Table Cᵃ (Continued)
CRITICAL VALUES OF F

DEGREES OF FREEDOM IN NUMERATOR

Each cell shows light number (top, $p=.05$) / dark number (bottom, $p=.01$).

Denom. df	1	2	3	4	5	6	7	8	9	10	11	12	14	16	20	24	30	40	50	75	100	200	500	∞
14	4.60/8.86	3.74/6.51	3.34/5.56	3.11/5.03	2.96/4.69	2.85/4.46	2.77/4.28	2.70/4.14	2.65/4.03	2.60/3.94	2.56/3.86	2.53/3.80	2.48/3.70	2.44/3.62	2.39/3.51	2.35/3.43	2.31/3.34	2.27/3.26	2.24/3.21	2.21/3.14	2.19/3.11	2.16/3.06	2.14/3.02	2.13/3.00
15	4.54/8.68	3.68/6.36	3.29/5.42	3.06/4.89	2.90/4.56	2.79/4.32	2.70/4.14	2.64/4.00	2.59/3.89	2.55/3.80	2.51/3.73	2.48/3.67	2.43/3.56	2.39/3.48	2.33/3.36	2.29/3.29	2.25/3.20	2.21/3.12	2.18/3.07	2.15/3.00	2.12/2.97	2.10/2.9	2.08/2.89	2.07/2.80
16	4.49/8.53	3.63/6.23	3.24/5.29	3.01/4.77	2.85/4.44	2.74/4.20	2.66/4.03	2.59/3.89	2.54/3.78	2.49/3.69	2.45/3.61	2.42/3.55	2.37/3.45	2.33/3.37	2.28/3.25	2.24/3.18	2.20/3.10	2.16/3.01	2.13/2.96	2.09/2.89	2.07/2.86	2.04/2.80	2.02/2.77	2.01/2.75
17	4.45/8.40	3.59/6.11	3.20/5.18	2.96/4.67	2.81/4.34	2.70/4.10	2.62/3.93	2.55/3.79	2.50/3.68	2.45/3.59	2.41/3.52	2.38/3.45	2.33/3.35	2.29/3.27	2.23/3.16	2.19/3.08	2.15/3.00	2.11/2.92	2.08/2.86	2.04/2.79	2.02/2.76	1.99/2.70	1.97/2.67	1.96/2.65
18	4.41/8.28	3.55/6.01	3.16/5.09	2.93/4.58	2.77/4.25	2.66/4.01	2.58/3.85	2.51/3.71	2.46/3.60	2.41/3.51	2.37/3.44	2.34/3.37	2.29/3.27	2.25/3.19	2.19/3.07	2.15/3.00	2.11/2.91	2.07/2.83	2.04/2.78	2.00/2.71	1.98/2.68	1.95/2.62	1.93/2.59	1.92/2.57
19	4.38/8.18	3.52/5.93	3.13/5.01	2.90/4.50	2.74/4.17	2.63/3.94	2.55/3.77	2.48/3.63	2.43/3.52	2.38/3.43	2.34/3.36	2.31/3.30	2.26/3.19	2.21/3.12	2.15/3.00	2.11/2.92	2.07/2.84	2.02/2.76	2.00/2.70	1.96/2.63	1.94/2.60	1.91/2.54	1.90/2.51	1.88/2.49
20	4.35/8.10	3.49/5.85	3.10/4.94	2.87/4.43	2.71/4.10	2.60/3.87	2.52/3.71	2.45/3.56	2.40/3.45	2.35/3.37	2.31/3.30	2.28/3.23	2.23/3.13	2.18/3.05	2.12/2.94	2.08/2.86	2.04/2.77	1.99/2.69	1.96/2.63	1.92/2.56	1.90/2.53	1.87/2.47	1.85/2.44	1.84/2.42
21	4.32/8.02	3.47/5.78	3.07/4.87	2.84/4.37	2.68/4.04	2.57/3.81	2.49/3.65	2.42/3.51	2.37/3.40	2.32/3.31	2.28/3.24	2.25/3.17	2.20/3.07	2.15/2.99	2.09/2.88	2.05/2.80	2.00/2.72	1.96/2.63	1.93/2.58	1.89/2.51	1.87/2.47	1.84/2.42	1.82/2.38	1.81/2.36
22	4.30/7.94	3.44/5.72	3.05/4.82	2.82/4.31	2.66/3.99	2.55/3.76	2.47/3.59	2.40/3.45	2.35/3.35	2.30/3.26	2.26/3.18	2.23/3.12	2.18/3.02	2.13/2.94	2.07/2.83	2.03/2.75	1.98/2.67	1.93/2.58	1.91/2.53	1.87/2.46	1.84/2.42	1.81/2.37	1.80/2.33	1.78/2.31
23	4.28/7.88	3.42/5.66	3.03/4.76	2.80/4.26	2.64/3.94	2.53/3.71	2.45/3.54	2.38/3.41	2.32/3.30	2.28/3.21	2.24/3.14	2.20/3.07	2.14/2.97	2.10/2.89	2.04/2.78	2.00/2.70	1.96/2.62	1.91/2.53	1.88/2.48	1.84/2.41	1.82/2.37	1.79/2.32	1.77/2.28	1.76/2.26
24	4.26/7.82	3.40/5.61	3.01/4.72	2.78/4.22	2.62/3.90	2.51/3.67	2.43/3.50	2.36/3.36	2.30/3.25	2.26/3.17	2.22/3.09	2.18/3.03	2.13/2.93	2.09/2.85	2.02/2.74	1.98/2.66	1.94/2.58	1.89/2.49	1.86/2.44	1.82/2.36	1.80/2.33	1.76/2.27	1.74/2.23	1.73/2.21
25	4.24/7.77	3.38/5.57	2.99/4.68	2.76/4.18	2.60/3.86	2.49/3.63	2.41/3.46	2.34/3.32	2.28/3.21	2.24/3.13	2.20/3.05	2.16/2.99	2.11/2.89	2.06/2.81	2.00/2.70	1.96/2.62	1.92/2.54	1.87/2.45	1.84/2.40	1.80/2.32	1.77/2.29	1.74/2.23	1.72/2.19	1.71/2.17
26	4.22/7.72	3.37/5.53	2.98/4.64	2.74/4.14	2.59/3.82	2.47/3.59	2.39/3.42	2.32/3.29	2.27/3.17	2.22/3.09	2.18/3.02	2.15/2.96	2.10/2.86	2.05/2.77	1.99/2.66	1.95/2.58	1.90/2.50	1.86/2.41	1.82/2.36	1.78/2.28	1.76/2.25	1.72/2.19	1.70/2.15	1.69/2.13

(Denominator df is "DEGREES OF FREEDOM IN DENOMINATOR.")

Table C[a] (Continued)
CRITICAL VALUES OF F

df																								
27	4.21 **7.68**	3.35 **5.49**	2.96 **4.60**	2.73 **4.11**	2.57 **3.79**	2.46 **3.56**	2.37 **3.39**	2.30 **3.26**	2.25 **3.14**	2.20 **3.06**	2.16 **2.98**	2.13 **2.93**	2.08 **2.83**	2.03 **2.74**	1.97 **2.63**	1.93 **2.55**	1.88 **2.47**	1.84 **2.38**	1.80 **2.33**	1.76 **2.25**	1.74 **2.21**	1.71 **2.16**	1.68 **2.12**	1.67 **2.10**
28	4.20 **7.64**	3.34 **5.45**	2.95 **4.57**	2.71 **4.07**	2.56 **3.76**	2.44 **3.53**	2.36 **3.36**	2.29 **3.23**	2.24 **3.11**	2.19 **3.03**	2.15 **2.95**	2.12 **2.90**	2.06 **2.80**	2.02 **2.71**	1.96 **2.60**	1.91 **2.52**	1.87 **2.44**	1.81 **2.35**	1.78 **2.30**	1.75 **2.22**	1.72 **2.18**	1.69 **2.13**	1.67 **2.09**	1.65 **2.06**
29	4.18 **7.60**	3.33 **5.42**	2.93 **4.54**	2.70 **4.04**	2.54 **3.73**	2.43 **3.50**	2.35 **3.33**	2.28 **3.20**	2.22 **3.08**	2.18 **3.00**	2.14 **2.92**	2.10 **2.87**	2.05 **2.77**	2.00 **2.68**	1.94 **2.57**	1.90 **2.49**	1.85 **2.41**	1.80 **2.32**	1.77 **2.27**	1.73 **2.19**	1.71 **2.15**	1.68 **2.10**	1.65 **2.06**	1.64 **2.03**
30	4.17 **7.56**	3.32 **5.39**	2.92 **4.51**	2.69 **4.02**	2.53 **3.70**	2.42 **3.47**	2.34 **3.30**	2.27 **3.17**	2.21 **3.06**	2.16 **2.98**	2.12 **2.90**	2.09 **2.84**	2.04 **2.74**	1.99 **2.66**	1.93 **2.55**	1.89 **2.47**	1.84 **2.38**	1.79 **2.29**	1.76 **2.24**	1.72 **2.16**	1.69 **2.13**	1.66 **2.07**	1.64 **2.03**	1.62 **2.01**
32	4.15 **7.50**	3.30 **5.34**	2.90 **4.46**	2.67 **3.97**	2.51 **3.66**	2.40 **3.42**	2.32 **3.25**	2.25 **3.12**	2.19 **3.01**	2.14 **2.94**	2.10 **2.86**	2.07 **2.80**	2.02 **2.70**	1.97 **2.62**	1.91 **2.51**	1.86 **2.42**	1.82 **2.34**	1.76 **2.25**	1.74 **2.20**	1.69 **2.12**	1.67 **2.08**	1.64 **2.02**	1.61 **1.98**	1.59 **1.96**
34	4.13 **7.44**	3.28 **5.29**	2.88 **4.42**	2.65 **3.93**	2.49 **3.61**	2.38 **3.38**	2.30 **3.21**	2.23 **3.08**	2.17 **2.97**	2.12 **2.89**	2.08 **2.82**	2.05 **2.76**	2.00 **2.66**	1.95 **2.58**	1.89 **2.47**	1.84 **2.38**	1.80 **2.30**	1.74 **2.21**	1.71 **2.15**	1.67 **2.08**	1.64 **2.04**	1.61 **1.98**	1.59 **1.94**	1.57 **1.91**
36	4.11 **7.39**	3.26 **5.25**	2.86 **4.38**	2.63 **3.89**	2.48 **3.58**	2.36 **3.35**	2.28 **3.18**	2.21 **3.04**	2.15 **2.94**	2.10 **2.86**	2.06 **2.78**	2.03 **2.72**	1.98 **2.62**	1.93 **2.54**	1.87 **2.43**	1.82 **2.35**	1.78 **2.26**	1.72 **2.17**	1.69 **2.12**	1.65 **2.04**	1.62 **2.00**	1.59 **1.94**	1.56 **1.90**	1.55 **1.87**
38	4.10 **7.35**	3.25 **5.21**	2.85 **4.34**	2.62 **3.86**	2.46 **3.54**	2.35 **3.32**	2.26 **3.15**	2.19 **3.02**	2.14 **2.91**	2.09 **2.82**	2.05 **2.75**	2.02 **2.69**	1.96 **2.59**	1.92 **2.51**	1.85 **2.40**	1.80 **2.32**	1.76 **2.22**	1.71 **2.14**	1.67 **2.08**	1.63 **2.00**	1.60 **1.97**	1.57 **1.90**	1.54 **1.86**	1.53 **1.84**
40	4.08 **7.31**	3.23 **5.18**	2.84 **4.31**	2.61 **3.83**	2.45 **3.51**	2.34 **3.29**	2.25 **3.12**	2.18 **2.99**	2.12 **2.88**	2.07 **2.80**	2.04 **2.73**	2.00 **2.66**	1.95 **2.56**	1.90 **2.49**	1.84 **2.37**	1.79 **2.29**	1.74 **2.20**	1.69 **2.11**	1.66 **2.05**	1.61 **1.97**	1.59 **1.94**	1.55 **1.88**	1.53 **1.84**	1.51 **1.81**
42	4.07 **7.27**	3.22 **5.15**	2.83 **4.29**	2.59 **3.80**	2.44 **3.49**	2.32 **3.26**	2.24 **3.10**	2.17 **2.96**	2.11 **2.86**	2.06 **2.77**	2.02 **2.70**	1.99 **2.64**	1.94 **2.54**	1.89 **2.46**	1.82 **2.35**	1.78 **2.26**	1.73 **2.17**	1.68 **2.08**	1.64 **2.02**	1.60 **1.94**	1.57 **1.91**	1.54 **1.85**	1.51 **1.80**	1.49 **1.78**
44	4.06 **7.24**	3.21 **5.12**	2.82 **4.26**	2.58 **3.78**	2.43 **3.46**	2.31 **3.24**	2.23 **3.07**	2.16 **2.94**	2.10 **2.84**	2.05 **2.75**	2.01 **2.68**	1.98 **2.62**	1.92 **2.52**	1.88 **2.44**	1.81 **2.32**	1.76 **2.24**	1.72 **2.15**	1.66 **2.06**	1.63 **2.00**	1.58 **1.92**	1.56 **1.88**	1.52 **1.82**	1.50 **1.78**	1.48 **1.75**
46	4.05 **7.21**	3.20 **5.10**	2.81 **4.24**	2.57 **3.76**	2.42 **3.44**	2.30 **3.22**	2.22 **3.05**	2.14 **2.92**	2.09 **2.82**	2.04 **2.73**	2.00 **2.66**	1.97 **2.60**	1.91 **2.50**	1.87 **2.42**	1.80 **2.30**	1.75 **2.22**	1.71 **2.13**	1.65 **2.04**	1.62 **1.98**	1.57 **1.90**	1.54 **1.86**	1.51 **1.80**	1.48 **1.76**	1.46 **1.72**
48	4.04 **7.19**	3.19 **5.08**	2.80 **4.22**	2.56 **3.74**	2.41 **3.42**	2.30 **3.20**	2.21 **3.04**	2.14 **2.90**	2.08 **2.80**	2.03 **2.71**	1.99 **2.64**	1.96 **2.58**	1.90 **2.48**	1.86 **2.40**	1.79 **2.28**	1.74 **2.20**	1.70 **2.11**	1.64 **2.02**	1.61 **1.96**	1.56 **1.88**	1.53 **1.84**	1.50 **1.78**	1.47 **1.73**	1.45 **1.70**
50	4.03 **7.17**	3.18 **5.06**	2.79 **4.20**	2.56 **3.72**	2.40 **3.41**	2.29 **3.18**	2.20 **3.02**	2.13 **2.88**	2.07 **2.78**	2.02 **2.70**	1.98 **2.62**	1.95 **2.56**	1.90 **2.46**	1.85 **2.39**	1.78 **2.26**	1.74 **2.18**	1.69 **2.10**	1.63 **2.00**	1.60 **1.94**	1.55 **1.86**	1.52 **1.82**	1.48 **1.76**	1.46 **1.71**	1.44 **1.68**
55	4.02 **7.12**	3.17 **5.01**	2.78 **4.16**	2.54 **3.68**	2.38 **3.37**	2.27 **3.15**	2.18 **2.98**	2.11 **2.85**	2.05 **2.75**	2.00 **2.66**	1.97 **2.59**	1.93 **2.53**	1.88 **2.43**	1.83 **2.35**	1.76 **2.23**	1.72 **2.15**	1.67 **2.06**	1.61 **1.96**	1.58 **1.90**	1.52 **1.82**	1.50 **1.78**	1.46 **1.71**	1.43 **1.66**	1.41 **1.64**
60	4.00 **7.08**	3.15 **4.98**	2.76 **4.13**	2.52 **3.65**	2.37 **3.34**	2.25 **3.12**	2.17 **2.95**	2.10 **2.82**	2.04 **2.72**	1.99 **2.63**	1.95 **2.56**	1.92 **2.50**	1.86 **2.40**	1.81 **2.32**	1.75 **2.20**	1.70 **2.12**	1.65 **2.03**	1.59 **1.93**	1.56 **1.87**	1.50 **1.79**	1.48 **1.74**	1.44 **1.68**	1.41 **1.63**	1.39 **1.60**
65	3.99 **7.04**	3.14 **4.95**	2.75 **4.10**	2.51 **3.62**	2.36 **3.31**	2.24 **3.09**	2.15 **2.93**	2.08 **2.79**	2.02 **2.70**	1.98 **2.61**	1.94 **2.54**	1.90 **2.47**	1.85 **2.37**	1.80 **2.30**	1.73 **2.18**	1.68 **2.09**	1.63 **2.00**	1.57 **1.90**	1.54 **1.84**	1.49 **1.76**	1.46 **1.71**	1.42 **1.64**	1.39 **1.60**	1.37 **1.56**

Table C[a] (Continued)
CRITICAL VALUES OF F

FINDING p-VALUE
If observed F is
...smaller than light number, p > .05
...between light and dark numbers, p < .05
...larger than dark number, p < .01

DEGREES OF FREEDOM IN NUMERATOR

Values shown as light number / dark number.

DEGREES OF FREEDOM IN DENOMINATOR	1	2	3	4	5	6	7	8	9	10	11	12	14	16	20	24	30	40	50	75	100	200	500	∞
70	3.98 / 7.01	3.13 / 4.92	2.74 / 4.08	2.50 / 3.60	2.35 / 3.29	2.23 / 3.07	2.14 / 2.91	2.07 / 2.77	2.01 / 2.67	1.97 / 2.59	1.93 / 2.51	1.89 / 2.45	1.84 / 2.35	1.79 / 2.28	1.72 / 2.15	1.67 / 2.07	1.62 / 1.98	1.56 / 1.88	1.53 / 1.82	1.47 / 1.74	1.45 / 1.69	1.40 / 1.62	1.37 / 1.56	1.35 / 1.53
80	3.96 / 6.96	3.11 / 4.88	2.72 / 4.04	2.48 / 3.56	2.33 / 3.25	2.21 / 3.04	2.12 / 2.87	2.05 / 2.74	1.99 / 2.64	1.95 / 2.55	1.91 / 2.48	1.88 / 2.41	1.82 / 2.32	1.77 / 2.24	1.70 / 2.11	1.65 / 2.03	1.60 / 1.94	1.54 / 1.84	1.51 / 1.78	1.45 / 1.70	1.42 / 1.65	1.38 / 1.57	1.35 / 1.52	1.32 / 1.49
100	3.94 / 6.90	3.09 / 4.82	2.70 / 3.98	2.46 / 3.51	2.30 / 3.20	2.19 / 2.99	2.10 / 2.82	2.03 / 2.69	1.97 / 2.59	1.92 / 2.51	1.88 / 2.43	1.85 / 2.36	1.79 / 2.26	1.75 / 2.19	1.68 / 2.06	1.63 / 1.98	1.57 / 1.89	1.51 / 1.79	1.48 / 1.73	1.42 / 1.64	1.39 / 1.59	1.34 / 1.51	1.30 / 1.46	1.28 / 1.43
125	3.92 / 6.84	3.07 / 4.78	2.68 / 3.94	2.44 / 3.47	2.29 / 3.17	2.17 / 2.95	2.08 / 2.79	2.01 / 2.65	1.95 / 2.56	1.90 / 2.47	1.86 / 2.40	1.83 / 2.33	1.77 / 2.23	1.72 / 2.15	1.65 / 2.03	1.60 / 1.94	1.55 / 1.85	1.49 / 1.75	1.45 / 1.68	1.39 / 1.59	1.36 / 1.54	1.31 / 1.46	1.27 / 1.40	1.25 / 1.37
150	3.91 / 6.81	3.06 / 4.75	2.67 / 3.91	2.43 / 3.44	2.27 / 3.14	2.16 / 2.92	2.07 / 2.76	2.00 / 2.62	1.94 / 2.53	1.89 / 2.44	1.85 / 2.37	1.82 / 2.30	1.76 / 2.20	1.71 / 2.12	1.64 / 2.00	1.59 / 1.91	1.54 / 1.83	1.47 / 1.72	1.44 / 1.66	1.37 / 1.56	1.34 / 1.51	1.29 / 1.43	1.25 / 1.37	1.22 / 1.33
200	3.89 / 6.76	3.04 / 4.71	2.65 / 3.88	2.41 / 3.41	2.26 / 3.11	2.14 / 2.90	2.05 / 2.73	1.98 / 2.60	1.92 / 2.50	1.87 / 2.41	1.83 / 2.34	1.80 / 2.28	1.74 / 2.17	1.69 / 2.09	1.62 / 1.97	1.57 / 1.88	1.52 / 1.79	1.45 / 1.69	1.42 / 1.62	1.35 / 1.53	1.32 / 1.48	1.26 / 1.39	1.22 / 1.33	1.19 / 1.28
400	3.86 / 6.70	3.02 / 4.66	2.62 / 3.83	2.39 / 3.36	2.23 / 3.06	2.12 / 2.85	2.03 / 2.69	1.96 / 2.55	1.90 / 2.46	1.85 / 2.37	1.81 / 2.29	1.78 / 2.23	1.72 / 2.12	1.67 / 2.04	1.60 / 1.92	1.54 / 1.84	1.49 / 1.74	1.42 / 1.64	1.38 / 1.57	1.32 / 1.47	1.28 / 1.42	1.22 / 1.32	1.16 / 1.24	1.13 / 1.19
1000	3.85 / 6.66	3.00 / 4.62	2.61 / 3.80	2.38 / 3.34	2.22 / 3.04	2.10 / 2.82	2.02 / 2.66	1.95 / 2.53	1.89 / 2.43	1.84 / 2.34	1.80 / 2.26	1.76 / 2.20	1.70 / 2.09	1.65 / 2.01	1.58 / 1.89	1.53 / 1.81	1.47 / 1.71	1.41 / 1.61	1.36 / 1.54	1.30 / 1.44	1.26 / 1.38	1.19 / 1.28	1.13 / 1.19	1.08 / 1.11
∞	3.84 / 6.64	2.99 / 4.00	2.60 / 3.78	2.37 / 3.32	2.21 / 3.02	2.09 / 2.80	2.01 / 2.64	1.94 / 2.51	1.86 / 2.41	1.83 / 2.32	1.79 / 2.24	1.75 / 2.18	1.69 / 2.07	1.64 / 1.99	1.57 / 1.87	1.52 / 1.79	1.46 / 1.69	1.40 / 1.59	1.35 / 1.52	1.28 / 1.41	1.24 / 1.36	1.17 / 1.25	1.11 / 1.15	1.00 / 1.00

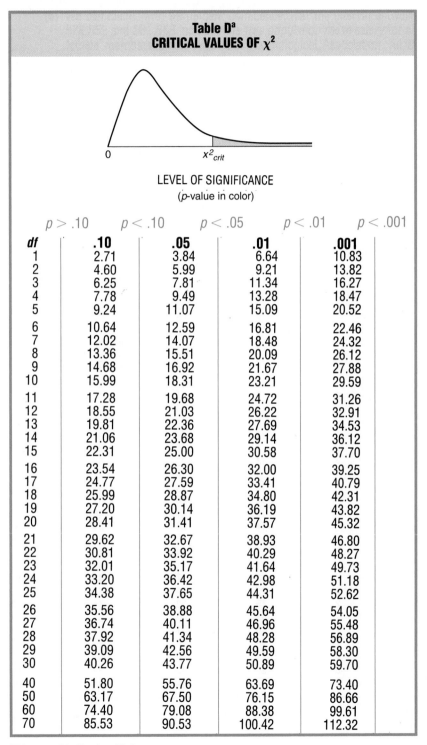

Table D[a]
CRITICAL VALUES OF χ^2

LEVEL OF SIGNIFICANCE
(*p*-value in color)

	$p > .10$	$p < .10$	$p < .05$	$p < .01$	$p < .001$
df	**.10**	**.05**	**.01**	**.001**	
1	2.71	3.84	6.64	10.83	
2	4.60	5.99	9.21	13.82	
3	6.25	7.81	11.34	16.27	
4	7.78	9.49	13.28	18.47	
5	9.24	11.07	15.09	20.52	
6	10.64	12.59	16.81	22.46	
7	12.02	14.07	18.48	24.32	
8	13.36	15.51	20.09	26.12	
9	14.68	16.92	21.67	27.88	
10	15.99	18.31	23.21	29.59	
11	17.28	19.68	24.72	31.26	
12	18.55	21.03	26.22	32.91	
13	19.81	22.36	27.69	34.53	
14	21.06	23.68	29.14	36.12	
15	22.31	25.00	30.58	37.70	
16	23.54	26.30	32.00	39.25	
17	24.77	27.59	33.41	40.79	
18	25.99	28.87	34.80	42.31	
19	27.20	30.14	36.19	43.82	
20	28.41	31.41	37.57	45.32	
21	29.62	32.67	38.93	46.80	
22	30.81	33.92	40.29	48.27	
23	32.01	35.17	41.64	49.73	
24	33.20	36.42	42.98	51.18	
25	34.38	37.65	44.31	52.62	
26	35.56	38.88	45.64	54.05	
27	36.74	40.11	46.96	55.48	
28	37.92	41.34	48.28	56.89	
29	39.09	42.56	49.59	58.30	
30	40.26	43.77	50.89	59.70	
40	51.80	55.76	63.69	73.40	
50	63.17	67.50	76.15	86.66	
60	74.40	79.08	88.38	99.61	
70	85.53	90.53	100.42	112.32	

[a] *Discussed in Section 19.4.*

Table Eᵃ
CRITICAL VALUES OF MANN-WHITNEY U

NONDIRECTIONAL TEST
.05 level of significance (light numbers)
.01 level of significance (dark numbers)

n_2\n_1	1	2	3	4	5	6	7	8	9	10	11	12	13	14	15	16	17	18	19	20
1	—	—	—	—	—	—	—	—	—	—	—	—	—	—	—	—	—	—	—	—
	—	—	—	—	—	—	—	—	—	—	—	—	—	—	—	—	—	—	—	—
2	—	—	—	—	—	—	—	0	0	0	0	1	1	1	1	1	2	2	2	2
	—	—	—	—	—	—	—	—	—	—	—	—	—	—	—	—	—	—	**0**	**0**
3	—	—	—	—	0	1	1	2	2	3	3	4	4	5	5	6	6	7	7	8
	—	—	—	—	—	—	—	—	**0**	**0**	**0**	**1**	**1**	**1**	**2**	**2**	**2**	**2**	**3**	**3**
4	—	—	—	0	1	2	3	4	4	5	6	7	8	9	10	11	11	12	13	13
	—	—	—	—	—	**0**	**0**	**1**	**1**	**2**	**2**	**3**	**3**	**4**	**5**	**5**	**6**	**6**	**7**	**8**
5	—	—	0	1	2	3	5	6	7	8	9	11	12	13	14	15	17	18	19	20
	—	—	—	—	**0**	**1**	**1**	**2**	**3**	**4**	**5**	**6**	**7**	**7**	**8**	**9**	**10**	**11**	**12**	**13**
6	—	—	1	2	3	5	6	8	10	11	13	14	16	17	19	21	22	24	25	27
	—	—	—	**0**	**1**	**2**	**3**	**4**	**5**	**6**	**7**	**9**	**10**	**11**	**12**	**13**	**15**	**16**	**17**	**18**
7	—	—	1	3	5	6	8	10	12	14	16	18	20	22	24	26	28	30	32	34
	—	—	—	**0**	**1**	**3**	**4**	**6**	**7**	**9**	**10**	**12**	**13**	**15**	**16**	**18**	**19**	**21**	**22**	**24**
8	—	0	2	4	6	8	10	13	15	17	19	22	24	26	29	31	34	36	38	41
	—	—	—	**1**	**2**	**4**	**6**	**7**	**9**	**11**	**13**	**15**	**17**	**18**	**20**	**22**	**24**	**26**	**28**	**30**
9	—	0	2	4	7	10	12	15	17	20	23	26	28	31	34	37	39	42	45	48
	—	—	**0**	**1**	**3**	**5**	**7**	**9**	**11**	**13**	**16**	**18**	**20**	**22**	**24**	**27**	**29**	**31**	**33**	**36**
10	—	0	3	5	8	11	14	17	20	23	26	29	33	36	39	42	45	48	52	55
	—	—	**0**	**2**	**4**	**6**	**9**	**11**	**13**	**16**	**18**	**21**	**24**	**26**	**29**	**31**	**34**	**37**	**39**	**42**
11	—	0	3	6	9	13	16	19	23	26	30	33	37	40	44	47	51	55	58	62
	—	—	**0**	**2**	**5**	**7**	**10**	**13**	**16**	**18**	**21**	**24**	**27**	**30**	**33**	**36**	**39**	**42**	**45**	**48**
12	—	1	4	7	11	14	18	22	26	29	33	37	41	45	49	53	57	61	65	69
	—	—	**1**	**3**	**6**	**9**	**12**	**15**	**18**	**21**	**24**	**27**	**31**	**34**	**37**	**41**	**44**	**47**	**51**	**54**
13	—	1	4	8	12	16	20	24	28	33	37	41	45	50	54	59	63	67	72	76
	—	—	**1**	**3**	**7**	**10**	**13**	**17**	**20**	**24**	**27**	**31**	**34**	**38**	**42**	**45**	**49**	**53**	**56**	**60**
14	—	1	5	9	13	17	22	26	31	36	40	45	50	55	59	64	67	74	78	83
	—	—	**1**	**4**	**7**	**11**	**15**	**18**	**22**	**26**	**30**	**34**	**38**	**42**	**46**	**50**	**54**	**58**	**63**	**67**
15	—	1	5	10	14	19	24	29	34	39	44	49	54	59	64	70	75	80	85	90
	—	—	**2**	**5**	**8**	**12**	**16**	**20**	**24**	**29**	**33**	**37**	**42**	**46**	**51**	**55**	**60**	**64**	**69**	**73**
16	—	1	6	11	15	21	26	31	37	42	47	53	59	64	70	75	81	86	92	98
	—	—	**2**	**5**	**9**	**13**	**18**	**22**	**27**	**31**	**36**	**41**	**45**	**50**	**55**	**60**	**65**	**70**	**74**	**79**
17	—	2	6	11	17	22	28	34	39	45	51	57	63	67	75	81	87	93	99	105
	—	—	**2**	**6**	**10**	**15**	**19**	**24**	**29**	**34**	**39**	**44**	**49**	**54**	**60**	**65**	**70**	**75**	**81**	**86**
18	—	2	7	12	18	24	30	36	42	48	55	61	67	74	80	86	93	99	106	112
	—	—	**2**	**6**	**11**	**16**	**21**	**26**	**31**	**37**	**42**	**47**	**53**	**58**	**64**	**70**	**75**	**81**	**87**	**92**
19	—	2	7	13	19	25	32	38	45	52	58	65	72	78	85	92	99	106	113	119
	—	**0**	**3**	**7**	**12**	**17**	**22**	**28**	**33**	**39**	**45**	**51**	**56**	**63**	**69**	**74**	**81**	**87**	**93**	**99**
20	—	2	8	13	20	27	34	41	48	55	62	69	76	83	90	98	105	112	119	127
	—	**0**	**3**	**8**	**13**	**18**	**24**	**30**	**36**	**42**	**48**	**54**	**60**	**67**	**73**	**79**	**86**	**92**	**99**	**105**

ᵃ Discussed in Section 20.3. To be significant, the observed U must equal or be less than the value shown in the table. Dashes in the table indicate that no decision is possible at the specified level of significance.

DIRECTIONAL TEST
.05 level of significance (light numbers)
.01 level of significance (**dark numbers**)

n_2 \ n_1	1	2	3	4	5	6	7	8	9	10	11	12	13	14	15	16	17	18	19	20
1	—	—	—	—	—	—	—	—	—	—	—	—	—	—	—	—	—	—	0	0
	—	—	—	—	—	—	—	—	—	—	—	—	—	—	—	—	—	—	—	—
2	—	—	—	—	0	0	0	1	1	1	1	2	2	2	3	3	3	4	4	4
	—	—	—	—	—	—	—	—	—	—	—	—	**0**	**0**	**0**	**0**	**0**	**0**	**1**	**1**
3	—	—	0	0	1	2	2	3	3	4	5	5	6	7	7	8	9	9	10	11
	—	—	—	—	—	—	**0**	**0**	**1**	**1**	**1**	**2**	**2**	**2**	**3**	**3**	**4**	**4**	**4**	**5**
4	—	—	0	1	2	3	4	5	6	7	8	9	10	11	12	14	15	16	17	18
	—	—	—	**0**	**0**	**1**	**1**	**2**	**3**	**3**	**4**	**5**	**5**	**6**	**7**	**7**	**8**	**9**	**9**	**10**
5	—	0	1	2	4	5	6	8	9	11	12	13	15	16	18	19	20	22	23	25
	—	—	—	**0**	**1**	**2**	**3**	**4**	**5**	**6**	**7**	**8**	**9**	**10**	**11**	**12**	**13**	**14**	**15**	**16**
6	—	0	2	3	5	7	8	10	12	14	16	17	19	21	23	25	26	28	30	32
	—	—	—	**1**	**2**	**3**	**4**	**6**	**7**	**8**	**9**	**11**	**12**	**13**	**15**	**16**	**18**	**19**	**20**	**22**
7	—	0	2	4	6	8	11	13	15	17	19	21	24	26	28	30	33	35	37	39
	—	—	**0**	**1**	**3**	**4**	**6**	**7**	**9**	**11**	**12**	**14**	**16**	**17**	**19**	**21**	**23**	**24**	**26**	**28**
8	—	1	3	5	8	10	13	15	18	20	23	26	28	31	33	36	39	41	44	47
	—	—	**0**	**2**	**4**	**6**	**7**	**9**	**11**	**13**	**15**	**17**	**20**	**22**	**24**	**26**	**28**	**30**	**32**	**34**
9	—	1	3	6	9	12	15	18	21	24	27	30	33	36	39	42	45	48	51	54
	—	—	**1**	**3**	**5**	**7**	**9**	**11**	**14**	**16**	**18**	**21**	**23**	**26**	**28**	**31**	**33**	**36**	**38**	**40**
10	—	1	4	7	11	14	17	20	24	27	31	34	37	41	44	48	51	55	58	62
	—	—	**1**	**3**	**6**	**8**	**11**	**13**	**16**	**19**	**22**	**24**	**27**	**30**	**33**	**36**	**38**	**41**	**44**	**47**
11	—	1	5	8	12	16	19	23	27	31	34	38	42	46	50	54	57	61	65	69
	—	—	**1**	**4**	**7**	**9**	**12**	**15**	**18**	**22**	**25**	**28**	**31**	**34**	**37**	**41**	**44**	**47**	**50**	**53**
12	—	2	5	9	13	17	21	26	30	34	38	42	47	51	55	60	64	68	72	77
	—	—	**2**	**5**	**8**	**11**	**14**	**17**	**21**	**24**	**28**	**31**	**35**	**38**	**42**	**46**	**49**	**53**	**56**	**60**
13	—	2	6	10	15	19	24	28	33	37	42	47	51	56	61	65	70	75	80	84
	—	**0**	**2**	**5**	**9**	**12**	**16**	**20**	**23**	**27**	**31**	**35**	**39**	**43**	**47**	**51**	**55**	**59**	**63**	**67**
14	—	2	7	11	16	21	26	31	36	41	46	51	56	61	66	71	77	82	87	92
	—	**0**	**2**	**6**	**10**	**13**	**17**	**22**	**26**	**30**	**34**	**38**	**43**	**47**	**51**	**56**	**60**	**65**	**69**	**73**
15	—	3	7	12	18	23	28	33	39	44	50	55	61	66	72	77	83	88	94	100
	—	**0**	**3**	**7**	**11**	**15**	**19**	**24**	**28**	**33**	**37**	**42**	**47**	**51**	**56**	**61**	**66**	**70**	**75**	**80**
16	—	3	8	14	19	25	30	36	42	48	54	60	65	71	77	83	89	95	101	107
	—	**0**	**3**	**7**	**12**	**16**	**21**	**26**	**31**	**36**	**41**	**46**	**51**	**56**	**61**	**66**	**71**	**76**	**82**	**87**
17	—	3	9	15	20	26	33	39	45	51	57	64	70	77	83	89	96	102	109	115
	—	**0**	**4**	**8**	**13**	**18**	**23**	**28**	**33**	**38**	**44**	**49**	**55**	**60**	**66**	**71**	**77**	**82**	**88**	**93**
18	—	4	9	16	22	28	35	41	48	55	61	68	75	82	88	95	102	109	116	123
	—	**0**	**4**	**9**	**14**	**19**	**24**	**30**	**36**	**41**	**47**	**53**	**59**	**65**	**70**	**76**	**82**	**88**	**94**	**100**
19	0	4	10	17	23	30	37	44	51	58	65	72	80	87	94	101	109	116	123	130
	—	**1**	**4**	**9**	**15**	**20**	**26**	**32**	**38**	**44**	**50**	**56**	**63**	**69**	**75**	**82**	**88**	**94**	**101**	**107**
20	0	4	11	18	25	32	39	47	54	62	69	77	84	92	100	107	115	123	130	138
	—	**1**	**5**	**10**	**16**	**22**	**28**	**34**	**40**	**47**	**53**	**60**	**67**	**73**	**80**	**87**	**93**	**100**	**107**	**114**

Table F[a]
CRITICAL VALUES OF WILCOXON T

FINDING p-VALUE
If observed T is
…larger than .05 number, $p > .05$
…between .05 and .01 numbers, $p < .05$
…smaller than .01 number, $p < .01$

LEVEL OF SIGNIFICANCE

| | NONDIRECTIONAL TEST | | | | | | DIRECTIONAL TEST | | | | |
	.05	.01		.05	.01		.05	.01		.05	.01
n			n			n			n		
5	—	—	28	116	91	5	0	—	28	130	101
6	0	—	29	126	100	6	2	—	29	140	110
7	2	—	30	137	109	7	3	0	30	151	120
8	3	0	31	147	118	8	5	1	31	163	130
9	5	1	32	159	128	9	8	3	32	175	140
10	8	3	33	170	138	10	10	5	33	187	151
11	10	5	34	182	148	11	13	7	34	200	162
12	13	7	35	195	159	12	17	9	35	213	173
13	17	9	36	208	171	13	21	12	36	227	185
14	21	12	37	221	182	14	25	15	37	241	198
15	25	15	38	235	194	15	30	19	38	256	211
16	29	19	39	249	207	16	35	23	39	271	224
17	34	23	40	264	220	17	41	27	40	286	238
18	40	27	41	279	233	18	47	32	41	302	252
19	46	32	42	294	247	19	53	37	42	319	266
20	52	37	43	310	261	20	60	43	43	336	281
21	58	42	44	327	276	21	67	49	44	353	296
22	65	48	45	343	291	22	75	55	45	371	312
23	73	54	46	361	307	23	83	62	46	389	328
24	81	61	47	378	322	24	91	69	47	407	345
25	89	68	48	396	339	25	100	76	48	426	362
26	98	75	49	415	355	26	110	84	49	446	379
27	107	83	50	434	373	27	119	92	50	466	397

[a] *Discussed in Section 20.4. To be significant, the observed* T *must equal or be less than the value shown in the table. Dashes in the table indicate that no decision is possible at the specified level of significance.*

Table G[a]
CRITICAL VALUES OF q FOR TUKEY'S HSD TEST

.05 level of significance (light numbers)
.01 level of significance (dark numbers)

ERROR df	α	NUMBER OF MEANS (k) 2	3	4	5	6	7	8	9	10	11
2	.05	6.08	8.33	9.80	10.9	11.7	12.4	13.0	13.5	14.0	14.4
	.01	**14.0**	**19.0**	**22.3**	**24.7**	**26.6**	**28.2**	**29.5**	**30.7**	**31.7**	**32.6**
3	.05	4.50	5.91	6.82	7.50	8.04	8.48	8.85	9.18	9.46	9.72
	.01	**8.26**	**10.6**	**12.2**	**13.3**	**14.2**	**15.0**	**15.6**	**16.2**	**16.7**	**17.8**
4	.05	3.93	5.04	5.76	6.29	6.71	7.05	7.35	7.60	7.83	8.03
	.01	**6.51**	**8.12**	**9.17**	**9.96**	**10.6**	**11.1**	**11.5**	**11.9**	**12.3**	**12.6**
5	.05	3.64	4.60	5.22	5.67	6.03	6.33	6.58	6.80	6.99	7.17
	.01	**5.70**	**6.98**	**7.80**	**8.42**	**8.91**	**9.32**	**9.67**	**9.97**	**10.24**	**10.48**
6	.05	3.46	4.34	4.90	5.30	5.63	5.90	6.12	6.32	6.49	6.65
	.01	**5.24**	**6.33**	**7.03**	**7.56**	**7.97**	**8.32**	**8.61**	**8.87**	**9.10**	**9.30**
7	.05	3.34	4.16	4.68	5.06	5.36	5.61	5.82	6.00	6.16	6.30
	.01	**4.95**	**5.92**	**6.54**	**7.01**	**7.37**	**7.68**	**7.94**	**8.17**	**8.37**	**8.55**
8	.05	3.26	4.04	4.53	4.89	5.17	5.40	5.60	5.77	5.92	6.05
	.01	**4.75**	**5.64**	**6.20**	**6.62**	**6.96**	**7.24**	**7.47**	**7.68**	**7.86**	**8.03**
9	.05	3.20	3.95	4.41	4.76	5.02	5.24	5.43	5.59	5.74	5.87
	.01	**4.60**	**5.43**	**5.96**	**6.35**	**6.66**	**6.91**	**7.13**	**7.33**	**7.49**	**7.65**
10	.05	3.15	3.88	4.33	4.65	4.91	5.12	5.30	5.46	5.60	5.72
	.01	**4.48**	**5.27**	**5.77**	**6.14**	**6.43**	**6.67**	**6.87**	**7.05**	**7.21**	**7.36**
11	.05	3.11	3.82	4.26	4.57	4.82	5.03	5.20	5.35	5.49	5.61
	.01	**4.39**	**5.15**	**5.62**	**5.97**	**6.25**	**6.48**	**6.67**	**6.84**	**6.99**	**7.13**
12	.05	3.08	3.77	4.20	4.51	4.75	4.95	5.12	5.27	5.39	5.51
	.01	**4.32**	**5.05**	**5.50**	**5.84**	**6.10**	**6.32**	**6.51**	**6.67**	**6.81**	**6.94**
13	.05	3.06	3.73	4.15	4.45	4.69	4.88	5.05	5.19	5.32	5.43
	.01	**4.26**	**4.96**	**5.40**	**5.73**	**5.98**	**6.19**	**6.37**	**6.53**	**6.67**	**6.79**
14	.05	3.03	3.70	4.11	4.41	4.64	4.83	4.99	5.13	5.25	5.36
	.01	**4.21**	**4.89**	**5.32**	**5.63**	**5.88**	**6.08**	**6.26**	**6.41**	**6.54**	**6.66**
15	.05	3.01	3.67	4.08	4.37	4.59	4.78	4.94	5.08	5.20	5.31
	.01	**4.17**	**4.84**	**5.25**	**5.56**	**5.80**	**5.99**	**6.16**	**6.31**	**6.44**	**6.55**
16	.05	3.00	3.65	4.05	4.33	4.56	4.74	4.90	5.03	5.15	5.26
	.01	**4.13**	**4.79**	**5.19**	**5.49**	**5.72**	**5.92**	**6.08**	**6.22**	**6.35**	**6.46**
17	.05	2.98	3.63	4.02	4.30	4.52	4.70	4.86	4.99	5.11	5.21
	.01	**4.10**	**4.74**	**5.14**	**5.43**	**5.66**	**5.85**	**6.01**	**6.15**	**6.27**	**6.38**
18	.05	2.97	3.61	4.00	4.28	4.49	4.67	4.82	4.96	5.07	5.17
	.01	**4.07**	**4.70**	**5.09**	**5.38**	**5.60**	**5.79**	**5.94**	**6.08**	**6.20**	**6.31**
19	.05	2.96	3.59	3.98	4.25	4.47	4.65	4.79	4.92	5.04	5.14
	.01	**4.05**	**4.67**	**5.05**	**5.33**	**5.55**	**5.73**	**5.89**	**6.02**	**6.14**	**6.25**
20	.05	2.95	3.58	3.96	4.23	4.45	4.62	4.77	4.90	5.01	5.11
	.01	**4.02**	**4.64**	**5.02**	**5.29**	**5.51**	**5.69**	**5.84**	**5.97**	**6.09**	**6.19**
24	.05	2.92	3.53	3.90	4.17	4.37	4.54	4.68	4.81	4.92	5.01
	.01	**3.96**	**4.55**	**4.91**	**5.17**	**5.37**	**5.54**	**5.69**	**5.81**	**5.92**	**6.02**
30	.05	2.89	3.49	3.85	4.10	4.30	4.46	4.60	4.72	4.82	4.92
	.01	**3.89**	**4.45**	**4.80**	**5.05**	**5.24**	**5.40**	**5.54**	**5.65**	**5.76**	**5.85**
40	.05	2.86	3.44	3.79	4.04	4.23	4.39	4.52	4.63	4.73	4.82
	.01	**3.82**	**4.37**	**4.70**	**4.93**	**5.11**	**5.26**	**5.39**	**5.50**	**5.60**	**5.69**
60	.05	2.83	3.40	3.74	3.98	4.16	4.31	4.44	4.55	4.65	4.73
	.01	**3.76**	**4.28**	**4.59**	**4.82**	**4.99**	**5.13**	**5.25**	**5.36**	**5.45**	**5.53**
120	.05	2.80	3.36	3.68	3.92	4.10	4.24	4.36	4.47	4.56	4.64
	.01	**3.70**	**4.20**	**4.50**	**4.71**	**4.87**	**5.01**	**5.12**	**5.21**	**5.30**	**5.37**
∞	.05	2.77	3.31	3.63	3.86	4.03	4.17	4.29	4.39	4.47	4.55
	.01	**3.64**	**4.12**	**4.40**	**4.60**	**4.76**	**4.88**	**4.99**	**5.08**	**5.16**	**5.23**

[a] *Discussed in Section 16.10.*

ROW NUMBER

00000	10097	32533	76520	13586	34673	54876	80959	09117	39292	74945
00001	37542	04805	64894	74296	24805	24037	20636	10402	00822	91665
00002	08422	68953	19645	09303	23209	02560	15953	34764	35080	33606
00003	99019	02529	09376	70715	38311	31165	88676	74397	04436	27659
00004	12807	99970	80157	36147	64032	36653	98951	16877	12171	76833
00005	66065	74717	34072	76850	36697	36170	65813	39885	11199	29170
00006	31060	10805	45571	82406	35303	42614	86799	07439	23403	09732
00007	85269	77602	02051	65692	68665	74818	73053	85247	18623	88579
00008	63573	32135	05325	47048	90553	57548	28468	28709	83491	25624
00009	73796	45753	03529	64778	35808	34282	60935	20344	35273	88435
00010	98520	17767	14905	68607	22109	40558	60970	93433	50500	73998
00011	11805	05431	39808	27732	50725	68248	29405	24201	52775	67851
00012	83452	99634	06288	98033	13746	70078	18475	40610	68711	77817
00013	88685	40200	86507	58401	36766	67951	90364	76493	29609	11062
00014	99594	67348	87517	64969	91826	08928	93785	61368	23478	34113
00015	65481	17674	17468	50950	58047	76974	73039	57186	40218	16544
00016	80124	35635	17727	08015	45318	22374	21115	78253	14385	53763
00017	74350	99817	77402	77214	43236	00210	45521	64237	96286	02655
00018	69916	26803	66252	29148	36936	87203	76621	13990	94400	56418
00019	09893	20505	14225	68514	46427	56788	96297	78822	54382	14598
00020	91499	14523	68479	27686	46162	83554	94750	89923	37089	20048
00021	80336	94598	26940	36858	70297	34135	53140	33340	42050	82341
00022	44104	81949	85157	47954	32979	26575	57600	40881	22222	06413
00023	12550	73742	11100	02040	12860	74697	96644	89439	28707	25815
00024	63606	49329	16505	34484	40219	52563	43651	77082	07207	31790
00025	61196	90446	26457	47774	51924	33729	65394	59593	42582	60527
00026	15474	45266	95270	79953	59367	83848	82396	10118	33211	59466
00027	94557	28573	67897	54387	54622	44431	91190	42592	92927	45973
00028	42481	16213	97344	08721	16868	48767	03071	12059	25701	46670
00029	23523	78317	73208	89837	68935	91416	26252	29663	05522	82562
00030	04493	52494	75246	33824	45862	51025	61962	79335	65337	12472
00031	00549	97654	64051	88159	96119	63896	54692	82391	23287	29529
00032	35963	15307	26898	09354	33351	35462	77974	50024	90130	39333
00033	59808	08391	45427	26842	83609	49700	13021	24892	78565	20106
00034	46058	85236	01390	92286	77281	44077	93910	83647	70617	42941
00035	32179	00597	87379	25241	05567	07007	86743	17157	85394	11838
00036	69234	61406	20117	45204	15956	60000	18743	92423	97188	96338
00037	19565	41430	01758	75379	40419	21585	66674	36806	84962	85207
00038	45155	14938	19476	07246	43667	94543	59047	90033	20826	69541
00039	94864	31994	36168	10851	34888	81553	01540	35456	05014	51176
00040	98086	24826	45240	28404	44999	08896	39094	73407	35441	31880
00041	33185	16232	41941	50949	89435	48581	88695	41944	37548	73043
00042	80951	00406	96382	70774	20151	23387	25016	25288	94624	61171
00043	79752	49140	71961	28296	69861	02591	74852	20539	00387	59579
00044	18633	32537	98145	06571	31010	24674	05455	61427	77938	91936
00045	74029	43902	77557	32270	97790	17119	52527	58021	80814	51748
00046	54178	45611	80993	37143	05335	12969	56127	19255	36040	90324
00047	11664	49883	52079	84827	59381	71539	09973	33440	88461	23356
00048	48324	77928	31249	64710	02295	36870	32307	57546	15020	09994
00049	69074	94138	87637	91976	35584	04401	10518	21615	01848	76938
00050	09188	20097	32825	39527	04220	86304	83389	87374	64278	58044
00051	90045	85497	51981	50654	94938	81997	91870	76150	68476	64659
00052	73189	50207	47677	26269	62290	64464	27124	67018	41361	82760
00053	75768	76490	20971	87749	90429	12272	95375	05871	93823	43178
00054	54016	44056	66281	31003	00682	27398	20714	53295	07706	17813
00055	08358	69910	78542	42785	13661	58873	04618	97553	31223	08420
00056	28306	03264	81333	10591	40510	07893	32604	60475	94119	01840
00057	53840	86233	81594	13628	51215	90290	28466	68795	77762	20791
00058	91757	53471	61613	62669	50263	90212	55781	76514	83483	47055
00059	89415	92694	00397	58391	12607	17646	48949	72306	94541	37408

ª Discussed in Section 8.4.

APPENDIX D

Glossary

Glossary

Numbers in parentheses indicate the section in which the term is introduced.

Addition rule: Add together the separate probabilities of several mutually exclusive events to find the probability that any one of these events will occur. (8.8)

Alpha (α): The probability of a type I error, that is, the probability of rejecting a true null hypothesis. (11.7) Also see *level of significance*.

Alternative hypothesis (H_1): The opposite of the null hypothesis. Often identified with the research hypothesis. (10.6)

Analysis of variance (ANOVA): An overall test of the null hypothesis for more than two population means. (16.1)

Approximate numbers: Occur whenever numbers are rounded off, as is always the case with values for continuous variables. (1.6)

Bar graph: Bar-type graph for qualitative data with gaps between adjacent bars. (2.10)

Beta (β): The probability of a type II error, that is, the probability of retaining a false null hypothesis. (11.8)

Bimodal: Describes any distribution with two obvious peaks. (3.1)

Central limit theorem: Regardless of the population shape, the shape of the sampling distribution of the mean will approximate a normal curve if the sample size is sufficiently large. (9.6)

Conditional probability: The probability of one event, given the occurrence of another event. (8.9)

Confidence interval (CI): A range of values that, with a known degree of certainty, includes an unknown population characteristic, such as a population mean. (12.2)

Confidence interval for $\mu_1 - \mu_2$ (or μ_D): A range of values that, in the long run, includes the unknown effect (difference between population means) a certain percent of the time. (14.8)

Confounding variable: An uncontrolled variable that compromises the interpretation of a study. (1.6)

Constant: A characteristic or property that can take on only one value (1.6)

Continuous variable: A variable that consists of numbers whose values, at least in theory, have no restrictions. (1.6)

Correlation coefficient: See *Pearson correlation coefficient.*

Correlation matrix: A table showing correlations for all possible pairs of variables. (6.8)

Counterbalancing: Reversing the order of conditions for equal numbers of all subjects. (15.1)

Critical z score: A z score that separates common from rare outcomes and hence dictates whether the null hypothesis should be retained or rejected. (10.7)

Cumulative frequency distribution: A frequency distribution showing the total number of observations in each class and all lower-ranked classes. (2.5)

Curvilinear relationship: A relationship that can be described best with a curved line. (6.2)

Data: A collection of observations or scores from a survey or an experiment. (1.4)

Decision rule: Specifies precisely when the null hypothesis should be rejected (because the observed value qualifies as a rare outcome). (10.7)

Degrees of freedom (df): The number of values free to vary, given one or more mathematical restrictions. (4.6)

Dependent variable: A variable that is believed to have been influenced by the independent variable. (1.6)

Descriptive statistics: The area of statistics concerned with organizing and summarizing information about a collection of actual observations. (1.2)

Difference score (*D*): The arithmetic difference between each pair of scores in repeated measures or, more generally, in two related samples. (15.1)

Directional test: See *One-tailed test.*

Discrete variable: A variable that consists of isolated numbers separated by gaps. (1.6)

Distribution-free tests: Tests, such as *U*, *T*, and *H*, that make no assumptions about the form of the population distribution. (20.2)

Effect: Any difference between a true and a hypothesized population mean. (11.8) Also, any difference between two (or more) population means. (14.1) See also *Treatment effect.*

Estimated standard error of difference between sample means ($s_{\bar{x}_1 - \bar{x}_2}$): The standard deviation of the sampling distribution of difference between means used whenever the unknown variance common to both populations must be estimated. (14.5)

Estimated standard error of the mean ($s_{\bar{x}}$): The standard deviation of the sampling distribution of the mean used whenever the unknown population standard deviation must be estimated. (13.6)

Estimated standard error of the mean difference ($s_{\bar{D}}$): The standard deviation of the sampling distribution of the mean difference used whenever the unknown population standard deviation for difference scores must be estimated. (15.5)

Expected frequency (*f*_e): The hypothesized frequency for each category, given that the null hypothesis is true. Used with the chi-square test. (19.3)

Experiment: A study in which the investigator decides who receives the special treatment. (1.6)

Frequency distribution: A collection of observations produced by sorting observations into classes that show their frequency (f) of occurrence. (2.1)

Frequency distribution for grouped data: A frequency distribution produced whenever observations are sorted into classes of *more than one* value. (2.1)

Frequency distribution for ungrouped data: A frequency distribution produced whenever observations are sorted into classes of *single* values. (2.1)

Frequency polygon: A line graph for quantitative data that emphasizes the continuity of continuous variables. (2.8)

***F* ratio:** Ratio of the between-group mean square (for subjects treated differently) to the within-group mean square (for subjects treated similarly). (16.5)

F_{se} test for simple effects: A test of the effect of one factor on the dependent variable at a single level of another factor. (18.9)

Histogram: A bar-type graph for quantitative data, with no gaps between adjacent bars. (2.8)

Hypothesized sampling distribution: Centered about the hypothesized population mean, this distribution is used to generate the decision rule. (11.8)

Independent events: The occurrence of one event has no effect on the probability that the other event will occur. (8.9)

Independent variable: The treatment that is manipulated by the investigator in an experiment. (1.6)

Inferential statistics: The area of statistics concerned about generalizing beyond actual observations. (1.2)

Interaction: The product of inconsistent simple effects. (18.3)

Interquartile range (IQR): The range for the middle 50 percent of all scores. (4.7)

Interval/ratio measurement: Locates observations along a scale having equal intervals and a true zero. (1.5)

Kruskal-Wallis *H* test: A test for ranked data when there are more than two independent groups. (20.5)

Least squares regression equation: The equation that minimizes the total of all squared predictive errors for known *Y* scores in the original correlation analysis. (7.3)

Level of confidence: The percent of time that a series of confidence intervals includes the unknown population characteristic, such as the population mean. (12.4)

Level of measurement: Rules that specify the extent to which a number actually represents some attribute. (1.5)

Level of significance (α): The degree of rarity required of an observed outcome to reject the null hypothesis. (H_0) (10.7)

Linear relationship: A relationship that can be described best with a straight line. (6.2)

Main effect: The effect of a single factor when any other factor is ignored. (18.1)

Mann-Whitney U test: A test for ranked data when there are two independent groups. (20.3)

Margin of error: That which is added to and subtracted from some sample value, such as the sample proportion or sample mean, to obtain the limits of a confidence interval. (12.7)

Mean: See *Population mean* or *Sample mean*.

Mean of the sampling distribution of the mean ($\mu_{\bar{x}}$): The mean of all sample means always equals the population mean. (9.4)

Mean square (MS): A variance estimate obtained by dividing a sum of squares by its degrees of freedom. (16.4)

Measures of central tendency: A general term for the various averages that attempt to describe the middle or typical value in a distribution. (3.1)

Measures of variability: A general term for various measures of the amount by which scores are dispersed or scattered. (4.1)

Median: The middle value when observations are ordered from least to most. (3.2)

Mode: The value of the most frequent observation or score. (3.1)

Multiple comparisons: The possible comparisons whenever more than two population means are involved. (16.10)

Multiple regression equation: A least squares equation that contains more than one predictor or X variable. (7.6)

Multiplication rule: Multiply together the separate probabilities of several independent events to find the probability that these events will occur together. (8.9)

Mutually exclusive events: Events that cannot occur together. (8.8)

Negative relationship: Occurs insofar as pairs of observations tend to occupy dissimilar and opposite relative positions in their respective distributions. (6.1)

Negatively skewed distribution: A distribution that includes a few extreme observations in the negative direction. (2.9)

Nominal measurement: Sorts observations into different classes or categories. (1.5)

Nondirectional test: See *Two-tailed test*.

Nonparametric tests: Tests, such as U, T, and H, that evaluate entire population distributions rather than specific population characteristics. (20.2)

Normal curve: A theoretical curve noted for its symmetrical bell-shaped form. (5.1)

Null hypothesis (H_0): A statistical hypothesis that usually asserts that nothing special is happening with respect to some characteristic of the underlying population. (10.5)

Observational study: A study that focuses on the detection of relationships between variables not manipulated by the investigator. (1.6)

Observed frequency (f_0): The obtained frequency for each category. Used with the chi-square test. (19.3)

Odds ratio (OR): Indicates the relative occurrence of one value of the dependent variable across the two categories of the independent variable. (19.12)

One-factor ANOVA: The simplest type of analysis of variance that tests for differences among population means categorized by only one independent variable. (16.1)

One-tailed (or directional) test: The rejection region is located in just one tail of the sampling distribution. (11.3)

One-variable χ^2 test: Evaluates whether observed frequencies for a single qualitative variable are adequately described by hypothesized or expected frequencies. (19.1)

Ordinal measurement: Arranges observations in terms of order. (1.5)

Outlier: A very extreme observation. (2.3)

Partial squared curvilinear correlation (η_p^2): The proportion of explained variance in the dependent variable after one or more sources have been eliminated from the total variance. (17.8)

Pearson correlation coefficient (r): A number between -1.00 and $+1.00$ that describes the linear relationship between pairs of quantitative variables. (6.3)

Percentile rank of an observation: Percentage of scores in the entire distribution with similar or smaller values than that score. (2.5)

Point estimate: A single value that represents some unknown population characteristic, such as the population mean. (12.1)

Pooled variance estimate (s_p^2): The most accurate estimate of the population variance (assumed to be the same for both populations) based on a combination of two sample sums of squares and their degrees of freedom. (14.5)

Population: Any complete set of observations. (1.3)

Population correlation coefficient (ρ): A number between -1.00 and 1.00 that describes the linear relationship for all paired observations in a population. (15.9)

Population mean (μ): The balance point for a population, found by dividing the total value of all scores in the population by the number of scores in the population. (3.3)

Population size (N): The total number of scores in the population. (3.3)

Population standard deviation (σ): A rough measure of the average amount by which scores deviate from the population mean. (4.5)

Positively skewed distribution: A distribution that includes a few extreme observations in the positive direction. (2.9)

Positive relationship: Occurs insofar as pairs of observations tend to occupy similar relative positions in their respective distributions. (6.1)

Power ($1 - \beta$): The probability of detecting a particular effect. (11.11)

Power curve: Shows how the likelihood of detecting any possible effect varies for a fixed sample size. (11.11)

Probability: The proportion or fraction of times that a particular event is likely to occur. (8.7)

p-Value: The degree of rarity of a test result, given that the null hypothesis is true. (14.6)

Qualitative data: A set of observations where any single observation is a word, letter, or code that represents a class or category. (1.4)

Quantitative data: A set of observations where any single observation is a number that represents an amount or a count. (1.4)

Random assignment: A procedure designed to ensure that each person has an equal chance of being assigned to any group in an experiment. (1.3)

Random error: The combined effects of all uncontrolled factors on the scores of individual subjects. (16.2)

Random sampling: A sample produced when all potential observations in the population have an equal chance of being selected. (1.3)

Range: The difference between the largest and smallest scores. (4.2)

Ranked data: A set of observations where any single observation is a number that indicates relative standing. (1.4)

Ratio measurement: See *Interval/ratio measurement.*

Real limits: Located at the mid-point of the gap between adjacent tabled boundaries. (2.2)

Regression equation: See *Least squares regression equation.*

Regression fallacy: Occurs whenever regression toward the mean is interpreted as a real, rather than a chance, effect. (7.7)

Regression toward the mean: A tendency for scores, particularly extreme scores, to shrink toward the mean. (7.7)

Relative frequency distribution: A frequency distribution showing the frequency of each class as a part or fraction of the total frequency for the entire distribution. (2.4)

Repeated measures: Whenever the same subject is measured more than once. (15.1)

Repeated-measures ANOVA: A type of analysis that tests whether differences exist among population means with measures on the same subjects. (17.1)

Research hypothesis: Usually identified with the alternative hypothesis, this is the informal hypothesis or hunch that inspires the entire investigation. (10.6) See *Alternative hypothesis.*

Sample: Any subset of scores from a population. (1.3)

Sample correlation coefficient (*r*): A number between −1.00 and 1.00 that describes the linear relationship between paired observations in a sample. (6.3)

Sample mean ($\bar{X}$): The balance point for the sample, found by dividing the total value of all scores in the sample by the number of scores. (3.3)

Sample size (*n*): The total number of scores in the sample. (3.3)

Sample standard deviation (*s*): A rough measure of the average amount by which scores in the sample deviate from their mean. (4.5)

Sample standard deviation of difference scores (s_D): A rough measure of the average amount by which difference scores in the sample deviate from the mean difference score. (14.5)

Sampling distribution of the mean: The probability distribution of means for all possible random samples of a given size from some population. (9.1)

Sampling distribution of *t*: The distribution that would be obtained if a value of *t* were calculated for each sample mean for all possible random samples of a given size from some population. (13.2)

Sampling distribution of $\bar{X}_1 - \bar{X}_2$: Differences between sample means based on all possible pairs of random samples from two underlying populations. (14.3)

Sampling distribution of *z*: The distribution of *z* values that would be obtained if a value of *z* were calculated for each sample mean for all possible random samples of a given size from some population. (10.2)

Scatterplot: A special graph containing a cluster of dots that represents all pairs of observations. (6.2)

Simple effect: The effect of one factor on the dependent variable at a single level of another factor. (18.3)

Squared Cramer's phi coefficient (ϕ_c^2): A very rough estimate of the proportion of explained variance (or predictability) between two qualitative variables. (19.11)

Squared curvilinear correlation (η^2): The proportion of variance in the dependent variable that can be explained by or attributed to the independent variable. (16.9)

Squared partial curvilinear correlation. See *Partial squared curvilinear correlation.*

Standard deviation: A rough measure of the average amount by which observations deviate from their mean. (4.4)

Standard error of estimate ($s_{Y|X}$): A rough measure of the average amount of predictive error. (7.4)

Standard error of the difference between means, ($\sigma_{\bar{X}_1 - \bar{X}_2}$): A rough measure of the average amount by which any sample mean difference deviates from the difference between population means. (14.3)

Standard error of the mean ($\sigma_{\bar{X}}$): A rough measure of the average amount by which sample means deviate from the population mean. (9.5)

Standard error of the mean difference ($\sigma_{\bar{D}}$): The standard deviation of the sampling distribution for the mean difference. (15.3)

Standard normal curve: The one tabled normal curve for *z* scores with a mean of 0 and a standard deviation of 1. (5.3)

Standard score: Unit-free score expressed relative to a known mean and a known standard deviation. (5.7)

Standardized effect estimate, Cohen's *d*: Describes effect size by expressing the observed mean difference in standard deviation units. (14.9)

Statistical significance: Implies only that the null hypothesis is probably false, but not whether it's false because of a large or small effect. (14.7)

Stem and leaf display: A device for sorting quantitative data on the basis of leading and trailing digits. (2.8)

Sum of squares (*SS*): The sum of squared deviation scores. (4.5)

***t* ratio:** A replacement for the z ratio whenever the unknown population standard deviation must be estimated. (13.3)

Transformed standard score (*z′*): A standard score that, unlike a z score, usually lacks negative signs and decimal points. (5.7)

Treatment effect: The existence of at least one difference between the population means. (16.2)

True sampling distribution: Centered about the true population mean, this distribution produces the one observed mean (or z). (11.8)

Tukey's *HSD* test: A multiple comparison test for which the cumulative probability of at least one type I error never exceeds the specified level of significance. (16.10)

Two independent samples: Observations in each sample are based on different (and unmatched) subjects. (14.1)

Two-factor ANOVA: A more complex type of analysis of variance that tests whether differences exist among population means categorized by two factors or independent variables. (18.1)

Two related samples: Each observation in one sample is paired, on a one-to-one basis, with a single observation in the other sample. (15.1)

Two-tailed (or nondirectional) test: Rejection regions are located in both tails of the sampling distribution. (11.3)

Two-variable χ^2 test: Evaluates whether observed frequencies reflect the independence of two qualitative variables. (19.7)

Type I error: Rejecting a true null hypothesis. (11.6)

Type II error: Retaining a false null hypothesis. (11.6)

Unit of measurement: The smallest possible difference between scores. (2.2)

Variability between groups (in ANOVA): Variability among scores of subjects who, being in different groups, receive different experimental treatments. (16.2)

Variability within groups (in ANOVA): Variability among scores of subjects who, being in the same group, receive the same experimental treatment. (16.2)

Variable: A characteristic or property that can take on different values. (1.6)

Variance: The mean of all squared deviation scores. (4.3)

Variance estimate (in ANOVA): See *Mean square*.

Wilcoxon *T* test: A test for ranked data when there are two related groups. (20.4)

***z* score:** A unit-free score that indicates how many standard deviations an observation is above or below the mean of its distribution. (5.2)

***z* test for a population mean:** A hypothesis test that evaluates how far the observed sample mean deviates, in standard error units, from the hypothesized population mean. (10.2)

Photo Credits

Index